D1499770

THE ONE SHOW

THE ONE SHOW

Judged To Be Advertising's Best Print, Radio, TV. Volume 8
A Presentation of The One Club for Art and Copy

Published by Rotovision S.A. Geneva

The One Club For Art and Copy

Ron Berger
PRESIDENT

Angela Dominguez
DIRECTOR

Michelle Michelman
MEMBERSHIP COORDINATOR
DIRECTOR OF PUBLIC RELATIONS

Earl Cavanah
DESIGNER

Ryuichi Minakawa
ART DIRECTOR

Frank DeLuca
LAYOUT AND PRODUCTION

Izabella Piestrzynska
EDITOR

Carolyn Dempsey
ASSISTANT EDITOR

Jerry Friedman
PHOTOGRAPHER

George Sell
MODELMAKER

Spano-Roccanova
RETOUCHER

Fisher Composition, Inc.
TYPESETTING

Toppan Printing Co., Ltd., Tokyo, Japan
COLOR SEPARATIONS, PRINTING AND BINDING

PUBLISHED AND DISTRIBUTED BY
Rotovision S.A.
10, Rue de l'Arquebuse
Case Postale 434
CH - 1211 Geneve 11
Switzerland
Telephone 22 - 21 21 21
IN ASSOCIATION WITH
The One Club for Art and Copy, Inc.
3 West 18th Street
New York, New York 10011
(212) 255-7070

First Printing.
ISBN 0-9602628-8-1
ISSN 0273-2033

Contents

The Board of Directors

President's Message

To all of those creative people who in spite of things like concept testing, and animatics, and Burke, and Klucas, and McCullom-Spielman, and ASI, and who in spite of the fact that their agency may have just merged or been gobbled up by another agency, still have it in them to produce great creative work, we at The One Show offer our thanks.

Because without people like yourselves, going to work every morning (not to mention looking through this book) would be extremely depressing.

Ron Berger

Judges Panel

Stavros Cosmopulos
Chairman of the Board/Creative Director
Cosmopulos Crowley & Daly

Neil Drossman
Chief Executive Officer/Co-Creative Director
Drossman Lehman Marino

Roy Grace
Chairman
Grace & Rothschild

Dick Jackson
President
Jackson, Inc.

Marshall Karp
Creative Director
Lowe Marschalk

Lois Korey
President
Korey Kay & Partners

Andrew Langer
President
Lowe Marschalk

Bob Levenson
Chief Creative Officer
Saatchi Saatchi & Compton

Mike Mangano
Executive Vice President/Creative Director
Doyle Dane Bernbach

Ed McCabe
President/Creative Director Worldwide
Scali McCabe Sloves

Tom McElligott
Creative Director
Fallon McElligott

Curvin O'Rielly
Executive Vice President/Creative Director
McCann-Erickson

Dick Pantano
Creative Director
Hill Holliday Connors Cosmopulos

Dick Raboy
Chairman
Ephron Raboy Tsao Kernit

Nancy Rice
Partner
Rice & Rice

Bob Saabye
Executive Vice President of Art
Leonard Monahan Saabye

Ted Sann
Executive Vice President/Senior Creative Director
BBDO

Mike Tesch
Creative Director
Ally & Gargano

Mike Winslow
Senior Vice President/Creative Director
McKinney Silver Rockett

One Club Members

Michael Abadi
Jeffrey Abbott
Francine Abdow
Charles Abrams
Debbie Adelman
Norine Ader
Robin Albin
Carl Ally
Hal Altman
David Altschiller
Roy Andersen
Kathy Anderson
Jeffrey Antman
Sharon Appleman
Brian Arcarese
Frank Arcuri
Cathie Arquilla
Karen Armand
Jan Arnow
Thomas Augusta
Frank Aultman
Ellen Azorin
Catherine Bahlke
Carol Ann Baker
Thomas Baldinette
Maryann Barone
Brenda Basken
Clarence Bateman
Lisa Behnken
Brian Belefant
Garrett Bender
Ron Berger
Sandy Berger
Heidi Berghoff
Herbert Berkowitz
Kiri Bermack
David Bernstein
Debbie Bernstein
Peter Bertolami
Lee Ann Bezazian
Mel Black
Paul Blade
Ilene Block
Marylou Blomer
Jack Bloom
Chris Bodden
Frank Boehm
George Bonner Jr.
Deborah Bornstein
Kathy Botas
Kathleen Brady
Leslie Brand
Harry Braver
Jim Brodie
Jennifer Brooke
Isaac Brooks
Bryan Buckley
Richard Buckley
Ron Blurkhardt
Dirk Burrows
Penny Burrow
Ed Butler
Larry Cadman
Darlene Cah
Robert Calame
David Caliano
Michael Campbell
Marc Camporeale
John Caples
Bob Carducci
Patrick Carella
Robert Cargill
David Carlin
Michele Carlo
Margaret Carlson
Barbara Carmack
John Carrigan
Earl Carter
Cherly Casronuove
Christen Caudle
Earl Cavanah
Ronald Cesark
Susan Chaityn
Suzan Chang
Larry Chase
Sara Chereskin
Thomas Chiarello
Vincent Chieco
Joseph Chiffriller
Marcia Christ
Lisa Chu
Shelly Chung
Mikel Cirkus
John Clapps
Eric Claussen
Liz Coglianese
Andrew Cohen
Dale Cohen
Deanna Cohen
Cheryl Hall Cole
Adrienne Collier
John Colquhoun
Scott Coplen
Lynn Corley
David Corr
Jennifer Cott
Robert Cox
Allison Cross
Jane Cross
Bob Culver
Bruce Cumsky
Lisa Cushman
James Dale
Marlo Darden
Pearl DeFrancesco
Kathy Delaney
Crain DeLarge
Brian Dillon
Deborah Dilworth
Shelley Doppelt
Philip Doyle
Carol Dronsfield
Neil Drossman
Andrea Drozd
Lorraine Duffy
Kathleen Dunn
Paula Dunn
Laurence Dunst
Jim Durfee
Tina Dyes
Charles Eaton
Shannon Edwards
Victoria Eichinger
Bernadette Elias
Arthur Einstein
Jodi Evans
Keith Evans
Nancy Fairstone
Suzanne Falter
Meryl Fandman
Sherie Fas
Beth Federici
Gene Federico
Oksana Fedorenko
Bob Feig
Stephen Feinberg
Kerry Feuerman
Corinne Felder
Steve Feldman
Jerry Della Femina
Sarah Fendrick
Jerry Fields
Peggy Fields
Carole Anne Fine
Chuck Finkel
Carol Fiorino
Kathleen Fitzgerald
Marieve Fitzmaurice-Page
Daniel Flamberg
Susan Flynn
John Follis
Joyce Fox
Mel Freedman
Gay French
Kenneth Funk
Harvey Gabor
Bob Gage
Bertrand Garbassi

Amil Gargano
Thomas Garrett
Paul Gary
Robert Gerardi
Jan Gerding
Gary Geyer
Dona Gibbs
Frank Ginsberg
Jerry Giordano
Nina Glabman
Sharon Glazer
Rich Godfrey
Allison Gold
Leslie Goldberg
Amy Goldman
Charles Goldman
David Goldring
Jo Ann Goldsmith
Mark Goldstein
Nancy Goldstein
Todd Godwin
Alberto Gonzalez
Milt Gossett
Gary Graf
Herbert Graf
Alison Grant
John Grant
Donald Green
Paula Green
F. Sterling Grey
Dick Grider
Josclynne Grier
Mary Gross
Siegfried Gross
Brenda Seidler Guber
Olivia Gushin
Gary Gusick
Susan Gwardyak
Brown Hagood
Roberg Haigh
Jim Hallowes
Barbara Hamilton
Keith Harmeyer
Linda Harris
Joel Harrison
Nancy Hauptman
Karen Hawkins
Mary-Lynn Hedison
William Heinrich
Joan Helfman
Roy Herbert
Rony Herz
Joan Orlian Hillman
Peter Hirsch
Barri Lynn Hollander
Sandra Holtzman

Anna Horvat
Hugh Hough
Liz Howe
Mike Hughes
Kate Humphrey
Jeff Hunter
David Inana
George Jaccoma
Ellen Jacobs
Harry Jacobs Jr.
Corrin Jacobsen
Craig Jackson
Richard Jackson
Faith Johnson
Gary Johnson
Jean Johnson
James Johnston
Caroline Jones
Jennifer Jones
Jessica Josell
Charles Kane
Elizabeth Kaplan
Marshall Karp
Deborah Kasher
Linda Katz
Paul Kaufman
Richard Kaufman
Jane Kellner
Alison Kerner
Dana Warren King
Debra King
Nina Klein
Mary Kleve
Gary Kopervas
Lois Korey
Judy Kostuk
Stanley Kovics
Max Kovins
Denise Kresta
Helmut Krone
Andrew Krublit
Helen Kruger
Shep Kurnit
Henry Kwok
Eleanor Kyle
Janet LaCerra
Anthony La Petri
Larry Laiken
Lucille Landini
Andrew Langer
Deborah Langer
Patricia Sutula Langer
Doris Latino
Mary Wells Lawrence
Lisa Lebduska
Bruce Lee

Jean Lehman
Dany Lee Lennon
Robert Levenson
Robert Levers
Mark Levitt
Sharron Lewisy
Steven Libowitz
Lou Linder
Wallace Littman
Chana Locker
George Lois
Forrest Long
Allison Longo
Regina Lorenzo
Robert Lotterstein
Cecile Lozano
Peter Lubalin
Alden Ludlow III
Karen Lundstrem
David Luhn
Lisa Lurie
Ed McCabe
Ruth McCarthy
Bill McCullam
Ellie MacDougall
Malcolm MacDougall
Tom McElligott
Thomas McManus
Robert McPherson
Tony Macchia
Pamela Brooks Mace
Georgia Macris
Ira Madris
Joel Maliniak
Michael Mangano
Kathy Manuelian
Hope Manville
Howard Margulies
Hillary Martin
Marie Masciovecchio
Janice May
Mary Means
Leslie Stokes Mechanic
Jerome Meddick
Laura Meiselman
Sid Meltzer
Debra Mendel
Andy Merz
Mario Messina
Tom Messner
David Metcalf
Lyle Metzdorf
Lou Miano
Harold Michelson
Lucretia Miele
Mark Millar

Donald Miller
Matthew Miller
Pat Miller
Steven Miller
Jim Millman
Jonathan Mindell
Robert Mizrahi
Thomas Monahan
Kevin Mooney
Jeffrey Moore
Linda Morgenstern
Syl Morrone
Dina Morrongiello
Robert Mosconi
Norman Muchnick
Charles Mullen
Jeanne Chinard Mullen
Linda Mummiani
Ed Nagler
Thomas Nathan
James Nealey
Chris Nehlen
Bruce Nelson
Steve Nicholas
Bruce Nilson
Joyce Novotny
Madaleine Nulman
Coby O'Brian
Dick O'Brien
John O'Hara
Greg O'Neal
Joe O'Neill
Curvin O'Rielly
David Ogilvy
Bunmi Ojugbele
Don Olsen
Judy Olstein
Philip Orenstein
Sally Bond Ours
Maxine Paetro
Michelina Pagano
Rosemarie Pagano
Joanne Pateman
Mary Pax
Steve Penchina
Ellen Perless
Lynn Piasecki
David Piatowski
Dallene Pierce
Linda Pinero
Susan Pinke
Larry Plapler
Beth Player
Angelo Pocchia
Chris Pollock
Shirley Polykoff

Kay Pullen
Stan Quash
Elissa Querze
Brian Quinn
Douglas Raboy
Richard Raboy
Jim Raniere
Chris Ransick
Ted Regan
Michael Reid
Ann Reinertsen
Bob Reitzfeld
Robert Renk
Donn Resnick
Robert Resnick
Nancy Rice
Ruthann Richert
Cheryl Richman
Bruce Richter
Bill Ringler
Nancy Robbins
Judy Roberts
Anne Robertson
Peggy Robinson
Phyllis Robinson
Ashley Rogers
Ron Rosenfeld
Tom Rost
Mark Rothenberg
Carolyn Amorosi Rothseid
Leonard Ruben
Monique Rura
Dale Rushing
John Russo
Nat Russo
Trish Russoniello
Steve Rutter
Mike Rylander
Susan Sacks
Paul Safsel
Bonnie Salkow
Kenneth Sandbank
Laird Sanders
Jon Sandhaus
Harry Sandler
Neil Sanzari
Bob Sarlin
Herbert Satzman
Joanne Scannello
Carol Schaeffer
Agnes Schlenke
Joyce Schnaufer
Sy Schrekinger
Jay Schulberg
Craig Schwartz
Elsa Schwartz

Mary Schwartz
Nancy Schwartz
Robin Schwartz
Tom Schwartz
Lisa Schwartzman
Jamie Scott
Vicky Seidl
Melisse Shapiro
Amy Shaw
Renee Sheivachman
David Sherwood
Brett Shevack
Jamie Shevell
Jay Shmulevitz
Constantine Shoukas
Virgil Shutze
John Siddall
Katherine Siegmeth
Ronald Sigtermans
Jon Sills
Jon Silveira
Alan Silver
Sheralyn Silverstein
Ann Silvi
Susan Simmons
Karen Simon
Claudia Simpson
Tom Sinclair
Leonard Sirowitz
Bill Sklazie
George Slezak
Mike Slosberg
Chuck Smith
Gunther Smith
Jo Smith
Laurie Smith
Alan Solomon
Richard Solomon
Martin Solow
John Soltez
Dennis Soohoo
Blair Sorrel
Mark Spector
Susan Spelman
Helayne Spivak
Dean Stefanides
Robin Steinberg
Stan Stoj
Ray Stollerman
Ira Sturtevant
Andrea Stuzin
Len Sugarman
Tessa Super
Francis Szczesny
Norman Tanen
George Tannenbaum
Laura Tannenbaum
Jack Tauss
William Taylor
Donna Tedesco/Hartmann
Judy Teller
Marty Tempkin
Mike Tesch
Tom Thomas
Deepak Thosar
Daniel Tilles
Janice Tisch
Bill Tomlinson
James Tormey
Amy Tufel
Deborah Turner
Don Turner
Carol Turturro
Nancy Tynan
Diane Unger
Kathleen Unick
Ben Urman
William Uscatu
Sharon Vanderslice
Joan Van Der Veen
Margaret Van Sicklen
William Vartorella
Annette Vendryes
Ned Viseltear
Peter Vogt
Martha Voss
Nina Wachsman
Alita Wagner
Marvin Waldman
Teri Walker
Christopher Walther
Matt Warhaftig
Jane Warshaw
Nat Waterston
Wendy Wax
Mark Webb
Thomas Weber
Bruce Weinberg
Carol Weinfeld
Mary Weinraub
Riva Weinstein
Mimi Weisbond
Walter Weis
Paul Weiss
Mark Weitzman
Lynn Welsh
Bill Westbrook
David Wheeler
Anne Whitney
Richard Wilde
Clive Williamson
Cynthia Williamson
Kurt Willinger
Teresa Ann Willis
Tom Witt
Cindy Wojdyla
David Wojdyla
Connie Kail Wolf
Tracy Wong
Kenneth Woodard
Sandra Wright
Elizabeth Wynn
Terri Yenko
Joe Zagorski
Mark Zucker

GOLD, SILVER & BRONZE AWARDS

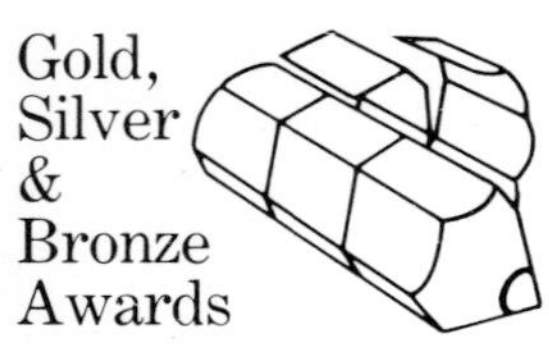

Consumer Newspaper Over 600 Lines: Single

1 GOLD
ART DIRECTOR
Bill Murphy
WRITER
Margaret Wilcox
PHOTOGRAPHER
Michael Pierce
CLIENT
The Boston Globe
AGENCY
Hill Holliday Connors Cosmopulos/Boston

2 SILVER
ART DIRECTOR
Helmut Krone
WRITER
Mike Rogers
CLIENT
Doyle Dane Bernbach
AGENCY
Doyle Dane Bernbach

3 BRONZE
ART DIRECTORS
Ted Barton
Geoff Roche
WRITER
Kirk Citron
PHOTOGRAPHER
Alan Krosnick
CLIENT
California Prune Board
AGENCY
Hal Riney & Partners/San Francisco

If you missed it on this empty page, imagine how easy it is to miss it in your kid's Halloween candy.

There. Up in the left hand corner. A pin. Just like the one your kids could bring home in a piece of their Halloween candy.

If you're going to find it before it finds your kid's mouth, you're going to have to look very carefully. Then look again. And not just for pins. For any breaks in a candy wrapper's surface.

Remember, when in doubt throw it out. Or your kids could get stuck with some Halloween candy they'll never forget.

The Boston Globe
A Public Affairs presentation of The Boston Globe.

1 GOLD

Some ads write themselves.

Gold Effies 1985

DOYLE DANE BERNBACH....14
Dancer Fitzgerald Sample....3
Advertising to Women....2
Bozell & Jacobs....2
Chiat/Day....2
D'Arcy MacManus Masius....2
NW Ayer....2
Ogilvy & Mather....2
Young & Rubicam....2
Benton & Bowles....1
Della Femina Travisano....1
Foote, Cone & Belding....1
J. Walter Thompson....1
keye/donna/pearlstein....1
Martin Agency....1
Moore, Hoch....1
Saatchi & Saatchi Compton....1
Shotwell....1
Siddall, Matus & Coughter....1
Smith Burke & Azzam....1
Ted Bates....1

Silver Effies

DOYLE DANE BERNBACH....7
Ogilvy & Mather....5
J. Walter Thompson....3
Young & Rubicam....3
BBDO....2
Grey....2
Mintz & Hoke....2
Patchen Brownfeld....2
Waring & LaRosa....2
W.B. Doner....2
Benton & Bowles....1
Bozell & Jacobs....1
Burton-Campbell....1
Campbell-Ewald....1
Cramer-Krasselt....1
Cunningham & Walsh....1
Dancer Fitzgerald Sample....1
Koehler Iversen....1
Kolker & Gill....1
Marschalk....1
McCann-Erickson....1
Metcalf....1
NW Ayer....1
Pringle Dixon Pringle....1
Salvati Montgomery Sakoda....1
Scali McCabe Sloves....1
Sieber & McIntyre....1
Tucker Wayne....1
William Esty....1

Bronze Effies

DOYLE DANE BERNBACH....7
SSC&B....4
NW Ayer....3
Benton & Bowles....2
Della Femina Travisano....2
Grey....2
J. Walter Thompson....2
Young & Rubicam....2
Ally & Gargano....1
Altschiller Reitzfeld Solin....1
BBDO....1
Clarity Coverdale....1
Dancer Fitzgerald Sample....1
Eisner....1
Epstein Raboy....1
Healy-Schutte & Comstock....1
Ketchum....1
Lott Walker....1
Marschalk....1
Mintz & Hoke....1
Needham Harper....1
Noble....1
Ogilvy & Mather....1
Price/McNabb....1
Saatchi & Saatchi Compton....1
Sage Marcom....1
Sieber & McIntyre....1
Stephan....1
Ted Bates....1

2 SILVER

There are five types of fiber your body uses. Here are four of them.

By now, you probably know most Americans don't eat enough fiber.

But what you may not have realized is that there's more than one kind.

And variety is important. Because your body actually uses five different types of dietary fiber. Cellulose, hemicellulose, lignin, pectin, and gums.

The first four are all found in the California prune. Which means prunes are a great way to balance your fiber diet.

Prunes are also one of the richest sources of fiber—they have nine grams per serving. Six prunes have more fiber than two bowls of bran flakes.*

And prunes are high in potassium. They're a good source of vitamin A. And they have no fat, no cholesterol, and almost no sodium. Not to mention a sweet, delicious, one-of-a-kind taste.

So if you've been trying to get more fiber in your diet, try prunes. Fiber never tasted so good.

*2/3 cup per serving

One way to serve your family prunes is in a fruit plate. You'll find more helpful serving suggestions in our free brochure. For your copy, write to Prune Ideas, P.O. Box 882168, San Francisco, CA 94188-2168

© CALIFORNIA PRUNE BOARD 1985

Prunes. The high fiber fruit.

3 BRONZE

Gold, Silver & Bronze Awards

Consumer Newspaper Over 600 Lines: Campaign

4 GOLD
ART DIRECTOR
Jerry Whitley
WRITERS
Mark Silveira
Joe O'Neill
PHOTOGRAPHERS
Jeffrey Zwart
Leon Kuzmanoff
CLIENT
BMW of North America
AGENCY
Ammirati & Puris

BMW PROVES THERE'S LIFE AFTER THE FIFTY PERCENT BRACKET.

Contrary to popular belief, all the members of the so-called "leisure class" do not pursue life at an entirely leisurely pace. Nor, for that matter, is all of the old money in old hands.

Thus, the shining examples of two- and four-wheeled wish fulfillment you see here.

The automobile, BMW's new 635CSi, you will probably recognize as the successor to the much-acclaimed 633CSi. The grand touring coupe AutoWeek once described as "the class of the field in a field of one."

A distinction that will doubtlessly endure, given the 635CSi's larger engine displacement and revised rear axle ratio. Both of which contribute to increased acceleration. And, working in concert with the coupe's fully independent suspension and ABS anti-lock braking system, make it, perhaps, the world's most elegant and well-mannered means of negotiating the fast lane.

Beside it, however, is a vehicle you may find somewhat less familiar. Unless you've recently been on the Continent, where BMW's new K100 RS was recently named Motorcycle of the Year in no less than five countries.

This is a motorcycle that gives new meaning to the expression "upwardly mobile." Possessing, as it does, a 4-cylinder engine that produces "a seamless crescendo of power" (Motorcyclist). Along with handling that "makes directional changes mere mentally inspired flicks" (Popular Science).

Of course, in neither case are these vehicles meant to be purchased solely as a means of transportation. But rather, they are for those individuals who find that, having provided for the family, the future and (albeit unwillingly) the federal budget, there are funds remaining for experiences of pure transport.

THE ULTIMATE DRIVING MACHINE.

4 GOLD

FOR THOSE WHO KNOW THE VALUE OF A DOLLAR, A CAR THAT JUSTIFIES SPENDING FORTY THOUSAND OF THEM.

The old adage, "If you have to ask what it costs, you can't afford it," seems to be rapidly slipping out of date.

And with it, a certain breed of luxury car whose lavish prices have always

gone unquestioned.

Today's enlightened car buyer not only is asking "How much?" but "Why so much?" A state of affairs that has left many car makers groping for answers. And placed a record number of buyers behind the wheel of a BMW 735i.

THE DIFFERENCE BETWEEN A CLASSIC CAR AND A DATED CAR.

Peer beneath the glimmering hood ornaments and multilayered enamel of certain age-old status symbols and you'll unveil a car that is just that: age-old.

Examine the inner workings of a BMW 735i and you'll find quite the reverse.

Its new 3.5-liter engine is the successor to a power plant that Road & Track hailed as "the most refined in-line six in the world."

Working in tandem with that engine is the third generation of an electronic fuel management system that, in its original state, was among the world's most advanced. So advanced, it was used to govern the BMW engine that powered a Formula One champion race car.

The result? A veritable paradox—a six-cylinder automobile that is not only fuel-efficient* but also out-accelerates many eight-cylinder cars in its class.

A CAR THAT DOES NOT ACCEPT THE INEVITABLE.

BMW engineers are passionate believers in the theory that, in driving, "forewarned is forearmed."

They've endowed the new 735i with an electronic Service Interval Indicator that signals you the moment service is recommended.

With an onboard computer that informs you of everything from range on remaining fuel to the potential of road icing.

With an ABS braking system that helps provide you with infinitely more control over your fate during stopping. A system that helps prevent the wheels from locking (a prime cause of skidding) and enables steering even in panic stops. One whose concept has been applied not just on roadways but on runways where, day-in and day-out, it brings the most sophisticated passenger jet aircraft to a controlled, secure halt.

Does the BMW 735i possess the luxuries befitting a car in its price range? Indeed. It's just that the 735i's luxuries are not there in lieu of necessities.

You will find everything that one, in good taste, could require. Eight-way power seats of hand-stitched leather. Walnut paneling. A cockpit-like dash that sweeps out to meet you. A telescopically-adjustable steering column. Electrically-controlled right-and-left mirrors. An electrically-controlled, dual position sun roof.

The 735i is, in the end, a car that single-handedly justifies having expensive taste in cars.

An automobile that doesn't require rationalizations for its lofty $40,000 purchase price** because it comes fully equipped with a long list of superbly engineered reasons.

A list that your BMW dealer will be more than pleased to continue at your earliest convenience.

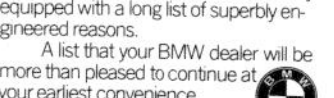

AS LONG AS THERE ARE PEOPLE WHO CAN AFFORD PERFECTION, BMW WILL CONTINUE TO PURSUE IT.

"Life," the accountants often say, "is a series of compromises."

If you can afford to ignore this wisdom, BMW would like to draw your attention to a car that disdains it, too: the new 635CSi sports coupe.

Justifiably priced at about $40,000,* the BMW 635CSi demonstrates precisely what can be achieved when automotive engineers are free from the usual cost constraints and the importunities of mass production.

And when, of course, they have an ideal worth pursuing in the first place.

THE GRAND COUPE THAT IS UNABASHEDLY GRAND.

In the case of the 635CSi, the ideal is an aristocratic one: the European Grand Touring tradition, combining uncommon style and luxury with definitive performance.

The BMW 635CSi manages to fulfill the first two criteria even before you turn the ignition key.

Its finely honed body panels and exterior surfaces, meticulously hand-fitted and hand-examined, add up to a virtually objective definition of automotive beauty. "As automotive sculpture, it's a Rodin" (Road & Track magazine).

Its amenities include supple hand-stitched leather seats, an electronic two-way sunroof, and cockpit-like ergonomics. "And everything is put together as if lives depended on the coupe's solidity" (Car and Driver).

Its front and rear carpeting is a molded single piece for a perfectly tailored fit. Even its trunk is lined and plushly carpeted on the notion that fine objects are carried in a fine car.

However, it's when you actually turn the ignition key that you discover exactly how far the 635CSi advances the cause of Grand Touring.

BMW ENHANCES GOING AND STOPPING ALIKE.

The BMW coupe's new 3.5-liter, fuel-injected engine propels it from 0 to 60 in 7.8 seconds. A prowess abetted by the latest generation of BMW's Digital Motor Electronics, which sustains peak performance by adjusting fuel delivery and ignition timing literally hundreds of times a second. As well as via a new rear-axle ratio that further improves acceleration.

Because stopping is just as important as going, however, we'd like to call your attention to another new 635CSi feature: a computerized ABS anti-lock braking system.

Operating on the same principle that brings 287-ton 747 jet aircraft to a safe, secure halt, the ABS system helps prevent the brakes from locking. Thus, permitting the car to be maneuvered even during emergency stops. And, equally important, even on rain-slicked or icy roadways.

The new 635CSi, in sum, serves to confirm the BMW coupe's position as "the benchmark" without which "you won't know how to judge anything else" (AutoWeek magazine).

And, not incidentally, the managerial astuteness of a car company where even the head of finance is an engineer.

A handful are at your nearby BMW dealers now, awaiting automotive enthusiasts who also do not have to report to accountants.

THE ULTIMATE DRIVING MACHINE.

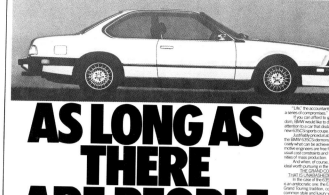

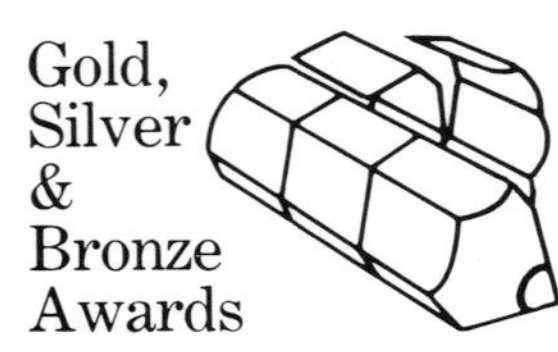

Gold,
Silver
&
Bronze
Awards

Consumer Newspaper Over 600 Lines: Campaign

5 SILVER
ART DIRECTORS
Ted Barton
Geoff Roche
WRITER
Kirk Citron
PHOTOGRAPHERS
J. Stainsbury
Alan Krosnick
Bernard Phillips
Laurie Rubin
CLIENT
California Prune Board
AGENCY
Hal Riney & Partners/San Francisco

There are five types of fiber your body uses. Here are four of them.

By now, you probably know most Americans don't eat enough fiber.

But what you may not have realized is that there's more than one kind.

And variety is important. Because your body actually uses five different types of dietary fiber. Cellulose, hemicellulose, lignin, pectin, and gums.

The first four are all found in the California prune. Which means prunes are a great way to balance your fiber diet.

Prunes are also one of the richest sources of fiber—they have nine grams per serving. Six prunes have more fiber than two bowls of bran flakes.*

And prunes are high in potassium. They're a good source of vitamin A. And they have no fat, no cholesterol, and almost no sodium. Not to mention a sweet, delicious, one-of-a-kind taste.

So if you've been trying to get more fiber in your diet, try prunes. Fiber never tasted so good.

One way to serve your family prunes is in a fruit plate. You'll find more helpful serving suggestions in our free brochure. For your copy, write to Prune Ideas, P.O. Box 882168, San Francisco, CA 94188-2168.

*2/3 cup per serving.

Prunes. The high fiber fruit.

5 SILVER

Some news about fiber you'll find easy to swallow.

California prunes are dried plums.
That's what makes them such a sweet way to get fiber.

You've heard a lot of news lately about fiber. How it's good for your health. How a high-fiber, low-fat diet may reduce the risk of some kinds of cancer.*

Unfortunately, most high fiber foods just aren't very appetizing.

There is, however, a sweet way to get fiber. A bowl of prunes.

Prunes have more dietary fiber, ounce-for-ounce, than almost any other food. A serving of six prunes has more fiber than two bowls of bran flakes.

The difference is, prunes are a spoonful of natural sweetness. Which means they're fiber you can actually enjoy.

And there's more. Prunes also give you potassium, vitamin A, no fat, no cholesterol, and almost no sodium.

One way to serve your family prunes is at breakfast. You'll find more serving suggestions in our free brochure. Write to Prune Ideas, 103 World Trade Center, San Francisco, California 94111.

**According to the National Cancer Institute, NIH publication No. 85-77111.*

So if you'd like to get more fiber in your diet, remember. Good nutrition doesn't have to put your taste buds to sleep.

Prunes. The high fiber fruit.

Which has the most fiber?

We'll give you a little hint. The fruit with the most fiber isn't a banana. Or an apple. Or an orange, a peach or a pear.

It's the humble prune. Which has more dietary fiber than almost any fruit— or any food—you can name.

To get the same dietary fiber as a serving of six prunes,

ORANGES have 2.6 grams of fiber per serving.
PEARS have 3.8 grams of fiber per serving.
BANANAS have 4.1 grams of fiber per serving.
PRUNES have 9.3 grams of fiber per serving.
PEACHES have 1.4 grams of fiber per serving.
APPLES have 3.0 grams of fiber per serving.

you'd have to eat four slices of whole wheat bread. Or six peaches. Or three apples. Or two and a half bowls of bran flakes.

And prunes don't just have fiber. They're one of the richest sources of potassium, and a good source of Vitamin A. With no fat, no cholesterol, almost no sodium, and a delicious, one-of-a-kind taste.

All of which makes prunes one of the most nutritious fruits you can buy.

One way to serve your family prunes is at breakfast. They're delicious stewed, with a cinnamon stick and a slice of lemon. You'll find more helpful serving suggestions in our free brochure. For your copy, write to Prune Ideas, 103 World Trade Center, San Francisco, CA 94111.

So if you're looking for a sweet way to get more fiber in your diet, try California prunes.

Proof, once again, that good things come in small packages.

Prunes. The high fiber fruit.

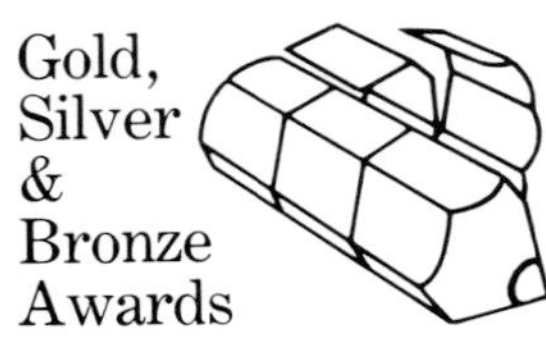

Consumer Newspaper Over 600 Lines: Campaign

6 BRONZE
ART DIRECTORS
Michael Fazende
Tom Lichtenheld
WRITERS
Bill Miller
Rod Kilpatrick
John Stingley
PHOTOGRAPHERS
Carl Fischer
Buck Holzemer
Bettman Archives
CLIENT
American Association of Advertising Agencies
AGENCY
Fallon McElligott/Minneapolis

PEOPLE HAVE BEEN TRYING TO FIND THE BREASTS IN THESE ICE CUBES SINCE 1957.

The advertising industry has been accused of many things over the years. Among them, witchcraft.

Whether it's called "subliminal advertising" or "hidden persuasion," the gist of the accusation is always the same.

Advertisers are charged with sneaking seductive little pictures into their ads. It's claimed that these pictures can somehow get you to buy a product without your even seeing them.

Consider the photograph above. According to some people, there's a pair of female breasts hidden in the patterns of light refracted by the ice cubes.

Well, if you looked hard enough and long enough you probably *could* find the breasts. For that matter, you could also find Millard Fillmore, a stuffed pork chop and a 1946 Dodge.

It's a bit like looking at the night sky. If you squint your eyes and your imagination just right, you can see constellations. But regardless of what you see, they're really just stars.

In the same way, our ads are just ads. They're intended to inform, not hypnotize. And we wouldn't waste your time or ours with such laughable nonsense as subliminal images.

So if anyone claims to see breasts in that drink up there, they aren't in the ice cubes.

They're in the eye of the beholder.

ADVERTISING
ANOTHER WORD FOR FREEDOM OF CHOICE.
American Association of Advertising Agencies.

6 BRONZE

DESPITE WHAT SOME PEOPLE THINK, ADVERTISING CAN'T MAKE YOU BUY SOMETHING YOU DON'T NEED.

Some people would have you believe that you are putty in the hands of every advertiser in the country.

They think that when advertising is put under your nose, your mind turns to oatmeal.

It's mass hypnosis. Subliminal seduction. Brain washing. Mind control. It's advertising.

And you are a pushover for it.

It explains why your kitchen cupboard is full of food you never eat.

Why your garage is full of cars you never drive.

Why your house is full of books you don't read, TV's you don't watch, beds you don't use, and clothes you don't wear.

You don't have a choice. You are forced to buy.

That's why this message is a cleverly disguised advertisement to get you to buy land in the tropics.

Got you again, didn't we? Send in your money.

ADVERTISING

ANOTHER WORD FOR FREEDOM OF CHOICE.

American Association of Advertising Agencies

HOWEVER POWERFUL A MESSAGE IS, SOME PEOPLE MAY NOT BUY IT.

People have an overwhelming tendency to question what they're told. Even when it's cast in stone.

That's what makes us human. We make our own decisions. Sometimes right. Sometimes wrong. But always our own.

So it's hard to believe when people claim that advertising made them buy something they didn't want.

Sure, we'd like to think that the advertising we create has a powerful impact on you.

But the truth is we simply present facts. Try to make them interesting and entertaining. Then sit back and hope we got through.

As for having some kind of power over people's actions, greater forces than the advertising industry have tried.

And God only knows, no one does everything they're told.

ADVERTISING

ANOTHER WORD FOR FREEDOM OF CHOICE.

American Association of Advertising Agencies

Gold, Silver & Bronze Awards

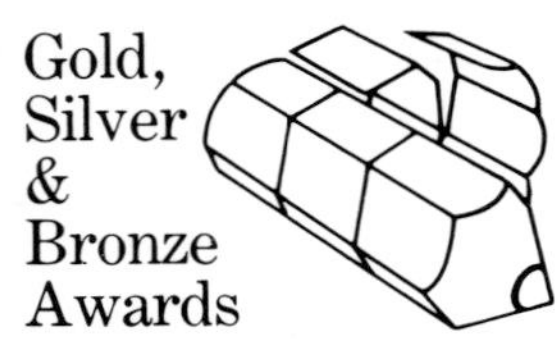

Consumer Newspaper 600 Lines Or Less: Single

7 GOLD
ART DIRECTOR
Tony Angotti
WRITER
Tom Thomas
DESIGNER
Tony Angotti
PHOTOGRAPHER
Robert Ammirati
CLIENT
Barron's
AGENCY
Angotti Thomas Hedge

8 SILVER
ART DIRECTORS
Bob Phillips
Jeff Vogt
WRITER
Mark Silveira
DESIGNER
Bob Phillips
PHOTOGRAPHER
Jeffrey Zwart
ARTIST
R & V Studio
CLIENT
BMW of North America
AGENCY
Ammirati & Puris

9 BRONZE
ART DIRECTOR
Jerry Gentile
WRITER
Barbara DeSantis
CLIENT
Adventist Health System
AGENCY
Doyle Dane Bernbach/Los Angeles

Let wealth pursue you for a change.

Subscribe to Barron's.

Every week we'll bring to your doorstep the earnings updates, company reports, market analysis, interviews and technical data you need to make better decisions.

Which can help make the difference between pursuing wealth and catching up with it.

See for yourself by picking up a copy at a newsstand this weekend. And to subscribe, call 800-345-8501 (in PA, 800-662-5180).*

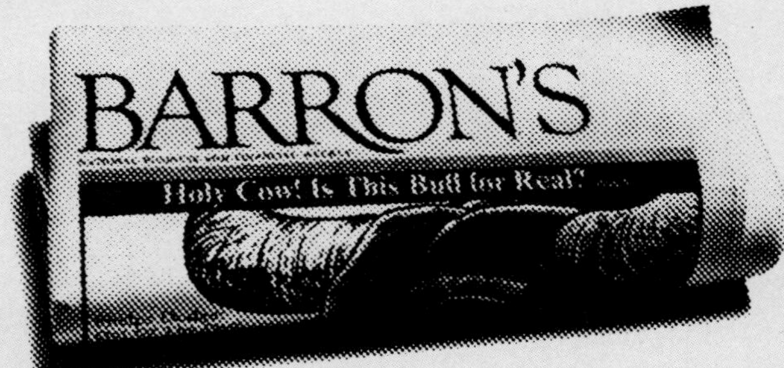

HOW THE SMART MONEY GETS THAT WAY.

*In the continental U.S. only.
© 1986 DOW JONES & COMPANY, INC.

7 GOLD

THE LUXURY SEDAN THAT MADE RADAR DETECTORS A MULTIMILLION DOLLAR INDUSTRY.

Some automobiles inspire comment. Others praise. But precious few spawn entire industries.

Yet such would seem to be the case with the nearly simultaneous appearance of a boom in radar detectors and the now legendary BMW 5-Series.

But then, what choice does a car like the 535i leave the spirited driver? Those drivers who, in the immortal words of a famous actress, "can resist anything...except temptation."

Temptation which here takes the form of BMW's exuberant 3.5-liter in-line six. A power plant fully capable of accelerating beyond the current national speed limit in a mere 7.7 seconds.

Exhilarating performance that's perfectly mated to the fully independent suspension system Motor Trend simply calls "a delight." Performance that's governed by a microprocessor-based engine management system. And reined in by BMW's ABS anti-lock braking system.

But despite the 535i's clear performance bias, inside it's every bit a luxury sedan. Replete with leather seats, every conceivable power-assist feature, and a new, high-performance sound system.

All of which should provide more than ample incentive to hurry (observing all local speed limits, please) to your authorized BMW dealer.

For a driving experience so utterly satisfying, some might say, there ought to be a law.

THE ULTIMATE DRIVING MACHINE.

LET YOUR LOCAL BMW DEALERS ARRANGE A THOROUGH TEST DRIVE.

City	City	City	City	City	City
DEALER NAME	**DEALER NAME**	**DEALER NAME**	**DEALER NAME**	**DEALER NAME**	**DEALER NAME**
Dealer Address	Dealer Address	Dealer Address	Dealer Address	Dealer Address	Dealer Address
Phone Number	Phone Number	Phone Number	Phone Number	Phone Number	Phone Number

8 SILVER

What happens after "after"?

Before

After

?

You've seen the ads. Read the testimonials. Heard the tales of pounds shed painlessly; figures streamlined overnight.

They're good stories. Except for the endings. Because four out of five dieters eventually gain back all the weight they lose—and more.

You can get off the see-saw: with the Weight Program at St. Helena Hospital. We don't promise miracles. Just a workable plan that can take weight off for good. So give us a call at (800) 862-7575. We'll give you before-and-after story a very happy ending.

THE WEIGHT PROGRAM AT:
St. Helena
HOSPITAL AND HEALTH CENTER OF NAPA VALLEY

9 BRONZE

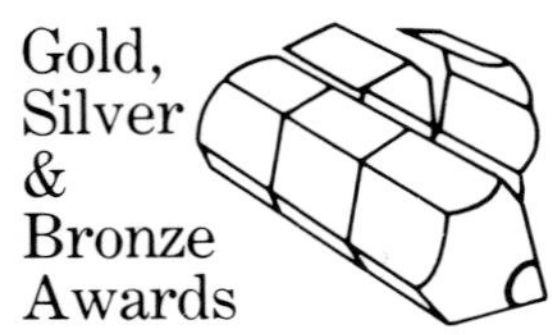

Consumer Newspaper 600 Lines Or Less: Campaign

10 GOLD
ART DIRECTOR
Michael Fazende
WRITER
Phil Hanft
CLIENT
Country Cottage
AGENCY
Fallon McElligott/Minneapolis

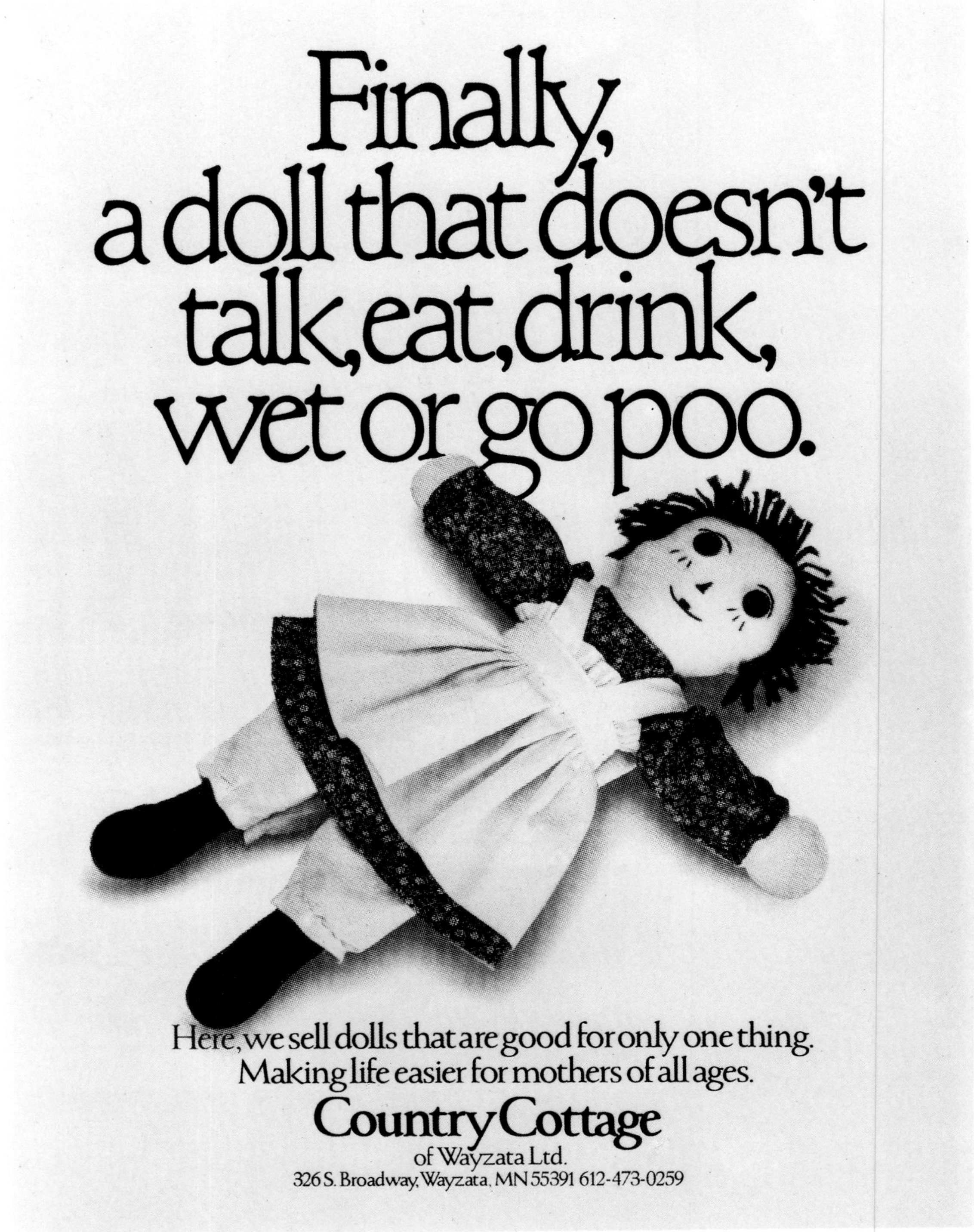

Finally, a doll that doesn't talk, eat, drink, wet or go poo.

Here, we sell dolls that are good for only one thing.
Making life easier for mothers of all ages.

Country Cottage
of Wayzata Ltd.
326 S. Broadway, Wayzata, MN 55391 612-473-0259

10 GOLD

We take plastic. We don't sell it.

Here, we prefer to live in the past. But due to overwhelming pressure from many of our customers, we have made one concession to the present. Visa, American Express and MasterCard.

Country Cottage
of Wayzata Ltd.
326 S. Broadway, Wayzata, MN 55391 612-473-0259

For under $40 you too can have an odd duck in your family.

Even the most perfect families need their resident quacks. Something a little different, but not strange enough to hide in a closet.

Country Cottage
of Wayzata Ltd.
326 S. Broadway, Wayzata, MN 55391 612-473-0259

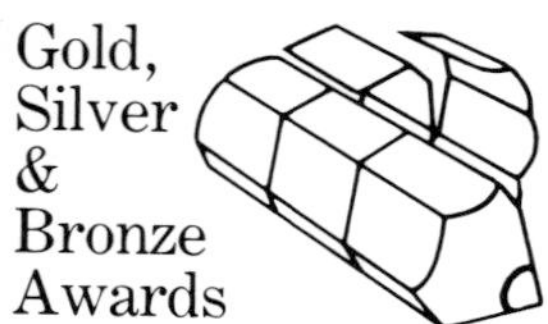

Consumer Newspaper 600 Lines Or Less: Campaign

11 SILVER
ART DIRECTORS
John Morrison
Steve Beaumont
WRITER
David Lubars
ARTIST
Cynthia Shern
PHOTOGRAPHERS
Lamb & Hall
CLIENT
Apple Computer
AGENCY
Chiat/Day - Los Angeles

How to break into the library.

It's the middle of the night. You're working on your paper, "Identifying Kafkaesque Symbolism In The Film, 'Porky's II: The Next Day.'" You have no idea who Kafka is. You need information. Your library is closed. You'll get an F. You are depressed.

Don't be.

Because with a Macintosh™ and an Apple® Modem, you can access databanks and receive information worldwide. Not to mention scour the Library of Congress at 3 am.

Which just goes to show, Macintosh helps students work smarter, quicker and more creatively. And the beauty of Macintosh is, you don't have to know diddley about computers to use one.

So get a Macintosh. And head straight for the library.

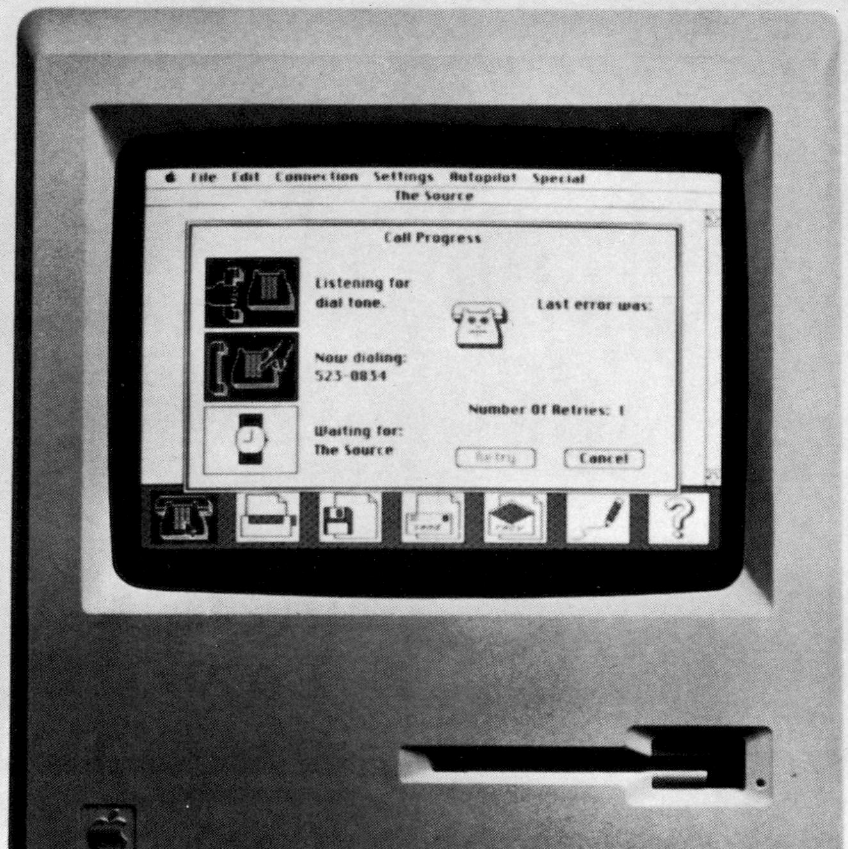

11 SILVER

Bring order to the Middle East.

If your term paper on The Middle East Crisis is suffering its own border skirmishes, we recommend a Macintosh.™

With programs like Think Tank,™ you can build exhaustively detailed outlines that prevent the rewriting and retyping that can turn a six day war into a three month project.

Another example of how Macintosh helps students work smarter, quicker and more creatively.

And the beauty of Macintosh is, you don't have to know diddley about computers to use one. If only Kissinger had it this easy.

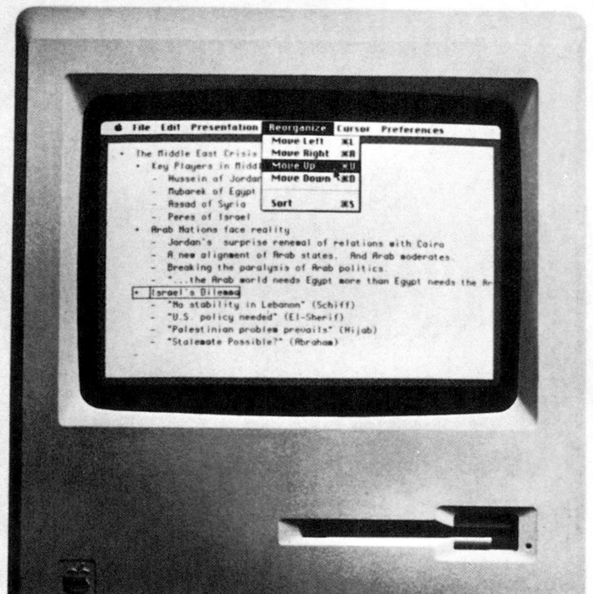

Use it to alter your grades.

You just got a C+ in *Post-War Foreign Policy.* You just got a B— in *Communications Law.* You just got an F+ in *Advanced Physics.*

An F+? Boy, you could use some help.

From a Macintosh™ personal computer.

A Macintosh can help you with your homework. Help you with your term papers. Help you with your research projects. And help you organize your study time and think more clearly.

And at last count, Macintosh could run hundreds of software programs to help you with everything from linguistics to law. Physics to philosophy. Medicine to Medieval history.

The point being, when you bring a Macintosh home with you, there's a good chance you'll be bringing home something else. Better grades.

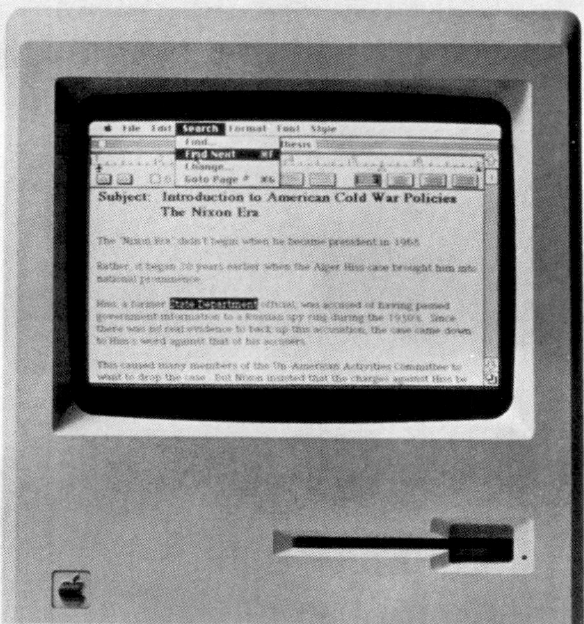

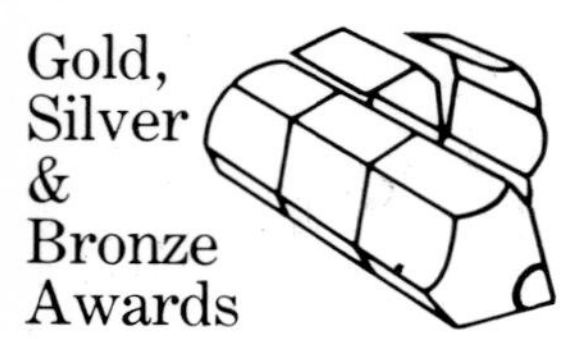

Consumer Newspaper 600 Lines Or Less: Campaign

12 BRONZE
ART DIRECTOR
Bob Barrie
WRITER
Mike Lescarbeau
CLIENT
Mountain Chiropractic
AGENCY
Fallon McElligott/Minneapolis

What kind of slouch won't see a chiropractor?

Delaying treatment for a back injury can be as harmful as the injury itself. Don't put it off. Call Mountain Chiropractic. Because if your back feels like it's killing you, maybe it is.

Mountain Chiropractic

104 N. Ash, Cortez, CO 565-7817 (T, Th); 3211 Main Ave., Durango, CO 259-6540 (M, W, F)

12 BRONZE

Back again?

Chronic back pain can be a sign of serious health problems anywhere in the body. Come to Mountain Chiropractic for a complete examination. We'll break our backs to fix yours.

Mountain Chiropractic

104 N. Ash, Cortez, CO 565-7817 (T, Th); 3211 Main Ave., Durango, CO 259-6540 (M, W, F)

We refurbish run-down joints.

Proper chiropractic treatment can make you look and feel good all over. Call Mountain Chiropractic and let us make a joint effort on your behalf.

Mountain Chiropractic

104 N. Ash, Cortez, CO 565-7817 (T, Th); 3211 Main Ave., Durango, CO 259-6540 (M, W, F)

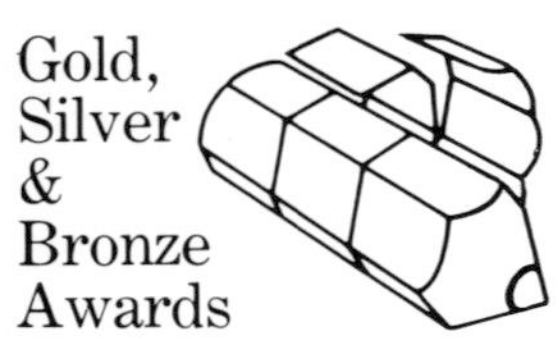

Gold, Silver & Bronze Awards

Consumer Magazine B/W: 1 Page Or Spread Including Magazine Supplements

13 GOLD
ART DIRECTOR
Frank Haggerty
WRITER
Jack Supple
ARTIST
Larry Tople
CLIENT
Blue Fox Tackle Company
AGENCY
Carmichael-Lynch/
Minneapolis

14 SILVER
ART DIRECTOR
Michael Fazende
WRITER
Mike Lescarbeau
PHOTOGRAPHER
Craig Perman
CLIENT
American Association of
Advertising Agencies
AGENCY
Fallon McElligott/Minneapolis

15 BRONZE
ART DIRECTORS
Don Easdon
Ralph Moxley
WRITER
Bill Heater
PHOTOGRAPHER
Larry Robbins
CLIENT
John Hancock
AGENCY
Hill Holliday Connors
Cosmopulos/Boston

THE MAN WHO CATCHES FISH ON A SHRED OF CLOTH.

This extraordinarily true story is based on one simple fact. In the jungles of Central America, you do not fish for fun. You fish to catch fish. And this is how you do it.

THE BEST KEPT SECRET IN FISHING. UNTIL DR. JUICE GOT A WHIFF OF IT.

Dr. Gregory Bambanek, discoverer of "Dr. Juice," has learned how to dial in the elements of scent to provoke feeding.

In 1978, an American anthropologist named Dr. Gregory Bambanek, M.D. was studying the primitive people of Central America. They are the mixed blood descendants of English pirates, Mayan Indians and African slaves. There is powerful magic there.

He befriended the medicine man, Dzacar, who not only healed the sick but kept the healthy well-fed. In this meat-poor tribe, Dzacar was the number one fisherman.

Dzacar's magic was in his uncanny ability to catch fish on nothing but a hook, line and a shred of cloth. With this unlikely rig, he would pole out into the tropical river and return with snook, tarpon and bandarootoo.

One drop of Dr. Juice Fish Scent attracts gamefish and camouflages human scent.

It was one such night that Dr. Gregory Bambanek, himself a fisherman, went along with Dzacar and first got a whiff of the potent stuff Dzacar had on that lure.

ONE DROP IS DETECTABLE IN A 30,000 GALLON POOL.

What Bambanek brought home was a secret formulation of scents derived from living jungle plants, fish and animals. Back in America, in his laboratory, he analyzed the chemical makeup of the potion.

Kairomones were the scientific base of the formula. To the gamefish, this hormonal substance indicates a living organism such as live baitfish.

By dialing in other hormonal "communicators" he found he could send other messages like a hot line to the fish's brain.

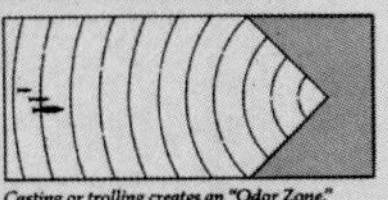

Casting or trolling creates an "Odor Zone."

He added *Fear Pheromones*, the smell of fear given off by prey species that attracts and excites predators. He added *Schooling Pheromones*, the scent baitfish use to home in on their school and gamefish use to find them. He added traces of *Sex Pheromones* which, in small doses, make gamefish very aggressive and territorial.

And finally, he added *Attractant Amino Acids* which camouflage the repellent scent of human finger prints without alerting the fish to any smell out of the ordinary.

Incredibly, in a dilution of one part per 10,000,000,000, Dr. Juice Fish Scent will register its powerful messages of food, fear and sexual aggression deep in the fish's brain, triggering the desired strike response.

PICK UP THE SCENTS THE FISH DO.

Dr. Juice Fish Scents are a total approach to attracting and triggering fish that will significantly improve the size of your catch.

Outdoor Life called it, "a far cry from the run-of-the-mill, anise oil based, licorice-smelling fish 'attractors.'"

One drop squeezed onto a bare lure will remain potent for as long as an hour. And with "Juicers," the special time release tabs of cloth, the scent will not wash away for as long as 3 hours.

At that rate, one 30 gram bottle should last you one whole season. Or one whole village.

Look for Dr. Juice One Drop Fish Scent in your tackle stores.

Available in 9 formulations for the 9 most popular species of gamefish. Unless you have a taste for bandarootoo.

DR. JUICE ONE DROP FISH SCENT.

13 GOLD

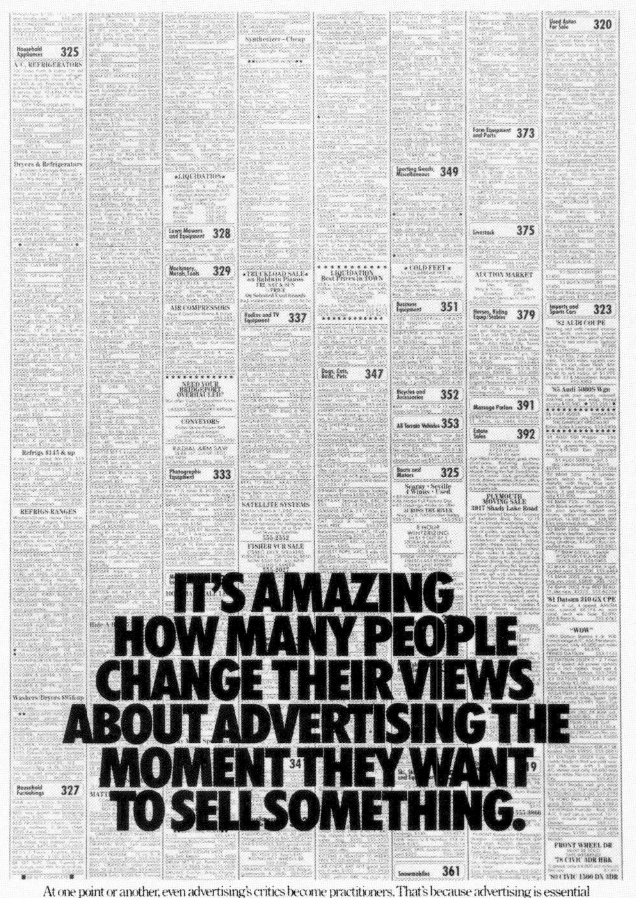

14 SILVER

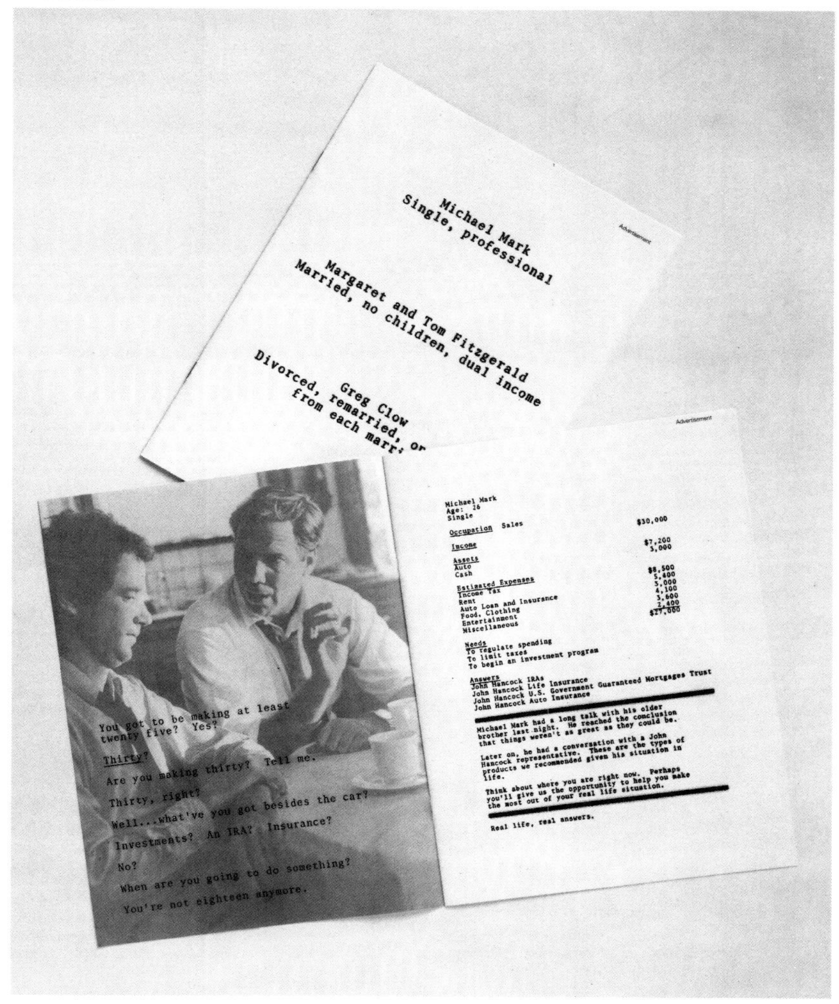

15 BRONZE

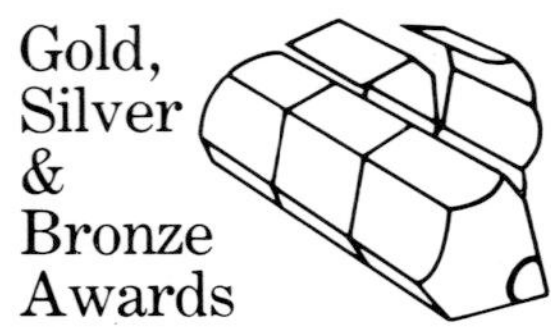

Consumer Magazine Color: 1 Page Or Spread Including Magazine Supplements

16 GOLD
ART DIRECTORS
Charlie Piccirillo
Matt Rao
WRITER
Barry Greenspon
PHOTOGRAPHER
Chuck Lamonica
CLIENT
Chivas Regal
AGENCY
Doyle Dane Bernbach

17 SILVER
ART DIRECTOR
Jerry Whitley
WRITER
Joe O'Neill
DESIGNER
William Hartwell
PHOTOGRAPHER
Jeffrey Zwart
CLIENT
BMW of North America
AGENCY
Ammirati & Puris

18 BRONZE
ART DIRECTORS
Gerald Andelin
Bruce Campbell
WRITER
Hal Riney
PHOTOGRAPHER
Jim Wood Photography
CLIENT
E&J Gallo Winery
AGENCY
Hal Riney & Partners/San Francisco

12 YEARS OLD WORLDWIDE • BLENDED SCOTCH WHISKY • 86 PROOF
© 1985 375 SPIRITS COMPANY. NEW YORK, N.Y.

CHIVAS REGAL
FOUNDED 1801
BLENDED SCOTCH WHISKY

Who says you can't get a great bottle of Scotch for under $5?

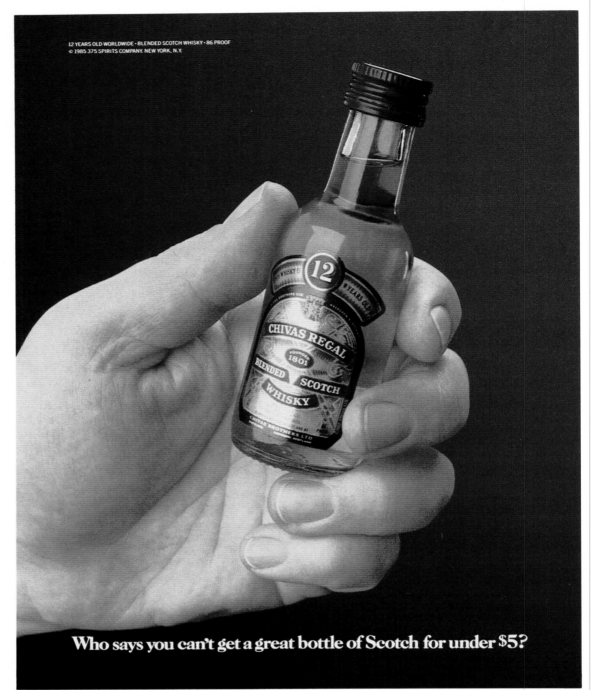

16 GOLD

PANIC IS A HUMAN TRAIT. CORRECTING IT IS A BMW'S.

Before today is over, a scenario like the one above is apt to take place.

The driver of the car, out of pure instinct, will probably jam on his brakes.

A perfectly normal reaction.

After the brakes lock, he'll try to steer clear of the truck.

Another perfectly normal reaction.

Perfectly normal, and yet, hopelessly wrong. Because once a car's brakes have locked, it is no longer possible to steer it.

It is precisely because of "normal" responses like these that every BMW is now equipped with a braking system designed, quite literally, to save a driver from himself. The ABS anti-lock system.

With ABS, no matter how hard you hit the brakes, electronic sensors automatically "pump" them—faster than humanly possible—and prevent locking.

This may not only help you elude an accident but also decreases stopping distances by up to 15% on dry roads. And by up to 40% on wet or icy roads.

But BMW's do more than react to emergencies. They help anticipate them.

The moment temperatures approach freezing, you'll be given notice by an onboard computer that sounds a warning.

Another system called Check Control alerts you to the fitness of everything from headlights to taillights to the brakes.

Yet another device advises you when routine service is recommended.

Every BMW is, in fact, a long list of such systems and devices—exquisitely melded into a car.

Your nearby BMW dealer will be happy to take you on a tour of these systems, as well as the surrounding neighborhood, by arranging a thorough and spirited test drive at your convenience.

In addition, comprehensive financing and leasing programs are now available at all participating BMW dealers through the BMW Credit Corporation.

THE ULTIMATE DRIVING MACHINE.

17 SILVER

Our neighborhood is the finest in the world.

But it's getting a little crowded.

Years ago, when Gallo first came to California's famed Sonoma and Napa growing regions, the neighborhood wasn't quite so crowded.

There were the Beaulieus, the Mondavis, and the Martinis.

And just over the hill, lived the Kenwoods.

But when the rest of the world discovered the extraordinary quality of our wine grapes from Sonoma County and the Napa Valley, we had folks moving in from just about everywhere.

Now there are the Heitzes, and the Jordans, and the Montelenas, and some folks with rather odd names, like the Duckhorns, and the Stag's Leaps.

Yet today, even though there are more folks around, Gallo still makes more wine with premium Sonoma and Napa grapes than any other vintner.

And we still continue to experiment with new strains of varietal grapes, better methods of growing our grapes, and improved harvesting and winemaking techniques, as we have since we first came here.

Because we're never satisfied with being just the same as folks next door.

We want to keep improving the neighborhood.

Today's Gallo.

18 BRONZE

Gold, Silver & Bronze Awards

Consumer Magazine B/W: Campaign Including Magazine Supplements

19 GOLD
ART DIRECTOR
Frank Haggerty
WRITER
Jack Supple
PHOTOGRAPHER
Gary Silberman
CLIENT
Blue Fox Tackle Company
AGENCY
Carmichael-Lynch/
Minneapolis

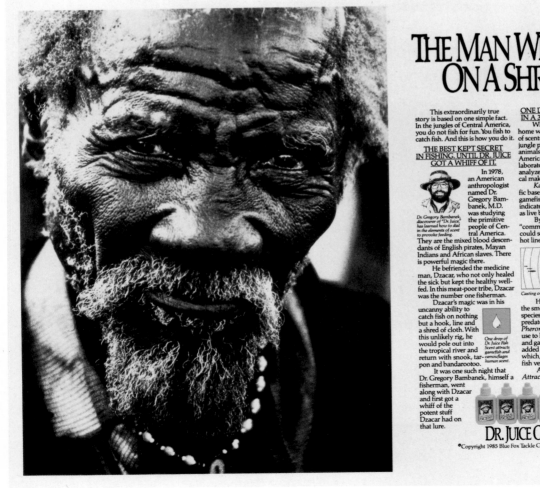

THE MAN WHO CATCHES FISH ON A SHRED OF CLOTH.

This extraordinarily true story is based on one simple fact. In the jungles of Central America, you do not fish for fun. You fish to catch fish. And this is how you do it.

THE BEST KEPT SECRET IN FISHING. UNTIL DR. JUICE GOT A WHIFF OF IT.

Dr. Gregory Bambanek, discoverer of "Dr. Juice," has learned how to dial in the elements of scent to provoke feeding.

In 1978, an American anthropologist named Dr. Gregory Bambanek, M.D. was studying the primitive people of Central America. They are the mixed blood descendants of English pirates, Mayan Indians and African slaves. There is powerful magic there.

He befriended the medicine man, Dzacar, who not only healed the sick but kept the healthy well-fed. In this meat-poor tribe, Dzacar was the number one fisherman.

Dzacar's magic was in his uncanny ability to catch fish on nothing but a hook, line and a shred of cloth. With this unlikely rig, he would pole out into the tropical river and return with snook, tarpon and bandarootoo.

One drop of Dr. Juice Fish Scent attracts gamefish and camouflages human scent.

It was one such night that Dr. Gregory Bambanek, himself a fisherman, went along with Dzacar and first got a whiff of the potent stuff Dzacar had on that lure.

ONE DROP IS DETECTABLE IN A 30,000 GALLON POOL.

What Bambanek brought home was a secret formulation of scents derived from living jungle plants, fish and animals. Back in America, in his laboratory, he analyzed the chemical makeup of the potion.

Kairomones were the scientific base of the formula. To the gamefish, this hormonal substance indicates a living organism such as live baitfish.

By dialing in other hormonal "communicators" he found he could send other messages like a hot line to the fish's brain.

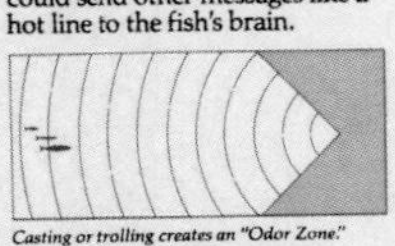

Casting or trolling creates an "Odor Zone."

He added *Fear Pheromones*, the smell of fear given off by prey species that attracts and excites predators. He added *Schooling Pheromones*, the scent baitfish use to home in on their school and gamefish use to find them. He added traces of *Sex Pheromones* which, in small doses, make gamefish very aggressive and territorial.

And finally, he added *Attractant Amino Acids* which camouflage the repellent scent of human finger prints without alerting the fish to any smell out of the ordinary.

Incredibly, in a dilution of one part per 10,000,000,000, Dr. Juice Fish Scent will register its powerful messages of food, fear and sexual aggression deep in the fish's brain, triggering the desired strike response.

PICK UP THE SCENTS THE FISH DO.

Dr. Juice Fish Scents are a total approach to attracting and triggering fish that will significantly improve the size of your catch.

Outdoor Life called it, "a far cry from the run-of-the-mill, anise oil based, licorice-smelling fish 'attractors.'"

One drop squeezed onto a bare lure will remain potent for as long as an hour. And with "Juicers,®" the special time release tabs of cloth, the scent will not wash away for as long as 3 hours.

At that rate, one 30 gram bottle should last you one whole season. Or one whole village.

Look for Dr. Juice One Drop Fish Scent in your tackle stores. Available in 9 formulations for the 9 most popular species of gamefish. Unless you have a taste for bandarootoo.

DR. JUICE ONE DROP FISH SCENT.

WHY TROUT AVOID THE AMAZON RIVER.

Discovered by an anthropologist, "Dr. Juice" combines the secret of tribal fishermen with biological science. Bait kairomones attract gamefish. Sex pheromones excite aggression. Attractant aminos mask human scent. And baitfish "fright" pheromones draw deadly strikes. One drop is powerful magic.

DR. JUICE ONE DROP FISH SCENT.®

Available in Bass, Walleye, Musky/Northern, Salmon, Trout/Steelhead, Lake Trout, Panfish, Catfish and Saltwater scents. ©1985 Blue Fox Tackle Company, 645 North Emerson, Cambridge, Minnesota 55008.

THE BEST WALLEYE FISHERMAN IN THE WORLD DOESN'T EVEN KNOW WHAT A WALLEYE IS.

Discovered by an anthropologist, "Dr. Juice" combines the secret of tribal fishermen with biological science. Bait kairomones attract gamefish. Sex pheromones excite aggression. Attractant aminos mask human scent. And baitfish "fright" pheromones draw deadly strikes. One drop is powerful magic.

DR. JUICE ONE DROP FISH SCENT.®

Available in Bass, Walleye, Musky/Northern, Salmon, Trout/Steelhead, Lake Trout, Panfish, Catfish and Saltwater scents. ©1985 Blue Fox Tackle Company, 645 North Emerson, Cambridge, Minnesota 55008.

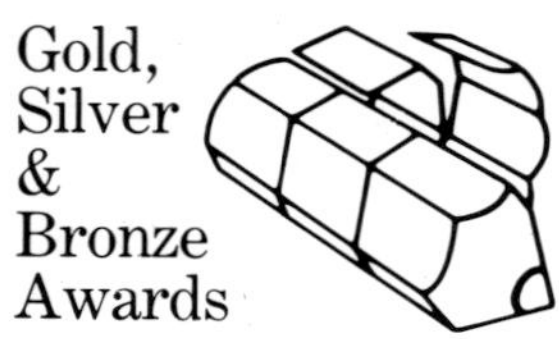

Consumer Magazine B/W: Campaign Including Magazine Supplements

20 SILVER
ART DIRECTORS
Rob Dalton
Michael Fazende
WRITERS
John Stingley
Mike Lescarbeau
CLIENT
WFLD-TV
AGENCY
Fallon McElligott/Minneapolis

WHEN A NUCLEAR WAR STARTS, THE BEST PLACE TO BE IS UNDERGROUND.

The biggest losers in a nuclear war will be the survivors. Facing horrors that will span generations. "Threads" is a shockingly realistic, BBC film which makes us face the truth. We're digging ourselves into a hole. And if we don't find a solution soon, that may be the best place to be. A live, call-in panel discussion will follow.

"THREADS" MONDAY AT 7 PM./PANEL DISCUSSION AT 9 PM.

20 SILVER

JOIN US SUNDAY EVENING AND WE'LL STRAIGHTEN THIS OUT.

Jacques and Jean-Michel Cousteau correct misconceptions and reveal fascinating facts about the mighty Mississippi. There's history, folklore and a look at the river's present and future. And if all that leaves you dizzy, just be glad you weren't on the trip.

"COUSTEAU: MISSISSIPPI" SUNDAY AT 8 PM.

THIS MAN HAS A SERIOUS HEART PROBLEM. HE DOESN'T HAVE ONE.

He's cold. He's cruel. He's James Munroe. Follow the saga of this man's rise to fame, fortune and the destruction of all those who stand in his way. Don't miss Empire Inc., Sunday 5-7, Monday 8-10 and Tuesday 8-10.

EMPIRE INC. STARTS SUNDAY AT 5 PM.

Gold,
Silver
&
Bronze
Awards

Consumer Magazine Color: Campaign Including Magazine Supplements

21 GOLD
ART DIRECTOR
Andy Arghyrou
WRITER
Derek Day
DESIGNER
Andy Arghyrou
PHOTOGRAPHER
Steve Cavalier
CLIENT
Cow & Gate
AGENCY
Abbott Mead Vickers/SMS - London

How come they don't need identical milks?

Because, although they're identical twins, they don't have identical appetites.

Gemma on the left (the elder by 27 minutes) has a normal appetite.

Young Gail, however, is something of a budding Oliver Twist. Hard to satisfy. She often wakes up earlier, and cries with hunger before normal meal times.

So if you were asked to recommend milks for each of them, which would you choose?

Obviously, the ideal recommendation would be breastmilk.

(Perhaps a little extra for Gail.)

Breastmilk, as you know, is by far the most suitable for a baby. In the real world, of course, some mothers cannot, or choose not to breastfeed.

So for Gemma – the one with the normal appetite – you'd want to suggest a milk that's as close as possible to the real thing.

Cow & Gate Premium, like most other babymilks, meets all the latest DHSS guidelines for nutritional composition.

At Cow & Gate we have also given very thorough consideration to how our babymilks are absorbed.

And independent tests have proved that babies absorb the major nutrients in Premium in much the same way as they do those of mother's milk.

But what about Gail, the hungrier twin?

Well, Cow & Gate's Plus also meets all the DHSS recommendations.

But it's a slightly less modified babymilk than Premium, and has a higher proportion of casein to whey.

Casein, nutritionists agree, is digested more slowly by baby.

It's for this reason that we believe Plus leaves a baby feeling satisfied for longer.

If you'd like further nutritional information on our infant formulae, write to the address below for a copy of the free brochures we have prepared.

In the meantime, it's good to know that there are three milks you can recommend with confidence to almost any mother.

The two that Cow & Gate make.

And better still, the one that mother makes.

Breastmilk is the best food for newborn babies. The purpose of infant milk formula is to replace or supplement breastmilk when a mother cannot, or chooses not to breastfeed. The cost of infant formula should be considered before deciding how to feed a baby. For more information write to Cow and Gate Ltd., Trowbridge, Wiltshire BA14 8YX

How much does a baby's brain depend on a baby's stomach?

A baby's brain grows faster in the first year of life than at any other time.

So much so that, by baby's first birthday, the brain will have reached 65% of its eventual adult size.

To maintain this rate of growth a baby requires energy and nutrients which, obviously, must come from milk and the first solids.

So the role that a baby's digestive system plays could hardly be more vital, because it has to absorb the goodness that's in the milk and food.

The key word there is 'absorb'.

Just think how important that is to a growing baby.

Yet because a baby's tiny digestive system is immature, absorbing certain nutrients is quite difficult.

Fat is an interesting example. A young baby gets roughly half of the required energy intake from fat.

But there are two main kinds of fat: saturated and unsaturated.

Broadly speaking, a baby finds unsaturated fat much easier to absorb.

This is one of the reasons mother's milk is so perfect: a high proportion of the fat it contains is unsaturated.

But what about mothers who can't or prefer not to breastfeed?

Will baby get the right kind of fat from babymilk?

You can rest assured that at Cow & Gate we've taken this problem very seriously indeed.

That's why Cow & Gate Premium, like breastmilk, contains a high proportion of unsaturated fat.

Because of this, it's easily absorbed by baby.

Independent clinical tests showed that babies absorb between 87 and 95 per cent of the fat in Premium.

This compared with 89 and 96 per cent for breastmilk.

Of course, fat is just one source of energy in a baby's diet.

The other sources are carbohydrate and protein.

Here again, clinical trials confirm that absorption levels for Premium closely resemble those for breastmilk.

Between them the easily-absorbed fat, protein and carbohydrate in Premium

SOURCES

Widdowson, E.M. Absorption and excretion of fat, nitrogen and minerals from 'filled' milks by babies one week old. Lancet [illegible]

Southgate, D.A.T. and Barrett I.M. The intake and excretion of calorific constituents of milk by babies. Br J Nutr 20:363 1966

Senterre J. unpublished data

Hanna F.K., Navarrette D.A. and Hsu F.A. Calcium-fatty acid absorption in term infants fed human milk and prepared formulas simulating human milk. Paediatrics 45:216-224 1970

can supply all the energy required by a young baby.

Not just for the brain, but for all the other vital organs and tissues as well.

After all, at Cow & Gate we haven't set out to produce a nation of Einsteins.

We simply want to see exactly the same thing as you do: normal, healthy, thriving babies.

Cow & Gate

Breastmilk is the best food for babies. The purpose of infant milk formula is to replace or supplement breastmilk when a mother cannot, or chooses not to breastfeed. The cost of infant formula should be considered before deciding how to feed a baby. For more information write to Cow and Gate Ltd., Trowbridge, Wiltshire BA14 8YX

We could feed them all on something different.

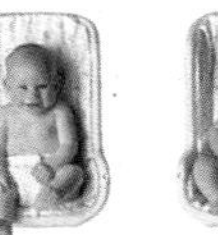

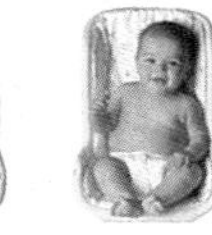

Stage 1 Fruit & Cereal Breakfast for Holly

Stage 1 Creamed Porridge for Jennifer

Stage 1 Bacon Egg & Tomato Breakfast for Alex

Stage 1 Muesli Breakfast for Grace

Stage 1 Beef Dinner for Arthur

Stage 1 Lamb Dinner for Candice

Stage 1 Chicken Dinner for Lauren

Stage 1 Beef & Bone Broth for Alice

Stage 1 Vegetable & Rice Casserole for Jenny

Stage 1 Fish in Cheese Sauce for Richard

Stage 1 Cheese & Tomato Savoury for Katrina

Stage 1 Chicken Risotto for Ricki

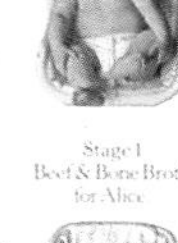

Stage 1 Spaghetti Bolognaise for Cloe

Stage 1 Prune and Apple Dessert for Katie

Stage 1 Peach Melba for Daisy

Stage 1 Fruit Delight Dessert for Amanda

Stage 1 Apple Dessert for Hazeline

Stage 1 Chocolate Pudding for Lea

Stage 1 Apple & Banana Dessert for Sarah

Stage 1 Cherry Treat Dessert for Ashley

Stage 1 Crème Caramel for Charlotte

Stage 1 Strawberry Fool for Ruth

Stage 1 Apple & Orange Dessert for Giovanni

Raspberry Yogurt for Judy

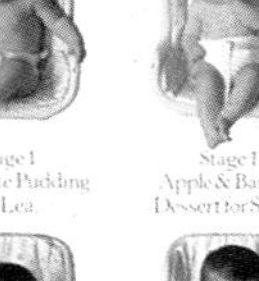

Pear Yogurt for Henry

Banana Yogurt for Rosemary

Strawberry Yogurt for Stephanie

Cherry Yogurt for Jean-Pierre

Apple & Blackcurrant Yogurt for Nina

Peach Melba Yogurt for Jessie

Apple Yogurt for Boadicea

Mixed Fruit Yogurt for John

Stage 2 Bacon Egg & Tomato Breakfast for Nicholas

Stage 2 Muesli Breakfast for Jamie

Stage 2 Fruit & Cereal Breakfast for Christopher

Stage 2 Creamed Porridge for James

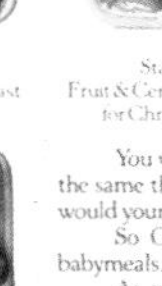

Stage 2 Beef & Kidney Dinner for Georgina

Stage 2 Chicken Dinner for Clare

Stage 2 Beef Dinner for Louise

Stage 2 Lamb Dinner for Robin

Stage 2 Vegetable Casserole with Pasta for Leila

Stage 2 Lamb & Noodle Casserole for Andrew

Stage 2 Spaghetti Bolognaise for Martin

Stage 2 Fish in Cheese Sauce for David

Stage 2 Cheese and Tomato Savoury for Timothy

Stage 2 Chicken Risotto for Aaron

Stage 2 Peach Melba for Michael

Stage 2 Fruit Delight Dessert for Lucy

Stage 2 Apple Dessert for Robert

Stage 2 Strawberry Fool for Naomi

Stage 2 Apple & Banana Dessert for Julie

Stage 2 Cherry Treat Dessert for Melvyn

Stage 2 Chocolate Pudding for Julian

Stage 2 Apple & Orange Dessert for Estee

Stage 2 Crème Caramel for William

Stage 2 Pineapple Dessert for Tara

You wouldn't take too kindly to eating the same thing day in, day out. And neither would your baby.

So Cow & Gate make 47 different babymeals, and nine yogurts in all.

As well as preventing boredom setting in, a wide menu makes sure your baby enjoys a balanced and healthy diet.

You've probably noticed that Cow & Gate varieties come in two stages. This is because babies go through two stages of weaning.

Our Stage 1 meals are all finely sieved and puréed, so they're the perfect texture for babies from about three to seven months, who just suck and swallow.

(Our yogurts are also suitable from about three months.)

Our Stage 2 meals are made with little, soft meaty or fruity pieces. They help teach babies from about seven months how to chew.

And the next stage? Real grown-up food in all its variety.

Cow & Gate

Two short steps to grown-up food.

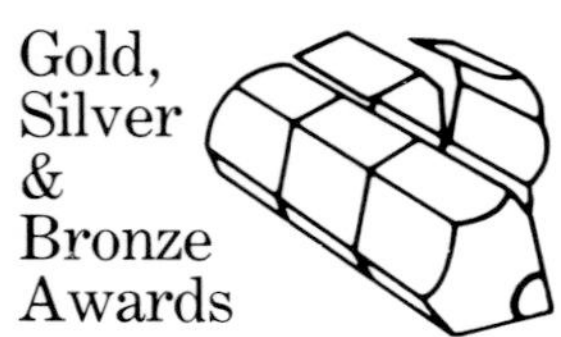

Consumer Magazine Color: Campaign Including Magazine Supplements

22 SILVER
ART DIRECTOR
Larry Bennett
WRITER
Harriet Frye
PHOTOGRAPHERS
Barbara Bordnick
Tim Olive
CLIENT
Royal Caribbean Cruise Line
AGENCY
McKinney Silver & Rockett/
Raleigh, NC

The water slides by in blue-white ripples, punctuated now and then by the leap of a flying fish.

The breeze, as it skims past you down the open deck, seems to carry all your worries right out to sea.

And the sun, high in a tropical sky, warms parts of your psyche you didn't even know were cold.

On a Royal Caribbean cruise, you can leave the pressures behind.

And renew the energies sapped by all those years of full-speed-ahead.

We'll take you to mountains that rise out of turquoise seas, only to lose themselves in layers of cloud.

To fortifications once guarded by the Conquistadores. To old churches whose mosaics arch toward vaulted stone ceilings. To islands where the beaches stretch for miles.

We'll cater to your taste for good food and good company. Entertain you. Indulge you. Totally spoil you. For seven, eight, ten or fourteen days.

Just see your travel agent about a Royal Caribbean cruise.

It may be exactly what you need to get yourself in high gear again.

ROYAL CARIBBEAN
Song of Norway, Song of America, Nordic Prince, Sun Viking
Ships of Norwegian Registry

Our Ships Don't Have Sails, But They Could Put The Wind Back Into Yours.

22 SILVER

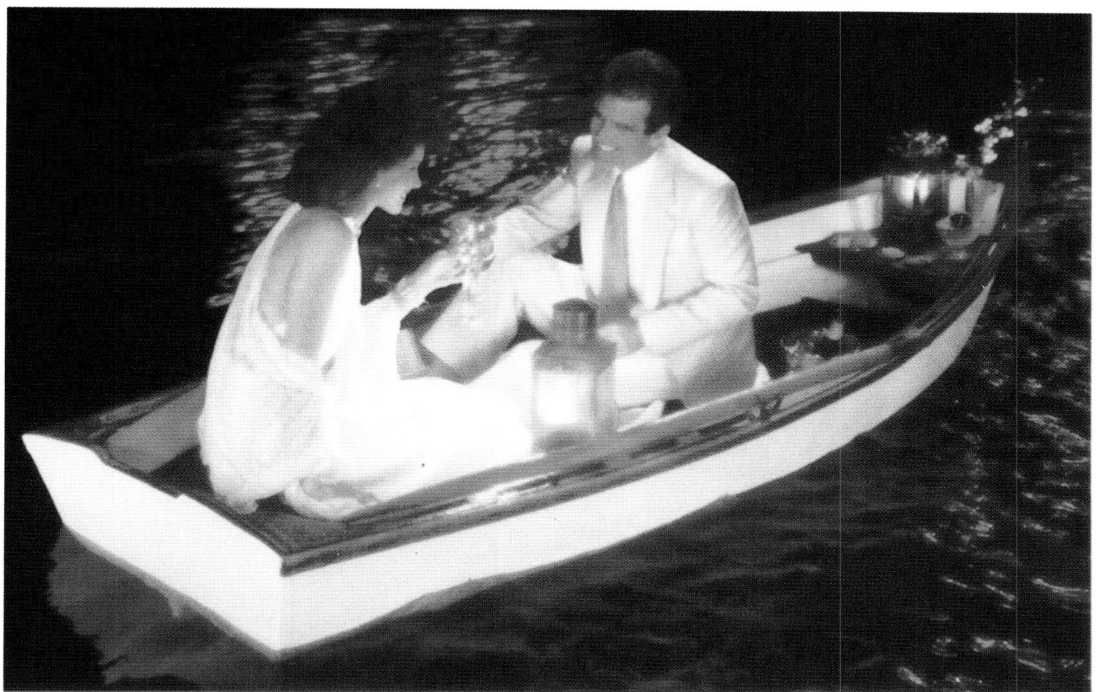

The decks are strung with lights that soar high above the sea, framing the deepening indigo of the night.

Far below you, on the water, the reflection of a tropical moon scatters into a thousand glowing bits.

When evening comes, on a Royal Caribbean cruise, you'll see that all the romantic stories you've heard about cruising are absolutely true.

You'll sip a vintage Bordeaux, savor a perfectly prepared leg of lamb, indulge yourself in Cherries Jubilee flamed right at your table.

You'll watch the silent passing of a freighter, far out on the horizon. And dance under more stars than you ever thought the sky could hold.

And you'll find that the warmth of the islands lingers in your mind, long after the sun goes down.

So talk to your travel agent about a Royal Caribbean cruise. For seven, eight, ten or fourteen days.

After all, some things are just too good to be left to your imagination.

ROYAL CARIBBEAN

Song of Norway, Song of America, Nordic Prince, Sun Viking
Ships of Norwegian Registry

Now Imagine The Same Idea, On A Slightly Larger Scale.

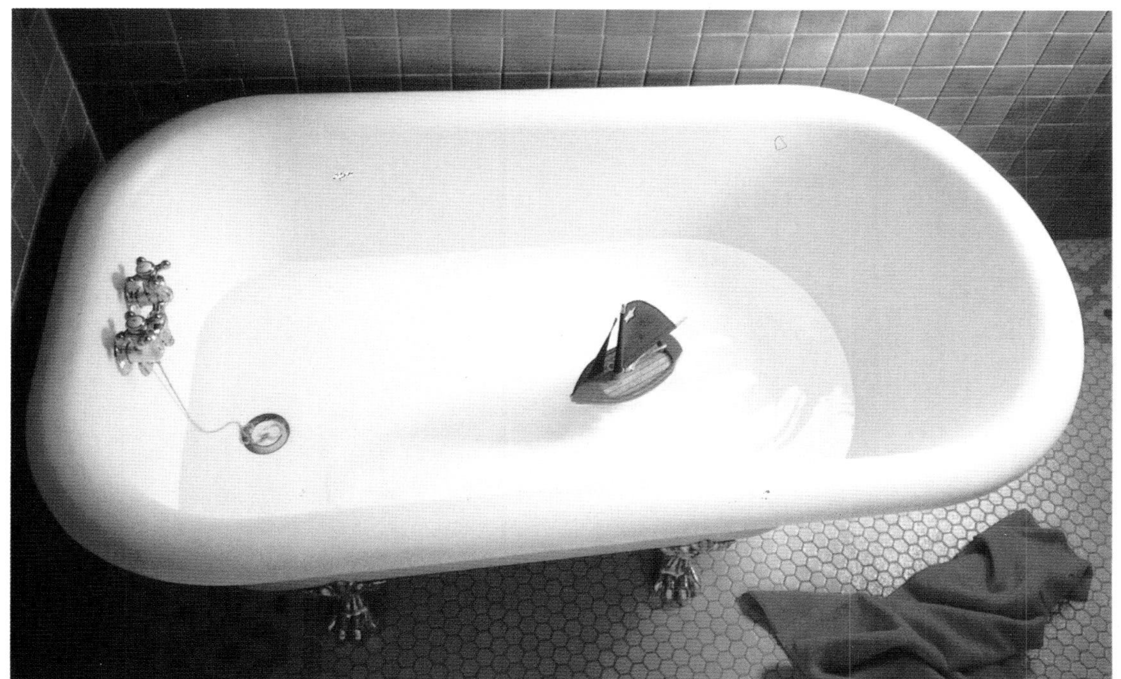

Somewhere, deep in your mind, is a child who grew up with dreams of adventure and romance.

A child who could turn a toy boat into a sailing ship. And a bathtub into the bounding main.

On a Royal Caribbean cruise, you could find yourself getting to know that child all over again.

You could spend seven, eight, ten, or even fourteen days discovering storybook islands ringed with palm trees and scented with hibiscus.

You could dance to the pulsating rhythm of steel drums. Dine on fresh pineapple and flaming babalu. Meet a neon-blue fish, face to face, in the lacy shadows of a coral reef.

Or stand high on a polished deck, with a warm breeze in your face, as your ship glides through an indigo sea that stretches all the way to the edges of your imagination.

Just see your travel agent about a Royal Caribbean cruise.

It can take you away to some of the most beautiful places on earth.

And take you back to some of the most beautiful times of your life.

ROYAL CARIBBEAN

Song of Norway, Song of America, Nordic Prince, Sun Viking
Ships of Norwegian Registry

Ever Since You Were A Kid, You've Wanted To Take A Cruise.

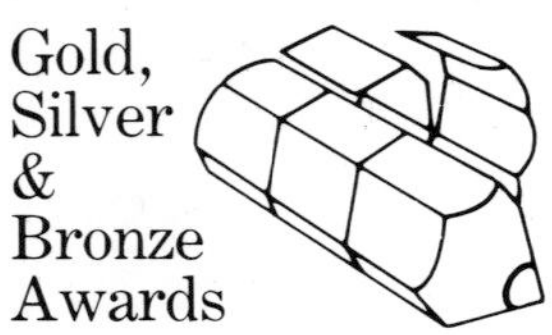
Gold,
Silver
&
Bronze
Awards

Consumer Magazine Color: Campaign Including Magazine Supplements

23 BRONZE
ART DIRECTOR
Gail Bartley
WRITER
David Tessler
DESIGNER
Gail Bartley
PHOTOGRAPHER
Barney Edwards
CLIENT
Waterford Crystal
AGENCY
Ammirati & Puris

In a disposable world, is there a place for a vase designed to last centuries?

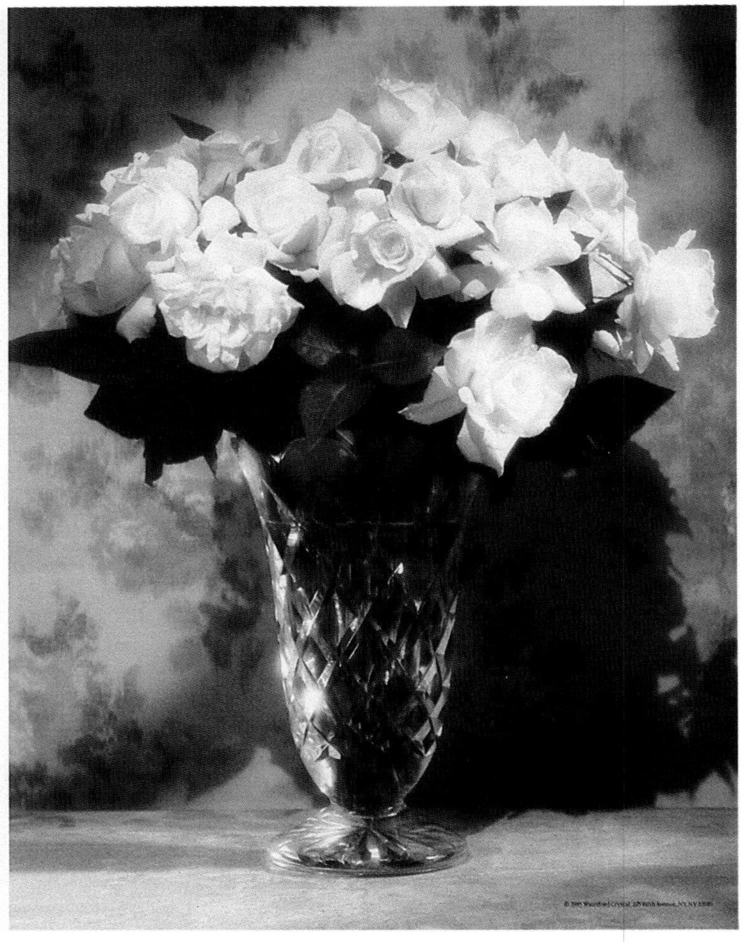

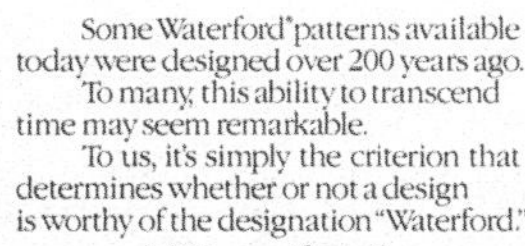
Some Waterford® patterns available today were designed over 200 years ago.
To many, this ability to transcend time may seem remarkable.
To us, it's simply the criterion that determines whether or not a design is worthy of the designation "Waterford."
Waterford
Steadfast in a world of wavering standards.

23 BRONZE

At Waterford, we take 1,120 times longer than necessary to create a glass.

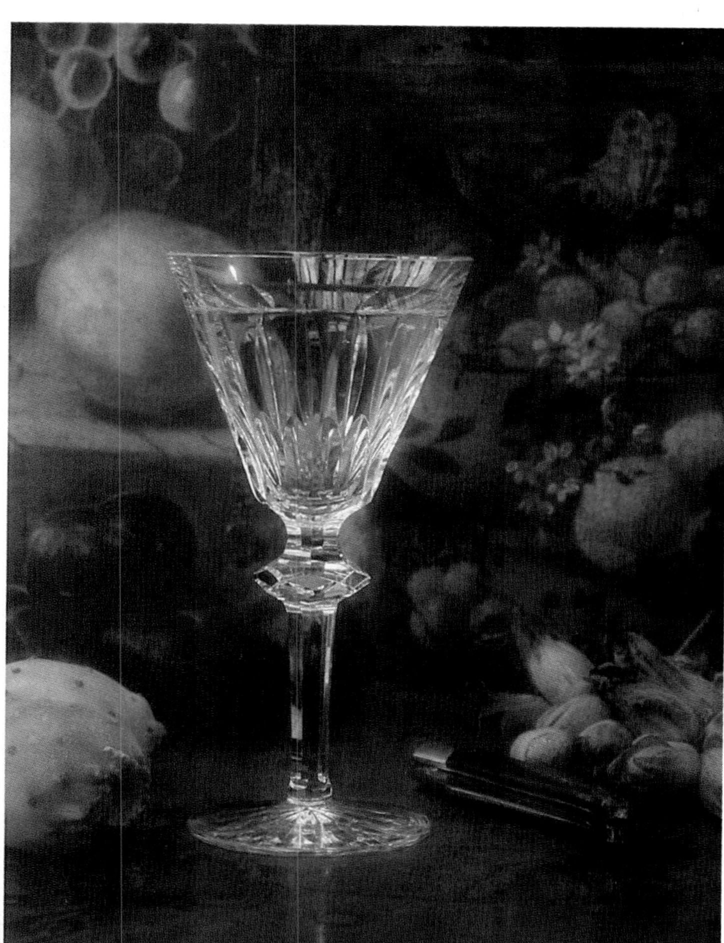

Every glass is blown by mouth, every wedge and diamond cut by hand, and every step of the way, it's all scrutinized by some of the world's most unforgiving eyes.

That is why, while a machine can churn out a glass in only 45 seconds, it takes upward of 14 hours to craft a single piece of Waterford® stemware.

Maintaining Waterford standards means resisting quite a few temptations —including the opportunity to increase our output by 112,000 percent.

Waterford

Steadfast in a world of wavering standards.

Sometimes perfume can be seductive without ever leaving the bottle.

Perfume can be thought of as fantasy in liquid form.

And when it's kept in a Waterford® scent bottle—mouth-blown and hand-cut from the world's most luminous crystal—the fantasy becomes a visual one.

It's perhaps the only instance where the sensual delights of perfume aren't limited to one sense only.

Waterford

Steadfast in a world of wavering standards.

Consumer Magazine Less Than A Page B/W Or Color: Single

24 GOLD
ART DIRECTOR
John Vitro
WRITER
Martha Shaw
DESIGNER
John Vitro
ARTIST
Ron Van Buskirk
PHOTOGRAPHER
Marshall Harrington
CLIENT
WD40
AGENCY
Phillips-Ramsey/San Diego

25 SILVER
ART DIRECTOR
Joe Staluppi
WRITER
James Jordan
PHOTOGRAPHER
Charles Gold
CLIENT
Procter & Gamble/Crest
AGENCY
D'Arcy Masius Benton & Bowles

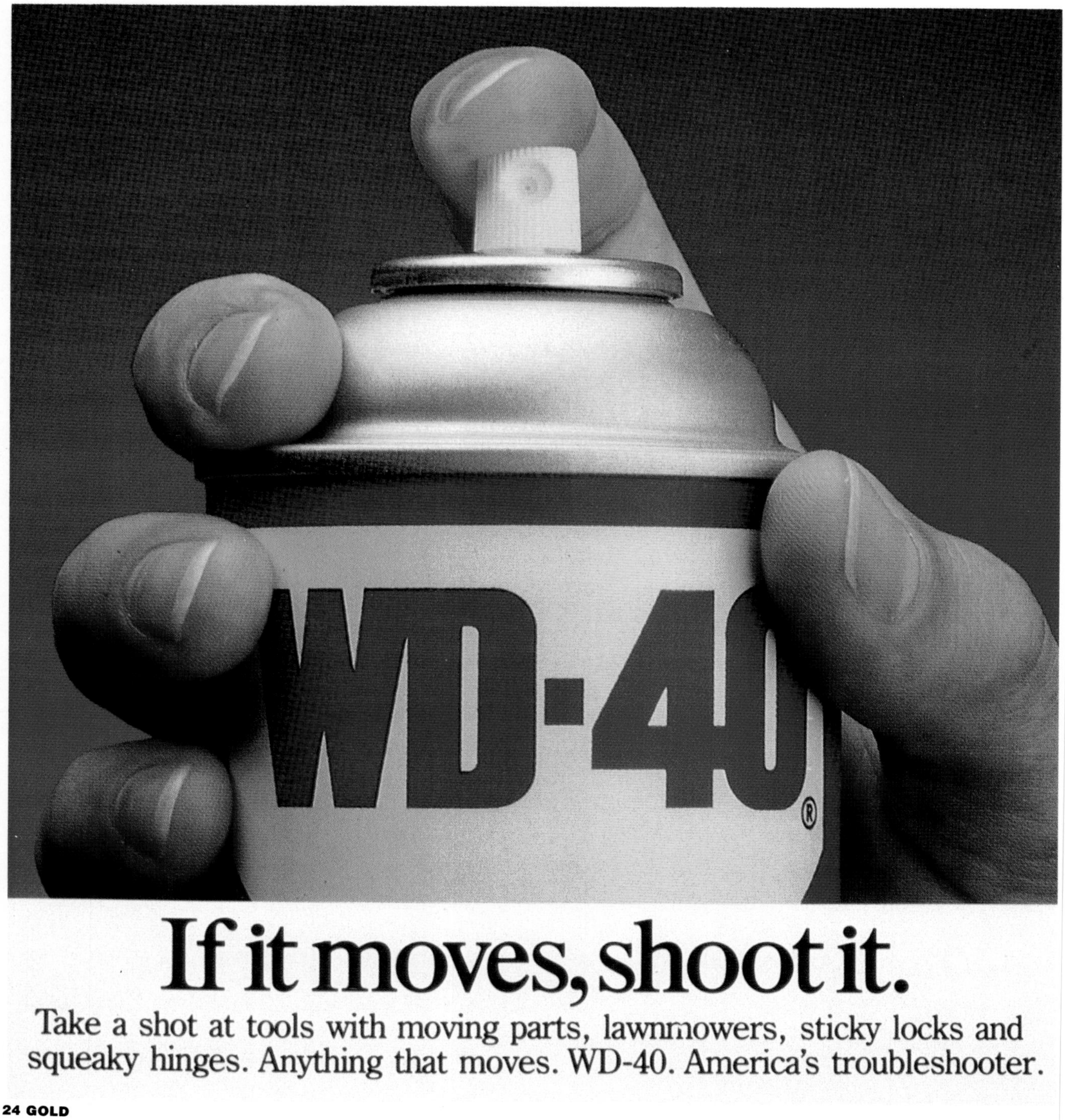

WD-40®

If it moves, shoot it.

Take a shot at tools with moving parts, lawnmowers, sticky locks and squeaky hinges. Anything that moves. WD-40. America's troubleshooter.

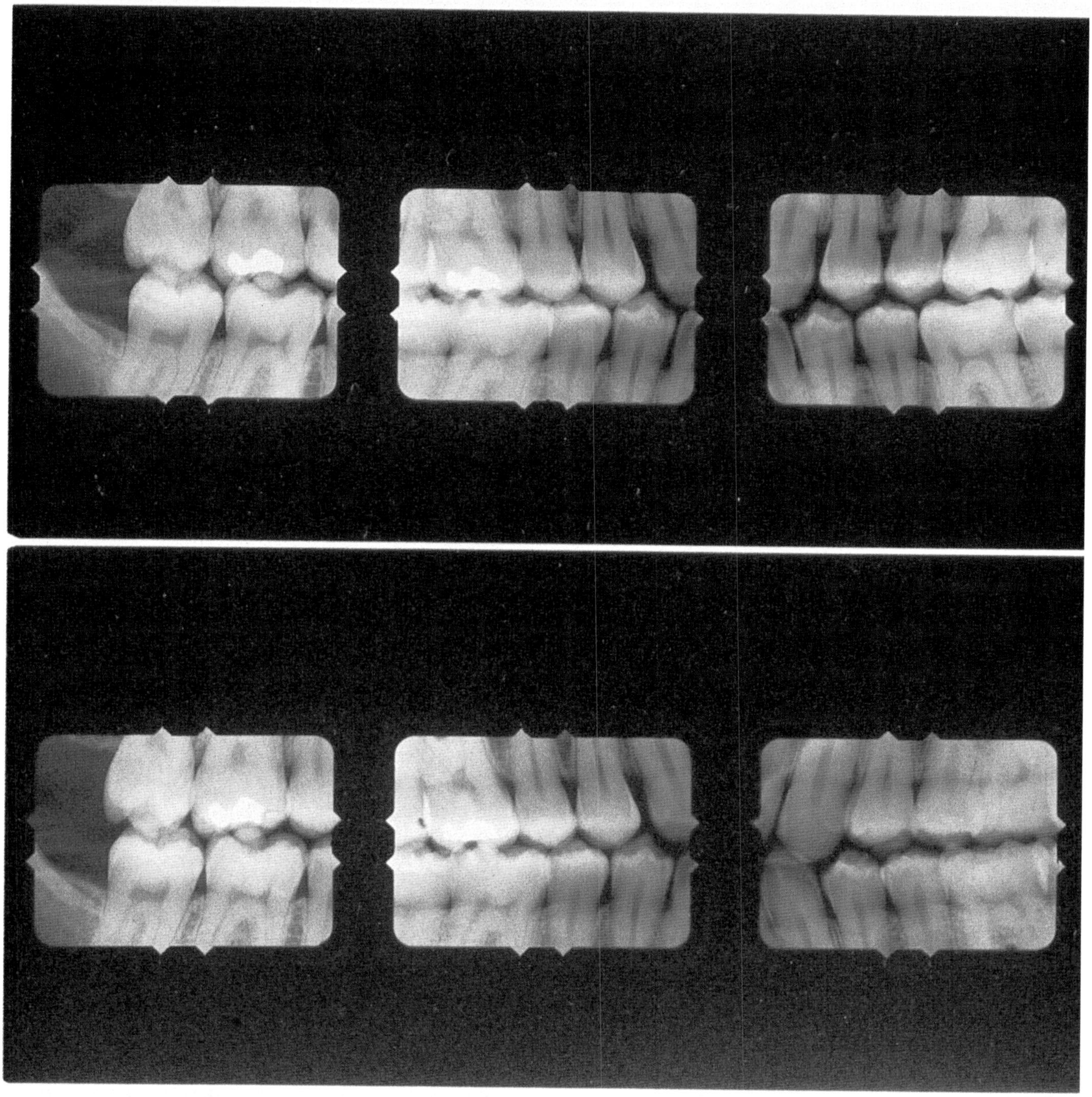

Get positive negatives.

When your X-rays come back, you want good news. And you can help make that happen. By brushing with Crest. Because, when it comes to toothpaste, Crest is the most cavity protection you can get.

More dentists use Crest than any other toothpaste. Shouldn't you?

"Crest has been shown to be an effective decay-preventive dentifrice that can be of significant value when used in a conscientiously applied program of oral hygiene and regular professional care." Council on Dental Therapeutics, American Dental Association. © P&G 1985

Gold,
Silver
&
Bronze
Awards

Consumer Magazine Less Than A Page B/W Or Color: Campaign

26 SILVER
ART DIRECTOR
Joe Staluppi
WRITER
James Jordan
PHOTOGRAPHER
Charles Gold
CLIENT
Procter & Gamble/Crest
AGENCY
D'Arcy Masius Benton & Bowles

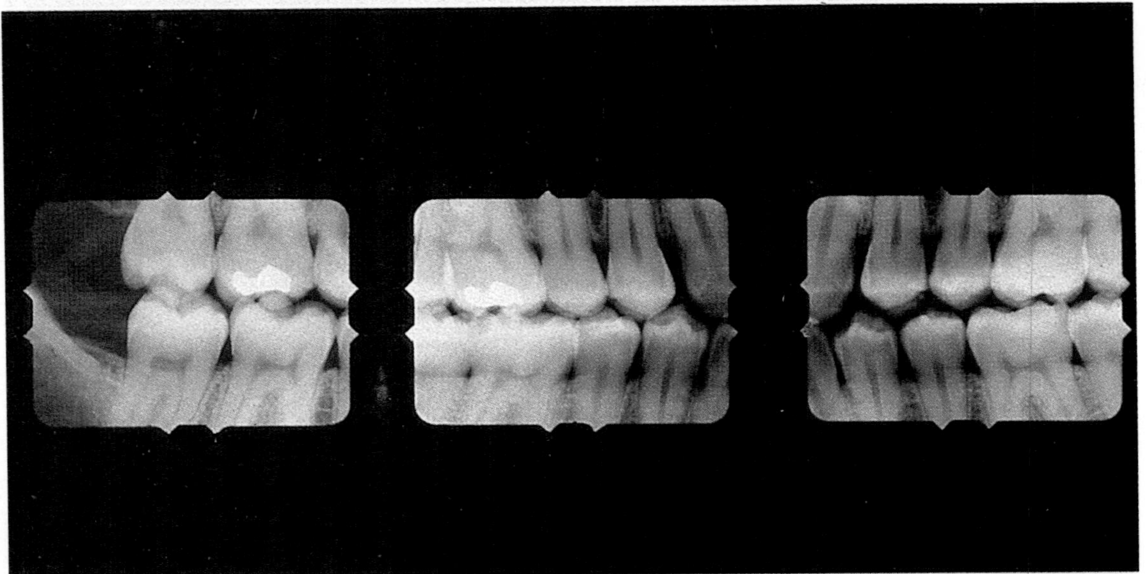

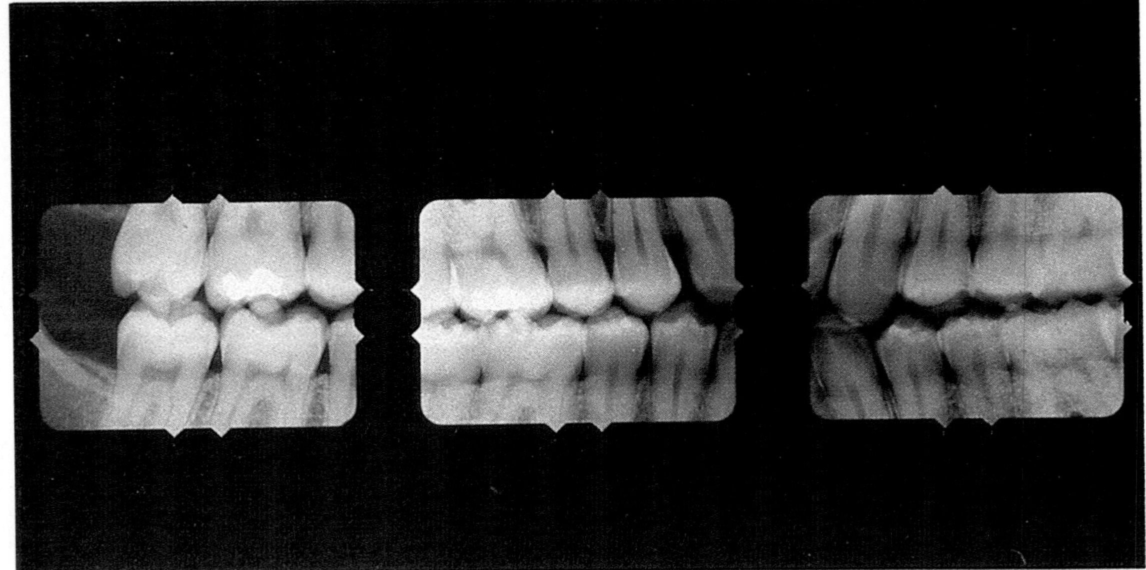

Get positive negatives.

When your X-rays come back, you want good news. And you can help make that happen. By brushing with Crest. Because, when it comes to toothpaste, Crest is the most cavity protection you can get.

More dentists use Crest than any other toothpaste. Shouldn't you?

"Crest has been shown to be an effective decay-preventive dentifrice that can be of significant value when used in a conscientiously applied program of oral hygiene and regular professional care." Council on Dental Therapeutics, American Dental Association. © P&G 1985

26 SILVER

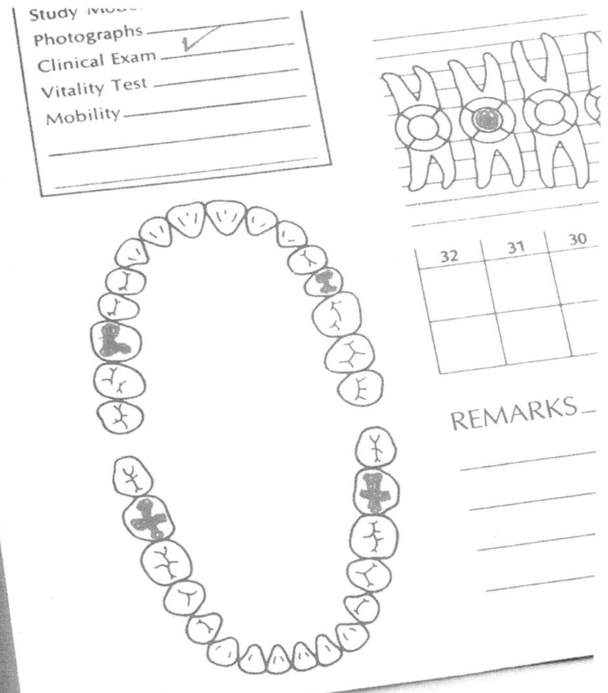

Don't let your kids get bad marks.

To make sure your kids do as well as they can at the dentist's office, you've got to make sure they do their homework. And that means brushing with Crest. Because, when it comes to toothpaste, Crest is the most cavity protection they can get.

More dentists' families use Crest than any other toothpaste. Shouldn't yours?

"Crest has been shown to be an effective decay-preventive dentifrice that can be of significant value when used in a conscientiously applied program of oral hygiene and regular professional care." Council on Dental Therapeutics, American Dental Association. © P&G 1985

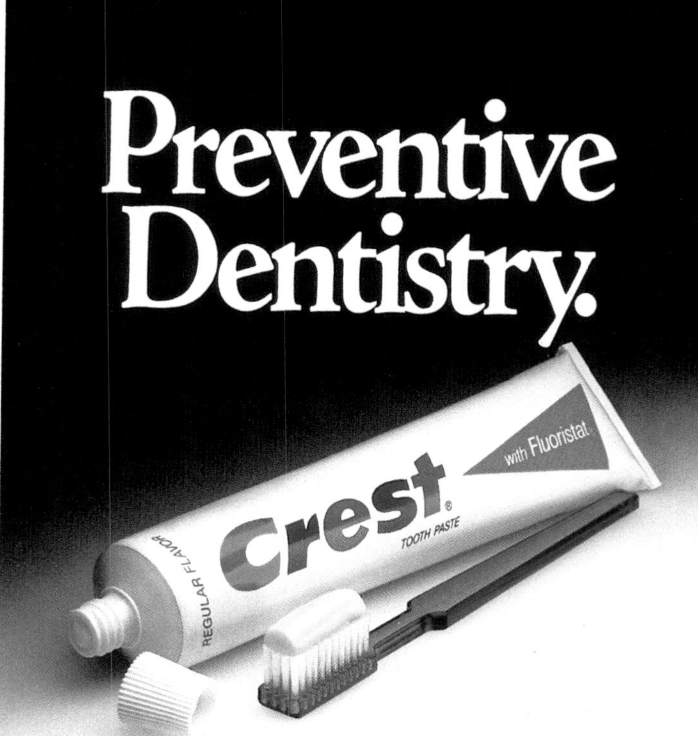

When your dentist catches a little problem and keeps it from becoming a big one, that's preventive dentistry. So is brushing regularly with Crest. Crest's Fluoristat® actually helps strengthen teeth and makes them more resistant to decay. And that helps prevent problems before they start.

More dentists use Crest than any other toothpaste. Shouldn't you?

"Crest has been shown to be an effective decay-preventive dentifrice that can be of significant value when used in a conscientiously applied program of oral hygiene and regular professional care." Council on Dental Therapeutics, American Dental Association. © P&G 1985

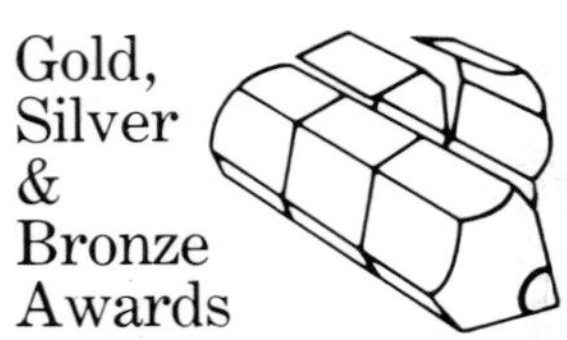

Gold, Silver & Bronze Awards

Consumer Magazine Less Than A Page B/W Or Color: Campaign

27 BRONZE

ART DIRECTOR
Paul Debes

WRITER
Stephen Crane

PHOTOGRAPHER
Ken Buschner

CLIENT
Shimano American Corporation

AGENCY
Perri Debes Looney & Crane/ Rochester, NY

Last year, we broke tradition.
This year, we 're burying it.
SHIMANO Magnumlite GT-2593 FIGHTIN' ROD
Our new improved Fightin' Rod™ grips are made from a softer, more comfortable material that makes this year's Fightin' Rods easier to handle—even when they're wet.
This is the first rod ever fitted with a Titanium composite insert, to provide the incredible power in our Power Butt and the strongest reel-mounting base ever.
All fourteen models feature our revolutionary handle-less design that lets you actually grip the blank itself, for greater sensitivity than ever before.
We use only the genuine article—top-of-the-line Fuji Hardloy guides.
The Magnumlite GT Fightin' Rod features our exclusive BRG (Boron Reinforced Graphite) Construction. Used at critical pattern changes, it provides unmatched strength where most rods break.
A moment of silence, please.
For all those traditional rods soon to take up their rightful place among history's curiosities.
Because if last year's introduction of our revolutionary Magnumlite® GT Fightin' Rod didn't lay to rest the myth that worn-out designs and wacky gimmicks catch fish, *this* year's version surely will.
Not only does it incorporate all the tradition-shattering innovations we introduced last year—like "through-the-*hand*" blank design for unbelievable sensitivity, a Titanium composite insert that puts the kick in our Power Butt, BRG (Boron Reinforced Graphite) Construction for unmatched strength where other rods break and computer designed actions for use with a host of lure and line weights—it now features an even wider range of models and actions, for everything from ultra light spinning to heavy-duty baitcasting.
Improved grips made from a softer, more comfortable material. So they're easier to handle, even when they're wet.
Dynamite new cosmetics designed to out-class every other rod on the rack.
And if that doesn't make the traditional rod extinct, it also comes with a price tag that's even lower than last year's.
So hurry down to your local Shimano dealer's for a new and improved Magnumlite GT Fightin' Rod.
Pick it up, hold it in your hands, and you'll realize there's only one thing that can be said for all those traditional rods gathering dust on the rack: R.I.P.
For a copy of our Shimano Catalog and Team Shimano patch, send $2.00 to: Shimano American Corp., 205 Jefferson Road, Parsippany, NJ 07054.
SHIMANO®
TOMORROW'S TACKLE TODAY

27 BRONZE

How to separate the men from the toys.
All eleven Shimano Graphite Fightin' Rods feature our "through-the-hand" blank construction—for unequaled sensitivity and power.
SHIMANO Graphite SF-1602 FIGHTIN' ROD
SHIMANO Graphite SF-2593 FIGHTIN' ROD
Count on Shimano to use nothing but the best—genuine Fuji guides featuring aluminum oxide inserts.
Graphite Fightin' Rod blanks are made with reinforced Graphite construction, at points where ordinary rods are likely to break. The result is smoother transmission of casting energy.
Our computer designed tips are so precise, so powerful, they practically do your casting for you.
Last year, we brought out the little kid in a lot of grown men when we introduced our Magnumlite® GT Fightin' Rods.
They cried when they discovered they couldn't afford one.
Instead, they had to keep fishing with traditional rods. Rods that, when compared to a Fightin' Rod,™ looked, felt and acted like fishing toys. It was simply more than a lot of them could bear.
Wipe away the tears, fellas. Because this year there's a Fightin' Rod anyone can afford. The new Shimano® Graphite Fightin' Rod.
But just because it's less expensive doesn't mean it's any less a Fightin' Rod.
Like our original GT, it's stronger, faster and more powerful than any traditional rod you've ever fished, with all the hook-setting, hawg-hauling power that has become our trademark.
It features our exclusive, ultra-sensitive "through-the-hand" design. Our revolutionary reinforced Graphite construction. Genuine Fuji guides. And a whole rod-rack-full of lengths and actions.
So take heart!
Rush down to your local Shimano dealer for a Fightin' Rod that's everything those "toy" rods aren't, yet costs about the same.
The new Shimano Graphite Fightin' Rod.
Do it today. If you wait, there might not be any left when you arrive.
And that would be a crying shame.
For a copy of our Shimano Catalog and Team Shimano patch, send $2.00 to: Shimano American Corp., 205 Jefferson Road, Parsippany, NJ 07054.
SHIMANO®
TOMORROW'S TACKLE TODAY

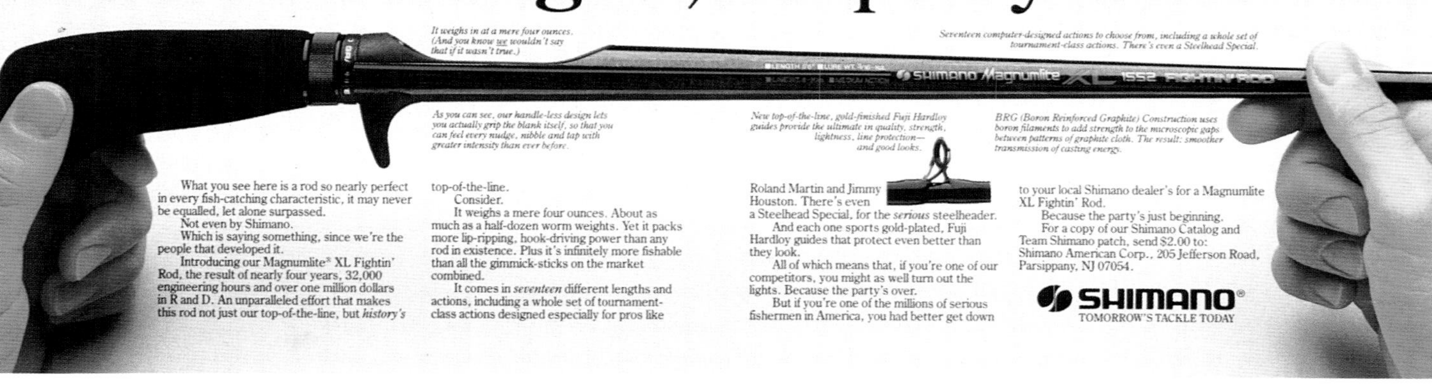

Turn out the lights, the party's over.
It weighs in at a mere four ounces. (And you know we wouldn't say that if it wasn't true.)
Seventeen computer-designed actions to choose from, including a whole set of tournament-class actions. There's even a Steelhead Special.
SHIMANO Magnumlite XL 1552 FIGHTIN' ROD
As you can see, our handle-less design lets you actually grip the blank itself, so that you can feel every nudge, nibble and tap with greater intensity than ever before.
New top-of-the-line, gold-finished Fuji Hardloy guides provide the ultimate in quality, strength, lightness, line protection—and good looks.
BRG (Boron Reinforced Graphite) Construction uses boron filaments to add strength to the microscopic gaps between patterns of graphite cloth. The result: smoother transmission of casting energy.
What you see here is a rod so nearly perfect in every fish-catching characteristic, it may never be equalled, let alone surpassed.
Not even by Shimano.
Which is saying something, since we're the people that developed it.
Introducing our Magnumlite® XL Fightin' Rod, the result of nearly four years, 32,000 engineering hours and over one million dollars in R and D. An unparalleled effort that makes this rod not just our top-of-the-line, but history's top-of-the-line.
Consider.
It weighs a mere four ounces. About as much as a half-dozen worm weights. Yet it packs more lip-ripping, hook-driving power than any rod in existence. Plus it's infinitely more fishable than all the gimmick-sticks on the market combined.
It comes in seventeen different lengths and actions, including a whole set of tournament-class actions designed especially for pros like Roland Martin and Jimmy Houston. There's even a Steelhead Special, for the serious steelheader.
And each one sports gold-plated, Fuji Hardloy guides that protect even better than they look.
All of which means that, if you're one of our competitors, you might as well turn out the lights. Because the party's over.
But if you're one of the millions of serious fishermen in America, you had better get down to your local Shimano dealer's for a Magnumlite XL Fightin' Rod.
Because the party's just beginning.
For a copy of our Shimano Catalog and Team Shimano patch, send $2.00 to: Shimano American Corp., 205 Jefferson Road, Parsippany, NJ 07054.
SHIMANO®
TOMORROW'S TACKLE TODAY

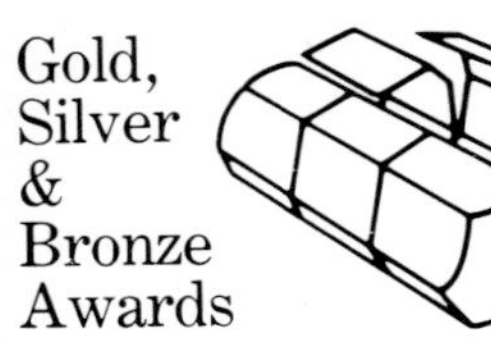

Gold,
Silver
&
Bronze
Awards

Trade B/W: 1 Page Or Spread

28 GOLD
ART DIRECTOR
Marc Marvin
WRITER
Seth Warner
DESIGNER
Marc Marvin
CLIENT
Levi Strauss & Company
AGENCY
Foote Cone & Belding/San Francisco

29 SILVER
ART DIRECTOR
Pat Burnham
WRITER
Bill Miller
PHOTOGRAPHER
Jim Arndt
CLIENT
PYTKA
AGENCY
Fallon McElligott/Minneapolis

30 BRONZE
ART DIRECTOR
Abie Sussman
WRITER
Jody Shrager
CLIENT
Toshiba
AGENCY
Calet Hirsch & Spector

You're looking at the most respected designer in the clothing business today.

Recently, the American Society of Quality Control held a survey to find out consumers' confidence in American products. And using the word quality as a benchmark for confidence, they asked more than 1000 American consumers to select products and companies they associate with the word, "quality."

Of the Fortune 500, thirty companies were selected. Twenty-six of which were American. But only one of which was a clothing designer. And you're looking at him.

His name is Levi Strauss. And even though his designs date back to the 1850's, so does the quality associated with them.

After all, long before it was in style to put rivets in the pockets of jeans, Levi Strauss used them to keep the pockets from falling apart.

And while fancy stitching in jeans may be trendy today, Strauss used the bar stitch to keep his jeans from splitting at the seams.

In fact, this spirit of endless commitment to quality led to 12 new improvements to his jeans in just the past year alone. And as Levi Strauss himself used to say, "Levi's denim jeans are the standard of quality that all Levi's clothing must be judged against."

So while the man in the funny suit may not look like a respected clothing designer of today, just remember that no other designer earned the same respect from American consumers. Besides, you're looking at the first man to ever wear a pair of designer jeans.

QUALITY NEVER GOES OUT OF STYLE®

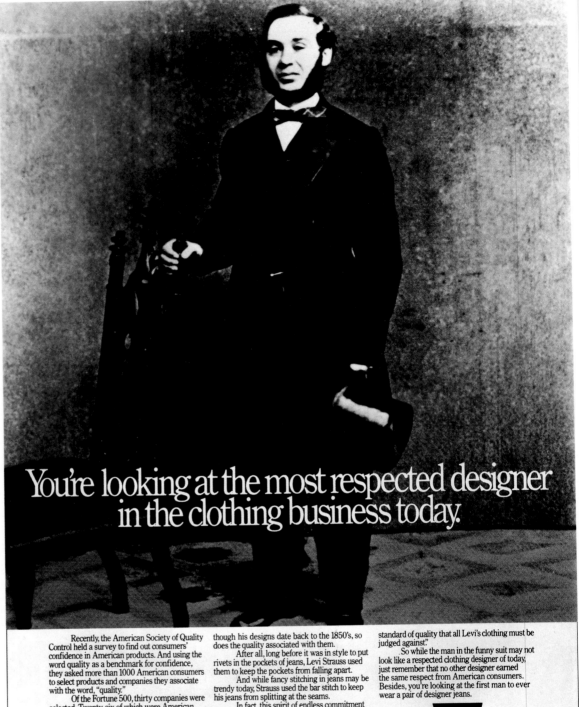

28 GOLD

THANK GOD WE DIDN'T USE FUJI FILM.

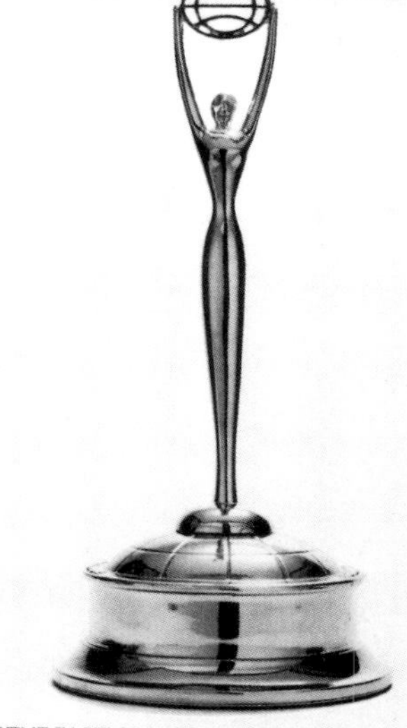

WINNER OF THE EASTMAN KODAK AWARD FOR CINEMATOGRAPHY,
1985 CLIOS , WANG "CATHEDRAL."

Special thanks to Dick Pantano, Tony Winch, Anne Funicane and Jay Hill.

PYTKA

721 B, Hampton Drive, Venice, California 90291 • 213/392-8451

29 SILVER

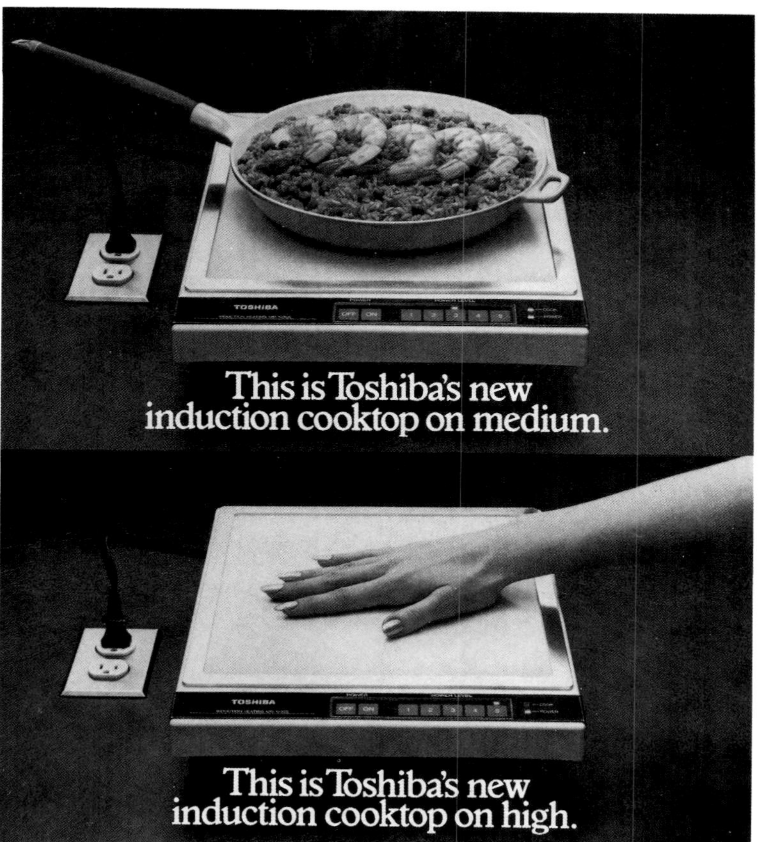
TOSHIBA
OFF ON
This is Toshiba's new induction cooktop on medium.
TOSHIBA
OFF ON
This is Toshiba's new induction cooktop on high.

Toshiba's new induction cooktop will cook all sorts of things. But what makes it so remarkable is what it won't cook.

There are no open flames and no redhot electric coils. It works by creating a magnetic field that heats the inside of any iron or steel pan directly. Instead of heating the cooking surface.

Naturally, a cooktop like this is perfect for a lot of your customers—especially those with young kids.

It's also a great idea for anyone who wants to save energy—since it doesn't waste any, heating up the cooking surface.

It has some other helpful features, too. Like electronic touch controls, an LED display that tells your customers what power level they're on, and a glass cooking top that's easier to clean.

So offer your customers Toshiba's induction cooktop. Or they may get burned.

In Touch with Tomorrow
TOSHIBA
Toshiba America, Inc., 82 Totowa Road, Wayne, NJ 07470

30 BRONZE

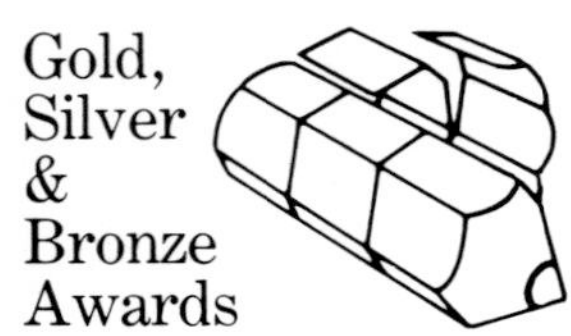

Trade Color: 1 Page Or Spread

31 GOLD
ART DIRECTOR
Cabell Harris
WRITER
Luke Sullivan
DESIGNER
Cabell Harris
PHOTOGRAPHER
John Whitehead
CLIENT
Meredith Corporation
AGENCY
Drinking Buddies Advertising/Richmond, VA

32 SILVER
ART DIRECTOR
Nancy Rice
WRITER
Bill Miller
PHOTOGRAPHER
Jim Marvy
CLIENT
Rolling Stone
AGENCY
Fallon McElligott/Minneapolis

33 BRONZE
ART DIRECTOR
Nancy Rice
WRITER
Bill Miller
PHOTOGRAPHER
Mark Hauser
CLIENT
Rolling Stone
AGENCY
Fallon McElligott/Minneapolis

FOR 4 MONTHS OUT OF THE YEAR, THE WEATHER MAKES FARMING IMPOSSIBLE. DURING THE OTHER 8, THE GOVERNMENT DOES.

Imagine what it would be like if the weather kept you from buying media for four months out of every year.

Then imagine that during the other eight, your hands were tied. Tied while trade deficits, tight money, and foreign policy dictated how you'd buy your media.

Essentially, that's what running a farm is like these days.

Given all that, wouldn't you look for the best advice you could find? Sure you would.

That's why so many farmers read Successful Farming® every month. Successful Farming ties together the total farm operation. Not with long-winded feature articles, but with concise, informative how-to articles on contemporary management practices.

They also read the ads as proved by the high Chilton readership scores. Which is great for our advertisers, considering that our magazine reaches the high-income farmers responsible for 85% of all production expenses in America.

Which is why if you have a product that can help today's farmers make a better living off the land, there's no better place to tell them about it than Successful Farming.

For more information, contact your nearest Successful Farming sales executive. Or call Gil Spears, collect, at 515-284-3118. Successful Farming. Meredith Corporation, Locust at Seventeenth. Des Moines, Iowa 50336.

31 GOLD

Perception.

Reality.

If you think you can calculate the net worth of a Rolling Stone reader by emptying his right front pocket, you should check what he's carrying around in his right rear pocket. One and a half million Rolling Stone readers are card carrying capitalists. Cash in on the action in Rolling Stone. Source: Simmons 1984

32 SILVER

Perception.

Reality.

If your idea of a Rolling Stone reader looks like a holdout from the 60's, welcome to the 80's. Rolling Stone ranks number one in reaching concentrations of 18-34 readers with household incomes exceeding $25,000. When you buy Rolling Stone, you buy an audience that sets the trends and shapes the buying patterns for the most affluent consumers in America. That's the kind of reality you can take to the bank. Source: Simmons 1984

33 BRONZE

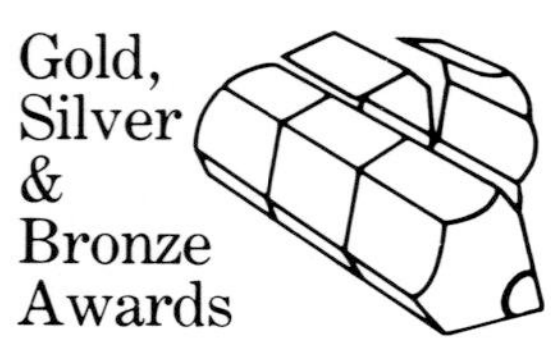

Trade Less Than A Page B/W Or Color: Single

34 SILVER
ART DIRECTORS
Yvonne Smith
Marc Deschenes
WRITERS
Marc Deschenes
Yvonne Smith
DESIGNERS
Yvonne Smith
Marc Deschenes
ARTIST
Gina Norton
PHOTOGRAPHERS
Lamb & Hall
CLIENT
Noritsu
AGENCY
(213) 827-9695 & Associates/
Venice, CA

35 BRONZE
ART DIRECTOR
Steve Williams
WRITER
Mark Travers
DESIGNER
Steve Williams
ARTIST
Steve Williams
PHOTOGRAPHER
Steve Williams
CLIENT
Kerlick Switzer & Johnson
AGENCY
Kerlick Switzer & Johnson/
St. Louis

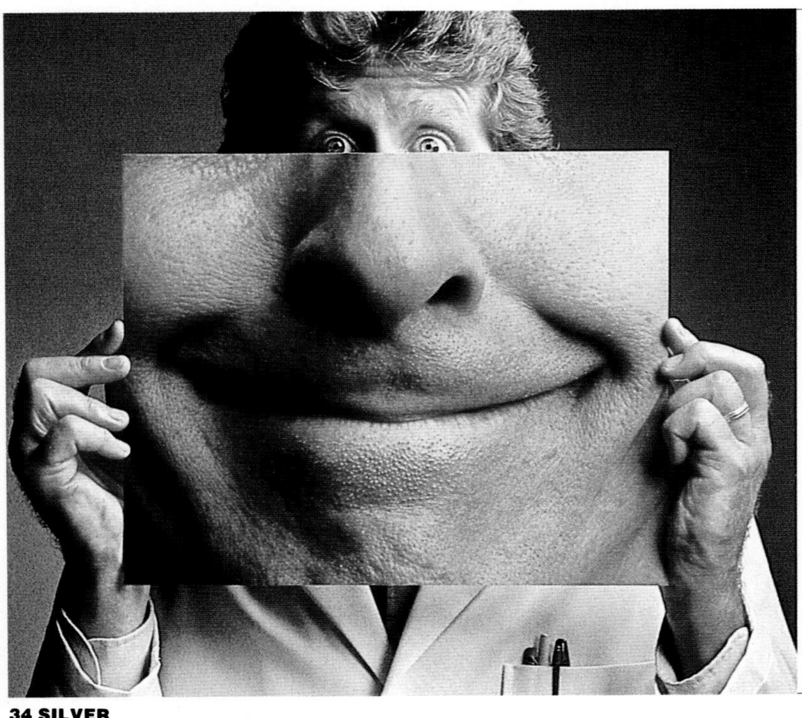

IF YOU MADE $9.95 ON ONE PRINT, YOU'D BE HAPPY, TOO.

With our little QSS-602U daylight enlarging system you can make $2.38 profit on a 5x7 print. About $4.25 on an 8x10. And almost $10 on an 11x14.
For more information, see us in booth 549. Or call (714) 521-9040. So you can be all smiles, too.

THE QSS-602U BY NORITSU

Noritsu America Corporation, 6900 Noritsu Avenue, Buena Park, CA 90620
QSS is a registered trademark of the Noritsu America Corporation.

34 SILVER

WANTED: WRITER FOR A SLIMEBUCKET ACCOUNT.

Oh sure, we have the typical complement of glitzy high technology and packaged goods accounts and junkets to the coast to overproduce TV spots. And of course, the Writer/Producer we hire will work on many of them.

But he or she will also work on one of the nation's largest manufacturers of sanitary equipment. That's right, slimebuckets. We're talking trash here. And this Writer will have his or her pretty head in trash for a few days every month. Sound exciting? We think so.

The Writer we want is an excellent conceptual thinker. He or she brings at least 5 years of agency experience—and a closetful of awards for print, radio and television advertising.

We offer a terrific compensation package. So if you'd like to explore the possibility of working for a slimebucket agency, call Mark Travers, Executive Creative Director.

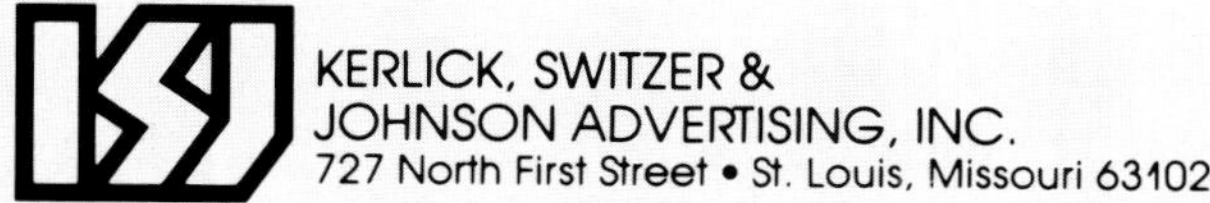

(314) 241-4656

35 BRONZE

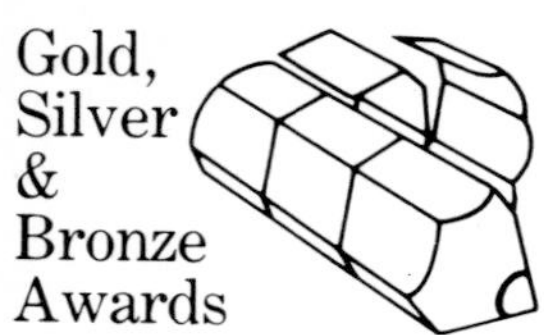

Trade Any Size B/W Or Color: Campaign

36 GOLD
ART DIRECTOR
Nancy Rice
WRITER
Bill Miller
PHOTOGRAPHERS
Mark Hauser
Jim Marvy
CLIENT
Rolling Stone
AGENCY
Fallon McElligott/Minneapolis

Perception.

Reality.

If your idea of a Rolling Stone reader looks like a holdout from the 60's, welcome to the 80's. Rolling Stone ranks number one in reaching concentrations of 18-34 readers with household incomes exceeding $25,000. When you buy Rolling Stone, you buy an audience that sets the trends and shapes the buying patterns for the most affluent consumers in America. That's the kind of reality you can take to the bank.

Source: Simmons 1984

Perception.

Reality.

If you still think a Rolling Stone reader's idea of standard equipment is flowers on the door panels and incense in the ashtrays, consider this: Rolling Stone households own 5,199,000 automobiles. If you've got cars to sell, welcome to the fast lane. Source: Simmons 1984

Perception.

Reality.

If you think the pages of Rolling Stone are filled with left wing politics and music to make your hair stand on end, call 1-212-PL8-3800 and we'll send you a copy of America's #1 lifestyle publication for 18-34 year olds, featuring the latest and most respected information about what's happening in music and entertainment today. If you're not on the cover of Rolling Stone, don't worry, there's still room inside. Source: Simmons 1984

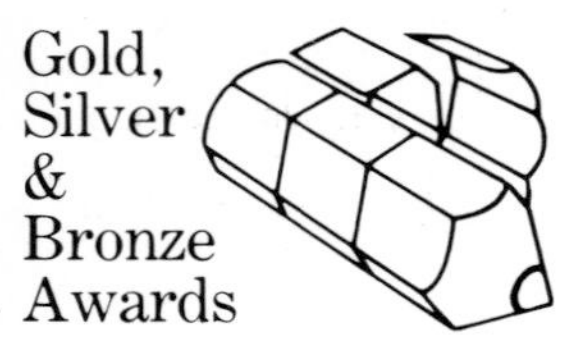

Trade Any Size B/W Or Color: Campaign

37 SILVER
ART DIRECTOR
Cabell Harris
WRITER
Luke Sullivan
DESIGNER
Cabell Harris
PHOTOGRAPHER
John Whitehead
CLIENT
Meredith Corporation
AGENCY
Drinking Buddies
Advertising/Richmond, VA

NO MATTER WHAT THE FARMER'S ALMANAC SAYS, THE NEXT 365 DAYS ARE GOING TO BE HELL ON FARMERS.

There are few things in a farmer's life that he can count on. Good interest rates? Nope. Good yields? Good weather? Good prices? Forget it.

Fortunately, there's one thing he can count on 365 days a year. Successful Farming® Magazine.

The one magazine he can count on for reliable information on how to run a farm and make an honest dollar off of it. Information on production, management and marketing.

Our readers also count on ads that they read in our magazine. At least according to our high Chilton Ad-Chart scores they do. Which is great for our advertisers, considering that our magazine is aimed at the high-income farmers responsible for 85% of all production expenses in America.

All of which means that if you have a product that can help farmers weather the elements more efficiently, there's no better place to tell them about it than Successful Farming.

For more information, contact your nearest Successful Farming sales executive. Or call Gil Spears, collect, at 515-284-3118. Successful Farming Magazine, Meredith Corporation, Locust at Seventeenth, Des Moines, Iowa 50336.

37 SILVER

SOMETHING IS WRONG WHEN THE PEOPLE WHO PUT FOOD ON AMERICA'S TABLES HAVE TROUBLE PUTTING SOME ON THEIR OWN.

Make that a lot of things are wrong.

Trade deficits. Tight money. Huge surpluses. Bad weather. Low prices. You name it.

Yet while running a farm these days can be next to impossible, reaching the right farms is easier than ever. Through Successful Farming®.

In fact, Successful Farming is aimed at the farmers responsible for 85 percent of all production expenses in America.

And according to our high Chilton scores, farmers are reading us too. Because Successful Farming ties together the total farm operation. Not with long-winded "feature" articles, but with concise, informative how-to articles on contemporary management practices.

So if you have a product that will make owning a farm more profitable, there's no better place to tell an owner about it than Successful Farming.

Contact your nearest Successful Farming sales executive for more details. Or call Gil Spears, collect, at 515-284-3118. Successful Farming. Meredith Corporation, Locust at Seventeenth. Des Moines, Iowa 50336.

FOR 4 MONTHS OUT OF THE YEAR, THE WEATHER MAKES FARMING IMPOSSIBLE. DURING THE OTHER 8, THE GOVERNMENT DOES.

Imagine what it would be like if the weather kept you from buying media for four months out of every year.

Then imagine that during the other eight, your hands were tied. Tied while trade deficits, tight money, and foreign policy dictated how you'd buy your media.

Essentially, that's what running a farm is like these days.

Given all that, wouldn't you look for the best advice you could find? Sure you would.

That's why so many farmers read Successful Farming® every month. Successful Farming ties together the total farm operation. Not with long-winded feature articles, but with concise, informative how-to articles on contemporary management practices.

They also read the ads as proved by the high Chilton readership scores. Which is great for our advertisers, considering that our magazine reaches the high-income farmers responsible for 85% of all production expenses in America.

Which is why if you have a product that can help today's farmers make a better living off the land, there's no better place to tell them about it than Successful Farming.

For more information, contact your nearest Successful Farming sales executive. Or call Gil Spears, collect, at 515-284-3118. Successful Farming. Meredith Corporation, Locust at Seventeenth. Des Moines, Iowa 50336.

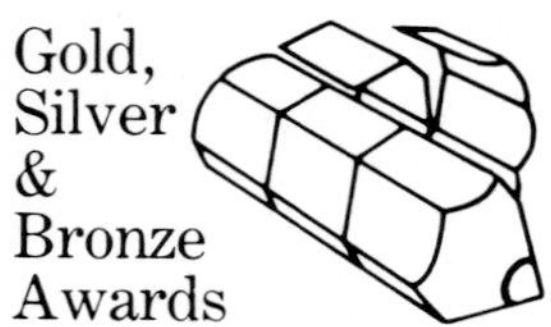

Gold, Silver & Bronze Awards

Trade Any Size B/W Or Color: Campaign

38 BRONZE
ART DIRECTORS
Bob Saabye
Tom Monahan

WRITER
Jeff Abbott

DESIGNER
Sharon Collins

PHOTOGRAPHERS
Clint Clemens
Gene Dwiggins

CLIENT
Siebe North

AGENCY
Leonard Monahan Saabye/
Providence, RI

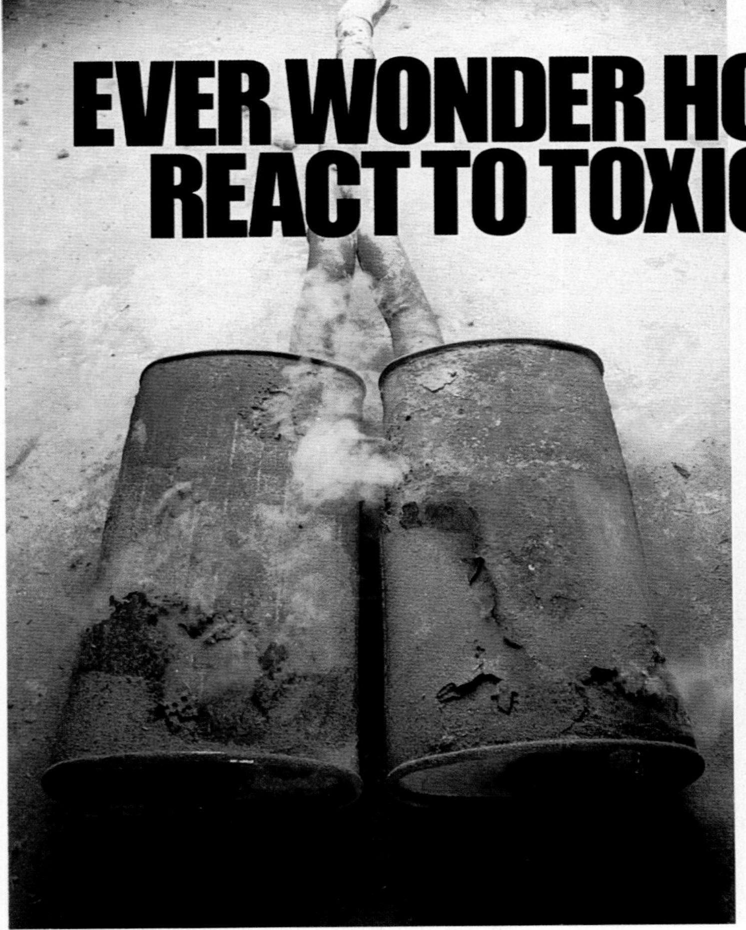

EVER WONDER HOW YOUR LUNGS REACT TO TOXIC MATERIALS?

The fact-of-the-matter is that lungs allow most toxic agents to penetrate their walls, enter the bloodstream and affect other vulnerable organs. Like the liver or kidneys.

This can happen when you're using a respirator that doesn't fit well. Take a deep breath and think about that.

It's not a very comforting thought, especially since respirators are a fact of life in industry today. And when there are gaps in protection, more than just your lungs are at stake.

7700 Series Respirator

Providing the best protection without sacrificing comfort is no simple matter. It takes real expertise, innovation and a commitment to research and development.

In short, it takes a company like North Safety Equipment.

Self-Contained Breathing Apparatus

COMFORT YOU CAN LIVE WITH.

A good example is our 7700 respirator. It's fitting to say it's the most comfortable high performance respirator made today.

We designed it using anthropometric data from the armed services supplemented by numerous tests on workers with a wide variety of facial features.

The final product was made with a soft, hypoallergenic silicone rubber so that the 7700 would further conform to the face.

This resulted in a superior fit. And that means greater comfort and better protection. This was confirmed in nationwide tests.

HOW TO THROW AWAY A GOOD IDEA.

We took this knowledge and developed another innovative product. The North 100 Series disposable cartridge respirator.

It's an economical alternative to cleaning and maintenance. Just throw it out after it's done its job.

But even though it's disposable, we didn't compromise comfort or protection. It has many features of North's 7700 including the cradle suspension system and low nose profile.

North's expertise also includes self-contained breathing apparatus. As a matter of fact, our affiliate, Siebe Gorman & Co. Ltd. produced the first SCBA in 1879.

100 Series Disposable Respirator

And we've just kept improving our SCBA. The North 800 Series was engineered for simplicity and has a unique fail-open valve design that assures a supply of air in case of malfunction, as long as there's air in the cylinder.

These three products; the North 7700 dual cartridge respirator, 100 Series disposable respirator, and 800 Series SCBA, are just part of our broad line of respiratory protective devices.

So if you've been holding your breath for better respiratory protection, contact North Safety Equipment, 2000 Plainfield Pike, Cranston, RI 02920 (401) 943-4400. Siebe North Canada, Ltd., Rexdale, Ontario, Canada M9W 5V8 (416) 675-2810.

Safety Equipment

38 BRONZE

THIS IS WHAT YOUR HAND LOOKS
LIKE TO MOST TOXIC CHEMICALS.

It's been said that ignorance is bliss. Unfortunately, when you're handling dangerous materials, that bliss can be rather short-lived.

You see, despite their rugged appearance, hands need protection. But, it isn't just a matter of providing a pair of gloves. The gloves have to be designed for the particular situation.

It takes expertise to do that in today's industrial environment. And that's exactly what we offer at North Hand Protection.

Viton Glove

A good example is what we're doing in gloves that resist permeation. We're the only producer of industrial gloves of Butyl and Viton® elastomers. These two formulations provide the best protection against many toxic chemicals.

Even these gloves, however, aren't always appropriate. That's why we produce different gloves, such as Nitrile Latex, for a variety of other chemical applications. So no matter what you're working with, we can deliver the best protection possible.

Nitrile Latex Glove

As a matter of fact, we offer the same level of quality in our industrial gloves as the U.S. Government demands in the gloves we supply for protection against chemical warfare agents. You'll find no other manufacturer can match North's capabilities.

But industrial hand protection doesn't end with chemical resistant gloves. And neither does our expertise.

We were leaders in developing the coated knit glove. This innovation performs so well that it's becoming the industry standard.

And while everyone else was cutting and sewing their gloves, we began knitting them on machines to eliminate the seams and make our gloves more comfortable. This also gives them longer life and added value.

Butyl Glove

It's easy to see why industrial workers should put their hands in North gloves. Before they put them in anything else.

We'd like to tell you more. Contact North Hand Protection, 4090 Azalea Drive, P.O. Box 70729, Charleston, SC 29405. (803) 554-0660. North Hand Protection products are sold through authorized distributors.

NORTH
Hand Protection

Viton is a registered trademark of E.I. Dupont.

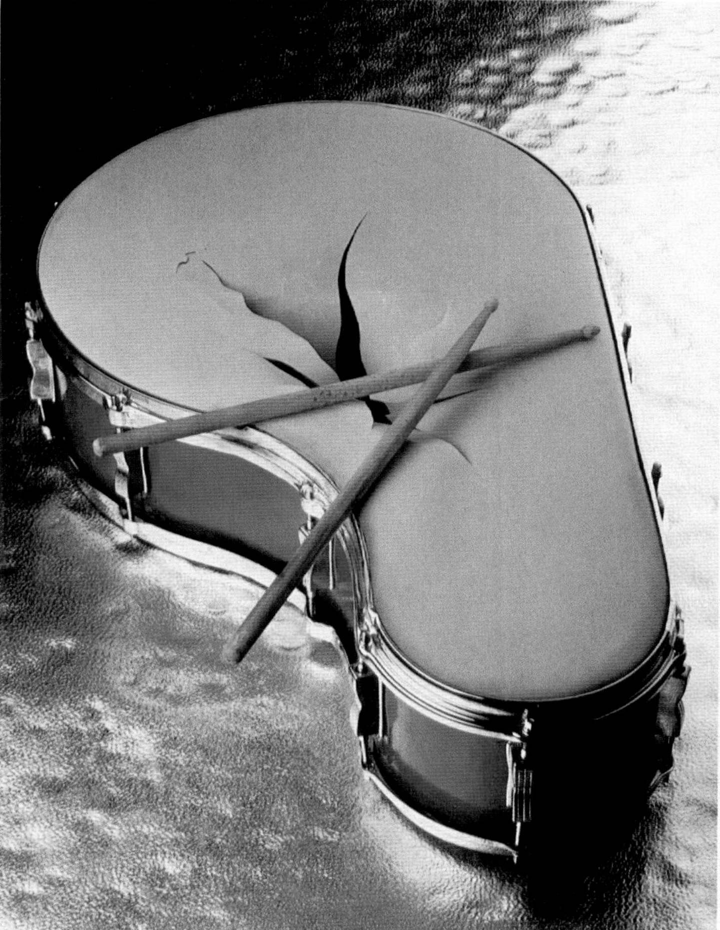

WAS THE EAR MADE TO TAKE A BEATING?

Not from what we hear.

You see, the ear is a delicate instrument that's rather unforgiving of abuse. It has to be protected from hazardous noise.

That's not as easy as it sounds, since all ears are different.

To provide comfortable protection you must first have an understanding of the ear and then the technical expertise to translate that into effective protection.

North has both of those qualities.

Sound-Off™ Earmuff

Because of our experience in hearing protection, we know there isn't any one solution. So we offer many.

Com-Fit® Ear Plugs

One example is our DeciDamp® disposable ear plug. It's made of polymer foam that expands smoothly in the ear to form a snug, comfortable fit. It's found throughout industry because it provides such an effective noise barrier.

Another type of ear plug is our Com-Fit® It's a reusable silicone ear plug insert that also offers excellent protection and comfort, since it comes with its own inserter device which insures a proper fit.

For other applications we have ear muffs. For instance, our Sound-Off™ muff reduces dangerous noise while permitting workers to hear conversations. And it does this with a minimum of pressure on the head.

We make other hearing protectors as well, including one that's molded to the worker's ear.

As a matter of fact, North Health Care is the only manufacturer who offers a complete line of hearing protectors. Each of which meets the most rigid specifications.

They are inspected at every stage of development to insure that proper standards are met.

Most companies would be satisfied to offer such a line.

We're not. We go a step further to insure that workers will get the most benefit out of our hearing protection products.

We've had all our Territory Managers certified as industrial Audiometric Technicians, so they can assist you with your audiometric testing.

North Health Care Territory Managers are trained in measuring the sensitivity of workers' ears to different frequencies as well as giving otoscopic examinations.

DeciDamp® Ear Plugs

In this way, they're able to recommend and fit hearing protectors that will be the most effective and the most comfortable for the industrial worker.

So no matter what your workers are listening to, North will make it easy on their ears.

If you'd like to hear more, contact North Health Care, Rockford, IL 61103 (815) 877-2531. Or Siebe North Canada Ltd., Rexdale, Ontario, Canada M9W 5V8 (416) 675-2810.

NORTH
Health Care

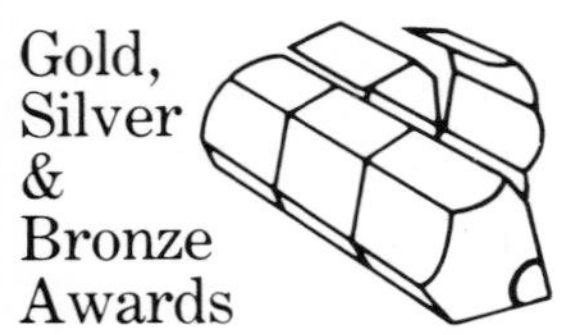

Collateral Brochures Other Than By Mail

39 GOLD
ART DIRECTOR
Nancy Rice
WRITER
Bill Miller
CLIENT
Rolling Stone
AGENCY
Fallon McElligott/Minneapolis

40 SILVER
ART DIRECTOR
Simon Bowden
WRITER
Marty Cooke
DESIGNER
Simon Bowden
PHOTOGRAPHERS
Pete Turner
Eric Meola
Sara Moon
NASA
Neil Leifer
David Kennerly
CLIENT
Nikon
AGENCY
Scali McCabe Sloves

41 BRONZE
ART DIRECTOR
James Sebastian
DESIGNERS
James Sebastian
Pen-Ek Ratanaruang
William Walter
PHOTOGRAPHER
Bruce Wolf
CLIENT
Martex/West Point Pepperell
AGENCY
Designframe Incorporated

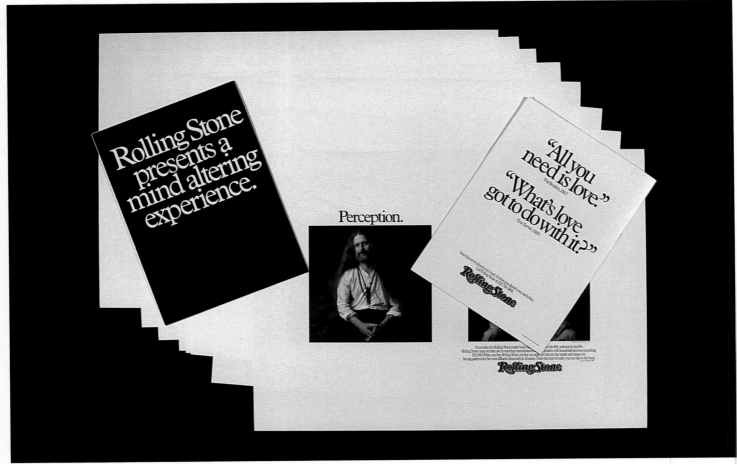

39 GOLD

Pete Turner,
Eric Meola,
David Hume Kennerly,
Sarah Moon,
Neil Leifer
and NASA
on Nikon lenses.

40 SILVER

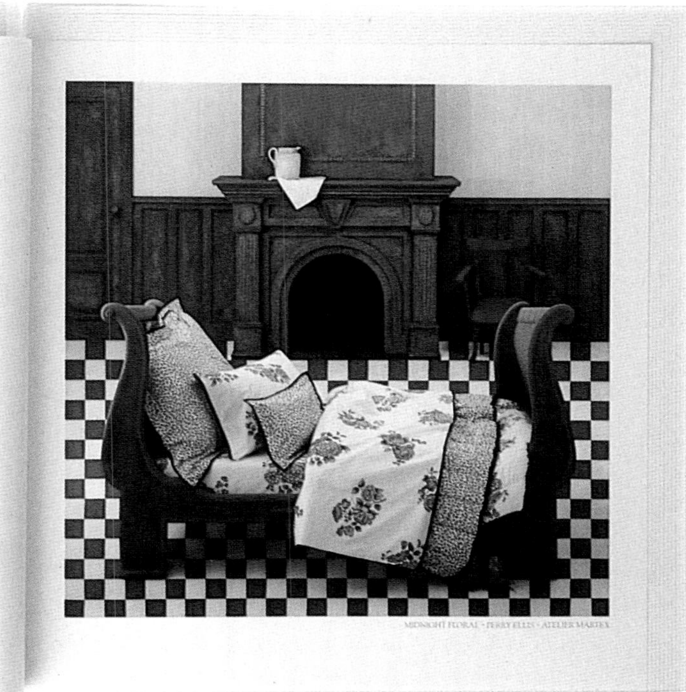

41 BRONZE

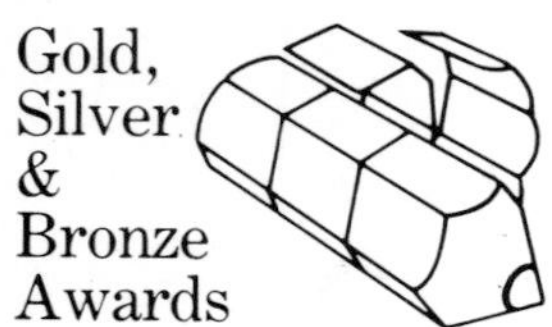

Collateral Sales Kits

42 SILVER
ART DIRECTOR
Beth Jeffe
WRITER
Norah Delaney
DESIGNER
Beth Jeffe
CLIENT
BMW of North America
AGENCY
Ammirati & Puris

43 BRONZE
ART DIRECTOR
Frank Schulwolf
WRITER
Arthur Low
ARTIST
Ted Lodigensky
CLIENT
Aviation Sales Company
AGENCY
Susan Gilbert & Company/
Coral Gables, FL

Collateral Direct Mail

44 GOLD
ART DIRECTOR
Nancy Rice
WRITER
Mike Lescarbeau
CLIENT
Michael & Linda Ehrlich
AGENCY
Fallon McElligott/Minneapolis

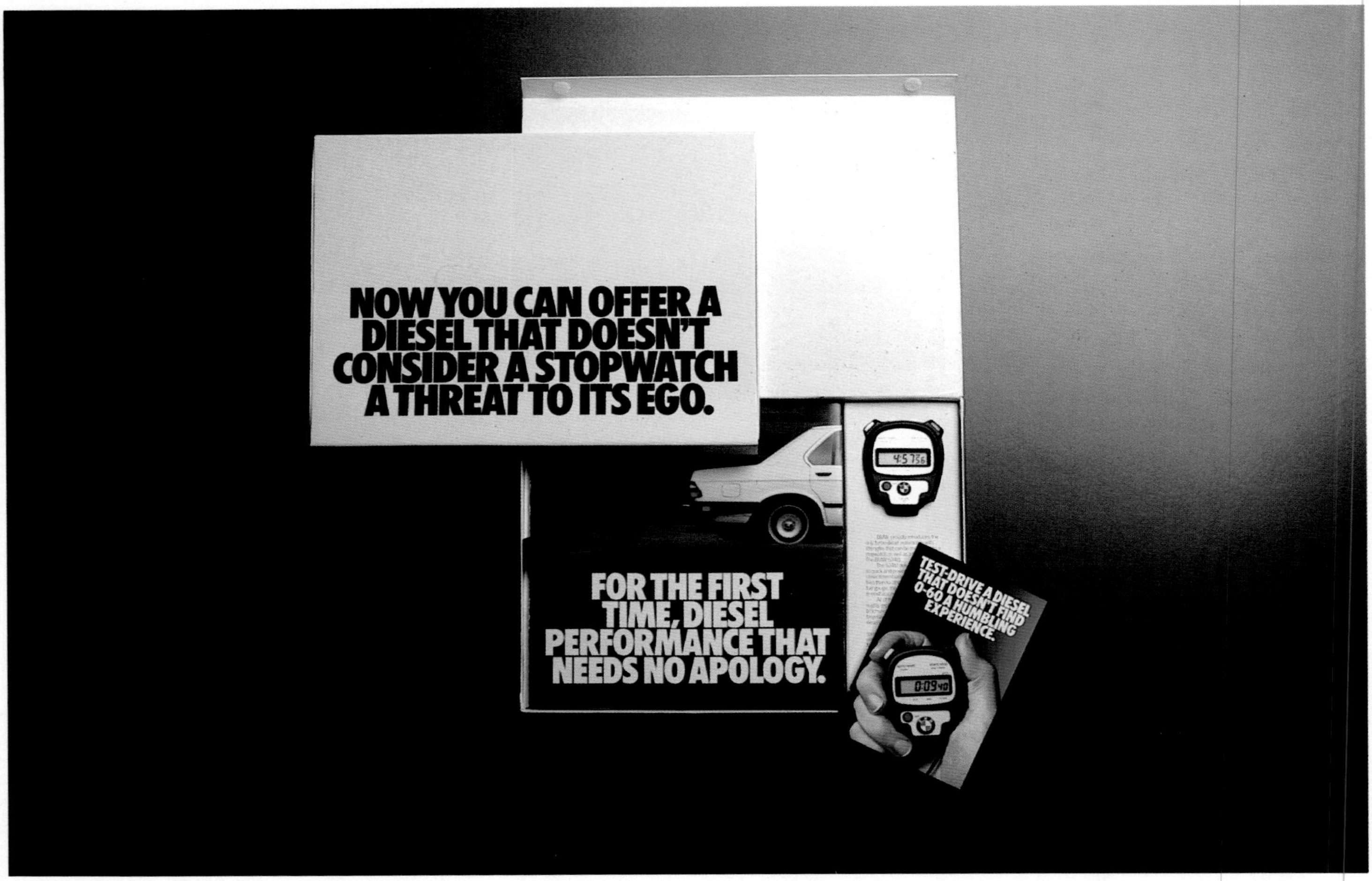

42 SILVER

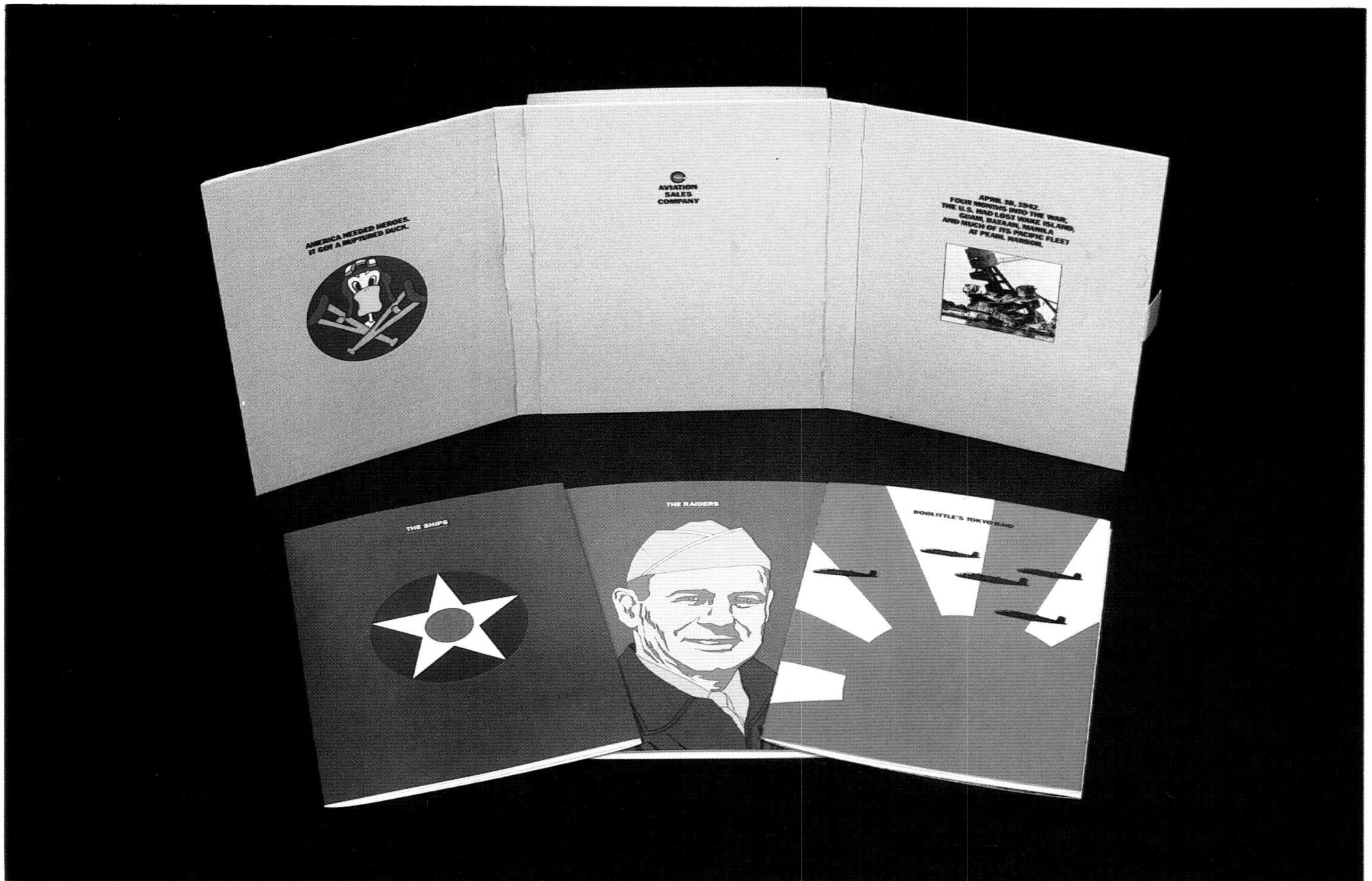

43 BRONZE

ON WEDNESDAY, JANUARY SIXTEENTH, MICHAEL AND LINDA EHRLICH'S FIRST CHILD WAS BORN WITHOUT A PENIS.

44 GOLD

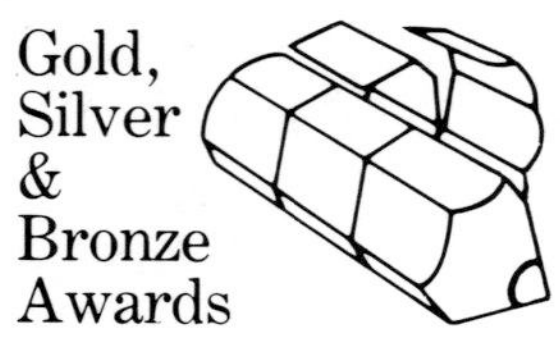

Collateral Direct Mail

45 SILVER
ART DIRECTOR
Bryan Buckley
WRITER
Bryan Buckley
CLIENT
Bryan Buckley
AGENCY
Grace & Rothschild

46 BRONZE
ART DIRECTOR
Dean Hanson
WRITER
Dean Hanson
DESIGNER
Dean Hanson
CLIENT
Mary Hanson
AGENCY
Fallon McElligott/Minneapolis

Collateral P.O.P.

47 GOLD
ART DIRECTOR
Mark Haumersen
WRITER
John Garvis
CLIENT
Army Surplus Store
AGENCY
Martin/Williams - Minneapolis

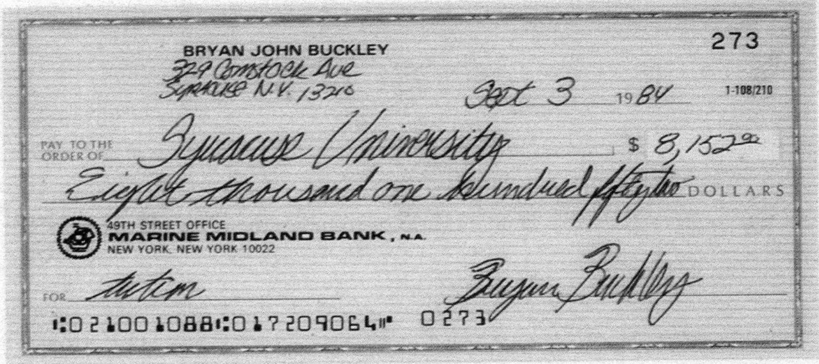

Thanks to your Volkswagen ads I'm $25,000 in debt.

My name is Bryan Buckley. Your legendary ads didn't inspire me to buy a Volkswagen. They inspired me to go into advertising.

I spent four years at college trying to come up with visuals for toilet bowl cleaners and headlines for the illiterate.

Now I have loan payments into the next century, a '69 Pontiac with 162,000 on it, and a choice of hot-dogs or tuna for dinner.

Sound depressing?

It isn't.

Now, I've got a good book.

Mr. Grace, if you're interested in hiring the assistant art director you brought into the business, please drop me a line.

If not, please stop doing great ads. I'd hate to see you ruin anyone else's credit rating.

B U C K L E Y

45 SILVER

SYDNEY KATHERINE
7 lbs. 1 oz.

Twins.

WILLIAM LEONARD
6 lbs. 4 oz.

Mary Hanson Just Solved The Mystery Of Why Mother Nature Gives Us Two Of Everything.

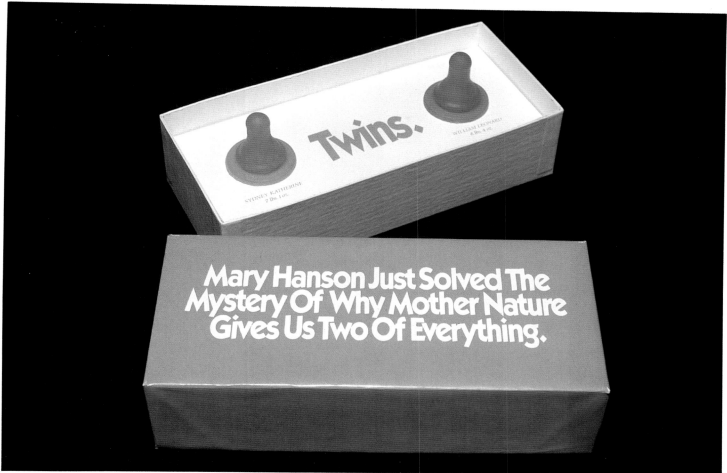

46 BRONZE

YOU MAY HAVE SEEN OUR FASHIONS ON THE STREETS OF PARIS.

47 GOLD

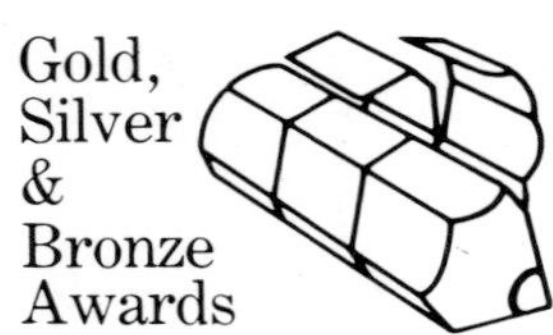
Gold,
Silver
&
Bronze
Awards

Collateral P.O.P.

48 SILVER
ART DIRECTOR
Bob Barrie
WRITER
John Stingley
DESIGNER
Bob Barrie
ARTISTS
Dick Hess
Mark Hess
CLIENT
Prince Spaghetti Sauce
AGENCY
Fallon McElligott/Minneapolis

49 BRONZE
ART DIRECTOR
Bob Barrie
WRITER
Sam Avery
DESIGNER
Bob Barrie
PHOTOGRAPHER
Rick Dublin
CLIENT
Davanni's
AGENCY
Fallon McElligott/Minneapolis

Outdoor: Single

50 GOLD
ART DIRECTOR
Rob Dalton
WRITER
Sam Avery
DESIGNER
Rob Dalton
CLIENT
WFLD-TV
AGENCY
Fallon McElligott/Minneapolis

PRINCE
SPAGHETTI SAUCE
Original.

PRINCE
CHUNKY HOMESTYLE
Chunky.
When we make Prince Spaghetti Sauce, we give you a choice. Because no two people have quite the same taste.
PRINCE

48 SILVER

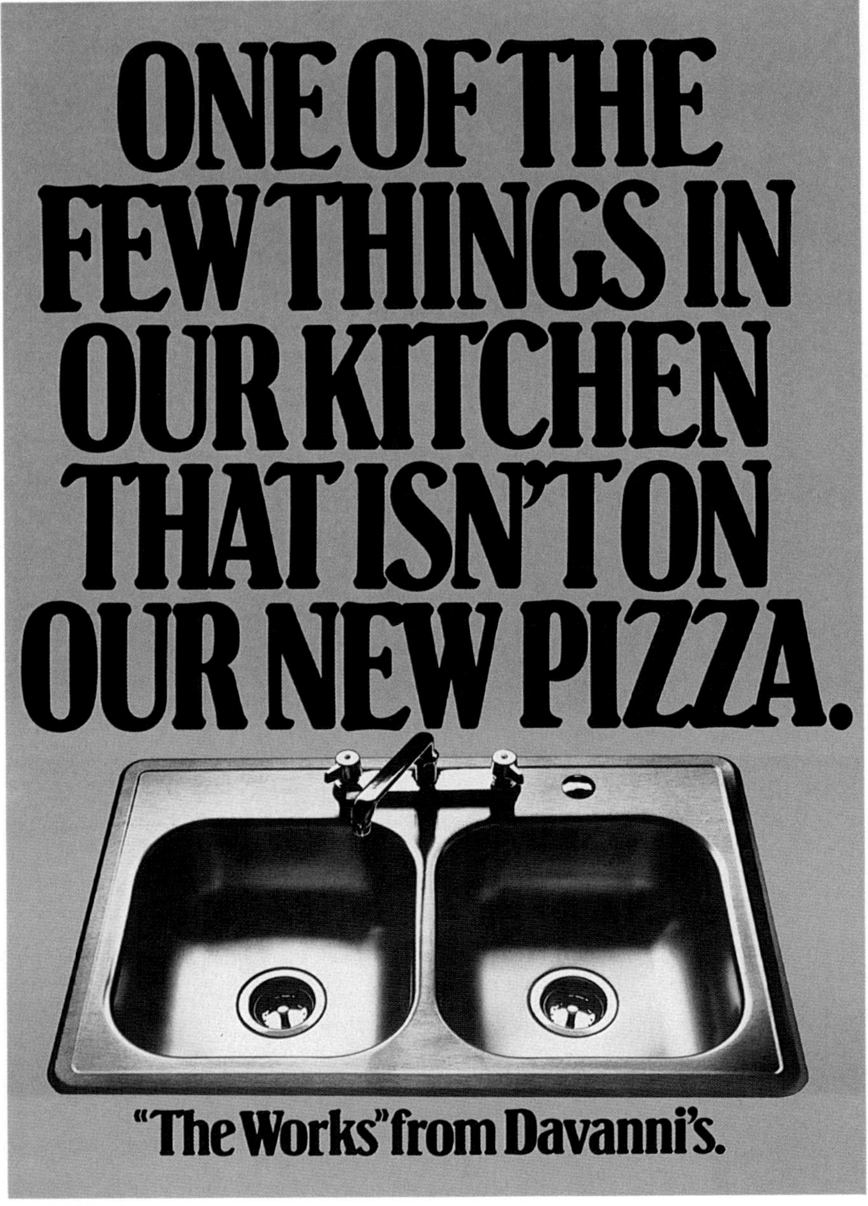
ONE OF THE FEW THINGS IN OUR KITCHEN THAT ISN'T ON OUR NEW PIZZA.
"The Works" from Davanni's.

49 BRONZE

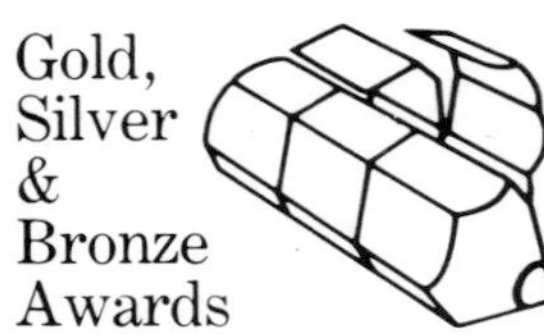

Outdoor: Single

51 SILVER
ART DIRECTOR
Kathleen Lee
WRITER
Charles Bromley
DESIGNER
Kathleen Lee
CLIENT
Israel Government Tourist Office
AGENCY
Biederman & Company

52 BRONZE
ART DIRECTOR
Rob Dalton
WRITER
Sam Avery
DESIGNER
Rob Dalton
CLIENT
WFLD-TV
AGENCY
Fallon McElligott/Minneapolis

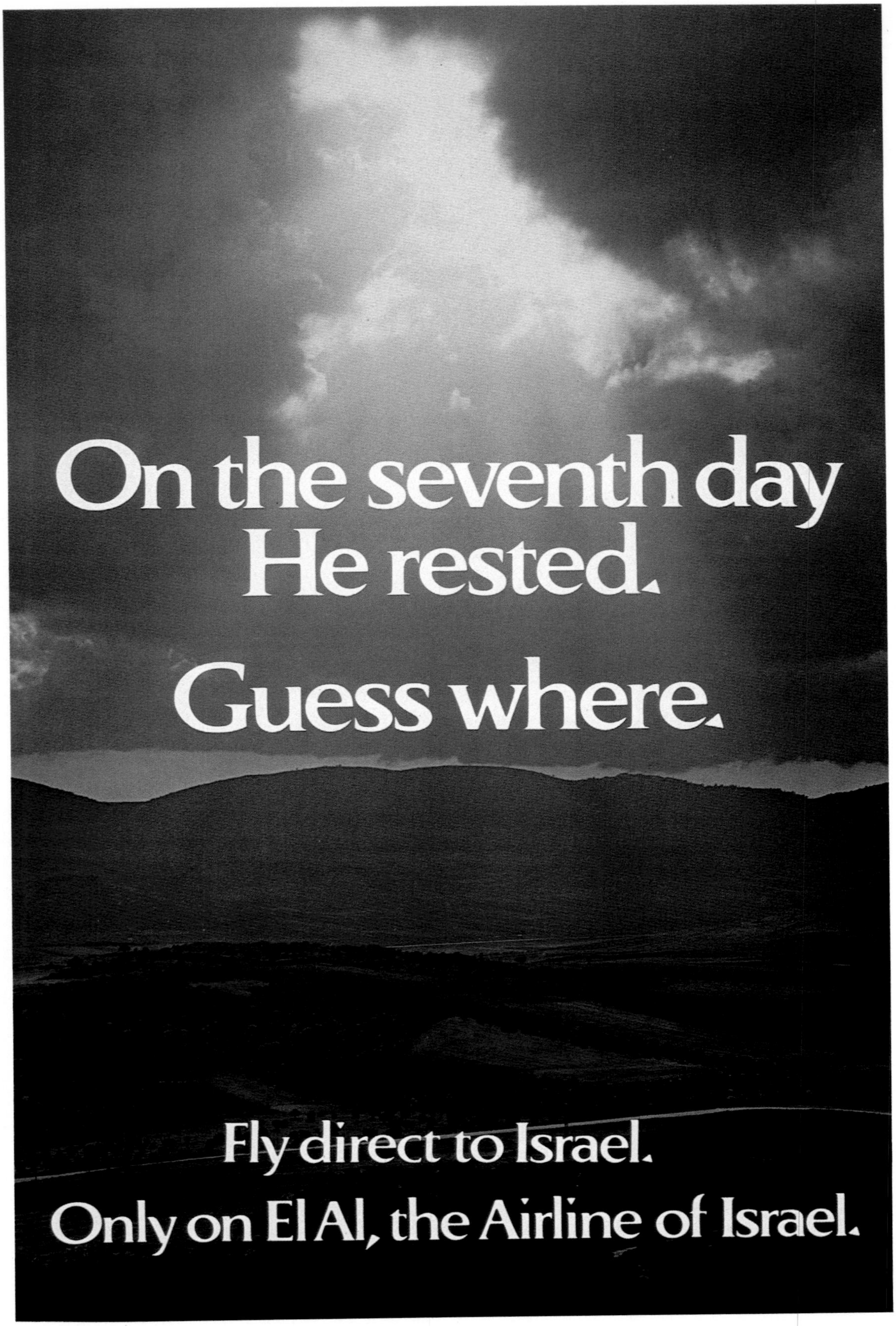

On the seventh day He rested.

Guess where.

Fly direct to Israel.

Only on El Al, the Airline of Israel.

51 SILVER

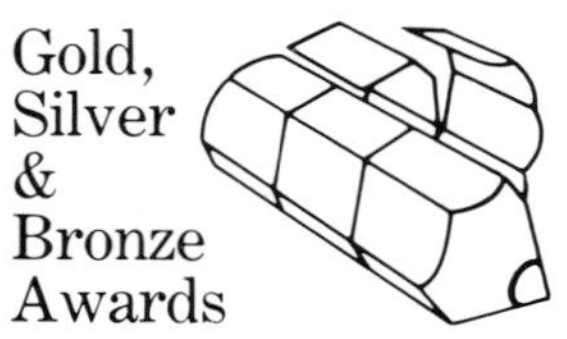

Outdoor: Campaign

53 GOLD
ART DIRECTORS
Rob Dalton
Tom Lichtenheld
WRITERS
Sam Avery
Jarl Olsen
DESIGNER
Rob Dalton
CLIENT
WFLD-TV
AGENCY
Fallon McElligott/Minneapolis

BITCH, BITCH, BITCH.

Dynasty. Weeknights at 9.

32
WFLD TV

53 GOLD

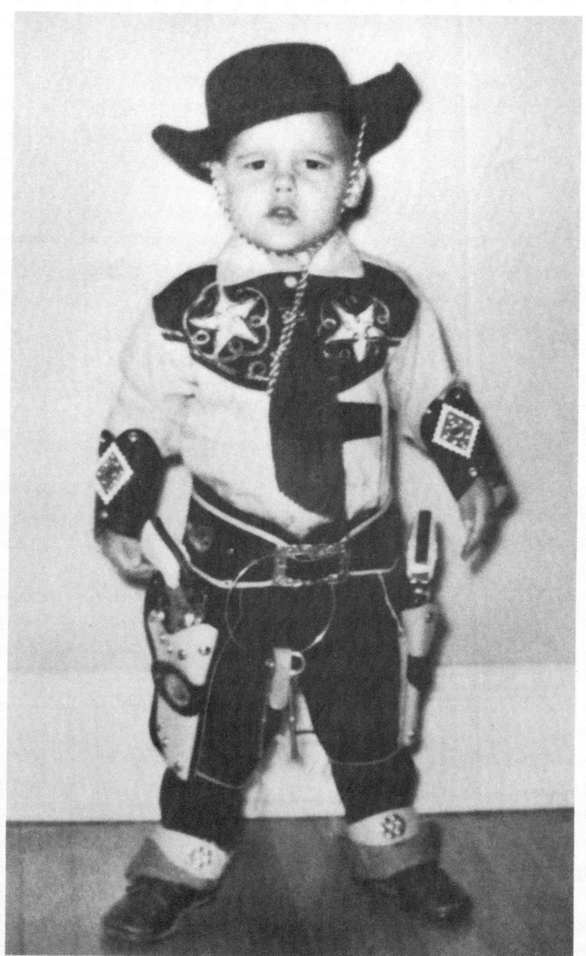

"GO AHEAD, MAKE MY LUNCH."

See the young Clint Eastwood in "For a Few Dollars More" Monday, November 11 at 7pm.

32
WFLDTV

IT SEEMS THE KENNEDYS MAY HAVE SHARED MORE THAN THEIR POLITICAL BELIEFS.

Discover the truth about an extraordinary woman. And the men who loved her.

"THE LAST DAYS OF MARILYN MONROE." WEDNESDAY, DECEMBER 4, AT 7 PM.

32
WFLDTV

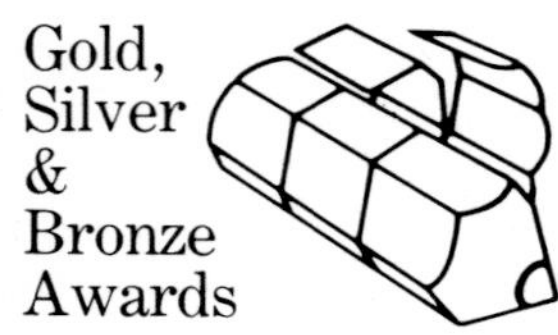

Outdoor: Campaign

54 SILVER
ART DIRECTOR
Bob Barrie
WRITER
Rod Kilpatrick
DESIGNER
Rob Barrie
CLIENT
Musicland
AGENCY
Fallon McElligott/Minneapolis

55 BRONZE
ART DIRECTORS
Cliff Goodenough
Ron Sandilands
WRITER
Bernie Hafeli
DESIGNERS
Cindy Ward
Anne Henry
CLIENT
Woodland Park Zoo
AGENCY
Livingston & Company/
Seattle

To an Ethiopian it's dinner music.

A public service message from
musicland

Who says music only nourishes the soul?

A public service message from
musicland

An entire nation is eating up the profits.

A public service message from
musicland

54 SILVER

VOTE FOR A SNAKE.
YES ON ZOO BONDS.

VOTE FOR A BABOON.
YES ON ZOO BONDS.

VOTE FOR A TURKEY.
YES ON ZOO BONDS.

55 BRONZE

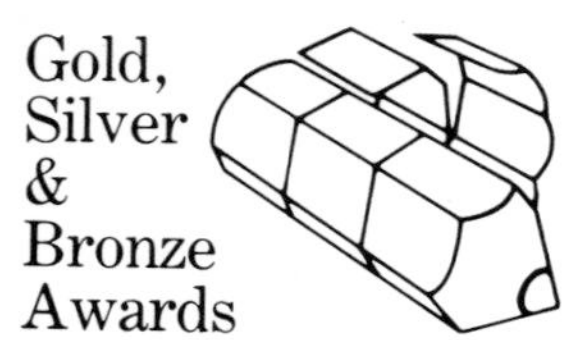

Public Service Newspaper Or Magazine: Single

56 GOLD
ART DIRECTOR
Amy Watt
WRITER
Edward Boches
PHOTOGRAPHER
Frank Rapp
CLIENT
Greater Media Cable TV Company
AGENCY
Mullen Advertising & Public Relations/Prides Crossing, MA

57 SILVER
ART DIRECTOR
Nancy Rice
WRITER
Tom McElligott
CLIENT
Episcopal Church
AGENCY
Fallon McElligott/Minneapolis

58 BRONZE
ART DIRECTOR
Nancy Rice
WRITER
Tom McElligott
ARTIST
Dürer
CLIENT
Episcopal Church
AGENCY
Fallon McElligott/Minneapolis

If your child were missing, could you describe his laugh, his smile? What about the way he shrugs his shoulders? Or nods his head?

We could.

We'll videotape your children for free. September 14, between 11 am and 6 pm at the Fairfield Mall in Chicopee.
On September 18, from 6:30 pm to 8 pm; and September 21, from 11 am to 4 pm at our offices, 16 Ames Ave., off Front St.

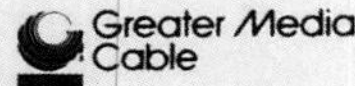

If you think church is only for families, remember Jesus was single.

The Episcopal Church believes there's more than enough room for singles in the family of God.
We invite you to join us in faith and fellowship every Sunday.
The Episcopal Church

57 SILVER

Now that your kids can name the nine reindeer shouldn't they be able to name the twelve apostles?

To help your children discover some of the most unforgettable characters they'll ever meet,
join us in The Episcopal Church each Sunday as we read from the greatest story ever told.
The Episcopal Church

58 BRONZE

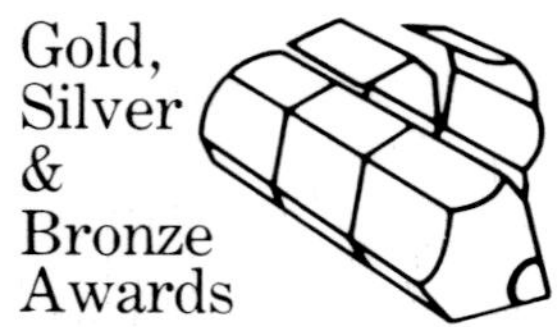

Public Service Newspaper Or Magazine: Campaign

59 GOLD
ART DIRECTOR
Nancy Rice
WRITERS
Tom McElligott
Mike Lescarbeau
CLIENT
Episcopal Church
AGENCY
Fallon McElligott/Minneapolis

Where women stand in the Episcopal Church.

If you believe that men and women should share equally in the sacraments and service of Christianity, join us where God's calling can be answered by anyone.
The Episcopal Church

59 GOLD

Does Easter mean beans to your kids?

If you agree that Easter should do more for your children than raise their blood sugar level, we invite you and your family to experience the true miracle of Easter in The Episcopal Church.

The Episcopal Church

If you think church is only for families, remember Jesus was single.

The Episcopal Church believes there's more than enough room for singles in the family of God. We invite you to join us in faith and fellowship every Sunday.

The Episcopal Church

Gold,
Silver
&
Bronze
Awards

Public Service Newspaper Or Magazine: Campaign

60 BRONZE
ART DIRECTOR
Cabell Harris
WRITER
Mike Hughes
PHOTOGRAPHER
Pat Edwards
CLIENT
Manchester Rescue Squad
AGENCY
Drinking Buddies
Advertising/Richmond, VA

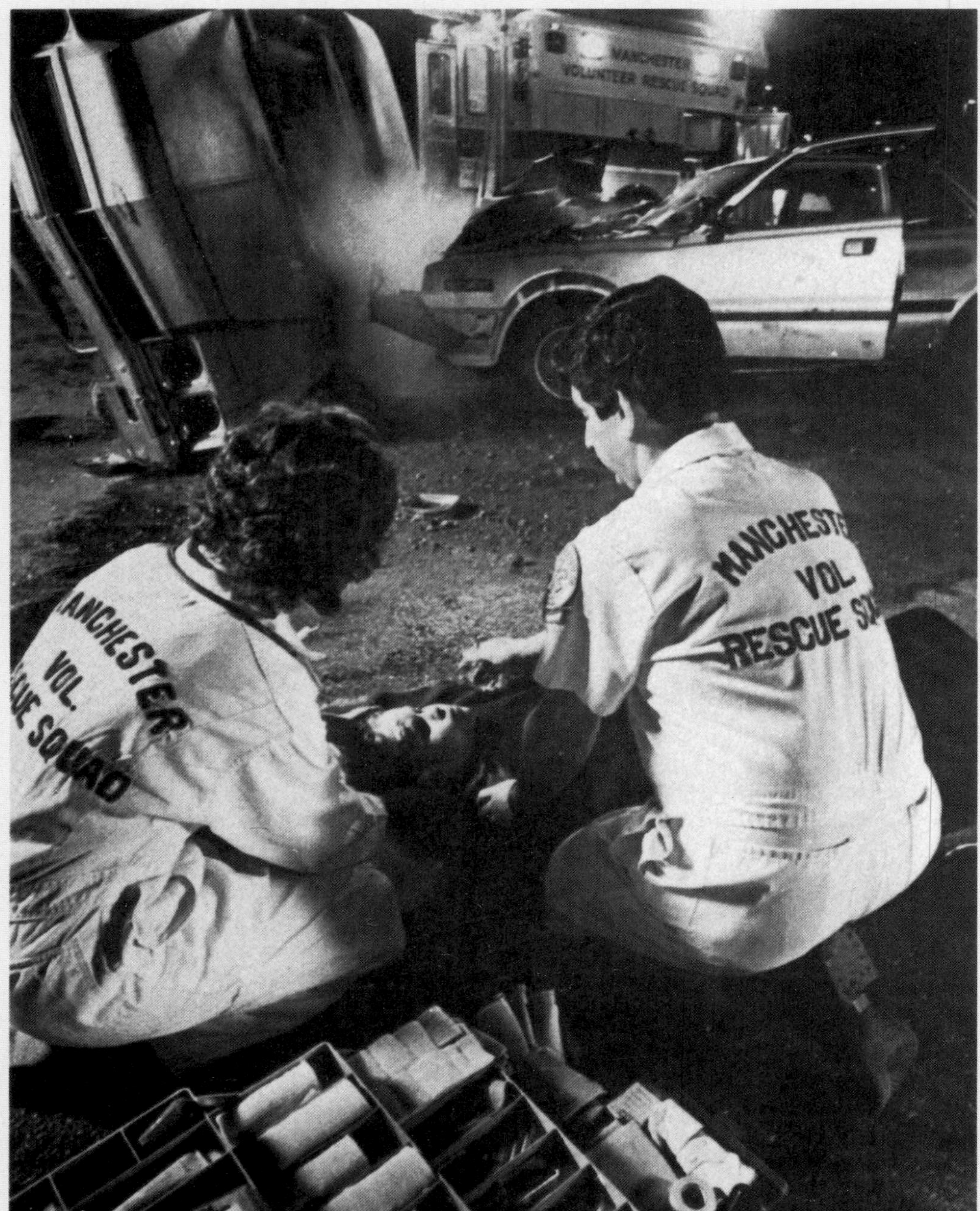

NOT ALL SUPERHEROES LIVE IN COMIC BOOKS.

You can't leap tall buildings in a single bound. And there's a good chance you'll never stop a mad scientist from blowing up the world.

But you can make a big difference. You really can be somebody's hero.

Sign up for the Manchester Volunteer Rescue Squad. We'll train you to help your neighbors and friends through some of life's biggest emergencies.

Every week of the year, someone on our squad makes an important difference in someone else's life. Every week.

Maybe they provide CPR. Maybe they rush someone to a hospital. Maybe they help after an accident.

But whatever they do, their actions are nothing less than heroic.

BE SOMEBODY'S HERO.

60 BRONZE

THE MANCHESTER RESCUE SQUAD IS FOR ALL THOSE PEOPLE WHO GREW UP WANTING TO BE SOMEBODY'S HERO.

Ever since you were a kid, you've wanted to do something special with your life. Something important.

Of course, you're very important now, both at home and on the job. But, still, something's missing in your life.

A sense of commitment, maybe. A sense of adventure. Or maybe even some little sense of heroism.

Maybe you should sign up for the Manchester Volunteer Rescue Squad. If you do, you'll learn nothing less than the skills you need to save people's lives.

But we don't want to mislead you. You'll work hard, you'll work for no pay and you'll work a lot of crazy hours. You see, unless you can leap tall buildings in a single bound, being a hero isn't easy.

Call 276-4344 to learn more. If you're not in our area, we'll direct you to another volunteer rescue squad close to you.

BE SOMEBODY'S HERO.

Join The Manchester Volunteer Rescue Squad.

OUR VOLUNTEERS LIVE LIFE IN THE FAST LANE.

For sheer drama, your nine-to-five job can't touch our round-the-clock job.

For example, last Sunday, while you were home reading the newspaper, Manchester Rescue Squad volunteers were helping their neighbors through some of life's biggest emergencies.

They were responding to accident calls. Administering aid to stroke victims. Rushing someone to the hospital.

If you were a volunteer, you'd be trained to handle these emergencies, too. (Just think, incidentally, how much more confident you'll be around your own family once you have these skills.)

We're looking for volunteers right now. So please give us a call at 276-4344. If you're not in our area, we'll direct you to the volunteer squad nearest you.

After all, we're not the only ones around here living life in the fast lane.

BE SOMEBODY'S HERO.

Join The Manchester Volunteer Rescue Squad.

Gold, Silver & Bronze Awards

Public Service Outdoor: Single

61 GOLD
ART DIRECTOR
Bob Barrie
WRITER
Mike Lescarbeau
DESIGNER
Bob Barrie
PHOTOGRAPHER
Bobby Holland
CLIENT
Reader's Digest
AGENCY
Fallon McElligott/Minneapolis

62 SILVER
ART DIRECTOR
Rob Boezewinkel
DESIGNER
Rob Boezewinkel
PHOTOGRAPHER
Nick Koudis
CLIENT
American Cancer Society

63 BRONZE
ART DIRECTOR
Nancy Rice
WRITER
Tom McElligott
ARTIST
Hans Holbein
CLIENT
Episcopal Church
AGENCY
Fallon McElligott/Minneapolis

"Before I'll ride with a drunk, I'll drive myself." —Stevie Wonder
Driving after drinking, or riding with a driver who's been drinking, is a big mistake. Anyone can see that.

61 GOLD

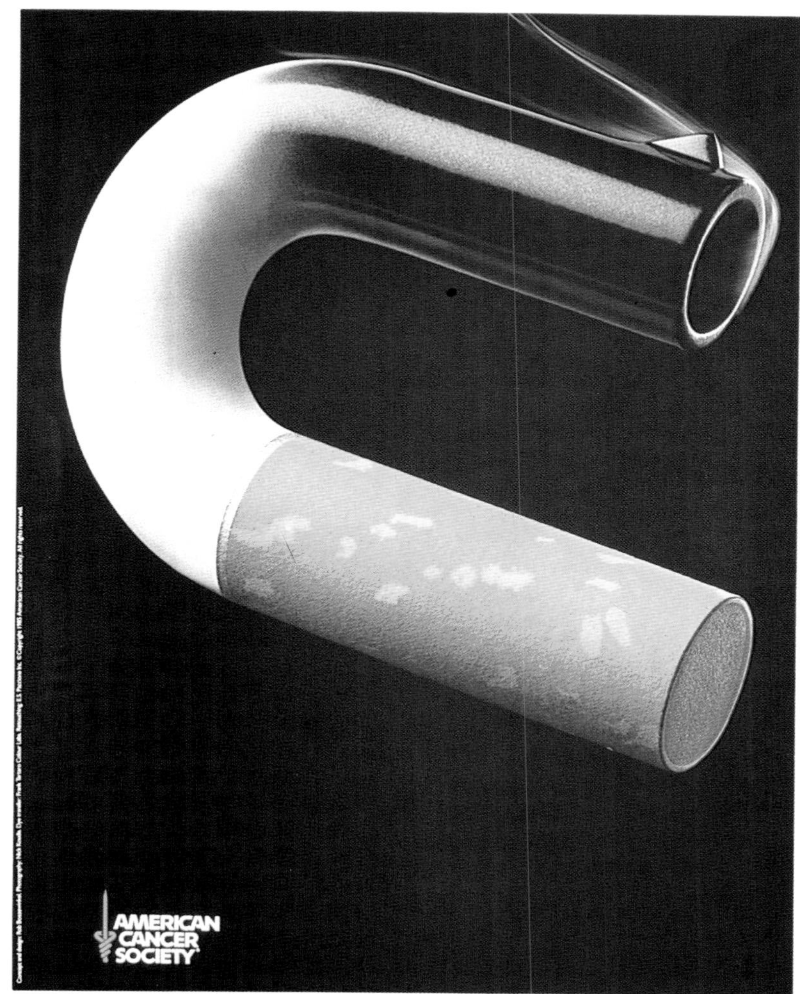

62 SILVER

63 BRONZE

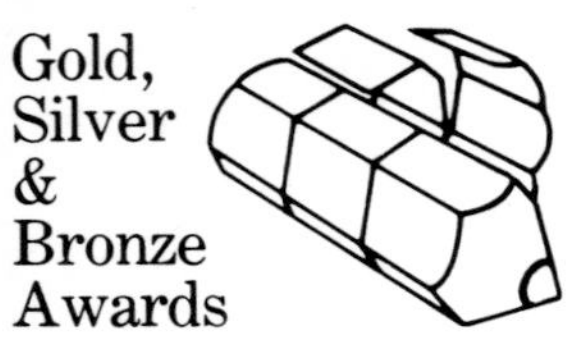

College Competition

64 GOLD
ART DIRECTOR
David Ring
CLIENT
The CIA
COLLEGE
East Texas State University, Commerce

Read it.

Now
eat it.

Pssst. The CIA wants you.

Gold, Silver & Bronze Awards

College Competition

65 SILVER
ART DIRECTOR & WRITER
Blake W. Zipoy
CLIENT
The CIA
COLLEGE
East Texas State University, Commerce

IF YOU'RE INTO
VANDALISM,
BRIBERY,
HAZING,
KIDNAPPING,
LYING,
CHEATING,
THIEVERY,
HACKING,
AND
DIRTY TRICKS,

YOUR COUNTRY NEEDS YOU.

sed diam nonumy eiusmod te
nostrud exercitation ullamcorpor susci
in reprehenderit in voluptate velit esse molestaie son c
o dignissim qui blandit prasesent lu
or sunt in culpa qui officia d
ber a tempor cum soluta nobis elig
s assumenda est, omnis dolor r
diand sint et molest
riore repellat. Hanc ego cum tene
ante cum memorite it tum etia ergat. Nos amice
civiuda. Et tamen in.

THE C.I.A.
AMERICA'S NON-DECORATED HEROS.

65 SILVER

AMERICA
NEEDS
TOP COLLEGE
GRADUATES
FOR

VANDALISM,
BRIBERY,
HAZING,
KIDNAPPING,
LYING,
CHEATING,
THIEVERY,
HACKING,
AND
DIRTY TRICKS.

sed diam nonumy eiusmod te
nostrud exercitation ullamcorper susc
in reprehenderit in voluptate velit esse molestæ son c
o dignissim qui blandit prasesent lu
or sunt in culpa qui officia d
ber a tempor cum soluta nobis elig
s assumenda est, omnis dolor r
diand sint et molest
nore repellat. Hanc ego cum tene
ante cum memorite it tum etia ergat. Nos amice
civiuda. Et tamen in.

THE C.I.A.
AMERICA'S NON-DECORATED HEROS.

College Competition

66 BRONZE
ART DIRECTOR & WRITER
Tom Hudder

CLIENT
The CIA

COLLEGE
Pasadena Art Center College
of Design, CA

When you apply for a job, consider not only who you'll be working for, but also who you'll be working against.

Now is the time to investigate
a career with the C.I.A.
See a recruiter today.

Apply for a job with our company. We may offer you a roomy company car,

secluded company housing,

maybe even a chance to fly on one of our sophisticated company aircraft.

Best of all, someday you might get a chance to work with our President.

Now is the time to investigate a career with the C.I.A. See a recruiter today.

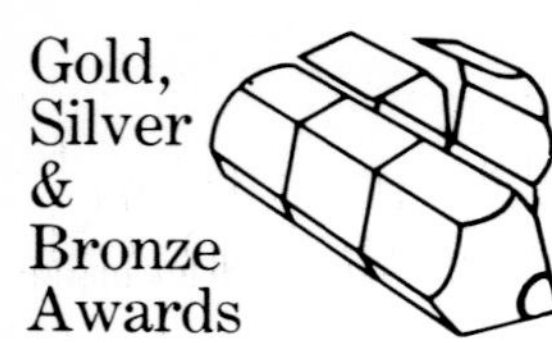

Gold, Silver & Bronze Awards

Consumer Radio: Single

67 GOLD
WRITERS
Robin Raj
John Crawford
CLIENT
NYNEX Information Resources
AGENCY
Chiat/Day

68 SILVER
WRITERS
Charles Mullen
John Clapps
AGENCY PRODUCER
Richard Goldstein
CLIENT
Suntory Beer
AGENCY
Isidore & Paulson

69 BRONZE
WRITER
Jarl Olsen
AGENCY PRODUCER
Jarl Olsen
CLIENT
WFLD-TV
AGENCY
Fallon McElligott/Minneapolis

Consumer Radio: Campaign

70 GOLD
WRITERS
Mark Fenske
Emo Phillips
AGENCY PRODUCER
Laurie Berger
CLIENT
Dovebar International
AGENCY
Zechman & Associates/Chicago

71 SILVER
WRITERS
Robin Raj
John Crawford
CLIENT
NYNEX Information Resources
AGENCY
Chiat/Day

72 BRONZE
WRITER
James Parry
AGENCY PRODUCER
Bertelle Selig
CLIENT
Reader's Digest
AGENCY
James Parry, Inc.

67 GOLD

(INTERVIEWER SPEAKING WITH NECKTIE RENOVATOR. HE IS NOT THE EASIEST PERSON TO INTERVIEW. SEWING MACHINES AND FACTORY SOUNDS IN BACKGROUND.)

INTVR: We're here with Ed Leber, who runs another one of those unusual businesses in the Nynex Yellow Pages. Ed, you restore neckties.

ED: That's right. We're necktie renovators.

INTVR: Now what exactly does that involve?

ED: We take the ties and resize them, reshape them . . . um . . . (WITH INTERVIEWER) Renovate them.

INTVR: Mmmm, that's fascinating. So as the styles change, you might take somebody's wide ties and make them narrow.

ED: We do that, yes.

INTVR: Ever make a narrow tie wide?

ED: No, we can't do that.

INTVR: Your ad in the NYNEX Yellow Pages says you've been in business since 1947. How'd you get started in business, Ed?

ED: Well, I started out doing this in 1947 and I just kind of . . . uh . . .

INTVR: Kept at it?

ED: Yeah.

INTVR: Well, what is it you like about the necktie renovation business?

ED: The people.

INTVR: Ed Leber. Necktie renovator. Just another reason the NYNEX Yellow Pages helps more people in New England find more goods and services.

ED: I do have one funny story . . .

INTVR: Well, we're out of time, Ed.

ED: Oh.

INTVR: The NYNEX Yellow Pages. No matter what you need, it's always there when you need it.

68 SILVER

(SFX: COTO PLAYS INTRODUCTION)

JAPANESE ADMAN: Honorable client. We make presentation of TV storyboard to introduce Suntory Draft Beer overseas in America.

JAPANESE CLIENT: Proceed. Please.

ADMAN: First, we see famous athletes on camping trip—sitting around camp fire.

CLIENT: Hi. Yes.

ADMAN: Headman say, you guys ready for another Suntory Draft Beer in a bottle.

CLIENT: Good . . . Good.

ADMAN: Now get this: man tells dog, Alex go get beer. Dog comes back with Crysdal horses who have whole wagon load of Suntory.

CLIENT: Crysdal?

ADMAN: You know horse with funny feet.

TOGETHER: Oh, Crysdals.

ADMAN: Man starts to play hard basketball game—loser to buy Suntory Beer . . . but get this: as they play we hear Crysdals drinking up all the Suntory Beer . . . How do you like?

CLIENT: Hmmm . . . Maybe TV no such good idea. How 'bout radio.

ANNCR: Introducing Suntory's new advertising campaign: we have a lot of catching up to do.

69 BRONZE

JACQUES COUSTEAU (SINGING IN FRENCH):
Old man river, that old man river,
He must know somethin'
But he don't say nothing
He just keeps rollin'
He just keeps rollin' along
(HUMS)

ANNCR: Jacques Cousteau sings the praises of the Mighty Mississippi, Sunday at 8. Explore America's greatest waterway with the crew of the Calypso on Cousteau: Mississippi on WFLD Metromedia 32.

JACQUES: *Lift that barge! Tote that bale . . .*

70 GOLD

EMO PHILLIPS: It's always been a tradition in our house that when it's your birthday, you get . . . presents.
Once my mom said, 'Son, what do you want for your birthday?'
I said, 'I want an icy cold chocolate-covered kooky crazy DoveBar.'
She said, 'Don't use alliteration with me, young man. You'll get a regular ice cream bar.'
I said, 'Mom, it's my birthday!
'I'm lucky if it comes once a year.
'And I don't want a regular ice cream bar, I want a DoveBar.
'I don't care if it is a bit harder for you to slip under the closet door.
'Hmphh.'

VO: The DoveBar. In your grocer's freezer.

70 GOLD

EMO PHILLIPS: Once, my dad said, 'Son, who ate that chocolate DoveBar I had in the freezer?'
I said, 'Oh, er, um, uh . . . Princess Edwina of Norway!'
And my dad grabbed a blender and some two-by-fours and gave me the spanking of my life.
Crying, I ran into my room, and there was Edwina, eating a DoveBar and laughing hysterically.
I screamed, 'Daddy! I found your DoveBar!'
But the Princess jumped out the window and sped off in a waiting car, leaving just a shiny brown wrapper to remind us of the excitement that only a DoveBar can bring.

VO: The DoveBar. In your grocer's freezer.

70 GOLD

EMO PHILLIPS: One morning, as I was skipping merrily to school, I saw a DoveBar beckoning to me through a supermarket window.
Suddenly, a little devil appeared over my head saying, 'Use the money your mom gave you for the class field trip to buy the DoveBar.'
Then a little angel appeared over my head and said, 'He's right, that is a good idea.'
Well, although that DoveBar was fantastic, just as I was finishing it I saw the school bus leaving for the field trip.
A lump rose in my throat.
And I learned a lesson that day.
No matter how tasty a DoveBar is . . . never swallow the stick.

VO: The DoveBar. In your grocer's freezer.

71 SILVER

(INTERVIEWER SPEAKING WITH NECKTIE RENOVATOR. HE IS NOT THE EASIEST PERSON TO INTERVIEW. SEWING MACHINE AND FACTORY SOUNDS IN BACKGROUND.)

INTVR: We're here with Ed Leber, who runs another one of those unusual businesses in the Nynex Yellow Pages. Ed, you restore neckties.

ED: That's right. We're necktie renovators.

INTVR: Now what exactly does that involve?

ED: We take the ties and resize them, reshape them . . . um . . . (WITH INTERVIEWER) Renovate them.

INTVR: Mmmm, that's fascinating. So as the styles change, you might take somebody's wide ties and make them narrow.

ED: We do that, yes.

INTVR: Ever make a narrow tie wide?

ED: No, we can't do that.

INTVR: Your ad in the NYNEX Yellow Pages says you've been in business since 1947. How'd you get started in business, Ed?

ED: Well, I started out doing this in 1947 and I just kind of . . . uh . . .

INTVR: Kept at it?

ED: Yeah.

INTVR: Well, what is it you like about the necktie renovation business?

ED: The people.

INTVR: Ed Leber. Necktie renovator. Just another reason the NYNEX Yellow Pages helps more people in New England find more goods and services.

ED: I do have one funny story . . .

INTVR: Well, we're out of time, Ed.

ED: Oh.

INTVR: The NYNEX Yellow Pages. No matter what you need, it's always there when you need it.

72 BRONZE

ANNCR: A certain football coach praised his players by saying . . .

1ST COACH: It shows what the guys can do when they get their dandruff up.

ANNCR: After a brutal game, a hockey coach praised his players by saying . . .

2ND COACH: They didn't go by the Queen of Marksberry Rules tonight.

ANNCR: But another coach, concerned about sloppy defense, said . . .

3RD COACH: We've got to nip it in the butt.

ANNCR: And a player, tired of being reminded of an embarrassing incident, said . . .

PLAYER: C'mon, let a dead horse rest.

ANNCR: Want one more? When it was rumored that Yogi Berra might become manager of the Mets, a sportswriter asked, 'Yogi, have you made up your mind yet?' Answered Yogi . . .

"YOGI": Not that I know of.

ANNCR: Memorable malapropisms of sports—recounted in the October Reader's Digest. Every month, more people read—really *read*—The Digest than anything else . . . and learn it's not how you play the game, it's how you talk about it. We make a difference in more than 50 million lives. Oh, and then there was the college football coach who was told one of his players had charisma. Said the coach . . .

4TH COACH: What? Will he be okay by Saturday?

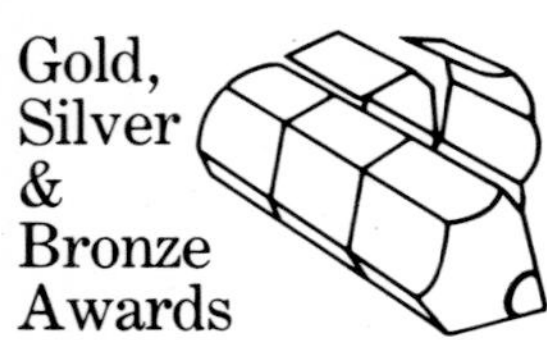

Consumer Television Over :30 (:45/:60/:90) Single

73 GOLD
ART DIRECTOR
Bruce Campbell
WRITER
Hal Riney
AGENCY PRODUCER
Barbro Eddy
PRODUCTION CO.
PYTKA
DIRECTOR
Joe Pytka
CLIENT
E&J Gallo Winery
AGENCY
Hal Riney & Partners/San Francisco

74 SILVER
ART DIRECTOR
Saskia Mossel
WRITER
Steve Baer
AGENCY PRODUCER
Al Gay
PRODUCTION CO.
David Ashwell Film Company
DIRECTOR
David Ashwell
CLIENT
General Foods Shake 'N Bake
AGENCY
Ogilvy & Mather

75 BRONZE
ART DIRECTOR
Don Easdon
WRITER
Bill Heater
AGENCY PRODUCER
Mary Ellen Argentieri
PRODUCTION CO.
PYTKA
DIRECTOR
Joe Pytka
CLIENT
John Hancock
AGENCY
Hill Holliday Connors Cosmopulos/Boston

73 GOLD

ANNCR: There are no better ways to make wine . . .
No better land to grow wine . . .
No better wines, than Gallo wines today.
Today's Gallo . . .
All the best a wine can be.

74 SILVER

DAUGHTER 1: Hi, mom, what's for dinner?
MOTHER: A new recipe for crispier . . . chicken.
SON: What's for dinner?
MOTHER: A new shake and bake recipe.
SON: Does that like make us guinea pigs?
MOM: No, your table manners do that.
DAUGHTER 2: What's for dinner?
MOM: A new shake and bake recipe.
SON: It's experimental.
MOM: It's new.
DAD: Hello.
MOM: Hi.
DAD: What's for dinner?
GRANDMA: Bird seed.
DAUGHTER 2: What's in it?
MOM: Everything.
DAUGHTER 2: What's everything?
DAD: What?
DAUGHTER 2: What's everything?
MOM: Basil, paprika, peppers . . .
SON: Dead leaves . . .

Income
Salary . . . $30,000

Needs
To limit tax liability
To build investments

DAD: What?

DAUGHTER 1: Dead leaves?

SON: Swamp grass . . .

DAD: What?

DAUGHTER 1: What's for dinner?

GRANDMA: A new recipe for crispier chicken.

DAD: What . . . chicken, thank you.

DAUGHTER 2: Will I . . .

MOM: What?

DAUGHTER 2: Like it.

MOM: If it goes in your mouth, it stays in your mouth.

DAUGHTER 2: I like this.

SON: I didn't get enough.

DAUGHTER 1: That's mine.

ANNCR.: New Shake And Bake coating mixture . . .

(DAUGHTER LOOKS TOWARD THE RINGING PHONE)

DAUGHTER 1: Hmph.

ANNCR: The complete recipe for success.

75 BRONZE

DAVE: Grace sure looked good tonight, didn't she?

MIKE: Yeah.

DAVE: So . . . how much you making now? Hunh? (CHUCKLE)

MIKE: I'm doing fine.

DAVE: You gotta be making at least 25.

MIKE: I'm fine. Maybe a little better than that.

DAVE: 30? Tell me . . . yes or no . . . are you making 30?

MIKE: Yes.

DAVE: 30?

MIKE: Around 30.

DAVE: You got any investments, any stuff?

MIKE: Got the car.

DAVE: That's not an investment. You got an IRA, life insurance?

MIKE (SIGH): Not really.

DAVE: You're making 30 and you don't have anything like that? What d'ya think? You're 18 years old or something?

Gold, Silver & Bronze Awards

Consumer Television Over :30 (:45/:60/:90) Campaign

76 GOLD
ART DIRECTOR
Gerald Andelin
AGENCY PRODUCER
Deborah Martin
PRODUCTION CO.
PYTKA
DIRECTOR
Joe Pytka
CLIENT
E&J Gallo Winery
AGENCY
Hal Riney & Partners/San Francisco

77 SILVER
ART DIRECTOR
Don Easdon
WRITER
Bill Heater
AGENCY PRODUCER
Mary Ellen Argentieri
PRODUCTION CO.
PYTKA
DIRECTOR
Joe Pytka
CLIENT
John Hancock
AGENCY
Hill Holliday Connors Cosmopulos/Boston

76 GOLD

FRANK: Hello there. My name is Frank Bartles, and this is Ed Jaymes. You know, it occurred to Ed the other day that between his fruit orchard and my premium wine vineyard, we could make a truly superior, premium grade wine cooler.
It sounded good to me, so Ed took out a second on his house and wrote to Harvard for an MBA, and now we're preparing to enter the Wine Cooler business.
We will try to keep you posted on how it's going.
Thank you very much for your support.

76 GOLD

FRANK: Hello again. I'm Frank Bartles, and you remember Ed Jaymes, my partner.
We have selected a bottle for our new premium wine cooler, and we were about to print up a label when Ed called my attention to the fact that we did not yet have a name for our product.
We were lucky he noticed that, as that would have been a big mistake.
So if you have any good ideas for a wine cooler name, we'd really appreciate your sending them along.
Thank you again for your support.

Needs

To protect
housing investment

Long-term
investment strategy

76 GOLD

FRANK: We want to thank you for all the name suggestions for our new wine cooler. There were some really clever ones.
But we decided just to call it 'The Bartles and Jaymes Wine Cooler' because my last name is Bartles, and Ed's is Jaymes.
If you don't like the name, please don't tell us, because we have already printed up our labels.
Anyway, you could always just call it Bartles and skip the Jaymes all together.
Ed says that is okay with him.
Thanks for your continued support.

77 SILVER

LAWYER: There's a lot of paperwork here. There's always paperwork when you buy a house. First one says that you lose the house if you don't make your payments. You probably don't want to think about that but . . . you do have to sign it.
Next says the property is insured for the amount of the note. And you sign that in the lower left corner.
This pretty much says that nobody's got a gun to your head . . . that you're entering this agreement freely.
Next is the house is free of termites. Last one says that the house will be your primary residence and that you won't be relying on rental income to make the payments.
I hope you brought your checkbook. This is the fun part. I say that all the time though most people don't think so. (CHUCKLE)

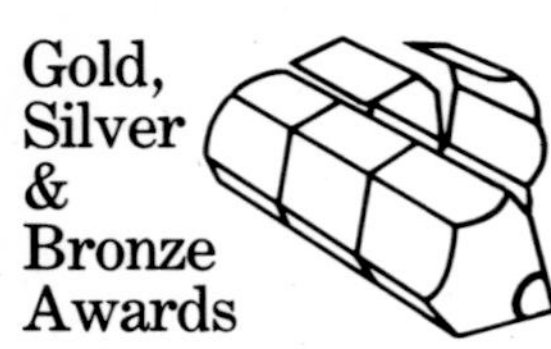

Consumer Television Over: 30 (:45/:60/:90) Campaign

78 BRONZE
ART DIRECTOR
Gerald Andelin
WRITER
Hal Riney
AGENCY PRODUCER
Deborah Martin
PRODUCTION CO.
PYTKA
DIRECTOR
Joe Pytka
CLIENT
E&J Gallo Winery
AGENCY
Ogilvy & Mather/San Francisco

Consumer Television :30 Single

79 GOLD
ART DIRECTOR
Rich Silverstein
WRITERS
Jeff Goodby
Andy Berlin
AGENCY PRODUCER
Debbie King
PRODUCTION CO.
Jon Francis Films
DIRECTOR
Jon Francis
CLIENT
San Francisco Examiner
AGENCY
Goodby Berlin & Silverstein/ San Francisco

80 SILVER
ART DIRECTOR
Gerald Andelin
WRITER
Hal Riney
AGENCY PRODUCER
Deborah Martin
PRODUCTION CO.
PYTKA
DIRECTOR
Joe Pytka
CLIENT
Henry Weinhard
AGENCY
Ogilvy & Mather/San Francisco

81 BRONZE
ART DIRECTOR
Rob Tomnay
WRITERS
Bob Isherwood
Jack Vaughan
AGENCY PRODUCER
Lois McKenzie
PRODUCTION CO.
Ian MacDonald Productions
DIRECTORS
Ian MacDonald
Wayne Maule
CLIENT
Allied Grocery Products
AGENCY
The Campaign Palace/ Australia

78 BRONZE

FRANK: Well, the new Bartles and Jaymes premium wine cooler is finally in the bottle, and our marketing director Gary Cox is now getting ready to put it into distribution in major markets. Please buy some, because frankly from our point of view there's no other wine cooler anywhere that's nearly as good at any price.
It would also be a personal favor to Ed, because he took out that second on his house and pretty soon he's got a big balloon payment coming up. Thank you and we hope you enjoy our new premium wine cooler

79 GOLD

(MUSIC UNDER THROUGHOUT)

WILL: I'm Will Hearst, publisher of The Examiner. And this is David Burgin . . . our editor. David's got a reputation as sort of a tough guy. But I think that's blown way out of proportion. Firm, sure . . . take charge, you bet. What I see in David is just a nice guy who commands a healthy respect. He's forcing us all to set our sights a little higher. And hey, what's wrong with that?

ANNCR: The next generation at the San Francisco Examiner.

80 SILVER

ANNCR: A hundred years ago, Henry Weinhard was making the West's finest premium beer . . . . . . serving it in the West's finest eating and drinking establishments . . .

COWBOY: Beer . . .

ANNCR: and charging just a little more

BARTEND: A nickel.

ANNCR: than the price of ordinary beers . . .

COWBOY: A *nickel*?

ANNCR: Because Henry made his beer just 400 barrels at a time . . .

BARTEND: It's Henry's.

ANNCR: Just like we still do today . . .

COWBOY: Ya' know, when I come in, I coulda swore you was a girl I knew back in Kansas City . . .

ANNCR: Isn't it nice to know there are still a few things that have never changed?

COWBOY: What's your sign?

81 BRONZE

(NATURAL SFX THROUGHOUT: CHAINS, SIGHS ETC.)
(SFX: HAWAIIAN MUSIC)

VO: Lolly Gobble Bliss Bombs. Everyone's idea of bliss.

Consumer Television :30 Campaign

82 GOLD
ART DIRECTORS
Bernie Guild
Leslie Caldwell
WRITER
Mike Koelker
AGENCY PRODUCER
Steve Neely
PRODUCTION CO.
Petermann Dektor
DIRECTOR
Leslie Dektor
CLIENT
Levi's 501 Jeans
AGENCY
Foote Cone & Belding/San Francisco

83 SILVER
ART DIRECTOR
Michael Tesch
WRITER
Patrick Kelly
AGENCY PRODUCER
Maureen Kearns
PRODUCTION CO.
Kelly Pictures
DIRECTOR
Patrick Kelly
CLIENT
Federal Express
AGENCY
Ally & Gargano

82 GOLD

(MUSIC: UP)

SINGER: *I've been crazy for you girl since we were terrible two's.*
In our buttonfly, shrink-to-fit 501 blues.
Now, our bodies grew up different, and I love your ways and means.
Because Levi's always understood . . . it's all in the jeans.

(MUSIC: UNDER)

SINGER: *It's all in the jeans.*
The 501 jeans.

(MUSIC: UNDER AND OUT)

82 GOLD

(MUSIC: UP)

SINGER: *She has this thing about her*
Levi's 501 jeans.
The way they curve every curve,
that I've had the nerve to notice.
They've been through stormy weather,
wind to a feather.
From good to bad and back together.
They have shrunk to fit her
exceptional form, that I've been
sincerely interested in keeping warm.
Cause I got this thing about her
and her Levi's 501 jeans.

(MUSIC: OUT)

82 GOLD

(MUSIC: UP)

SINGER: *Have you heard the news about 501 blues?*
It's a personal jean fit especially for you.
When you walk that walk, tell the world you're the greatest.
Man these blue jeans just can't lose.
I've got to get the blues on my body. Levi's button-fly blues.
So blue, so blue, so blue, so blue, 501 blue.

(MUSIC: OUT)

83 SILVER

(MUSIC: UNDER)

ANNCR VO: Some air express companies must have special training classes. Otherwise, where would they come up with their excuses?

TEACHER (UNDER ANNCR): O.K., Bernard, what's your excuse?

STUDENT: I know the package is late, but there's a lot of traffic between here and the airport!

TEACHER: Excellent!

STUDENT 2: Delivery by 10:30 a.m.? We'll make every conceivable effort!

TEACHER: Very good!

STUDENT 3: I've got a man out sick and another one just quit on me. (LAUGHS)

TEACHER: Wonderful!

ANNCR VO: There's only one reason to choose an air express company. Reliability. And that means Federal Express. Why fool around with anyone else?

Gold, Silver & Bronze Awards

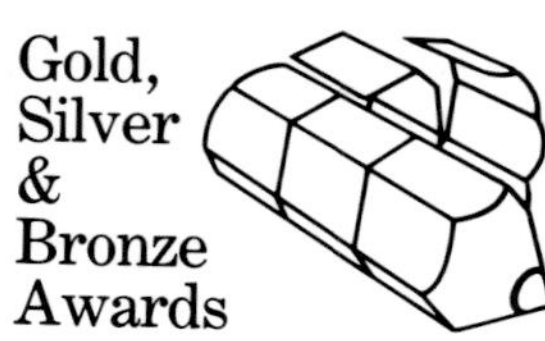

Consumer Television :30 Campaign

84 BRONZE
ART DIRECTOR
Gerald Andelin
WRITER
Hal Riney
AGENCY PRODUCER
Deborah Martin
PRODUCTION CO.
PYTKA
DIRECTOR
Joe Pytka
CLIENT
E&J Gallo Winery
AGENCY
Hal Riney & Partners/San Francisco

Consumer Television :10 Single

85 GOLD
ART DIRECTOR
Michael Tesch
WRITER
Patrick Kelly
AGENCY PRODUCER
Maureen Kearns
PRODUCTION CO.
Kelly Pictures
DIRECTOR
Patrick Kelly
CLIENT
Federal Express
AGENCY
Ally & Gargano

86 SILVER
ART DIRECTOR
Earl Cavanah
WRITER
Larry Cadman
AGENCY PRODUCER
Jean Muchmore
PRODUCTION CO.
Kelly Pictures
DIRECTOR
Patrick Kelly
CLIENT
Nikon
AGENCY
Scali McCabe Sloves

87 BRONZE
ART DIRECTOR
Bob Barrie
WRITER
Phil Hanft
AGENCY PRODUCER
Judy Brink
PRODUCTION CO.
James Productions
DIRECTOR
Jim Lund
CLIENT
Minnesota Zoo
AGENCY
Fallon McElligott/Minneapolis

84 BRONZE

FRANK: Hello again.
You know, people often complain that they cannot find enough Bartles & Jaymes Premium Wine Coolers in their stores' cold boxes.
So Ed has designed a special kind of bottle which will stay cold all by itself.
This works fine except for the $211 cost of each bottle, and also the fact that you must have a place to plug it in.
So for now, you should probably just ask your store manager to keep plenty of Bartles & Jaymes in his cold box.
Thank you again for your support.

85 GOLD

GUY: Listen, if I don't have that package by 10:30 a.m. tomorrow, my whole business will collapse.

(SFX: BOOM)

ANNCR VO: Next time, send it Federal Express.

86 SILVER

MAN: The new Nikon One-Touch is not only easy to use, it's so compact, you can slip it in your pocket. That way, you won't look like a tourist.

87 BRONZE

VO: The Minnesota Zoo proudly announces the arrival of 3 Cheetahs, the world's fastest land animal.

(SFX: SWOOOOOOSH)

VO: Want to see them again?

Consumer Television :10 Campaign

88 GOLD
ART DIRECTOR
Paul Figg
WRITER
Terry Comer
AGENCY PRODUCER
Sean Ascroft
PRODUCTION CO.
Ian MacDonald Productions
DIRECTOR
Ian MacDonald
CLIENT
Hoover (Australia)
AGENCY
John Clemenger/Australia

89 SILVER
ART DIRECTOR
Michael Tesch
WRITER
Patrick Kelly
AGENCY PRODUCER
Maureen Kearns
PRODUCTION CO.
Kelly Pictures
DIRECTOR
Patrick Kelly
CLIENT
Federal Express
AGENCY
Ally & Gargano

88 GOLD

MVO: Because of its soil deposit eliminator . . . the Hoover Elite 900 gets clothes cleaner and brighter.
Taaaaaadaaaaa.
That's why Hoover is ahead of the rest.

88 GOLD

P: The new Hoover President dishwasher is so quiet.
It's quieter than . . .
. . . it's quieter than a mouse.
That's why Hoover is ahead of the rest.

88 GOLD

P: For difficult spots the new Hoover Turbopower comes complete with a unique 'burst of power' switch.
That's why Hoover is ahead of the rest.

89 SILVER

GUY: Listen, if I don't have that package by 10:30 a.m. tomorrow, my whole business will collapse.

(SFX: BOOM)

ANNCR VO: Next time, send it Federal Express.

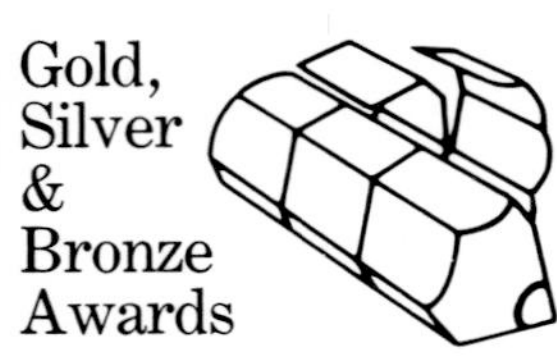

Gold, Silver & Bronze Awards

Public Service Television: Single

90 GOLD
ART DIRECTORS
Rich Silverstein
Jeff Goodby
WRITERS
Jeff Goodby
Andy Berlin
AGENCY PRODUCER
Deborah King
PRODUCTION CO.
Jon Francis Films
CLIENT
Mill Valley Film Festival
AGENCY
Goodby Berlin & Silverstein/
San Francisco

91 SILVER
ART DIRECTOR
Steve Feldman
WRITER
Frank Anton
AGENCY PRODUCER
Michael Pollock
PRODUCTION CO.
Cinematic Directions
DIRECTOR
Vilmos Zsigmond
CLIENT
UNICEF
AGENCY
TBWA

92 BRONZE
ART DIRECTOR
Geoff Hayes
WRITER
Evert Cilliers
AGENCY PRODUCER
Michael Pollock
PRODUCTION CO.
Cinematic Directions
DIRECTOR
Vilmos Zsigmond
CLIENT
UNICEF
AGENCY
TBWA

90 GOLD

(START WITH PAN & PUSH IN ON BOY ON SKATEBOARD DELIVERING *CAHIERS DU CINEMA* NEWSPAPERS TO NEIGHBORHOOD)

ANNCR VO: Once a year, the eyes of the international film community turn to the tiny town of Mill Valley, California, and its glorious cinematic celebration.

(CUT TO SCENE OF MILL VALLEY. VENTURES "PIPELINE" MUSIC IS UNDER)

(CUT TO LADIES IN BEAUTY PARLOR)

LADY 1: Of course, we had the debut of "Paris, Texas" last year, and that was very nice.

LADIES (CHORUS): Very nice.

(QUICK CUT OF MILL VALLEY SCENE WITH MUSIC UNDER)

(CUT TO TWO GARBAGE COLLECTORS IN BACK OF GARBAGE TRUCK)

MAN 1: I guess we're all looking forward to the film noir retrospective.

MAN 2: Yeah. We like that deep focus.

MAN 1: Well, there's a surface to the genre that, if anything, improves with age.

(CUT TO MILL VALLEY SCENE & MUSIC)

(CUT TO COUPLE BEHIND COUNTER IN HARDWARE STORE)

MAN: They're bringing back that Jane Russell Movie, "Hot Blood."

(QUICK CUTS OF MILL VALLEY SCENES & MUSIC UNDER)

(CUT TO MOM, DAD, BOY & GIRL AT DINNER TABLE)

MOM: Ellen & Bob want an answer about the video-fest. Are we going or not . . . (CONTINUE UNDER)

DAD: What's the matter?

GIRL: Aaron says that the recent New Zealand films are better than the French new wave.

BOY: I did not! I just said they were reminiscent.

GIRL: That's stupid, Daddy. Where's their Truffaut? Where's their Goddard?

MOM: . . . Rich . . . Rich?

(CUT TO 2 SUSHI CHEFS AT SUSHI BAR)

SUSHI 1: We are going to see the premiere of Haskell Wexler's film, "Latino."

SUSHI 2: We are Haskell Wexler fans from way back.

SUSHI 1: "Medium Cool."

(TWO CUTS OF LADIES IN BEAUTY PARLOR)

LADY 2: That Vim Venders is such a nice young director.

LADY 1: There should be more like him.

(CUT TO CUE OF JACK-IN-THE-BOX DRIVE UP SPEAKERPHONE & GIRL IN CORVETTE ANSWERING BACK)

SPEAKER: So, uh, am I gonna see you at the premiere of that new Paul Schrader film?

GIRL: "Mashima"?

SPEAKER: Yeah!

GIRL: No, I can't. My dad's taking us to Africa.

SPEAKER: Well, can't you get out of it?!

(MORE MILL VALLEY CUTS & MUSIC)

(CUT TO 2 COPS PARKED IN A CAR AT SPEEDTRAP WITH RADAR GUN)

COP 1: I was tellin' Morris, get this, we got the world premiere of Joseph Papp's new film starring Meryl Streep and John Gielgud, and he says, 'Who's Joseph Papp?'

COP 2: You gotta be kiddin' me.

COP 1: I don't know how that guy ever made sargeant.

(QUICK CUT OF MILL VALLEY SCENE & MUSIC)

(CUT TO BUTCHER CUTTING UP CHICKEN)

BUTCHER: Of course, Eisenstein really wrote *the* book on film cutting. Everything since has more or less been a footnote. But some footnotes are more interesting than others. This year, we're having a panel discussion with some of the best editors in the business . . . Marsha Lucas, Bob Dalva, Michael Chandler, Tom Standford.

(MILL VALLEY SCENES & MUSIC)

(CUT TO MECHANICS IN GARAGE WORKING ON A MERCEDES. SPEAKER IS UNDER CAR, TELLING JOKES)

MECHANIC: So God's up in heaven. He looks down at his calendar and he sees the end of the world coming up and he decides that somebody should film it, right? He asks St. Peter to go down and shop the property for a director . . .

(CUT TO VARIOUS TITLES & CREDITS)

St. Peter comes back and says he can't find a director and God says, 'What about Lucas?' And St. Peter says, 'He won't do it. He'll produce it, but he won't direct it.' 'That's no good,' God says. 'How about Spielburg?' 'He can't do it, it has something to do with his contract. How about Coppola?' says St. Peter. God says, 'Coppola! Coppola! I got to make a profit on this thing!'

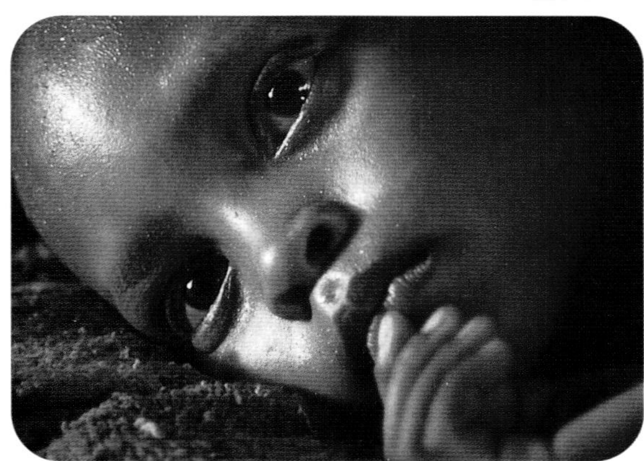

91 SILVER

VO: This year in the world's poor countries, parents will bury a million children who will die from tetanus.
A million and a half who will die from whooping cough.
Three million who will die from measles.
And 5 million more children who will die from dehydration often caused by diarrhea. You can help end this tragedy every time you buy UNICEF Greeting Cards.
Last year, the cards helped provide the clean drinking water that saved millions of children.
This year, the one you buy could help even more villages be like this one. Where they are digging wells. Instead of graves.
UNICEF Greeting Cards. Every time you buy them you help save a child's life.

92 BRONZE

ANNCR VO: Sometimes all a mother has to give is love. And sometimes even that is not enough. This woman's children are sick and suffering from malnutrition. She is too weak to carry more than one of them to a place where she can get help—5 days walk away. She has to choose which one to take—even though she knows the others may not survive.
You have a choice, too. UNICEF Cards. Every time you buy them, you help save a child's life—by bringing vaccines and medicines to the millions who need them.
Call now.
The choice you make can help others have a better choice than this.

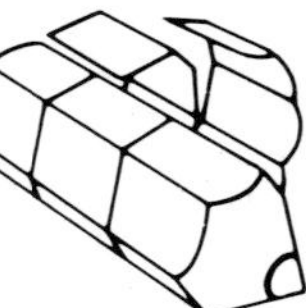

Public Service Television: Campaign

93 SILVER
ART DIRECTOR
B. A. Albert
WRITER
Cleve Willcoxon
AGENCY PRODUCER
Carol Hardin
PRODUCTION CO.
Jayan/Crawford Productions
CLIENT
The Alliance Theatre
AGENCY
D'Arcy Masius Benton & Bowles/Atlanta

Political Television: Single

94 GOLD
ART DIRECTOR
Pat Burnham
WRITER
Bill Miller
AGENCY PRODUCER
Judy Brink
PRODUCTION CO.
James Productions
CLIENT
American Association of Advertising Agencies
AGENCY
Fallon McElligott/Minneapolis

95 SILVER
ART DIRECTOR
Jamie Mambro
WRITERS
Jonathan Plazonja
Ray Welch
AGENCY PRODUCERS
Jamie Mambro
Jonathan Plazonja
PRODUCTION CO.
Viz Wiz
DIRECTOR
Peter Fasciano
CLIENT
Union of Concerned Scientists
AGENCY
Welch/Currier - Boston

THAT WITHOUT COMMERCIAL INTERRUPTIONS,

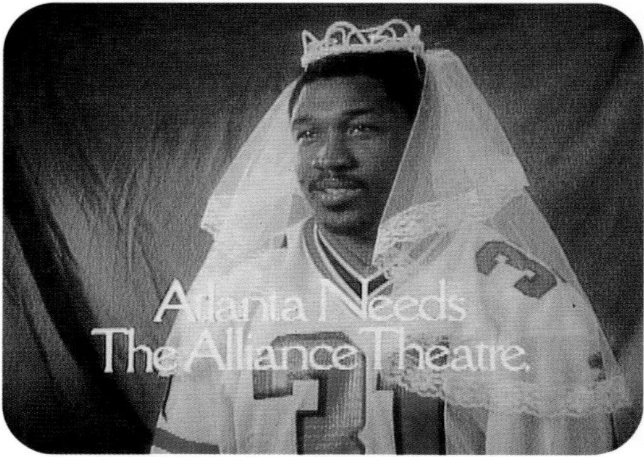

THERE WOULDN'T BE ANYTHING

TO INTERRUPT.

93 SILVER

MAYOR ANDREW YOUNG: 76 trom-, 76 trombones, nope. 76 trombones lead the big parade.

VINCE DOOLEY: A horse, a horse, my kingdom for a horse.

WILLIAM ANDREWS: What light through yonder window breaks.

ANNCR VO: Atlanta needs the Alliance Theatre and Atlanta Children's Theatre to produce the best. The alternative is to depend on this kind of talent and that would be a tragedy.

JIMMY CARTER: To be or not to be, that is the question.

94 GOLD

VO: This commercial interruption is brought to you . . .
. . . on behalf of the people who make commercial interruptions . . .
. . . as a reminder that without commercial interruptions . . .
. . . there wouldn't be anything . . .

(SFX: CLICK)

. . . to interrupt

SILENCE

95 SILVER

RAY: Mr. President, respectfully, I . . . I don't know much about bombs or 'Star Wars' . . . I'm just a working man with a bad haircut. But I do believe in something:
That maybe the best thing you could do on November 19, is drop a bomb on the Russians . . . a *verbal* bomb . . . a real proposal to end the arms race.
This Summit is a chance to do something bold, maybe even something brave. And to waste it could be as tragic as dropping the bomb itself.
So for God's sake, Sir, please don't blow it.

(SFX: DRUM ROLL)

THE GOLD AWARD WINNERS ON THE GOLD AWARD WINNERS

The Gold Award Winners on The Gold Award Winners

Consumer Newspaper Over 600 Lines: Campaign

AGENCY: Ammirati & Puris
CLIENT: BMW of North America

Oddly enough, having a great deal of money doesn't necessarily make a person any more eager to part with it. On the contrary, in fact.

Thus, we make a special effort to remind the buyers of BMW's most expensive cars of what they are getting for the money. While simultaneously reminding the rest of the world that these individuals have the money to begin with.

It's what you might call a 'value campaign' for people who pinch Kruggerands.

Joe O'Neill
Mark Silveira
Jerry Whitley

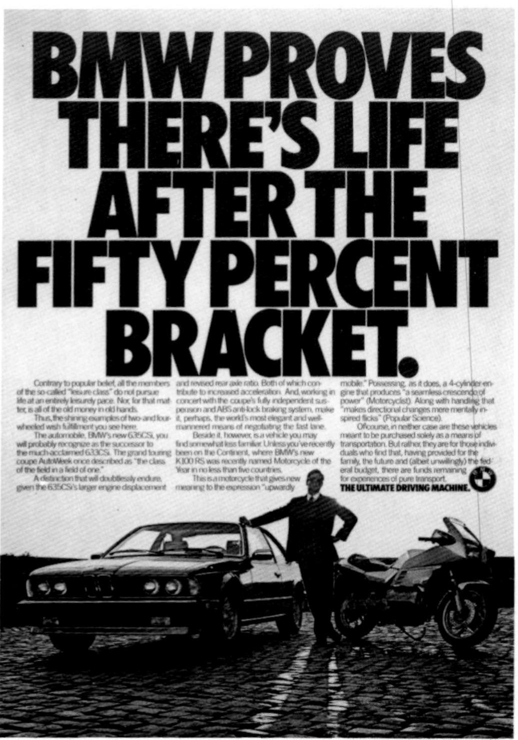

4 GOLD

Consumer Newspaper
600 Lines Or Less:
Single

AGENCY: Angotti Thomas Hedge
CLIENT: Barron's

We began our agency in January of 1985.

Our earliest days were spent dispersing 19 imitation Breuer chairs, bought on sale someplace in Westchester, throughout a space that an Ad Age reporter later called 'closet-like.'

Every few days delivery men would show up and leave a pile of boxes. This was our office furniture. For some reason the most desirable (not to mention affordable) furniture was made in Europe and arrived unassembled. The assembly instructions were a triumph of Global Communications: they were written in 4 different languages, the least intelligible of which was English.

Besides building desks, we spent much time arranging for insurance, meeting with lawyers and trying to reason with a temperamental phone system. (There's something about calling your very own agency's very own number and hearing yourself described as non-working.)

Somehow during all this we managed to do some advertising. The ad shown here is for Barron's, an absolutely first-rate publication for people who enjoy investing. We reasoned that since you bought Barron's to pursue wealth, you wouldn't mind if we arranged for *it* to pursue *you*—which is exactly what happens when you subscribe.

Somewhere in a closet at home, both of us have piles of One Show Gold and Silver pencils. These were given for work on such big-budget accounts as BMW and Xerox, in such glamorous categories as Color Magazine Campaign and TV Campaign.

None of these was more satisfying than this one.

Tom Thomas
Anthony Angotti

Let wealth pursue you for a change.

Subscribe to Barron's.

Every week we'll bring to your doorstep the earnings updates, company reports, market analysis, interviews and technical data you need to make better decisions.

Which can help make the difference between pursuing wealth and catching up with it.

See for yourself by picking up a copy at a newsstand this weekend. And to subscribe, call 800-345-8501 (in PA, 800-662-5180).*

HOW THE SMART MONEY GETS THAT WAY.

*In the continental U.S. only.
©1986 DOW JONES & COMPANY, INC

7 GOLD

Consumer Newspaper
600 Lines Or Less:
Campaign

AGENCY: Fallon McElligott/Minneapolis
CLIENT: Country Cottage

With a big client like this, the hardest part was getting the campaign past the stiffs on the creative review board.

Phil Hanft
Michael Fazende

Finally, a doll that doesn't talk, eat, drink, wet or go poo.

Here, we sell dolls that are good for only one thing. Making life easier for mothers of all ages.

Country Cottage
of Wayzata Ltd.
326 S. Broadway, Wayzata, MN 55391 612-473-0259

10 GOLD

Consumer Magazine B/W: 1 Page Or Spread Including Magazine Supplements

AGENCY: Carmichael-Lynch/Minneapolis
CLIENT: Blue Fox Tackle Company

A lot of people have asked us whether the story of 'The Man Who Catches Fish On A Shred of Cloth' is completely true.

Truth is, the same medicine man also catches fish on a strip of taboo chicken (a chicken killed by a vampire bat).

But we had to draw the line somewhere.

Frank Haggerty
Jack Supple

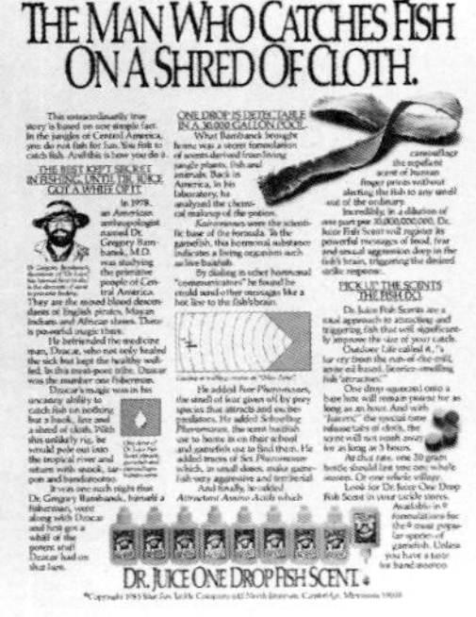

13 GOLD

Consumer Magazine Color: 1 Page Or Spread Including Magazine Supplements

AGENCY: Doyle Dane Bernbach
CLIENT: Chivas Regal

First you arrive at a strategy. (Actually, the Chivas strategy was arrived at back when advertising people still called strategies 'ideas.')

Then you do about 85 executions.

Then you kill about 70 of those executions yourself.

Then the client kills 10 more.

Then you run what's left.

Then you get lucky.

Charlie Piccirillo
Barry Greenspon
Matt Rao

16 GOLD

Consumer Magazine B/W: Campaign Including Magazine Supplements

AGENCY: Carmichael-Lynch/Minneapolis
CLIENT: Blue Fox Tackle Company

Dr Juice has such a great product story that all we had to do was tell it.
Truth is stranger than fishin'.

Frank Haggerty
Jack Supple

19 GOLD

Consumer Magazine Color: Campaign Including Magazine Supplements

AGENCY: Abbott Mead Vickers/SMS - London
CLIENT: Cow & Gate

Perhaps it's ironic that we're both single yet the concepts (after we got to grips with the complicated products) proved relatively easy.
So some credit must go to the account team and the planner.
The executions were a different story (it's incredible how mothers insist their very young babies can perform on command).
We're grateful to Steve Cavalier, the photographer, for his endless patience, because at the end of the session we almost ended up screaming and being sick along with all the babies.
We're still not sure if it has put us off becoming fathers but it certainly hasn't put us off working on future Cow & Gate ads.

Andy Arghyrou
Derek Day

How come they don't need identical milks?

21 GOLD

Consumer Magazine Less Than A Page B/W Or Color: Single

AGENCY: Phillips-Ramsey/San Diego
CLIENT: WD-40

It was a bleak afternoon that had turned to night even before we noticed. The walls of the creative conference room were creeping in on all sides, like an encroaching deadline.

We sat staring at a can of WD-40.

Visions of rusting hinges and corroding mechanisms haunted us as the clock ticked away. The world appeared in a hopeless state of deterioration.

But we knew WD-40 could save it, if only . . . if only we could reach people and warn them. Before it was too late.

The ad was aimed at WD-40 owners. It was to remind them to use it more often, rather than let the can itself rust away in the garage or under the sink. An ironic thought.

The ad hit its target. And we hit ours.

That's a great feeling.

Thank you to all the people involved—the agency, the client and the judges. And of course, the guy who shot the guy shooting.

Martha Shaw
John Vitro

24 GOLD

Trade B/W: 1 Page Or Spread

AGENCY: Foote Cone & Belding/San Francisco
CLIENT: Levi Strauss & Company

We had a better ad, but the client killed it.

Seth Warner

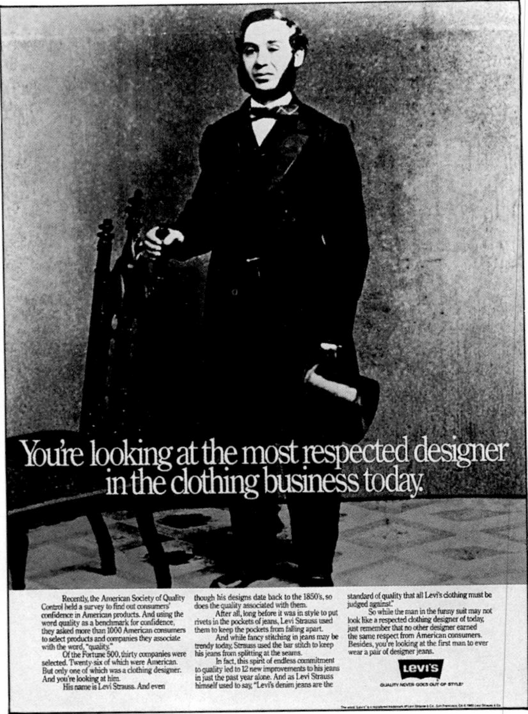

28 GOLD

Trade Color: 1 Page Or Spread

AGENCY: Drinking Buddies Advertising/Richmond, VA
CLIENT: Meredith Corporation

How did we come up with this year's Successful Farming campaign? Well . . . uh . . . we were in our offices here in Virginia . . . in Jamaica, yeahhhh, that's it! But we couldn't get any work done because . . . all the naked native women there, they were all over us, yeahhhhh, that's the ticket! So we, uh, we walked to . . . no, we flew back to Virgini . . . to London, yeahhhh, that's it! In our own personal Lear Je . . . our own Concorde. Then we worked on the ads in our hotel roo . . . I mean at David Ogilvy's château for 8 solid hours, er 8 solid minutes and the ideas came to us just like that. Then we sold and produced the campaign all by ourselves. Took the photos ourselves, too. Yeahhhh! And now that we've won a Gold in the One Sho . . . er, the Nobel Peace Pri . . . I mean, the Cannes Film Festival (We won Oscars, too. Swept the show!), well, Tom McElligott called . . . no, flew to Ogilvy's place just to offer us jobs as writer and art direc . . . as senior vice-pres . . . as partners, yeahhhh! At Fallon McElligott Sullivan & Harri . . . at Sullivan Harris & Partners. Yeahhhh, that's it! That's the ticket!

Luke Sullivan
Cabell Harris

FOR 4 MONTHS OUT OF THE YEAR, THE WEATHER MAKES FARMING IMPOSSIBLE. DURING THE OTHER 8, THE GOVERNMENT DOES.

31 GOLD

Trade Any Size B/W Or Color: Campaign

AGENCY: Fallon McElligott/Minneapolis
CLIENT: Rolling Stone

It's reward enough that in a year in which I was terribly distracted I didn't let my client or my craft down.

But the gold is sure nice.

Nancy Rice
Bill Miller

Perception.

Reality.

36 GOLD

Collateral
Brochures
Other Than By Mail

AGENCY: Fallon McElligott/Minneapolis
CLIENT: Rolling Stone

1985 was a 'mind-altering experience' for me.

Working with a great client like The Rolling Stone, a great writer like Bill Miller, and a great support team helped me through.

Thanks Jann W., Kent B., Les Z., Kevin B., Jim M., Mark H., Bob M., Peggy L., and Bill M.

Nancy Rice
Bill Miller

39 GOLD

Collateral
Direct Mail

AGENCY: Fallon McElligott/Minneapolis
CLIENT: Michael & Linda Ehrlich

Mike and I did 2 announcements for the Ehrlichs.

One went to the relatives, one went to friends.

One made it into the baby book, one made it into the One Show book.

Guess which one.

Nancy Rice
Mike Lescarbeau

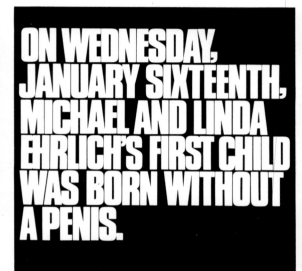

ON WEDNESDAY, JANUARY SIXTEENTH, MICHAEL AND LINDA EHRLICH'S FIRST CHILD WAS BORN WITHOUT A PENIS.

44 GOLD

Collateral P.O.P.

AGENCY: Martin/Williams - Minneapolis
CLIENT: Army Surplus Store

The American Surplus Store, located on the fringe of downtown Minneapolis, is not exactly in a position to give Dayton's department stores a run for their money.

It's the kind of place where a cigar-chewing salesman is likely to glue himself to you as soon as you open the door. (There's also a sign on the door asking if the place looks like a bank. No? Then don't bother asking about change for the bus.) The merchandise, new and used, is stacked from floor to ceiling. The stuff in the windows has faded from years of display, and they used to have a bomb in the window until we bought it for a direct mail piece to a prospective client. (We didn't get the business.)

In short, not a popular hangout for the fashion plates in town.

Until Army fashions became the cat's pajamas.

Then it was easy.

We came up with the idea like we would any other. Mark and I got together, tossed around a few ideas, discussed the previous night's Letterman show, considered which agency people we'd cast as the characters in 'Gilligan's Island,' tossed around a few more ideas, talked about our latest remodeling projects, the new receptionist, finished off with another idea or two, and broke for lunch.

Isn't that how great advertising is always done?

John Jarvis
Mark Haumersen

YOU MAY HAVE SEEN OUR FASHIONS
ON THE STREETS OF PARIS.
AMERICAN SURPLUS STORE

47 GOLD

Outdoor: Single

AGENCY: Fallon McElligott/Minneapolis
CLIENT: WFLD-TV

Thanks, Thanks, Thanks.

Sam Avery
Rob Dalton

BITCH, BITCH, BITCH.
Dynasty. Weeknights at 9.
32
WFLDTV

50 GOLD

Outdoor: Campaign

AGENCY: Fallon McElligott/Minneapolis
AGENCY: WFLD-TV

They're smart. They have a neat product. They want good work. They aren't afraid to take risks. We wouldn't be surprised if they even pay their bills.

Sound like any client you have? We thought not.

Sam Avery
Rob Dalton
Tom Lichtenheld
Jarl Olsen

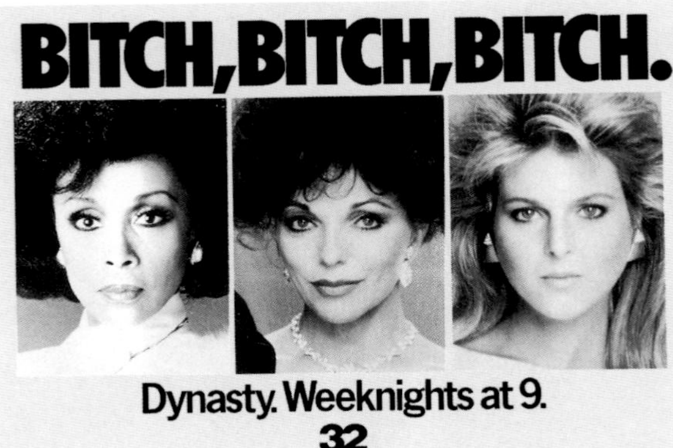
BITCH, BITCH, BITCH.
Dynasty. Weeknights at 9.
32
WFLDTV

53 GOLD

Public Service Newpaper Or Magazine: Single

AGENCY: Mullen Advertising/Prides Crossing, MA
CLIENT: Greater Media Cable TV Company

This was one of those assignments we dread. The agency's public relations department went and sold the client a community service program and then informed the creative team that we had to produce the materials. In 5 days. With no budget.

Oh, and by the way, there has to be an ad, a poster and a direct mail piece.

That gave us the rest of the morning to come up with one idea that would work for all 3 executions.

Anyway, we learned 2 things from the exercise. The first is that we shouldn't hide every time the pr people show up in the creative department. The second is that we should have entered the poster and direct mail piece, too.

Edward Boches
Amy Watt

If your child were missing, could you describe his laugh, his smile? What about the way he shrugs his shoulders? Or nods his head?

We could.

We'll videotape your children for free. September 14, between 11 am and 6 pm at the Fairfield Mall in Chicopee. On September 18, from 6:30 pm to 8 pm; and September 21, from 11 am to 4 pm at our offices, 16 Ames Ave., off Front St.

Greater Media Cable

56 GOLD

Public Service Newspaper Or Magazine: Campaign

AGENCY: Fallon McElligott/Minneapolis
CLIENT: Episcopal Church

I have an admission to make. And it's rather overdue.

Someone's name is missing from the credits on this campaign.

Someone who has contributed for years in quiet, humble anonymity.

Through 4 art directors.

Four copywriters.

Four photographers.

And 3 illustrators.

Someone whose unstoppable optimism, courage, and bright ideas have over the years turned a modest little advertising campaign on behalf of one Episcopal church into an international advertising campaign used by hundreds of churches in different denominations and even different languages.

That someone is
The Reverend George Martin,
Executive Director of
The Episcopal Ad Project.
A very special client.
God knows.

Tom McElligott

Where women stand in the Episcopal Church.

If you believe that men and women should share equally in the sacraments and service of Christianity, join us where God's calling can be answered by anyone.
The Episcopal Church

59 GOLD

Public Service Outdoor: Single

AGENCY: Fallon McElligott/Minneapolis
CLIENT: Reader's Digest

This poster was developed as an entry for the Reader's Digest Anti-Drunk Driving Creative Challenge.

We were allowed only 2 entries in this contest and had to choose from around 20 that we had created.

We asked our co-workers to help us pick the 2 strongest posters, and after getting opinions from Sam Avery, Jamie Barrett, Greg Beaupre, Bruce Bildsten, Pat Burnham, Sandra Cyronek, Rob Dalton, Mike Fazende, George Gier, Phil Hanft, Dean Hanson, Rod Kilpatrick, Tom Lichtenheld, Tom McElligott, Bill Miller, Jarl Olsen, Houman Pirdavari and John Stingley, we chose this one and another.

We would like to thank Mr. Lynn Mapes of the Reader's Digest for his patience as we tried to get in touch with Stevie Wonder to clear using his photograph.

We'd also like to thank Stevie Wonder for saying yes when we did finally reach him. And, of course, we are very grateful to The One Show for honoring this poster with a gold award.

Bob Barrie
Mike Lescarbeau

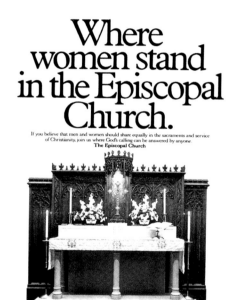

"Before I'll ride with a drunk, I'll drive myself." –Stevie Wonder
Driving after drinking, or riding with a driver who's been drinking, is a big mistake. Anyone can see that.

61 GOLD

The Gold Award Winners on The Gold Award Winners

College Competition

COLLEGE: East Texas State University
AGENCY: The CIA

As a student at East Texas State University, I knew the 2 brothers, Henry and Steve Popp who were the last 2 consecutive college gold winners.

They and my instructor Rob Lawton urged me to compete. Rob told me that I better win the gold this year to hopefully disprove the assumption that 2 consecutive gold medals from a small east Texas town was a mere coincidence.

In the brainstorming process, I researched many actual CIA ads. They seemed to ignore the actual job and focused on travel, meeting new people, and learning a foreign language. However, everyone knows America gets its James Bonds from the CIA. So I went from there. With 4 days until the deadline, I went through a lot of coffee and pencils. And at 10:30 PM, 11 hours before the deadline I sent them from Dallas via Federal Express.

David Ring

64 GOLD

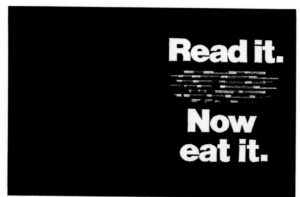

Consumer Radio: Single

AGENCY: Chiat/Day
CLIENT: Nynex Information Resources

Everyone knows you can find anything in the phone book. Right?

Since we happened to be advertising a brand of Yellow Pages that blankets the most densely populated area in the country, we decided to test that hypothesis.

The result is a campaign that uncovers some rather unusual businesses. (Lifted straight from the Pages. Scout's honor.) Most are even stranger than we imagined.

Only in New York. Right?

Robin Raj
John Crawford

SEE GOLD AWARD WINNER 67

Consumer Radio: Campaign

AGENCY: Zechman and Associates/Chicago
CLIENT: Dovebar International

This was a team effort all the way. Everything funny, Emo did. Everything else is stuff I stuck in.

Mark Fenske

SEE GOLD AWARD WINNER 70

Consumer Television Over :30 (:45/:60/:90) Single

AGENCY: Hal Riney & Partners/San Francisco
CLIENT: E&J Gallo Winery

Well, let me think now.

I was facing my one hundred-and-third wine commercial, the last hundred-and-two having been turned down. Ernest just didn't agree with anything I wrote. So I asked Bruce Campbell, my art director, 'Why don't we just say nothing at all? That way, nobody can disagree!'

We tried it.

Ernest agreed. Compared to what I'd been writing, a better solution was no writing at all.

The public agreed, as well. In the first few weeks, the campaign got thousands of calls and letters. It still does.

Oh, I finally did get in a few words, at the end of the spot.

(Residuals.)

Hal Riney

73 GOLD

The Gold Award Winners on The Gold Award Winners

Consumer Television
Over :30 (:45/:60/:90)
Campaign

AGENCY: Hal Riney & Partners/San Francisco
CLIENT: E&J Gallo Winery

While Gallo and ourselves were trying to figure out whether there really *was* such a business as wine coolers, our 2 biggest potential competitors were trying to figure out what sort of advertising wine cooler advertising should be.

Because, while wine coolers had evolved into a major category, no one had ever *done* a major wine cooler advertising campaign before.

Our best guess was that the competition would focus on the usual youthful lifestyle stuff. So we spent our time looking for something else.

Bartles and Jaymes were the result.

Jerry Andelin, my partner and art director, and I had 2 different approaches. The first was a pair of farmers. The second was a couple of down-at-the-heels sherry and madeira merchants from London.

The farmers won.

Don't ever do a Bartles and Jaymes campaign, unless you're prepared to write and produce a commercial a week.

Hal Riney

76 GOLD

Consumer Television
:30 Single

AGENCY: Goodby Berlin & Silverstein/San Francisco
CLIENT: San Francisco Examiner

As we worked on the new campaign for William Randolph Hearst III's *San Francisco Examiner*, it only seemed natural to include a spot about their newly-hired editor, David Burgin.

When we asked people at the paper what kind of guy Burgin was, however, the blood would drain out of their faces and they'd start patting their pockets for a cigarette.

That was all we needed to know.

Jeffrey Goodby
Andy Berlin
Rich Silverstein

79 GOLD

Consumer Television :30 Campaign

AGENCY: Foote Cone & Belding/San Francisco
CLIENT: Levi's 501 Jeans

It started with a belief that reality can't be re-created. Reality must be captured. So, a different kind of campaign was born, 501 Blues, capturing real people in real situations having the unique blend of personal fun. The campaign revitalized the jeans business and made the 501 jean the largest selling garment in the world, ever!

Denny Wilkinson

82 GOLD

Public Service Television: Single

AGENCY: Goodby Berlin & Silverstein/San Francisco
CLIENT: Mill Valley Film Festival

The most famous film festival in the world—Cannes—gets a lot of coverage in the American media (especially via PBS).

We thought, then, that it might be interesting to imagine what would happen if a small American film festival were to be covered by the French media: What kind of reactions the French might get from 'everyday' American citizens when they asked them about esoteric cinematic issues.

From there, it wasn't much of a leap to realize that the French weren't really necessary. (In fact, when you really think about it, they never are.) So we figured the point we had in mind could be made better by putting the sensibilities of film academicians into unlikely containers.

That, more or less, was the idea.

Jeffrey Goodby
Andy Berlin
Rich Silverstein

90 GOLD

PRINT FINALISTS

Consumer Newspaper Over 600 Lines: Single

96
ART DIRECTOR
Bob Barrie
WRITER
Rod Kilpatrick
DESIGNER
Bob Barrie
CLIENT
MedCenters Health Plan
AGENCY
Fallon McElligott/Minneapolis

97
ART DIRECTORS
Jeff Roll
Yvonne Smith
WRITERS
Dave Butler
Mark Monteiro
PHOTOGRAPHERS
Lamb & Hall
CLIENT
Porsche Cars North America
AGENCY
Chiat/Day - Los Angeles

98
ART DIRECTOR
Gary Lancaster
WRITER
Stephen Heller
ARTIST
Christy Sheets Mull
PHOTOGRAPHER
Charlie Latham
CLIENT
American Medical International
AGENCY
Ogilvy & Mather/Atlanta

We've Been Caring For Seniors Since They Were Juniors.

When the Nicollet Clinic opened its doors in 1921, you were only a child.

You've done a lot of growing since then. And so has the clinic. Today, Park Nicollet Medical Center is one of the cornerstones of MedCenters MediCare—a senior health care plan with a tradition of quality that's been around almost as long as you have.

So at MedCenters MediCare, we don't have to guess about your health-care needs. We know them from experience.

But that doesn't mean we're resting on our laurels. Instead, we're constantly looking for ways to make our plan even better.

For example, our Division of Geriatric Medicine and Health is entirely dedicated to research and programs that can benefit you today and tomorrow.

And our Senior Advisory Board keeps us in touch with some of the top experts in the field: Seniors just like you.

There are many more good reasons to choose MedCenters MediCare. To find out about them, call us at 927-3995. (Outside the Twin Cities, call 1-800-642-0091 toll-free.) Or mail the coupon.

Even if you didn't visit one of our clinics back in 1921, get in touch with us today.

After all, it's never too late to make up for lost time.

For more information, call 927-3995.
(Outside the Twin Cities, call 1-800-642-0091 toll-free.)
Or mail coupon to: MedCenters MediCare, 4951 Excelsior Boulevard, St. Louis Park, MN 55416

☐ *I'd like to know more about MedCenters MediCare.*

Name ____________________
Address ____________________
City ____________________
State __________ *Zip* __________
Phone (   ) ____________________

MEDCENTERS MEDICARE

43 locations including Park Nicollet Medical Center.

No other luxury car comes with this interior.

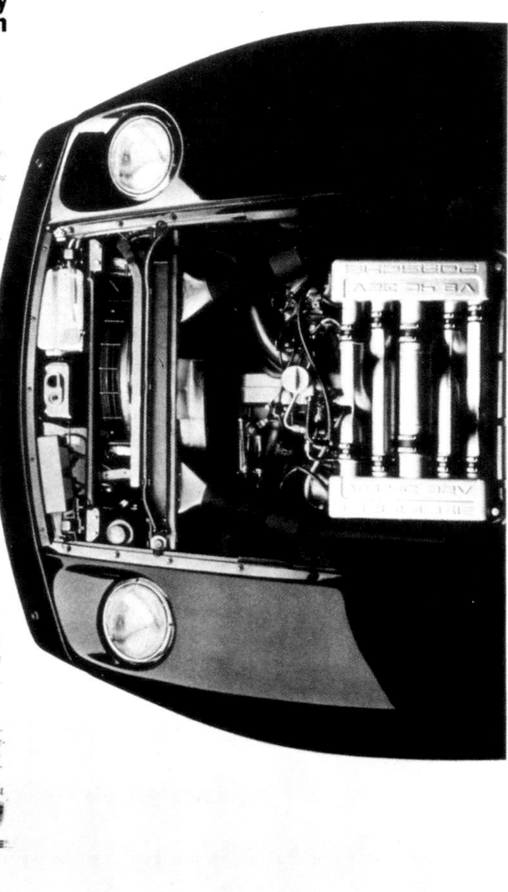

In short, what's most important about the Porsche 928S four-valve—or any Porsche—is what's most difficult to measure: thirty-seven years of strict adherence to a philosophy which holds that building fast cars cannot be accomplished by building cars fast.

PORSCHE

A health service for your family from AMI St. Jude Medical Center

Working while you're pregnant

Many women today keep working up until a very short time before they have their babies. All it takes is a little planning and following the suggestions you'll find below.

It used to be that when a woman became pregnant she quit her job. But no more.

That doesn't mean, however, a woman won't go through all the bodily and emotional changes that take place during pregnancy.

But it needn't be a problem. All it takes is a few simple steps such as the ones we've listed here.

How to cope with morning sickness

It's more than difficult to work up to your full potential when you're nauseated.

But there are some ways of controlling your out-of-sorts stomach.

Most doctors, for example, recommend you keep some sort of non-acid, non-greasy food handy. You might try keeping a box of crackers in your desk.

Choose the childbirth courses that suit you

We offer a number of courses and services that can make having a baby a more enjoyable experience. Pregnagym™ gives you a chance to exercise while you're pregnant (464-4581). And all the resources of the Women's Health Foundation (464-0012) are here to meet your needs.

And in cases when you're "morning sick" all day, you might try eating several small, bland meals instead of a larger one.

In any case, it's important you do eat properly.

Don't forget about good nutrition

It's easy to get so caught up in your work that you don't eat the way you should. That's always bad. When you're pregnant, it can be disastrous.

Force yourself to eat a well-balanced diet of proteins and vegetables. Stay as far as possible from fatty foods.

Eat food high in fiber to calm hunger pangs and keep you regular.

Avoid beverages that are high in sodium or caffeine. And eat plenty of cheese, yogurt, cottage cheese and milk.

Control your cravings! As hard as it may be, it can be a source of too much of a good thing, and a lot of extra calories.

Your doctor will probably also recommend prenatal vitamins. Take them religiously. You and your baby both need the extra help.

Smoking

Don't do it. Smoking isn't good for anybody, but it can be especially bad for your baby.

We know it won't be easy to quit. You're under the pressure of work and surrounded by smoking co-workers.

But here are the facts. Smoking has been directly related to spontaneous miscarriages, stillbirths, premature births and labor complications.

Smoking can also prevent you and your body from using certain vitamins and minerals in the foods you eat.

Women who smoke often have smaller babies, and there's an increased chance of brain damage.

You've probably always wanted to quit smoking. Now you have the best reason ever to do it.

Exercise

Years ago, pregnant women went to bed. But that's not you, or you wouldn't be working.

In any case, doctors say you need to get exercise. Don't sit at your desk too long. Walk to lunch, or take a walk when you get home.

At the same time, we're not recommending you start jogging. And if you feel fatigued or uncomfortable, take it easy.

Can work make pregnancy easier?

A recent study indicates that you might actually be better off physically and emotionally if you work while you're pregnant.

According to the study, working can reduce backache, vomiting, insomnia, loss of appetite, fear, depression and anxiety.

Work helps you concentrate on more than how you feel, so you become less aware of the symptoms of pregnancy. In fact, it seems that the more prestigious a woman's job, the less pregnancy may affect her.

There is a trade-off though. Women who work during pregnancy reportedly have more leg cramps, fatigue and job-related stress.

Avoid stress

This may be the hardest part of working while you're pregnant. You have to learn to relax.

We suggest you plan a time each day to sit back, forget about the problems of business, and spend a few minutes with your baby.

You'll feel better and your baby will be better off. And your work will still get done.

Never forget that even though you are working, you're pregnant. The world will need to adjust a little for you.

Be easy on yourself

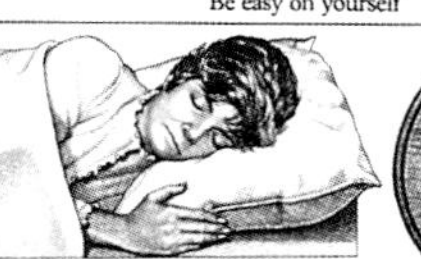

Rest
You will need to rest more. Your body is going through a great many changes and you have a life growing inside you. That takes a lot of energy.

Don't work too late
Keep an eye on the time. There's nothing you can't finish tomorrow. (If there is, you need to change your schedule until the baby's born.)

Stay away from stressful situations
This is one time in life when you need to control the stress of the work place. Set aside time to take it easy on yourself each day.

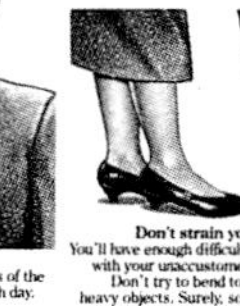

Don't strain yourself
You'll have enough difficulty getting around with your unaccustomed new figure. Don't try to bend too far or lift heavy objects. Surely, someone will be more than willing to help you out.

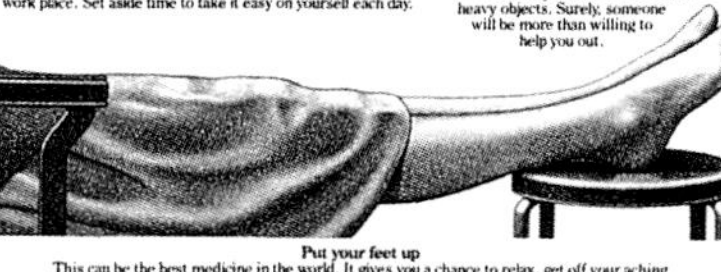

Put your feet up
This can be the best medicine in the world. It gives you a chance to relax, get off your aching feet, and spend a little time with your thoughts and what's going on inside you.

Who is AMI?

American Medical International, AMI, is one of the largest health care organizations in the world, now employing over 40,000 health care professionals. We provide a variety of services in 500 different communities in six countries, including yours.

At AMI, we're dedicated to providing the best health care possible for our patients.

In addition to hospital care, AMI facilities worldwide provide occupational health services, out-patient care, and psychiatric care.

Due to our years of experience, we at AMI are able to bring your family health care in an efficient and cost-effective way.

For more information call 468-8600 or your doctor

Whatever information you need to know about working while you're pregnant, we can help (chances are, there's someone in the same condition here at the hospital).

That includes helping you find an obstetrician or a pediatrician, or any other kind of doctor. You can reach our Physician Referral service at 468-8600. We can provide you with a list of qualified doctors in the area.

If you'd like, we can arrange a peek at our LDR's, specially designed rooms where labor, delivery, and recovery all take place.

AMI St. Jude Medical Center is conveniently located near the Kenner Center by the corner of West Esplanade and Loyola Drive

AMI St. Jude Medical Center

180 West Esplanade Avenue, Kenner, Louisiana 70065

For a reprint of this ad, contact AMI St. Jude Medical Center

Pregnagym is a trademark of St. Anthony's Health Care Center.

Consumer Newspaper Over 600 Lines: Single

99
ART DIRECTOR
Tom Lichtenheld
WRITER
Sam Avery
ARTIST
Tom Lichtenheld
CLIENT
MedCenters Health Plan
AGENCY
Fallon McElligott/Minneapolis

100
ART DIRECTORS
Gail Bartley
William Hartwell
WRITER
David Tessler
DESIGNER
William Hartwell
PHOTOGRAPHER
Jeffrey Zwart
ARTIST
R & V Studio
CLIENT
BMW of North America
AGENCY
Ammirati & Puris

101
ART DIRECTOR
Marten Tonnis
WRITER
Steve Rabosky
PHOTOGRAPHER
Bo Hylen
CLIENT
Apple Computer
AGENCY
Chiat/Day - Los Angeles

When You Have A Problem This Big, You'd Better Have More Than One Doctor.

When you're a member of MedCenters Health Plan you get more than the MedCenters personal physician of your choice. You get a team of more than 600 doctors, all working together toward a single goal.

To maintain your health at the highest possible level.

So your personal physician never works in isolation.

Whether you're suffering from the common cold, or a serious medical problem, your doctor is backed up by a carefully selected team that includes specialists in every medical field.

That means a second opinion can be arranged at a moment's notice.

Of course, while you'll benefit from MedCenter's unique coordinated care, you'll also benefit from the other advantages of an HMO.

You never have to fill out claim forms. You never have to pay deductibles. And you never get a doctor bill.

Instead you get all the health care you need for one low monthly fee.

And we have economical plans for groups of every size. All the way down to one.

To find out how you can join MedCenters Health Plan, ask your employer.

Or call 927-3263 and ask us.

We can't promise that all your problems will be small. But we can promise you that all our doctors will work to solve them.

57 locations including Park Nicollet Medical Center

99

BMW. THE FIRST CAR COMPANY TO STAND BEHIND ITS CARS TWICE.

What is arguably the most widespread form of legalized gambling today takes place not in casinos or on racetracks, but on the used-car lots of America. Where billions of dollars are wagered yearly on what are hoped to be well-running automobiles.

At BMW dealerships, however, the odds have always been stacked heavily in favor of the used-car buyer. That's because BMW's are built to standards that are uncompromising in the extreme—enabling them to fulfill the needs of a succession of demanding owners.

And now, purchasing a previously-owned BMW is a surer thing than it ever was—thanks to the new, unique BMW Quality Continuation Plan.™

The cornerstone of the plan is the first factory-backed warranty ever offered at no extra cost on a used car. It's a 12-month/12,000-mile limited warranty that's virtually as comprehensive as the one protecting new BMW's—including coverage of everything from the engine and transmission to the air-conditioning system. It even covers roadside service.*

The automobiles that are available in the plan are BMW's built from model year 1981 through 1985 and driven for up to 75,000 miles. And in order to qualify for the warranty, they've had to pass a rigorous 42-point inspection and reconditioning program.

All of which results in previously-owned automobiles that adhere to the exacting standards of a BMW—in essence, used cars that are more rewarding to own than most new ones.

Of course, for most car manufacturers, such a program could be quite risky.

But considering the way we build BMW's in the first place, we're not really gambling at all.

BMW QUALITY CONTINUATION PLAN.™

SEE YOUR PARTICIPATING SACRAMENTO AREA BMW DEALER LISTED BELOW:

Roseville
ROSEVILLE BMW/SUBARU
901 Riverside Avenue
(916) 782-9434

Sacramento
NIELLO BMW
2020 Fulton Avenue
(916) 486-1011

Stockton
RAMFIELD MOTORS
4873 West Lane
(209) 473-3811

How to help your parents get through school.

You could get a Friday night job to go along with the after school job, all-day Saturday job and Sunday morning paper route you already have.

Or you could hope you grow 16 inches over the next three months and try out for the basketball team.

Or you could drag your folks kicking and screaming down to a participating authorized Apple dealer to enter our $1 Million Education Sweepstakes.

Top prize will be a $100,000 scholarship to use at the institution of your choice. Gratis. No grade points asked.

We also have five $5,000 scholarships to give away. Which will easily cover a couple of years at air conditioning and refrigeration repair school. Or two weeks at Brown.

There'll be 250 lucky winners of two Apple personal computers — one for you and one for your school.

1,000 winners of Apple school packs that contain an Apple T-shirt, calculator, mug, pen, and several other nifty things.

And, while their supplies last, participating authorized Apple dealers will be giving away a bunch of Apple T-shirts to everyone who gets their parents to enter our $1 Million Education Sweepstakes.

To do that, just bring them in by September 30th and have them fill out an entry blank.

Then, who knows, you could end up at college with 100,000 big ones in the bank.

And parents who call you up once a month to ask for spending money.

Apple's $1 Million Education Sweepstakes.

And now a word from our lawyers.

Consumer Newspaper Over 600 Lines: Single

102
ART DIRECTOR
Simon Bowden
WRITER
David Metcalf
DESIGNER
Simon Bowden
CLIENT
Volvo
AGENCY
Scali McCabe Sloves

103
ART DIRECTOR
Marvin Rich
WRITER
Bob Sundland
CLIENT
Net Air International
AGENCY
Chiat/Day - San Francisco

104
ART DIRECTOR
Constantine Shoukas
WRITER
Dorothy Linder
CLIENT
Eastern Airlines
AGENCY
Campbell-Ewald

IN AN ACCIDENT, COULD YOU SURVIVE YOUR CAR?
Does your car have front and rear energy absorbing crumple zones, like a Volvo?
Is your car equipped with three-point belts in the rear seats, like a Volvo?
Does your car have a back-up braking system that provides 80% of the original stopping power, like a Volvo?
Does your car have bumpers that will withstand a 5 mph collision, like a Volvo's?
Is your steering wheel designed to automatically collapse then fold upwards to help cushion impact, like a Volvo's?
©1985 VOLVO NORTH AMERICA CORPORATION
Is your fuel tank positioned near the rear axle, to help avoid rupturing in an accident, like a Volvo's?
Do the doors of your car have a rigid steel bar for side impact protection, like a Volvo's?
Is your car built around a steel safety cage to help protect the passengers, like a Volvo?
While no company can guarantee your safety in an accident, which would you rather be driving, your car or a Volvo?
VOLVO
A car you can believe in.

When you gotta go, you gotta go.

Airlines depart on a schedule.
Which is precisely where the airlines depart from the needs of business.

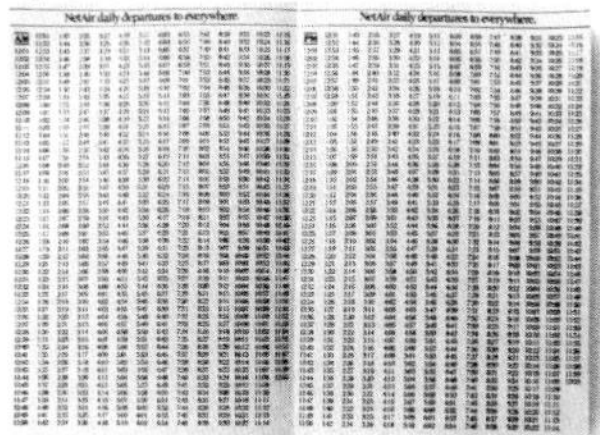

NetAir Flight Schedule

Because business demands don't always jibe with airline schedules.
NetAir® Jet-Taxi℠ service is different.
We don't fly on our schedule. We fly on your schedule.
8:01 a.m., 8:02, 8:03, whenever. The plane leaves when you get here.
And we not only fly anytime, we also fly anywhere. Direct to any destination.
Which seems destined to appeal to business because it can eliminate layovers when you need to fly to a smaller city that isn't an airline hub city.
When scheduled airlines can't, NetAir can.

Charters have been a "you never know" kind of thing up 'til now.
You never know their service standards. You never know their safety standards. You never even know their telephone number. (With thousands of charter services, who do you call?)
NetAir solves the problems of charters, as well as the problems of scheduled airlines.
NetAir is a network of Flight Centers, coordinated to bring uniformly high standards to on-demand flights.
We'll be national soon. Right now, we're in the western half of the country.
It costs more than regular airlines.
Cab rides cost more than bus rides.
And personal computers cost more than calculators.
For reservations or a brochure describing the various factors that can make a NetAir flight cost-effective, as well as other information about us, call 800-NETAIR-1. In Colorado, call direct 825-1000. (NASDAQ: NTARU)
Because getting where you want when you want is important if you want to get anywhere in business these days.

For reservations or information, please call 800-NETAIR-1. In Colorado, **call direct 825-1000.**

103

TO THE AIRLINES WHO MATCHED OUR $99 FARE TO FLORIDA: MATCH THIS.

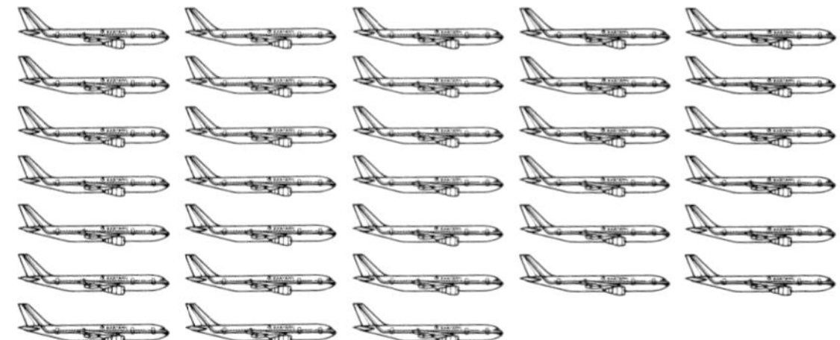

THE MOST DAILY NONSTOPS. NO ADVANCE PURCHASE AND NO MINIMUM/MAXIMUM STAY REQUIREMENTS.

While it's possible for an airline to come down to our price, it's not so easy to come up to our service.

Eastern flies more nonstops to Florida than any other airline. 33 every day. To Miami, Ft. Lauderdale, Orlando, Tampa/St. Petersburg and West Palm Beach.

Monday through Thursday for only $99 each way in Coach. Friday through Sunday for only $10 more.

And there's no advance purchase. Also, you can make your visit as long as you wish. Or as short, for that matter.

In addition, almost all our flights to Florida are wide-bodies.

But we don't just give you unparalleled service, we give you all the amenities.

So get complete details from your Travel Agent, or Eastern Airlines at 212-986-5000 in New York or 201-621-2121 in Newark.

It's futile to bother with any other airline.
They can't match Eastern.

EASTERN
WE EARN OUR WINGS EVERY DAY®

Seats are limited. Travel must be completed by 12/16/85. Fare not valid for travel on 11/27/85.

104

Consumer Newspaper Over 600 Lines: Single

105
ART DIRECTOR
Bob Barrie
WRITER
Phil Hanft
DESIGNER
Bob Barrie
PHOTOGRAPHER
Rick Dublin
CLIENT
MAX Long Distance
AGENCY
Fallon McElligott/Minneapolis

106
ART DIRECTOR
Jerry Whitley
WRITER
Joe O'Neill
PHOTOGRAPHER
Jeffrey Zwart
CLIENT
BMW of North America
AGENCY
Ammirati & Puris

107
ART DIRECTOR
Mark Decena
WRITERS
Ken Musto
Larry Plapler
CLIENT
People Express
AGENCY
Plapler Russo

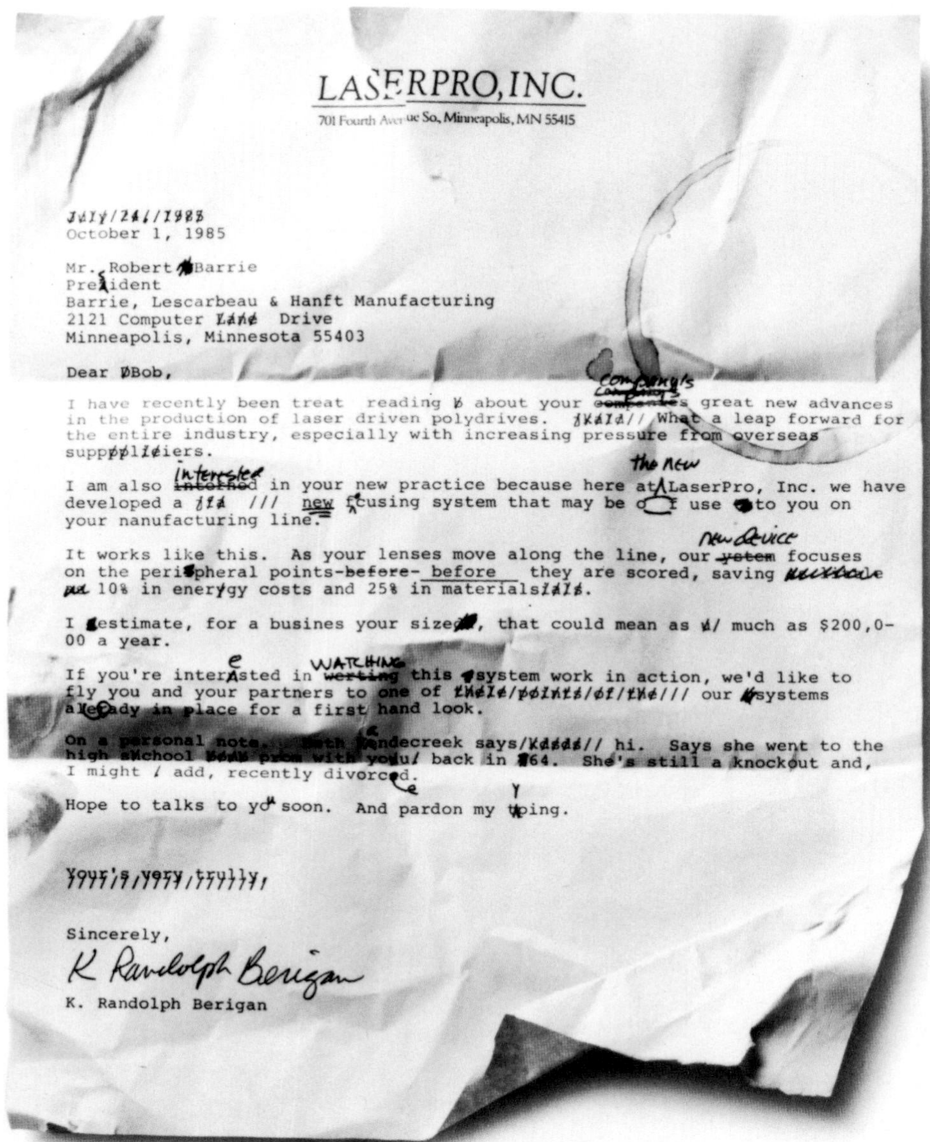

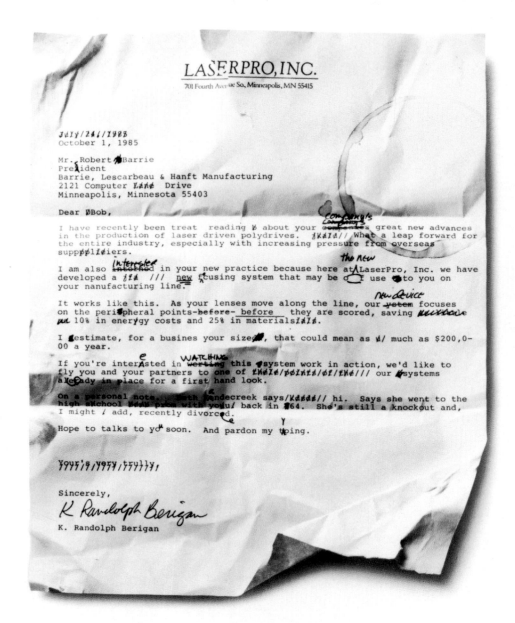

LASERPRO, INC.
701 Fourth Avenue So, Minneapolis, MN 55415

October 1, 1985

Mr. Robert Barrie
President
Barrie, Lescarbeau & Hanft Manufacturing
2121 Computer Drive
Minneapolis, Minnesota 55403

Dear Bob,

I have recently been treat reading about your company's great new advances in the production of laser driven polydrives. What a leap forward for the entire industry, especially with increasing pressure from overseas suppppliers.

I am also interested in your new practice because here at the new LaserPro, Inc. we have developed a /// new focusing system that may be of use to you on your nanufacturing line.

It works like this. As your lenses move along the line, our new device focuses on the peripheral points- before they are scored, saving 10% in enerygy costs and 25% in materials.

I estimate, for a busines your size, that could mean as much as $200,0-00 a year.

If you're interested in WATCHING this system work in action, we'd like to fly you and your partners to one of /// our systems already in place for a first hand look.

On a personal note. Beth Vendecreek says// hi. Says she went to the high school prom with you back in 64. She's still a knockout and, I might add, recently divorced.

Hope to talks to you soon. And pardon my typing.

Your's very trully,

Sincerely,

K Randolph Berigan

K. Randolph Berigan

You wouldn't mail a business letter that looks like this. Why make long distance calls that sound like it?

In this new age of business communications, clear and static-free long distance calls are just as important as clear and error-free letters.

Perhaps even more so.

Which is why, during Equal Access Balloting, it makes sense to seriously consider MAX Business Long Distance.

At MAX, we conceived and designed our system specifically to serve businesses first.

The result is long distance that delivers quiet, clear transmissions. Guarantees open lines, even during peak hours. Plus offers business options like our MAX Wats and 800 Travel Service.

In fact, you get everything you'd expect from a company like AT&T. But at rates you'd pay MCI or Sprint.

For an explanation of Equal Access and MAX Long Distance that's as clear and static-free as our phone lines, call 1-800-631-4000 toll free. Or mail the coupon.

MAX Business Long Distance. You pay less. You don't get less.

Vote MAX during Equal Access.

☐ I'd like a clearer picture before I vote. Please send all the facts.
☐ Consider this coupon our company's vote for MAX.

Name ______
Position ______ Company ______
Address ______
City ______ State ______ Zip ______
Phone ______

Mail to: MAX Long Distance
Corporate Sales Center
26877 Northwestern Hwy, Suite 320
Southfield, MI 48034

MAX Long Distance

FOR THOSE WHO KNOW THE VALUE OF A DOLLAR, A CAR THAT JUSTIFIES SPENDING FORTY THOUSAND OF THEM.

The old adage, "If you have to ask what it costs, you can't afford it," seems to be rapidly slipping out of date.

And with it, a certain breed of luxury car whose lavish prices have always gone unquestioned.

Today's enlightened car buyer not only is asking "How much?" but "Why so much?" A state of affairs that has left many car makers groping for answers. And placed a record number of buyers behind the wheel of a BMW 735i.

THE DIFFERENCE BETWEEN A CLASSIC CAR AND A DATED CAR.

Peer beneath the glimmering hood ornaments and multilayered enamel of certain age-old status symbols and you'll unveil a car that is just that: age-old.

Examine the inner workings of a BMW 735i and you'll find quite the reverse.

Its new 3.5-liter engine is the successor to a power plant that Road & Track hailed as "the most refined in-line six in the world."

Working in tandem with that engine is the third generation of an electronic fuel management system that, in its original state, was among the world's most advanced. So advanced, it was used to govern the BMW engine that powered a Formula One champion race car.

The result? A veritable paradox—a six-cylinder automobile that is not only fuel-efficient* but also out-accelerates many eight-cylinder cars in its class.

A CAR THAT DOES NOT ACCEPT THE INEVITABLE.

BMW engineers are passionate believers in the theory that, in driving, "forewarned is forearmed."

They've endowed the new 735i with an electronic Service Interval Indicator that signals you the moment service is recommended.

With an onboard computer that informs you of everything from range on remaining fuel to the potential of road icing.

With an ABS braking system that helps provide you with infinitely more control over your fate during stopping. A system that helps prevent the wheels from locking (a prime cause of skidding) and enables steering even in panic stops. One whose concept has been applied not just on roadways but on runways where, day-in and day-out, it brings the most sophisticated passenger jet aircraft to a controlled, secure halt.

Does the BMW 735i possess the luxuries befitting a car in its price range? Indeed. It's just that the 735i's luxuries are not there in lieu of necessities.

You will find everything that one, in good taste, could require. Eight-way power seats of hand-stitched leather. Walnut paneling. A cockpit-like dash that sweeps out to meet you. A telescopically-adjustable steering column. Electrically-controlled right-and-left mirrors. An electrically-controlled, dual position sun roof.

The 735i is, in the end, a car that single-handedly justifies having expensive taste in cars.

An automobile that doesn't require rationalizations for its lofty $40,000 purchase price** because it comes fully equipped with a long list of superbly engineered reasons.

A list that your BMW dealer will be more than pleased to continue at your earliest convenience.

THE ULTIMATE DRIVING MACHINE.

SAVE AS YOU GO.

3 NON STOPS DAILY TO NEW YORK/NEWARK–$53/$80					
FROM MONTREAL-MIRABEL VIA NEWARK TO:		ONE-WAY PRICE			
ALBANY		$80/$121	HOUSTON-HOBBY		$148/$175
ATLANTA		$135/$162	JACKSONVILLE		$135/$162
BALTIMORE		$80/$121	MELBOURNE, FL		$162/$203
BIRMINGHAM		$135/$162	MIAMI		$162/$203
BOSTON		$80/$121	MINNEAPOLIS/ST. PAUL		$148/$203
CHARLOTTE		$107/$135	NASHVILLE		$135/$162
CHICAGO		$135/$162	NEW ORLEANS		$89
CINCINNATI		$107/$135	NORFOLK/VIRGINIA BEACH		$80/$121
CLEVELAND		$107/$135	ORLANDO		$147/$203
COLUMBIA, SC		$107/$135	PITTSBURGH		$107/$135
COLUMBUS		$107/$135	PROVIDENCE		$80/$121
DALLAS/FT. WORTH		$175/$203	RALEIGH/DURHAM		$107/$135
DAYTON		$107/$135	SAN DIEGO		$129
DENVER		$148/$175	SARASOTA/BRADENTON		$162/$203
DETROIT		$107/$135	ST. LOUIS		$79
FT. LAUDERDALE		$162/$203	ST. PETERSBURG/TAMPA		$162/$203
FT. MYERS		$162/$203	WASHINGTON-DULLES INT'L		$53/$80
GREENSBORO		$107/$134	WASHINGTON-NATIONAL		$80/$121
HARTFORD/SPRINGFIELD		$80/$121	WEST PALM BEACH		$162/$203
SAN FRANCISCO/ OAKLAND	COACH	$230/$298	LONDON, ENGLAND	COACH	$324/$351
	PREMIUM	$476		PREMIUM	$665/$692
LOS ANGELES	COACH	$230/$298	BRUSSELS, BELGIUM	COACH	$188/$215 (9/8-9/30) $256/$283 (10/1-11/13)
	PREMIUM	$476		PREMIUM	$665/$692

Prices effective through 11/13/85. Fares are quoted in Canadian dollars and are subject to government approval.
All flights arrive at Terminal C—Newark International Airport.

PEOPLExpress

FLY SMART

PEOPLE EXPRESS AIRLINES/FOR RESERVATIONS, PHONE: IN MONTREAL, QUEBEC **(514) 875-6787**; IN BURLINGTON, VT **(802) 863-2509** OR CALL YOUR TRAVEL AGENT.

Consumer Newspaper Over 600 Lines: Single

108
ART DIRECTOR
Yvonne Smith
WRITER
Mark Monteiro
PHOTOGRAPHERS
Lamb & Hall
CLIENT
Porsche Cars North America
AGENCY
Chiat/Day - Los Angeles

109
ART DIRECTOR
Tim Delaney
WRITER
John Malecki
DESIGNER
Tim Delaney
PHOTOGRAPHER
Stu Peltz
CLIENT
Perdue
AGENCY
Scali McCabe Sloves

110
ART DIRECTOR
Duncan Milner
WRITER
Hal Maynard
ARTIST
Diane Denny
PHOTOGRAPHER
Chris Wimpey
CLIENT
The Tribune
AGENCY
WFC/San Diego

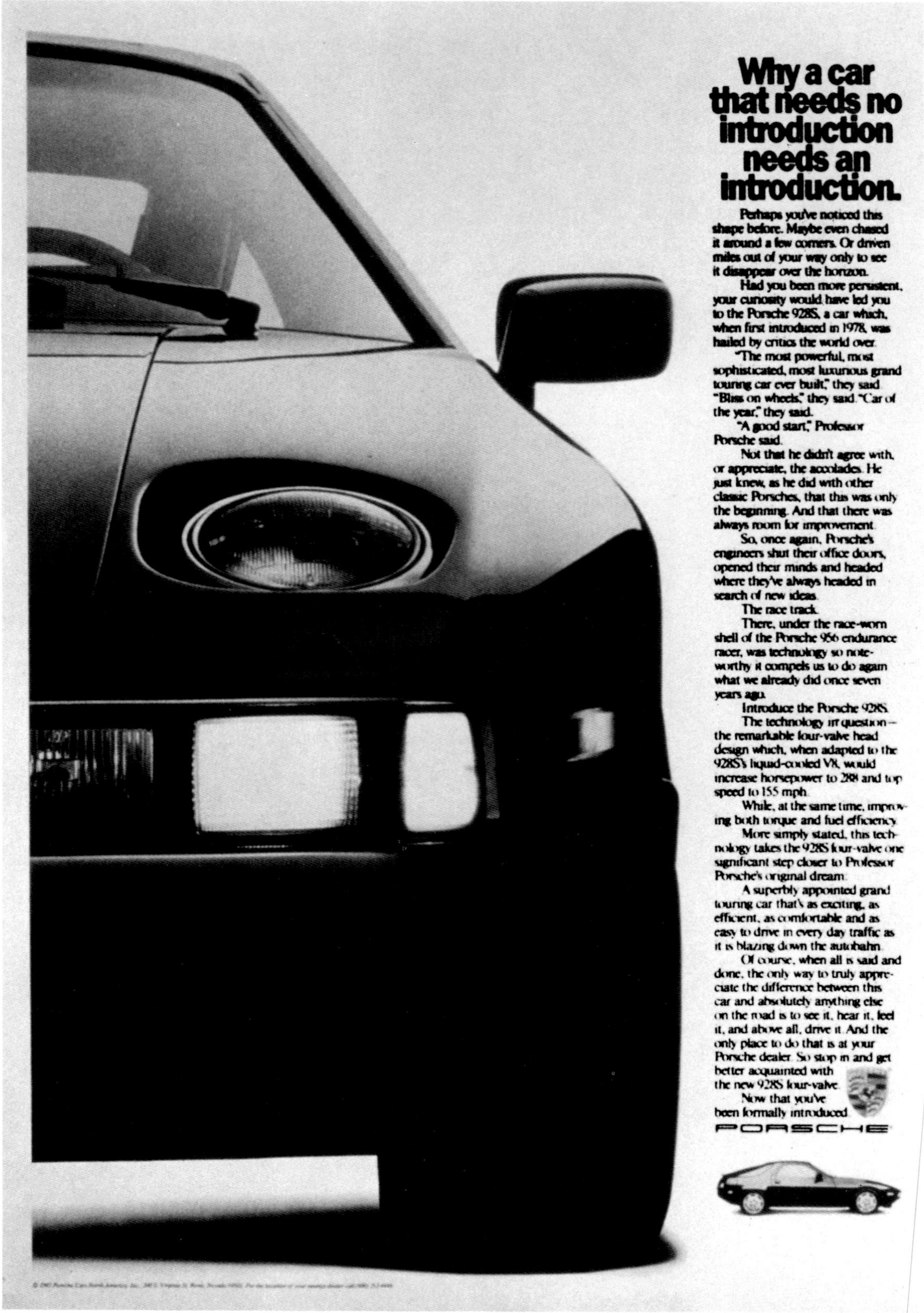

Why a car that needs no introduction needs an introduction.

Perhaps you've noticed this shape before. Maybe even chased it around a few corners. Or driven miles out of your way only to see it disappear over the horizon.

Had you been more persistent, your curiosity would have led you to the Porsche 928S, a car which, when first introduced in 1978, was hailed by critics the world over.

"The most powerful, most sophisticated, most luxurious grand touring car ever built," they said. "Bliss on wheels," they said. "Car of the year," they said.

"A good start," Professor Porsche said.

Not that he didn't agree with, or appreciate, the accolades. He just knew, as he did with other classic Porsches, that this was only the beginning. And that there was always room for improvement.

So, once again, Porsche's engineers shut their office doors, opened their minds and headed where they've always headed in search of new ideas.

The race track.

There, under the race-worn shell of the Porsche 956 endurance racer, was technology so noteworthy it compels us to do again what we already did once seven years ago.

Introduce the Porsche 928S.

The technology in question—the remarkable four-valve head design which, when adapted to the 928S's liquid-cooled V8, would increase horsepower to 288 and top speed to 155 mph.

While, at the same time, improving both torque and fuel efficiency.

More simply stated, this technology takes the 928S four-valve one significant step closer to Professor Porsche's original dream:

A superbly appointed grand touring car that's as exciting, as efficient, as comfortable and as easy to drive in every day traffic as it is blazing down the autobahn.

Of course, when all is said and done, the only way to truly appreciate the difference between this car and absolutely anything else on the road is to see it, hear it, feel it, and above all, drive it. And the only place to do that is at your Porsche dealer. So stop in and get better acquainted with the new 928S four-valve.

Now that you've been formally introduced.

PORSCHE

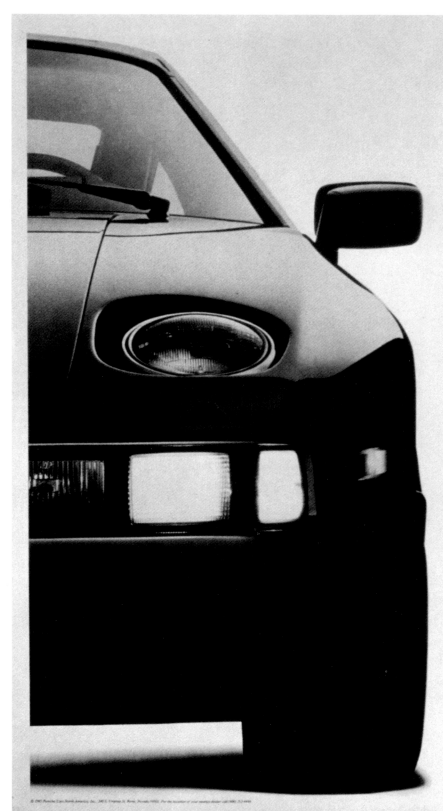

108

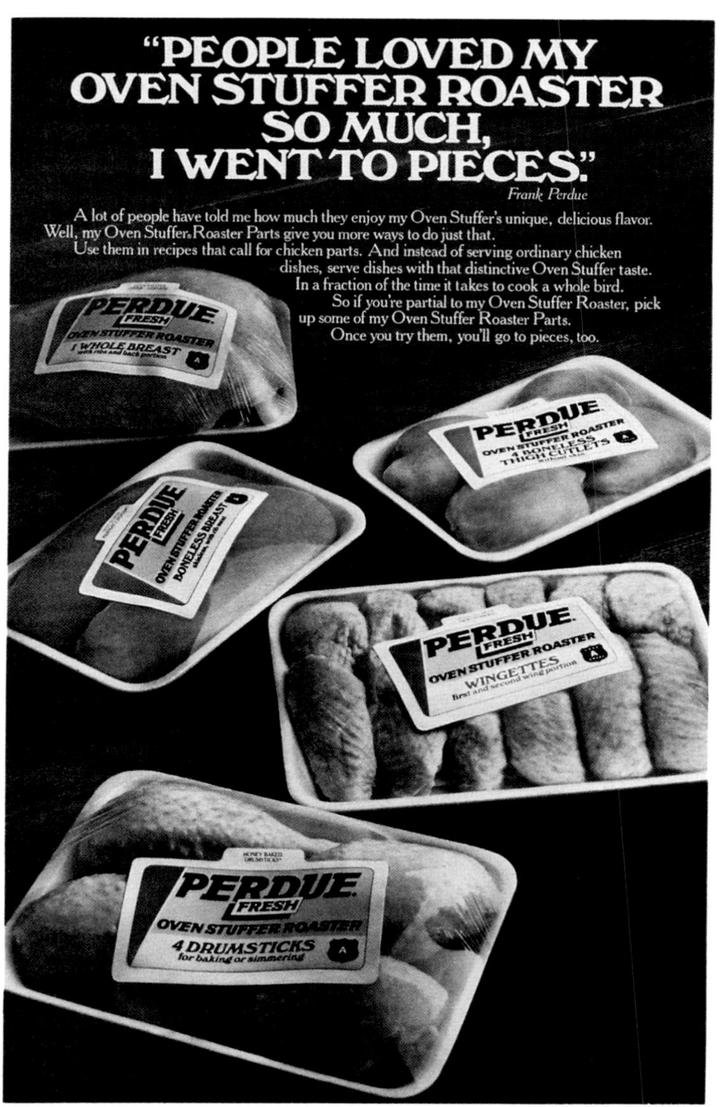

109

From now on, you won't have to work for Peanuts.

Or any of your other favorite features.

Because they won't be jumping all over the paper. We've reorganized The Tribune so that most things you like to read will be in the same section every day.

Now The Tribune will come to you on most days as six sections: News, Financial, Metro, Sports, Scene/Entertainment/TV and Classified. Each with its own familiar format, designed to make reading The Tribune much easier for you.

And just in case you haven't found Charlie Brown or any other comics yet today, check their new home, in the Sports section.

THE TRIBUNE
It hits home.

110

Consumer Newspaper Over 600 Lines: Single

111
ART DIRECTOR
Michelle Weibman
WRITER
Emma Hayward
DESIGNER
Michelle Weibman
ARTIST
Michelle Weibman
CLIENT
TWA
AGENCY
Ogilvy & Mather

112
ART DIRECTOR
Tom Lichtenheld
WRITER
Sam Avery
CLIENT
MedCenters Health Plan
AGENCY
Fallon McElligott/Minneapolis

113
ART DIRECTOR
Steve Beaumont
WRITER
Penny Kapousouz
PHOTOGRAPHER
Bob Grigg
CLIENT
Apple Computer
AGENCY
Chiat/Day - Los Angeles

Imagine this page is the Atlantic Ocean.
See those black lines? That's us.

Those black lines going back and forth across the page are the number of times TWA flies across the Atlantic each week.

About four hundred times in fact. (Don't count them, they didn't all fit.)

That, by the way, is more than anyone else.

And on April 28th, we even discover three brand-new places. Copenhagen, Geneva and Bombay.

(The latter, you may feel, is something of an exciting departure from our traditional destinations.)

You'll be able to get to Copenhagen and Geneva from J.F.K. every day. And to Bombay three times a week.

We're also starting a new Gateway to Europe at St. Louis which will make your life a great deal easier if you happen to live in the West and want to go nonstop to London or Paris or even Frankfurt.

And we'll have a new nonstop from J.F.K. to Tel Aviv. And from June 15th, a nonstop to Munich, and a 747 on our nonstop to Amsterdam.

That, of course, is on top of all the existing ones.

Twenty-eight opportunities a week to get to London from J.F.K. Twenty-one to get to Paris. Fourteen to get to Rome, Frankfurt and Athens. Twelve to get to Madrid. Daily flights from Boston to London, Rome and Paris. Three times a week to Cairo and Tel Aviv. The list is endless.

The only important thing you really need to know is that we fly nonstop from the U.S. to more places in Europe than any other airline.

Then, next time you need to go, all those little black lines will begin to make a lot of sense.

TWA

LEADING THE WAY. TWA.

111

With MedCenters Health Plan, You're Covered No Matter Where It Hurts.

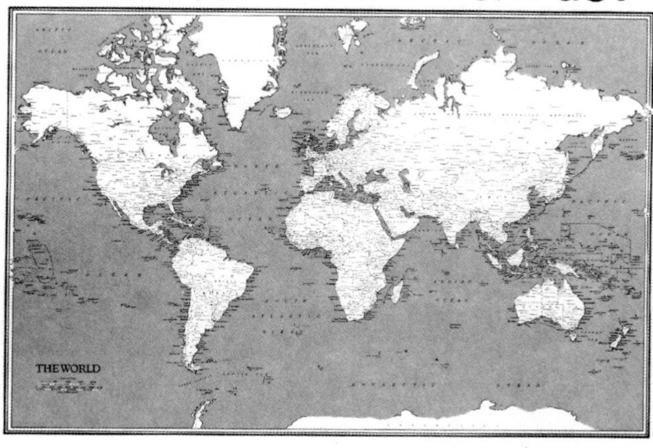

Next time you plan a vacation, bear in mind that MedCenters Health Plan covers you in any emergency whether you're vacationing in Paris or Pequot Lakes. For more information about our comprehensive HMO benefits, talk to your employer. Or give us a call at 927-3263.

MEDCENTERS HEALTH PLAN

112

What's your problem?

We've devised this simple chart to show you just a few of the business problems The Macintosh Office can handle.

The chart works much the same way Macintosh does. If you can put your index finger on your problem, you can put your finger on our solutions.

113

114
ART DIRECTOR
John Clapps
WRITER
Charles Mullen
PHOTOGRAPHER
Scott Laperruque
CLIENT
Custom Communications Systems
AGENCY
Clapps & Mullen

115
ART DIRECTOR
Jim Mountjoy
WRITER
Steve Lasch
PHOTOGRAPHER
Tom Walters
CLIENT
Direct Express
AGENCY
Loeffler Mountjoy/North Carolina

116
ART DIRECTOR
Mark Decena
WRITERS
John Russo
Larry Plapler
CLIENT
People Express
AGENCY
Plapler Russo

Any moron can install a computer. And usually one does.

It's a well known fact that the people who design computers are very bright. Sometimes brilliant.

But it's not so well known that the people who install computers are usually just the opposite.

If you want proof, just look at the maze of cables and balls and balls of wire behind your computers now.

And with each new computer you add, or repair you make—things get more complicated. And more expensive.

That's where we come in.

Custom Communications Systems. (201-342-1288)

We make things simple. We organize the computers that organize your life.

In fact, we specialize in condensing hundreds of cables into just a manageable few. In addition, we sell and install all types of data communication equipment.

We're not saying you have to be a genius to install computers. But it helps.

CUSTOM COMMUNICATIONS SYSTEMS.

114

ARE YOU STILL SUPPORTING THE FEDERAL BUDGET?

Direct Express offers guaranteed next morning delivery at a down-to-earth price. (For two pounds, Federal's rate is $25.00. Ours? Still $9.65.) We serve the Greater Atlanta, Charleston, Columbia, Greenville, Charlotte, Greensboro and Raleigh areas. So, make a huge Federal budget cut. Start going Direct.

DIRECT EXPRESS

Nothing Beats Going Direct.

115

THE BEST THING FOR YOUR UNPREDICTABLE SCHEDULE IS OUR PREDICTABLE SCHEDULE.

NEW YORK

TO NEW YORK	TO BUFFALO
7:20 AM	6:35 AM
8:20 AM	7:35 AM
9:20 AM	8:35 AM
10:20 AM	9:35 AM
11:20 AM	10:45 AM
12:25 PM	12:35 PM
2:20 PM	2:35 PM
4:20 PM	4:35 PM
6:20 PM	5:35 PM
7:20 PM	6:35 PM
8:20 PM	7:35 PM
9:20 PM	8:35 PM
10:20 PM	9:35 PM (Friday and Sunday only)
11:20 PM (Friday and Sunday only)	10:35 PM

Eleven non stops to New York. A schedule that's tailored to yours. And an 85% on-time performance in September.

All for $35 off peak, $49 peak. And our low, unrestricted prices apply every seat, every flight, every day—as you might have predicted from People Express.

PEOPLExpress
FLY SMART

NEW YORK/NEWARK, BOSTON, CHICAGO, DETROIT, WASHINGTON, BALTIMORE, HOUSTON, SYRACUSE, BUFFALO, NORFOLK, COLUMBUS, PITTSBURGH, HARTFORD/SPRINGFIELD, BURLINGTON, MINNEAPOLIS/ST. PAUL, PORTLAND, JACKSONVILLE, SARASOTA, MELBOURNE, MIAMI, WEST PALM BEACH, ST. PETERSBURG, LOS ANGELES, SAN FRANCISCO/OAKLAND, LONDON, ENGLAND. PEOPLE EXPRESS AIRLINES/FOR RESERVATIONS, PHONE: **(312) 374-4139** OR CALL YOUR TRAVEL AGENT. FOR PREMIUM CLASS RESERVATIONS CALL **(201) 596-6070.**

116

Consumer Newspaper Over 600 Lines: Single

117
ART DIRECTOR
Raul Pina
WRITER
Chris Messner
CLIENT
Health America
AGENCY
Della Femina Travisano & Partners

118
ART DIRECTOR
Simon Bowden
WRITER
David Metcalf
DESIGNER
Simon Bowden
PHOTOGRAPHER
Jerry Friedman
CLIENT
Volvo
AGENCY
Scali McCabe Sloves

119
ART DIRECTOR
Rob Oliver
WRITER
Tom Jenkins
PHOTOGRAPHER
Snowden
CLIENT
Volkswagen Audi Group
AGENCY
Doyle Dane Bernbach/London

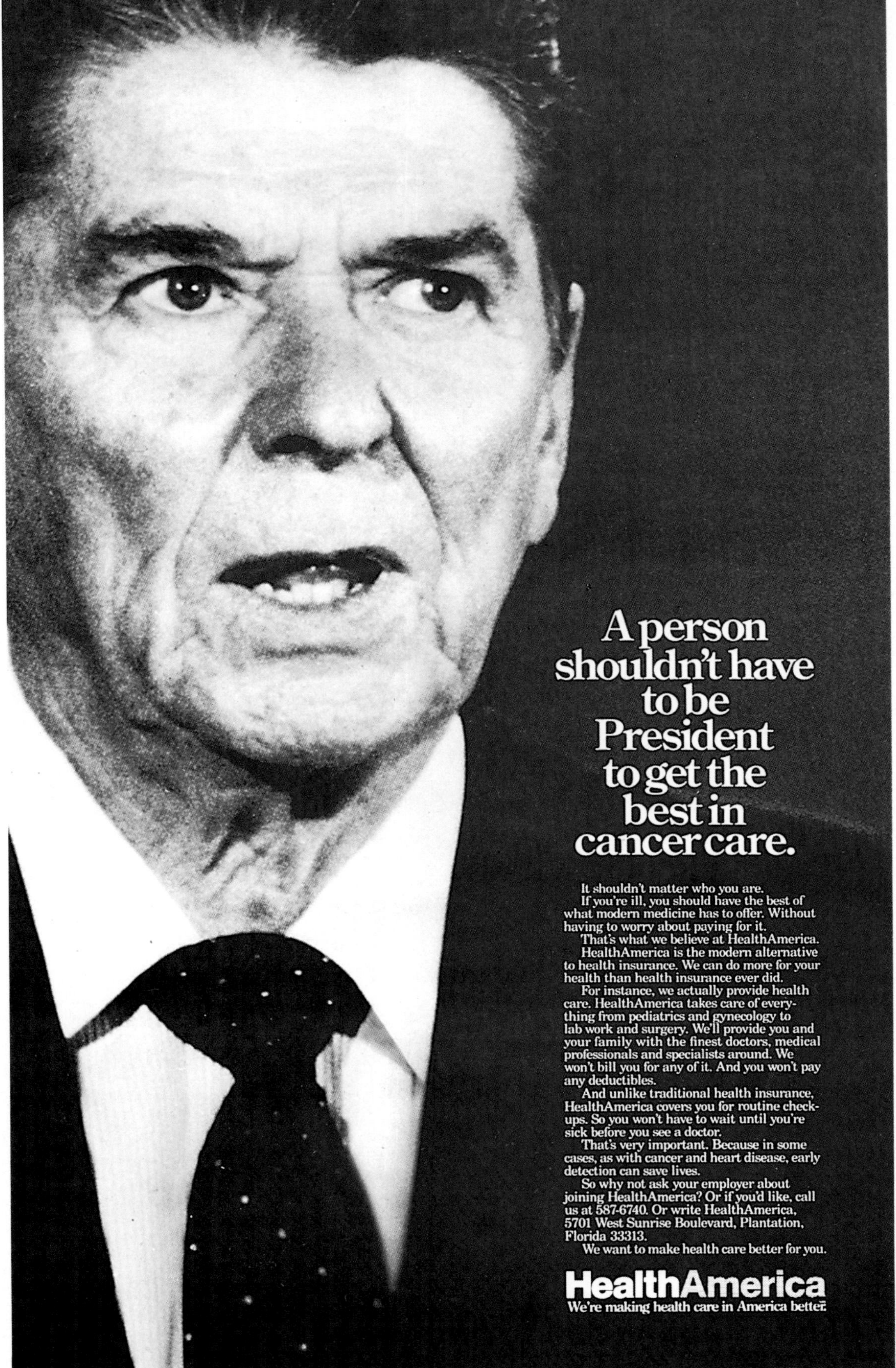
A person shouldn't have to be President to get the best in cancer care.
It shouldn't matter who you are.
If you're ill, you should have the best of what modern medicine has to offer. Without having to worry about paying for it.
That's what we believe at HealthAmerica.
HealthAmerica is the modern alternative to health insurance. We can do more for your health than health insurance ever did.
For instance, we actually provide health care. HealthAmerica takes care of everything from pediatrics and gynecology to lab work and surgery. We'll provide you and your family with the finest doctors, medical professionals and specialists around. We won't bill you for any of it. And you won't pay any deductibles.
And unlike traditional health insurance, HealthAmerica covers you for routine check-ups. So you won't have to wait until you're sick before you see a doctor.
That's very important. Because in some cases, as with cancer and heart disease, early detection can save lives.
So why not ask your employer about joining HealthAmerica? Or if you'd like, call us at 587-6740. Or write HealthAmerica, 5701 West Sunrise Boulevard, Plantation, Florida 33313.
We want to make health care better for you.
HealthAmerica
We're making health care in America better.

117

IN AN ACCIDENT, COULD YOU SURVIVE YOUR CAR?

Does your car have front and rear energy absorbing crumple zones, like a Volvo?
Does your car have bumpers that will withstand a 5 mph collision, like a Volvo's?
Is your car equipped with three-point belts in the rear seats, like a Volvo?
Is your steering wheel designed to automatically collapse then fold upwards to help cushion impact, like a Volvo's?
Does your car have a back-up braking system that provides 80% of the original stopping power, like a Volvo?
Do the doors of your car have a rigid steel bar for side impact protection, like a Volvo's?
Is your car built around a steel safety cage to help protect the passengers, like a Volvo?
Is your fuel tank positioned near the rear axle, to help avoid rupturing in an accident, like a Volvo's?
While no company can guarantee your safety in an accident, which would you rather be driving, your car or a Volvo?
VOLVO
A car you can believe in.

D-86-247—4 Col. x 14"

118

When they become optional extras, so will our rear seat belts.

On January 31st 1983 the wearing of front seat belts became law.

It saved the lives of countless people who were lucky enough to be in the front seats.

Alas, the law didn't apply to back seats.

By the end of that year 1,300 children, most of them travelling in the back, had been killed or seriously injured inside cars.

In spite of this, almost all the leading car manufacturers still classify rear seat belts as extras on cars costing less than £8,000. (In other words, cars most likely to be carrying families.)

At Volkswagen if something makes a car safer we don't call it an extra. And we don't charge extra for it.

All Volkswagens, regardless of price, come with rear seat belts. As standard.

All four door Volkswagens are fitted with child proof locks. As standard.

And all Volkswagens have self-stabilising steering to help keep the car in a straight line during a blow-out or an emergency stop. This too is standard.

All Volkswagens, however, do not come with rally seats or leather steering wheels.

These are our extras.

It's your option.

119

Consumer Newspaper Over 600 Lines: Single

120
ART DIRECTOR
Michael Fazende
WRITER
John Stingley
PHOTOGRAPHER
Bettman Archive
CLIENT
American Association of Advertising Agencies
AGENCY
Fallon McElligott/Minneapolis

121
ART DIRECTOR
Mark Fuller
WRITER
Ed Jones
ARTIST
Brian Leister
PHOTOGRAPHER
Pat Edwards
CLIENT
Martha Jefferson Hospital
AGENCY
Finnegan & Agee/Virginia

122
ART DIRECTOR
Mark Decena
WRITER
John Russo
ARTISTS
Todd Schorr
Kathy Schorr
CLIENT
People Express
AGENCY
Plapler Russo

HOWEVER POWERFUL A MESSAGE IS, SOME PEOPLE MAY NOT BUY IT.

People have an overwhelming tendency to question what they're told. Even when it's cast in stone.

That's what makes us human. We make our own decisions. Sometimes right. Sometimes wrong. But always our own.

So it's hard to believe when people claim that advertising made them buy something they didn't want.

Sure, we'd like to think that the advertising we create has a powerful impact on you.

But the truth is we simply present facts. Try to make them interesting and entertaining. Then sit back and hope we got through.

As for having some kind of power over people's actions, greater forces than the advertising industry have tried.

And God only knows, no one does everything they're told.

ADVERTISING
ANOTHER WORD FOR FREEDOM OF CHOICE.
American Association of Advertising Agencies

120

OUR LASER CAN TREAT MANY OPTIC DISORDERS IN THE BLINK OF AN EYE.

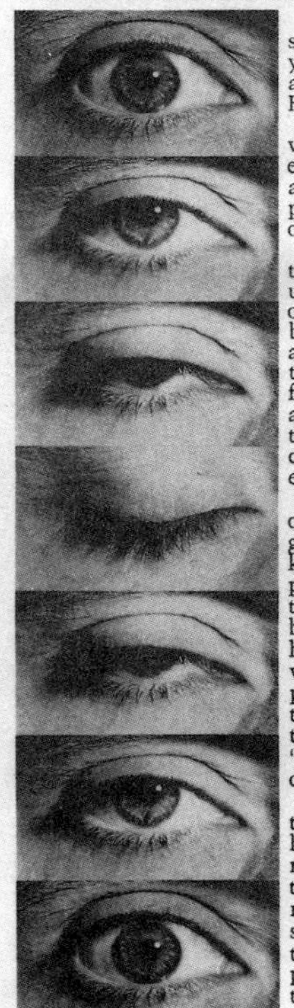

An argon-krypton laser sounds like something you'd find in a distant galaxy, not at Martha Jefferson Hospital.

But for many patients with certain diseases of the eye, treatment with our argon-krypton laser has proven to be the best thing on earth.

It seems appropriate that lasers should be used to treat eye disorders. The laser beam is, after all, a type of light, though far more intense and concentrated than the light that colors our daily environment.

The beam of our argon-krypton laser enters the eye the way ordinary light does. Treatment is fast and virtually painless.

In the hands of trained ophthalmologists, the beam generated by our argon-krypton laser becomes a precise medical instrument that can seal abnormal blood vessels that cause hemorrhaging and loss of vision in some diabetic patients. It can be used to treat and prevent certain types of glaucoma. Or to "weld" many tears and detachments of the retina.

Beyond the successful treatment it can provide, laser surgery offers significant advantages over traditional eye surgery techniques. For one thing, no surgical incision is required, thus reducing both surgical preparation and recovery time. In fact, laser procedures usually last only a few minutes to an hour or so, depending on the problem being treated.

What's more, most patients who undergo laser eye treatment experience no pain whatsoever.

Needless to say, providing the level of health care exemplified by laser surgery requires major investments on the part of Martha Jefferson. Investments in new and highly skilled personnel. Investments in new equipment. Investments in continuous staff training.

We're happy to make those investments because they're an extension of the investment we've been making in the well-being of this community for over eighty years.

We'd like you to know more about the role Martha Jefferson could play in your well-being. Call 293-0508 for more information about the range of services we offer or to arrange a personal tour of the hospital.

We'll show you things that are so amazing, you may not believe your eyes.

MARTHA JEFFERSON HOSPITAL
Charlottesville, Virginia

121

OUR 50¢ CUP OF COFFEE VS. THEIR $15 BAGEL.

At People Express, we charge a nominal price for things like coffee. A snack. Or checking a bag. You see, at People Express, you never pay for the things you don't want. Which is one reason you pay so little for the things you do want. Like frequent flights—21 a day to Boston—on clean, comfortable Boeing jets. And service by owners.

In fact our price is so low to Boston that on any business morning you pay $15 less than the next lowest price; New York Air's.

That means 3 round trips to Boston on People Express saves you $90—that's a lot of bagels. It's also enough to fly us almost everywhere we fly to—and that's a lot of places. 36 cities in all.

On People Express, we don't give away "free" snacks. Which is one reason we charge so little.

TO BOSTON		TO NEW YORK	
7:00 AM	3:00 PM	6:40 AM	3:40 PM
8:00 AM	3:30 PM	7:40 AM	4:10 PM
9:00 AM	4:00 PM	8:40 AM	4:40 PM
10:00 AM	4:30 PM	9:40 AM	5:10 PM
11:00 AM	5:00 PM	10:40 AM	5:40 PM
12:00 PM	6:00 PM	11:40 AM	6:10 PM
1:00 PM	7:00 PM	12:40 PM	6:40 PM
1:30 PM	8:00 PM	1:40 PM	7:40 PM
2:00 PM	9:00 PM	2:40 PM	8:40 PM
2:30 PM	10:00 PM	3:10 PM	9:40 PM
	11:00 PM		10:40 PM

PEOPLExpress
FLY SMART

PEOPLE EXPRESS AIRLINES/FOR RESERVATIONS, PHONE ONE OF OUR FIVE NEW YORK NUMBERS. IN MANHATTAN: (212) 432-9494, (212) 319-9494, (212) 772-0344 IN QUEENS: (718) 204-5353 IN BROOKLYN: (718) 499-9090 IN NEW JERSEY (201) 596-6000 ON LONG ISLAND (516) 542-1120 IN WESTCHESTER/ROCKLAND (914) 328-0329 IN STAMFORD, CONN. (203) 348-9504 IN TRENTON, N.J. (609) 393-1031 OR CALL YOUR TRAVEL AGENT. FOR PREMIUM CLASS RESERVATIONS CALL 1 (800) 344-4000.

122

Consumer Newspaper Over 600 Lines: Single

123
ART DIRECTOR
Bob Kasper
WRITER
Kathy Kiley
CLIENT
The Provident
AGENCY
HBM/MacDonald - Boston

124
ART DIRECTOR
Corrin Jacobsen
WRITER
Dick Jackson
DESIGNER
Corrin Jacobsen
PHOTOGRAPHER
Ulf Skogsbergh
CLIENT
The Post House Restaurant
AGENCY
Dick Jackson Inc.

125
ART DIRECTOR
Pat Epstein
WRITER
John Swartzwelder
DESIGNER
Pat Epstein
PHOTOGRAPHER
Dan Wolff
CLIENT
Continental Airlines
AGENCY
Scali McCabe Sloves

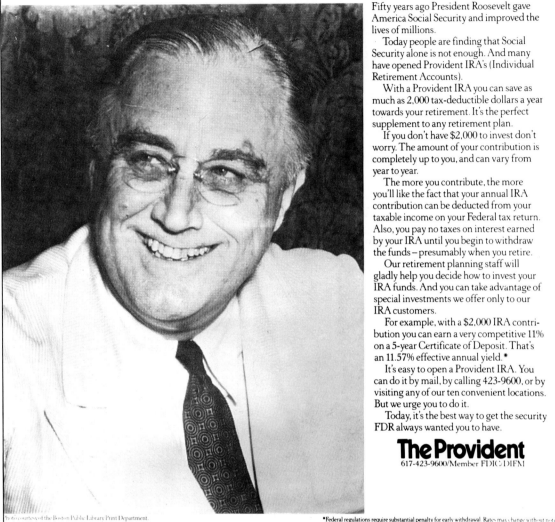

ARE YOU STILL RELYING ON THIS MAN TO PLAN FOR YOUR RETIREMENT?

Fifty years ago President Roosevelt gave America Social Security and improved the lives of millions.

Today people are finding that Social Security alone is not enough. And many have opened Provident IRA's (Individual Retirement Accounts).

With a Provident IRA you can save as much as 2,000 tax-deductible dollars a year towards your retirement. It's the perfect supplement to any retirement plan.

If you don't have $2,000 to invest don't worry. The amount of your contribution is completely up to you, and can vary from year to year.

The more you contribute, the more you'll like the fact that your annual IRA contribution can be deducted from your taxable income on your Federal tax return. Also, you pay no taxes on interest earned by your IRA until you begin to withdraw the funds – presumably when you retire.

Our retirement planning staff will gladly help you decide how to invest your IRA funds. And you can take advantage of special investments we offer only to our IRA customers.

For example, with a $2,000 IRA contribution you can earn a very competitive 11% on a 5-year Certificate of Deposit. That's an 11.57% effective annual yield.*

It's easy to open a Provident IRA. You can do it by mail, by calling 423-9600, or by visiting any of our ten convenient locations. But we urge you to do it.

Today, it's the best way to get the security FDR always wanted you to have.

The Provident
617-423-9600/Member FDIC/DIFM

Photo courtesy of the Boston Public Library Print Department.

*Federal regulations require substantial penalty for early withdrawal. Rates may change without notice.

WHAT TO ORDER AT THE POST HOUSE IF YOU HAVE THE TEMERITY TO RESIST ORDERING STEAK.

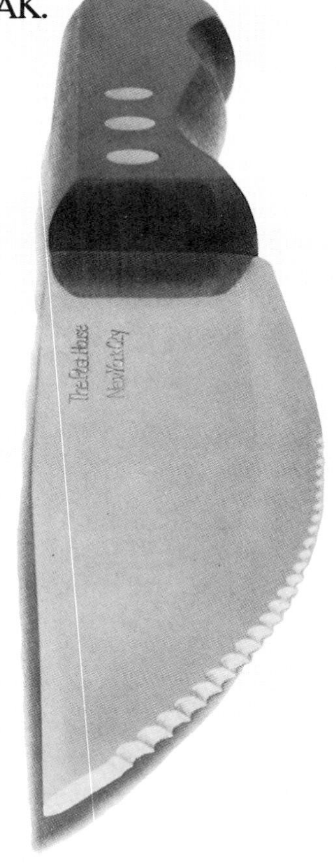

The Post House
New York City

"The best choice on the menu is the pungent lemon-and-pepper burnished chicken. The meat is moist, well protected by the veneer of crisp skin."
—*N.Y. Times*, September 1982

"The best appetizer is a fresh lumpmeat cocktail, but don't fail to try the stone crabs in season.
"...and luscious New York cheesecake that James Beard and I raved about one evening."
—*Town & Country*, September 1982

"The Post House serves the most delicious fresh sourdough rolls in Manhattan, so delicious that one has to guard against overdoing it before the giant steaks arrive. The Post House also serves some of the best onion rings and hash browns anywhere, the onions greaseless and light as a feather, and the spuds crusty and properly greasy."
—*WNCN-FM*, February 1985

"A prime cut above the usual, plus the widest and freshest variety of seafood in New York City's steakhouse milieu. Its raisin bread alone is worth the visit."
—*Forbes*, October 1982

And, oh, yes:
"Your steak will be properly aged and tender, and will arrive precisely as you describe your wishes to the waiter. Your salad will be crisply fresh, your vegetables will be lightly cooked, and the service will make you feel that you will almost enjoy paying the premium steak house prices."
—*WNCN-FM*, February 1985

"Steaks and chops are seared to juicy perfection, including one of the best chopped sirloins in town, and I defy anyone to find better onion rings."
—*Town & Country*, September 1982

THE POST HOUSE
New York's most elegant steakhouse.
28 East 63rd Street, N.Y.C. (Between Park & Madison.)
Open 7 days. Reservations (212) 935-2888

124

UNITED CHARGES YOU $50 WHEN YOU MISS YOUR FLIGHT. CONTINENTAL DOESN'T.
CONTINENTAL TO CHICAGO, $99.
When you get one of those "special low fares" on an airline like United you're taking a big chance.
Because if you miss your flight—for any reason—United will charge you a $50 penalty.
Continental offers you low fares and great service with no penalties at all.
With our Advance Off-Peak℠ fare you book your ticket 14 days in advance, and you can fly any day of the week. And never worry about penalties.
So don't take any chances. Next time fly Continental.
For information or reservations, call your travel agent. Or call 398-3000 or 1-800-525-0280.
DENVER TO:
ADVANCE OFF-PEAK FARE
N.Y./Newark $109
Houston $99
Los Angeles $99
Chicago $99
Washington, D.C. $129
CONTINENTAL.
THE ONLY AIRLINE WORTH FLYING.™
48 U.S. CITIES • MEXICO • CANADA • LONDON • THE SOUTH PACIFIC • MICRONESIA • INDONESIA • HAWAII • THE FAR EAST
Call early for our Advance Off-Peak fares, as seats may be limited. Fares subject to change. © 1985 Continental Air Lines, Inc.

125

Consumer Newspaper Over 600 Lines: Single

126
ART DIRECTOR
Rob Oliver
WRITER
Tom Jenkins
ARTIST
Steve Dell
CLIENT
Volkswagen
AGENCY
Doyle Dane Bernbach/London

127
ART DIRECTOR
Marten Tonnis
WRITER
Steve Rabosky
ARTIST
Barbara Banthien
PHOTOGRAPHER
Bo Hylen
CLIENT
Apple Computer
AGENCY
Chiat/Day - Los Angeles

128
ART DIRECTOR
Bob Wilvers
WRITER
Larry Plapler
CLIENT
People Express
AGENCY
Plapler Russo

You may be surprised to learn that Volkswagens aren't expensive.

They go down hill slower than most cars. (Test drive one and you'll realise why they hold their price so well.)

Yet most Volkswagen Polos and Passats actually cost less than Ford Fiestas and Sierras.

Any colour, so long as it's Volkswagen's, is covered by a three year paint warranty.

Every Volkswagen has negative roll radius to help it stop in a straight line even when the road is wet or greasy.

And every Volkswagen is fitted with dual circuit brakes for fail-safe stopping. (GTi models have disc brakes all-round.)

This is one of the few ways of getting from 0–60 faster than a Volkswagen Golf GTi or Scirocco GTX.

This is one of the few ways of getting around town using less petrol than a Volkswagen Formel E.

And this is a smooth road if you're driving a Golf, Jetta or Passat. They all have thinking rear axles for maximum stability on every surface.

Some manufacturers consider these to be optional extras. We don't. That's why every Volkswagen car is fitted with rear seat belts.

If you don't already drive a Volkswagen, this is the most reliable way to travel to your nearest dealer.

For the address of your nearest dealer write to Volkswagen Sales Enquiries, Yeomans Drive, Blakelands, Milton Keynes MK14 5AN.

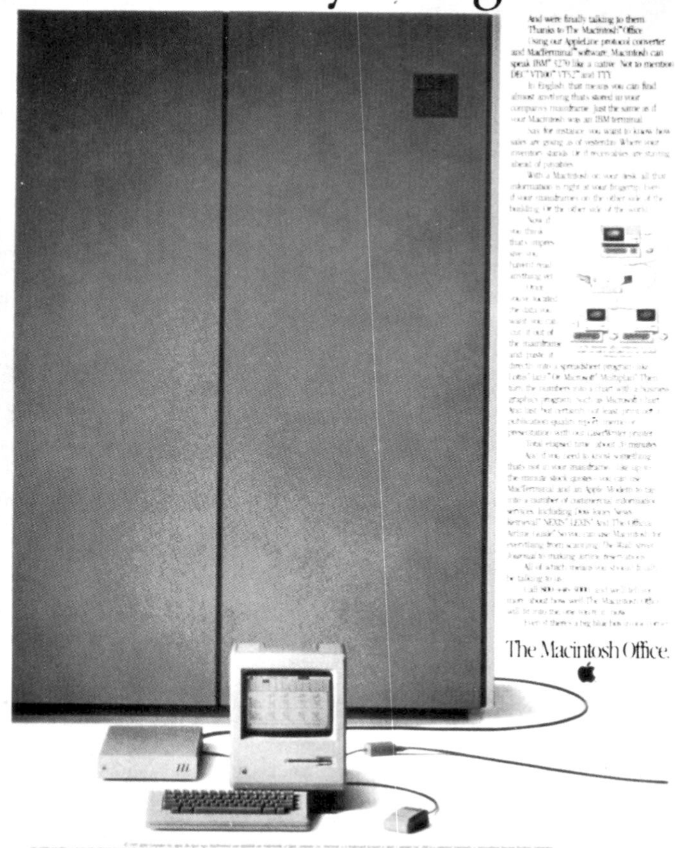

IBM is finally talking to us.
And we're finally talking to them. Thanks to The Macintosh™ Office.
Using our AppleLine protocol converter and MacTerminal™ software, Macintosh can speak IBM® 3270 like a native. Not to mention DEC™ VT100™ VT52™ and TTY.
The Macintosh Office.

127

THE OLD WORLD, THE NEW WAY. $99.

NON STOP TO BRUSSELS, THE GATEWAY TO EUROPE.

Starting September 8, we're flying from convenient Newark International Airport to Brussels National Airport in Belgium, for one of those mind-boggling People Express prices: $99. (October 1, the price becomes $149.)

What's more, clean, comfortable Boeing 747s will be flying every single day of the week.

As if Brussels isn't spectacular enough, from there you have easy access to France, Germany, Holland and Switzerland.

And if all this isn't spectacular enough—for only $450, you can fly our luxurious Premium Class.

As long as we have you thinking about Europe, we'd like to remind you that we also fly to London, England for just $199 Coach or $450 Premium Class.

People Express. We think you should be able to fly whenever you want, wherever you want.

Even if that "wherever" is Europe.

PEOPLExpress
FLY SMART

128

Consumer Newspaper Over 600 Lines: Single

129
ART DIRECTOR
Gary Larsen
WRITER
Rick Colby
ARTIST
Jerry Fruchtman
CLIENT
Protype Corporation
AGENCY
Larsen Colby Koralek/Los Angeles

130
ART DIRECTORS
Tony Siracusa
Paul Regan
WRITER
Lynn Schweikart
CLIENT
Worcester Telegram & Gazette
AGENCY
Ingalls Quinn & Johnson/Boston

131
ART DIRECTOR
Chris Armstrong
WRITER
Emma Hayward
DESIGNER
Chris Armstrong
PHOTOGRAPHER
Beth Galton
CLIENT
TWA
AGENCY
Ogilvy & Mather

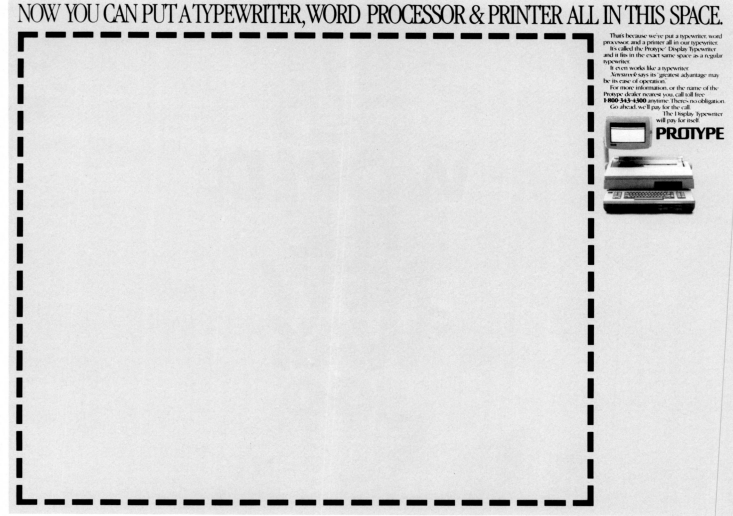

129

HIS EYES HOW THEY SPARKLED, HIS DIMPLES HOW MERRY, AND THE NOSE ON HIS FACE WAS AS RED AS A CHERRY.

Imagine how he'll be behind the wheel.

Please don't drink and drive
this Holiday Season

Worcester
TELEGRAM & GAZETTE

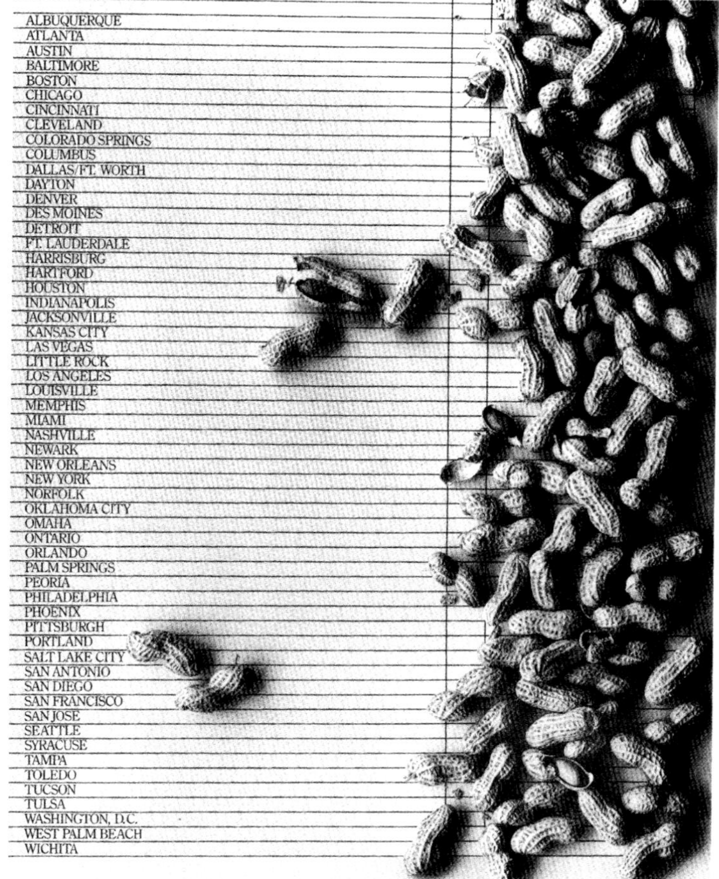

This is all you need to know about our fares.

We don't know how it started, but it seems that some people think our fares aren't as low as the other airlines here in Lambert Field.

After thinking about it, we decided that maybe it was because TWA is, well, sort of the "big" airline here.

We have the biggest schedules, for instance. Two hundred flights to fifty-seven places in the United States every day. And two hundred back.

And we have more big, comfy widebodies from Lambert Field than any other airline.

And we're big on things like training.

And big on service.

And we're big on ideas to help get you through the airport fast. Like curbside check-in. And Airport Express.® (We can give you your boarding passes in advance.)

And we have the only frequent flyer program at Lambert Field that gets you around the big wide world absolutely free.

So in some senses we are sort of "big."

But when it comes to fares, we have some of the very littlest you can get. Like the ones in our fare box. (You won't find any lower.)

You see, we don't believe in doing business by charging premium prices. Even though we offer premium service.

Perhaps we're a little nuts. But it's better than being expensive.

Our latest little fares

Chicago – 7 flights a day* Little Rock – 4 flights a day*
$49 Peak & $34 Off-Peak

Houston – 4 flights a day* New Orleans – 3 flights a day*
$75 Peak & $60 Off-Peak

*Mon.–Fri. Fares and schedules subject to change. Seats are limited.

For reservations, call your travel agent, or TWA at (314) 291-7500.

LEADING THE WAY. TWA.

Consumer Newspaper Over 600 Lines: Single

132
ART DIRECTOR
Irv Klein
WRITER
Stephanie Arnold
DESIGNER
Irv Klein
CLIENT
Management Science America
AGENCY
Levine Huntley Schmidt & Beaver

133
ART DIRECTOR
Mark Johnson
WRITER
Martin Kaufman
DESIGNER
Mark Johnson
PHOTOGRAPHERS
Leon Kuzmanoff
Robert Ammirati
ARTIST
R & V Studio
CLIENT
United Parcel Service
AGENCY
Ammirati & Puris

134
ART DIRECTOR
Jessica Welton
WRITER
Rebecca Flora
PHOTOGRAPHERS
Mark Waldo
David Hale
CLIENT
Midlothian Enterprises
AGENCY
Siddall Matus Coughter/ Virginia

SOMETIMES THIS ORGANIZATION GETS OUR GOVERNMENT'S INFORMATION FASTER THAN OUR GOVERNMENT.

In the interests of detente, when a high official of their government requests information from a high official in our government, they usually get it. And quickly, too.

Unfortunately, if you're not the President of the United States, but merely work for him, you can wait forever before you get the information you need. You're left playing catch-up because there's never been a standardized software system.

Which is exactly where we come in. We're Management Science America, Inc. The largest independent applications software company in the world.

And we've just spent five years and 20 million dollars developing a system that makes getting the information you need as simple as asking for it.

It's called INFORMATION EXPERT.™ The fourth generation technology that allows all your software systems to talk to one another. In English. Whether it's with existing or new software.

Which proves what five thousand customers in both government and business already know about us.

We're not only the industry's standard but a single source for financial and human resource products as well.

For example, our Budgetary Control System which manages budgeting, fund accounting and the procurement process, also picks up where other budgeting systems leave off. Ours provides multiple levels of funds availability checking.

And just by using our General Ledger and Accounts Payable Systems you can control your entire flow of funds. From budget preparation through disbursement.

Now if MSA sounds like a good way to run the government, don't write your congressman. Call Robert Carpenter at 404-239-2000.

MSA SOFTWARE
INTELLIGENCE OF A HIGHER ORDER.

The first package delivery company to fly anywhere is now the first to fly everywhere.

In 1929, UPS pioneered the notion of overnight air delivery between cities on America's West Coast.
Today, June 3, 1985, UPS becomes the first company to deliver overnight to every address in the 48 states. Service is also available to Hawaii* and Puerto Rico.
United Parcel

Now UPS can deliver overnight to more places in the U.S. than anyone else.

And that's not the only new advantage UPS gives you. INTRODUCING THE UPS NEXT DAY AIR LETTER AND PAK.

The new UPS Next Day Air Letter at $8.50 is the lowest-priced overnight letter in the business.

And at $11.50,** the new UPS Next Day Air Pak costs about 50% less than everyone else's.

Yet both our Letter and our Pak are delivered with the unsurpassed reliability businesses have come to expect from UPS Next Day Air.

So now UPS can offer you overnight air delivery to places no other company goes, for prices so low no other company matches them.

In short, when it comes to overnight delivery, there's no substitute for experience.

FIND THE HOMES HIDDEN IN THIS PICTURE.

Look very closely. You can almost detect the chimney of a four-bedroom Colonial just beyond an elm. The deck of a contemporary, patio home between two pines. Or the spire of a classic Victorian rising above an oak bough.

All in all, there are over 200 new homes at Evergreen, products of some of the finest builders in the area. So while you may have trouble locating the houses in the photograph, once at Evergreen, uncovering the right one is a breeze.

You will find them nestled along shaded cul-de-sacs. Not far from future shopping, medical and recreational centers. Only a little further from the highly regarded schools of Chesterfield County. And eventually, with the Powhite Parkway extension, a short, civilized drive from downtown Richmond. But first, you have to find Evergreen.

Take Route 60 West to Coalfield Road (across from Sycamore Square). Turn left and go three miles to our signs on your left.

The homes at Evergreen are priced from the $50s to the $130s. The trees, of course, are free.

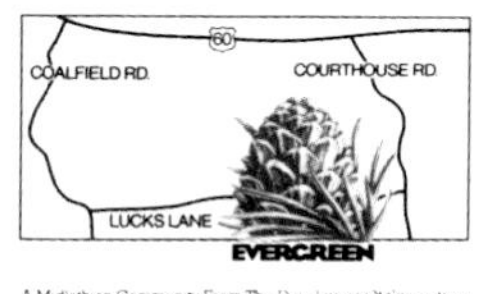

60
COALFIELD RD.
COURTHOUSE RD.
LUCKS LANE
EVERGREEN

A Midlothian Community From The Developers Of Smoketree

Consumer Newspaper Over 600 Lines: Single

135
ART DIRECTOR
Bob Barrie
WRITER
Rod Kilpatrick
DESIGNER
Bob Barrie
ARTIST
Henry Winkles
CLIENT
MedCenters Health Plan
AGENCY
Fallon McElligott/Minneapolis

136
ART DIRECTOR
Julian Scott
WRITER
Richard Carman
ARTIST
Character Photosetting
CLIENT
ITT
AGENCY
KMP Humphreys Bull & Barker/London

137
ART DIRECTOR
Steve Ohman
WRITER
Harold Karp
CLIENT
W.R. Grace
AGENCY
Lowe Marschalk

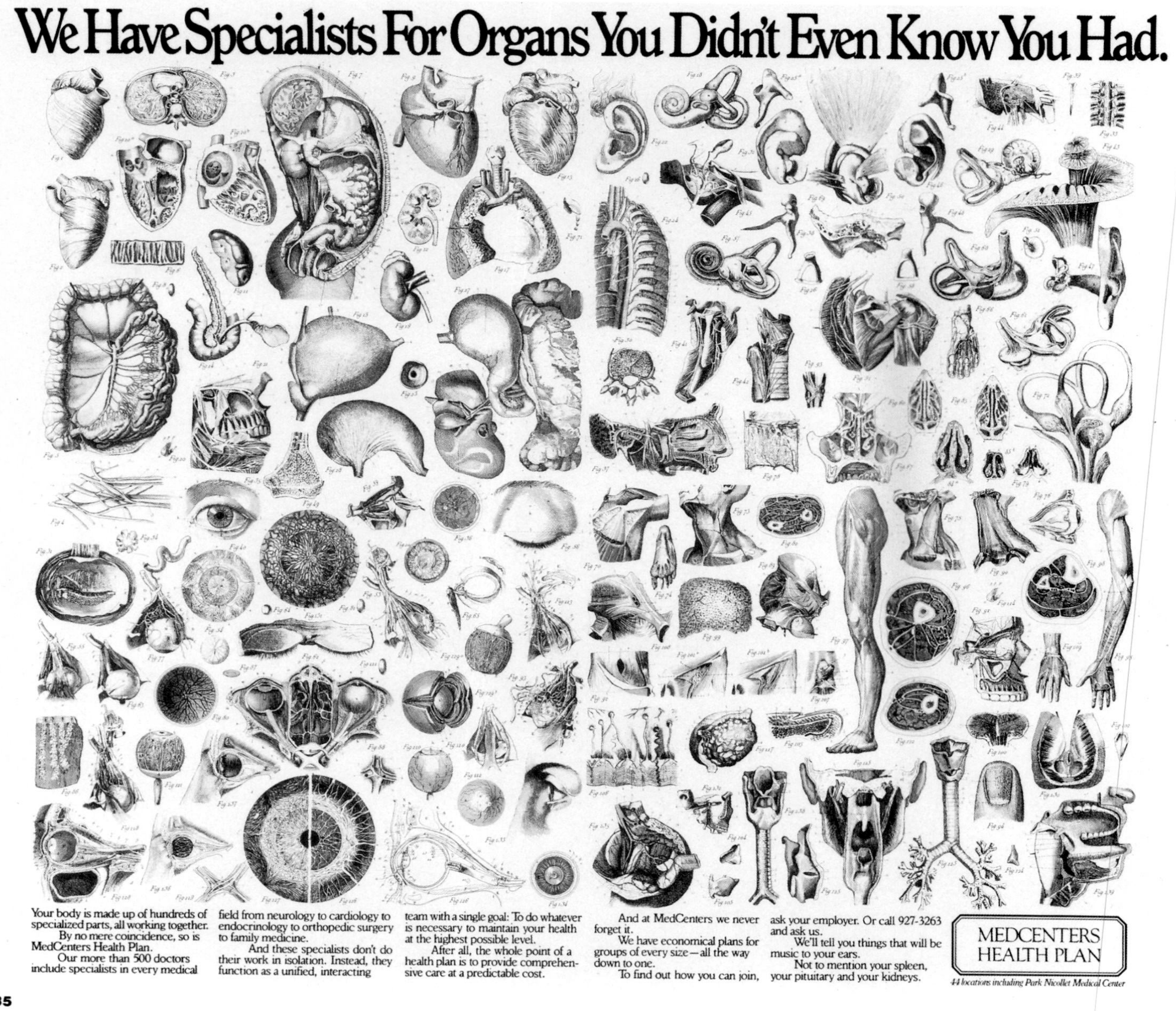

We Have Specialists For Organs You Didn't Even Know You Had.

Your body is made up of hundreds of specialized parts, all working together.

By no mere coincidence, so is MedCenters Health Plan.

Our more than 500 doctors include specialists in every medical field from neurology to cardiology to endocrinology to orthopedic surgery to family medicine.

And these specialists don't do their work in isolation. Instead, they function as a unified, interacting team with a single goal: To do whatever is necessary to maintain your health at the highest possible level.

After all, the whole point of a health plan is to provide comprehensive care at a predictable cost.

And at MedCenters we never forget it.

We have economical plans for groups of every size—all the way down to one.

To find out how you can join, ask your employer. Or call 927-3263 and ask us.

We'll tell you things that will be music to your ears.

Not to mention your spleen, your pituitary and your kidneys.

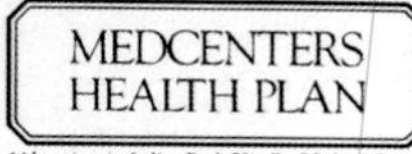

44 locations including Park Nicollet Medical Center

Consumer Newspaper Over 600 Lines: Single

138
ART DIRECTOR
Woody Litwhiler
WRITER
Ted Charron
CLIENT
Eastern Airlines
AGENCY
Campbell-Ewald

139
ART DIRECTOR
Yvonne Smith
WRITER
Mark Monteiro
PHOTOGRAPHERS
Lamb & Hall
CLIENT
Porsche Cars North America
AGENCY
Chiat/Day - Los Angeles

140
ART DIRECTOR
Michael Lawlor
WRITER
Richard Russo
CLIENT
Health America
AGENCY
Della Femina Travisano & Partners

SAVE THE BUFFALO.

IN FACT, SAVE A WHOLE HERD OF THEM.
EASTERN HAS JUST LOWERED ITS FARE TO THE WEST.

$150* LOS ANGELES SAN DIEGO SAN JOSE SAN FRANCISCO ALBUQUERQUE PHOENIX SALT LAKE CITY ONTARIO, CA.
EACH WAY IN COACH

$59† HOUSTON
NO ADVANCE PURCHASE REQUIRED
EACH WAY IN COACH

Call your Travel Agent or Eastern Airlines at 435-1111 in Atlanta.

WE EARN OUR WINGS EVERY DAY®

Fares valid from Atlanta only and subject to change without notice. *Reservations must be made and tickets purchased 3 days in advance. Travel must be completed by 11/15/85. †Valid through 10/31/85 to Houston on flight #657 only; return to Atlanta on flight #552 only. Valid 11/1-25/85 to Houston on flight #454 only Sun-Fri., return to Atlanta on flight #316 only. Travel must be completed by 11/25/85.

138

139

Last year 25,000 people died of "just a little indigestion."

Every year thousands of men and women die from what they think is just a little indigestion.

Unfortunately, most of them didn't see their doctor, simply because their insurance didn't cover it. And they just couldn't afford to pay for it out of their own pocket.

Had their insurance covered routine checkups, they might have found that what they had wasn't just a little indigestion but the early signs of a heart attack.

At HealthAmerica, we don't think you should wait until you're too sick to see a doctor. That's why at HealthAmerica, you're covered for preventive medicine and unlimited routine checkups. Not to mention everything from pediatrics and gynecology to lab work and surgery.

And with HealthAmerica you only see the doctors, you never see their bills.

So ask your employer about joining HealthAmerica. Or call us at 587-6740, or write 5701 West Sunrise Blvd., Plantation, FL 33313.

HealthAmerica

We're making health care in America better.

140

Consumer Newspaper Over 600 Lines: Single

141
ART DIRECTOR
Houman Pirdavari
WRITER
Jarl Olsen
DESIGNER
Houman Pirdavari
PHOTOGRAPHER
Jim Arndt
CLIENT
The Brief Encounter
AGENCY
Fallon McElligott/Minneapolis

142
ART DIRECTOR
Trevor McConnell
WRITER
Marta Cutler
DESIGNER
Words Over North America
ARTIST
Stephen Quinlan
CLIENT
Cunard Line
AGENCY
Saatchi & Saatchi Compton Hayhurst/Toronto

143
ART DIRECTORS
Mike Campbell
Jerry Sukenick
WRITER
Bob Culver
CLIENT
NYNEX Mobile Communications
AGENCY
Scali McCabe Sloves Direct

141

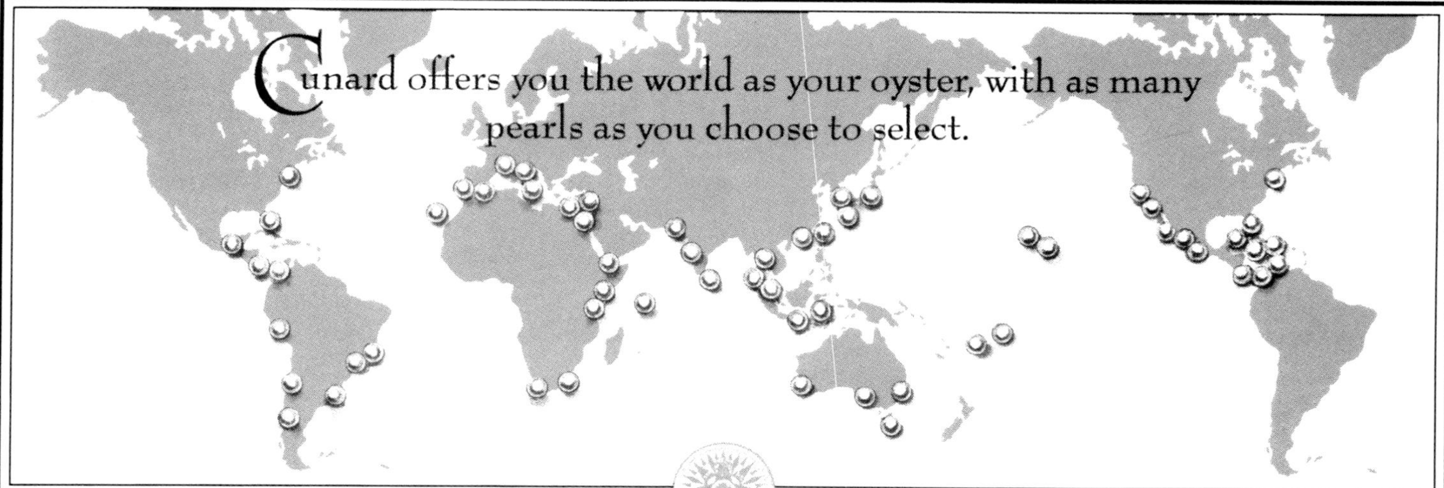
Cunard offers you the world as your oyster, with as many pearls as you choose to select.

Capture the Spirit of the Explorers'. 'Voyage to the Citadels of Civilization'. Two world cruises, one aboard QE2, the latter aboard Sagafjord, that sail the seven seas to the four corners of the earth. Two voyages that offer you the world. Or a part of it. For you can still treasure its pearls by choosing portions of either cruise if your time is limited.

'Capture the Spirit of the Explorers' aboard QE2.

Only two ships in the world have been awarded the coveted 5 Plus Star rating in Fielding's 1985 Guide. QE2's legendary elegance and luxury have earned her that honor. On January 15 she sails southbound from New York in the spirit of the explorers, destined for 33 ports of call on 4 continents. For the first time she'll transit the Strait of Magellan near the tip of South America, with maiden arrivals in Peru and Chile amongst others.

Decide from her itinerary which part of the world you wish to see and how many days you wish to see it in, anywhere from 6 to 95. As an example, join the ship in Tokyo and sail to Los Angeles on an 11-day journey for as little as $2,095 U.S.* Or embark in Hong Kong for a 19-day passage to Los Angeles from just $4,125 U.S.* Or sail from Fort Lauderdale to Rio de Janeiro for carnival time, a 23-day voyage that costs as low as $5,515 U.S.* A generous air allowance or return airfare to and from your point of departure is included in your fare depending upon the length of voyage you choose.

QUEEN ELIZABETH 2
CUNARD
British registry

'Voyage to the Citadels of Civilization' aboard Sagafjord.

The second ship to receive the coveted 5 Plus Star rating in Fielding's 1985 Guide is Sagafjord. She sails westbound from Fort Lauderdale on January 6, destined for the great civilizations of the world. For 102 days she circumnavigates the globe, calling at 28 ports in the Orient, Middle East, India and Western Europe. She is the only ship to include the Australian Loop in her travels.

Again, choose which of her destinations appeal to you most, then decide upon your length of voyage, anywhere from 14 to 102 days. Perhaps meet the ship in Haifa and sail for 19 days to Fort Lauderdale for as little as $4,110 U.S.* Or depart from Hong Kong on a 29-day journey to Haifa from just $7,390 U.S.* Or set sail from Fort Lauderdale for Sydney in 34 days and pay as low as $7,420 U.S.* All fares include return airfare from 71 gateway cities in North America.

With the world yours for the taking, choose which of its enchanting pearls you wish to collect. Consider how much time you have, anywhere from 6 to 102 days, then decide upon your cruise. And enjoy the magic of QE2 or Sagafjord as you sail on a voyage of discovery to the intoxicating riches the world and Cunard have to offer.

CUNARD/NAC
SAGAFJORD
Bahamian registry

For More Information, See or Call Your Travel Agent.

*Fares quoted per person, double occupancy.

C U N A R D

142

If you're about to get a mobile phone, you probably assume it will work wherever you drive.

But contrary to popular belief, mobile phones only work in what is called a *coverage area.*

That's why it's important to choose a mobile phone service with a wide coverage area. One with good coverage will get you a lot farther.

In the northeastern United States, no one offers better coverage than NYNEX Mobile Communications. We cover more than 4,400 square miles in and around New York. Including as far north as White Plains. As far east as Hauppauge. As far south as New Brunswick. And as far west as Morristown.

CURRENT COVERAGE
FUTURE COVERAGE
NEW YORK

What's more, with NYNEX you can use your mobile phone in major cities all the way from Boston to Washington, D.C.

NYNEX Mobile Communications has something else most mobile phone companies can't lay claim to.

Experience.

We not only helped invent the cellular mobile phone system. We introduced it in New York, and provide service in Boston, Providence, Albany, and other cities. In a high tech business like mobile communications, experience is an important consideration.

NYNEX also offers detailed billing at no extra charge. A toll-free customer service number. The most direct routing of your calls to save you money. And soon, we'll have the most extensive network of transmitters of any mobile communications system in the U.S.

Which means if you drive with us, you'll get better mileage out of your phone.

For more information, simply call 1-800-292-BELL.

What good is a mobile phone if it doesn't go where you want to drive?

NYNEX
Mobile Communications

143

Consumer Newspaper Over 600 Lines: Single

144
ART DIRECTOR
Robert Reitzfeld
WRITER
David Altschiller
DESIGNER
Robert Reitzfeld
PHOTOGRAPHER
Robert Ammirati
CLIENT
Boar's Head Provisions
AGENCY
Altschiller Reitzfeld

145
ART DIRECTOR
Carolyn Tye
WRITERS
Bill Westbrook
Robin Konieczny
PHOTOGRAPHER
Pat Edwards
CLIENT
Ukrop's Super Markets
AGENCY
Westbrook/Virginia

146
ART DIRECTOR
Bob Marberry
WRITER
Ben Vergati
DESIGNER
Bob Marberry
PHOTOGRAPHER
Neal Vance
CLIENT
Downtown Flowers
AGENCY
Vergati & Associates/Texas

Something's not kosher in the ham business.

It has recently come to our attention that there has been some flim-flam surrounding the sale of our ham.

Specifically, when you ask for Boar's Head you may not always be getting it. You may be getting lower-priced,

What you see isn't always what you get.

lesser-quality ham instead (the latest twist on the old switcheroo).

At Boar's Head, this makes us extremely unhappy. First, we didn't work for 80 years to gain the reputation as one of the world's great hams, only to have someone pawn off a run-of-the-mill substitute as us. Second, if you are going to pay a little more to get the best, you shouldn't end up with anything less than the best.

Mind you, we don't suspect this bit of delicatessen petty larceny is of epidemic proportions. Most deli owners are decent, hardworking folks like the rest of us. But we have taken some precautions to protect you from those who aren't.

Next time you go in to buy Boar's Head ham, ask the deli man to show you the brand on the ham itself. (Even after the wrapper is off the ham, the Boar's Head brand remains.) Then make sure that the ham he just showed you is the ham that ends up on the slicer.

If the man says it is Boar's Head but won't show you the Boar's Head brand, walk.

A man who cheats you on quality on one thing will certainly do it on others. Then call us at 1-718-456-3600, and let us know who the culprit is. He will soon be an ex-Boar's Head dealer.

Simple as that.

In the ham business, nothing is worse than a few bad eggs.

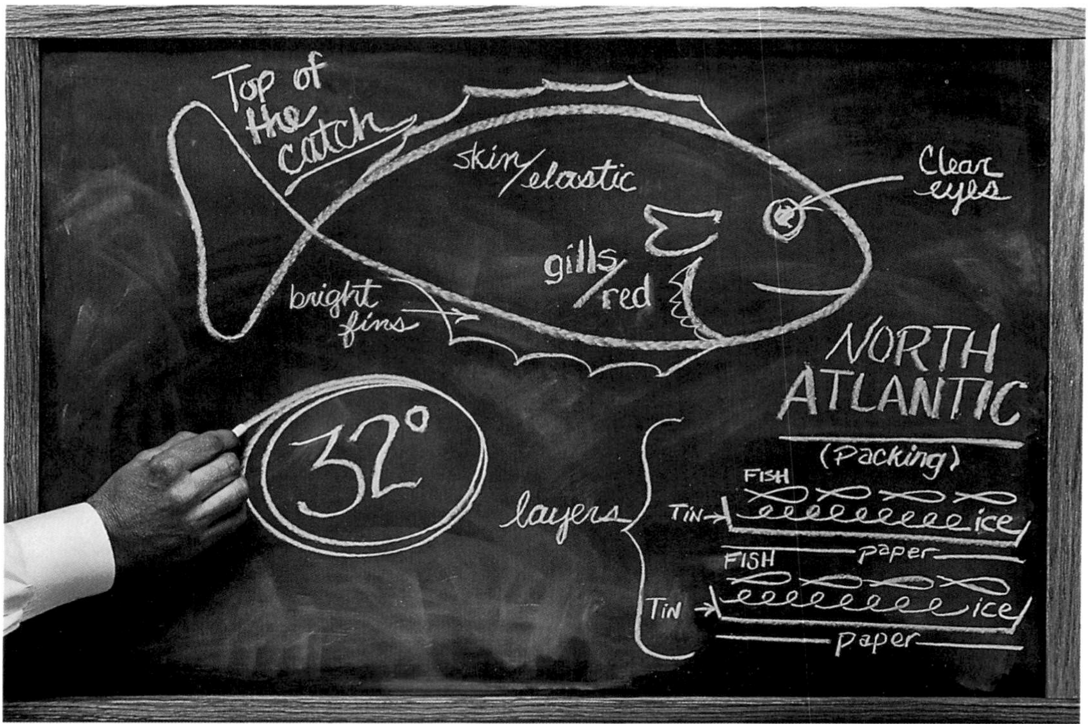

Top of the catch
skin/elastic
Clear eyes
gills/red
bright fins
NORTH ATLANTIC
32°
(Packing)
layers
FISH
TIN
ice
FISH
paper
TIN
ice
paper

To learn about fresh seafood we actually enrolled in a school of fish.

At Ukrops, we recently made a commitment to bring the freshest and best quality seafood to Richmond.

So we went to Boston.

There we went to a fish school taught by one of the country's most respected suppliers of fresh fish from the North Atlantic, M.F. Foley, Inc. Their seafood is considered good enough for the White House.

We hoped it would be good enough for Richmond.

In school we learned that the last fish to be caught are called the top of the catch, the freshest fish on the boat. And now, that's all we buy.

We learned how to tell if "fresh fish" is really fresh. The gills must be bright red. The skin must be firm. And if we still aren't sure, we look each fish straight in the eye. If it's cloudy, we throw it back.

And then we learned the single most important thing about fresh fish: Temperature. From the time a fish comes out of the water until it comes out of your refrigerator, it should be kept as close to 32° Fahrenheit as possible.

So we chose a supplier who understands temperature. They clean, cut, pack and fly our fish in fresh from New England on the very same day.

Our South Atlantic fish is handled in the same careful way. In fact, our local supplier even went to school with us.

So whether you buy cod from Cape Cod or flounder from Hatteras, at Ukrops it's almost as good as buying them at the dock itself.

We also learned how to make sure our fish stay fresh. We refrigerate them so freshness stays in, and we seal them in plastic wrap so harmful bacteria stay out. Whenever we sell seafood that's been previously frozen you'll know it. Because we always mark it right on each package.

Today, Ukrops offers enough fresh fish to make your head swim. From salmon and sole to monkfish and mackerel. We have trout, croaker, and haddock. And when they're available we have halibut, red snapper, bluefish, rockfish, swordfish and even shark.

So come to Ukrops. Once you've tasted our fresh seafood you won't want to be caught serving anything else.

Ukrops

145

Give a Wandering Jew a home.
They make wonderful roommates. They love good music. And they're always there to listen to your problems.
They're easy to care for, too. Just give them a little water and occasionally wave a warm bagel under their leaves.
Of course, the wandering Jew is only one of many house plants you'll find living at Downtown Flowers.
We also have one of the best selections of fresh cut flowers you'll find anywhere. And if we don't have what you want, we'll get it for you.
So if you want to add some instant warmth to your living room, do something kosher. Adopt a wandering Jew.
DOWNTOWN FLOWERS
1525 Elm St. (in the LTV Tower Lobby) 698-1090

146

Consumer Newspaper Over 600 Lines: Single

147
ART DIRECTOR
Brandt Wilkins
WRITER
Paul Wolfe
DESIGNER
Brandt Wilkins
ARTIST
R & V Studio
CLIENT
BMW of North America
AGENCY
Ammirati & Puris

148
ART DIRECTORS
John Housley
Brian Murphy
WRITER
Bob Mariani
DESIGNER
John Housley
PHOTOGRAPHER
Bob Oliveira
CLIENT
Brooks
AGENCY
Wooding & Housley/Rhode Island

149
ART DIRECTOR
Judy Austin
WRITER
Tom Pedulla
ARTIST
Rob Bolster
CLIENT
The Boston Globe
AGENCY
Hill Holliday Connors Cosmopulos/Boston

Send us $2 and we'll send you a quarterback.

Not just any quarterback, ours.

We're talking about a handsome 16 x 24 poster of Dan Marino. *The* Quarterback of 1984.

The man who threw 48 touchdown passes in a single season.

The man who threw for over 5,000 yards in a single season.

The man named MVP in the AFC by the players themselves.

Dan Marino.

This poster is Brooks' tribute to a superior athletic performer. From the company who knows all about high performance. From the ground up.

Send $2 to cover shipping and handling for your Dan Marino wall poster to: Brooks Shoe, Inc., Dept. 13, Blettner Avenue, Hanover, PA 17331.

BROOKS

High performance from the ground up.

Do not send cash. Make check or money order payable to Brooks Shoe, Inc. Pennsylvania residents add 6% sales tax. Offer void where prohibited. Offer ends 1/31/85. Allow 3-4 weeks for delivery.

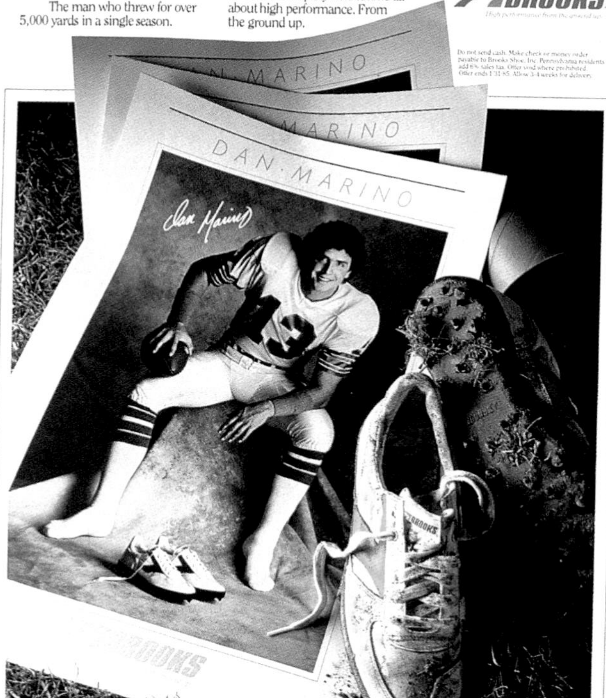

Kids who take candy from strangers should have their heads examined.

It's probably not a good idea to let your children go trick or treating in unfamiliar neighborhoods. But if they do–and even if they don't–be sure to inspect their candy carefully before it gets eaten. Discard all unwrapped treats. And check candy packages and fruits for surface breaks. When in doubt, throw it out.

And have a happy, safe Halloween.

The Boston Globe

A Public Affairs presentation of The Boston Globe

Consumer Newspaper Over 600 Lines: Single

150
ART DIRECTOR
Jac Coverdale
WRITER
Jerry Fury
CLIENT
Audio King
AGENCY
Clarity Coverdale Rueff/ Minneapolis

151
ART DIRECTOR
Tom Lichtenheld
WRITER
Bill Miller
DESIGNER
Tom Lichtenheld
CLIENT
WFLD-TV
AGENCY
Fallon McElligott/Minneapolis

152
ART DIRECTOR
David Nathanson
WRITER
Neal Gomberg
DESIGNER
David Nathanson
PHOTOGRAPHER
Dennis Gottlieb
CLIENT
Mitsubishi Electric Sales America
AGENCY
Chiat/Day

WHEN WE INSTALL YOUR YOUR CAR CAR STE RE O WE GUARANTEE THISSSSS WILL NEVER HAPPEN

If you have your car stereo installed by just anyone, you could end up listening to a lot of excuses on why it doesn't work the way it should. Not at Audio King.
When we install a car stereo, car alarm, or mobile phone, we guarantee our work for as long as you own your car. And, we guarantee your satisfaction.

We can do that because we have the largest, most sophisticated installation centers in the area. And our installers have an average of *seven years* experience installing mobile electronics. With every make and model imaginable.

So if you want to listen to music rather than who-knows-what, come to Audio King for your car stereo installation.

The Adult Electronics Store
AUDIO KING

EDINA 920-4272, 7101 France Ave. S., 2 blks. S. of Southdale Center · **BURNSVILLE** 435-8933, 14232 Burnhaven Dr., Just W of Burnsville Center · **MINNETONKA** 546-4040, 1808 S. Plymouth Rd., Just W of Ridgedale Center · **ROSEVILLE** 636-3686, 1723 W Cty Rd. B-2, Just N. of Rosedale Center · **BROOKLYN CENTER** 566-2360, 5515 Xerxes Ave. N., Just W of Brookdale Center **Car Stereo Installation Centers: GOLDEN VALLEY** 546-0800, 1 block N. of Hwy. 55 on Winnetka · **BURNSVILLE** 435-8933, Behind our Burnsville store at Burnhaven Dr. · **MAPLEWOOD** 770-0108, 2310 Hazelwood N. at Hwy. 36 · **ELECTRONICS REPAIR CENTER** 560-3860

WATCH & WEAR.
Turn your favorite TV show into your favorite T-shirt with these iron-on decals.
Then, watch and wear your favorite superstars on WFLD-TV Metromedia 32.
32
WFLD TV

151

You do things your way.
We do things our way.
Except for when you do things our way.
And we do things your way.
In an effort to blend the best of both ways.
And produce the best products.
Like projection televisions. (The ones with the big screens.)
And Diamond-Vision. (The ones with the very big screens.)
This blending of cultures works when we send engineers to study here and you send engineers to study with us in Japan.
And we expect it to work at the plant we're planning in Braselton, Georgia. Where the Far East will meet the Deep South.
Sayonara. Y'all.
MITSUBISHI ELECTRIC

152

153
ART DIRECTOR
Karen Howe
WRITER
Peter Byrne
CLIENT
Chase Manhattan Bank of Canada
AGENCY
Scali McCabe Sloves/Toronto

154
ART DIRECTORS
Ted Barton
Geoff Roche
WRITER
Kirk Citron
ARTIST
Dugald Stermer
PHOTOGRAPHER
Laurie Rubin
CLIENT
California Prune Board
AGENCY
Hal Riney & Partners/San Francisco

155
ART DIRECTOR
Jessica Welton
WRITER
Leslie Trinite Clark
PHOTOGRAPHERS
Gary Kufner
Eric Meola
CLIENT
Mobil Land Development
AGENCY
Siddall Matus Coughter/Virginia

EVERY INVESTMENT PAYS INTEREST SOONER OR LATER.

SOONER.

1. Chase Manhattan Instant Interest Certificate (interest paid upon deposit)

LATER.

1. Bank of Commerce Short Term Deposits (interest paid upon maturity)
2. Bank of Commerce Certificates (interest paid semi-annually)
3. Bank of Montreal Short Term Deposits (interest paid upon maturity)
4. Bank of Montreal Certificates (interest paid semi-annually)
5. National Bank Short Term Deposits (interest paid upon maturity)
6. National Bank Certificates (interest paid semi-annually)
7. Bank of Nova Scotia Short Term Deposits (interest paid upon maturity)
8. Bank of Nova Scotia Certificates (interest paid semi-annually)
9. Royal Bank Short Term Deposits (interest paid upon maturity)
10. Royal Bank Certificates (interest paid semi-annually)
11. Toronto Dominion Short Term Deposits (interest paid upon maturity)
12. Toronto Dominion Certificates (interest paid semi-annually)
13. Canada Trust Short Term Deposits (interest paid upon maturity)
14. Canada Trust Certificates (interest paid annually)
15. Credit Foncier Trust Short Term Deposits (interest paid upon maturity)
16. Credit Foncier Trust Certificates (interest paid annually)
17. First City Trust Short Term Deposits (interest paid upon maturity)
18. First City Trust Certificates (interest paid annually)
19. Guaranty Trust Short Term Deposits (interest paid upon maturity)
20. Guaranty Trust Certificates (interest paid annually)
21. Guardian Trust Short Term Deposits (interest paid upon maturity)
22. Guardian Trust Certificates (interest paid annually)
23. Montreal Trust Short Term Deposits (interest paid upon maturity)
24. Montreal Trust Certificates (interest paid annually)
25. Royal Trust Short Term Deposits (interest paid upon maturity)
26. Royal Trust Certificates (interest paid annually)
27. Government of Canada Savings Bonds (interest paid upon redemption or annually whichever comes first)
28. Government of Canada Treasury Bills (interest paid at redemption)

From the Chase Manhattan Bank of Canada, a member of one of the world's largest banks, comes one of the world's most innovative investment opportunities.

The Chase Instant Interest Certificate.

Unlike ordinary certificates of deposit, the Chase Instant Interest Certificate pays all your interest up front. You make your deposit by a certified cheque and we issue a cheque for your interest. All your interest. Instantly.

For example, if you deposit $60,000 for one year at a rate of 7%, you'll walk away with a cheque for $4,200.

That means you can earn interest on your interest by re-investing it. Or you can use it to make that special purchase you've been putting off.

You can do anything you please with your interest, because it's all yours. The day you make your deposit.

The Chase Instant Interest Certificate pays highly competitive rates. And of course, deposits up to $60,000 are fully insured by the Canada Deposit Insurance Corporation.

CHASE INSTANT INTEREST CERTIFICATE RATES

Term*	Rate**
30-59 days	6¾
60-89 days	7
90-179 days	7¼
180-365 days	7¾

*Minimum 30 days, maximum 1 year **Rates are as of November 15, 1985 and are subject to change without notice

If you've got between $10,000 and $60,000 to invest, invest five minutes and get all the details of the Chase Instant Interest Certificate by calling Chase at (416) 365-2409.

CHASE

Which has the most fiber?

We'll give you a little hint. The fruit with the most fiber isn't a banana. Or an apple. Or an orange, a peach or a pear.

It's the humble prune. Which has more dietary fiber than almost any fruit— or any food—you can name.

ORANGES have 2.6 grams of fiber per serving.
PEARS have 3.8 grams of fiber per serving.
BANANAS have 4.1 grams of fiber per serving.
PRUNES have 9.3 grams of fiber per serving.
PEACHES have 1.4 grams of fiber per serving.
APPLES have 3.0 grams of fiber per serving.

To get the same dietary fiber as a serving of six prunes, you'd have to eat four slices of whole wheat bread. Or six peaches. Or three apples. Or two and a half bowls of bran flakes.

And prunes don't just have fiber. They're one of the richest sources of potassium, and a good source of Vitamin A. With no fat, no cholesterol, almost no sodium, and a delicious, one-of-a-kind taste.

One way to serve your family prunes is at breakfast. They're delicious stewed, with a cinnamon stick and a slice of lemon. You'll find more helpful serving suggestions in our free brochure. For your copy, write to Prune Ideas, 103 World Trade Center, San Francisco, CA 94111.

All of which makes prunes one of the most nutritious fruits you can buy.

So if you're looking for a sweet way to get more fiber in your diet, try California prunes.

Proof, once again, that good things come in small packages.

Prunes. The high fiber fruit.

154

A point of land
for people who can't
live without water.

If being close to the water makes you feel more alive, your life could go on forever at Sailfish Point.

Here, you are surrounded by the ocean you love. As well as the luxuries you demand. And because the entire peninsula is private, you can drink in its pleasures without taking in the rest of the world.

You can race with the wind just beyond the seawalled marina. Where ocean-going yachts can turn without cutting corners. You can drive down fairways that seem to sail into the sea. On a par 72 course designed by Jack Nicklaus. You can even watch the waves unfold while you dine. Because the elegant Sailfish Point Country Club overlooks the ocean's edge.

For more information about Florida's most opulent private residence, just write or call our exclusive sales agent. Or arrange for a personal appointment. Only a few will share this secluded point of land. And the endless supply of water that comes with it.

Sailfish Point.

155

Consumer Newspaper
Over 600 Lines: Single

156
ART DIRECTOR
Tim Hannell
WRITER
Jim Glynn
ARTIST
Tim Hannell
CLIENT
Frontier Airlines
AGENCY
Tracy-Locke/Denver

157
ART DIRECTOR
Lester Feldman
WRITER
Mike Mangano
DESIGNER
Lester Feldman
ARTIST
Lester Feldman
PHOTOGRAPHER
Bruno
CLIENT
Chivas Regal
AGENCY
Doyle Dane Bernbach

158
ART DIRECTOR
Sal DeVito
WRITER
Amelia Rosner
DESIGNER
Sal DeVito
PHOTOGRAPHER
Jerry Friedman
CLIENT
Drexel Burnham Lambert
AGENCY
Chiat/Day

If you want to see something fly for less than Frontier, fold up this ad.

Fold

Fold

Fold

Fold

Fold

Fold

Cut on dotted line

$39
Albuquerque
Billings
Casper
Grand Junction
Jackson
Lincoln
Oklahoma City
Omaha
Rapid City
Salt Lake City
Sioux Falls
Wichita

$59
Bismarck
Boise
Bozeman
Cedar Rapids
Dallas/Fort Worth
Des Moines
El Paso
Eugene
Fargo
Great Falls
Houston
Kalispell
Kansas City
Las Vegas
Los Angeles
Madison
Midland/Odessa
Milwaukee
Minneapolis/St. Paul
Minot
Missoula
Oakland
Orange County
Palm Springs
Phoenix
Reno
Rockford
Sacramento
St. Louis
San Diego
Seattle
Spokane
Springfield
Stockton
Tucson
Tulsa

All year long we've been telling you no one flies for less than Frontier. And we're not about to change that now. That's why we're offering you these incredibly low prices to every city Frontier flies. Prices no other airline can beat. With service they can only hope to match.

So call your travel agent or Frontier at 399-0808. But call today. Seats are limited. Advance roundtrip purchase required. Prices reflect one-half of roundtrip fare. Prices are effective for travel Dec. 31 through Jan. 3 only.

Why pay more? Take off with an old friend.

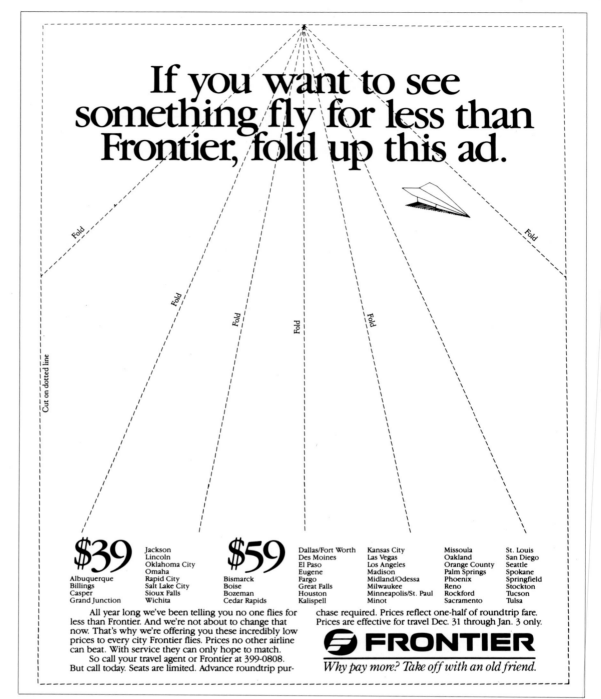

CHIVAS REGAL
12
What else would you give
a special Daddy for Father's Day?
Daddy Warbucks © 1985 Tribune Media Services, Inc.
Chivas Regal © 1985 375 Spirits Co., N.Y.C. 12 Years Old Worldwide • Blended Scotch Whisky • 86 Proof

157

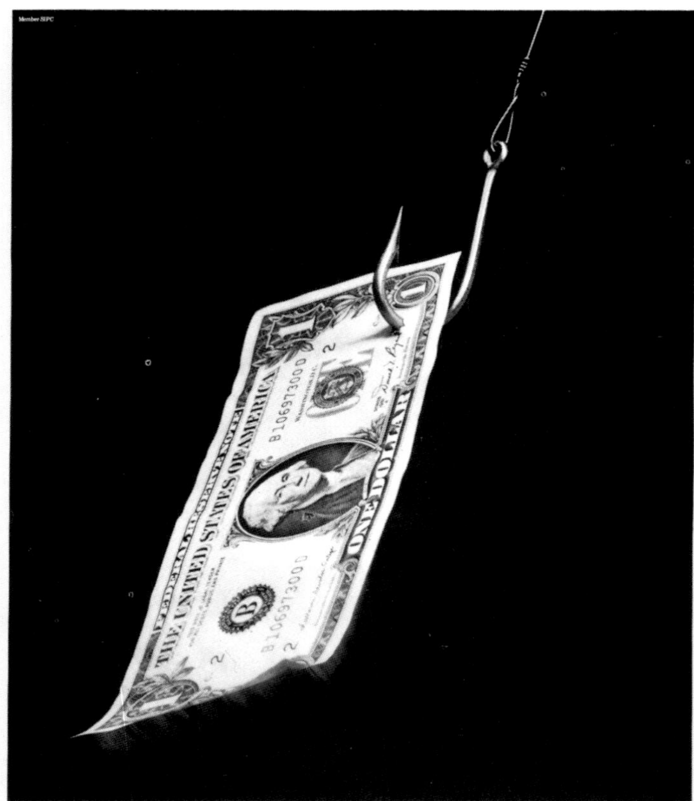

WE DON'T THROW THE SMALL ONES BACK.

We don't refuse Fortune 500 companies when they come to us for capital. That's unthinkable.

By the same token, we don't turn our backs on companies whose fortunes have yet to be made.

For one good reason.

Small companies have a way of turning into big companies overnight. And, along the way, the million dollar deals become multi-million dollar deals. Or even billion dollar deals.

The way we see it, promising young firms are long on vision. They're chock full of brilliant ideas. And enthusiasm they have plenty of. All they need is someone to lend them support.

If your company sounds like that, give Andrew Frost a call at (212) 480-4972.

And if you're still skeptical, consider MCI, Charter Medical, Golden Nugget, or Kinder-Care. Right now, they're some of our biggest clients.

At one time, they were among our smallest.

Drexel Burnham

Drexel Burnham Lambert Incorporated

158

Consumer Newspaper Over 600 Lines: Single

159
ART DIRECTOR
Michael Fazende
WRITER
Mike Lescarbeau
PHOTOGRAPHER
John Cascarano
CLIENT
American Association of Advertising Agencies
AGENCY
Fallon McElligott/Minneapolis

160
ART DIRECTOR
Michael Thomas
WRITER
John Malecki
PHOTOGRAPHER
Chuck Lamonica
CLIENT
Perdue
AGENCY
Scali McCabe Sloves

161
ART DIRECTOR
Ted Shaine
WRITER
Diane Rothschild
PHOTOGRAPHER
Walter Iooss
CLIENT
CIGNA
AGENCY
Doyle Dane Bernbach

ADVERTISING MAKES THINGS COST MORE, RIGHT?

We admit it. Advertising has a tremendous impact on prices. But you may be surprised by what *kind* of impact.

In addition to being informative, educational and sometimes entertaining, advertising can actually lower prices.

It works like this: Advertising spurs competition which holds down prices. And since advertising also creates a mass market for products, it can bring down the cost of producing each product, a savings that can be passed on to consumers.

Moreover, competition created by advertising provides an incentive for manufacturers to produce new and better products.

Which means advertising can not only reduce prices, but it can also help you avoid lemons.

ADVERTISING
ANOTHER WORD FOR FREEDOM OF CHOICE.
American Association of Advertising Agencies.

159

I put my fresh, tender Perdue chickens through 57 quality inspections. And any chicken that fails to pass even one of them fails to earn the Perdue label.

That's why my chickens don't have pinfeathers, feathers, wing hairs, scrapes and bruises like you'll find on other chickens.

And why I can confidently print a money-back guarantee on every Perdue label. Something you *won't* find on most other chickens.

If you do buy another bird that's not as good as one of mine, there is something you can do.

Just return it to the store. Squawk. And ask for your money back.

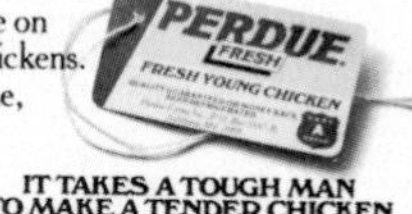
PERDUE
FRESH
FRESH YOUNG CHICKEN

IT TAKES A TOUGH MAN TO MAKE A TENDER CHICKEN.

"THE ONLY TOUGH THING ABOUT A PERDUE CHICKEN IS BECOMING ONE." *Frank Perdue*

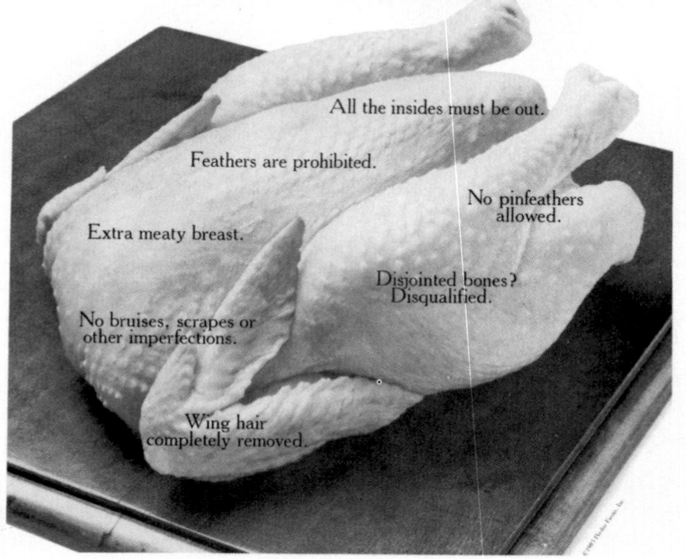
All the insides must be out.
Feathers are prohibited.
No pinfeathers allowed.
Extra meaty breast.
Disjointed bones? Disqualified.
No bruises, scrapes or other imperfections.
Wing hair completely removed.

UNFORTUNATELY, THIS IS ONE OF THE FEW DOCTORS AMERICANS SEE REGULARLY.

SIXERS
6

While everybody recognizes the value of preventive health care, the reality is that very few people see a doctor unless something is wrong.

In fact, millions of Americans don't even have their own doctor to see.

As a result, even easily correctable conditions go uncorrected.

And treatable illnesses become untreatable.

It's a senseless, all too frequently tragic problem.

It's also an expensive one.

Because people without doctors tend to use emergency rooms, at emergency room prices, for any medical problem they have.

Whether it's a bad cold or a broken leg.

What it all amounts to is that too many people are getting too little care.

At too high a price.

And that's why we've made a serious commitment to a new form of health care delivery.

At CIGNA Healthplan, we operate Health Maintenance Organizations that deliver high quality, accessible and affordable health care.

For a small monthly payment, plus a few dollars a visit, CIGNA Healthplan provides members with a comprehensive package of health benefits. As well as ready access to a CIGNA physician of their own.

This obviously encourages the kind of preventive care that can stop small medical problems from becoming big ones.

In fact, a recent Rand Corporation study showed that membership in an HMO reduced hospitalization by as much as 40% over a five-year period.

And reduced health care expenses by close to 25% during that same time.

Not surprisingly, we already have over 750,000 members enrolled nationwide. If you think we might be of value to your company, please write to CIGNA Corporation, Department R2, One Logan Square, Philadelphia, PA 19103.

That way your employees would have two doctors to see.

One of ours. And Dr. J.

CIGNA

Consumer Newspaper Over 600 Lines: Single

162
ART DIRECTORS
Ted Barton
Geoff Roche

WRITER
Kirk Citron

PHOTOGRAPHER
Barry Robinson

CLIENT
California Prune Board

AGENCY
Hal Riney & Partners/San Francisco

163
ART DIRECTOR
Mike Campbell

WRITER
Bob Culver

PHOTOGRAPHER
Dennis Chalkin

CLIENT
NYNEX Mobile Communications

AGENCY
Scali McCabe Sloves Direct

164
ART DIRECTOR
Tom Lichtenheld

WRITER
Mike Lescarbeau

DESIGNER
Tom Lichtenheld

CLIENT
Wall Street Journal

AGENCY
Fallon McElligott/Minneapolis

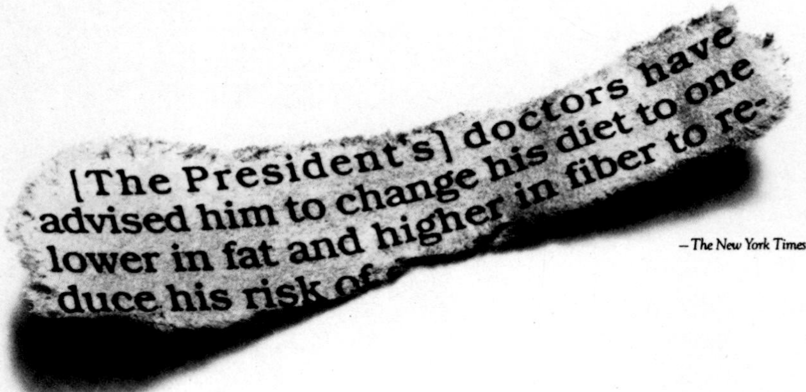
[The President's] doctors have
advised him to change his diet to one
lower in fat and higher in fiber to reduce his risk of

—The New York Times

A word to the wise. Prunes have more dietary fiber per serving than almost any other food. Including bran flakes and whole wheat bread.

Prunes. The high fiber fruit.

162

Over the years the mobile phone has developed a reputation as a plaything of the idle rich.

Those who had one were usually seen comfortably ensconced in the backseat of a limousine.

But with the introduction of the cellular mobile phone, everything changed.

Now the mobile phone is no longer a jet set accoutrement, but a practical working tool. Thousands of people use them every day.

And of all the accessories you can get for your car, a mobile phone is one that might actually pay for itself down the road.

Which is something that rich Corinthian leather upholstery, for example, will never do.

ONE OF THOSE RARE CASES IN WHICH THE BIGGEST ALSO HAPPENS TO BE THE BEST.

You wouldn't buy a car without looking under the hood, would you?

The same principle applies to choosing a mobile phone company.

You're not just buying a phone, but an extensive telecommunications network. And NYNEX has the largest mobile communications network in the entire northeastern United States.

What's more, unlike some mobile phone companies that are new to the business, we have a lot of experience.

We helped invent the cellular mobile phone system more than ten years ago.

WE GIVE YOU MORE BOSTON FOR YOUR MONEY.

In the Boston area, no one offers better service than NYNEX Mobile Communications.

We cover nearly 4,000 square miles in and around the city. That's more of the metropolitan area for your money than anyone else gives you.

And with NYNEX you can drive to Connecticut, New York, New Jersey, Philadelphia, and Washington, DC. and still make calls without making any special arrangements.

Some companies cover only a single city.

What good is a mobile phone if it isn't truly mobile?

THE MOBILE PHONE HAS EVOLVED FROM A PERK TO A PREREQUISITE.

Ever since the introduction of cellular mobile phones, you've been hearing how nicely one would complement all the technology that went into your high-performance car.

However, the new mobile phones should not be thought of as executive perks, but standard business equipment.

Depending on how much time you spend in your car, it's the phone on your desk that may be a luxury. And that's not an idle claim.

An independent study[1] recently showed that mobile phones pay for themselves in a surprising number of situations.

After all, don't you think your time could be more productively spent talking to clients than listening to the radio?

And if your mobile phone qualifies as a deductible business expense, our free detailed billing could provide you with what the IRS fondly refers to as an "adequate contemporaneous record" of your business calls.

NYNEX MOBILE COMMUNICATIONS. THE WAY TO GO.

Every new technology has its share of companies that noisily rush into the marketplace, making their claims to anyone who will listen.

But when the dust settles, you need a company that not only offers the highest quality of service now, but the expertise to pioneer innovations in the future.

At NYNEX, we're committed to offering mobile phone service that sets the standard by which other mobile phone companies are measured.

By the way, while the mobile phone may no longer be a luxury, it's guaranteed to make an impression.

Just imagine leaving a business card with the number for your car phone on it.

For information, call 1-800-292-BELL.

NYNEX
Mobile Communications

Business weeklies are fine if you only do business weekly.

The Wall Street Journal.
The daily diary of the American dream.

Consumer Newspaper Over 600 Lines: Single

165
ART DIRECTOR
Charlie Clark
WRITER
Rebecca Flora
PHOTOGRAPHER
Dennis Manarchy
CLIENT
Virginia Dept. of Economic Development
AGENCY
Siddall Matus Coughter/ Virginia

166
ART DIRECTOR
Rick Carpenter
WRITER
Jaci Sisson
PHOTOGRAPHERS
David Leach
Bill Werts
CLIENT
ISUZU
AGENCY
Della Femina Travisano & Partners

167
ART DIRECTOR
Burt Blum
WRITER
Todd Heyman
PHOTOGRAPHER
Charles Gold
CLIENT
Redbook Magazine
AGENCY
Rosenfeld Sirowitz & Humphrey

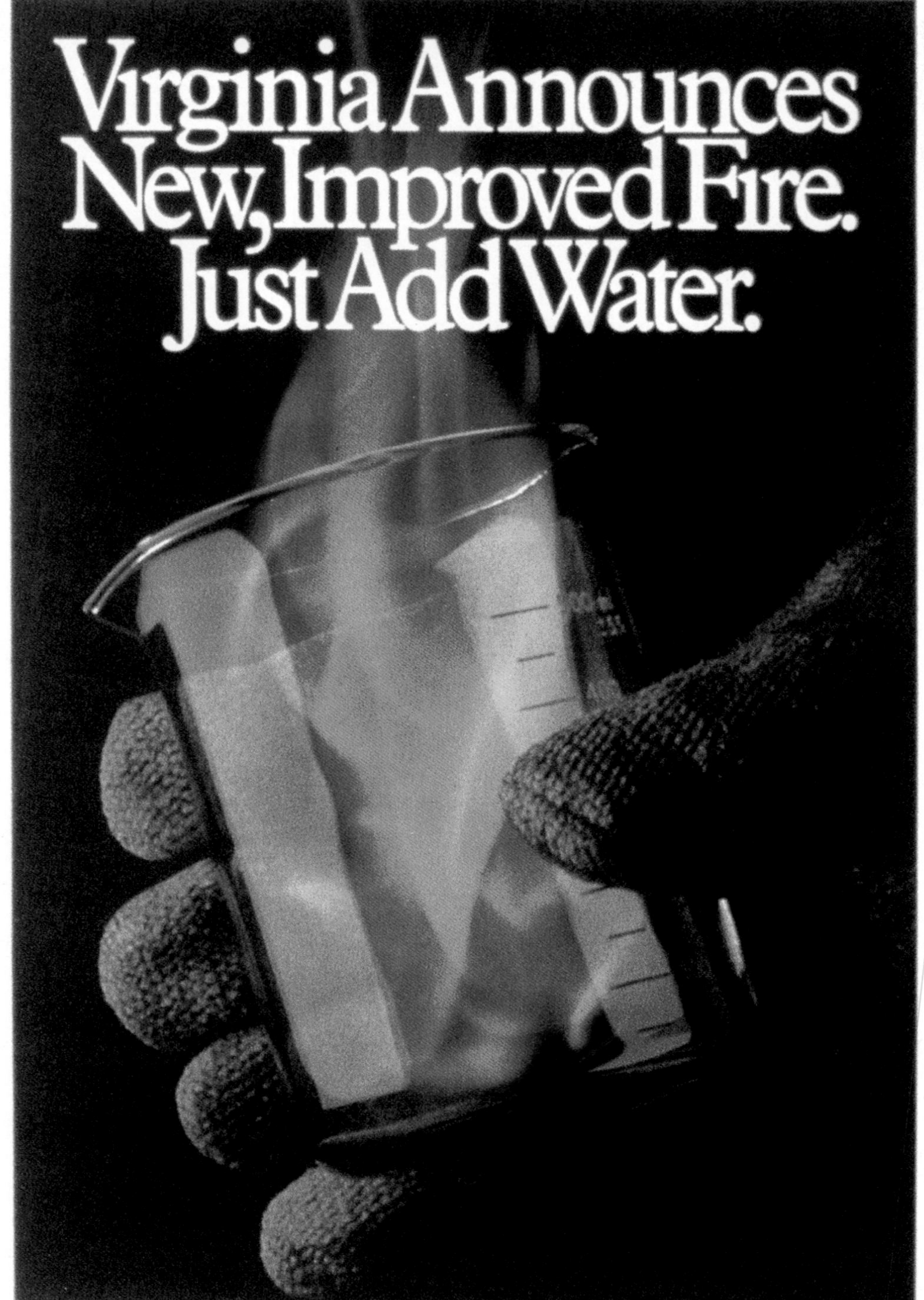

Ever since man discovered fire, he's searched for better ways to fuel it.

One such way was only recently discovered in Virginia. It uses an element more basic than fire itself. Because a key ingredient of the new fuel is water.

Two companies, Atlantic Research Corporation in Northern Virginia and United Coal Company in Southwestern Virginia, have each developed a fuel that combines water with the State's vast coal reserves. A mixture that looks, burns and handles like No. 6 fuel oil. Yet it's cheaper, safer and potentially far more abundant.

Innovative solutions like these are common in Virginia, as are the bright minds that produce them. Virginia has the nation's second highest concentration of doctoral scientists and engineers. That's more than California or Massachusetts.

And Virginia's 71 institutions of higher learning work closely with business to ensure Virginia maintains that lead.

The State government also gets high marks. A conservative fiscal policy earns Virginia a AAA bond rating and keeps both business and employee taxes well below the national average. In fact, Virginia boasts a corporate tax rate that hasn't increased since 1972.

But these are just a few of the reasons companies like AT&T, Ingersoll Rand, COMSAT TeleSystems and IBM have chosen Virginia for research and development. If you'd like more reasons, write Scott Eubanks, Director, Virginia Department of Economic Development, Governor's Office, Washington Building, Richmond, VA 23219. Or call (804) 786-3791.

Virginia
We're Doing Some Of America's Most Exciting Work.

In the Baja 1000, we had the competition right where we wanted them.
Isuzu wins the Stock Mini-Pickup Class in the Baja 1000.
For a long time, Nissan, Toyota, Chevrolet, Mitsubishi and Ford have pretty much dominated the stock mini-pickup class of the Baja 1000.
But that's all behind us now.
Because when the first truck in Class 7S crossed the finish line it wasn't one of theirs. It was one of ours.
Gallery Racing Team's Isuzu Baja Truck.
What's even more amazing than winning the Baja 1000 is how we won it.
While the other teams had years of experience off-road racing in Baja, we had only one. And while the other teams sent extensive crews and in some cases, fleets of trucks, we sent only one.
Of course, it takes more than a truck to win a thousand kilometer off-road race. So we'd like to thank the people who supported us every kilometer of the way.
Our sponsors, B.F. Goodrich and Gallery Racing. And our drivers, Mike Leon, Javier Tiznado, Bob Vander Kamp and Bill Petersen.
With their help we've made it a little harder for the competition. Especially when it comes to looking at themselves in the mirror.
ISUZU
ISUZU
RACING TEAM
BFGoodrich

IF YOU COULD MARRY ANY MAN WOULD YOU CHOOSE YOUR HUSBAND AGAIN?
Let's face it—juggling a job, a home, children, and a husband is, to put it mildly, challenging. A perfect partner can make your juggling a joy. But a less-than-perfect mate can ter even the most capable juggler to drop everything.
In our July issue, Dr. Richard B. Stuart, noted specialist in marital relations, reveals the four essential rules for picking the perfect partner. Test yourself:
Can the two of you be too much alike?
Did you choose him to please yourself…or others?
Do you know the difference between real love and infatuation?
To what extent do you recognize and support each other's independence?
Tough test! But, then again, who ever told you marriage would be easy?
Stop spreading! Win the battle of the bulge!
Have you noticed that dieting and exercising just don't budge your bulges like they used to? Don't despair, help is at hand!
Here are 48 easy-to-use tips from the experts. (Surprise! They don't involve drastic dieting or even heavy sweating.)
Remember, you have nothing to lose but what you've gained.
Summer shorts that make any body better.
You can look good in shorts. The right style can trim those thighs, diminish that derriere, even stretch short legs.
Learn what's right for you in our timely guide to the season's most flattering shorts.
There's no better way to feel cool. Or look hot.
Sit down with a sweetie pie.
Picture luscious vanilla ice cream surrounded by a scrumptious chocolate-coconut shell, or mouthwatering frozen cappuccino, topped with whipped cream and grated chocolate.
You'll love how quick and easy our 7 tempting icebox pies are to make. And, best of all, no oven, no baking!
And that's not the half of it.
We'll inspire you with 13 spectacular pages of country decorating ideas. Advise you what to do when you're in the mood for love… and he isn't. Help you look better than ever with new hairdos that will trim off years. And lots more.
It's all in our July Redbook. Pick up your copy now.
REDBOOK
REDBOOK. THE ONE AND ONLY BABYBOOMERBOOK FOR WOMEN.

Consumer Newspaper Over 600 Lines: Single

168
ART DIRECTOR
Sal DeVito
WRITER
Amelia Rosner
DESIGNER
Sal DeVito
CLIENT
Drexel Burnham Lambert
AGENCY
Chiat/Day

169
ART DIRECTOR
Dean Hanson
WRITER
Mike Lescarbeau
PHOTOGRAPHER
Craig Perman
CLIENT
Minnesota Federal
AGENCY
Fallon McElligott/Minneapolis

170
ART DIRECTOR
Rob Tomnay
WRITER
Jack Vaughan
DESIGNER
Tony Langmead
CLIENT
Apple Computer
AGENCY
The Campaign Palace/
Australia

Member SIPC

WAITING FOR A TAX BILL COULD PUT A LOT OF AMERICANS TO SLEEP.

There's only one thing worse than tax reform.

And that's waiting for it.

Because while the country waits for the arduous process to be finished, the country suffers.

Investors become wary investors. Industries stop making decisions to wait for the outcome.

It's no wonder it drags on. For a plan that aims for simplification, it's mighty complex.

And there's certainly enough to quibble about.

But any good piece of legislation has both supporters and opponents. Without them, the system wouldn't be working the way it was designed to.

No one would argue that tax reform has to be done right. Because down the road, no one wants to go through tax reform reform. But one thing is certain.

It must also be done quickly.

Because if we put our economy to sleep, we may have to shake it hard to wake it up again.

For a copy of *Tax Reform and Corporate America: A Preliminary Analysis*, call 1-800-237-8000, Ext.55.

Drexel Burnham

Drexel Burnham Lambert Incorporated

168

JUST HOW ARE YOU GOING TO PAY FOR YOUR NEW BATHROOM?

Of all the creative ways to finance a home improvement, a loan from Minnesota Federal is one of the more practical.

Our interest rates are very competitive and our application process is simple and painless.

So check the Yellow Pages for the Minnesota Federal near you. Then stop in and see us about a home improvement loan today. We promise to process your request quickly, because we know how difficult waiting for a bathroom can be.

Minnesota Federal

The Apple Christmas Packages from only $2,295. The computers will be around a long time. We wish we could say the same about the prices.

It has been something of a tradition with Apple to offer special packages at special prices over Christmas.

Computers make wonderful gifts and the Festive Season is one time such a purchase can be justified.

(Although your child's development and your own productivity should be priorities at any time.)

At this time of year, however, we like to play Santa.

And put together packages which place a complete computer system within closer reach.

This year is no exception.

We have put together two different packages around two different models, to cater for both family and professional home computing.

What is exceptional this year is the value of the offers.

The Family Package Offer.

Between now and February 6 (unless we happen to sell out beforehand), we are offering a special price on a complete solution for family use.

It centres around the Apple IIc personal computer and includes a high-resolution monochrome monitor, a mouse, four self-teaching disks, a graphics package, and a bundle of four software programs.

This is not superseded equipment or obscure software, this is the very latest and most popular product, some only newly released.

The entire package would normally set you back a good $2,800.

This Christmas we offer it for just $2,295; $500 worth of extra value.

But perhaps the true value is that it offers serious home computing.

Not the fast-fading novelty of an overpriced toy.

The IIc Computer.

Introduced in 1984, the IIc is a powerful (128K), yet very compact and portable unit. (The disk drive is actually built in.)

It's simple to use and simple to set up.

Plug the monitor into the computer, plug the computer into the power socket and away you go.

Some killjoys wonder if serious computing shouldn't be harder than this.

We think that only a serious computer has the power to be this simple.

Learning is easy; the IIc comes with a self-teaching, four-disk tutorial as a matter of course.

Adding accessories is as easy as plugging them in. All the necessary circuitry is already inside, bought and paid for.

The IIc is also very stylish to look at.

When you design a computer to be around for a while, those are important considerations. (See separate box.)

'Tis the night after Christmas, and all through the house, every creature is stirring, including our mouse.

The Family Package comes complete with a mouse.

An exciting by-product of our revolutionary Macintosh technology, the mouse makes it possible to control the computer without using the keyboard.

Together with the accompanying MousePaint graphics package, you can create pictures on the screen of your IIc.

MasterType's Writer.

Word processing is fundamental to personal computing.

We give you one of the best examples, MasterType's Writer from Scarborough Systems.

It features dual windows, help files, sorting, macros, a selection of typefaces and a tutorial disk.

Despite quite sophisticated functions, its operation is remarkably easy.

The first word processing program capable of performing in colour, it perfectly suits an optional colour monitor and colour printer.

Giving you not just the ability to process words, but the power to express yourself colourfully.

Mind Over Minors. How well do you know your kids?

Mind Over Minors is software that helps you manage and motivate youngsters.

You can identify your child's (and your own) personality traits to improve communication and handling.

Sounds like the sinister side of computers they warned us about, but far from it.

Fascinating to the point of being addictive, it's a sometimes funny, sometimes thought-provoking program.

Microzine.

Microzine is a complete activity magazine in electronic form, providing you with eight complete programs on two separate disks.

Teachers cite it as a most exciting innovation in electronic learning.

Microzine challenges your children's minds while it captures their imaginations.

Kids can talk to Microzine and it talks back.

Adventures and mysteries let kids become the stars of their own stories.

Microzine also comes complete with student's handbook.

Hitchhiker's Guide to the Galaxy. See the Universe the safe, sure money-saving way!

Recreates the highly popular ABC TV series as an adventure/time travel game.

Co-written by the incorrigible author himself, Douglas Adams.

For the first time you're more than a passive reader. You can actually shape the course of the story.

Hitchhiker's package contains your Don't Panic! Button, authentic fluff, peril-sensitive sunglasses, microscopic space fleet and no tea.

Consumer Newspaper Over 600 Lines: Single

171
ART DIRECTOR
George Halvorsen
WRITER
Bill Johnson
PHOTOGRAPHER
Frank Miller
CLIENT
Metropolitan Medical Center
AGENCY
Ruhr/Paragon - Minneappolis

172
ART DIRECTOR
Alan Lerner
WRITER
Indra Sinha
CLIENT
British War Museum
AGENCY
Ogilvy & Mather/London

173
ART DIRECTOR
Gary Greenberg
WRITER
Peter Seronick
DESIGNER
Gary Greenberg
ARTIST
Arthur Matson
CLIENT
Old Neighborhood
AGENCY
Rossin Greenberg Seronick & Hill/Boston

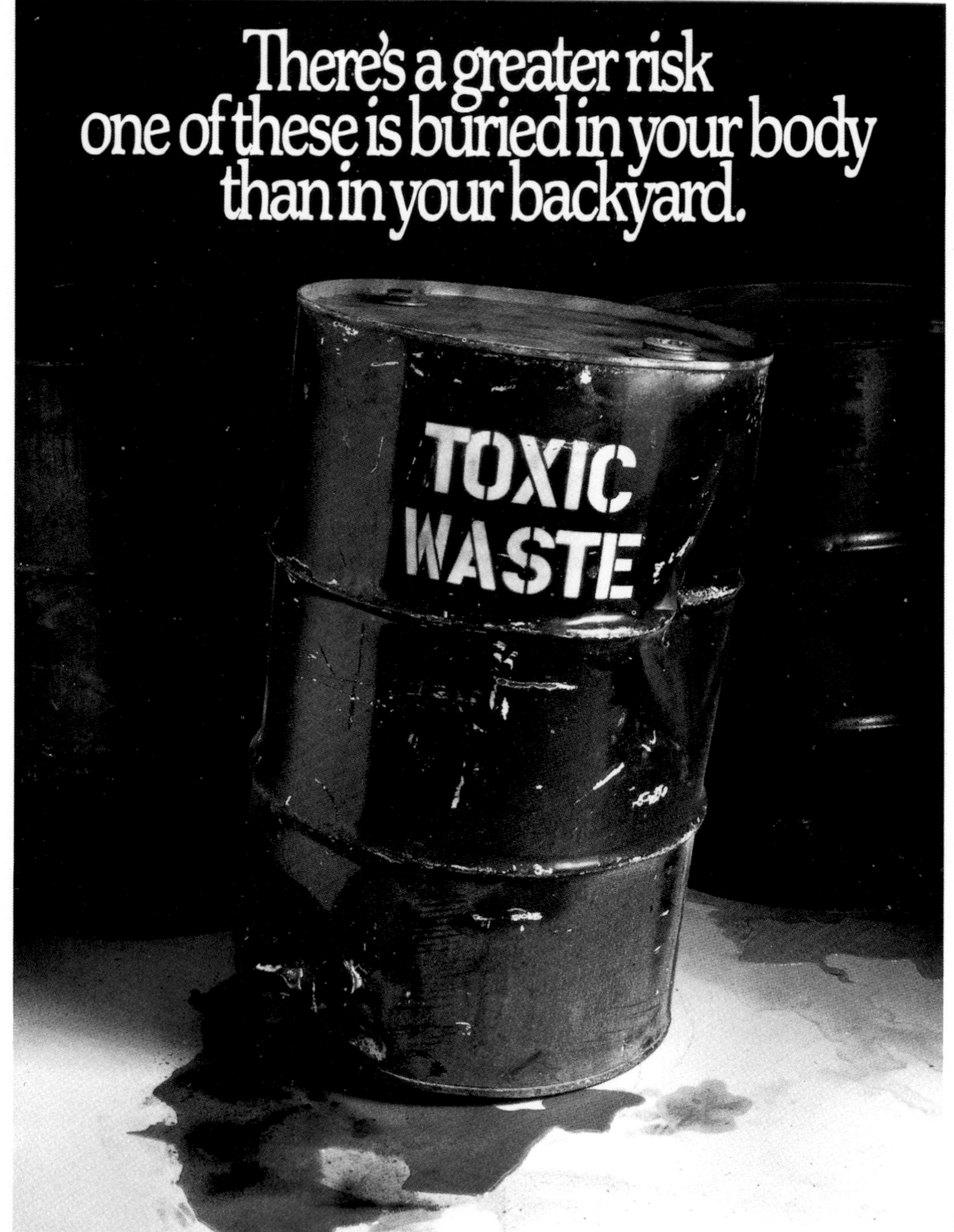
There's a greater risk
one of these is buried in your body
than in your backyard.
TOXIC
WASTE

Without your knowing about it, toxic wastes may be building up in your body as a result of kidney disease.

Normally, the kidneys remove these wastes from the body. But sometimes the kidneys fail to function properly because of the effects of heart conditions, high blood pressure, or diabetes. Untreated, the problem can lead to death.

Many hospitals treat kidney disease, but at Metropolitan Medical Center and Hennepin County Medical Center, we specialize in it.

Through our joint efforts, we've established the largest kidney treatment center in the state. We offer superior capabilities for diagnosing the illness. We provide the widest range of treatment options and services, including financial and nutritional counseling. Most importantly, we've developed specialized training and educational programs.

Thanks to these efforts, which began 20 years ago, we've been able to develop our technical expertise and have made significant advances in treating the disease.

We're developing a fast dialysis process that reduces the amount of time patients have to spend undergoing treatment.

We're learning new ways to prevent infections, formerly a common problem among dialysis patients.

We're working with urologists to provide state-of-the-art treatments for kidney stones, including the use of shock waves to dissolve kidney stones within the body.

For more information talk to your physician or call us at (612) 347-5000 or write the Program Office.

Kidney disease. It's just one more area of critical care that we specialize in, for the health of the community.

MMC

Metropolitan Medical Center
900 South Eighth Street, Minneapolis, MN 55404
A HealthOne Company

171

16th Middlesex retreating with heavy losses from Hawthorn Ridge, 7.45am.
SOMEWHERE IN THIS PICTURE, 2nd Lt. ERIC HEATON LIES DYING.
By 4am, there was enough light to see the German lines.
Near the rivers, mist still lingered, but the wooded ridges were clear.
A light rain began to fall and the men in the trenches held out their helmets to catch the water. Their throats were dry.
The rain gave way to a cloudless blue sky, without a breath of wind. It was going to be hot: a perfect summer's day.
Tangles of yellow weed marked the enemy trenches and the grassy fields of No Man's Land were covered in scarlet poppies.
At 6.25am, the British guns opened fire on the German positions.
It was July 1st 1916. The Battle of the Somme was about to begin.
A walk-over
All along the 18 mile front, British infantrymen were preparing for the coming action.
They did not expect a tough fight. Their generals had promised them that the German trenches would be empty, wiped out by the British artillery.
One Brigadier-General assured his troops they would not need rifles. They could go over the top with walking sticks.
During the previous week, the German lines had been hit by 1,508,652 British shells and mortar bombs.
People in the south of England heard the bombardment and wondered if a naval battle was being fought in the Channel.
Few realised that the far off thunder was the beginning of the Big Push which would win The War To End Wars.
Fix bayonets
Not every soldier believed it would be a walk-over.
Some men, peering out across their parapets, could see that the barbed wire entanglements opposite them were still intact.
One sergeant in the Middlesex could not stop the shaking in his body growing worse and worse as Zero Hour approached.
Others were in high spirits. Captain Neville, of the 8th East Surreys, gave each of his platoons a football to kick off towards the German trenches.
A rum ration was served and some men became tipsy. "Fix Bayonets" was carried out with much laughter.
A letter home
In his front line trench in the Beaumont Hamel sector, 2nd Lt. Eric Heaton of the 16th Middlesex was nerving himself up for his first action.
He was 20 years old and had been in France four months. On the eve of battle he had written to his parents:
"I cannot quite express my feelings on this night . . . My greatest concern is that I may have the courage and determination necessary to lead my platoon well".
Eric Heaton had a crucial task.
At 7.20am, ten minutes before Zero Hour, a gigantic mine: a tunnel packed with explosives, would detonate beneath the German redoubt at Hawthorn Ridge.
His men were to cross 500 yards of No Man's Land and quickly occupy the newly formed crater.
Zero hour
At 7.20, the mine at Hawthorn Ridge blew, spewing a huge column of chalk and earth thousands of feet into the air.
Seconds later, shock waves rocked the trench where Eric Heaton and his platoon waited, throwing men to the ground.
German artillery immediately opened fire on the nearest British trenches and shrapnel rattled like hail above the heads of the 16th Middlesex.
The men could not understand where the enemy fire was coming from – weren't the Germans all supposed to be dead?
When the last seconds had ticked away, Lt. Heaton blew his whistle and started up the ladder to No Man's Land.
The 9th Platoon of the 16th Middlesex scrambled up after him, weighed down by their heavy packs.
Slowly, they fanned out into a long line and began to move towards the smoking Hawthorn Ridge crater.
The new tactics
Because the generals expected little German resistance, they had altered the normal rules of an infantry attack.
The British soldiers were to advance slowly in waves.
Each wave was to walk forward at a steady pace, covering no more than 100 yards in two minutes. A speed of rather less than two miles an hour.
As the leading waves paced farther into No Man's Land, they started hares that were still living there among the long grasses and wild summer flowers.
Then the German machine gunners opened up.
'Tac Tac Tac'
Too late, it became clear that their deep shelters and dugouts had preserved the Germans from the British artillery.
The waves of soldiers, following orders, came walking slowly forward and toppled like dominoes as the machine guns swept their lines.
The dead lay in long rows where they had fallen. As the few survivors continued to advance, German howitzers began to pound No Man's Land.
A man in Eric Heaton's battalion described what it was like.
"Imagine stumbling over a ploughed field in a thunderstorm, the incessant roar of the guns and flashes as the shells exploded. Multiply all this and you have some idea of the Hell into which we were heading."
The fate of the 16th Middlesex
Eric Heaton's men were unlucky. In the ten minutes between the blowing of the Hawthorn Ridge mine and the start of the attack, the Germans had already occupied the newly formed crater.
The 16th Middlesex were swept by machine gun fire and blown apart by artillery shells. The leading wave had almost disappeared, but individual survivors kept to their steady, disciplined pace.
The following waves met the same fate, yet always a few men survived and kept going.
2nd Lt. Eric Heaton was last seen alive in the maelstrom of exploding metal near the German front line.
"I saw him in No Man's Land not far from the German lines and at that time he was quite alright in company with Mr Jack." Pte A.J. Bird. The two officers were exhorting their men to push on through the German barbed wire.
Oranges and lemons
The enemy's barbed wire entanglements, like his trenches and his troops, were supposed to have been utterly destroyed by the British artillery bombardment.
Yet all along the front, men who had survived the holocaust of No Man's Land reached the German wire to find it still intact.
At Gommecourt, five miles to the north of Eric Heaton's sector, the reason for this was plain to see.
Unexploded British mortar bombs, large and round as footballs and painted bright orange, lay in drifts against the wire.
They were, in the soldiers' slang, 'napoo'. No good. Duds.
Most of those who tried to cut or thread their way through the German wire got caught on the long barbs.
One by one, as they struggled there, they were shot.
Missing believed Killed
No one knows for certain what happened to 2nd Lt. Eric Heaton.
One report stated that he had been wounded by a machine gun and later killed by a shell. But one of his platoon said that he saw him hit in the knee – it was almost blown off – and thought that he had bled to death.
Eric Heaton was one of 57,470 men listed killed, wounded or missing on that first day of the Somme.
Unmentioned in despatches
You will not find 2nd Lt. Eric Heaton in the history books. His moment of glory went unrecorded. His last remains are a bundle of letters and photographs kept in a cardboard box in our vaults.
From them we have pieced together his story.
Our Museum contains thousands of such stories. Not just from the Somme but every battle of the First and Second World Wars.
Not just the stories of soldiers, airmen and sailors, but of civilians who found themselves caught up in war. We would like to tell their stories. But without your help many of our cardboard boxes will never be opened.
Will you help us?
The Imperial War Museum is in urgent need of help.
Our building leaks. Plumbing, wiring, heating and drains must all be completely replaced. The glass roofs above our main galleries are beyond repair.
Facilities for visitors, particularly the disabled, are poor.
Worst of all, the Museum is simply too small to display its collections properly.
We have very little money. In fact, we could not have published this advertisement but for the generosity of the newspapers in which it appears.
The first phase of our redevelopment scheme will cost £9,000,000. If we can raise £2,500,000, the Government have said that they will give us the rest.
You can help us by making a donation or a covenant. Every £10 covenanted will produce £14.30. Please address donations and enquiries about covenants to the Director, Imperial War Museum, Lambeth Rd, London SE1 6HZ. Cheques should be made payable to "The Imperial War Museum Trust Redevelopment Appeal". Thank you.
IMPERIAL WAR MUSEUM APPEAL

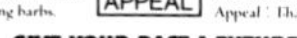
GIVE YOUR PAST A FUTURE

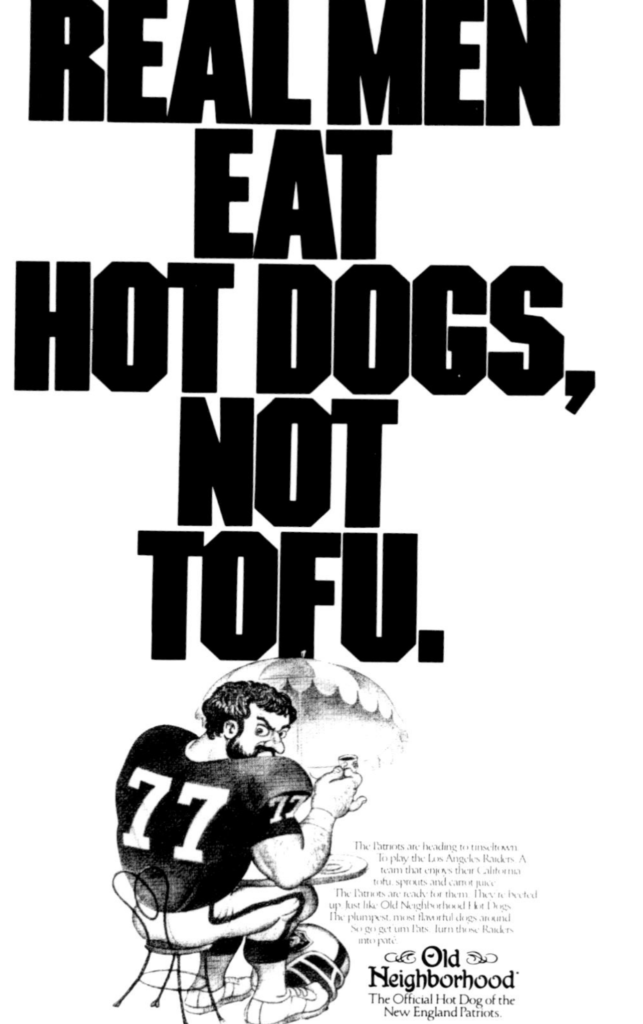
REAL MEN
EAT
HOT DOGS,
NOT
TOFU.
77
The Patriots are heading to tinseltown.
To play the Los Angeles Raiders. A
team that enjoys their California
tofu, sprouts and carrot juice.
The Patriots are ready for them. They're beefed
up. Just like Old Neighborhood Hot Dogs.
The plumpest, most flavorful dogs around.
So go get 'um Pats. Turn those Raiders
into paté.
Old
Neighborhood
The Official Hot Dog of the
New England Patriots.

Consumer Newspaper Over 600 Lines: Single

174
ART DIRECTOR
Michael Fazende
WRITER
John Stingley
ARTIST
David Langley
CLIENT
Marine Midland Bank
AGENCY
Fallon McElligott/Minneapolis

175
ART DIRECTORS
Geoff Hayes
Michel Roux
WRITER
Evert Cilliers
DESIGNER
Geoff Hayes
ARTIST
Andy Warhol
PHOTOGRAPHER
Michel Roux
CLIENT
Carillon Importers
AGENCY
TBWA

176
ART DIRECTOR
Chris Vice
WRITER
Bill Johnson
PHOTOGRAPHER
Jim Arndt
CLIENT
United Hospital
AGENCY
Ruhr/Paragon - Minneapolis

Considering the fickleness of the American car buyer, how long can you afford to wait for loan approval?
American car buyers have never been noted for their loyalty. Or their contentment.
With each changing whim of style, they change their mind about what they want.
So once a dealer makes a sale, how long can they wait for loan approval without a customer changing his or her mind?
At Marine Midland Automotive Financial, we realize that to move cars, you have to move fast.
So we do. Approving most loan applications in just hours.
And since automotive financing is all we do, dealers don't have to wait for us to get up to speed while impatient customers are getting up to leave.
We can also offer more innovative financing options, to help make monthly payments more affordable.
At Automotive Financial, we understand the car dealer's business, because it's our business. Our only business.
Call 800-448-3400, ext. 334, for the name and number of your local representative.
If you're losing deals because of financing, maybe we can help salvage them.
AUTOMOTIVE FINANCIAL
A MARINE MIDLAND COMPANY

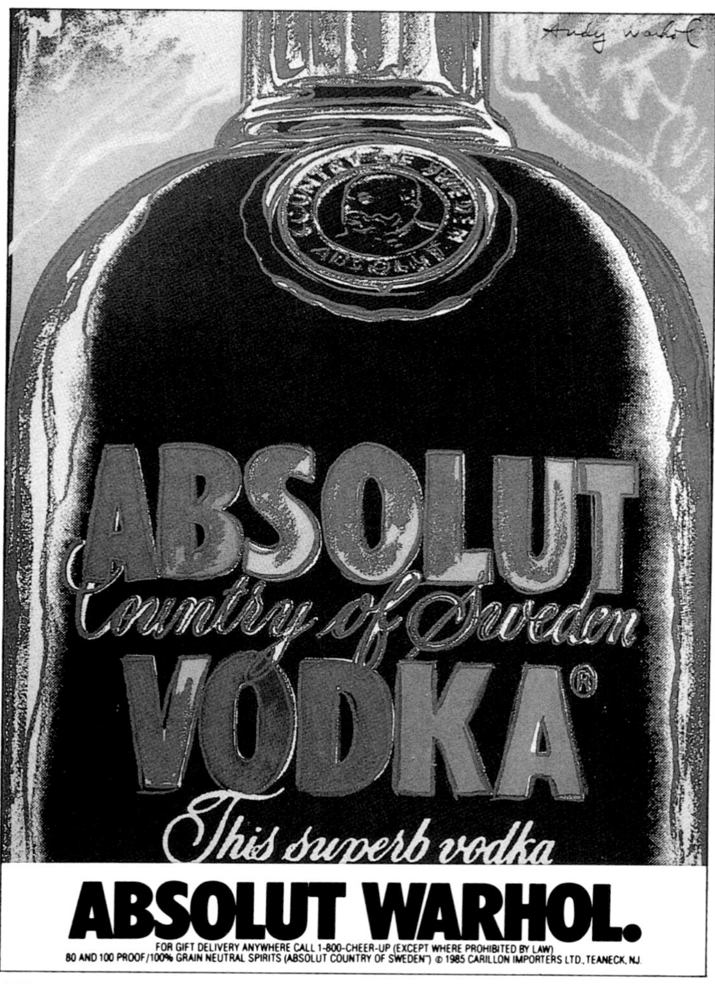
Andy Warhol
COUNTRY OF SWEDEN
ABSOLUT
ABSOLUT
Country of Sweden
VODKA®
This superb vodka
ABSOLUT WARHOL.
FOR GIFT DELIVERY ANYWHERE CALL 1-800-CHEER-UP (EXCEPT WHERE PROHIBITED BY LAW)
80 AND 100 PROOF/100% GRAIN NEUTRAL SPIRITS (ABSOLUT COUNTRY OF SWEDEN™) © 1985 CARILLON IMPORTERS LTD., TEANECK, NJ.

175

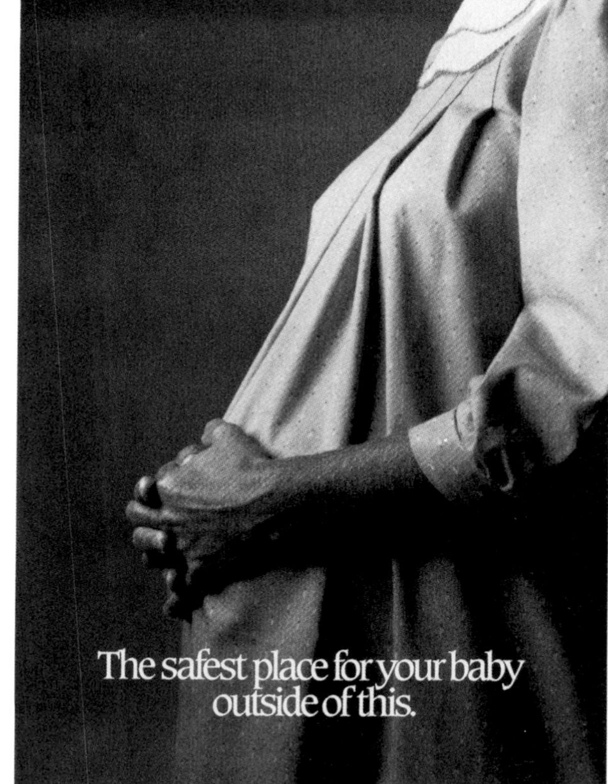
The safest place for your baby
outside of this.

When it's time for your baby to leave the womb, you want to make sure that it's born in the safest, most comfortable environment possible.

That's why you should consider having your baby at the Perinatal Center of United Hospital and Children's Hospital of St. Paul.

The combined resources of these two hospitals make it possible for us to offer you the comfort of knowing that you're in one of the region's leading medical facilities. We are specially prepared to deal with difficult pregnancies, high-risk births and on-the-spot intensive care for babies.

We offer many other unique services, such as a Regional Pregnancy Diabetes Clinic and genetic testing and counseling. We offer infertility assessments and testing, as well as advanced infant pulmonary capabilities. In short, the most advanced care possible for mother and child.

We can also offer you the widest variety of birthing options available locally, from traditional labor and delivery rooms to home-like settings in the Family Birth Center where you choose the family and medical personnel in attendance.

You decide how much or how little you want the hospital to be involved. You participate in deciding whether and how much medication to use. You decide whether to keep your baby in your room with you. And whether to have your partner stay with you. Your choices are many.

Hopefully, you'll never need any of our high-risk facilities. But won't you feel safer just knowing that they're there?

For more information about our perinatal services, talk to your doctor. Or call us at (612) 298-8868.

At our Perinatal Center, every birth is a special delivery.

PERINATAL CENTER
United Hospital and Children's Hospital of St. Paul

176

Consumer Newspaper Over 600 Lines: Single

177
ART DIRECTOR
Marcus Kemp
WRITER
Jim Copacino
CLIENT
Alaska Airlines
AGENCY
Livingston & Company/
Seattle

178
ART DIRECTOR
Chris Vice
WRITER
Bill Johnson
PHOTOGRAPHER
Jim Arndt
CLIENT
United Hospital
AGENCY
Ruhr/Paragon - Minneapolis

179
ART DIRECTORS
G. Oliver White
Steve Davis
WRITER
Charles Ashby
DESIGNERS
G. Oliver White
Steve Davis
ARTIST
GraphicsGroup
PHOTOGRAPHERS
Tim Olive
Pat Patterson
CLIENT
NCNB
AGENCY
McKinney Silver & Rockett/
North Carolina

ALASKA
SEATTLE
LAX
You may not have realized it, but Los Angeles is a big part of Alaska. Because now Alaska Airlines offers four nonstop flights each day from LAX to Seattle: Including a direct flight to Anchorage, plus convenient connections to other cities throughout Alaska. We also fly to many major West Coast cities from the suburban Burbank, Long Beach and Ontario airports. So if your clients are looking for a better way to travel in and out of L.A., the only sensible thing to do is book them on an airline called Alaska.
Alaska Airlines

177

When you're having a baby,
we can give you every choice except one:
boy or girl.

Not so long ago families didn't have a lot of choices available to them when starting their families. But today families are being offered a host of alternatives.

To help families make the most of their options we've set up the Family Birth Center within the Perinatal Center at United Hospital and Children's Hospital of St. Paul.

The Family Birth Center allows families to experience childbirth in a warm homelike setting with as little or as much involvement by the hospital as the family requires. Yet if necessary all the technology and expertise of a state-of-the-art medical facility is only steps away.

At the Family Birth Center the entire process can take place in a single room. Husbands, children, parents and other support persons may participate in the care of the mother. Both the baby and the support person may stay in the mother's room throughout.

All of the major decisions are left up to your family. You decide whether to use your own physician or a certified nurse midwife. You decide how long to stay in the center after delivery. You pay only for the services you require. As a result the cost is generally lower.

For more information talk to your doctor. Or call us at 298-8470.

You'll discover we have all the birthing options you can conceive of.

FAMILY BIRTH CENTER
United Hospital and Children's Hospital of St. Paul

178

179

Consumer Newspaper Over 600 Lines: Single

180
ART DIRECTORS
Dave Gardiner
Gary Greenberg
WRITER
Tom O'Connor
DESIGNERS
Dave Gardiner
Gary Greenberg
ARTIST
Arthur Matson
CLIENT
Old Neighborhood
AGENCY
Rossin Greenberg Seronick & Hill/Boston

181
ART DIRECTOR
Rob Dalton
WRITER
Jarl Olsen
DESIGNER
Rob Dalton
ARTIST
Maureen Kenny
CLIENT
WLOL
AGENCY
Fallon McElligott/Minneapolis

182
ART DIRECTOR
Mark Erwin
WRITER
Rhonda Peck
CLIENT
Chase Manhattan Bank
AGENCY
Scali McCabe Sloves

THE HOT DOG NEW ENGLAND CAN'T WAIT TO GET ITS HANDS ON.
99
99
Normally, Old Neighborhood is the hot dog the Patriots want to get their hands on. And who can blame them. Old Neighborhood makes the plumpest, most flavorful hot dogs around. But tomorrow the Patriots will be after another kind of hot dog altogether.
We wish them luck.
Old Neighborhood
The Official Hot Dog of the New England Patriots.

180

Togetanymore intothirtysecondswe'd havetotalklikethis.

A very full half-minute of news, gossip and entertainment trivia.
The Thirty Second Scoop, heard every other hour at ten minutes to the hour.

181

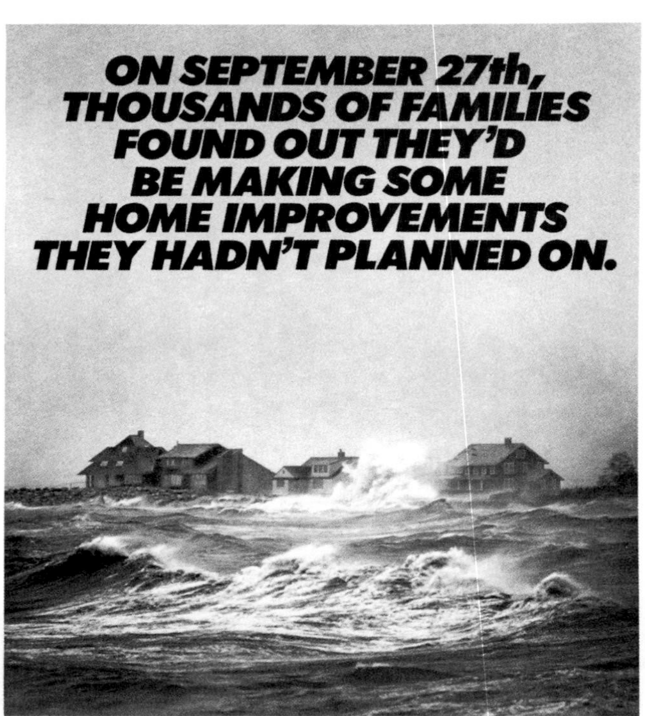

ANNOUNCING SPECIAL HOME IMPROVEMENT LOANS, NOW THROUGH NOVEMBER 15TH.

If you were one of the thousands of people whose home didn't make it through Hurricane Gloria without a scratch, Chase has some welcome news.

Chase Home Improvement Loan **13%** ANNUAL PERCENTAGE RATE Not available for all amounts

We know that your insurance may not cover all of your losses. That's why we're doing everything we can to help make your repairs more affordable.

To begin, we've lowered our rate on Home Improvement loans to a 13% Annual Percentage Rate.

You can borrow amounts up to $20,000, if you qualify. And take up to seven years to pay us back. Just as an example, a $10,000 loan over seven years at this low rate means your payments will be $181.92 a month.

All you have to do to apply for a loan is come into any Chase branch. Or, if time is of the essence, call our emergency Loan-By-Phone team at (718) 423-8600 or (516) 352-3316.

Of course, you don't have to be a hurricane victim to take advantage of our special rate. Which makes it a good time to make any kind of home improvements.

The ones you've always wanted. And the ones you have to have.

EQUAL HOUSING LENDER

182

Consumer Newspaper Over 600 Lines: Single

183
ART DIRECTOR
Bob Brihn
WRITER
Dana Offerman
PHOTOGRAPHER
Rick Dublin Photography
CLIENT
Twin City Federal
AGENCY
Ruhr/Paragon - Minneapolis

184
ART DIRECTORS
Ed Tajon
David Price
WRITER
Jeremy Wolff
DESIGNER
Ed Tajon
CLIENT
Holland America Line
AGENCY
Elgin Syferd Advertising/
Seattle

185
ART DIRECTOR
Gregory Elkin
WRITER
Mike Rogers
DESIGNER
Gregory Elkin
PHOTOGRAPHER
Larry Sillen
CLIENT
Michelin Tire Corporation
AGENCY
Doyle Dane Bernbach

If we don't answer your loan request in 4 to 48 hours, we'll give you 2 notes of apology.

At TCF, we're so confident of our fast response on loan requests, that we'll pay you $25 if we don't meet these deadlines:

For Passcard reserve loans, we guarantee an answer within four hours.

For installment loans, such as a home improvement or auto loan, we guarantee an answer within eight hours.

And, for home equity loans, we guarantee an answer within 48 hours.

So if you need a loan, come to TCF. And if your loan request takes a little longer than expected, we know you'll accept our apologies. With both hands.

EQUAL HOUSING LENDER

WHERE MINNESOTA BANKS

183

HOLLAND AMERICA CRUISES
CARIBBEAN & MEXICO

It doesn't take a lot of money for your clients to go a long way on a Holland America cruise to the Caribbean or Mexico.

Consider all they get. For 7 or 14 days aboard the Noordam, the Nieuw Amsterdam or the Rotterdam, they'll have magnificent accommodations and gourmet cuisine. On-board activities ranging from tennis, swimming and golf to intimate lounges, a casino and a theatre. Staterooms that are larger than most. Plus they'll be treated to Holland America's exclusive Ocean Liner Service℠, and receive the expert attention of our experienced Dutch officers and world-renowned crew every mile of the way.

And those miles take them to some of the most exotic ports of call in the world. Places like St. Thomas, Montego Bay and Grand Cayman in the Caribbean. Puerto Vallarta, Zihuatanejo/Ixtapa, and Acapulco along the Mexican Riviera.

Guests booking before August 1 qualify for our unique Dutch Incentive Savings of up to $400 per couple. That means 7-day cruise fares can start as low as $895.*

Our 7- and 14-day cruises include free air** from most major gateways. And on Holland America ships, unlike any other luxury cruise, *no tipping is required.*

So the next time you're planning a trip for a client, remember, they'll get it all on a Holland America cruise. For 38¢ a mile, it's the most luxurious vacation value on land or sea.

Call today for cruise reservations: (800) 426-0327 or (206) 281-1970. For sales service: (800) 626-9900 or (206) 281-3535. For brochures: (800) 225-1451. In New Jersey, (800) 225-1452.

* Prices are per person, double occupancy, space available basis, plus port charges. **Does not include Christmas cruises to the Caribbean. Ships' registry: Netherlands Antilles.

THIS SHOULD STOP THE COMPETITION FROM INFLATING THEIR TIRES.

THE NEW YORK TIMES, TUESDAY, JULY 30, 1985

Michelin Tire Rated as Best In Federal Testing Program

Group Makes Ratings Public

The National Highway Traffic Safety Administration has just confirmed what we've been saying all along:

A Michelin doesn't tire.

Manufacturers' tests, conducted according to NHTSA's specifications, proved Michelin lasts longer than any other radial.

Not only did the Michelin XH outperform its closest competitor by 10,000 miles. The full line of Michelin radials did better than the full line of any other manufacturer.

Of course, the competition may continue to inflate the merits of their tires. But if they do, you'll know their claims are a little flat.

MICHELIN® BECAUSE SO MUCH IS RIDING ON YOUR TIRES.™

Consumer Newspaper Over 600 Lines: Single

186
ART DIRECTOR
Don Harbor
WRITER
Ken Hines
DESIGNER
Jeff France
PHOTOGRAPHER
Jamie Cook
CLIENT
Norfolk General Hospital
AGENCY
Lawler Ballard/Virginia

187
ART DIRECTOR
Jerry Whitley
WRITER
Mark Silveira
ARTIST
R & V Studio
CLIENT
BMW of North America
AGENCY
Ammirati & Puris

188
ART DIRECTOR
Ron Sandilands
WRITER
Bernie Hafeli
DESIGNER
Cindy Ward
PHOTOGRAPHER
Chuck Kuhn
CLIENT
Pacific Northwest Bell
AGENCY
Livingston & Company/Seattle

You don't have to be a musician to appreciate this.

A Chopin waltz played for the first time since a traumatic injury to one hand. Not a flawless performance, mind you, but the most satisfying one of the pianist's career.

It's a performance that could never have taken place without some remarkable advances in the field of reconstructive surgery.

Today, physicians around the world are perfecting surgical techniques that would have seemed like science fiction a generation ago.

Many of those techniques were developed right here in our corner of the globe. At Norfolk General Hospital and Eastern Virginia Medical School (EVMS).

This innovative work began more than 25 years ago when two talented specialists, a urologist and a plastic surgeon, teamed up to devise a new way to repair hypospadias, a genital deformity affecting one in 350 baby boys.

Then, a few years later, other physicians at Norfolk General applied those techniques to mending the urethra — the tube that carries urine from the bladder — when it's damaged by injury or disease.

Since then, our hospital has encouraged collaboration among specialists in every field. In reconstructive surgery that teamwork has turned up a treasure of practical, reproducible results.

A good example is the use of myocutaneous flaps. Developed by surgeons working at Norfolk General, myocutaneous flaps are thick pieces of skin with underlying muscle and the vessels necessary to continue blood supply.

What makes them so valuable? These flaps can be moved successfully from one part of the body to another. And in their transplanted location, they look and work like the original, displaced tissue.

The applications of this technique are virtually limitless.

Myocutaneous flaps have been used to replace severely burned tissue. They've also been used with remarkable success in urogenital reconstruction. They've even been used to construct new breasts after mastectomies.

The vacularized nerve graft was another exciting breakthrough. This revolutionary technique, pioneered at EVMS's Microsurgical Research Center in 1981, enables physicians to replace damaged nerves with new ones.

The beneficiaries of these innovations are numberless.

Patients with facial paralysis can now undergo a surgical procedure in which nerves are grafted and muscles reinervated. So the face performs its special magic of smiling once again.

Using high-powered microscopes, surgeons can reattach severed fingers, hands, arms and legs.

When critically injured patients, victims of car wrecks and industrial accidents, are rushed to Norfolk General, specialists here don't stop at saving lives. They save the patient's appearance as well. Now it's even possible to build a new penis that looks, feels and functions normally.

The influence of reconstructive surgery at our hospital extends far beyond Hampton Roads. Patients come to us from other nations, other continents, when there is literally no one else in the world to turn to.

And every year physicians from around the world visit Norfolk General to observe and learn about reconstructive surgery. They hear lectures and read articles and books written by the leading specialists in the field.

When they return home, our visitors take with them new knowledge and skills they'll put to good use in the hospitals where they work. That way, patients who never see or hear about Norfolk General live happier, more active lives because of the work that goes on here.

The ingenious collaborative effort that has produced so many heartening results continues today.

And the promise of the future has never been brighter.

In one area, researchers at EVMS's Microsurgical Research Center are investigating substances that will speed up the healing of reattached nerves.

On another frontier, urologists and plastic surgeons are now researching new processes that could permit near normal bladder function in paraplegic patients.

And that's just the beginning.

For more information about reconstructive surgery or any of the 41 specialities at Norfolk General Hospital, call us at 628-3518. We'll be glad to fill you in.

It's the least we can do for an encore.

Norfolk General, an Alliance hospital, leading the way in health care.

One Of These Hands Is A Work Of Art.

186

187

HEAVEN CAN WAIT.

Recently, Paul Henry had a heart attack in his home. When his wife Teresa found him, she immediately dialed 9-1-1.*

Within minutes a Renton Fire Department aid car arrived on the scene, thanks to the new enhanced 9-1-1 system and the Pacific Northwest Bell Network that makes it possible.

Even if a caller is unable to speak—even if a phone call is cut off—with enhanced 9-1-1, all necessary information instantly appears on a computer screen. Thereby enabling the emergency dispatcher to quickly send help—even if the dispatcher can't get a clear idea of the problem.

When King County implemented the enhanced 9-1-1 system in September, they relied on the dependability and technology of the Pacific Northwest Bell Network. How reliable is the enhanced 9-1-1 system?

Just ask Paul Henry.

The Pacific Northwest Bell Network. When the phone rings, it's us.

Pacific Northwest Bell

*Check for local availability before using this service.

188

Consumer Newspaper Over 600 Lines: Single

189
ART DIRECTORS
Scott Frederick
Cliff Schwandner
WRITER
Michael Farnam
PHOTOGRAPHER
Mike Capporale
CLIENT
Northlich Stolley
AGENCY
Northlich Stolley/Cincinnati

190
ART DIRECTOR
Steve Chase
WRITER
Terry O'Rielly
PHOTOGRAPHER
Mark Bird
CLIENT
Eastern Airlines
AGENCY
Campbell-Ewald/Toronto

IT DOESN'T DO ANY GOOD TO BE FAST ON THE DRAW IF YOU'RE A LOUSY SHOT.

The most responsive advertising agency in the world is useless if its creative doesn't stop you in your tracks. So if you're too busy to waste time on target practice, call us at 421-8840. We'll make sure that the advertising you get is fresh. Powerful. And squarely on target. Because we realize that in today's marketplace, you might not get a second shot. NORTHLICH, STOLLEY, INC.

200 West Fourth Street, Cincinnati, Ohio 45202

189

USE A FIVE YEAR OLD EXCUSE TO GO TO WALT DISNEY WORLD.

We know, we know. You're only doing this for the kids, right?

Right. Because they've always dreamed of going to Walt Disney World Magic Kingdom and EPCOT Center. Just the way you did when you were a kid, right? And won't they love being greeted by a Disney character when your Eastern flight arrives in Orlando.

And being that it's a special occasion and all, they can even borrow your Mickey Mouse ears. After all, you're only doing this for the kids, right?

Right.

WE EARN OUR WINGS EVERY DAY[SM]

FROM ONLY **$498***

Eastern's Orlando Value Plus Vacation includes • Round trip Coach airfare on Eastern • 8 days/7 nights in a quality hotel • Rental car, unlimited mileage • 3-day passport to Walt Disney World Magic Kingdom and EPCOT Center • Complimentary admission for 2 to Circus World or Wet 'n Wild attractions • Discounted prices for kids under 12 years of age.

Call your travel agent or Eastern 1-800-361-3020. In Toronto call 362-3461.

*Terms and Conditions: Prices effective until December 9th, 1985. Travel to Florida must originate Monday to Thursday. Seats limited and may not be available on every flight. Reservations must be made at least 14 days prior to departure and tickets must be purchased in advance. Rental cars available in Florida only. You pay gas. Optional collision damage waiver $6.95 (US) daily. Insurance not included. Prices based on double occupancy. They do not include meals, taxes or gratuities. There are cancellation penalties. Prices subject to availability and can change without notice.

Consumer Newspaper Over 600 Lines: Single

191
ART DIRECTOR
Carolyn Tye
WRITERS
Bill Westbrook
Kerry Feuerman
ARTIST
Carolyn Tye
CLIENT
Richmond Newspapers
AGENCY
Westbrook/Virginia

192
ART DIRECTOR
Cathi Mooney
WRITER
Ken Mandelbaum
DESIGNER
Cathi Mooney
PHOTOGRAPHER
Robert Ammirati
CLIENT
Federal Express
AGENCY
Ally & Gargano

Ever Heard Of A Parent Limiting The Time A Child Spends In Front Of A Newspaper?

When we found out that 67% of adults consider watching television mostly a waste of time compared to reading the newspaper, we weren't surprised. After all, parents have been limiting how much TV their kids watch for nearly three generations now.

Newspapers, on the other hand, are a whole different story.

The same Richmond area survey showed that over two-thirds of adults polled believe newspapers give you a lot of important information.

And they're right.

An average edition of the Richmond Times-Dispatch or News Leader contains hundreds of stories, ranging from international politics to local weather conditions.

You get science reports, gardening tips, medical advice, recipes. And when was the last time you cut a coupon out of your TV?

When you read the Richmond Times-Dispatch and The News Leader you are literally getting an encyclopedia of current events, 7 days a week, 365 days a year.

We tell you when the space shuttle is going up, when interest rates are going down and when arms negotiations are going nowhere fast.

It's news you can use. Financial reports, help wanted ads, financial advice, book reviews, movie reviews, editors' views.

It's entertainment. Comics, sports scores, crossword puzzles, even your horoscope.

In fact, there's only one thing you won't get with a newspaper that even a child eventually gets with television: bored.

Nothing Delivers Information Like The Richmond Newspapers.

191

IF MONEY WERE NO OBJECT WHICH WOULD YOU USE?

WELL IT ISN'T.

$10.75 **$11.00**

With Federal Express' Drop-Off discount, you can send an Overnight Letter℠ for only twenty-five cents more than Express Mail.®

To take advantage of the discount, you do something you're probably pretty good at already.

Walking.

Just walk your Overnight Letter to any of the 48 Federal Express Drop-Boxes or Service Centers in the Phoenix area.

Then, instead of having to stand for Express Mail's 3:00 PM delivery commitment, you'll get delivery by 10:30* in the morning, and the reliability of Federal Express.

Instead of having to settle for the limited number of locations that Express Mail delivers to overnight, you'll be able to send something to any of 121,000.

And, instead of having to wait up to a week for proof that what you sent actually got there, you'll get it the same day.

The discount is also good for Federal Express Courier-Paks,® Priority-One℠ packages, and Standard Air.℠ We'll even let you pay with any major credit card (as long as it's yours).

Before we announced Drop-Off discounts, it might have been worth putting up with Express Mail to save yourself some money.

But really, is it worth it now?

For more information, call Federal Express at 254-4662.

FEDERAL EXPRESS ANNOUNCES DROP-OFF DISCOUNTS

Consumer Newspaper Over 600 Lines: Campaign

193

ART DIRECTOR
Joe Pendergast

WRITER
James Parry

CLIENT
Reader's Digest

AGENCY
James Parry, Inc.

194

ART DIRECTORS
Jeff Roll
Yvonne Smith

WRITERS
Dave Butler
Mike Monteiro

PHOTOGRAPHERS
Lamb & Hall

CLIENT
Porsche Cars North America

AGENCY
Chiat/Day - Los Angeles

Presenting an ordinary day of drinking on America's highways. From the first death to the 55th.

Every day of every year, hundreds of thousands of Americans drink and then drive. So, every year, an estimated 23,500 Americans are killed in alcohol-related highway accidents. On average, that's 64 such deaths per day.

The September Reader's Digest reviews one day: January 21, 1984—a day picked at random, a day on which 55 people died this way, a perfectly ordinary, horrible day.

Drinking—And Dying—On America's Highways

By Joseph P. Blank

12:10 a.m. Colbert County, Ala. Nineteen-year-old Brian Posey, blood-alcohol content (bac) .14,* is speeding south on U.S. 43 in a Chevy Camaro. He tries to pass Harold Mann, 19, who, according to the police report, was also speeding and under the influence of alcohol. Posey sideswipes Mann's Ford, careens off the road and overturns. Posey and two passengers, Benny Michael Burleson, 20, and Barry Hill, 19, are killed, and a third passenger is injured.

Benny Burleson

12:40 a.m. near Kernville, Calif. Linda Kissack, 27, is killed when her car caroms off a tree and smashes into boulders. Her bac: .18. Twenty minutes later, near Santa Barbara, a car driven by Cynthia Espinoza, 19, bac .13, jumps a curb and flattens a 60-foot chain-link fence. Espinoza, a mother of two, is killed.

1:15 a.m. Poultney, Vt. Bruce Reynolds, 25, has been drinking at two bars. At around 12:30 a.m., a woman sees him leave the Ragtime Bar. He appears "loaded," but she makes no attempt to stop him or report his condition to authorities.

Reynolds's car rounds a bend, jumps an embankment and smashes into a tree. Reynolds, who is not wearing his seat belt, is ejected and killed. His bac: a sky-high .30.

* In most states, a driver is "under the influence" with a blood-alcohol content of .10 percent or higher.

1:15 a.m. Riverside County, Calif. Candi Lynn Easter, 20, is driving about 65 m.p.h. along an I-15 straightaway. Suddenly her car crosses two lanes, vaults an embankment and rolls over several times. Passenger Jacqueline Hachee, also 20, is thrown beneath the car. She dies three days later. Easter walks away from the accident. Her bac is .11. Although convicted of driving while under the influence, Easter is fined only $680 and put on three years' probation.

Jacqueline Hachee

1:30 a.m. Yuba City-Sutter area, Calif. Fifty-year-old Navis Lowery, intoxicated, is killed when her car overturns on Route 20. At the same time in Mt. Jackson, Va., Victor Barb, 44, bac .24, loses control of his pickup—which strikes a tree head-on, killing him. He leaves a wife, four children and two grandchildren.

1:40 a.m. Nanakuli, Hawaii. Navy man Thomas Fitzgerald, 20, is speeding when he hits and kills pedestrian Omaha Lutu, 30, bac .20. Fitzgerald, bac .16, is convicted of negligent homicide in the first degree and sentenced to five years' probation.

1:40 a.m. Hampton, Va. Glenn Sprouse, 37, has spent Friday night in Mitch's Pub shooting pool. Now, with a bac of .18, he is rushing to another bar with two friends in his pickup. At 80 m.p.h., Sprouse veers off the road and slams into a tree. The pickup's roof is torn open. Passenger Troy Bass, 23, soars through the opening and lands in some bushes. He survives. Driver Sprouse and passenger Ronald Kanaday, 22, are killed.

More than a year after the accident, Bass has trouble putting weight on his left leg. On doctor's orders, he has quit his job in a garden nursery. Nerve damage in his back prevents him from lifting heavy objects. "I'm just glad I'm alive," he says. "I haven't had a drink since the accident. I don't drive, and don't know if I'll drive again. No matter who I'm with, I'm still scared of the road."

According to his father, Kanaday was "a quiet kind of boy who loved to fish and shoot pool. He was my baby. I never saw him drink." He considered the long months since the tragedy and said, "Life hasn't been the same."

1:45 a.m. Goldsboro, N.C. Jeffrey Mark Lee, 22, is killed when he misses a curve, strikes a ditch bank and rolls his car over several times. Police estimate his speed at 85 m.p.h. and believe he had been drag racing. His bac: .14.

Lee's father was killed when Lee was just 18 months old—in a car accident involving alcohol.

Sometime after 2 a.m. outside Red Bluff, Calif. David Walker, 19, who has been drinking, is killed after his car plummets into a ravine.

2:29 a.m. Fresno, Calif. Linda Bogenreif, 23, is driving under the influence, bac .22. At an intersection, she collides with a car driven by Kelly Moen, 19, who has also been drinking. Bogenreif suffers head injuries; Moen is killed. Bogenreif is fined $673 and sentenced to three years' probation. Moen's family, stunned by the loss of their "sunshine-filled" daughter, moves to a new location.

Kelly Moen

2:30 a.m. Rush Township, Ohio. Richard Cade, 19, has been drinking. He is alone in a '74 Olds and driving at an unsafe speed. He drives off the road, strikes a mailbox, fence and culvert, continues across a yard and over a driveway, and finally hits a large tree. The car overturns and catches fire. Cade is burned beyond recognition.

A friend had cautioned Cade not to drink and drive, and had offered to put him up for the night. But Cade said he had to get home.

2:35 a.m. Burton, Mich. Frank Adams, 24, bac .21, dies when his car slams into a tractor-trailer.

2:45 a.m. near Hamlet, N.C. Royce Britt, 24, who has been drinking, is speeding and misses a curve. He is injured when his car rolls over; his passenger, Linda Norton, 23, dies two days later. Britt is sentenced to three years' probation, with 30 days and four weekends in jail.

3:10 a.m. Westminster, Texas. Juan Hernandez, 29, loses control of his car. He swerves onto the road's shoulder, tries to regain the road, veers into the opposite lane, piles into a truck. One passenger, Juan Balderas, 19, is ejected from the right-front seat onto the shoulder, and is killed. Witnesses tell police that Hernandez has been drinking. Hernandez flees the scene. He is still wanted by police for failure to stop and render aid.

3:44 a.m. Springdale, Ark. A car driven by Samuel Pianalto, 23 and intoxicated, collides with a pickup driven by Richard Edens, 35, also intoxicated. Edens is killed. Pianalto's car contains 13 beer cans and one in a thermal holder. An open can is also found in Edens's car.

And so it went. The September Reader's Digest recounts each alcohol-related highway death of January 21, 1984, up to and including the 55th and last...

11:54 p.m. near Ottumwa, Iowa. Brian McDaniel, 16, is driving his brother's Pontiac Firebird with passenger Jay Fite, 17. McDaniel, who has been issued his driver's license that very day, is driving fast. He passes four cars on the left in a no-passing zone and, swerving behind the fifth car, passes on the right shoulder. Re-entering the lane, he loses control and skids sideways across the highway. Steven Lord, 30, has no time to avoid the collision. He almost cuts the Firebird in half.

Jay Fite

McDaniel, Lord and Lord's passenger, Stephen Throckmorton, 32, die at the scene. (Throckmorton, a machine operator, leaves a wife and four children.) Fite, hospitalized with injuries, dies two days later. Both drivers had been drinking.

For January 21, 1984, the carnage is over. But six minutes later, another day will begin. And at 12:01 a.m. on January 22, 1984, in Visalia, Calif., Karen Wonacott, 18, will be killed when...

...and on and on, until Americans decide to stop it. How? Later this year, Reader's Digest will challenge students in nearly every high school in America to devise programs against drunk driving; to help motivate them, the Reader's Digest Foundation will give away $500,000 in college scholarships. And for a free copy of the new Reader's Digest booklet "Stop Drunk Driving Now!" call (914) 241-5372 or write Reprint Manager, Reader's Digest, Box 25, Pleasantville, NY 10570.

Reader's Digest

We make a difference in more than 50 million lives.

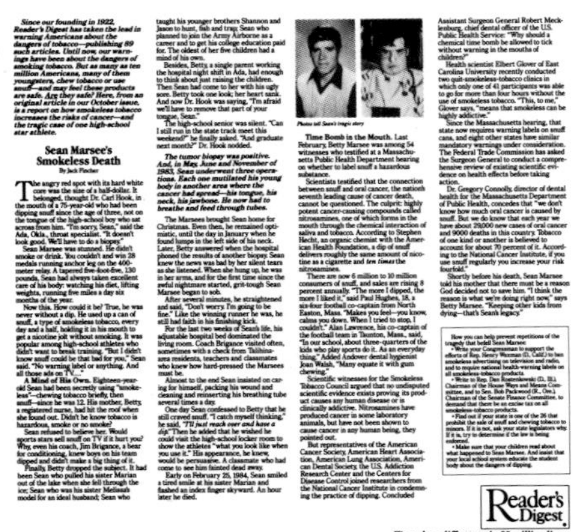

Why a car that needs no introduction needs an introduction.

Perhaps you've noticed this shape before. Maybe even chased it around a few corners. Or driven miles out of your way only to see it disappear over the horizon.

Had you been more persistent, your curiosity would have led you to the Porsche 928S, a car which, when first introduced in 1978, was hailed by critics the world over.

"The most powerful, most sophisticated, most luxurious grand touring car ever built," they said. "Bliss on wheels," they said. "Car of the year," they said.

"A good start," Professor Porsche said.

Not that he didn't agree with, or appreciate, the accolades. He just knew, as he did with other classic Porsches, that this was only the beginning. And that there was always room for improvement.

So once again, Porsche's engineers shut their office doors, opened their minds and headed where they've always headed in search of new ideas.

The race track.

There, under the race-worn shell of the Porsche 956 endurance racer, was technology so noteworthy it compels us to do again what we already did once seven years ago.

Introduce the Porsche 928S.

The technology in question — the remarkable four-valve head design which, when adapted to the 928S's liquid-cooled V8, would increase horsepower to 288 and top speed to 155 mph.

While, at the same time, improving both torque and fuel efficiency.

More simply stated, this technology takes the 928S four-valve one significant step closer to Professor Porsche's original dream.

A superbly appointed grand touring car that's as exciting, as efficient, as comfortable and as easy to drive in every day traffic as it is blazing down the autobahn.

Of course, when all is said and done, the only way to truly appreciate the difference between this car and absolutely anything else on the road is to see it, hear it, feel it, and above all, drive it. And the only place to do that is at your Porsche dealer. So stop in and get better acquainted with the new 928S four-valve.

Now that you've been formally introduced.

PORSCHE

No other luxury car comes with this interior.

You're looking at the new Porsche 928S.

Or, to be more precise, its front-mounted, fuel injected, 32 valve, twin-cam, liquid-cooled, aluminum alloy, V8 engine.

An engine whose basic design, since its introduction seven years ago, has been considered as close to perfection as anything ever mounted to the front, middle or rear end of a car. And one which, this year, comes even closer to that ideal.

The reason: a new four-valve head design borrowed from our 956 endurance racer.

The 956 represents a new school of thought in race car design. One which is more attuned to real world driving considerations (i.e. fuel consumption and aerodynamics) and, therefore, more useful in the development of real world road cars.

Like the Porsche 928S.

By adapting its already legendary V8 engine to the 956's four-valve technology, the 928S not only saw an increase in horsepower (234 to 288) and top speed (144 to 155), but an increase in fuel efficiency as well.

These are incredible figures for any sports car. But they become even more impressive after you drive the 928S and discover that it's also one of the most comfortable, most sophisticated cars ever built.

Of course, not everything about the Porsche 928S can be measured in miles-per-hour, miles-per-gallon or by the number of creature comforts.

Not heritage. Not pride. Not craftsmanship. And not the kind of spirit that possessed Professor Porsche to adopt such time consuming testing and manufacturing procedures that the production of this car is limited to fewer than 15 a day.

In short, what's most important about the Porsche 928S four-valve — or any Porsche — is what's most difficult to measure: thirty-seven years of strict adherence to a philosophy which holds that building fast cars cannot be accomplished by building cars fast.

PORSCHE

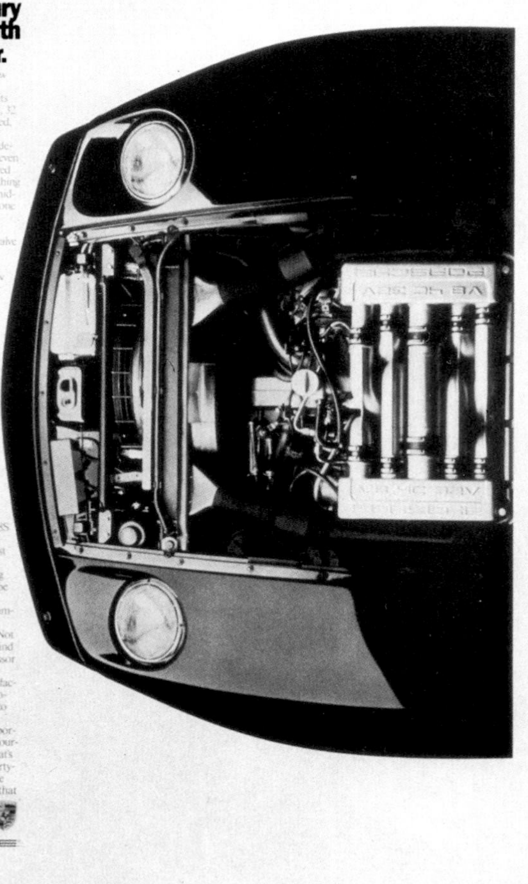

It was easier to turn a Porsche into a luxury car than vice versa.

Ever since the first 356 rolled off the assembly line and into automotive history, enthusiasts have associated the name Porsche with one thing.

Performance.

So it's no wonder that, when words like comfortable and luxurious started showing up next to our 928S, more than one eyebrow was raised.

Was this sacrilege? Had Porsche finally given in? Had they gotten soft?

The answer was, as always, an emphatic no.

Because the 928S was, in fact, exactly what Professor Porsche meant it to be: a grand touring car which would offer superb appointments and unparalleled comfort. Yet still deliver all the exhilarating performance you'd expect of any car which bears the Porsche marque.

This year, the 928S is better than ever. Faster, quieter, smoother and more efficient.

Thanks, in large part, to a new four-valve head design which, when adapted to an already legendary V8 engine, not only

increased both horsepower (234 to 288) and top speed (144 to 155), but fuel economy as well.

Facts which, while certainly impressive, tell only part of the 928S story.

If you'd like to experience the rest, stop by your Porsche dealer and drive the new 928S four-valve.

You'll soon learn that this Porsche, like those that came before, wasn't created to support accepted notions of what a car should be, but to create new ones.

You'll also understand why it's easier to convert owners of other cars into Porsche enthusiasts than vice versa.

PORSCHE

Consumer Newspaper Over 600 Lines: Campaign

195
ART DIRECTOR
Tod Seisser
WRITER
Stephanie Arnold
DESIGNER
Tod Seisser
PHOTOGRAPHERS
Greg Gorman
Francesco Scavullo
Jean Pagliuso
CLIENT
McCall's
AGENCY
Levine Huntley Schmidt & Beaver

196
ART DIRECTORS
Tod Seisser
Irv Klein
WRITERS
Jay Taub
Stephanie Arnold
DESIGNERS
Tod Seisser
Irv Klein
ARTIST
Robert Grossman
CLIENT
New York Air
AGENCY
Levine Huntley Schmidt & Beaver

195

49 TIMES A DAY, WE RUN POLITICIANS OUT OF WASHINGTON.

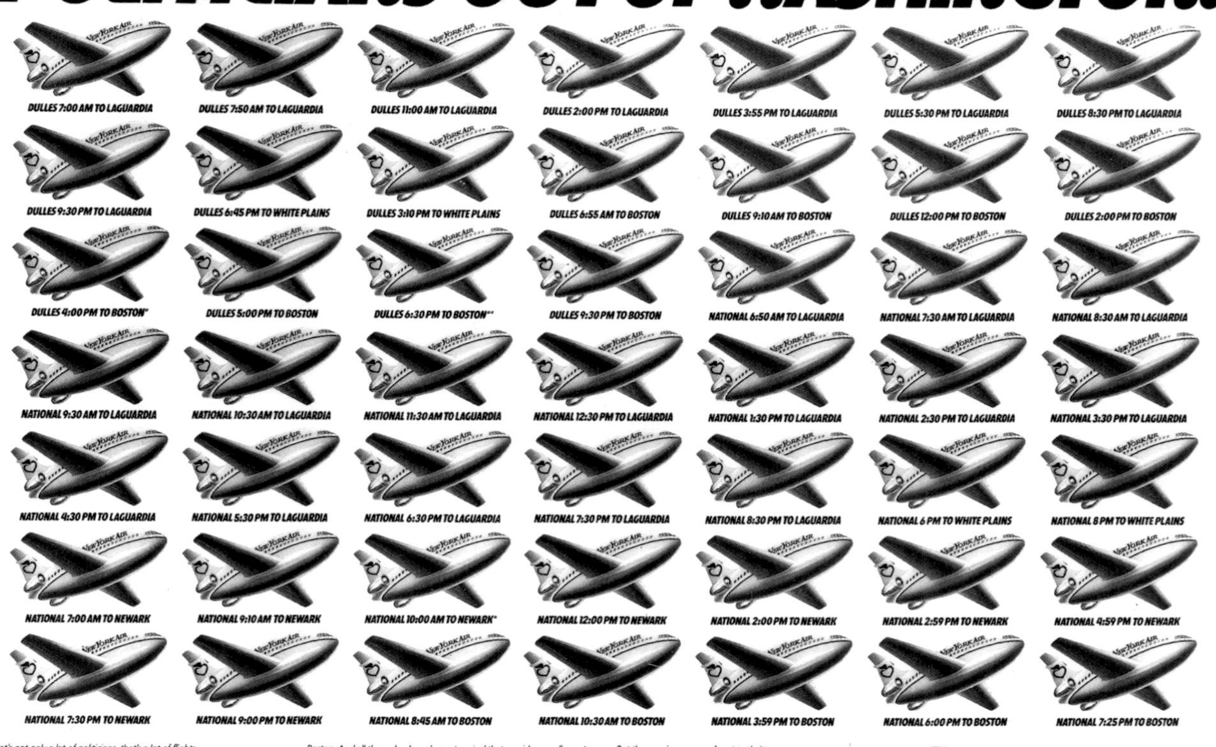

That's not only a lot of politicians, that's a lot of flights.

Because in addition to our 31 flights every weekday from National, we now offer 18 flights every weekday from Dulles. Ten to New York. Eight to Boston. And all through a brand-new terminal that provides a walkway to the plane. Not a crowded bus.

Of course, running politicians out of town isn't always an easy job. But then again, someone's got to do it.

For further information, call your travel agent or New York Air at 202-588-2300 or 800-221-9300.

NEW YORK AIR

Schedules subject to change without notice. *Effective October 2. **Except Fridays.

STOP BY THE HOUSE ANYTIME.

NEW YORK TO WASHINGTON

LA GUARDIA	7:30 AM	TO NATIONAL	WHITE PLAINS	7:30 PM	TO DULLES
LA GUARDIA	8:30 AM	TO NATIONAL	NEWARK	7:00 AM	TO NATIONAL
LA GUARDIA	9:30 AM	TO NATIONAL	NEWARK	8:00 AM	TO NATIONAL
LA GUARDIA	10:30 AM	TO NATIONAL	NEWARK	9:00 AM	TO NATIONAL
LA GUARDIA	11:30 AM	TO NATIONAL	NEWARK	12:00 PM	TO NATIONAL
LA GUARDIA	12:30 PM	TO NATIONAL	NEWARK	2:00 PM	TO NATIONAL
LA GUARDIA	1:30 PM	TO NATIONAL	NEWARK	4:00 PM	TO NATIONAL
LA GUARDIA	2:30 PM	TO NATIONAL	NEWARK	6:00 PM	TO NATIONAL
LA GUARDIA	3:30 PM	TO NATIONAL	NEWARK	7:00 PM	TO NATIONAL
LA GUARDIA	4:30 PM	TO NATIONAL	LA GUARDIA	6:59 AM	TO DULLES
LA GUARDIA	5:30 PM	TO NATIONAL	LA GUARDIA	8:00 AM	TO DULLES
LA GUARDIA	6:30 PM	TO NATIONAL	LA GUARDIA	9:15 AM	TO DULLES
LA GUARDIA	7:30 PM	TO NATIONAL	LA GUARDIA	10:30 AM	TO DULLES
LA GUARDIA	8:30 PM	TO NATIONAL	LA GUARDIA	2:30 PM	TO DULLES
LA GUARDIA	10:00 PM	TO NATIONAL	LA GUARDIA	4:59 PM	TO DULLES
WHITE PLAINS	7:20 AM	TO NATIONAL	LA GUARDIA	7:25 PM	TO DULLES
WHITE PLAINS	4:59 PM	TO NATIONAL	LA GUARDIA	9:00 PM	TO DULLES
WHITE PLAINS	8:00 AM	TO DULLES			

WASHINGTON TO NEW YORK

NATIONAL	6:50 AM	TO LA GUARDIA	DULLES	3:10 PM	TO WHITE PLAINS
NATIONAL	7:30 AM	TO LA GUARDIA	NATIONAL	7:00 AM	TO NEWARK
NATIONAL	8:30 AM	TO LA GUARDIA	NATIONAL	9:10 AM	TO NEWARK
NATIONAL	9:30 AM	TO LA GUARDIA	NATIONAL	10:00 AM	TO NEWARK
NATIONAL	10:30 AM	TO LA GUARDIA	NATIONAL	12:00 PM	TO NEWARK
NATIONAL	11:30 AM	TO LA GUARDIA	NATIONAL	2:00 PM	TO NEWARK
NATIONAL	12:30 PM	TO LA GUARDIA	NATIONAL	2:59 PM	TO NEWARK
NATIONAL	1:30 PM	TO LA GUARDIA	NATIONAL	4:40 PM	TO NEWARK
NATIONAL	2:30 PM	TO LA GUARDIA	NATIONAL	7:30 PM	TO NEWARK
NATIONAL	3:30 PM	TO LA GUARDIA	NATIONAL	9:00 PM	TO NEWARK
NATIONAL	4:30 PM	TO LA GUARDIA	DULLES	7:00 AM	TO LA GUARDIA
NATIONAL	5:30 PM	TO LA GUARDIA	DULLES	7:50 AM	TO LA GUARDIA
NATIONAL	6:30 PM	TO LA GUARDIA	DULLES	11:00 AM	TO LA GUARDIA
NATIONAL	7:30 PM	TO LA GUARDIA	DULLES	2:00 PM	TO LA GUARDIA
NATIONAL	8:30 PM	TO LA GUARDIA	DULLES	3:55 PM	TO LA GUARDIA
NATIONAL	6:00 PM	TO WHITE PLAINS	DULLES	5:45 PM	TO LA GUARDIA
NATIONAL	8:00 PM	TO WHITE PLAINS	DULLES	7:30 PM	TO LA GUARDIA
DULLES	6:45 AM	TO WHITE PLAINS	DULLES	9:30 PM	TO LA GUARDIA

The best way to visit the seat of your government is by booking a seat on New York Air. So call your travel agent. Or New York Air at 718-565-1100 or 800-221-9300. And don't be a stranger. Come see the family once in a while.

NEW YORK AIR

THE BEST ECONOMIC NEWS TO COME OUT OF WASHINGTON IN YEARS.

FROM WASHINGTON (DULLES) TO:	
TAMPA/ST. PETE	$69
JACKSONVILLE	$69
ORLANDO	$89
FT. LAUDERDALE	$89
NEW ORLEANS	$89

There's a new economic trend coming out of Washington. And it's coming out of our airline. New York Air. For we can now fly you from Washington to Florida or New Orleans at prices that sound more like campaign promises than actual airfares. And with the kind of service that makes our competition look like it's standing still.

Now we're not saying there aren't any restrictions. Because with some of our fares there are. Just call your travel agent or New York Air (202-588-2300 or 800-221-9300) and see how they apply.

You see, anyone in Washington who'd like to cut costs can start by cutting the cost of flying.

NEW YORK AIR

Consumer Newspaper Over 600 Lines: Campaign

197
ART DIRECTOR
Carolyn Tye
WRITERS
Bill Westbrook
Kerry Feuerman
Robin Konieczny
ARTIST
Carolyn Tye
CLIENT
Richmond Newspapers
AGENCY
Westbrook/Virginia

Consumer Newspaper 600 Lines Or Less: Single

198
ART DIRECTORS
Kevin Kearns
Amy Watt
WRITER
Edward Boches
PHOTOGRAPHER
Frank Rapp
CLIENT
Greater Media Cable Company
AGENCY
Mullen Advertising & Public Relations/Prides Crossing, MA

199
ART DIRECTOR
Brent Ladd
WRITER
Shelly Rubin
CLIENT
Decker Foods
AGENCY
Bozell Jacobs Kenyon & Eckhardt

If The 6 O'clock News Reported Everything We Report, It Would Last Until The 11 O'clock News.

To give you all the news the newspaper does, television news programs would have to last 5 hours. Or their newscasters would have to talk very, very fast.

Each Richmond newspaper fills page after page with stories that report hundreds of newsworthy events: from secretive space shots in Russia to the frightening gun shots in El Salvador, from bold New York fashions to old-fashioned recipes from Europe.

Both The Richmond News Leader and Times-Dispatch give you an encyclopedia of news. Yet it's not just more stories, it's more of each story. It's reporting that takes you behind the scenes at the General Assembly, through the scenes of a new Broadway play or throughout the scene of the crime.

You'll get writing that is clear, concise and accurate. The kind of reporting that only happens when journalists are more interested in informing than entertaining.

And you'll get more than news, you'll also get views. There are columnists like Art Buchwald, William F. Buckley, Bob Greene and Miss Manners. There are previews of local sales, reviews of movies, theaters and books.

And best of all, with the newspaper you can always get as much or as little news and information as you want, whenever you want. Not when television wants.

So pick up a Times-Dispatch and a News Leader. They're everything TV news should be. And much, much more.

Nothing Delivers News Like The Richmond Newspapers.

Ever Heard Of A Parent Limiting The Time A Child Spends In Front Of A Newspaper?

Nothing Delivers Information Like The Richmond Newspapers.

When Was The Last Time A Newspaper Underestimated Your Intelligence?

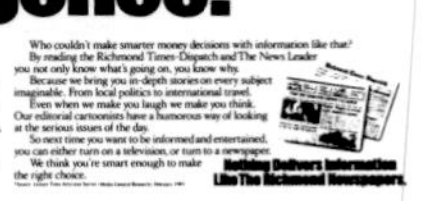

Nothing Delivers Information Like The Richmond Newspapers.

The only rabbit population that's declining.

To tune into major movies, top comedy, superstar concerts, and up-to-the-minute news, sports and weather, more and more people are subscribing to Greater Media Cable.

We guarantee great reception, quality programming and a variety of entertainment choices to fit any family or lifestyle. Our introductory offer includes free installation, a 15-day money-back guarantee and a monthly rate that's about equal to the price of two movie tickets.

We also have an extensive choice of premium networks. Including HBO, Cinemax, Showtime and The Movie Channel.

Call us today. And find out why Greater Media Cable subscribers are multiplying faster than you know what.

Greater Media Cable

198

LOW.

AND BEHOLD.

Now you can bring home our bacon and leave the salt behind. That's right. All the flavor of Decker Bacon, with a third less salt. What's more, you can take it home for even less. So save on our new Lower Salt Bacon. And behold our old great taste.

199

Consumer Newspaper 600 Lines Or Less: Single

200
ART DIRECTOR
Daniel Varon
WRITER
Dalton O'Sullivan
PHOTOGRAPHER
Weststock
CLIENT
Chevron
AGENCY
J. Walter Thompson/San Francisco

201
ART DIRECTOR
Mark Crim
WRITERS
Jim Ferguson
Mark Crim
DESIGNER
Mark Crim
CLIENT
Cantina Laredo Restaurant
AGENCY
Keller Crescent Company/Irvine, TX

202
ART DIRECTOR
Dabni Harvey
WRITERS
Linda Bugaj Young
Dabni Harvey
CLIENT
Sizzler
AGENCY
BBDO/Los Angeles

203
ART DIRECTOR
Ron Sandilands
WRITER
Bernie Hafeli
DESIGNER
Carol Pica
CLIENT
Pacific Northwest Bell
AGENCY
Livingston & Company/Seattle

The Animals of the Santa Barbara Zoo would love to have you for lunch.

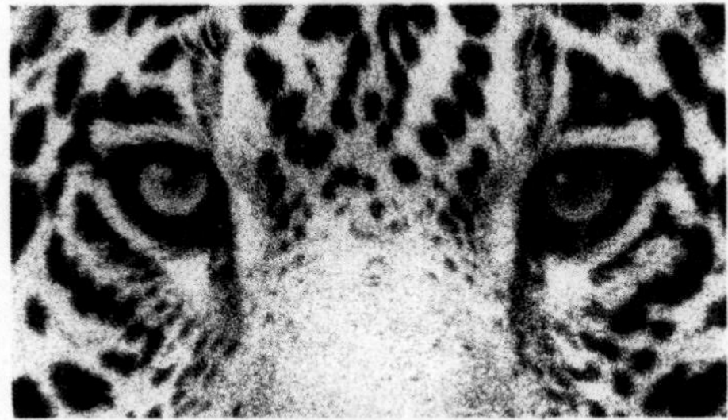

ZOO-B-QUE. Sunday, September 29 between noon and 4 P.M.

All the animals are hosting a mouth-watering barbecue, plus live music, dancers, puppet shows, and more — all for just six dollars per person, including zoo admission. So come enjoy the ways of the jungle. Both you and the animals will eat it up.

SANTA BARBARA ZOO

This Update brought to you by the people of Chevron.

200

THE LAST TIME SOMETHING THIS ENJOYABLE CAME FROM MEXICO IT WAS CONFISCATED BY THE POLICE.

Not even the Border Patrol could stop Cantina Laredo from bringing the great taste of Comida Casera across the Rio Grande to North Dallas.

But why would they? Afterall, Comida Casera is simply authentic, home-style Mexican cooking. And in Dallas, you can find it at Cantina Laredo. You'll discover dishes like tortilla soup, Tacos Al Pastor, Pollo a la Parilla, beef and chicken fajitas, and two kinds of cabrito (barbecued and baked). It's all this, plus more, that makes Cantina Laredo the most unique Mexican restaurant in Dallas.

Even our bar has a South of the Border flare with features like ten varieties of Mexican beer, eight brands of tequila, and the famous "El Patron" Margarita.

Come by Cantina Laredo today and taste homestyle Mexican cooking at its finest. It's so good, it should be illegal. But it's not.

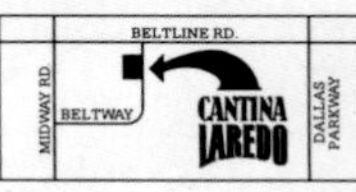

201

WE'VE CUT MILITARY SPENDING BY TEN PERCENT.

Now you can save 10% off lunch and dinner with Sizzler's military discount. It's good for any regular-priced item on our menu.

Choose from many different cuts of steak broiled to your order, delicious fresh fish, golden fried shrimp—even lobster. Plus our endless All-You-Can-Eat Fresh Fruit & Salad Bar.

So drop into Sizzler today. We're cutting prices so you can keep to your budget.

202

Yap, yap, yap, yap, yup, yup, nope, yup, nope, yup, nope, yup, yap, yap, yap.

Whether you agree or disagree, you'll find the conversation stimulating on Gabline. Up to 10 callers. 10 cents a minute. (Entire call only 5 cents a minute if over 15 minutes.)
3 PM—3 AM daily. 1-499-TALK.

203

Consumer Newspaper 600 Lines Or Less: Single

204
ART DIRECTOR
Terry Schneider
WRITER
Greg Eiden
PHOTOGRAPHER
Jim Piper
CLIENT
Red Lion Inns
AGENCY
Borders Perrin & Norrander/
Portland, OR

205
ART DIRECTOR
Bill Oakley
WRITER
Tim Kidwell
CLIENT
Dance St. Louis
AGENCY
D'Arcy Masius Benton &
Bowles/St. Louis

206
ART DIRECTOR
Sharon L. Occhipinti
WRITER
Dan Brooks
PHOTOGRAPHER
Irene Stern
CLIENT
GTE
AGENCY
Doyle Dane Bernbach

207
ART DIRECTOR
Sharon L. Occhipinti
WRITER
Larry Chase
DESIGNER
Sharon L. Occhipinti
CLIENT
GTE
AGENCY
Doyle Dane Bernbach

Repay the man you ate out of house and home.

Go ahead, pick it up. Treat your dad to brunch or dinner at any of our restaurants.

After all, June 16th is Father's Day. And he has been responsible for one or two of your meals.

Happy Father's Day

RED LION INNS
& THUNDERBIRD MOTOR INNS

204

AMAZING FEETS.

We bring the exciting world of dance to St. Louis.
For tickets - or other information on our '85-'86 season-call 968-3770.
Or stop by any Ticketmaster outlet.

205

If it breaks, it's ours.

Why buy? When you rent one of our phones and something goes wrong, we'll repair or replace it.

206

The angel behind the production of
Royal Shakespeare Company "Much Ado About Nothing."
Kennedy Center, January 25 through February 7

207

Consumer Newspaper 600 Lines Or Less: Single

208
ART DIRECTOR
Paul Schupanitz
WRITER
Tami Silesky
ARTIST
Warren Hansen
CLIENT
Chi-Chi's Consul Restaurant Corp.
AGENCY
Campbell-Mithun/Minneapolis

209
ART DIRECTOR
Randall Saitta
WRITER
Howard Gershen
CLIENT
Sony
AGENCY
Lowe Marschalk

210
ART DIRECTOR
Jeff Vogt
WRITER
Rich Pels
DESIGNER
Jeff Vogt
PHOTOGRAPHER
Jeffrey Zwart
ARTIST
R & V Studio
CLIENT
BMW of North America
AGENCY
Ammirati & Puris

211
ART DIRECTOR
Jim Mochnsky
WRITER
Peter Hinds
PHOTOGRAPHER
Dennis Johnson
CLIENT
Fairfax Hospital Association
AGENCY
Abramson Associates/ Washington DC

212
ART DIRECTOR
Jim Mochnsky
WRITER
Terry Coveny
PHOTOGRAPHER
Skip Brown
CLIENT
Fairfax Hospital Association
AGENCY
Abramson Associates/ Washington DC

If you don't get your lunch in 7 minutes, we'll do more than express our apologies.

At Chi-Chi's, we'll owe you more than an apology if you have to wait for your lunch.

Come in and try something from our Express Lunch menu. It'll take 7 minutes from the time you order until the time your lunch is served. If we make you wait longer, your next Express Lunch is free.

Express Lunch. 11-1:30 Weekdays.

© Consul Restaurant Corp

208

GET YOUR HEADS EXAMINED.

Or your belts.

Or your timer. Or several other sensitive areas in your Sony Betamax® VCR.

Just visit the free Sony Beta Clinic in your area and we'll conduct a special performance check of your recorder. It's an exclusive service for Sony Betamax customers, to show Sony's concern doesn't end when you take your VCR home and plug it in.

And while we're examining your machine, you can test our people. Ask us any questions you might have about Beta or the new Sony SuperBeta.™ How do I connect one to my cable system? Why is Beta's picture sharper than VHS? Why is SuperBeta 20% sharper than Beta? What are their special features, and how do I use them properly? We're here to make sure you get the most out of your Sony VCRs.

So join us at the free Sony Beta Clinic and get your heads examined.

You'd be crazy not to.

SONY®
BETA CLINIC

Offer good at participating dealers only.
©1985 Sony Corporation of America. Sony and Betamax are registered trademarks and SuperBeta is a trademark of Sony Corporation.

209

EVERY SUMMER, CAR DEALERS LOWER THEIR PRICES AND INVITE YOU TO DO THE SAME TO YOUR STANDARDS.
Now's the time of year most automobile dealers routinely display enthusiasm for cars whose main virtue is that they're "priced to move." If you can't share their enthusiasm, visit your BMW dealer. There you'll find cars that are engineered to move, as well.
Not that various other cars can't be coaxed to display reasonable speed and acceleration on long, dull interstates. But simply, BMW's are designed for a greater destiny.
To straighten serpentine mountain roads. An achievement that's made possible by such advances as a fully-independent suspension with components meriting numerous international patents.
As well as an engine whose parts are machined to tolerances of less than 4/100,000ths of an inch to power you effortlessly from 0 to 60. And a revolutionary anti-lock braking system engineered to bring you back to earth safe and sound.
Even so, BMW allows you to maintain exceptionally high standards at a cost made exceptionally reasonable by BMW's financing program—9.5% annual percentage rate for all 6- and 7-series BMW's purchased (or higher guaranteed leasing residuals).*
So if you still feel oddly compelled by the "unbelievable but true" offers most car dealers resort to, perhaps you should test-drive a BMW. It's a truly poignant reminder that high-pressure salesmanship is no substitute for high-performance engineering.
BMW
THE ULTIMATE DRIVING MACHINE.

*Through September 30, 1985. See your participating dealer for details. ©1985 BMW of North America, Inc. The BMW trademark and logo are registered.

LET YOUR LOCAL BMW DEALERS ARRANGE A THOROUGH TEST DRIVE.

City	City	City	City	City	City
DEALER NAME	**DEALER NAME**	**DEALER NAME**	**DEALER NAME**	**DEALER NAME**	**DEALER NAME**
Dealer Address	Dealer Address	Dealer Address	Dealer Address	Dealer Address	Dealer Address
Phone Number	Phone Number	Phone Number	Phone Number	Phone Number	Phone Number

210

You shouldn't have to choose a doctor the same way you choose a plumber.

What's the best way to find the family physician or specialist you need? Just call the Doctor's Appointment Desk.

We'll help you choose a physician in your area who is affiliated with The Fairfax Hospital. And we'll even make your first appointment, with the assurance that you'll be seen within 72 hours.

The Fairfax Hospital's Doctor's Appointment Desk

A DIVISION OF FAIRFAX HOSPITAL ASSOCIATION

698-3762

211

No rush hour traffic can stop our ambulance.

You're looking at ARIES (Air Rescue Intensive Emergency Service). One of two new emergency medical helicopters operated in association with Fairfax Hospital, Northern Virginia's only Level I Trauma Center.

Think of it. A person who has suffered traumatic injury has just minutes to get medical treatment. After that, their chances of survival get progressively worse.

ARIES increases those chances by flying over traffic at 120-150 MPH, delivering a team that's equipped to offer the advanced life support measures required and rushing the patient to our Trauma Center or other advanced care facility.

At Fairfax Hospital, caring goes beyond mere words. It's making that extra commitment. A commitment not only to the best people, but to the latest technology.

A commitment that can be the difference between life and death.

The Fairfax Hospital

A DIVISION OF FAIRFAX HOSPITAL ASSOCIATION

212

Consumer Newspaper 600 Lines Or Less: Single

213
ART DIRECTOR
Michael Winslow
WRITER
Barrett Rossie
CLIENT
Piedmont Airlines
AGENCY
McKinney Silver & Rockett/ North Carolina

214
ART DIRECTOR
Michael Fazende
WRITER
Phil Hanft
PHOTOGRAPHER
Craig Perman
CLIENT
Country Cottage
AGENCY
Fallon McElligott/Minneapolis

215
ART DIRECTOR
Tom Lichtenheld
WRITER
Jarl Olsen
DESIGNER
Tom Lichtenheld
CLIENT
WFLD-TV
AGENCY
Fallon McElligott/Minneapolis

Un-Fare.

It's tough to beat Piedmont's low fares to any of the cities listed below. Or, in fact, to any city we serve.

But, what really makes things unfare is that you can fly for these low prices, and still receive the kind of service that other airlines look up to.

In fact, a recent independent survey appearing in *USA Today* reports that frequent travelers rate Piedmont's service the best in America.

So, next time ask your travel agent to book Piedmont. Or call toll-free, 1-800-251-5720.

City	Fare	
BALTIMORE	$54.00	WE30
BOSTON	$66.50	WE30
BUFFALO	$59.00	BE70
CHARLOTTE	$66.50	WE30
CHICAGO	$89.00	WE30
CINCINNATI	$49.00	BE70
DALLAS/FT. WORTH	$99.00	WE30
DAYTONA BEACH	$99.00	WE30
DENVER	$109.00	WE30
FT. LAUDERDALE	$99.00	WE30
JACKSONVILLE, FL	$99.00	WE30
LOUISVILLE	$59.00	BE70
MIAMI	$109.00	WE30
NAPLES	$119.00	WE30
NEW YORK (LGA)	$59.00	HN
NEWARK	$49.00	HN
ORLANDO	$99.00	WE30
PHILADELPHIA	$54.00	WE30
TAMPA	$99.00	WE30

PIEDMONT

Fares shown may require up to a 30-day advance purchase and are half of the required round-trip purchase where applicable. Minimum/maximum stay, ticket time limit, seat limitation, time of day and/or day of week restrictions, and/or other restrictions may apply. Voluntary refund service charge penalty, cancellation penalty, or itinerary change penalty may apply. Fares may change or expire without notice. Fares shown may not be available on Mar. 21 – 23, Mar. 26 – 31, and Apr. 1 – 2. Fuel surcharge $2.50 per person from Boston. Fuel surcharge $1.00 per person from all Florida cities.

The stuff in our store is made by the most technologically imperfect methods known to man.

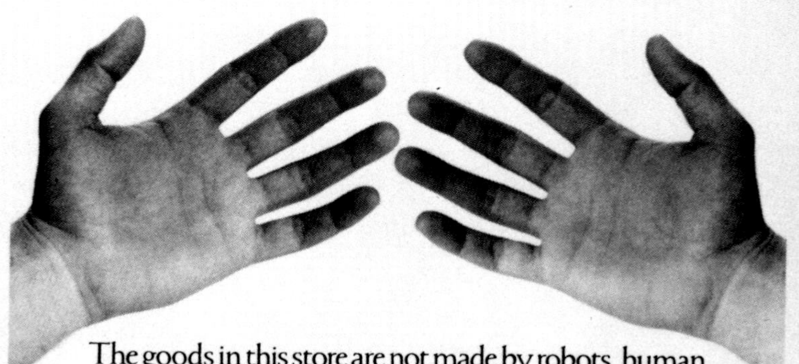

The goods in this store are not made by robots, human or otherwise. But carefully crafted by people who still believe in the beauty and character of things made by hand.

Country Cottage
of Wayzata Ltd.
326 S. Broadway, Wayzata, MN 55391 612-473-0259

214

THERE MAY BE EVEN MORE SHOOTING THAN NORMAL IN NEW YORK CITY TONIGHT.

The Chicago Bulls vs. The New York Knicks
Saturday, November 9 at 6:30 p.m.

215

Consumer Newspaper 600 Lines Or Less: Single

216
ART DIRECTOR
Steve Beaumont
WRITER
David Lubars
ARTIST
Cynthia Shern
PHOTOGRAPHER
Bob Randall
CLIENT
Apple Computer
AGENCY
Chiat/Day - Los Angeles

217
ART DIRECTOR
Tony Diamond
WRITER
Mike Renfro
DESIGNER
Tony Diamond
CLIENT
MBank
AGENCY
The Richards Group/Dallas

218
ART DIRECTOR
John McCafferty
WRITER
Larry Magnes
DESIGNER
John McCafferty
CLIENT
Intecon
AGENCY
Apple Advertising/Louisville, KY

Use it to alter your grades.

You just got a C+ in *Post-War Foreign Policy*. You just got a B— in *Communications Law*. You just got an F+ in *Advanced Physics*.

An F+? Boy, you could use some help.

From a Macintosh™ personal computer.

A Macintosh can help you with your homework. Help you with your term papers. Help you with your research projects. And help you organize your study time and think more clearly.

And at last count, Macintosh could run hundreds of software programs to help you with everything from linguistics to law. Physics to philosophy. Medicine to Medieval history.

The point being, when you bring a Macintosh home with you, there's a good chance you'll be bringing home something else. Better grades.

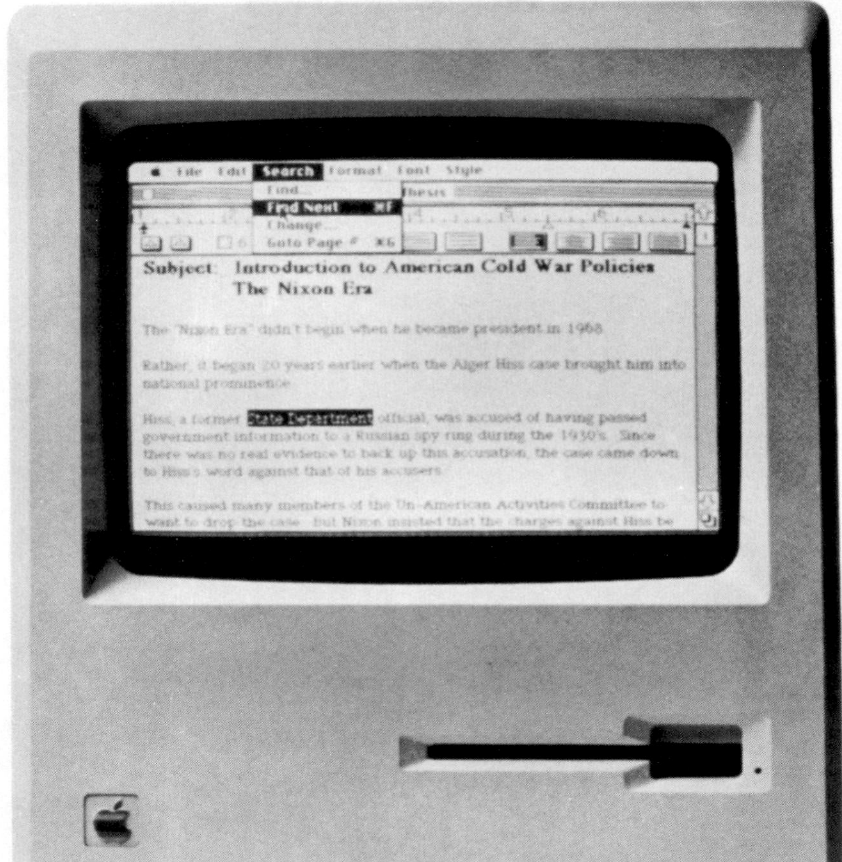

If it fits in this box, it'll fit in an MBank safe deposit box.

And even if it doesn't fit, chances are we've got a safe deposit box for you. There's no wait. Just call us. We'll be glad to show you something in your size.

MBank Port Arthur
A Momentum Bank

Memorial Freeway and Turtle Creek P.O. Box 1000 Port Arthur, TX 77641-1000 (409) 727-0123
Member MCorp, [illegible] and FDIC

217

Most offices are designed like this ad.

They waste space.

Some put too little in too much space. Some put too much in too little space. Most offices aren't planned at all; they just happen.

That's why there's Intecon.

We know what makes an office work. Our design staff has a step-by-step system to maximize your office floor space. To find out more, call 502/589-5522.

Louisville's exclusive Steelcase dealer.

INTECON

Interior concepts at work.

218

Consumer Newspaper 600 Lines Or Less: Single

219
ART DIRECTOR
Craig Pollock
WRITER
Robert McPherson
DESIGNER
Craig Pollock
PHOTOGRAPHER
Robert Ammirati
CLIENT
Barron's
AGENCY
Angotti Thomas Hedge

220
ART DIRECTOR
Bob Barrie
WRITER
Mike Lescarbeau
DESIGNER
Bob Barrie
CLIENT
Mountain Chiropractic
AGENCY
Fallon McElligott/Minneapolis

221
ART DIRECTOR
John Morrison
WRITER
David Lubars
PHOTOGRAPHERS
Lamb & Hall
CLIENT
Apple Computer
AGENCY
Chiat/Day - Los Angeles

Proof that money works harder given proper supervision.

Read Barron's and you'll see fresh evidence every week.

In dozens of pages of earnings updates and advance/decline statistics, in-depth business and investment reporting and incisive market analyses.

Precisely the sort of information you need to manage, guide and otherwise coax your portfolio into superior performance.

Pick up a copy at a newsstand this weekend.

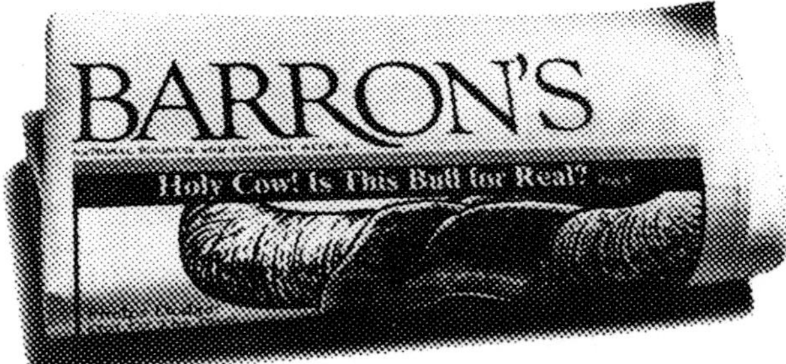

HOW THE SMART MONEY GETS THAT WAY.

219

Chronic back pain can be a sign of serious health problems anywhere in the body. Come to Mountain Chiropractic for a complete examination. We'll break our backs to fix yours.

Mountain Chiropractic

104 N. Ash, Cortez, CO 565-7817 (T, Th); 3211 Main Ave., Durango, CO 259-6540 (M, W, F)

How to break into the library.

It's the middle of the night. You're working on your paper, "Identifying Kafkaesque Symbolism In The Film, 'Porky's II: The Next Day.'" You have no idea who Kafka is. You need information. Your library is closed. You'll get an F. You are depressed.

Don't be.

Because with a Macintosh™ and an Apple® Modem, you can access databanks and receive information worldwide. Not to mention scour the Library of Congress at 3 am.

Which just goes to show, Macintosh helps students work smarter, quicker and more creatively. And the beauty of Macintosh is, you don't have to know diddley about computers to use one.

So get a Macintosh. And head straight for the library.

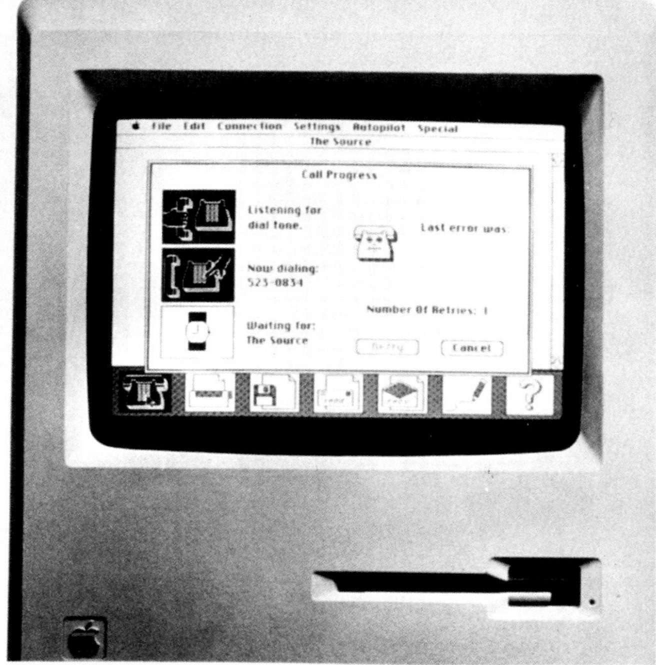

Consumer Newspaper 600 Lines Or Less: Single

222
ART DIRECTOR
Tony Diamond
WRITER
Mike Renfro
DESIGNER
Tony Diamond
CLIENT
MBank
AGENCY
The Richards Group/Dallas

223
ART DIRECTOR
John Morrison
WRITER
David Lubars
ARTIST
Cynthia Shern
PHOTOGRAPHERS
Lamb & Hall
CLIENT
Apple Computer
AGENCY
Chiat/Day - Los Angeles

224
ART DIRECTOR
Annette Osterlund
WRITER
Jamie Shevell
DESIGNER
Annette Osterlund
PHOTOGRAPHER
Rick Cohn
CLIENT
Western Union
AGENCY
Scali McCabe Sloves

Listed above are all the other banks you'll find open on Saturdays.

Only one bank in the Mid-County area is open on Saturdays, MBank. Our drive-in is open every Saturday from nine to noon. Weekdays from 6:30 a.m. to 7 p.m. So if your bank's hours don't fit your hours, call the bank with momentum. We keep going even when the week ends.

MBank Port Arthur
A Momentum Bank

Memorial Freeway and Turtle Creek P.O. Box 1000 Port Arthur, TX 77641-1000 (409) 727-0123
Member MCorp, MPACT and FDIC.

222

Bring order to the Middle East.

If your term paper on The Middle East Crisis is suffering its own border skirmishes, we recommend a Macintosh™

With programs like Think Tank,™ you can build exhaustively detailed outlines that prevent the rewriting and retyping that can turn a six day war into a three month project.

Another example of how Macintosh helps students work smarter, quicker and more creatively.

And the beauty of Macintosh is, you don't have to know diddley about computers to use one. If only Kissinger had it this easy.

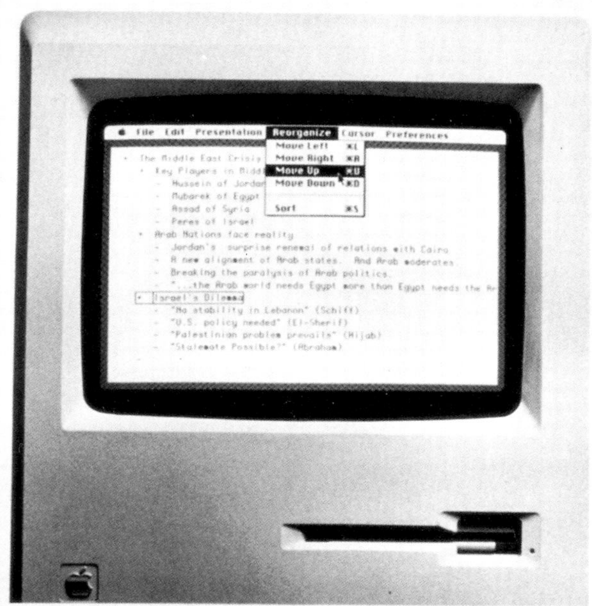

223

GET TWO PARENTS FOR THE PRICE OF ONE.

This Mother's and Father's Day, send both your parents a hand-delivered Western Union Telegram and Western Union will send you something. A check for $17.70—the price of one Telegram.*

You'll be giving your parents something no one else can get—your own special message. Not a card that thousands of other parents will receive.

And not only will it be opened before other letters, it'll be kept longer, too.

So call Western Union at 1-800-325-6000 and send your parents telegrams. You'll be giving them something that will last a lifetime.

WESTERN UNION

You don't just read a telegram. You feel it.

*The price of one ten words or less, physically delivered Telegram.

TWO FOR ONE REBATE CERTIFICATE

To receive a $17.70 refund on one of two Western Union Mother's—Father's Day Telegrams, use this certificate and mail in actual receipts or copies of the Western Union bills, telephone bills, or credit card charges covering both transactions. Telegrams must be sent between May 6 and May 14, 1985, and between June 6 and June 18, 1985.

Mail to: "Two for One"
RP-Two Railroad Place
Westport, CT 06880

Name ______________
(PLEASE PRINT)

Address ______________

City ______________

State ________ Zip ________

Offer expires 8/15/85. One refund per customer. Refund rights cannot be assigned. Void where prohibited by law. Allow 6-8 weeks for refund. Applies only to telegrams sent via telephone, tie-line or over-the-counter.

224

Consumer Newspaper 600 Lines Or Less: Campaign

225
ART DIRECTORS
Marianne Tombaugh
Roby Odom
WRITER
John Crawley
DESIGNER
Marianne Tombaugh
PHOTOGRAPHER
Robb Debenport
CLIENT
Wang Laboratories
AGENCY
The Hay Agency/Dallas

226
ART DIRECTOR
Ken Sakoda
WRITERS
Doug Reeves
Scott Montgomery
CLIENT
Wynn Oil
AGENCY
Salvati Montgomery Sakoda/California

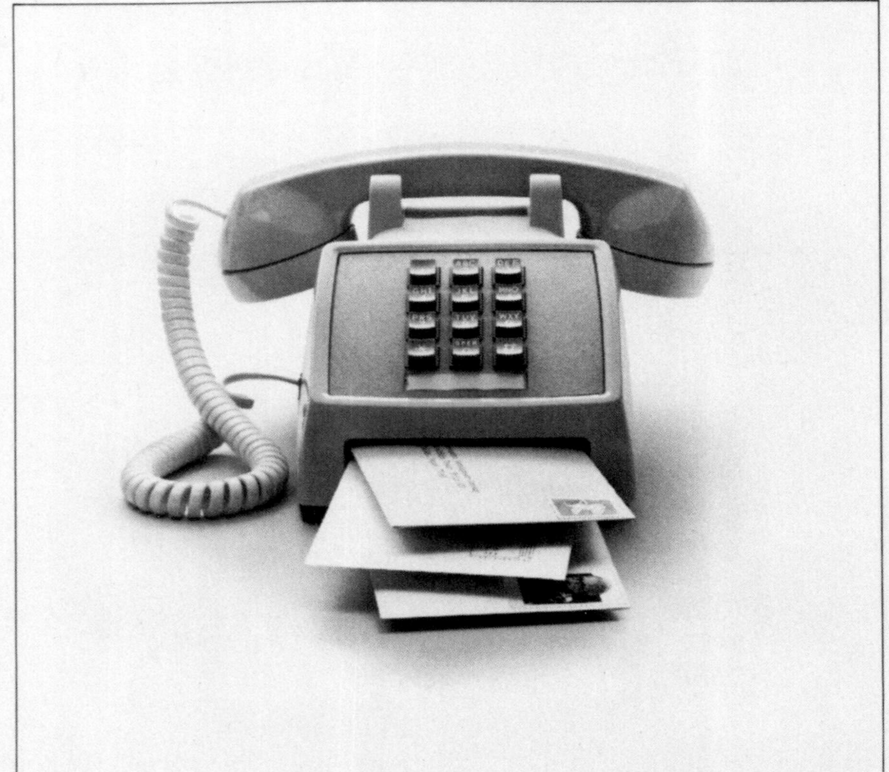

Reintroducing the mailbox.

The Wang DVX™ technology turns the telephone into a post office box.

Wang would like to introduce you to a new concept in mail. With our DVX™ Voice Mailbox, you can use most of the TOUCH-TONE telephones worldwide to deliver your messages.

It's fast. Secure. And it works 24 hours a day. Rain or shine, sleet or snow, gloom of night — it doesn't matter. The Wang DVX™ Voice Mailbox gets your communications through. On time. And to the right party.

The sending and retrieving of messages aren't affected by time zone differences or waiting for people who are away from their offices.

The Wang DVX™ Voice Mailbox does not call for capital expense in equipment. And there's no installation. All you do is subscribe to our Voice Communication Center at a low monthly cost. Learning to use our system is easy, too. Easy voice prompts take you through each step. If you can use a TOUCH-TONE telephone, you can use DVX.™

To find out more about how the Wang DVX™ Voice Mailbox is delivering more efficiency to the world of communications, ask for a free copy of our DVX™ brochure. Just drop us a line at 1-800-343-0664, ext. 5100. Our mailbox is always open.

WANG

We put people in front of computers.

© 1985 Wang Laboratories, Inc. DVX™ is a trademark of Wang Laboratories, Inc.

Neither rain nor snow, gloom or dark of night shall keep it from its appointed rounds.

Introducing the DVX™ Voice Mailbox from Wang.

Today, Wang can turn most of the TOUCH-TONE telephones worldwide into a mailbox. This means you can stay in touch anywhere. Anytime.

Because now with the Wang DVX™ Mailbox your messages can be sent across country or around the world instantaneously. At the push of a button.

This also means you don't have to wait for slow moving mail to deliver your communications. And you don't have to play telephone tag with people who are away from their offices. So your important information always gets through. And with the DVX™ Voice Mailbox from Wang, you won't suffer a communication lag caused by distant time zones. You can send and retrieve messages — 24 hours a day. All you need is a TOUCH-TONE telephone.

With the Wang DVX™ Voice Mailbox you don't buy any hardware — and there's no installation fuss. All you do is subscribe to our Voice Communication Center at a low monthly cost. Learning to use our system is as easy as using the phone.

To give you more information about this exciting new communications service, we've prepared a detailed DVX™ Voice Mail brochure. For your free copy drop us a line at 1-800-343-0664, extension 5100.

WANG

We put people in front of computers.

© 1985 Wang Laboratories, Inc. DVX™ is a trademark of Wang Laboratories, Inc.

It takes 5 minutes to write what you can say in 45 seconds.

The Wang DVX™ Voice Mailbox puts the power of the pen at the tip of your tongue.

Writing is time consuming. And in business your most important resource is your time. So Wang has devised a way to maximize your time while making your communications more efficient. We call it the Wang DVX™ Voice Mailbox. You'll call it amazing.

With our DVX™ you can pick up any TOUCH-TONE telephone, anywhere in the world and send messages, memos, letters and notes to employees or business associates across the office or around the globe.

Now time zones won't cause a communication lag. And you won't have to wait for people who are away from their offices. Simply leave your message and go about your work.

With the Wang DVX™ Voice Mailbox, you just speak your mind. Loud and clear. And your point will be communicated quickly with DVX.™

And with the Wang DVX™ Voice Mailbox, you won't have to buy any hardware or have your phone service interrupted with time-delaying installation. All you do is subscribe to our Voice Communication Center at a low monthly cost. We do all the programming.

To find out more about our exciting new communication tool and how it can make your office more productive, we've prepared a free brochure about the DVX.™ Just drop us a line at 1-800-343-0664, ext. 5100. All you have to say is, "I want one." We'll get the message.

WANG

We put people in front of computers.

© 1985 Wang Laboratories, Inc. DVX™ is a trademark of Wang Laboratories, Inc.

BOY SCOUT PUSHES OLD LADY

"He should be commended," declared Mrs. Alice Rickets. "Not many boys would've helped push my car out of that intersection."

"Shoot, easy as tying a bowline," chirped Tenderfoot Scout Jimmy Vickery. "But she should've used Wynn's® Spit Fire® Gas Treatment. It helps remove fuel system deposits that can cause engine after-run, rough idling, hard starting... even stalling."

"I'm kinda glad she didn't though. Now I'm that much closer to my Helping-Ladies-Stalled-In-Traffic Merit Badge."

HORSE FOUND DEAD ON INTERSTATE OFFRAMP

Authorities are still trying to locate the owner of a 1976 Mustang found near here recently. According to Mr. Bud Stevens of Bud's Towing, the hapless vehicle succumbed to "excessive wear" in the upper cylinder area of its engine.

"Happens all the time," Mr. Stevens continued. "See, back before unleaded gas, the lead used to help lubricate the valves and upper cylinders. Nowadays, no lead means less lubrication. Wear, friction. Engines dying quicker. Bingo."

Asked for a solution, Mr. Stevens responded "Wynn's® Top Oil. Really gets in there for additional lubrication. But don't tell anybody. I'll be out of business."

EX-CON HAULED IN FOR GOING STRAIGHT

"And I was trying so hard," confessed a still-stunned Stan Stevens as he watched his 1973 Cadillac being towed away. "I turned the steering wheel as hard as I could--like this--but I just kept going. Right past the turn and into old Mrs. Parker's tomatoes. She really gave me a piece of her mind. Also gave me Wynn's® Power Steering Fluid. Says it helps prevent leaks, wear and subsequent failure."

"I just can't believe that was a new car when I sto--uh--bought it. Boy, was I ripped off."

Consumer Newspaper 600 Lines Or Less: Campaign

227
ART DIRECTOR
Jim Mochnsky
WRITERS
Peter Hinds
Terry Coveny
DESIGNER
Jim Mochnsky
PHOTOGRAPHER
Len Rizzi
CLIENT
Fairfax Hospital Association
AGENCY
Abramson Associates/
Washington DC

228
ART DIRECTOR
Jerry Torchia
WRITER
Luke Sullivan
DESIGNER
Jerry Torchia
CLIENT
Henry Ford Museum & Greenfield Village
AGENCY
The Martin Agency/
Richmond, VA

You don't have to drink to have a drinking problem.

You can see it in your eyes. Maybe even on your face. You don't have a drinking problem, but you suffer as much as the one who does. Maybe you think it's too tough for you to face alone.

You don't have to wait for the problem to get worse. Talk to us at the Comprehensive Alcoholism Treatment Services of Fairfax Hospital Association. We help alcoholics recover. And we include the whole family in the healing process.

Our intensive approach uses the power of personal relationships and family involvement to help the alcoholic confront the effects of the disease. We strongly encourage friends and family members, including children, to play an active role in our therapeutic program. Our goal is to help the whole family recover.

Concerned family members or friends who want to find out more about our alcohol and drug treatment programs should call 462-HELP and speak to one of our professional staff. It's just a phone call. But it could help you all begin a new life.

Fairfax Hospital Association
COMPREHENSIVE ALCOHOLISM TREATMENT SERVICES

Every morning he wakes up with his wife's hangover.

If your wife is an alcoholic, she's not the only one who needs help. You live with the problem just as if it were your own, and it may be tearing you up, too.

You don't have to wait for the problem to get worse. Talk to us at the Comprehensive Alcoholism Treatment Services of Fairfax Hospital Association. We help alcoholics recover. And we include the whole family in the healing process.

Our intensive approach uses the power of personal relationships and family involvement to help the alcoholic confront the effects of the disease. We strongly encourage friends and family members, including children, to play an active role in our therapeutic program. Our goal is to help the whole family recover.

Concerned family members or friends who want to find out more about our alcohol and drug treatment programs should call 462-HELP and speak to one of our professional staff. It's just a phone call. But it could help you all begin a new life.

Fairfax Hospital Association
COMPREHENSIVE ALCOHOLISM TREATMENT SERVICES

It isn't easy being a third baseman with a drinking problem.

If Dad is an alcoholic, he's not the only one who's suffering. Losing a parent to alcohol can tear up the rest of the family, because everyone feels the pain.

Don't wait for the problem to get worse. Talk to us at the Comprehensive Alcoholism Treatment Services of Fairfax Hospital Association. We help alcoholics recover. And we include the whole family in the healing process.

Our intensive approach uses the power of personal relationships and family involvement to help the alcoholic confront the effects of the disease. We strongly encourage friends and family members, including children, to play an active role in our therapeutic program. Our goal is to help the whole family recover.

Concerned family members or friends who want to find out more about our alcohol and drug treatment programs should call 462-HELP and speak to one of our professional staff. It's just a phone call. But it could help you all begin a new life.

Fairfax Hospital Association
COMPREHENSIVE ALCOHOLISM TREATMENT SERVICES

George Washington Really Did Sleep Here.

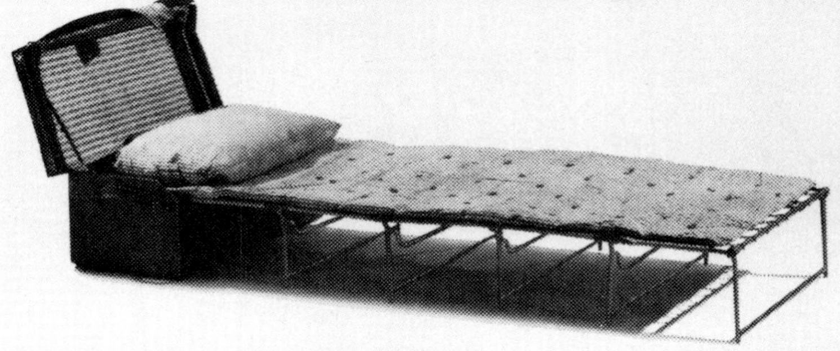

We cannot tell a lie. Washington's field bed is really here. Along with over a million other pieces of America's past. Call 1-800-835-2246 for a free brochure on the great American museum that's also great fun.

Henry Ford Museum & Greenfield Village In Dearborn, Michigan.

Flown To The South Pole By Admiral Brrrrd.

We have what made Byrd fly south for the winter, as well as over a million other pieces of America's past. Call 1-800-835-2246 for a free brochure on the great American museum that's also great fun.

Henry Ford Museum & Greenfield Village In Dearborn, Michigan.

It Weighs 600 Tons. And It'll Stop You In Your Tracks.

We have one of the largest locomotives in the world. But it's just a small part of all the tributes to American ingenuity on display here. Call 1-800-835-2246 for a free brochure on the great American museum that's also great fun.

Henry Ford Museum & Greenfield Village In Dearborn, Michigan.

Consumer Newspaper 600 Lines Or Less: Campaign

229
ART DIRECTOR
Diane Cook Tench
WRITER
Luke Sullivan
DESIGNER
Diane Cook Tench
PHOTOGRAPHERS
Dean Hawthorne
Pat Edwards
CLIENT
Barnett Bank
AGENCY
The Martin Agency/
Richmond, VA

230
ART DIRECTORS
Bob Phillips
William Hartwell
Jeff Vogt
WRITERS
Mark Silveira
Paul Wolfe
Rav Friedel
DESIGNERS
Bob Phillips
William Hartwell
Jeff Vogt
PHOTOGRAPHER
Jeffrey Zwart
ARTIST
R & V Studio
CLIENT
BMW of North America
AGENCY
Ammirati & Puris

1
2
3
GHI
4
MNO
6
WXY

Reach Out And Borrow Money From Someone.

Our new Loan-By-Phone service lets your fingers do the borrowing. In Palm Beach County, dial 965-LOAN. Or just call toll-free 1-800-245-3594. Loan-By-Phone hours are Monday-Friday 8-8; Saturday 8-5. Equal Opportunity Lender.

Barnett Bank
Barnett Is Florida's Bank.

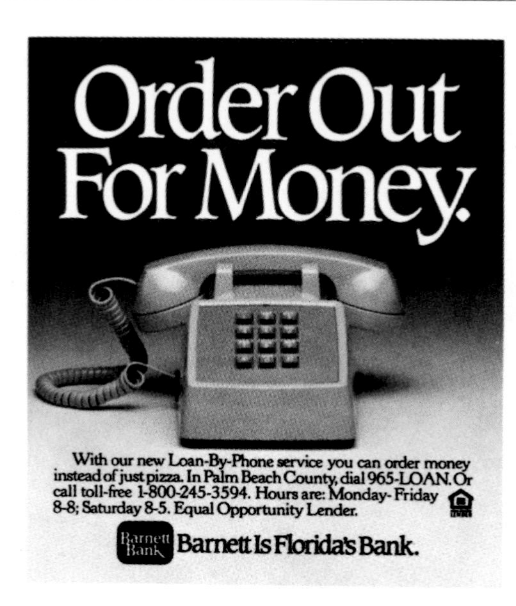
Order Out For Money.
With our new Loan-By-Phone service you can order money instead of just pizza. In Palm Beach County, dial 965-LOAN. Or call toll-free 1-800-245-3594. Hours are: Monday-Friday 8-8; Saturday 8-5. Equal Opportunity Lender.
Barnett Bank
Barnett Is Florida's Bank.

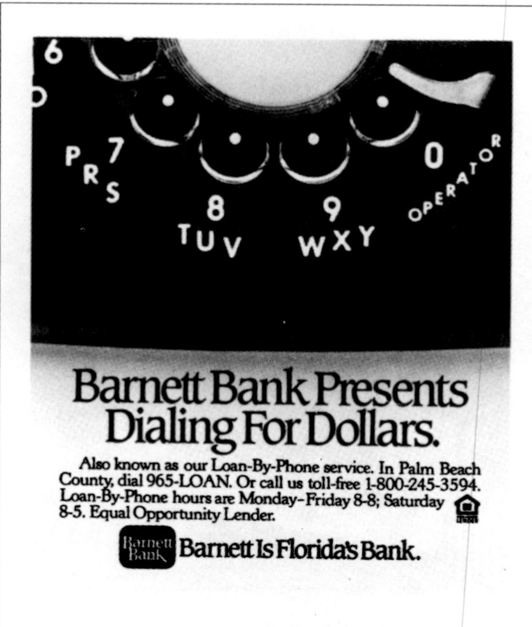
PRS 7
8 TUV
9 WXY
0 OPERATOR
Barnett Bank Presents Dialing For Dollars.
Also known as our Loan-By-Phone service. In Palm Beach County, dial 965-LOAN. Or call us toll-free 1-800-245-3594. Loan-By-Phone hours are Monday-Friday 8-8; Saturday 8-5. Equal Opportunity Lender.
Barnett Bank
Barnett Is Florida's Bank.

THE LUXURY SEDAN THAT MADE RADAR DETECTORS A MULTIMILLION DOLLAR INDUSTRY.

Some automobiles inspire comment. Others praise. But precious few spawn entire industries.

Yet such would seem to be the case with the nearly simultaneous appearance of a boom in radar detectors and the now legendary BMW 5-Series.

But then, what choice does a car like the 535i leave the spirited driver? Those drivers who, in the immortal words of a famous actress, "can resist anything...except temptation."

Temptation which here takes the form of BMW's exuberant 3.5-liter in-line six. A power plant fully capable of accelerating beyond the current national speed limit in a mere 7.7 seconds.

Exhilarating performance that's perfectly mated to the fully independent suspension system Motor Trend simply calls "a delight." Performance that's governed by a microprocessor-based engine management system. And reined in by BMW's ABS anti-lock braking system.

But despite the 535i's clear performance bias, inside it's every bit a luxury sedan. Replete with leather seats, every conceivable power-assist feature, and a new, high-performance sound system.

All of which should provide more than ample incentive to hurry (observing all local speed limits, please) to your authorized BMW dealer. For a driving experience so utterly satisfying, some might say, there ought to be a law.

THE ULTIMATE DRIVING MACHINE.

 European Delivery can be arranged through your authorized U.S. BMW dealer.

LET YOUR LOCAL BMW DEALERS ARRANGE A THOROUGH TEST DRIVE.

City	City	City	City	City	City
DEALER NAME	**DEALER NAME**	**DEALER NAME**	**DEALER NAME**	**DEALER NAME**	**DEALER NAME**
Dealer Address	Dealer Address	Dealer Address	Dealer Address	Dealer Address	Dealer Address
Phone Number	Phone Number	Phone Number	Phone Number	Phone Number	Phone Number

EMERGE FROM THE FREEWAY VICTORIOUS, NOT VICTIMIZED.

Highways extract a bitter toll from modern drivers. Not at the coin booths, but in the continual onslaught of noise, traffic jams and pollution.

For those forced to cope with such a demoralizing situation, BMW has engineered a most vivifying solution. The 528e.

A car whose high-torque, high-efficiency* Eta engine lets you power through traffic without endlessly shifting through the gears.

Whose orthopedically-designed seats and ergonomically-designed climate controls ensure you not only negotiate the highway nimbly, but navigate it in total comfort.

Whose ingenious ABS anti-lock braking system can actually mean the difference between emerging victorious from hazardous roads, and not emerging at all.

And whose parts and pieces mesh together so well that one automotive critic was moved to characterize the 528e as "sumptuous in a no-nonsense way and immaculately crafted" (Motor Trend).

Your local BMW dealer would be happy to arrange a thorough test drive of the BMW 528e. A triumph of technology in which every day you share in the victory.

THE ULTIMATE DRIVING MACHINE.

*EPA-estimated 20 mpg, 24 highway. Fuel efficiency figures are for comparison only. Your actual mileage may vary, depending on speed, weather and trip length.

LET YOUR LOCAL BMW DEALERS ARRANGE A THOROUGH TEST DRIVE.

City	City	City	City	City	City
DEALER NAME	**DEALER NAME**	**DEALER NAME**	**DEALER NAME**	**DEALER NAME**	**DEALER NAME**
Dealer Address	Dealer Address	Dealer Address	Dealer Address	Dealer Address	Dealer Address
Phone Number	Phone Number	Phone Number	Phone Number	Phone Number	Phone Number

THE CAR THAT WOULD FORCE ITS COMPETITORS TO RE-EXAMINE THEIR ENGINE TECHNOLOGY, IF THEY HAD ANY.

One manufacturer, with a reputation for performance, still gives you the very same engine they did in 1969.

Another, with a reputation for engineering, has failed to engineer data processing into their engines.

But there's one luxury sedan manufacturer that, despite a myriad of European and national championships, hasn't rested on their technological laurels: BMW.

In the power plant of a BMW 735i is the automotive equivalent of a central nervous system. A system that does nothing less than expand the possibilities of the internal combustion engine.

It's called Digital Motor Electronics, with sensors that monitor every vital engine function, and data such as outside air temperature, humidity, and engine load. And then orders the engine to deliver a superior balance of performance.

The computer reassesses this data every ten thousandth of a second.

As you would expect, this electronic self-analysis system extends to virtually every facet of a BMW 735i. From the ABS anti-lock brakes that help to prevent skidding and swerving in panic stops. To the Service Interval Indicator, which tells you, based on how the car has been driven, when routine service is advisable.

So if you'd like to own the world's most technologically advanced promise, there are several models to choose from.

If you'd like to own the world's most technologically advanced car, contact your BMW dealer for a thorough test drive of a 735i.

THE ULTIMATE DRIVING MACHINE.

 European Delivery can be arranged through your authorized U.S. BMW dealer.

LET YOUR LOCAL BMW DEALERS ARRANGE A THOROUGH TEST DRIVE.

City	City	City	City	City	City
DEALER NAME	**DEALER NAME**	**DEALER NAME**	**DEALER NAME**	**DEALER NAME**	**DEALER NAME**
Dealer Address	Dealer Address	Dealer Address	Dealer Address	Dealer Address	Dealer Address
Phone Number	Phone Number	Phone Number	Phone Number	Phone Number	Phone Number

Consumer Newspaper Over 600 Lines: Campaign

231
ART DIRECTOR
Michael Fazende
WRITER
Phil Hanft
PHOTOGRAPHER
Craig Perman
CLIENT
Country Cottage
AGENCY
Fallon McElligott/Minneapolis

232
ART DIRECTOR
Tom Lichtenheld
WRITER
Jarl Olsen
DESIGNER
Tom Lichtenheld
ARTIST
Bob Lambert
CLIENT
WFLD-TV
AGENCY
Fallon McElligott/Minneapolis

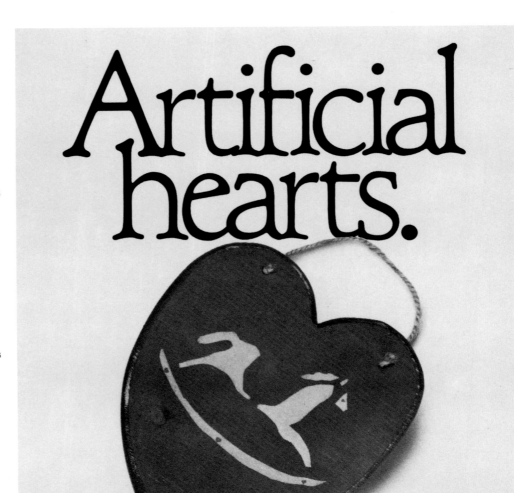

Artificial hearts.

Life is full of wonderful little oddities. And this is the place to find many of them. The Country Cottage. Charming, personal gifts for your family, your friends and yourself.

Country Cottage
of Wayzata Ltd.
326 S. Broadway, Wayzata, MN 55391 612-473-0259

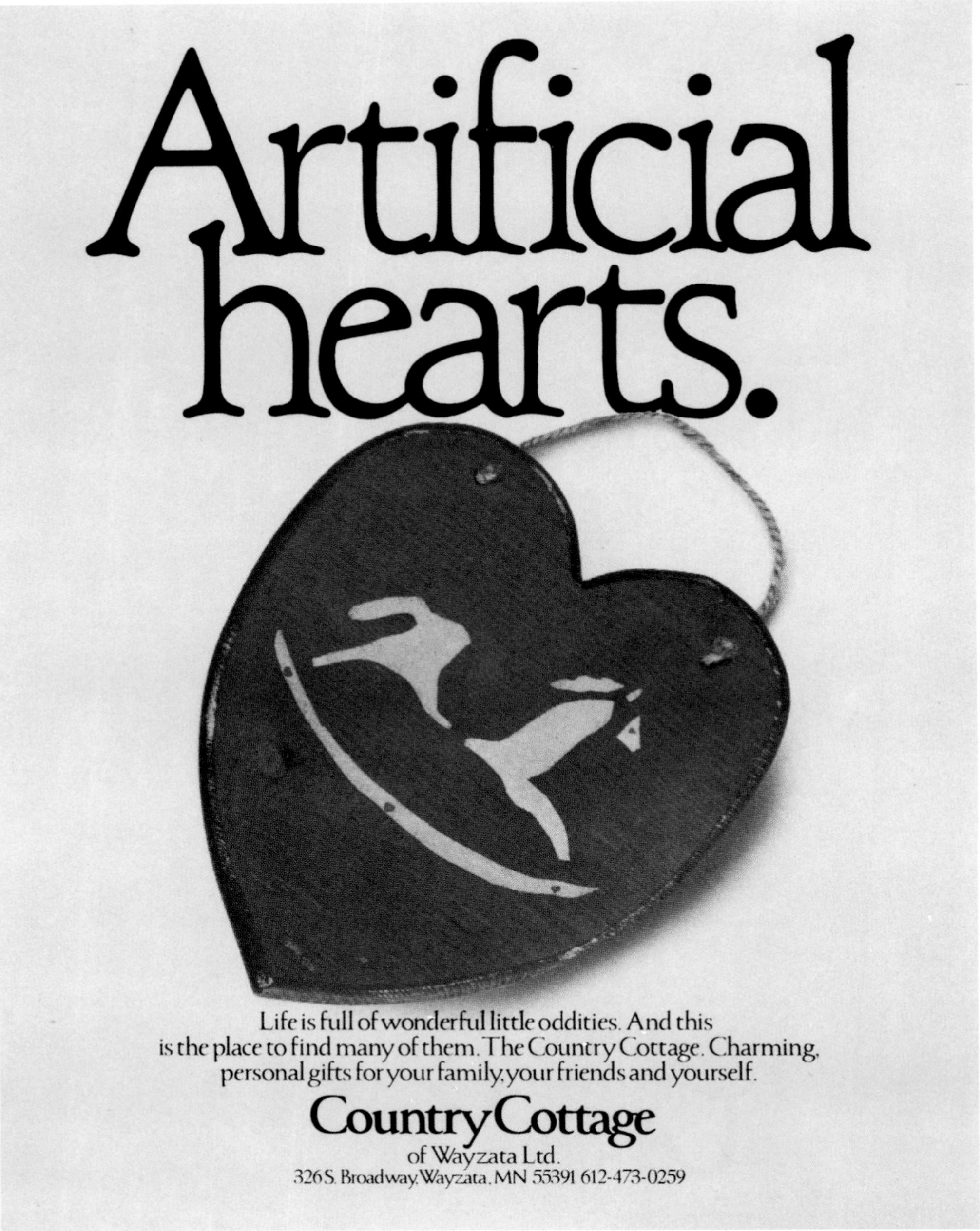

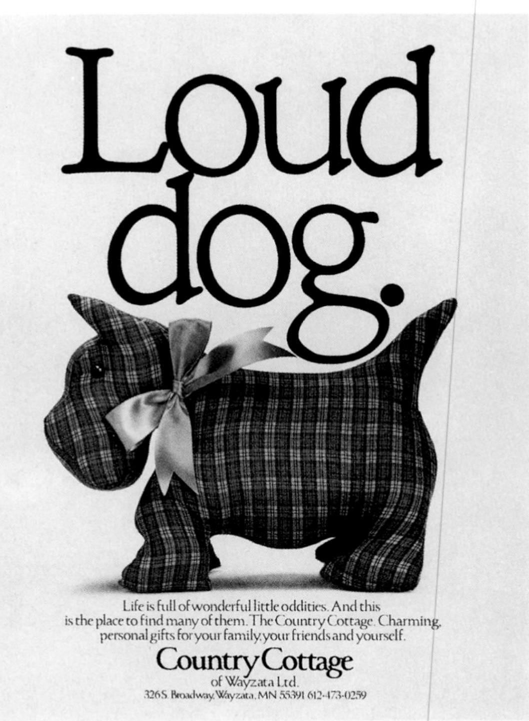

THERE MAY BE EVEN MORE SHOOTING THAN NORMAL IN NEW YORK CITY TONIGHT.

The Chicago Bulls vs. The New York Knicks
Saturday, November 9 at 6:30 p.m.

WE'RE GOING TO LOS ANGELES TO CLEAR THE AIR.

BULLS VS. LAKERS, TONIGHT AT 9:30 PM. 32 WFLDTV

IT WILL BE RAINING BUCKETS IN SAN ANTONIO TONIGHT.

See the Bulls in a shoot-out with the San Antonio Spurs.
Tonight at 7:30.

233
ART DIRECTORS
Kevin Kearns
Amy Watt
WRITER
Edward Boches
PHOTOGRAPHER
Frank Rapp
CLIENT
Greater Media Cable Company
AGENCY
Mullen Advertising & Public Relations/Prides Crossing, MA

234
ART DIRECTORS
Jeff Vogt
Brandt Wilkins
WRITERS
Rich Pels
David Tessler
Norah Delaney
DESIGNERS
Jeff Vogt
Brandt Wilkins
PHOTOGRAPHER
Jeffrey Zwart
ARTIST
R & V Studio
CLIENT
BMW of North America
AGENCY
Ammirati & Puris

The only rabbit population that's declining.

To tune into major movies, top comedy, superstar concerts, and up-to-the-minute news, sports and weather, more and more people are subscribing to Greater Media Cable.

We guarantee great reception, quality programming and a variety of entertainment choices to fit any family or lifestyle. Our introductory offer includes free installation, a 15-day money-back guarantee and a monthly rate that's about equal to the price of two movie tickets.

We also have an extensive choice of premium networks. Including HBO, Cinemax, Showtime and The Movie Channel.

Call us today. And find out why Greater Media Cable subscribers are multiplying faster than you know what.

Greater Media Cable

How come the best entertainment on network TV lasts only 30 seconds?

Often the best entertainment we see on network TV are the commercials. On some stations they're practically all we see.

That's why people everywhere are turning to Greater Media Cable. We've got entertainment that lasts all day long. All night too. With terrific movies, concerts, family shows and cultural specials. For a monthly rate that starts at the price of a case of beer.

We've also got the world's finest premium networks. HBO, Showtime, Cinemax and The Movie Channel. Delivering commercial-free entertainment 24 hours a day.

Call us today for information on free installation and our 15-day money-back guarantee. Greater Media Cable. It's everything you always wanted in TV. And more.

Immaculate Reception

If you've ever wished you could receive more stations than is possible with ordinary television, Greater Media Cable will seem like a miracle.

We give you all your local stations. Distant channels you can't pick up with an antenna. Plus a host of music, news and weather stations.

We also offer the premium networks. HBO, Showtime, Cinemax, The Movie Channel and Disney. Call us. Once you learn about Greater Media Cable, we're sure you'll want to convert.

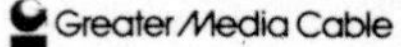

EVERY SUMMER, CAR DEALERS LOWER THEIR PRICES AND INVITE YOU TO DO THE SAME TO YOUR STANDARDS.
Now's the time of year most automobile dealers routinely display enthusiasm for cars whose main virtue is that they're "priced to move." If you can't share their enthusiasm, visit your BMW dealer. There you'll find cars that are engineered to move, as well.
Not that various other cars can't be coaxed to display reasonable speed and acceleration on long, dull interstates. But simply, BMW's are designed for a greater destiny.
To straighten serpentine mountain roads. An achievement that's made possible by such advances as a fully-independent suspension with components meriting numerous international patents.
As well as an engine whose parts are machined to tolerances of less than 4/100,000ths of an inch to power you effortlessly from 0 to 60. And a revolutionary anti-lock braking system engineered to bring you back to earth safe and sound.
Even so, BMW allows you to maintain exceptionally high standards at a cost made exceptionally reasonable by BMW's financing program—9.5% annual percentage rate for all 6- and 7-series BMW's purchased (or higher guaranteed leasing residuals).*
So if you still feel oddly compelled by the "unbelievable but true" offers most car dealers resort to, perhaps you should test-drive a BMW. It's a truly poignant reminder that high-pressure salesmanship is no substitute for high-performance engineering.
THE ULTIMATE DRIVING MACHINE.

*Through September 30, 1985. See your participating dealer for details. © 1985 BMW of North America, Inc. The BMW trademark and logo are registered.

LET YOUR LOCAL BMW DEALERS ARRANGE A THOROUGH TEST DRIVE.

City	City	City	City	City	City
DEALER NAME	**DEALER NAME**	**DEALER NAME**	**DEALER NAME**	**DEALER NAME**	**DEALER NAME**
Dealer Address	Dealer Address	Dealer Address	Dealer Address	Dealer Address	Dealer Address
Phone Number	Phone Number	Phone Number	Phone Number	Phone Number	Phone Number

FOR A THRILLING DEMONSTRATION ON THE BENEFITS OF THE MICROCHIP, SEE YOUR BMW DEALER.

The same fleck of silicon that controls virtually everything from worldwide telecommunications to pacemakers now controls automobile engines, as well.

Of which the most amazing example can be found under the hood of a BMW 528e. Deep within the recesses of the engine resides a network of sensors which constantly transmit data to microprocessors.

The information received is always used towards the same goal: a superior balance of performance with peak efficiency.*

This system is called Digital Motor Electronics. While it may be considered the most advanced system on the BMW 528e, it's hardly the only.

Another microprocessor-driven system called ABS helps you to make emergency stops (even on a sheet of ice) without locking your wheels. The microprocessor-governed Service Interval Indicator takes information, stores it, analyzes it and then recommends routine service to you as it's needed. And the Active Check Control acts like a computer, informing you of the operational readiness of the car.

You'll undoubtedly be thrilled by other aspects of the BMW 528e that have nothing whatsoever to do with microprocessors. And everything to do with agile suspension systems and luxurious interiors.

For a thorough demonstration, see your local authorized BMW dealer. Where you'll see the wonders of technology used to advance the automobile, instead of just the dashboard.

THE ULTIMATE DRIVING MACHINE.

*EPA estimated 20 mpg, 24 highway. Fuel efficiency figures are for comparison only. Your actual mileage may vary, depending on speed, weather, and trip length. © 1985 BMW of North America, Inc. The BMW trademark and logo are registered. European Delivery can be arranged through your authorized U.S. BMW dealer.

LET YOUR LOCAL BMW DEALERS ARRANGE A THOROUGH TEST DRIVE.

City	City	City	City	City	City
DEALER NAME	**DEALER NAME**	**DEALER NAME**	**DEALER NAME**	**DEALER NAME**	**DEALER NAME**
Dealer Address	Dealer Address	Dealer Address	Dealer Address	Dealer Address	Dealer Address
Phone Number	Phone Number	Phone Number	Phone Number	Phone Number	Phone Number

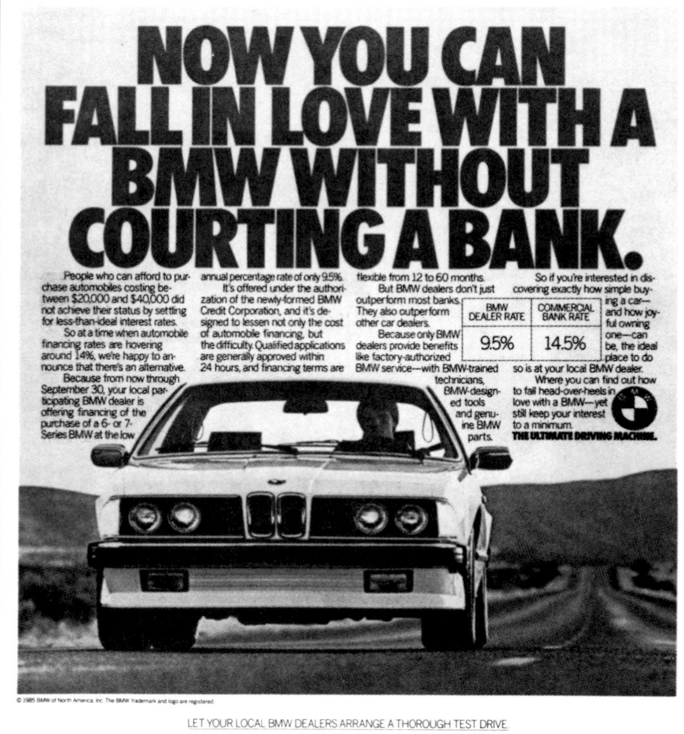
NOW YOU CAN FALL IN LOVE WITH A BMW WITHOUT COURTING A BANK.
People who can afford to purchase automobiles costing between $20,000 and $40,000 did not achieve their status by settling for less-than-ideal interest rates.
So at a time when automobile financing rates are hovering around 14%, we're happy to announce that there's an alternative.
Because from now through September 30, your local participating BMW dealer is offering financing of the purchase of a 6- or 7-Series BMW at the low annual percentage rate of only 9.5%.
It's offered under the authorization of the newly-formed BMW Credit Corporation, and it's designed to lessen not only the cost of automobile financing, but the difficulty. Qualified applications are generally approved within 24 hours, and financing terms are flexible from 12 to 60 months.
But BMW dealers don't just outperform most banks. They also outperform other car dealers.
Because only BMW dealers provide benefits like factory-authorized BMW service—with BMW-trained technicians, BMW-designed tools and genuine BMW parts.
BMW DEALER RATE
COMMERCIAL BANK RATE
9.5%
14.5%
So if you're interested in discovering exactly how simple buying a car—and how joyful owning one—can be, the ideal place to do so is at your local BMW dealer.
Where you can find out how to fall head-over-heels in love with a BMW—yet still keep your interest to a minimum.
THE ULTIMATE DRIVING MACHINE.

© 1985 BMW of North America, Inc. The BMW trademark and logo are registered.

LET YOUR LOCAL BMW DEALERS ARRANGE A THOROUGH TEST DRIVE.

City	City	City	City	City	City
DEALER NAME	**DEALER NAME**	**DEALER NAME**	**DEALER NAME**	**DEALER NAME**	**DEALER NAME**
Dealer Address	Dealer Address	Dealer Address	Dealer Address	Dealer Address	Dealer Address
Phone Number	Phone Number	Phone Number	Phone Number	Phone Number	Phone Number

Consumer Newspaper Over 600 Lines: Campaign

235
ART DIRECTORS
Gail Bartley
Brandt Wilkins
WRITER
Paul Wolfe
Steve Smith
DESIGNERS
Gail Bartley
Brandt Wilkins
ARTIST
Robert Grossman
CLIENT
Oppenheimer Management Corporation
AGENCY
Ammirati & Puris

236
ART DIRECTOR
Wayne Gibson
WRITER
Daniel Russ
ARTIST
Wayne Gibson
CLIENT
Matt's British Pub
AGENCY
Odd Couple Advertising/ Virginia

PEOPLE ARE JOINING OUR PREMIUM INCOME FUND AT A REMARKABLE RATE.

14.5%* DISTRIBUTION RETURN

The Oppenheimer Premium Income Fund shows that a fund can be conservative yet exciting at the same time.

On the one hand, the Fund has provided investors with a substantially higher return than many other income investments available.

On the other hand, this high return is unusual. Because it doesn't come with the degree of risk that's always a concern with equity investments. Due to the Fund's technique of writing covered call options, we can offer investors some protection against capital loss resulting from fluctuations in the equity market.

Of course, as market conditions change, there's no guarantee the present level of distribution can be maintained. However, the Premium Income Fund will strive to provide a higher return than fixed interest securities, such as bonds and money market accounts.**

For more information, mail the coupon, speak with your financial advisor, or call Oppenheimer at 1-800-222-0700 (in New Jersey, 1-800-222-0755).

We'll send you additional reasons why the Oppenheimer Premium Income Fund is gaining a lot of interest on the part of investors.

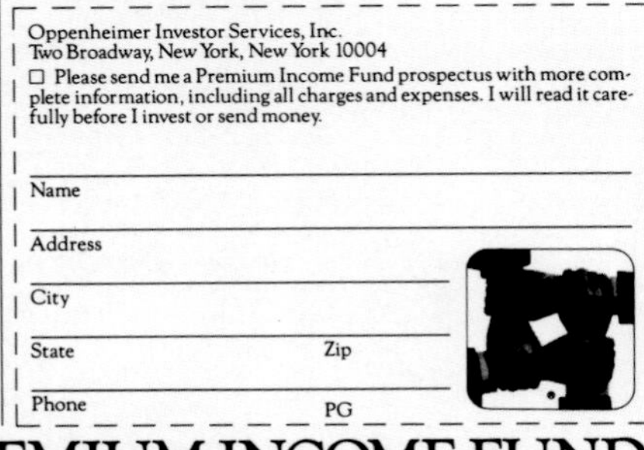

THE OPPENHEIMER PREMIUM INCOME FUND.

*Calculated by annualizing the daily dividends paid over the 20 days to August 15, and the August 15 offering price of $22.10. Past performance is not an indication of future yield, as net asset values fluctuate due to market conditions. **Fixed income investments may not fluctuate in value, and may pay a steady return. ©1985 Oppenheimer Investor Services, Inc.

HOW TO REDUCE YOUR TAXES WHILE CONGRESS WORKS AT REFORMING THEM.

Waiting to find out what Congress intends to do about tax reform could be a costly experience.

Investing in the Oppenheimer New York Tax-Exempt Fund can reduce your taxes right away while Congress debates and procrastinates.

And unlike many tax shelters, which only reduce or defer taxes, this fund eliminates federal, state and local taxes* on the income you earn. Right now the Fund's yield is 7.7%.** So, if you're in the 50% tax bracket, that's the equivalent of a 15.4% return on a taxable investment.

It means you may now earn a high return on your investment without having to pay the price of high risk.

If you're interested in more information on how to reduce your IOU to the IRS, mail the coupon, speak to your financial advisor or call Oppenheimer at 1-800-222-0700 (in New Jersey, call 1-800-222-0755).

You'll find that tax reform can begin at home.

Oppenheimer Investor Services, Two Broadway, New York, N.Y. 10004
☐ Please send me a N.Y. Tax-Exempt Fund prospectus with more complete information, including all charges and expenses. I will read it carefully before I invest or send money.
Name
Address
City State
Zip Phone
NH

THE OPPENHEIMER N.Y. TAX-EXEMPT FUND.

© 1985 Oppenheimer Investor Services, Inc. *A portion of your income may be subject to state and local taxes. **Calculated by annualizing the August 13 dividend and dividing by the August 15 offering price of $11.79.

NOW YOU CAN INVEST IN THE MARKET ARMED WITH SOMETHING BESIDES COURAGE.

$65,000 · $50,000 · $30,000 · $20,000 · $15,000 · $10,000
1975 · 1985
$64,097 Total Return
Income**
$36,875
Capital Growth***
Net Amount Invested: $9,150

Results of a $10,000 Investment (Net $9,150 after sales charge) January 1, 1975 to March 31, 1985 with all distributions reinvested.

To the cautious investors of the world who think entering the stock market takes nerve, Oppenheimer offers something that's been far more effective: the Equity Income Fund.

A conservative fund which since 1975 has provided a not-so-conservative average annual return of 19.9%.*

As the chart illustrates, this generous return has been composed of both capital growth and dividend income. And since the Fund invests primarily in blue-chip, high dividend paying stocks, that income has offered investors a cushion against fluctuations in the equity market.

For more information, mail the coupon, speak to your financial advisor, or call Oppenheimer at 1-800-222-0700 (in New Jersey, 1-800-222-0755).

Here's an investment tool that's proved more reliable than either a wing or a prayer.

Oppenheimer Investor Services, Inc., Two Broadway, New York, New York 10004
☐ Please send me an Equity Income Fund prospectus with more complete information, including all charges and expenses. I will read it carefully before I invest or send money.
Name
Address
City State
Zip Phone
EC

OPPENHEIMER EQUITY INCOME FUND

©1985 Oppenheimer Investor Services, Inc. *Past performance is not an indication of future results, as net asset values fluctuate due to market conditions. The period shown was one in which common stock prices fluctuated severely and were generally higher at the end than they were at the beginning. **Reinvested dividend income of $17,392. ***Capital Growth includes reinvested capital gains distributions of $30,711.

If Matt Ever Gives You Plain Fare, Fly Him Back To Britain.

Indeed, come eat at Matt's if you're really hungry, because he gives you hefty portions of some of Richmond's best fare, sauces and spirits. And after you've eaten, stop by the pub downstairs, or see live comedy from nationally acclaimed comedians in the Richmond Comedy Club.

We're just five minutes from Churchill, the Fan and Southside.

Matt's British Pub

109 S. 12th Street. 644-0848 Reservations. 323-1380 Comedy Club Reservations.

At Matt's British Pub, Humor Is Beneath Us.

Indeed, to humor our customers after a hearty meal and beverage, we send them downstairs, home of the Richmond Comedy Club where you see live comedy from the best headliners in the nation. Don't let anyone tell you the British are stuffy.

Matt's British Pub

109 S. 12th Street. 644-0848 Reservations. 323-1380 Comedy Club Reservations.

Thousands Die In Matt's Cellar.

Each week, thousands of perfectly sensible people head downstairs at Matt's British Pub to be killed by the nation's top comedians at the Richmond Comedy Club. Often they do it after a hearty meal at one of the city's top restaurants: Matt's. If you have nothing better to do and happen to have a death wish, why not call for reservations. We're five minutes away and plenty of parking.

Matt's British Pub

109 S. 12th Street. 644-0848 Reservations. 323-1380 Comedy Club Reservations.

Consumer Newspaper 600 Lines Or Less: Campaign

237
ART DIRECTOR
Bill Oakley
WRITER
Dave Henke
CLIENT
Southwestern Bell
AGENCY
D'Arcy Masius Benton & Bowles/St. Louis

Consumer Magazine B/W: 1 Page Or Spread Including Magazine Supplements

238
ART DIRECTOR
Steve Jaeger
WRITER
Cynthia Beck
DESIGNER
Steve Jaeger
PHOTOGRAPHER
Larry Sillen
CLIENT
Mobil
AGENCY
Doyle Dane Bernbach

239
ART DIRECTOR
John Morrison
WRITER
Rod Kilpatrick
PHOTOGRAPHER
Steve Umland
CLIENT
American Association of Advertising Agencies
AGENCY
Fallon McElligott/Minneapolis

How would you solve this problem?

☐ A. Deductive reasoning.

☐ B. Perseverance and dedication.

☐ C. A sword.

Mobil

We like people with fresh ideas.

238

YOUR REACTIONS TO ADVERTISING ARE TABULATED BY HIGHLY SOPHISTICATED EQUIPMENT.

$4 .90

Every time you shop, you have the opportunity to express your exact feelings about advertising. Not just by talking about them. But by putting your money where your mouth is.

Look at it this way. Whenever you go to the store, you make a cartload of buying decisions. And you're free to base those decisions on anything you choose. Including the advertising you've seen.

If you like a product's advertising—if you find it informative, honest and interesting—we suggest that you buy.

If you don't like the advertising—if it's misleading, tasteless or just plain boring—we suggest that you not buy.

In effect, you'll be casting your vote at the cash register. And by doing so, you'll be helping us create better advertising. More interesting advertising. More effective advertising. More tasteful advertising.

In short, the kind of advertising you've told us you want.

Some people may claim that the advertising industry doesn't care about your opinions.

But when you consider the facts, that argument just doesn't ring true.

ADVERTISING.

ANOTHER WORD FOR FREEDOM OF CHOICE.

American Association of Advertising Agencies.

239

Consumer Magazine B/W: 1 Page Or Spread Including Magazine Supplements

240
ART DIRECTOR
Mark Yustein
WRITER
Luke Sullivan
CLIENT
Book of the Month Club
AGENCY
Della Femina Travisano & Partners

241
ART DIRECTOR
Brian Kelly
WRITER
Jim Schmidt
PHOTOGRAPHERS
Jay Maisel
Dennis Manarchy
CLIENT
Wolverine Thermalites
AGENCY
Bozell Jacobs Kenyon & Eckhardt/Chicago

242
ART DIRECTOR
Raul Pina
WRITER
Chris Messner
CLIENT
WCBS-TV
AGENCY
Della Femina Travisano & Partners

243
ART DIRECTORS
Mitch Jackson
Leslie Davis
WRITER
Rich Flora
PHOTOGRAPHER
U.S. Marshall Clint Peoples' Collection
CLIENT
Dallas Times Herald
AGENCY
The Richards Group/Dallas

HARD SELL VS. SOFT SELL

QPB books are softcover editions in hardcover sizes. They're durably bound and printed on fine paper. Yet they cost up to 65% less than their hardcover counterparts.

In addition to our regular low prices, you can have any 3 books you see here for just 3 dollars. With absolutely no obligation to buy another book. Ever.

So, with an offer like this, who needs hard sell? Or hardcover prices?

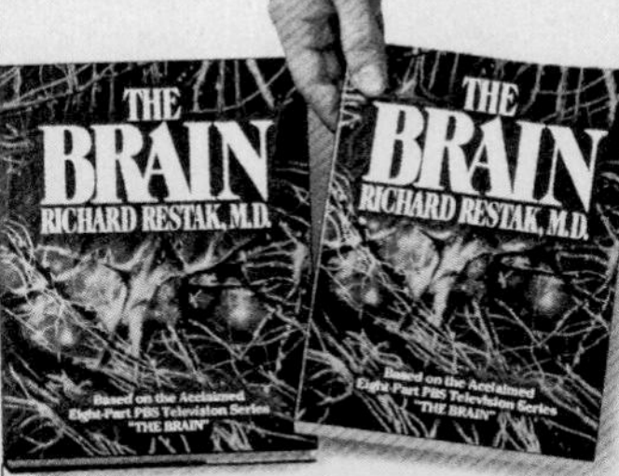

Hardcover: $24.95

QPB Softcover: $12.95

105. "...And Ladies of the Club" Helen Hooven Santmyer Hardcover: $19.95 **QPB Ed: $9.95**

632. The Kennedys An American Drama. Peter Collier and David Horowitz Hardcover: $20.95 **QPB Ed: $8.95**

171. The Discoverers Daniel J. Boorstin Hardcover: $25 **QPB: $7.95**

583. Him with His Foot in His Mouth and Other Stories. Saul Bellow Hardcover: $15.95 **QPB Ed: $7.95**

453. Beard on Bread and Beard on Pasta (2 Vols.) James Beard Hardcovers: $24.90 **QPB Ed: $9.95**

259. Russia: Broken Idols, Solemn Dreams. David K. Shipler Hardcover: $17.95 **QPB: $6.50**

100. The Best of Modern Humor Edited by Mordecai Richler Hardcover: $17.95 **QPB Ed: $9.95**

179. Calvino Set: *If on a Winter's Night a Traveler, Invisible Cities, The Baron in the Trees.* (3 Vols., Boxed) Italo Calvino. **QPB Ed: $10.95**

393. Vietnam: A History: The First Complete Account of Vietnam at War. Stanley Karnow Hardcover: $22.50 **QPB Ed: $8.95**

658. Sniglets and More Sniglets Rich Hall and Friends. **QPB: $9.95**

554. T. S. Eliot: A Life. Peter Ackroyd Hardcover: $24.95 **QPB Ed: $13.95**

584. Hugging the Shore: Essays and Criticisms. John Updike Hardcover: $19.95 **QPB: $8.95**

609. Doonesbury Dossier The Reagan Years. G. B. Trudeau. With an Introduction by Gloria Steinem Hardcover: $22.95 **QPB: $9.95**

359. How Life Imitates the World Series: An Inquiry into the Game. Thomas Boswell Hardcover: $14.95 **QPB: $5.95**

625. Late Night Thoughts on Listening to Mahler's Ninth Symphony. Lewis Thomas Hardcover: $12.95 **QPB: $5.95**

120. Brownies Linda Burum. **QPB: $5.95**

261. Make Your Money Grow (Revised Edition). Edited by Theodore J. Miller **QPB: $6.95**

231. Twentieth-Century Culture A Biographical Companion. Edited by Alan Bullock and R. B. Woodings Hardcover: $35 **QPB Ed: $12.95**

715. Outrageous Acts and Everyday Rebellions. Gloria Steinem Hardcover: $14.95 **QPB Ed: $6.95**

218. The Concise Columbia Encyclopedia Hardcover: $29.95 **QPB: $12.95**

199. The Word Processing Book Peter A. McWilliams. **QPB: $7.95**

571. The Brain (Inspired by the PBS television series). Richard M. Restak, M.D. Hardcover: $24.95 **QPB Ed: $12.95**

390. Rand McNally 1985 Road Atlas (United States, Canada, Mexico). **QPB: $5.95**

561. Love Medicine. Louise Erdrich Hardcover: $13.95 **QPB Ed: $6.95**

281. The Science Almanac 1985-1986 Edition. Edited by Bryan Bunch. **QPB: $10.95**

306. The Color Purple Alice Walker Hardcover: $11.95 **QPB Ed: $6.50**

104. A Passage to India E. M. Forster Hardcover: $11.95 **QPB: $5.95**

391. Between Ourselves: Letters between Mothers and Daughters, 1750-1982. Edited by Karen Payne Hardcover: $16.95 **QPB: $6.95**

264. Whole Earth Software Catalog. Stewart Brand **QPB: $13.50**

446. Omnibooth: The Best of George Booth. Hardcover: $18.95 **QPB Ed: $10.95**

310. The Beans of Egypt, Maine Carolyn Chute Hardcover: $15.95 **QPB: $5.95**

601. World Religions: From Ancient History to the Present. Editor: Geoffrey Parrinder Hardcover: $29.95 **QPB Ed: $13.95**

403. The Morrow Book of Quotations in American History Joseph R. Conlin Hardcover: $17.95 **QPB Ed: $7.95**

407. In Search of Excellence: Lessons from America's Best-Run Companies. Thomas J. Peters and Robert H. Waterman, Jr. Hardcover: $19.95 **QPB Ed: $6.95**

282. Irwin Shaw Short Stories Five Decades. Irwin Shaw Hardcover: $16.95 **QPB Ed: $9.95**

426. Geisha. Liza Crihfield Dalby Hardcover: $25 **QPB: $7.95**

717. Roget's International Thesaurus (Fourth Edition, Completely Revised and Redesigned). Revised by Robert L. Chapman **QPB: $8.95**

497. Ernest Hemingway on Writing Edited by Larry W. Phillips Hardcover: $12.95 **QPB Ed: $5.95**

507. Megatrends. John Naisbitt Hardcover: $17.50 **QPB Ed: $5.95**

Join now. Pick any 3 books or sets for $1 each—with no obligation to buy another book.

How membership works.
1. You receive the **QPB Review** 15 times each year (about every 3½ weeks). Each issue reviews a new **Selection,** plus scores of Alternates.
2. If you want the **Selection** do nothing. It will be shipped to you automatically. If you want one or more Alternate books—or no book at all—indicate your decision on the Reply Form always enclosed and return it by the date specified.
3. **Bonus books for Bonus Points.** For each softcover book or set you take (except for the books in this offer), you earn Bonus Points which entitle you to choose any of our softcover books. You pay only shipping and handling charges.
4. **Return privilege.** If the *QPB Review* is delayed and you receive the **Selection** without having had 10 days to notify us, you may return it for credit at our expense.
5. **Cancellations.** You may cancel membership at any time by notifying QPB. We may cancel your membership if you elect not to buy and pay for at least one book in every six-month period.

Let's try each other for 6 months.

Quality Paperback Book Club®, Camp Hill, PA 17012. Please enroll me in QPB and send the 3 choices I've listed below, billing me only $1 each, plus shipping and handling charges. I understand that I am not required to buy another book. You will send me the *QPB Review* (if my account is in good standing) for six months. If I have not bought and paid for at least one book in every six-month period, you may cancel my membership. A shipping and handling charge is added to each shipment.

Indicate by number the 3 books or sets you want. ☐ ☐ ☐

Name ______________________ 5-16
(Please print clearly) QB 67-5
Address ______________________ **Apt.** ______
City ______________ **State** ______ **Zip** ______
Prices generally higher in Canada.

The first book club for smart people who aren't rich.

240

In country like this, it's no wonder one man went through 150 pairs of Thermalites in just 3 months.

In Kittery, Maine, which is surrounded by the kind of country you see above, our Thermalites have been selling like hot cakes.

The fact is, Ernie Demsey, buyer at the Kittery Trading Post, started running out of his first order in just two weeks.

Two months and three orders later, over 70% of his inventory has been sold.

Quite obviously, the people of Kittery have taken a liking to our boot. And frankly, it's easy to see why.

Our Thermalites are designed to keep feet dry on the wettest days. Warm in the coldest temperatures. And comfortable on even the roughest terrain.

(If our Thermalites can do all this in country like Kittery, just imagine how well they'll perform in your area.)

So if you'd like to order some Thermalites, call **1-800-253-2184.**

But don't forget to write down our toll-free number. Chances are, you'll be calling it again.

WOLVERINE THERMALITES™

241

All Irish drink a lot.
All Chinese own laundries.
All Germans are Nazis.
All Italians are mafia.
All Russians are commies.
All Puerto Ricans drive Chevys.
All Jews are cheap.
All Greeks own diners.
All Poles are stupid.
All Blacks play basketball.

Ignorance.

Twenty years after the Civil Rights Act, there's enough of it around to keep prejudice and stereotyping alive in New York.

Starting May 13th, Channel 2's Tony Guida, Anthony Mason, and Randall Pinkston will present a series of special reports on how New York's racial and ethnic groups feel about each other. And about how those feelings affect our lives.

See "Race Relations in New York." A report that'll cause a lot of people to think twice.

2NEWS 6:00
WCBS-TV

242

WE WERE COVERING COWBOYS, RANGERS AND MAVERICKS
BACK WHEN THEY REALLY WERE COWBOYS, RANGERS AND MAVERICKS.

Dallas Times Herald

243

Consumer Magazine Color: 1 Page Or Spread Including Magazine Supplements

244
ART DIRECTOR
Robert Reitzfeld
WRITER
David Altschiller
DESIGNER
Martica Griffin
PHOTOGRAPHER
Cailor/Resnick
CLIENT
Pioneer Video
AGENCY
Altschiller Reitzfeld

245
ART DIRECTOR
Rick McQuiston
WRITER
Dan Wieden
PHOTOGRAPHER
Steve Bonini
CLIENT
Speedo
AGENCY
Wieden & Kennedy/Portland, OR

246
ART DIRECTOR
Ron Brello
WRITER
Jay Taub
DESIGNER
Ron Brello
PHOTOGRAPHER
Jerry Friedman
CLIENT
Citizen Watch
AGENCY
Levine Huntley Schmidt & Beaver

247
ART DIRECTORS
Jerry Whitley
Mark Johnson
WRITER
Paul Wolfe
DESIGNER
William Hartwell
PHOTOGRAPHER
Jeffrey Zwart
CLIENT
BMW of North America
AGENCY
Ammirati & Puris

ALL MONITORS ARE BETTER THAN TELEVISIONS. BUT SOME MONITORS ARE BETTER THAN OTHERS.

THERE'S NEVER BEEN A BETTER HOME MONITOR.

With the introduction of the Pioneer® SD-25A monitor/receiver, many of the classic, previously unsolved problems of video image reproduction have suddenly disappeared.

You merely have to see it side-by-side with other sets, and the difference is immediately obvious to your eyes. Since we can't offer you that comparison on the printed page, the facts will have to suffice.

A UNIQUE RED PHOSPHOR CRT.

Red has historically been a particularly difficult color for television to realize well. With the introduction of Pioneer's proprietary Red Phosphor CRT, red achieves a color accuracy never before possible. Because it is not accomplished at the expense of other colors. Simply put, at last true red can exist in the video company of true green.

AN EXCEPTIONAL BANDWIDTH OF 5.0 MHZ.

Today we hear much of comb filters. The presence of one, however, does not assure exceptional detail. Great resolution requires a comb filter that delivers wide video bandwidth. The Pioneer comb filter produces a remarkable luminance bandwidth of 5.0 MHz. Which in turn results in 400 horizontal lines and 450 vertical lines of video resolution.

BOTH A TINTED FACEPLATE AND A TINTED CRT.

Some manufacturers tint their faceplate to increase contrast. Others tint the front panel on their CRT. On the Pioneer SD-25A, we dramatically enhance contrast by tinting both. Every bit as important, a highly regulated switching power supply and black-level stabilizer create a dramatically wider video-dynamic range.

MORE DETAIL, LESS DISTORTION.

A unique velocity modulation circuit assures far better transient response. And a high-quality deflection yoke combined with a highly regulated power supply deliver exceptional geometric linearity.

In all, the edges are crisper, the shapes truer, the depth-of-field greater than you've probably ever seen in video before.

AUDIO THAT'S IN A LEAGUE WITH THE VIDEO.

As you would expect with a monitor/receiver of this quality, the audio is quite accomplished. A robust power supply produces a stereo/audio output 3 times that of conventional television. But what may be particularly meaningful to many of you is that there are 5 separate audio outputs that allow it to become part of the most sophisticated hi-fi system. There's a fixed output for recording; a Surround Sound output; and for your hi-fi there's a fixed output, a variable output for remote volume control, and there's even a separate sub-woofer output.

IT'S MORE THAN A MONITOR. IT'S AN EXPANDABLE RECEIVER.

Using a series of modules that are loaded into a port at the front of the set, the SD-25A is built to grow and improve with video's ever-changing technology.

A stereo TV tuner pack with built-in MTS decoder that's 139-channel cable capable, delivers the best of both cable and broadcast TV. (There are even 2 separate RF inputs.)

And there's a video-enhancer pack that increases the quality of transfers onto your VCR; an RGB control module; there's even a sing-along "Karaoke" module.

A REMOTE THAT EVEN CONTROLS LASERDISC.™

Given a monitor of this resolution and detail, it's not surprising that we've provided for the source that delivers the greatest resolution and detail: LaserDisc. Pioneer LaserDisc can be operated by the remote control, as can the Pioneer Super Beta Hi-Fi and 8 mm PCM VCRs.

YOU SIMPLY HAVE TO SEE IT.

Now that you understand what makes the Pioneer SD-25A perform so well, you should see it perform. Your eyes will understand instantly. It's the not-so-subtle difference between a monitor and a great monitor.

LaserDisc brand videodisc player is a trademark of Pioneer Electronics Corp.
© 1986 Pioneer Electronics (USA) Inc. All rights reserved.

Video for those who really care about audio.

244

For some reason, our best looking suits are often worn with accessories.

It is the most stunning collection of swimwear to ever hit the deck. Pick a print. Pick a panel. Either way, the colors are so hot that these season-to-season suits practically scorch water.

And if you think their looks will raise steam, wait until you take one to the blocks. Because at Speedo, we don't even think about fashion until we've perfected the fit. The fit that performs.

So contact your team dealer, or favorite sporting goods store. And see why a team doesn't have to dress like the U.S. Army to gather their share of medals.

SPEEDO

To locate the Speedo dealer nearest you, call toll free 800-347-8770.
Exclusive supplier of deck apparel to the U.S. National Swim Teams. Supplier to U.S. Diving, U.S. Water Polo and U.S. Synchronized Swimming.

245

We Bet You Can't Tell The World's Thinnest Water-Resistant Sport Watch From A Swizzle Stick.

You always thought you could tell them apart. And if you look very closely at them, maybe you can.

That's our whole point. You have to look closely. After all, who in the world has ever seen a sport watch this thin?

But the truth of the matter is, the object on the left hand side of the Baccarat glass is a finely cut crystal swizzle stick.

While the thinner object on the right, is the finely cut classic sport watch from Citizen.

Now, just how finely cut is our watch? 2.79 millimeters thin.

Yet it's made from tungsten carbide. An alloy that's five times harder than steel. And about one fifth its weight.

And as if that weren't enough, it even has a scratch resistant sapphire crystal.

When you couple all that with its fine sense of styling and attention to detail, you've got a classic example of our entire classic collection.

Then again, that's something anyone can tell.

CITIZEN

The Smartest Engineering Ever Strapped To A Wrist.

246

MOTORCYCLES ARE LIKE MUSIC. AFTER YEARS OF SHAKE, RATTLE AND ROLL, YOU START TO APPRECIATE THE GERMAN CLASSICS.

Like a vast hit parade of motorcycles, new bikes hit the road in swarms each year, destined to go from fashion to forgotten at an increasing clip.

Then there are the Legendary Motorcycles of Germany.™

BMW's classic road machines which, since 1923, have been famous for their endurance and reliability. And the motorcycles true enthusiasts turn to when their tastes mature.

"To ride a BMW R80 RT," Motorcyclist magazine wrote recently, "is to float, serene and slightly aloof, above both the road and the tacky, hard-sell paint jobs, feature lists and high-tech speed-first flash being thrown across the ocean by Japan, Inc."

That's more than a description of a motorcycle. It's the statement of a philosophy, in which minuscule production overrules the dictates of mass production.

Every BMW frame is aligned and scrutinized by a single craftsmen and bears his personal seal. Each bike is inspected every 72 seconds, with the pistons alone receiving 22 separate inspections.

And, when that pitiless regimen is finally complete, the finished motorcycles are then shipped to the testing facility—not the stores.

The new BMW R65 with Monolever™ Single Swing Arm Rear Suspension.

A result of such obsession, one critic wrote, is that "high-mileage, years-old BMW's retain their taut, solid feel when lesser motorcycles have long since gotten loose and rattly."

Another is that BMW bikes enjoy the most enduring warranty in the industry: 3 years and unlimited number of miles.*

Of course, behind such enduring bikes is enduring technology: BMW's classic flat-twin engine, which has powered BMW's through six decades and almost 200 track records. And whose light weight and low center of gravity place the R80 RT among the easiest handling touring bikes on the market.

BMW motorcycles are now available under convenient factory financing and leasing terms, and range from $3,800 to $7,650.**

A small price, indeed, for the kind of engineering that inspired Gaston Rahier to say, upon winning the legendary Paris-Dakar Rally on a BMW: "Sometimes the Dakar race seems as if it will go on forever. Fortunately, so do BMW's."

Your own journey into motorcycle immortality begins with a single step. To a BMW dealer for a thorough test ride.

THE LEGENDARY MOTORCYCLES OF GERMANY.

247

Consumer Magazine Color: 1 Page Or Spread Including Magazine Supplements

248
ART DIRECTOR
Susan Hoffman
WRITER
Jim Riswold
PHOTOGRAPHER
Pete Stone
CLIENT
Nike
AGENCY
Wieden & Kennedy/Portland, OR

249
ART DIRECTOR
Gary Johnston
WRITERS
Phil Lanier
Laurie Brandalise
PHOTOGRAPHERS
Ray Reding
Cindy Cooper
CLIENT
Apple Computer
AGENCY
Chiat/Day - Los Angeles

250
ART DIRECTOR
Sal DeVito
WRITER
Amelia Rosner
DESIGNER
Sal DeVito
PHOTOGRAPHER
Cailor/Resnick
CLIENT
Trump Casino Hotel
AGENCY
Chiat/Day

251
ART DIRECTOR
Joan Van Der Veen
WRITER
Sarah Humphrey
CLIENT
General Foods Corporation/ Jell-O Gelatin
AGENCY
Young & Rubicam

ONCE AGAIN, NIKE BRINGS A CROWD TO ITS FEET.

Athletes aren't the only ones rising to the occasion in our shoes.

But that doesn't come as a surprise to us. Because we've spent the last few years developing infants' shoes that make a little one's first steps easier.

How? Starting from the bottom, our shoes have flat outsoles to lessen those all-too-frequent wobbles and topples.

There's more to these outsoles. They're very light. And they're rubber. So they bend easily at the ball of the foot.

On top of all that, we made the uppers from either soft leather, canvas, or nylon. All of which are very flexible.

And very comfortable.

One last thing. Every Nike infants' shoe has an extra wide and deep toe box. To better complement the shape of a baby's foot. And make the shoe much easier to get in and out of.

Infants' shoes from Nike. Proof that what goes up doesn't have to come down.

At least not quite so often.

NIKE

248

Why every kid should have an Apple after school.

Today, there are more Apple® computers in schools than any other computer.

Unfortunately, there are still more kids in schools than Apple computers.

So innocent youngsters (like your own) may have to fend off packs of bully nerds to get some time on a computer.

Which is why it makes good sense to buy them an Apple IIc Personal Computer of their very own.

Send them home to a good school system.

The IIc is just like the leading computer in education, the Apple IIe. Only smaller. About the size of a three-ring notebook, to be exact.

Of course, since the IIc is the legitimate offspring of the IIe, it can access the world's largest library of educational software. Everything from Stickybear Shapes™ for preschoolers to SAT test preparation programs for college hopefuls.

In fact, the IIc can run over 10,000 programs in all. More than a few of which you might be interested in yourself.

For example, the best-selling AppleWorks™ 3-in-1 integrated software package. Personal finance and tax programs. Diet and fitness programs.

Not to mention fun programs for the whole family. Like "Genetic Mapping" and "Enzyme Kinetics."

One Apple that won't leave them hungry.

The Apple IIc is easy to set up and learn. And it comes complete with most everything you need to start computing in one box.

Including a free, easy-to-use 4-diskette course to teach you all about the IIc—when your kids get tired of your questions.

As well as a long list of built-in features that would add about $800 to the cost of a smaller-minded computer.

The features include: 128K of internal memory—as powerful as the average office computer.

A built-in disk drive that could drive up the price of a less-senior machine considerably.

And built-in adaptors for adding accessories, like our new ColorMonitor IIc, ImageWriter™ II printer and the Apple Personal Modem 300/1200.

A feast for their eyes.

The big 14-inch ColorMonitor IIc displays crisp, color graphics or a high resolution 80-column monochrome text for word processing.

You can print sharp color graphics, too, with our new ImageWriter II. It also prints near-letter-quality text in black and white, quickly and quietly. And, with its new SheetFeeder, you can switch to single sheets without removing the sprocket paper.*

If local color isn't enough, you can talk to the rest of the world through our new wall-mounted Apple Personal Modem 300/1200. With it, you can do your banking at home, check your stocks, gain access to all kinds of information libraries and much more.

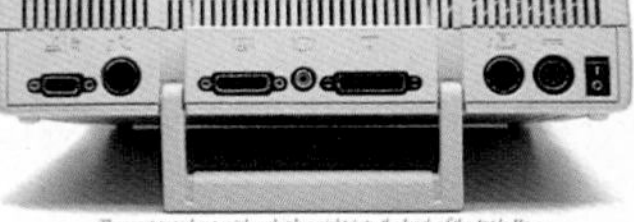

The most popular peripherals plug right into the back of the Apple IIc.

The ImageWriter II prints high quality color graphics.

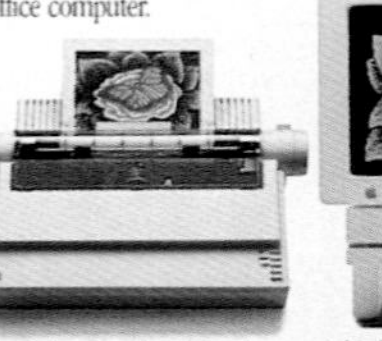

And speaking of high quality color, introducing ColorMonitor IIc.

Which would all add up to a very impressive list of expandable accessories if it weren't for all the others. Like an AppleMouse. And an extra disk drive when the time comes.

Avoid growing pains.

So while your children's shoe sizes and appetites continue to grow at an alarming rate, there's one thing you know can keep up with them. Their Apple IIc.

To learn more about it, visit any authorized Apple dealer. Or talk to your own computer experts.

As soon as they get home from school.

249

THE 1985 SUMMER GAMES HAVE BEGUN.

You don't have to wait another four years for the thrill of the competition. Just come to Trump Casino Hotel on the Boardwalk, where the games never stopped.

There's an event for everyone who wants to participate. Seven world-class restaurants to help you keep your strength up. And the kind of entertainment that leaves you entertained long after the show is over. But you'll have to come to Trump to be part of the fun.

Our summer games won't be televised.

TRUMP
CASINO HOTEL

How to dress a naked banana.

When you come across a banana in such an embarrassing condition, give it something exciting to wear. Jell-O® Brand Gelatin.

Just follow these fun, fruity new recipes. Before you know it, your family will be eating up the most luscious, most delicious banana creations around.

And if you think these treats are a big hit, wait till you see what we're up to next.

strawberry
ARTIFICIAL FLAVOR
JELL-O®
gelatin dessert
BRAND

Ever-So-Elegant Banana Trifle

1 package (3 oz.) JELL-O® Brand Strawberry Flavor Gelatin or Sugar Free Jell-O® Gelatin
$\frac{3}{4}$ cup boiling water
ice cubes
$\frac{1}{2}$ cup cold water
1 cup sliced bananas
1 cup sliced strawberries
2 cups $\frac{1}{2}$-inch pound cake cubes
$\frac{1}{4}$ cup orange juice
1 package (4-serving size) Jell-O® Vanilla Flavor Instant Pudding and Pie Filling
$1\frac{1}{2}$ cups cold milk
$\frac{1}{2}$ cup thawed Birds Eye® Cool Whip® Whipped Topping

Dissolve gelatin in boiling water. Add ice cubes to cold water to make $1\frac{1}{4}$ cups. Add to gelatin, stir until slightly thickened. Remove unmelted ice. Stir in bananas and strawberries. Place cake cubes in large serving bowl; sprinkle with orange juice. Spoon gelatin mixture over cake. Chill for 15 minutes. Prepare pudding mix with $1\frac{1}{2}$ cups milk as directed on package. Let stand a few minutes to thicken. Fold in whipped topping. Spoon into bowl over gelatin. Chill. Garnish. 10 servings. If you're counting calories, try making this recipe with Sugar Free Jell-O® Gelatin.

Stylishly Simple Banana Blend

1 package (3 oz.) JELL-O® Brand Gelatin, any flavor or Sugar Free Jell-O® Gelatin
1 cup boiling water
1 cup ice cubes and water
1 cup sliced bananas

Mix gelatin and boiling water in blender at low speed until gelatin is dissolved, about 30 seconds. Add ice cubes and water; stir until ice is partially melted; then blend at high speed 30 seconds. Pour into dessert glasses. Spoon in fruit. Chill until firm, 10-20 minutes. (This dessert layers as it chills: clear layer on bottom, frothy on top.) 6 servings. If you're counting calories, try making this recipe with Sugar Free Jell-O® Gelatin.

Fashionably Nutty Banana Salad

2 packages (3 oz. each) JELL-O® Brand Lime Flavor Gelatin or Sugar Free Jell-O® Gelatin
2 cups boiling water
$1\frac{1}{4}$ cups cold water
$\frac{3}{4}$ cup sliced banana
$\frac{1}{2}$ cup sour cream
$\frac{1}{4}$ cup diced celery
$\frac{1}{4}$ cup chopped walnuts

Dissolve 1 package gelatin in 1 cup boiling water. Add $\frac{3}{4}$ cup cold water. Chill until thickened. Add banana. Spoon into 6-cup mold. Chill until set but not firm, about 15 minutes. Dissolve remaining gelatin in 1 cup boiling water. Add $\frac{1}{2}$ cup cold water. Chill until slightly thickened. Blend in sour cream. Add celery and nuts. Spoon over clear layer in mold. Chill until firm, at least 4 hours. Unmold. Garnish. 10 servings. If you're counting calories, try making this recipe with Sugar Free Jell-O® Gelatin.

GENERAL FOODS

We're up to something good.

Consumer Magazine Color: 1 Page or Spread Including Magazine Supplements

252
ART DIRECTOR
Jack Mariucci
WRITER
Barry Greenspon
PHOTOGRAPHER
Henry Sandbank
CLIENT
Michelin Tire Corporation
AGENCY
Doyle Dane Bernbach

253
ART DIRECTOR
Paul Jervis
WRITER
Roger Feuerman
PHOTOGRAPHER
Jerry Friedman
CLIENT
Red Lobster Inns of America
AGENCY
Backer & Spielvogel

254
ART DIRECTOR
Tom Wolsey
WRITER
David Schneider
DESIGNER
Tom Wolsey
PHOTOGRAPHER
Bob Brody
CLIENT
Bank of New York
AGENCY
Ally & Gargano

255
ART DIRECTOR
Paul Jervis
WRITER
Roger Feuerman
PHOTOGRAPHER
Jerry Friedman
CLIENT
Red Lobster Inns of America
AGENCY
Backer & Spielvogel

252

THE NEW YORK TIMES, THURSDAY, MAY 9, 1985

Heart Risk Termed Lower With Fish in Diet

BOSTON, May 8 (UPI) — Eating fish once a week may significantly reduce the risk of heart attack and may even be beneficial to those suffering from rheumatoid arthritis and asthma, researchers said Wednesday.

Three separate studies published in The New England Journal of Medicine provided evidence of the healthy effects of saltwater fish oils, first seen in Eskimos and Japanese, who eat large amounts of fish and seldom have heart attacks...

Diets are Compared

The largest of the three studies conducted by researchers at the University of Leiden in the Netherlands, compared the diets of 852 men for more than 20 years with their risk of heart disease. It found that men who ate more than one ounce of fish a day were half as likely to suffer heart attacks.

A second study, conducted by researchers at the Oregon Health Sciences University, found that a diet rich in fish oil reduced very high levels of certain fats, triglycerides, which along with cholesterols seem to increase the risk of heart disease.

The doctors were surprised to find that fish high in fat, such as salmon and tuna, as well as fish low in fat, such as cod and flounder, were equally effective. In the past, doctors have only recommended their patients eat fish low in fat.

The third study, conducted at Brigham and Women's Hospital in Boston, had seven volunteers eat a diet high in fish fat for six weeks. The study found that the diet might have an anti-inflammatory effect on tissue in many areas of the body.

The discovery marked the first time researchers had found a potential way of influencing this type of swelling caused by the body's immune system.

Although the volunteers were all healthy, Dr. Frank Austen, chairman of Brigham and Women's department of immunology, said the finding could have important implications for people with rheumatoid arthritis and asthma.

Dr. Austen said the fish diet inhibited the production of leukotriene b4, an inflammatory agent 5,000 times more powerful than histamine, better known for its swelling effect in the hay fever season.

The three studies apply only to saltwater fish, and the researchers said they did not know if freshwater fish would produce the same results.

There's never been a better time for seafood.™

253

HAVE YOU OUTGROWN YOUR BANK, YOUR BANKER, YOUR CREDIT LINE, YOUR INVESTMENT STRATEGY?

Granted, everyone should have such problems.

On the other hand, if you happen to be suffering from this form of financial indigestion due to overachievement, you'll be gratified to learn that help is available. In the form of a Custom Banker at The Bank of New York.

Take, for example, the matter of credit. The arrangements your Custom Banker can work out with you may include the establishment of an unsecured credit line from $50,000 to $1 million or more, should your financial position and cash flow warrant it.

You can also establish a secured credit line of up to 80% of the market value of your investment portfolio, should you choose to place your marketable securities either in a custody account or in a personal investment account at The Bank of New York.

And since the basis of your relationship with a Custom Banker is predicated on knowing one another well, it goes without saying that if you need money fast, you can get money fast.

What's just as important, it is your Custom Banker's responsibility to apply this knowledge of your personal financial picture to his own breadth of knowledge in banking and finance. So that he or she can ably advise you on such matters as investment alternatives, tax-related instruments, and trust and estate needs.

To find out more about the credit and investment opportunities a Custom Banker can offer you, not to mention the banking-related tedium a Custom Banker can spare you, call Mr. Richard Freimuth, Vice President, Custom Banking Division, at 212-530-1971.

He'll be happy to have information sent to you, or arrange a comprehensive briefing at your convenience.

CUSTOM BANKING

THE BANK OF NEW YORK

MEMBER FDIC

254

The ocean rewrites our menu every day.

At Red Lobster® we don't chalk it up, if the ocean doesn't give it up. But that's your guarantee that the fish you see on our chalkboard is fresh, never frozen. And then broiled, to give you that healthy, good seafood taste. So what fresh fish will Red Lobster be serving up today? Only the ocean knows.

Red Lobster.

There's never been a better time for seafood.™

Most Major Credit Cards Accepted

255

Consumer Magazine Color: 1 Page Or Spread Including Magazine Supplements

256
ART DIRECTOR
Michael Dodson
WRITER
Karen Mallia
DESIGNER
Michael Dodson
PHOTOGRAPHER
Lynne St. John
CLIENT
Swanson Le Menu Dinners
AGENCY
Ogilvy & Mather

257
ART DIRECTOR
Ted Shaine
WRITER
Diane Rothschild
DESIGNER
Ted Shaine
PHOTOGRAPHER
Walter Iooss
CLIENT
CIGNA
AGENCY
Doyle Dane Bernbach

258
ART DIRECTOR
Sam Hurford
WRITER
Paul Grubb
PHOTOGRAPHER
Paul Bevitt
CLIENT
Holsten Distributors Ltd.
AGENCY
Gold Greenlees Trott/London

259
ART DIRECTOR
Paul Debes
WRITER
Stephen Crane
PHOTOGRAPHER
Ron Wu
CLIENT
Shimano American Corporation
AGENCY
Perri Debes Looney & Crane/ Rochester, NY

WHY SOME LE MENU DINNERS IMPROVE WITH AGE.

In our society, younger almost always means better. With the notable exception of wines, people and beef. Beef that has been aged is unquestionably superior. Connoisseurs lust for its mellow flavor and tender texture.

And while aged beef is a given in the better steakhouses of the world, it is something else again to find it in a frozen dinner.

For Le Menu, proper aging is an exact science, a balance of timing, humidity and temperature. Naturally, we cannot disclose the particulars which take our beef to perfection. Twelve locks—and several burly guards—stand between these culinary secrets and all of our competitors.

Suffice it to say that the aged beef contained in these Le Menu™ Dinners cannot be compared to the typical fare found elsewhere. We start with only grain-fed U.S. Choice sirloin, for it would be foolish to take this time and expense with inferior cuts.

Please judge our standards in one of Le Menu's newest beef dinners, Beef Stroganoff. We trust you will find it a noble tribute to Count Paul Stroganoff himself, the Russian diplomat for whom the dish was named.

Here, the beef is braised and steeped in stock, sherry and tomato paste; it is peppered, seasoned, then gently folded with sliced imported mushrooms and a generous dollop of sour cream.

This decadently rich main course is accompanied by egg noodles blended with two cheeses, butter and diced onion. You will also find a selection of julienne cut carrots, turnips and green beans, just barely touched with a light seasoned sauce.

You can also sample our aged beef in Le Menu Pepper Steak, tossed with strips of green pepper and onion, in a sauce of soy, sherry, teriyaki and beef stock, perked with a bit of ginger and garlic. It is served with long grain rice dotted with pimiento, and a medley of crisp oriental vegetables.

Outside better steakhouses, it is rare to find beef so carefully aged and artfully prepared. May we suggest *you* age not a day longer before you try it.

THERE'S ALWAYS SOMETHING SPECIAL ON LE MENU™

256

UNFORTUNATELY, THIS IS ONE OF THE FEW DOCTORS AMERICANS SEE REGULARLY.

While everybody recognizes the value of preventive health care, the reality is that few people see a doctor unless something is wrong.

In fact, millions of Americans don't even have their own doctor to see. As a result, correctable conditions go uncorrected.

And treatable illnesses become untreatable.

It's a senseless, all too frequently tragic problem.

It's also an expensive one.

Because people without doctors tend to use emergency rooms, at emergency room prices, for any medical problem they have.

Whether it's a bad cold or a broken leg.

What it all amounts to is that too many people are getting too little care. At too high a price.

And that's why we've made a serious commitment to a new form of health care delivery.

At CIGNA Healthplan, we operate Health Maintenance Organizations that deliver high quality, accessible and affordable health care.

For a small monthly payment, plus a few dollars a visit, CIGNA Healthplan provides members with a comprehensive package of health benefits.

As well as ready access to a CIGNA physician of their own.

This obviously encourages the kind of preventive care that can stop small medical problems from becoming big ones.

In fact, a recent Rand Corporation study showed that membership in an HMO reduced hospitalization by as much as 40% over a five-year period.

And reduced health care expenses by close to 25% during that same time.

Not surprisingly, we already have over 750,000 members enrolled nationwide.

If you think we might be of value to your company, please write to CIGNA Corporation, Department R2, One Logan Square, Philadelphia, PA 19103.

That way your employees would have two doctors to see. One of ours. And Dr. J.

CIGNA

257

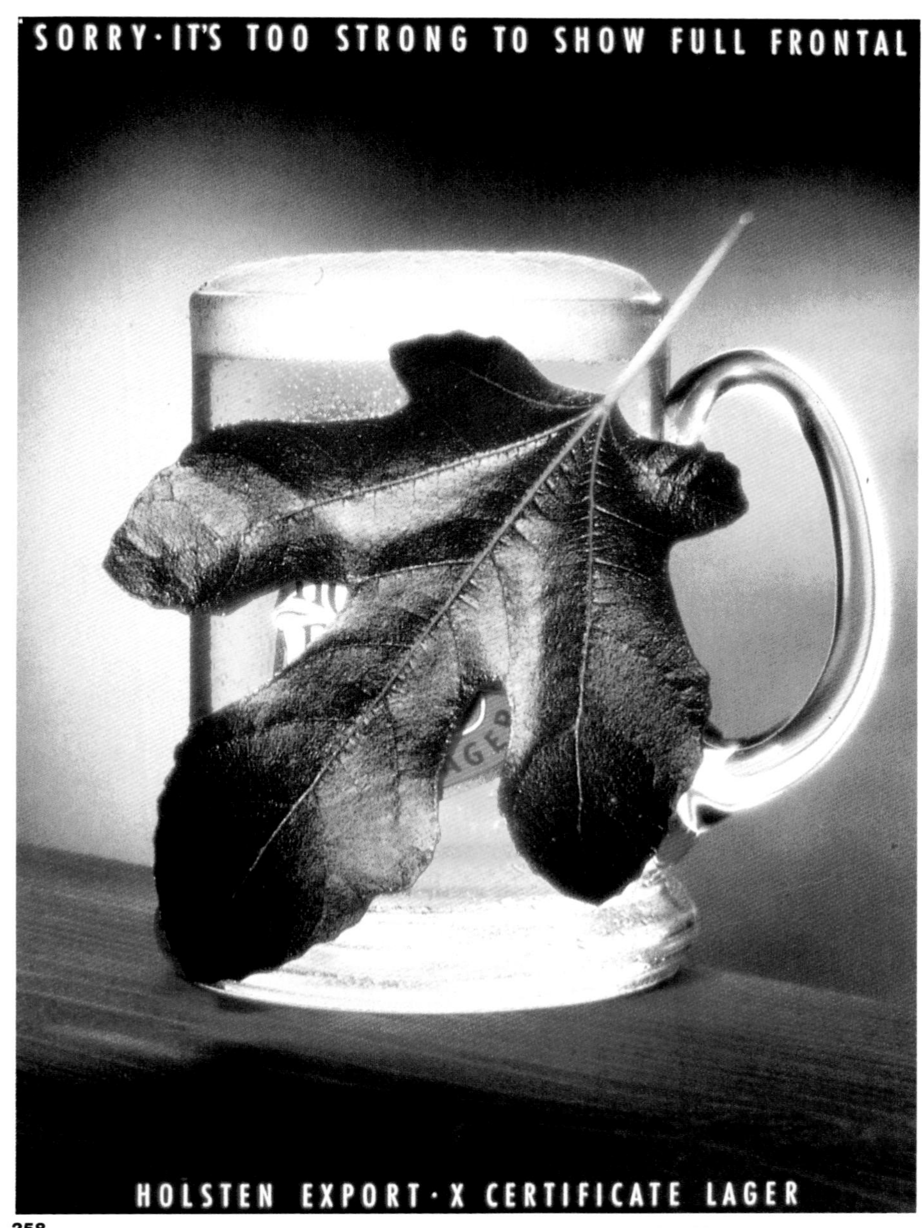
SORRY · IT'S TOO STRONG TO SHOW FULL FRONTAL
HOLSTEN EXPORT · X CERTIFICATE LAGER

258

Evolution. Revolution.
The reel on the left represents the highest rung on the evolutionary ladder of big game reels.
Triton® Trolling Series reels from Shimano.
Next to them, all other big game reels are still walking on their knuckles.
The reel on this page, however, represents a whole new species.
Triton® Lever Drag live bait, casting and trolling reels from Shimano.
In the long history of saltwater fishing, there's never been anything like them.
In fact, our Triton Lever Drags have more in common with our Triton Trolling Series than with any other live bait, casting or trolling reels you've ever fished.
Like our exclusive Ball Bearing Titanium Drag, the only drag in the world with a ball bearing for unmatched smoothness and Titanium-composite drag washers to keep the drag running cool when the fishing gets hot.
Four—count'em, four—stainless steel ball bearings to take the stress of hard-hitting, long-running game fish.
And a programmable lever drag that's so advanced, it has a patent pending.
So if you're after Giant Tuna or Marlin the size of small Caribbean islands, choose an evolutionary Triton Trolling Series reel, available in 4 sizes—TTS 30, TTS 50, TTS 50W, TTS 80W.
If you're into casting, trolling or live bait fishing for Albacore, Yellowtail, King Mackerel, or any other medium size saltwater fish, choose a revolutionary Triton Lever Drag reel, available in 3 sizes—TLD 5, TLD 10, TLD 15.
But whichever you choose, chances are it'll change the course of your personal fishing history forever.
And for the better.
For copies of our Triton owner's manuals, send $1.00 to: Triton Owner's Manuals, c/o Shimano American Corp., 205 Jefferson Rd., Parsippany, N.J. 07054.
SHIMANO®
TOMORROW'S TACKLE TODAY
SHIMANO
TRITON

259

Consumer Magazine Color: 1 Page Or Spread Including Magazine Supplements

260
ART DIRECTOR
Gary Yoshida
WRITER
Bob Coburn
PHOTOGRAPHERS
Dan Lamb
Jim Hall
CLIENT
American Honda Motor Company
AGENCY
Needham Harper Worldwide/ Los Angeles

261
ART DIRECTOR
Ted Shaine
WRITER
Diane Rothschild
PHOTOGRAPHER
Stock
CLIENT
CIGNA
AGENCY
Doyle Dane Bernbach

262
ART DIRECTOR
Jamie Mambro
WRITER
Gail Welch
DESIGNER
Jamie Mambro
ARTIST
John Burgoyne
PHOTOGRAPHER
Phil Porcella
CLIENT
Elizabeth Grady Face First
AGENCY
Welch/Currier - Boston

263
ART DIRECTORS
Bob Coburn
Gary Yoshida
WRITER
Bob Coburn
DESIGNERS
Bob Coburn
Gary Yoshida
PHOTOGRAPHERS
Lamb & Hall
CLIENT
American Honda Motor Company
AGENCY
Needham Harper Worldwide/ Los Angeles

A quick message from Honda.

We'll be brief. The car shown here is the most powerful Civic ever.

It's the new Honda Civic CRX Si. It has fuel injection. Driving enthusiasts will have no objection.

Fuel injection is just another way to get gasoline into the engine. Simply, it does the job more efficiently than a conventional carburetor.

Honda calls its new sequential-port system Programmed Fuel Injection. It times the exact moment to inject a precise measure of gasoline into each cylinder. The engine says when.

A 12-valve, cross-flow cylinder head makes effective use of the new fuel injection. Which makes it easier for you to get around slow moving traffic.

The CRX Si was designed for pure driving enjoyment. It comes only with a 5-speed manual transmission. Fifth gear is a true overdrive. It helps overall economy and reduces engine wear and interior noise level.

As always, you will find the engine and transmission up front for all the advantages of front-wheel drive. Less weight, more space, better traction.

One thing that makes the CRX Si a joy to drive is its suspension. Fore and aft stabilizer bars help control body lean while cornering. We've enclosed the rear bar inside the axle tube to keep everything neat underneath.

We've mounted nitrogen gas-filled rear shock absorbers to provide stable dampening. They help improve the ride.

Stopping power is trusted to power assisted brakes. Ventilated front discs help dissipate heat buildup. Rear brakes are drum type. Backing up everything is a dual diagonal hydraulic system.

Rack and pinion steering insures a positive feel to what's happening on the road. The car will positively turn on a dime, providing its diameter is no less than 29.5 feet. The Civic CRX has the tightest turning circle of any two seater sold in America. No wonder it's so easy to park.

In motion, the car is something else. A low 0.33 coefficient of aerodynamic drag. Honda designers shaped the car to direct air around it cleanly. To further improve total efficiency and help road holding ability.

Now you can see why there are so many aerodynamic features. Like a front air dam, flush windshield and door handles, low hoodline and rear spoiler. The CRX is slippery.

You can watch the air slipping by overhead. The CRX Si comes with a power sunroof. Just touch a button and the sunroof panel rises and retracts. Because of the special way it opens, its opening is larger than other designs would permit. And it takes up hardly any headroom. Only Honda has it.

You will find cast aluminum alloy wheels on the standard list. They are fitted with wide Michelin steel-belted radials. Anything less wouldn't be right.

There is a rear window washer and wiper. A big help with a window that's 980 square inches of glass. It also has an electric defroster.

All the windows are tinted to filter out sun rays. The windshield has a dark shaded upper area across the top.

You adjust the dual outside mirrors from inside the car. And you can turn on the headlights, signal turns, wipe and wash the windows quickly, slowly or intermittently. Without removing your hands from the steering wheel.

Tall people can sit in this car. The seatbacks recline and the bucket seats themselves adjust eight inches front or back. Legroom runs nearly 43 inches. The seats have adjustable headrests.

Right behind the bucket seats is a locking stowage compartment. For anything you don't want people to see. There is also 14.5 cubic feet of cargo space back there. With a wide rear hatch for easy loading and unloading.

On the dash panel you will see the instruments you need. These include a speedometer with odometer and trip odometer, tachometer, temperature and fuel gauges and functional warning lights. They are illuminated in high visibility orange for better night vision, like in airplane cockpits.

The rest of the instrument panel features door window defrosters, quartz digital clock, covered storage box. And finally, a coin box.

Certainly, by now, you must have gotten the message.

HONDA
The Civic CRX Si

260

WE KNOW A GREAT INVESTMENT WHEN WE SEE ONE.

Few things are more attractive to us than a run-down structure in an abandoned neighborhood.

Because while a crumbling wharf may not offer the obvious security of a suburban mall, what it does offer is the hope of a far greater return.

The key, of course, is to find the right run-down property in the right abandoned location.

And fortunately, CIGNA companies have had a great deal of success doing exactly that.

From Ghiardelli Square in San Francisco to Commercial Wharf in Boston, we've invested in projects that have rehabilitated not only neglected buildings, but whole neighborhoods. And earned substantial returns for our clients in the process.

Our interest in innovative properties hasn't been limited to renovations, either. Over the years we've invested in a range of nontraditional concepts, from suite hotels to rural malls.

We've also invested, successfully, in new inner-city commercial construction.

We were even among the first investors to invest in earthquake-resistant buildings.

So if you'd like more information on the real estate funds we manage for pension, individual or corporate investment, write to CIGNA Corporation, Department R5, One Logan Square, Philadelphia, Pennsylvania 19103.

While past performance, as everyone realizes, is not an indication of future results, we can promise you an investment approach that has provided exceptional returns even during periods of slow inflation.

We can promise you active management and ongoing evaluation of the property in our portfolio.

Most of all, we can promise you a tradition of investment boldness you might not expect from insurance companies.

In fact, we might even be able to offer you an investment every bit as inviting as the one you see here.

261

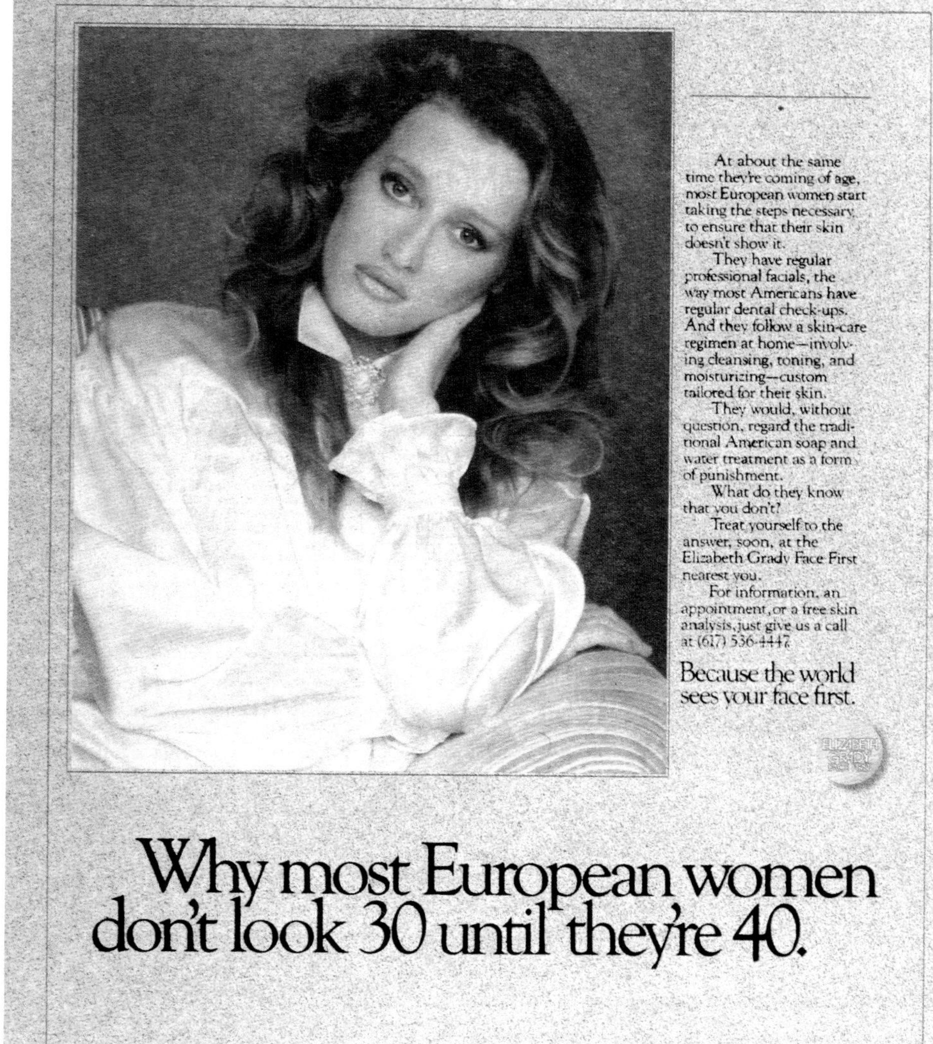

262

Comparisons haven't been made yet.

Honda has a way of bringing out the best in everyone. It's called the Accord.

Whenever we introduce a new Accord, everyone else returns to the drawing board. To try their best. Now we've done it again.

This is the new Honda Accord LX 4-Door Sedan. There's nothing else like it.

The hood is lower for aerodynamic efficiency. Also, you can see better over it. The reason we can make the hood so low is that, the car has a unique suspension. A double wishbone on all four wheels. It's the first time this suspension system has been used on a front-wheel-drive car. Race cars, however, have used it for years.

The new suspension does more than give the car a beautiful shape. It gives it a lovely ride, too. The handling is outstanding. We promise you'll be impressed.

You'll also be very comfortable. There is more headroom even though the roofline is lower. The car is also wider.

You'll also see through a lot more glass because the windows are larger. They all fit flush to the doors and body so there's less wind noise. The body itself is rigid and solid. The car is stable.

Conveniences have been well considered. This luxurious car comes with air conditioning. A new electronic stereo system with a cassette player. There are power windows and door locks. A power radio antenna. Dual power remote mirrors.

You might call the engine more of a powerhouse. Its size has been increased to two liters. And its mounts have been redesigned to absorb vibrations. It's smooth.

Variable-assist power steering takes the rough work out of parking. Cruise control makes long trips even more relaxing. And the trunk is substantially larger so you can carry more luggage.

While these extras might be available as optional equipment on other cars, they come standard on this car. We invite your comparison. HONDA

The New Accord

263

Consumer Magazine
Color: 1 Page Or Spread
Including Magazine
Supplements

264
ART DIRECTOR
Bob Butler
WRITERS
Tom McGuire
Peter Brown
Ron Berman
PHOTOGRAPHER
Terry Heffernan
CLIENT
Liquor Barn
AGENCY
Cole & Weber/Los Angeles

265
ART DIRECTOR
Ivan Horvath
WRITER
Bob Ancona
PHOTOGRAPHER
Mike Chesser
CLIENT
Yamaha Motor Corporation, USA
AGENCY
NW Ayer/Los Angeles

266
ART DIRECTOR
Earl Cavanah
WRITER
Larry Cadman
PHOTOGRAPHER
David Langley
CLIENT
Volvo
AGENCY
Scali McCabe Sloves

267
ART DIRECTOR
Susan Hoffman
WRITER
Ken Wieden
PHOTOGRAPHER
Steve Bonini
CLIENT
Nike
AGENCY
Wieden & Kennedy/Portland, OR

Château Gloria St. Julien
Château Mouton Rothschild
1984
PAUILLAC
We will sell these wines before their time.
Many of our most satisfied customers wait over a year for their wine to be delivered.
They've taken advantage of Liquor Barn's Bordeaux Futures Program and purchased the finest Bordeaux wines at low pre-release prices. How low? Well, our customers who had the foresight to buy 1982 Futures on Chateau Mouton Rothschild* saw the value of their investment rise from $33.16 to $85.00 or more a bottle in only 18 months.
A more modest example is the 1982 Chateau Gloria. Futures sold for just $6.98. The current price is over $14 per bottle.
Our wine buyers have recently returned from France with futures commitments on the 1984 vintage. They've carefully selected only the best wines from the best Chateaux. At the best prices. Stop in soon. It might be worth your time to buy some wine before its time, at Liquor Barn.
Fine wines, finally affordable.
Liquor Barn
Call 800-447-4700 for the Liquor Barn nearest you in California or Arizona, and for your free subscription to Good Libations. © 1985 Liquor Barn
Prices slightly higher in Arizona. *1982 label art shown; 1984 artist to be named.

264

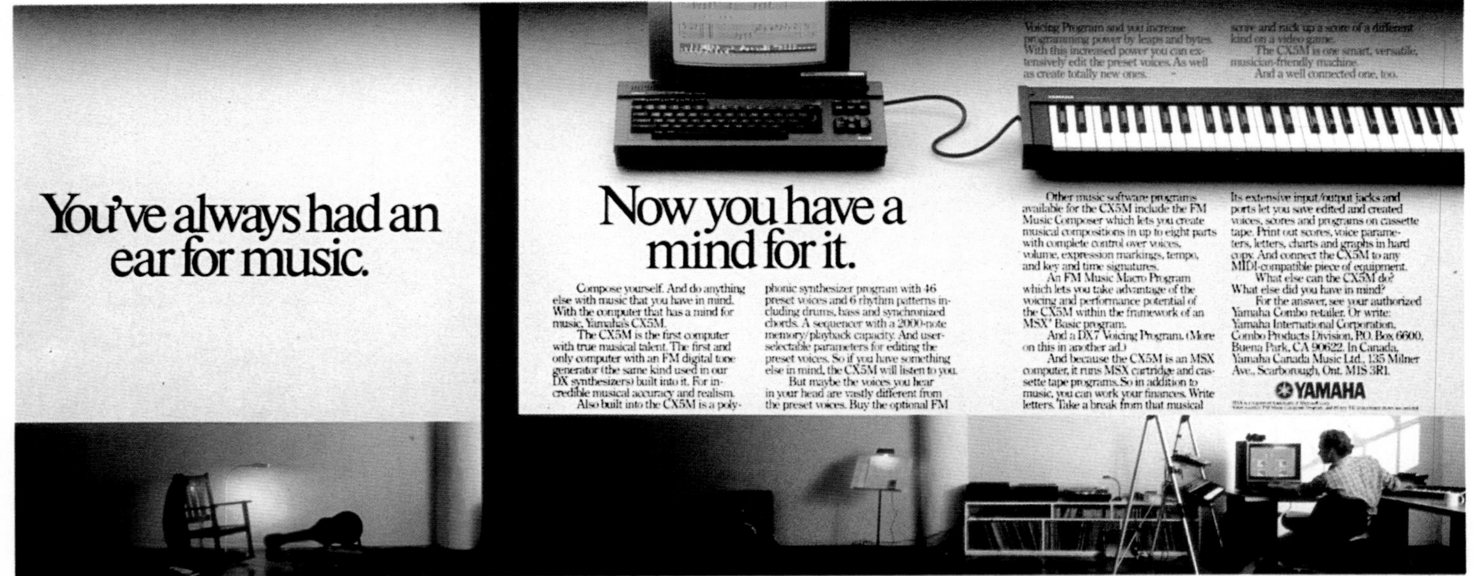

You've always had an ear for music.
Now you have a mind for it.
Compose yourself. And do anything else with music that you have in mind. With the computer that has a mind for music, Yamaha's CX5M.
The CX5M is the first computer with true musical talent. The first and only computer with an FM digital tone generator (the same kind used in our DX synthesizers) built into it. For incredible musical accuracy and realism.
Also built into the CX5M is a polyphonic synthesizer program with 46 preset voices and 6 rhythm patterns including drums, bass and synchronized chords. A sequencer with a 2000-note memory/playback capacity. And user-selectable parameters for editing the preset voices. So if you have something else in mind, the CX5M will listen to you.
But maybe the voices you hear in your head are vastly different from the preset voices. Buy the optional FM Voicing Program and you increase programming power by leaps and bytes. With this increased power you can extensively edit the preset voices. As well as create totally new ones.
Other music software programs available for the CX5M include the FM Music Composer which lets you create musical compositions in up to eight parts with complete control over voices, volume, expression markings, tempo, and key and time signatures.
An FM Music Macro Program which lets you take advantage of the voicing and performance potential of the CX5M within the framework of an MSX* Basic program.
And a DX7 Voicing Program. (More on this in another ad.)
And because the CX5M is an MSX computer, it runs MSX cartridge and cassette tape programs. So in addition to music, you can work your finances. Write letters. Take a break from that musical score and rack up a score of a different kind on a video game.
The CX5M is one smart, versatile, musician-friendly machine.
And a well connected one, too.
Its extensive input/output jacks and ports let you save edited and created voices, scores and programs on cassette tape. Print out scores, voice parameters, letters, charts and graphs in hard copy. And connect the CX5M to any MIDI-compatible piece of equipment.
What else can the CX5M do? What else did you have in mind?
For the answer, see your authorized Yamaha Combo retailer. Or write: Yamaha International Corporation, Combo Products Division, P.O. Box 6600, Buena Park, CA 90622. In Canada, Yamaha Canada Music Ltd., 135 Milner Ave., Scarborough, Ont. M1S 3R1.
YAMAHA

265

Turbo
YES, IT WILL FLY.
If you don't believe it, strap yourself into the cockpit of a Volvo 740 Turbo and take off.
This flying machine will rocket you from a standing start to legal speed in 6.7 seconds.* Faster than a BMW 325e. Faster than an Audi 5000S Turbo. Faster, even, than the much-touted Saab 16-valve Turbo.
"Enough juice to kick you squarely in the seat of the pants," exclaims *Autoweek*.
"...A brisk rush of surprise and pleasure.... Exemplary performance and handling," says *Road & Track*.
So check into your Volvo dealers and log some time in the intercooled 740 Turbo.
No pilot's license required.
*Based on tests conducted by Car And Driver.
THE 740 TURBO
By Volvo

266

JUST ADD ADRENALIN.
For distance running...
Zoom Air
For all-purpose running
Rival II
For cross country...
Zoom X II
For all-purpose running
Flame-Tech
For sprinting...
Zoom S II
For high jump...
High Jump
For long jump...
LJ III
For triple jump...
TJ 60
For javelin throw...
Javelin 88
For shot and discus...
SD Glide
NIKE
Beaverton, Oregon

267

Consumer Magazine Color: 1 Page Or Spread Including Magazine Supplements

268
ART DIRECTOR
Larry Bennett
WRITER
Harriet Frye
PHOTOGRAPHER
Barbara Bordnick
CLIENT
Royal Caribbean Cruise Line
AGENCY
McKinney Silver & Rockett/ North Carolina

269
ART DIRECTOR
Susan Hoffman
WRITER
Ken Wieden
PHOTOGRAPHER
Pete Stone
CLIENT
Nike
AGENCY
Wieden & Kennedy/Portland, OR

270
ART DIRECTORS
Gary Johns
Lee Clow
WRITER
Jeff Gorman
PHOTOGRAPHER
Carl Furuta
CLIENT
Nike
AGENCY
Chiat/Day - Los Angeles

271
ART DIRECTOR
Rick McQuiston
WRITER
Jim Riswold
PHOTOGRAPHERS
George Herrell
Gary McGuire
CLIENT
Honda Scooters
AGENCY
Wieden & Kennedy/Portland, OR

The decks are strung with lights that soar high above the sea, framing the deepening indigo of the night.

Far below you, on the water, the reflection of a tropical moon scatters into a thousand glowing bits.

When evening comes, on a Royal Caribbean cruise, you'll see that all the romantic stories you've heard about cruising are absolutely true.

You'll sip a vintage Bordeaux, savor a perfectly prepared leg of lamb, indulge yourself in Cherries Jubilee flamed right at your table.

You'll watch the silent passing of a freighter, far out on the horizon. And dance under more stars than you ever thought the sky could hold.

And you'll find that the warmth of the islands lingers in your mind, long after the sun goes down.

So talk to your travel agent about a Royal Caribbean cruise. For seven, eight, ten or fourteen days.

After all, some things are just too good to be left to your imagination.

ROYAL CARIBBEAN

Now Imagine The Same Idea, On A Slightly Larger Scale.

268

STILL CRAZY AFTER ALL THESE YEARS.

The Nike Sock Racer. A serious racing flat with a full length Nike-Air® midsole. Definitely not for everyone.

NIKE AIR

269

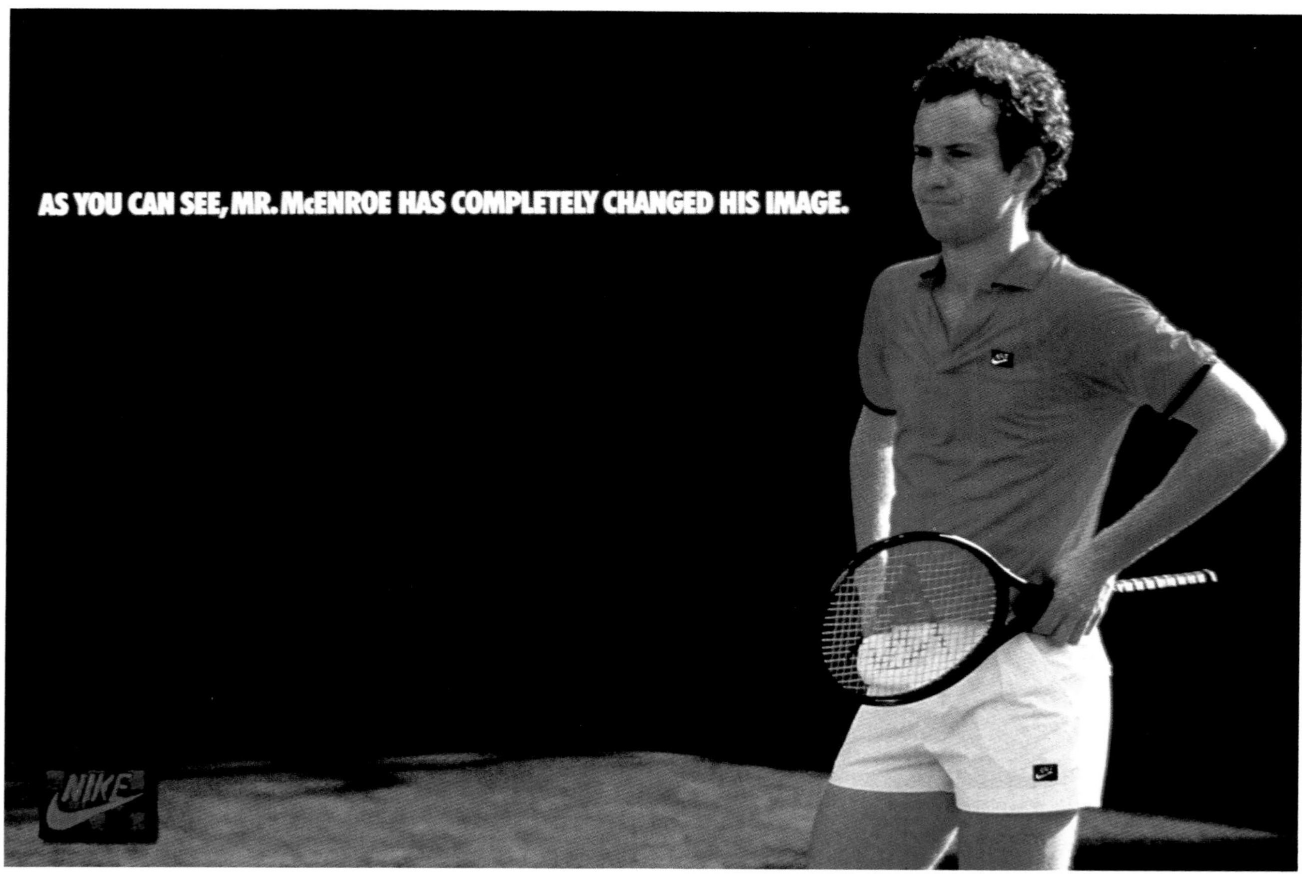

270

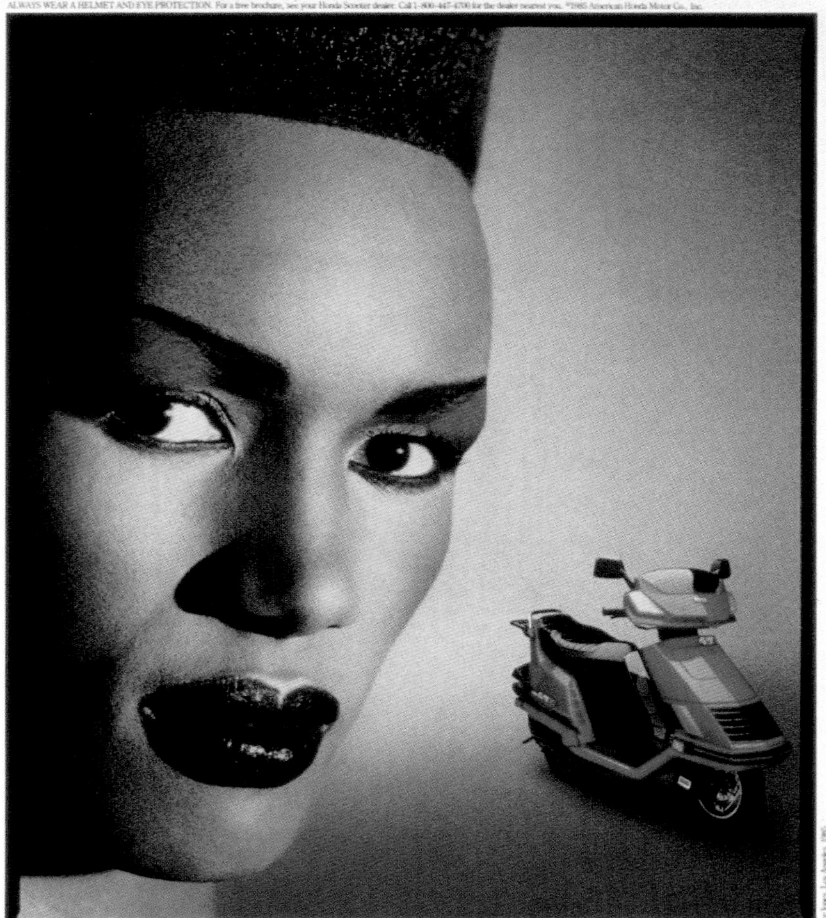

Make a radical departure.

271

Consumer Magazine Color: 1 Page Or Spread Including Magazine Supplements

272
ART DIRECTOR
Gary Johns
WRITER
Jeff Gorman
PHOTOGRAPHER
Carl Furuta
CLIENT
Nike
AGENCY
Chiat/Day - Los Angeles

273
ART DIRECTOR
Simon Bowden
WRITER
David Metcalf
DESIGNER
Simon Bowden
PHOTOGRAPHER
Jerry Friedman
CLIENT
Volvo
AGENCY
Scali McCabe Sloves

274
ART DIRECTOR
Hanna Mayer
WRITER
Sande Lohm
PHOTOGRAPHER
Michael Pohuski
CLIENT
McCormick & Company
AGENCY
W. B. Doner & Company/ Baltimore

275
ART DIRECTOR
Marten Tonnis
WRITER
Steve Rabosky
PHOTOGRAPHER
Bo Hylen
CLIENT
Apple Computer
AGENCY
Chiat/Day - Los Angeles

272

273

To reach Unjha, one must be willing to brave the 125 degree heat of the Great Indian Desert. That's why Unjha's only visitors are nomads and our spice buyers.

When the wind blows in Unjha, it's as if someone fanned a raging fire. The sky disappears behind a swirling mass of sand. And, in places, the land actually cracks from the searing heat.

Some find it merely oppressive. Others, hell on earth. In spite of the heat and blinding dust, here is where you'll find some of the most flavorful spices known to man.

2,000 years ago, camel caravans traveled whole countries for the cumin, dill and fennel seed this otherwise barren land produced. The trip took months, but those who made it found spices so rich, so full that to own them was as good as owning the world.

Not much has changed since then. Today, Unjha still produces spices so superior that to select them, a few are willing to travel the globe. Such is the task of the McCormick/Schilling spice buyer.

We regularly journey to remote spice capitals like Unjha. To smell, taste and select the most flavorful spices ourselves.

The fact is, our gourmet spices actually make your meals taste richer, make the flavor fuller. That's why we go to the ends of the earth for them.

McCormick®/Schilling® Gourmet. Quite simply, the best spices on earth.

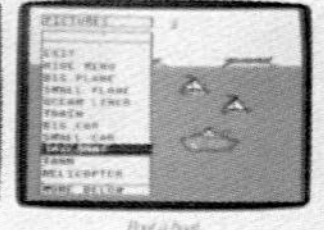

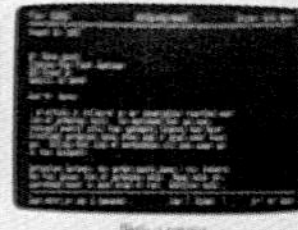

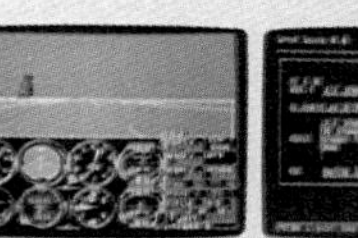

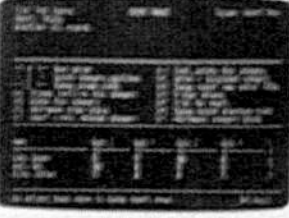

We have more good family programs than ABC, NBC and CBS combined.

You've taped every episode of the Bill Cosby Show. Twice.

You've flipped through the channels so often that it's worn the decals off your remote control.

And your eight-year-old just came downstairs wearing 12 of your best gold necklaces and asked you to give him a Mohawk haircut, *fool!*

If those are recurring plot themes around your house, maybe it's time you looked into an Apple® IIc Personal Computer.

It can run over 10,000 different programs, the world's largest library of personal computer software. So no matter what anyone in the family wants to do, an Apple IIc can help them do it.

If you can plug in a TV, you can hook up a IIc.

You can manage your personal finances with programs like Dollars and Sense and Tax Preparer.

Pop a program like AppleWorks™ into its disk drive, and you've got an integrated spreadsheet, word processor and data base to help you catch up with your work at home.

Or you can select from thousands of specialized programs for doctors, lawyers, contractors, farmers, brokers, screenwriters or just about any other legitimate business.

And the Apple IIc is a compact version of the computer that's used in schools more than all other computers combined—the Apple IIe.

So, unlike TV, it can teach kids more valuable lessons than how to drive a car through the side of a building without getting a scratch.

Of course, the Apple IIc isn't all work and no play. In fact, it can provide greater fun, adventure and excitement than the networks during the new season premieres.

There are programs that let you travel space, solve mysteries, explore jungles, become an instant millionaire, get elected president and save the world.

And an Apple IIc is easier to set up than the average VCR. Just take it out of the box, plug in two cords and you're ready to compute.

Plus you can just as easily add things like our new ImageWriter™ II printer, ColorMonitor II, Apple Personal Modem, mouse and external disk drive.

To see everything an Apple IIc can do live and in person, visit any authorized Apple dealer.

While they may not have all 10,000 software packages on hand, you'll find plenty of programs the whole family will want to run.

And rerun.

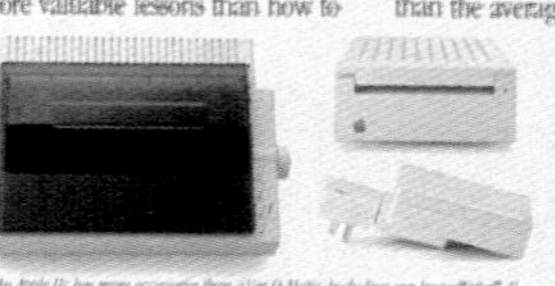

An Apple IIc has more accessories than a Veg-O-Matic. Including our ImageWriter™ II printer, Apple Personal Modem and UniDisk™ disk drive.

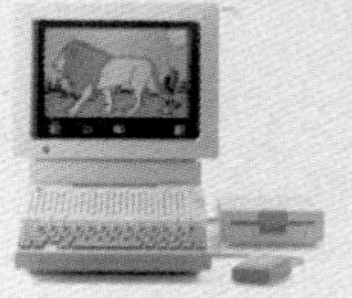

Consumer Magazine Color: 1 Page Or Spread Including Magazine Supplements

276
ART DIRECTOR
Harry Hartofelis
WRITER
Harriet Frye
PHOTOGRAPHER
Ralph Holland
CLIENT
North Carolina Travel & Tourism
AGENCY
McKinney Silver & Rockett/ North Carolina

277
ART DIRECTOR
Victoria Filice
WRITER
Susan Lee
PHOTOGRAPHERS
Lamb & Hall
CLIENT
American Honda Motor Company
AGENCY
Needham Harper Worldwide/ Los Angeles

278
ART DIRECTOR
Robert Joiner
WRITER
Rob Schapiro
DESIGNER
Robert Joiner
CLIENT
Potato Chip Snack Food Association
AGENCY
The Richards Group/Dallas

279
ART DIRECTOR
John Morrison
WRITER
Penny Kapousouz
ARTIST
Cynthia Shern
PHOTOGRAPHER
Dennis Manarchy
CLIENT
Apple Computer
AGENCY
Chiat/Day - Los Angeles

In North Carolina, We Take A Slightly Different Approach To Oceanfront High-Rises.

They have weathered the storms of nature, and stood tall through the storms of war. For nearly two centuries, they have beamed their silent warnings out across the rocky shoals.

And the land they guard remains much as it was when the first of the tall towers lit its first whale-oil lantern.

There are places, here, where the lighthouses are virtually the only man-made structures to be seen for miles around.

Where the white beaches are inhabited, not by high-rises and hot-dog stands, but by burrowing clams and an occasional pelican.

Close by, Victorian houses line the waterfronts. Tiny churchyards sleep in the dappled shadows of moss-hung oaks.

And the fishermen cast their nets, in the shimmering Atlantic sunrise, from boats hand-built no more than an island away.

Further inland, terraced fields disappear into dark groves of pine. Rivers twist their way through cool Appalachian forests.

And even the cities, with their flowered parks and lovingly restored old neighborhoods, seem to have escaped the modern-day notion that newer is better.

North Carolina. You'll find it filled with things that can lift your spirits to the skies.

And you'll find that very few of them are made of concrete.

For help in planning your vacation, just send us this coupon for your free North Carolina Travel Package.

NAME

ADDRESS

CITY STATE ZIP

NORTH CAROLINA

North Carolina Travel, Department 000, Raleigh, NC 27000
Call toll-free 1-800-VISIT NC, Operator 000

276

Is this the key to your car?

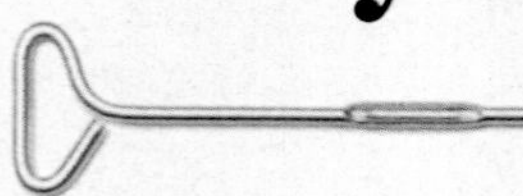

The Civic DX Hatchback is packed with space to keep you from feeling packed in.

The key is its innovative long-roof design. It makes this car remarkably big for its size.

In the rear, there's generous headroom so comfort doesn't take a back seat to economy. The rear seats slide back as well as recline so you can kick back. They also fold down one at a time to accommodate even odd-sized cargo.

Outside, the roof design makes the most of aerodynamics. So the exterior is as efficient as the interior.

And all around, there is a panoramic expanse of window area covering 319 degrees out of 360. Tinted glass and a rear wiper/washer help make sure the view stays clear.

This Civic is big on value, too. A 1.5 liter, 12-valve engine, 5-speed manual transmission, front-wheel drive, as well as an adjustable steering column are standard.

This year, there is 4-speed automatic transmission available.

If your small car leaves you open for suggestion, then we've got a suggestion. The 1986 Honda Civic DX Hatchback.

It's so big, it's uncanny.

HONDA
The Civic DX Hatchback

277

A potato has nutritional value.

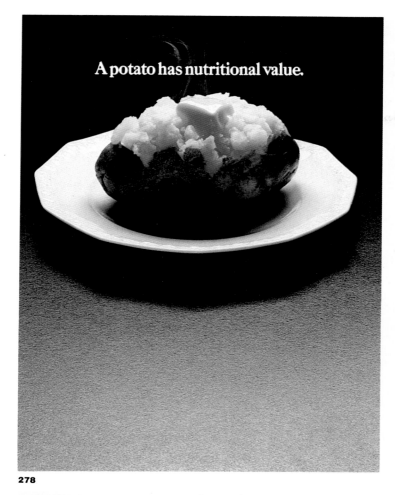

No matter how you slice it.

A potato is a potato is a potato. You can bake it. Boil it. Mash it. Or slice it up and quick-fry it into chips. It's still going to provide many of the same nutrients. As a matter of fact, a one-ounce serving of potato chips contains at least 15 essential nutrients. That includes about 10% of the U.S. RDA of Vitamin C and 8% of the U.S. RDA of Vitamin B_6.

A one-ounce bag of chips also contains 1.5 grams of dietary fiber. That's about how much you'll find in 1/2 cup of celery or cabbage. Which helps explain why potato chips are listed under the "vegetable" heading in USDA Handbook #8.

Of course, potato chips aren't a basic source of nutrients. But they do have more nutrients than most people realize. And fewer calories. Only 150 in a one-ounce bag.

It may also surprise people to know that a typical bag of chips has less than 1/8 of a teaspoon of salt* and 2¼ teaspoons of oil. A lot of people put more salt and butter on a baked potato. And, according to the Health and Nutrition Examination Study (HANES II)**, the fat in potato chips accounts for less than 1% of the daily calories in the average American diet.

As for cholesterol, most potato chips don't have any. That's because most chips are cooked only in vegetable oils***. And contrary to popular belief, most chips contain no preservatives.

Potato Chips
NUTRITION INFORMATION

Calories	150
Protein	2 grams
Carbohydrate	14 grams
Fat	10 grams
Cholesterol** (0 mg/100 g)	0 milligrams
Sodium	175 milligrams
Potassium	205 milligrams
Dietary Fiber	1.3 grams
Protein	2
Vitamin A	*
Vitamin C	10
Thiamine	2
Riboflavin	*
Niacin	4
Calcium	*
Iron	2
Vitamin B_6	8
Phosphorus	4
Magnesium	4
Copper	6

All this isn't to say that potato chips are for everyone. It's just a reminder that potato chips do come from potatoes. And, once a potato, always a potato.

"I may still run out of time. But at least now I know 30 days in advance."

When Informatics General was awarded a multi-million dollar, 60-man-year software development project for NASA, Project Director David Kaiser decided the colored yarn and push-pins had to go.

They had been one of many methods of constantly revising the PERT (scheduling) charts his projects so heavily depend on.

"I'd tried everything," David remembers. "I even pinned 3x5 index cards to a bulletin board and connected interdependent tasks with rubber bands. When anything changed, I'd move the cards by hand. The colored yarn indicated our critical path."

MacProject

Then David discovered a computer called Macintosh.™ And a powerful software program called MacProject.™

And according to David, project management hasn't been the same since.

"When I was scheduling on paper, I was limited to roughly 300 separately scheduled tasks. With Macintosh, we can work with 1600 separately scheduled tasks."

And scheduling at a greater level of detail is just one of the many differences Macintosh makes in David's work.

Unlike other scheduling programs, MacProject makes updating as easy as a point and click of Macintosh's mouse.

So David and his task managers are actually willing to do it. MacProject does the rest. Recalculates dates. Reformulates the critical path. And monitors all project resources.

So anyone on any project, from high-rise construction to film production, can refer to the most current information on people, money and time.

At a glance.

"We still wind up working a few weekends," David admits. "Only now we can calculate in advance exactly how many weekends we'll need to work to stay on schedule."

Another testimony to the fact that Macintosh not only helps work stay on schedule, but weekend ski trips, too.

Consumer Magazine Color: 1 Page Or Spread Including Magazine Supplements

280
ART DIRECTOR
Steve Beaumont
WRITERS
Penny Kapousouz
Steve Hayden
Brent Bouchez
PHOTOGRAPHER
Mark Coppos
CLIENT
Porsche Cars North America
AGENCY
Chiat/Day - Los Angeles

281
ART DIRECTOR
Annette Osterlund
WRITER
Jamie Shevell
DESIGNER
Annette Osterlund
PHOTOGRAPHER
Gary Perlweiler
CLIENT
Nikon
AGENCY
Scali McCabe Sloves

282
ART DIRECTOR
John Morrison
WRITER
David Lubars
PHOTOGRAPHER
Dennis Manarchy
CLIENT
Apple Computer
AGENCY
Chiat/Day - Los Angeles

283
ART DIRECTOR
Marcus Kemp
WRITER
Jim Copacino
CLIENT
Semiahmoo Resort
AGENCY
Livingston & Company/ Seattle

In 1948, Professor Porsche decided any car that merely got you from here to there, just didn't go far enough.

For Christmas 1920, Ferdinand Porsche Jr. received a toy car. Not the kind you push around on the floor or wind up and let go.

The kind you drive.

Fully operational, with headlights and an engine that would push it along at a brisk 30 miles per hour.

Of course, like most 11 year-olds, young Ferry had little understanding of the practical uses for the automobile. And cared even less.

Because his car provided him with countless hours of the one thing 11 year-olds value more than most anything else.

Fun.

Twenty-eight years later, the first 356 Porsche was introduced. Ferry Porsche was now Dr. Porsche, but the thrill of his first days behind the wheel was etched clearly in his memory.

And with his new silver convertible, he played a strong hunch. That while everyone else was building utilitarian cars for the masses, there must be at least a few people like himself who still felt eleven years old. And would want a car that did more than simply transport you from one place to another.

The kind of car you drive... just for the fun of it.

Seventeen years passed before the last 356 rolled off the assembly line. A white convertible with number 76,302 on its ID plate.

The hunch had become a legend. One that still thrives in the showrooms of Porsche dealerships today.

Be it the 944, 928 or 911. Somewhere in each, you can find a piece of that little silver car with the skinny tires and split-screen windshield.

As for Dr. Porsche, he's now a professor.

At the celebration of his 75th birthday, he was presented with another toy car. A scale model of the Le Mans winning 936 Porsche with just enough room for an eager 75-year-old man to squeeze into the cockpit.

And before any pictures could be snapped or toasts proposed, the little car had disappeared.

Along with Professor Porsche.

356-001 4-cylinder, horizontally opposed, air-cooled, pushrod, mid engine, 1131cc's, 40 hp. Weight: 1320 lbs. Top speed: 84 mph.

280

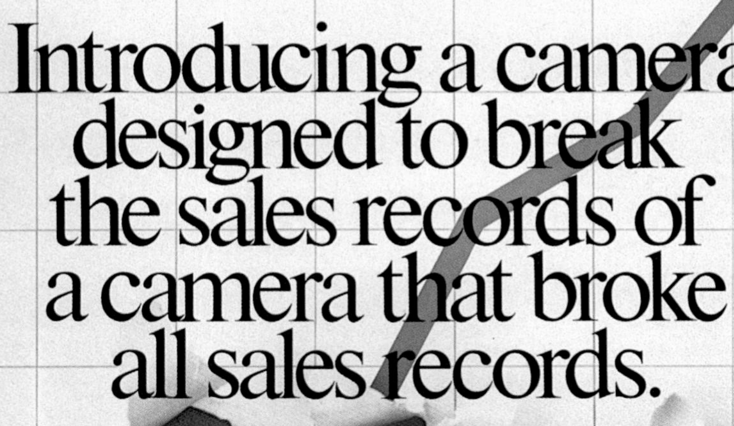
Introducing a camera designed to break the sales records of a camera that broke all sales records.

Nikon LENS
35mm 1:2.8
Nikon
One•Touch

Two years ago, when Nikon introduced the One-Touch, we expected sales to be good.

But what we didn't expect was that the One-Touch would become the hottest selling Nikon, breaking all our sales records ever.

Now, there's something that's going to send the sales curve right off the chart.

The new One-Touch. It still has auto-load, auto-wind, auto-focus and auto-flash, along with two new features—auto DX film speed set and built-in auto-lens cap. The only thing your customer has to do to get great, sharp pictures is turn it on and shoot.

To kick off the introduction, we'll be offering dealer video tapes to give you a detailed description of key features. And this year we'll be doing our most extensive advertising campaign ever, including network television and point-of-purchase displays. Even the packaging will help the camera sell itself because it shows examples of great One-Touch pictures, along with a description of its 11 automatic features.

The new One-Touch is available only in North America. And of course, your customers will be eligible to join the Nikon USA Club.

If your Nikon sales records were broken last year, expect them to be completely shattered this year.

Nikon.
We take the world's greatest pictures.®

© Nikon Inc., 1985

281

"There was never time to do it right, but always time to do it over. Now there's plenty of time for both."

Robert Kehoe had a problem. He'd been trying to put together a monthly newsletter for six months without much success.

Instead of a newsletter, he would wind up with typed pages covered with blotches of white-out. Smudgy illustrations made with not-so-magic markers. And more type bills than the newsletter had pages.

Robert is operations manager of Liberty Technologies, Inc. A Michigan-based company that specializes in developing cleaning products for the auto industry.

"It's my responsibility to communicate the benefits of using our products to the three biggest auto manufacturers," Robert says. "You know, how to keep your transmission assembly line spic and span . . . that kind of thing."

To Robert, a newsletter seemed like an efficient, simple way to do that.

Or so he thought.

"I'd get something pieced together to show the product support people. And by the time they'd all made changes, I'd be back to page one."

But somewhere between the running back and forth to the typesetter, the design shop, and the printer, Robert found time to order an Apple® Desktop Publishing System.

With his powerful new Macintosh™ personal computer, an Apple LaserWriter™ printer and software programs like Aldus PageMaker, MacDraw™ and MacWrite,™ Robert was able to set type. Cut graphics into text. Design border treatments. Make revisions in seconds. All by himself.

And faster than Robert used to spill white-out, the newsletter was done.

And printed.

And distributed. All within a few scant days.

He's also using his Macintosh to produce customized labels, business forms, fliers, price lists, sales reports and instruction manuals.

All within a few hours.

Another testimony to the fact that Macintosh is helping people like Robert work faster, smarter and more creatively.

Of course, that's hardly news to us.

Call (800) 446-3000 ext. 501 for the name of the nearest authorized Apple Desktop Publishing specialist in your area.

© 1985 Apple Computer, Inc. Apple and the Apple logo are registered trademarks of Apple Computer, Inc. LaserWriter, MacDraw and MacWrite are trademarks of Apple Computer, Inc. Macintosh is a trademark of McIntosh Laboratory, Inc. and is being used with its express permission. PageMaker is a trademark of Aldus Corporation.

AT OUR GOLF COURSE AT SEMIAHMOO YOU'LL SEE A LOT OF EAGLES.

Not the kind of eagles that drop into cups. The kind of eagles that soar through the air—high above evergreen forests, unspoiled shoreline and snow-capped mountains.

What we've just described is the Resort Semiahmoo. A planned community destined to be the next great resort in the West.

The managing partner of Semiahmoo is Centennial—a company whose principals have helped develop world-class resorts like Sea Pines on Hilton Head Island and Snowmass in Colorado. Semiahmoo will follow in this tradition.

Located near Blaine, Washington, Semiahmoo is coming to life along five miles of picture perfect beachfront—and acres of densely forested uplands.

This unique topography means Semiahmoo will have everything a great resort can offer: Starting with a challenging Arnold Palmer-designed, 18-hole golf course which is due to be completed in June, 1986. But golf is only the beginning.

Semiahmoo is already home of one of the finest marinas in the Northwest—putting you just a short sail from the picturesque San Juan Islands.

The centerpiece of Semiahmoo will be Lighthouse Square—a charming waterfront village which will bustle with restaurants, galleries, shops and an open-air market. Nearby, a 200-room inn and conference center will provide residents and visitors with year-round recreational facilities. Including a complete athletic club, indoor tennis, swimming, jogging and bicycle paths, as well as beachcombing and fishing.

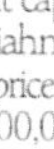

Perched above it all is Boundary Ridge, a prestigious neighborhood that captures the best of Semiahmoo.

Ranging in price from the low-$30,000s to over $100,000, these are one-third to one-half acre homesites—most with sweeping views of Semiahmoo Bay and the San Juan Islands.

Unquestionably, Boundary Ridge represents an important real estate opportunity. And the sooner you see it, the greater chance you'll have of owning a choice site.

Also, by this summer, fairway homesites and cottages, as well as beachfront condominiums will be offered.

For more information, mail the postcard. Or call Nick Blodgett, collect, at (206) 332-8588.

We're eager to give you a first-hand look at the next great resort community in the western United States.

And, more than likely, an eagle or two along the way.

THE RESORT SEMI·AH·MOO

Consumer Magazine Color: 1 Page Or Spread Including Magazine Supplements

284
ART DIRECTOR
Bob Barrie
WRITER
John Stingley
DESIGNER
Bob Barrie
ARTISTS
Dick Hess
Mark Hess
CLIENT
Prince Spaghetti Sauce
AGENCY
Fallon McElligott/Minneapolis

285
ART DIRECTOR
Grant Richards
WRITER
Glenn Gill
DESIGNER
Carl Warner
PHOTOGRAPHER
John Katz
CLIENT
Autry Industries
AGENCY
The Richards Group/Dallas

286
ART DIRECTOR
Ike Leonard
WRITER
Bob Solomon
PHOTOGRAPHER
Michael Watson
CLIENT
Cascade
AGENCY
Saatchi & Saatchi Compton

287
ART DIRECTOR
Al Colello
WRITERS
Yvonne Durant
Al Colello
ARTIST
Al Colello
PHOTOGRAPHER
Patrice Cassanova
CLIENT
Noxema Skin Cream
AGENCY
SSC&B: Lintas

Chunky.

Whether you choose our original sauce with imported olive oil and romano cheese, or our chunky homestyle with bits of tomato, herbs and spices, you'll get classic Italian taste.

284

How To Avoid Taking A Pounding At Tennis.

No matter how good your opponent is, two things should never take a pounding on the court. We're talking about your feet.

Autry recommends a preventative measure called the CLC.* A tennis shoe for men and women. One that allows you to concentrate on your game, instead of your feet.

Jim Autry's expertise goes into every pair of Autry shoes.

CLC stands for counter-lock-cord. An exclusive support system designed to grip your ankle for greater support and protection. Just as importantly, the CLC cradles your foot in comfort.

That's because its patented, removable Actionsorb* insole provides extra cushioning. Its innovative tread design improves traction and side-to-side adhesion. Its flex bars bend exactly where your foot does. And its silky smooth garment leather eliminates the usual break-in period. What's more, its unique heel counter keeps you on the balls of your feet, and relieves stress on the Achilles tendon.

Flex bars across the sole of your foot make the sole more flexible.

So it's not surprising that *Tennis* magazine touted the CLC as "a superbly designed shoe."

Take a pair out on the court and judge for yourself.

But when you do, we suggest challenging someone who's a graceful loser.

AUTRY

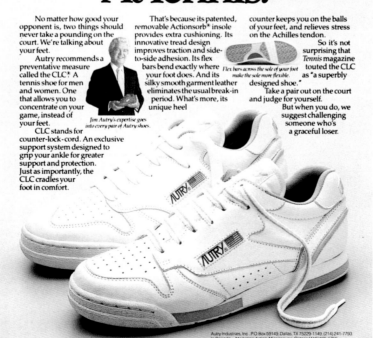

Autry Industries, Inc., P.O. Box 59149, Dallas, TX 75229-1149, (214) 241-7793.
In Canada—Marketing Action, Mississauga, Ontario (416) 625-6760

285

Nobody promotes better relations with china.
Cascade®
SAFE ON CHINA
CASCADE has been thoroughly tested for use on fine china patterns and bears the seal of approval of the American Fine China Guild.
AMERICAN FINE CHINA GUILD
For virtually spotless dishes.
Does your detergent have this seal?

286

ARE YOU
WASHING YOUR FACE
OR
DRYING YOUR SKIN?
The next time you wash your face, think about what you're doing to your skin.
Soap seems so innocent, but the truth is, it can leave your skin dry, tight and ready for a wrinkle.
Washing your face with Medicated Noxzema® Skin Cream is different. It cleans like no ordinary soap can.
Noxzema gets rid of dirt, oil, and make-up without leaving your skin dry. Instead, Noxzema leaves your skin silky smooth with a clear, healthy glow.
The next time you wash your face, think about it, are you drying your skin... or doing something beautiful for your skin?

Noxzema

BEAUTIFUL SKIN BEGINS
WITH NOXZEMA.

287

Consumer Magazine Color: 1 Page Or Spread Including Magazine Supplements

288
ART DIRECTOR
Tom Lichtenheld
WRITER
John Stingley
DESIGNER
Tom Lichtenheld
PHOTOGRAPHER
Steve Umland
CLIENT
WFLD-TV
AGENCY
Fallon McElligott/Minneapolis

289
ART DIRECTOR
David Nathanson
WRITER
Neal Gomberg
DESIGNER
David Nathanson
PHOTOGRAPHER
Dennis Gottlieb
CLIENT
Mitsubishi Electric Sales America
AGENCY
Chiat/Day

290
ART DIRECTOR
Dean Hanson
WRITER
Tom McElligott
PHOTOGRAPHER
Dave Jordano
CLIENT
Armour
AGENCY
Fallon McElligott/Minneapolis

291
ART DIRECTOR
Richard Osborn
WRITER
David Morris
DESIGNER
Richard Osborn
CLIENT
Peugeot - France
AGENCY
Weekes Morris & Osborn/ Australia

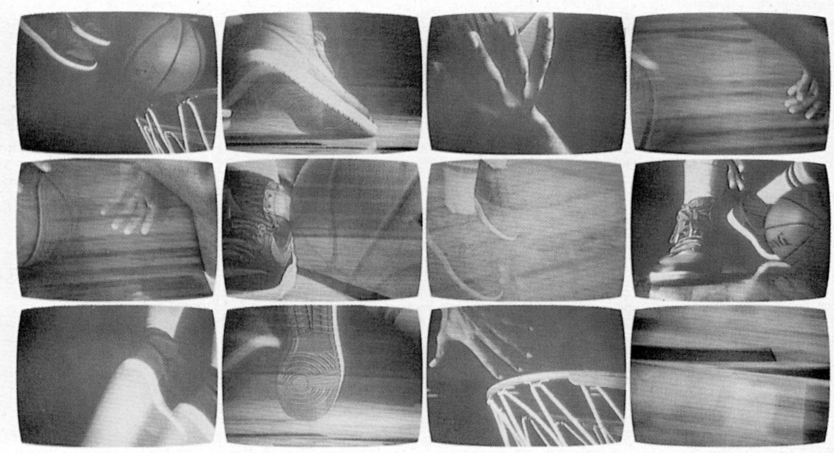

288

289

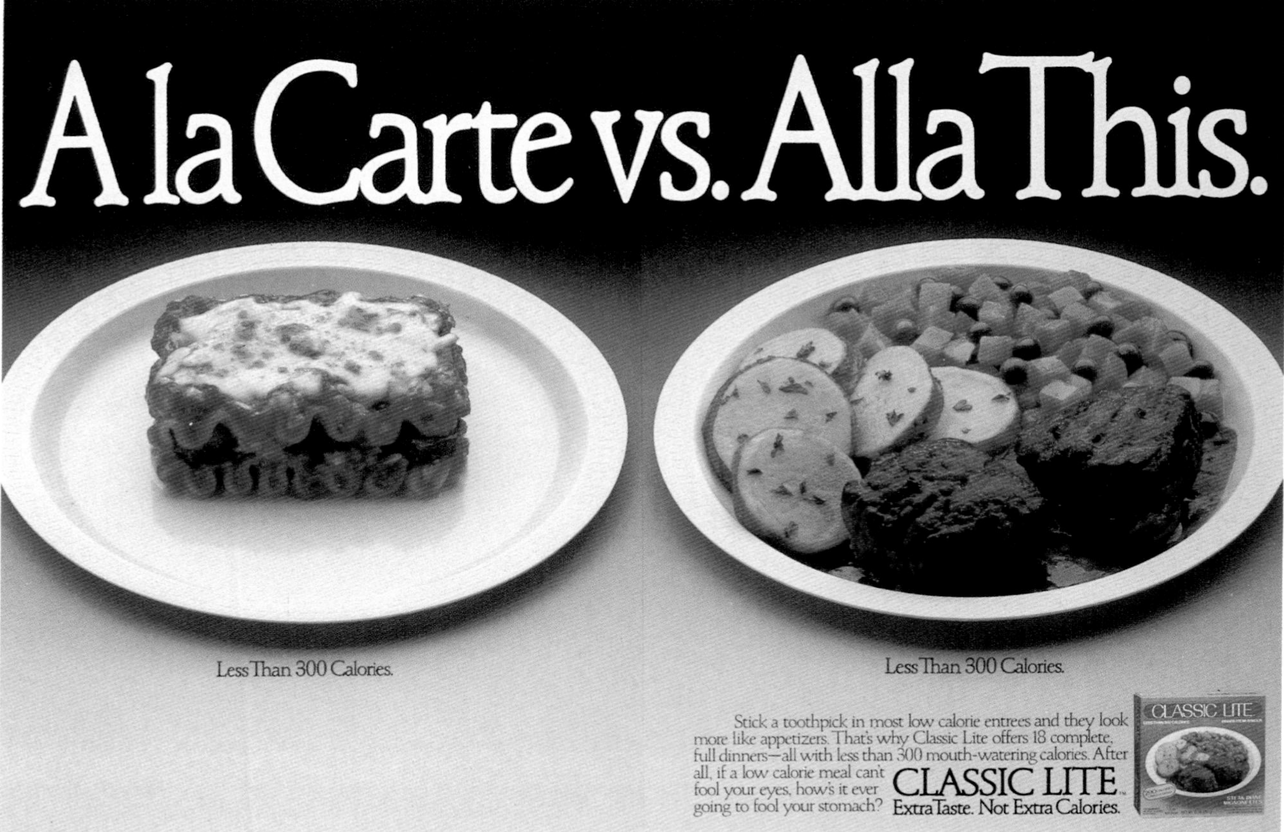
A la Carte vs. Alla This.
Less Than 300 Calories.
Less Than 300 Calories.
Stick a toothpick in most low calorie entrees and they look more like appetizers. That's why Classic Lite offers 18 complete, full dinners—all with less than 300 mouth-watering calories. After all, if a low calorie meal can't fool your eyes, how's it ever going to fool your stomach?
CLASSIC LITE.
Extra Taste. Not Extra Calories.
CLASSIC LITE

290

To most drivers this is a repair bill.
To Peugeot drivers it's just another road.

PEUGEOT

291

Consumer Magazine Color: 1 Page Or Spread Including Magazine Supplements

292
ART DIRECTOR
Steve Beaumont
WRITER
Penny Kapousouz
PHOTOGRAPHER
Mark Coppos
CLIENT
Porsche Cars North America
AGENCY
Chiat/Day - Los Angeles

293
ART DIRECTOR
Jerry Whitley
WRITER
Joe O'Neill
DESIGNER
William Hartwell
PHOTOGRAPHER
Jeffrey Zwart
ARTIST
Fred Greller
CLIENT
BMW of North America
AGENCY
Ammirati & Puris

294
ART DIRECTOR
Jerry Whitley
WRITER
Mark Silveira
PHOTOGRAPHER
Larry Dale Gordon
CLIENT
BMW of North America
AGENCY
Ammirati & Puris

Fun may be the most important discipline of all.

When Roland Kussmaul is tired of meetings, tired of wearing a tie, tired of hearing his phone ring, he leaves his office in the racing compound a few hundred yards west of the test track, to do the one thing he never gets tired of doing.

Driving.

Not driving as people who wear ties know it. But driving as Kussmaul knows it.

Putting the car a little bit sideways.

Kussmaul is a professional test driver. Which means he can detect a millimeter's difference in the thickness of a sway bar or a 5% adjustment in a spring rate. In a single test lap.

Kussmaul was Project Leader for our customer-owned 956 race cars. Project Manager on our SCCA 944 racer. And when he isn't helping tune the suspension of the Paris/Dakar 4-wheel drive car, he's out crossing African deserts in one.

Needless to say, a man like Roland Kussmaul isn't easily entertained.

Which says something about the Porsche 944.

A car Kussmaul drives not because it can do 0 to 60 mph in 8.3 seconds.

Not because its transaxle design helps make it the best handling production sports car on the market. Even when driven to Kussmaul's limit.

And no, not for its newly designed, 928-like interior. But for what may be the best reason of all to drive any Porsche.

The fun of it.

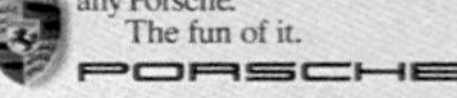

292

A MESSAGE TO MALCONTENTS EVERYWHERE: YOUR CAR IS READY.

To those of you who always fixate on tiny details others never seem to notice.

Who are routinely viewed as hypercritical. Difficult. Impossible to please.

To all of you so-called malcontents everywhere, a word of reassurance—there is one car company that understands you perfectly: BMW.

And our sentiments have taken the form, not just of kind words, but of a luxury sports coupe called the BMW 635CSi.

Produced in minuscule quantities, free from the usual constraints of time or cost, the 635CSi promises to arouse a long-awaited, elusive sensation in you known as contentment.

This contentment begins as you view the whole. "As automotive sculpture, it's a Rodin" (Road & Track). And only grows as you realize it is the sum of over 4,000 exquisitely sculpted parts.

Body panels, for instance, are routinely measured by computer. Engine components are controlled to tolerances one-fifth the thickness of a human hair.

The car's leather seat coverings are stitched by hand. Even the springs beneath the seat are calibrated to ensure their natural vibration will counter, and thus negate, that of the car.

Obsessive? Indeed, and you may be delighted to know this obsessiveness continues in the car's vital functions.

A 3.5-liter engine that "produces prodigious speeds" is watched over by an engine management system that alters performance according to variables as subtle as changes in the humidity.

A revolutionary electronic transmission can be programmed for high performance, high efficiency or manual shifting, according to your whims.

And the most "expensive and proven anti-lock braking system available" (AutoWeek), is standard equipment.

For a hands-on examination, we invite you to nitpick your way through a BMW dealer. Where such vices are considered to be virtues and where, at participating dealers, you can delve into the comprehensive leasing programs that are offered through the BMW Credit Corporation.

THE ULTIMATE DRIVING MACHINE.

293

THE FIRST HIGH-PERFORMANCE BIKE THAT RECOGNIZES THE WORLD ISN'T FLAT, STRAIGHT OR A QUARTER MILE LONG.

Glance at the cover of nearly any motorcycle magazine these days, and you might get the impression that the entire world of motorcycling starts at some dragstrip's "Christmas tree" and ends just 1,320 feet away.

Stories abound of the latest Japanese heavy metal—those bikes one journalist aptly described as "missiles with headlights and horns"—standing poised to break the 10-second barrier and capable of top speeds three times the national speed limit. All of which may make for exciting reading, but has little, if anything, to do with real riding.

On the other hand, there's the new BMW K100. A high-performance motorcycle whose performance is not only ballistic, but also balletic.

A motorcycle that Cycle Guide predicts "is going to dust some very good Japanese literbikes in sport tours." Not, however, with an engine whose output is devoted to the last 500 rpm's before redline. But rather, with an engine that makes 90 percent of its torque available at just 3,500 rpm's. For a "seamless crescendo of power that is exhilarating, yet tractable" (Motorcyclist).

A motorcycle whose low center of gravity and diminutive weight make it "a bike that can be herded along a twisty ribbon of road in the company of the best high-performance Japanese iron without losing its stately composure" (Cycle World).

A motorcycle whose ergonomics—the fundamental bar, seat and peg relationship—feel just right. So the BMW K100 is, as one motorcycle reviewer put it, "perfect for hours of the kind of riding that would be tiring in minutes on most bikes."

And perhaps most important, a motorcycle that offers something often missing in the world of high-performance bikes: repeat performances. A promise supported by the simplicity of the K100's design, the sophistication of its electronic engine management system and BMW's three-year warranty,* which is three times longer than most bike warranties.

Those who find the prospect of owning such a motorcycle appealing will no doubt find its $5,990** price all the more so. And wind down to their nearest BMW dealer for a thorough test ride.

THE LEGENDARY MOTORCYCLES OF GERMANY.

*Limited warranty protects against defects in workmanship and materials for three years and for an unlimited number of miles. It applies to motorcycles purchased from authorized U.S. dealers and BMW European Delivery only and is transferable within the period specified. See your dealer for details. **Manufacturer's suggested retail price. Actual price will depend on dealer. ©1984 BMW of North America, Inc. The BMW trademark and logo are registered.

Consumer Magazine Color: 1 Page Or Spread Including Magazine Supplements

295
ART DIRECTORS
Gail Bartley
William Hartwell
WRITER
David Tessler
DESIGNER
William Hartwell
PHOTOGRAPHER
Jeffrey Zwart
CLIENT
BMW of North America
AGENCY
Ammirati & Puris

296
ART DIRECTOR
Jim Andrews
WRITER
Melanie Early
PHOTOGRAPHER
Henry Bjoin
CLIENT
Sun-Maid Raisins
AGENCY
D'Arcy Masius Benton & Bowles/San Francisco

297
ART DIRECTORS
Jeff Vogt
William Hartwell
WRITER
Paul Wolfe
DESIGNER
William Hartwell
PHOTOGRAPHER
Jeffrey Zwart
ARTIST
R & V Studio
CLIENT
BMW of North America
AGENCY
Ammirati & Puris

298
ART DIRECTORS
Gary Johns
Rick Boyko
Andy Dijak
Yvonne Smith
WRITERS
Bill Hamilton
Jeff Gorman
Mark Monteiro
PHOTOGRAPHER
Mark Coppos
CLIENT
Nike
AGENCY
Chiat/Day - Los Angeles

BMW. THE FIRST CAR COMPANY TO STAND BEHIND ITS CARS TWICE.

INTRODUCING THE BMW QUALITY CONTINUATION PLAN.™

What is arguably the most widespread form of legalized gambling practiced today takes place not in casinos or on racetracks, but on the used-car lots of America.

Where billions of dollars are wagered yearly on what are hoped to be well-running automobiles.

At BMW dealerships, however, the odds have always been stacked heavily in favor of the used-car buyer. That's because BMW's are built to standards that are uncompromising in the extreme—enabling them to fulfill the needs of a succession of demanding owners.

And now, making an investment in a previously-owned BMW is a surer thing than it ever was—thanks to the new, unique BMW Quality Continuation Plan.

The cornerstone of the plan is the first factory-backed warranty ever offered at no extra cost on a used car. It's a 12-month / 12,000-mile limited warranty that's virtually as comprehensive as the one protecting new BMW's—including coverage of everything from the engine and transmission to the air-conditioning system. It even covers towing service.*

The automobiles that are available in the plan are BMW's built from model year 1981 through 1986 and driven for up to 75,000 miles. And in order to qualify for the warranty, they've had to pass a rigorous 42-point inspection and reconditioning program.

All of which results in previously-owned automobiles that adhere to the exacting standards of a BMW—in essence, used cars that are more rewarding to own than most new ones.

Of course, for most car manufacturers, such a plan could be quite risky.

But considering the way we build BMW's in the first place, we're not really gambling at all.

BMW QUALITY CONTINUATION PLAN.

*Program not available in all areas. Please contact your local authorized BMW dealer for details. © 1985 BMW of North America, Inc. The BMW trademark and logo are registered.

295

CREAMERY BUTTER
WHOLE GRAIN FLOUR
FARM FRESH EGGS
IMPORTED SPICES
WHIPPING CREAM.

WHY STOP NOW?

SUN-MAID® AMERICA'S FAVORITE RAISIN.

296

EMERGE FROM THE FREEWAY VICTORIOUS, NOT VICTIMIZED.

Highways extract a bitter toll from modern drivers. Not at the coin booths, but in the continual onslaught of noise, traffic jams and pollution.

For those forced to cope with such a demoralizing situation, BMW has engineered a most vivifying solution. The 528e.

A car whose high-torque, high-efficiency* Eta engine lets you power through traffic without endlessly shifting through the gears.

Whose orthopedically-designed seats and ergonomically-designed climate controls ensure you not only negotiate the highway nimbly, but navigate it in total comfort.

Whose ingenious ABS anti-lock braking system can actually mean the difference between emerging victorious from hazardous roads, and not emerging at all.

And whose parts and pieces mesh together so well that one automotive critic was moved to characterize the 528e as "sumptuous in a no-nonsense way and immaculately crafted" (Motor Trend).

Your local BMW dealer would be happy to arrange a thorough test drive of the BMW 528e. A triumph of technology in which every day you share in the victory.

BMW

THE ULTIMATE DRIVING MACHINE.

*EPA-estimated [20] mpg, 24 highway. Fuel efficiency figures are for comparison only. Your actual mileage may vary, depending on speed, weather and trip length. ©1985 BMW of North America, Inc. The BMW trademark and logo are registered.

LET YOUR LOCAL BMW DEALERS ARRANGE A THOROUGH TEST DRIVE

City	City	City	City	City	City
DEALER NAME	DEALER NAME	DEALER NAME	DEALER NAME	DEALER NAME	DEALER NAME
Dealer Address	Dealer Address	Dealer Address	Dealer Address	Dealer Address	Dealer Address
Phone Number	Phone Number	Phone Number	Phone Number	Phone Number	Phone Number

297

NIKE
FITNESS

298

Consumer Magazine Color: 1 Page Or Spread Including Magazine Supplements

299
ART DIRECTOR
Tom Wolsey
WRITER
Helayne Spivak
DESIGNER
Tom Wolsey
PHOTOGRAPHER
Henry Wolf
CLIENT
Karastan
AGENCY
Ally & Gargano

300
ART DIRECTORS
Cathi Mooney
Ken Mandelbaum
WRITERS
Ken Mandelbaum
Cathi Mooney
DESIGNER
Cathi Mooney
PHOTOGRAPHER
Hashi
CLIENT
Federal Express
AGENCY
Ally & Gargano

301
ART DIRECTOR
Ivan Horvath
WRITER
Bob Ancona
PHOTOGRAPHER
Mike Chesser
CLIENT
Yamaha Motor Corporation, USA
AGENCY
NW Ayer/Los Angeles

302
ART DIRECTORS
Jerry Whitley
Mark Johnson
WRITER
Mark Silveira
DESIGNER
William Hartwell
PHOTOGRAPHER
Jeffrey Zwart
CLIENT
BMW of North America
AGENCY
Ammirati & Puris

299

300

Johnny be good.

The full line of Yamaha electric guitars and basses, including the new SE200, are at your authorized Yamaha Combo Products dealer. For a complete catalogue, write: Yamaha International Corporation, Combo Products Division, P.O. Box 6600, Buena Park, CA 90622. In Canada, Yamaha Canada Music Ltd., 135 Milner Ave., Scarborough, Ont. M1S 3R1.

YAMAHA

301

IT'S SHAPED TO CUT THROUGH THE WIND, CLING TO THE ROAD AND NOT GET LOST IN THE PARKING LOT.

BMW INTRODUCES TRUE CLASS TO THE 750 CLASS: THE K75.

Over the last few years, 750cc riders have seen their choices dwindle down to basically two.

They could ride one of the Japanese hyperbikes, all of which often appear to have been extruded from the same tube of Stripe toothpaste. Or they could climb aboard something that looked like a malnutritioned "chopper."

Now, there's the BMW K75. A motorcycle shaped by the forces of nature rather than the forces of habit.

The K75 C cockpit fairing you see here is the product of extensive wind tunnel development. Which, not surprisingly, results in considerable weather protection, and lower drag.

Both highly relevant rider concerns.

A philosophy that's further developed in the K75's three-cylinder power plant, which, like the K100 Compact Drive™ it was derived from, produces the vast majority of its abundant torque at a low to midrange rpm level.

All-around performance that when coupled with BMW's low center of gravity and light weight predictably results in exceptional handling.

Also predictable is the extraordinary workmanship evident in the K75. But then, it was built to justify BMW's 3-year unlimited mileage warranty,* the industry's longest.

What may come as a surprise, however, is the remarkable shape the K75 leaves your finances in. BMW's range in price from $3,800 for the R65 to $7,650 for the K100RT** with leasing and factory financing available.

A premium price, to be sure. But one that virtually guarantees you an experience seldom enjoyed by the riders of other 750cc bikes. The chance to stand out in the crowd.

Just one of the K75's many outstanding features. The rest of which can best be explored via a thorough test ride at your BMW dealer.

THE LEGENDARY MOTORCYCLES OF GERMANY.

*See warranty at your dealer for details. **R65 not available in California. Manufacturer's suggested retail prices. Actual prices will depend on dealer. © 1985 BMW of North America, Inc. The BMW trademark and logo are registered. Ride safely. Always wear a helmet and eye protection. Call the Motorcycle Safety Foundation at 1-800-447-4700 for a riding course near you.

302

Consumer Magazine Color: 1 Page Or Spread Including Magazine Supplements

303
ART DIRECTOR
Marten Tonnis
WRITER
Steve Rabosky
ARTIST
Barbara Banthien
PHOTOGRAPHER
Bo Hylen
CLIENT
Apple Computer
AGENCY
Chiat/Day - Los Angeles

304
ART DIRECTOR
Cathi Mooney
WRITER
Ken Mandelbaum
DESIGNER
Cathi Mooney
PHOTOGRAPHER
Hashi
CLIENT
Federal Express
AGENCY
Ally & Gargano

305
ART DIRECTOR
Sal DeVito
WRITER
Amelia Rosner
DESIGNER
Sal DeVito
PHOTOGRAPHER
Jerry Friedman
CLIENT
Trump Casino Hotel
AGENCY
Chiat/Day

306
ART DIRECTOR
Ron Louie
WRITER
Patty Volk
DESIGNER
Ron Louie
PHOTOGRAPHER
Carl Furuta
CLIENT
Colombian Coffee
AGENCY
Doyle Dane Bernbach

303

304

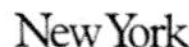

EVERY DAY THOUSANDS OF PEOPLE LEAVE THE MOST EXCITING CITY IN THE WORLD LOOKING FOR EXCITEMENT.

On the Boardwalk in Atlantic City.

305

Guess what coffee they serve at tea?

"The richest coffee in the world."

306

Consumer Magazine Color: 1 Page Or Spread Including Magazine Supplements

307
ART DIRECTOR
Cathi Mooney
WRITER
Ken Mandelbaum
DESIGNER
Cathi Mooney
PHOTOGRAPHER
Robert Ammirati
CLIENT
Timberland
AGENCY
Ally & Gargano

308
ART DIRECTOR
Tom Perkins
WRITER
Joe Anson
DESIGNER
Jerri Powers
PHOTOGRAPHER
Howard Waldron
CLIENT
Orlando Regional Medical Center
AGENCY
Anson-Stoner/Florida

309
ART DIRECTOR
Gail Bartley
WRITER
David Tessler
DESIGNER
Gail Bartley
PHOTOGRAPHER
Barney Edwards
CLIENT
Waterford Crystal
AGENCY
Ammirati & Puris

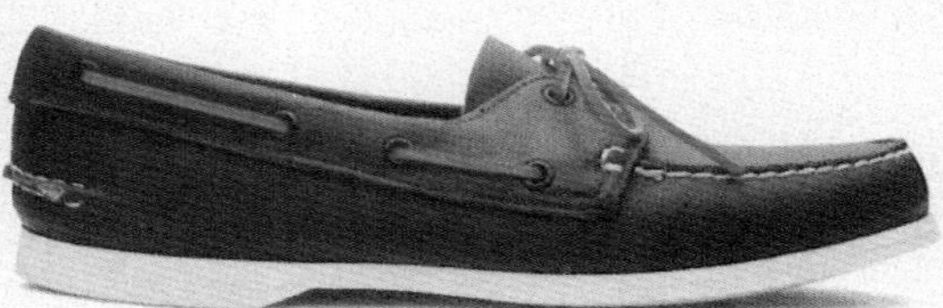

1930–THE INTRODUCTION OF THE BOAT SHOE.

1979–THE INTRODUCTION OF THE TIMBERLAND BOAT SHOE.
The classic boat shoe taken a giant step further.
More water-resistant. More comfortable. More durable.

1981–THE INTRODUCTION OF THE TIMBERLAND SUPER BOAT SHOE.
A shoe designed for world class sailors, but quickly adopted
by everyone else who wanted the best boat shoe money can buy.

1983–THE INTRODUCTION OF THE TIMBERLAND HI-TECH BOAT SHOE.
Here, we came to grips with the biggest problem confronting sailors: Water.
With a revolutionary sole design that virtually eliminated hydroplaning.

1984–THE INTRODUCTION OF THE TIMBERLAND SCUPPER.
Our latest launch: the high-performance sole of our
Hi-Tech boat shoe topped by our classic boat shoe upper.

WE'VE DONE MORE FOR THE BOAT SHOE IN THE LAST 5 YEARS THAN ANYONE ELSE HAS IN 50.

The Timberland Company, P.O. Box 7005, Portsmouth, New Hampshire 03801

*Registered trademarks of The Timberland Company

307

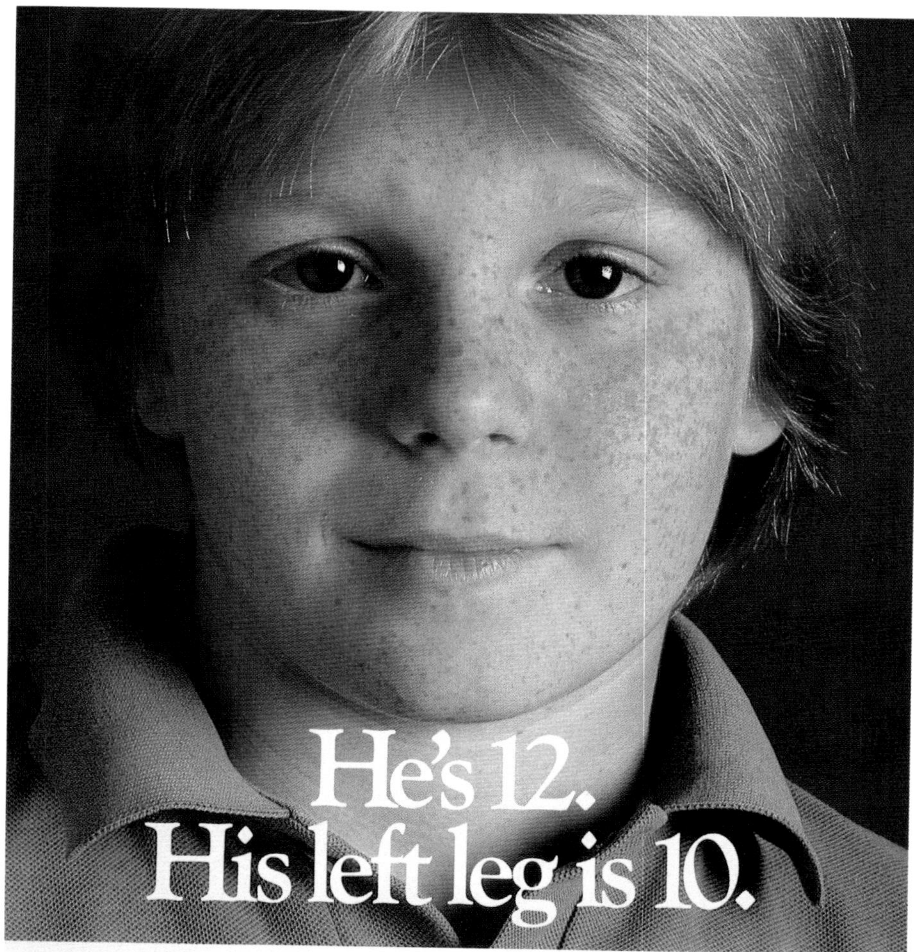

The little guy could actually range in age from newborn to teenager.

And he might just as easily be *she*.

He's one of thousands of youngsters who each year acquire a bone condition which restricts normal skeletal growth. In this case causing the bones of one leg to be shorter and thinner than the other. And to grow at a slower rate.

The condition once mandated that its victim would hobble through life — often developing curvature of the spine and severe backaches in the process. But today, thanks to developments in pediatric orthopedics, these once ill-fated bones are being lengthened, strengthened, and rebuilt in precision-like fashion. Even to the point that skeletal age and projected growth are being calibrated in terms of millimeters.

Yet, despite the advancements, it is still a condition which can cripple. One that, left untreated, can actually become worse as growth occurs. And difficult or impossible to correct once growth is complete.

First signs of a problem in children include leg pains, a slight limp, or an uneven hemline. Each of them worthy of simple testing by an orthopedic specialist.

Today victims of these bone disorders can be seen running and jumping on playgrounds all across America. Without limping. Without pain. Without braces and orthopedic shoes.

In an age of advancements, their once imperfect legs have been aged to perfection.

For referral information on orthopedic specialists, contact ORMC at 841-5221.

308

If a bride had chosen Waterford Crystal in 1783, she could still add to her collection today.

Every stemware pattern ever made by Waterford® is still available today.

And timelessness is a principle that governs not only what we make, but how we make it.

Our crystal is still blown by mouth and cut by hand—because whatever "advantages" might result from automation, the diamond-like fire and brilliance of Waterford are not among them.

Besides, while several days might seem long for the creation of a single glass, it's negligible compared to the generations that glass will endure.

Waterford

steadfast in a world of wavering standards

309

Consumer Magazine Color: 1 Page Or Spread Including Magazine Supplements

310
ART DIRECTOR
Jeff Roll
WRITER
Dave Butler
PHOTOGRAPHERS
Lamb & Hall
CLIENT
Porsche
AGENCY
Chiat/Day - Los Angeles

311
ART DIRECTOR
Jim Handloser
WRITER
David Schneider
DESIGNER
Jim Handloser
PHOTOGRAPHER
David Langley
CLIENT
Federal Express
AGENCY
Ally & Gargano

312
ART DIRECTOR
James Good
WRITER
John Gruen
PHOTOGRAPHER
Brian Lanker
CLIENT
Sports Illustrated
AGENCY
Ogilvy & Mather

313
ART DIRECTORS
Gus Tejerina
Tod Seisser
WRITER
Jay Taub
DESIGNER
Tod Seisser
PHOTOGRAPHER
Jerry Friedman
CLIENT
Citizen Watch
AGENCY
Levine Huntley Schmidt & Beaver

Keeping up with a Porsche 944 has just gone from difficult to impossible.

310

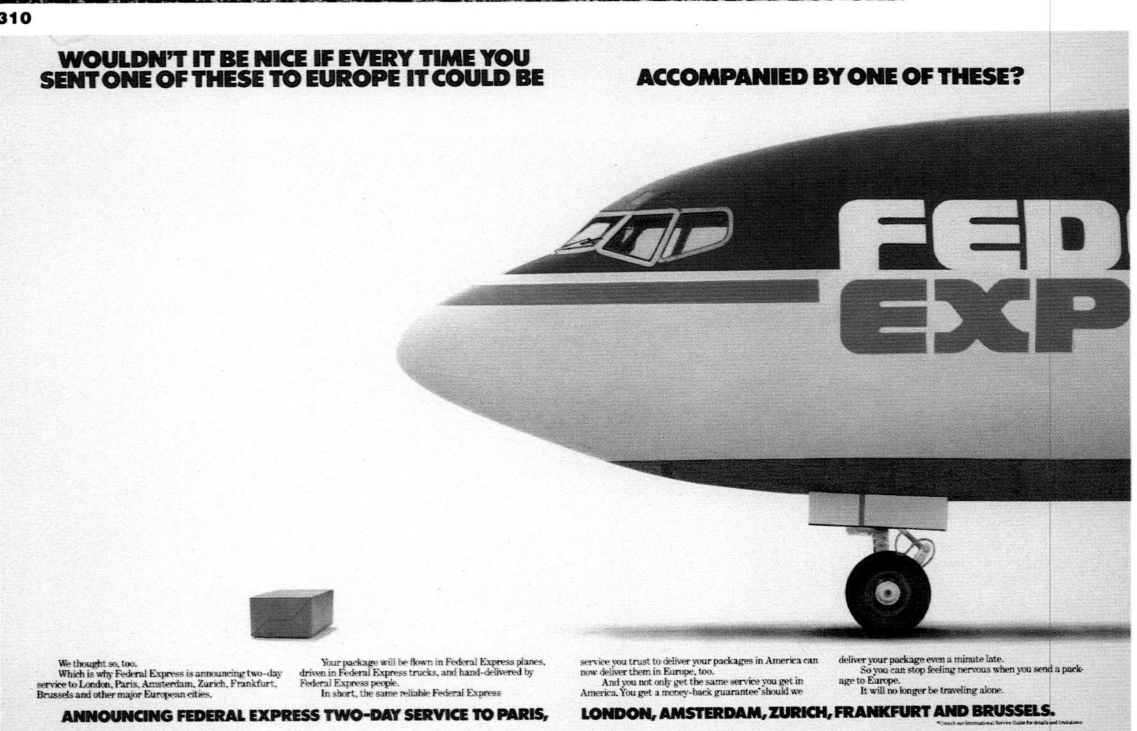
WOULDN'T IT BE NICE IF EVERY TIME YOU SENT ONE OF THESE TO EUROPE IT COULD BE
ACCOMPANIED BY ONE OF THESE?
FED
EXP
We thought so, too.
Which is why Federal Express is announcing two-day service to London, Paris, Amsterdam, Zurich, Frankfurt, Brussels and other major European cities.
Your package will be flown in Federal Express planes, driven in Federal Express trucks, and hand-delivered by Federal Express people.
In short, the same reliable Federal Express service you trust to deliver your packages in America can now deliver them in Europe, too.
And you not only get the same service you get in America. You get a money-back guarantee* should we deliver your package even a minute late.
So you can stop feeling nervous when you send a package to Europe.
It will no longer be traveling alone.
ANNOUNCING FEDERAL EXPRESS TWO-DAY SERVICE TO PARIS, LONDON, AMSTERDAM, ZURICH, FRANKFURT AND BRUSSELS.

311

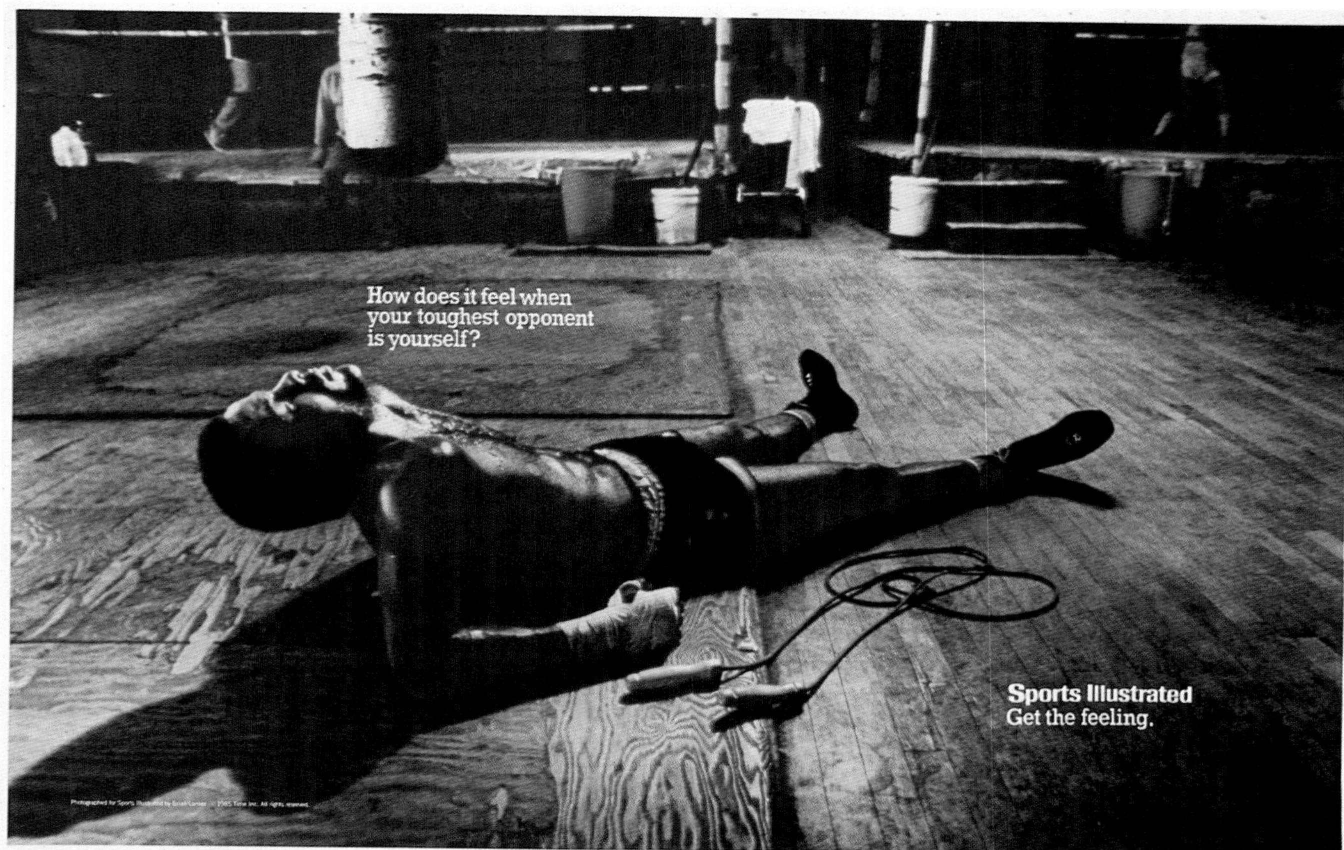

How does it feel when
your toughest opponent
is yourself?
Sports Illustrated
Get the feeling.

312

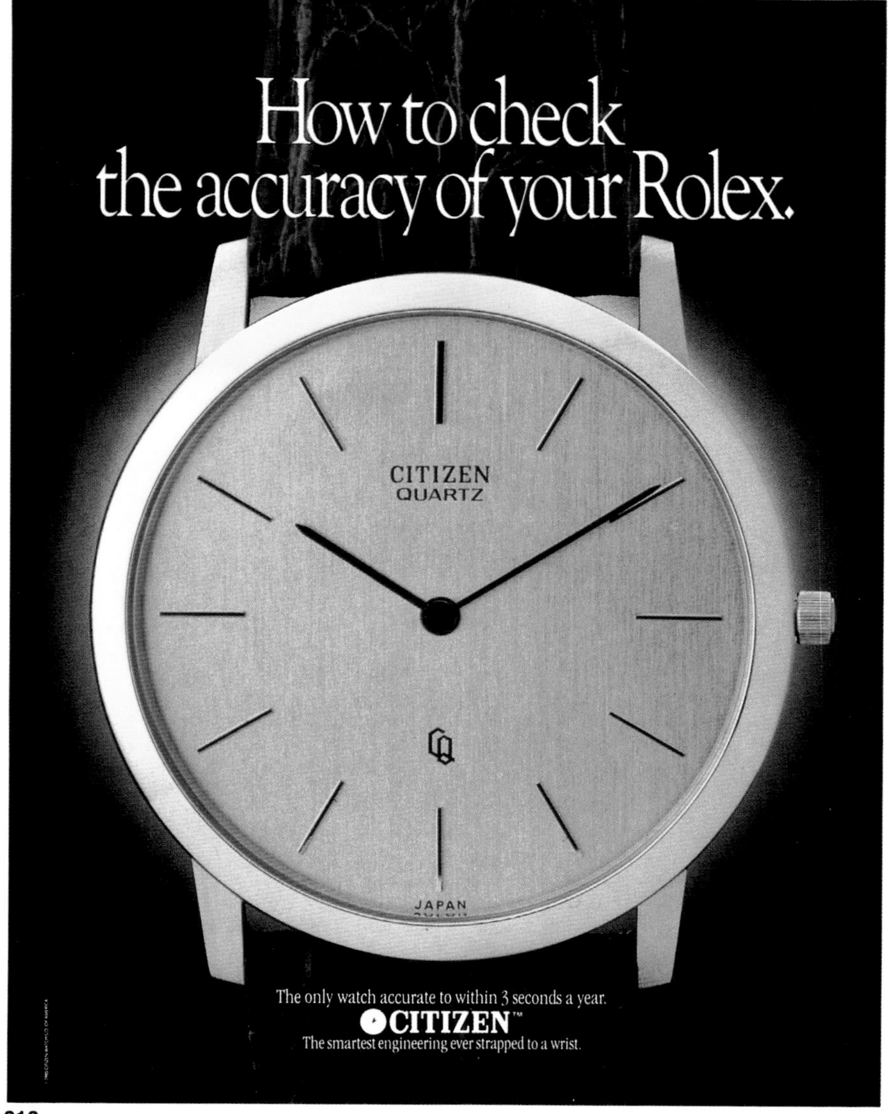

How to check
the accuracy of your Rolex.
CITIZEN
QUARTZ
JAPAN
The only watch accurate to within 3 seconds a year.
CITIZEN™
The smartest engineering ever strapped to a wrist.

313

Consumer Magazine Color: 1 Page Or Spread Including Magazine Supplements

314
ART DIRECTORS
Jerry Whitley
Mark Johnson
WRITER
Mark Silveira
DESIGNER
William Hartwell
PHOTOGRAPHER
Jeffrey Zwart
CLIENT
BMW of North America
AGENCY
Ammirati & Puris

315
ART DIRECTOR
Bob Saabye
WRITER
Ernie Schenck
DESIGNER
Bob Saabye
PHOTOGRAPHER
Myron
CLIENT
Foot-Joy
AGENCY
Leonard Monahan Saabye/
Providence, RI

316
ART DIRECTORS
Jeff Roll
Yvonne Smith
WRITERS
Dave Butler
Mark Monteiro
PHOTOGRAPHERS
Lamb & Hall
CLIENT
Porsche Cars North America
AGENCY
Chiat/Day - Los Angeles

317
ART DIRECTORS
Larry Bennett
Mark Oakley
WRITER
Charlie Ashby
PHOTOGRAPHER
Sovofoto
CLIENT
Fannie Mae
AGENCY
McKinney Silver & Rockett/
Raleigh, NC

314

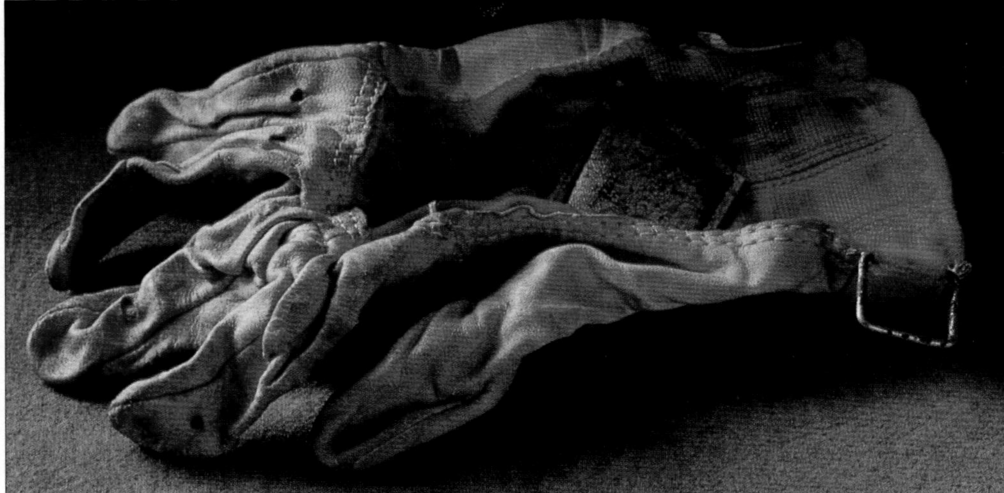

THERE'S A STIFF PENALTY FOR WEARING THE WRONG RACQUETBALL GLOVE.

You see, after a few games with most gloves, all that sweat you work up starts working its way into the leather.

Before you know it, an otherwise perfectly soft glove can become about as comfortable as wet cardboard.

Which is something that simply can't happen with Foot-Joy racquetball gloves.

You see, Foot-Joy gloves are made with a specially tanned Cabretta leather. So they're much more resistant to perspiration.

Which, in turn, means they stay soft and tacky far longer than other gloves.

And now, Foot-Joy racquetball gloves come in two styles. The Championship Player, our tournament glove. And the Tuff One, with a snug-fitting elasticized wrist, all-Spandex back and a lower price.

The Tuff One

The Championship Player

Both come in men's and women's sizes, including left and right hand versions, in a variety of colors.

Foot-Joy racquetball gloves. Quite bluntly, we think they're the best gloves in the game.

Even if they do have some stiff competition. Foot-Joy, 144 Field Street, Brockton, MA 02403.

Foot-Joy.

315

Why a car that needs no introduction needs an introduction.

Perhaps you've noticed this shape before. Maybe even chased it around a few corners. Or driven miles out of your way only to see it disappear over the horizon.

Had you been more persistent, your curiosity would have led you to the Porsche 928S, a car which, when first introduced in 1978, was hailed by critics the world over.

"The most powerful, most sophisticated, most luxurious grand touring car ever built," they said. "Bliss on wheels," they said. "Car of the year," they said.

"A good start," Professor Porsche said.

Not that he didn't agree with, or appreciate, the accolades. He just knew, as he did with other classic Porsches, that this was only the beginning. And that there was always room for improvement.

So, once again, Porsche's engineers shut their office doors, opened their minds and headed where they've always headed in search of new ideas.

The race track.

There, under the race-worn shell of the Porsche 956 endurance racer, was technology so noteworthy it compels us to do again what we already did once seven years ago.

Introduce the Porsche 928S.

The technology in question—the remarkable four-valve head design which, when adapted to the 928S's liquid-cooled V8, would increase horsepower to 288 and top speed to 155 mph.

While, at the same time, improving both torque and fuel efficiency.

More simply stated, this technology takes the 928S four-valve one significant step closer to Professor Porsche's original dream:

A superbly appointed grand touring car that's as exciting, as efficient, as comfortable and as easy to drive in every day traffic as it is blazing down the autobahn.

Of course, when all is said and done, the only way to truly appreciate the difference between this car and absolutely anything else on the road is to see it, hear it, feel it, and above all, drive it. And the only place to do that is at your Porsche dealer. So stop in and get better acquainted with the new 928S four-valve.

Now that you've been formally introduced.

PORSCHE

The Redistribution Of Capital Works, But Not The Way They Envisioned It.

In their system, the highest hope of the typical family is renting a two-room apartment. In America's, almost 65% of our people are in homes of their own.

One big story behind that statistic is a capital redistribution system called the "national secondary mortgage market."

Through it, lenders sold almost 7 out of every 10 new home mortgages to investors last year, accounting for some $140 billion.

And there's more to it than just big numbers: this market works for everyone.

Investors get good, solid yields with mortgage-backed securities and other mortgage-related products.

Lenders get the capital they need to meet the demand of their local market, no matter how fast it may grow.

And people who want to buy homes get a variety of options at affordable rates.

As the largest private investor in home mortgages, Fannie Mae is at the center of this dynamic market.

Our only business is getting capital to where it's needed in the housing market, which in turn helps millions of Americans realize their dream of owning a home.

So, if anyone wants to know about capital redistribution, they should look into our nation's secondary mortgage market.

Or they can ask us.

Fannie Mae. Where America gets the big ideas in home finance.

FannieMae

Consumer Magazine Color: 1 Page Or Spread Including Magazine Supplements

318
ART DIRECTOR
Gail Bartley
WRITER
David Tessler
DESIGNER
Gail Bartley
PHOTOGRAPHER
Barney Edwards
CLIENT
Waterford Crystal
AGENCY
Ammirati & Puris

319
ART DIRECTOR
David Kennedy
WRITERS
Dan Wieden
Jim Riswold
PHOTOGRAPHER
Harry DeZitter
CLIENT
Nike
AGENCY
Wieden & Kennedy/Portland, OR

320
ART DIRECTOR
Tony DeGregorio
WRITER
Lee Garfinkel
DESIGNER
Tony DeGregorio
PHOTOGRAPHER
Cailor/Resnick
CLIENT
Tel Plus Communications
AGENCY
Levine Huntley Schmidt & Beaver

321
ART DIRECTOR
Simon Bowden
WRITER
Marty Cooke
DESIGNER
Simon Bowden
PHOTOGRAPHER
Eric Meola
CLIENT
Nikon
AGENCY
Scali McCabe Sloves

At Waterford, we take 1,120 times longer than necessary to create a glass.

Every glass is blown by mouth, every wedge and diamond cut by hand, and every step of the way, it's all scrutinized by some of the world's most unforgiving eyes.

That is why, while a machine can churn out a glass in only 45 seconds, it takes upward of 14 hours to craft a single piece of Waterford stemware.

Maintaining Waterford standards means resisting quite a few temptations —including the opportunity to increase our output by 112,000 percent.

Waterford
Steadfast in a world of wavering standards.

318

319

At Tel Plus Communications, we believe the key to a successful telephone system isn't only state of the art technology.

It's state of the art people.

Which is why Tel Plus has assembled the most skilled and experienced professionals in the business.

People who will analyze your needs, and listen to your wants. Then recommend equipment (from phones and computers to integrated voice and data switching systems) that will satisfy both.

And our people don't just communicate with you. They communicate with each other. Ensuring that our engineers and installers work together to deliver a system that works for you. Not against you.

What's more, all of our systems come with this important back-up system: service people who are the best in the industry. Which means you'll get the service you need, and be spared the headaches you don't need.

How do you know we can keep these promises? Because we've been keeping them since 1972.

As the largest independent telecommunications company in United States, with over 65 offices nationwide, we have 25,000 phone systems already in place.

So if you're planning on installing a new phone system, or adding to a present one, make sure the company you choose is as advanced as their equipment.

Intelligent communication begins with intelligent people.
Call 1-800-TEL-PLUS

THIS ISN'T THE CAUSE OF COMMUNICATION PROBLEMS.

THIS IS.

A Telecom Plus International Company

320

Eric Meola on Nikon lenses:

"

"

Eric Meola, "Promised Land," Pasadena, California, 1977 Lens: 20mm f4 Nikkor

Nikon
We take the world's greatest pictures.

321

Consumer Magazine Color: 1 Page Or Spread Including Magazine Supplements

322
ART DIRECTOR
Rick McQuiston
WRITER
Jim Riswold
CLIENT
Nike
AGENCY
Wieden & Kennedy/Portland, OR

323
ART DIRECTOR
Cathi Mooney
WRITER
Ken Mandelbaum
DESIGNER
Cathi Mooney
PHOTOGRAPHERS
Robert Ammirati
Jim Salzano
CLIENT
Polaroid
AGENCY
Ally & Gargano

324
ART DIRECTOR
Woody Litwhiler
WRITER
Ted Charron
PHOTOGRAPHER
Carl Fischer
CLIENT
Tofu Time
AGENCY
Campbell-Ewald

325
ART DIRECTOR
John Porter
WRITER
Jim Offerman
PHOTOGRAPHER
Tom Bach
CLIENT
GNB Batteries
AGENCY
DBK&O/Minneapolis

A CRASH COURSE ON THE PRINCIPLE BEHIND NIKE-AIR CUSHIONING.

On the average, you'll crash 17,600 times during a 10-mile trip.

And, with every single impact, shock waves will be sent tearing through your body at speeds of up to 120 miles per hour.

We're talking about running. And the most important reason you need Nike-Air® cushioning.

Because if you buy a shoe with a conventional cushioning system, you stand a better chance of sidelining yourself with a painful injury.

What's really shocking is that the same shoe starts losing some of its cushioning almost immediately. And as much as 20 percent after just 500 miles.

But take heart.

It's because of these very reasons we developed Nike-Air cushioning.

Cushioning that reduces the impact and the pounding your body takes while running.

Cushioning that lessens your chance of injury.

Cushioning that won't break down, absorbing every bit as much shock on the first step as it does on the 999,999th.

Without a single leak. Or a single blow-out.

Now, where can you find this amazing cushioning system?

Currently, Nike-Air is available in 20 of our high-performance running shoes.

For occasional runners. Everyday runners. World-class runners. Long-distance runners. Men. Women. Children.

Nike-Air. Without it, you can tear up your body. With it, you can tear up the streets.

NIKE AIR

322

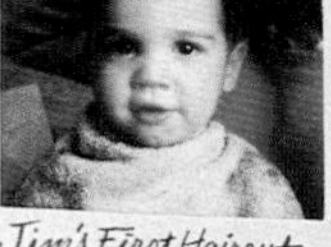

1 2 3

Jim Home From Hospital- 10/20/80

Jim's First Steps- 11/6/81

Allison's Dance Recital 12/27/82

Jim's First Haircut 4/25/83

A B C

Allison's First Day of School 9/20/84.

Jim's 4th Birthday 10/17/84

Katie's 7th Birthday 12/4/84.

Allison & Katie Christmas 1984.

HOW TO MAKE SURE YOUR KIDS TURN OUT ALL RIGHT.

All parents want the best for their children.

And while you do have some control over things like the schools they go to, the foods they eat, even what they watch on television, there are some things that will simply be out of your hands.

There is, however, one aspect of your son's or daughter's childhood that you can control completely: how you choose to record it.

With a Polaroid instant camera, you know within seconds if a shot came out the way you wanted it. And if it didn't, you get something you don't get with any other kind of camera: a second chance. So you can be absolutely sure that the shots of your son's first steps or your daughter's first birthday party are exactly the way you want to remember them.

Using a Polaroid camera can mean the difference between having photographs you'll look back on and cherish for the rest of your life.

Or having pictures that you'll look back on and regret.

Polaroid

We do what no other kind of camera can do.

For more information about Polaroid Photographic and Video products, call 1-800-225-1384. © 1985 Polaroid Corp. "Polaroid"®

323

THE MAN WHO LICKED ICE CREAM.

David Mintz must have a sweet disposition.

How else could you possibly explain a man who spent 9 years of his life, night after night, trying to invent the perfect dessert. And failed every single time.

Except one.

An August occasion that may be declared a national holiday by everyone who loves dessert.

On that summer night, in the back of his tiny 3rd Avenue deli, his enthusiasm for topping America's favorite dessert having dipped to an all time low, David Mintz discovered a dessert that was good and good for you. A magical blend of silky smooth tofu, flavors and fruits he called *Tofutti*.®

The Tofutti dessert David invented has only wholesome ingredients. No cholesterol, no lactose and absolutely no preservatives. Yet Tofutti tastes so rich, it's hard to believe it's good for you.

Has this taste of victory changed David Mintz? Not one bit. Chocolate or otherwise.

He's still the same humble, hard-working guy. And he's very thankful to everyone who's made Tofutti such a huge success.

In fact, as a little reward for you, he's back in the kitchen hard at work on yet another nutritional breakthrough.

A fudge brownie.

Visit our store at 336 Columbus Avenue near 76th Street.

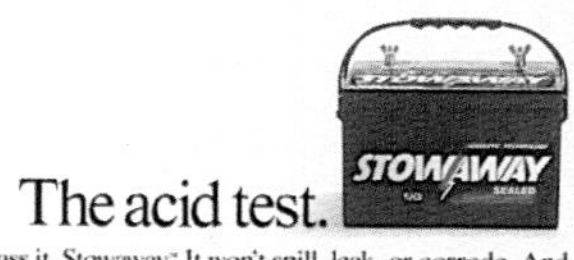

The acid test.

Only one battery can pass it. Stowaway.™ It won't spill, leak, or corrode. And it will never need maintenance. What's more, Stowaway is the most potent combination of deep-cycle and cranking power you can buy. For the dealer nearest you, call *1-800-447-4700.*

Consumer Magazine Color: 1 Page Or Spread Including Magazine Supplements

326
ART DIRECTOR
Matt Haligman
WRITER
Joe O'Neill
DESIGNER
Matt Haligman
PHOTOGRAPHER
Perry Ogden
CLIENT
Rose's Holland House
AGENCY
Ammirati & Puris

327
ART DIRECTOR
Ron Louie
WRITER
Alan Jacobs
DESIGNER
Ron Louie
PHOTOGRAPHER
George Holz
CLIENT
International Gold Corporation
AGENCY
Doyle Dane Bernbach

Rose's. A 19th-century lime juice—utterly steeped in tradition—that has always found its way into the drinks and cupboards of those who, if anything, prefer to part with tradition.
ROSE'S LIME JUICE.
THE UNCOMMON DENOMINATOR.
JAMES MATHERS PHOTOGRAPHED BY PERRY OGDEN. © 1985 Rose Holland House Inc.

326

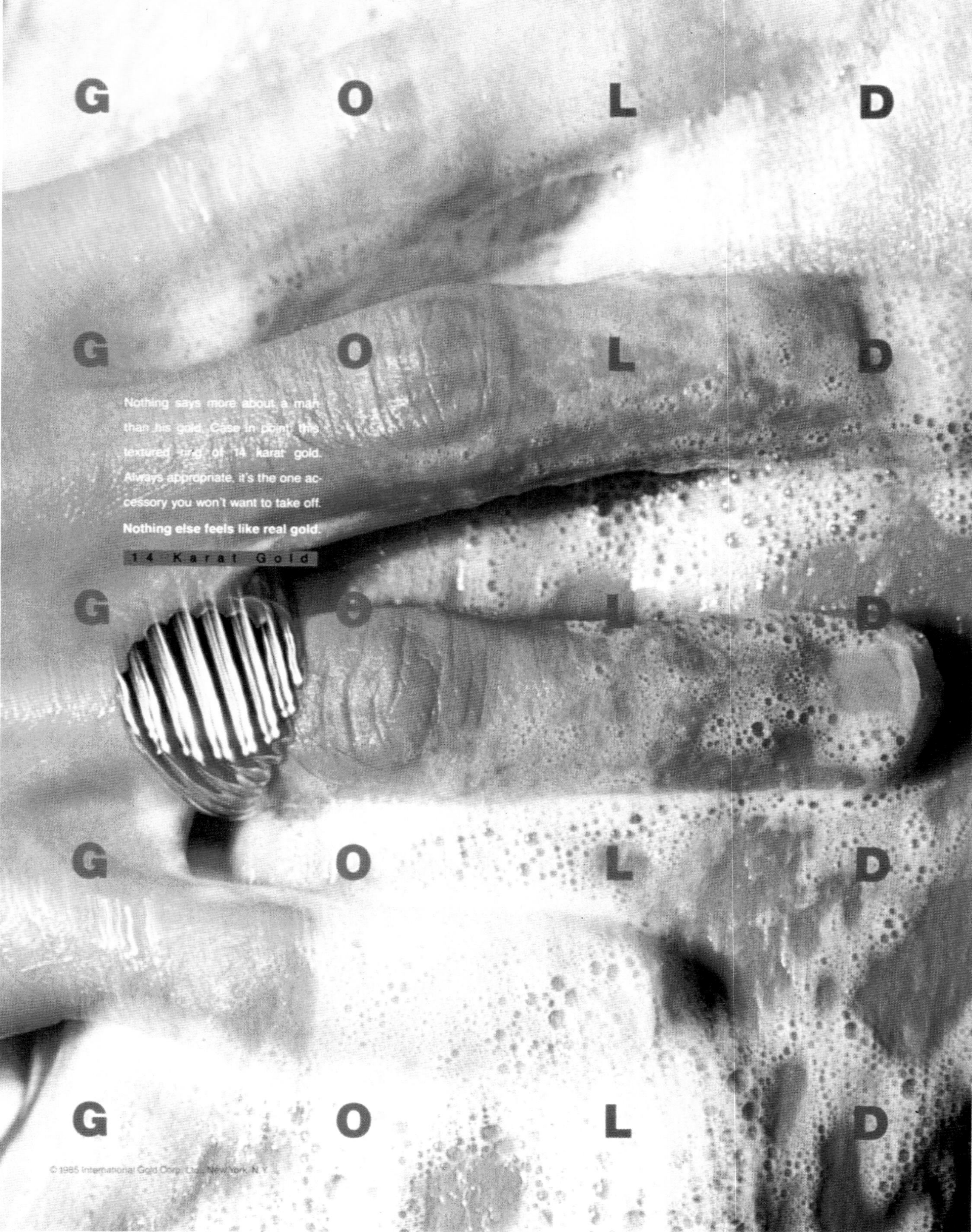

G O L D
G O L D
Nothing says more about a man than his gold. Case in point: this textured ring of 14 karat gold. Always appropriate, it's the one accessory you won't want to take off.
Nothing else feels like real gold.
14 Karat Gold
G O L D
G O L D
G O L D
© 1985 International Gold Corp. Ltd., New York, N.Y.

Consumer Magazine Color: 1 Page Or Spread Including Magazine Supplements

328
ART DIRECTOR
Tom Wolsey
WRITER
David Schneider
DESIGNER
Tom Wolsey
PHOTOGRAPHER
Dennis Chalkin
CLIENT
Bank of New York
AGENCY
Ally & Gargano

329
ART DIRECTOR
Simon Bowden
WRITER
David Metcalf
DESIGNER
Simon Bowden
PHOTOGRAPHER
Jerry Friedman
CLIENT
Volvo
AGENCY
Scali McCabe Sloves

330
ART DIRECTORS
Jeff Roll
Yvonne Smith
WRITERS
Dave Butler
Mark Monteiro
PHOTOGRAPHERS
Lamb & Hall
CLIENT
Porsche Cars North America
AGENCY
Chiat/Day - Los Angeles

GETTING TO THE TOP IS DIFFICULT ENOUGH. YOU SHOULDN'T HAVE TO DRAG SOME BANK UP WITH YOU.

Loyalty to a bank, like everything else, can be carried to excess.

If you are finding it more and more difficult to get the level of service, the level of credit, the investment expertise, indeed the simple understanding a person with your financial profile so obviously requires, then maybe it's time to unburden yourself to a Custom Banker at The Bank of New York.

You may already be aware of our Custom Bankers' long-standing reputation for offering more personal attention, more informed advice and quicker response to requests than their counterparts at other banks.

Well, there are reasons for that.

To begin with, no Custom Banker has all that many customers. So he or she can devote more time and attention to each individual.

Then there's The Bank of New York itself. Where your Custom Banker can tap sources of expertise in credit, investment, tax-related instruments, and trusts and estates with less red tape and far more speed than you'd ever expect to find in the gigantic banks.

For example, the credit arrangements your Custom Banker can work out for you may include the establishment of an unsecured credit line of $50,000 to $1 million or more. Or you can establish a secured credit line of up to 80% of the market value of your investment portfolio.

To find out more about Custom Banking, and the host of money management burdens it can get off your back, call Mr. Richard Freimuth, Vice President, Custom Banking Division, at 212-530-1971.

CUSTOM BANKING
THE BANK OF NEW YORK

MEMBER FDIC

328

IN AN ACCIDENT, COULD YOU SURVIVE YOUR CAR?

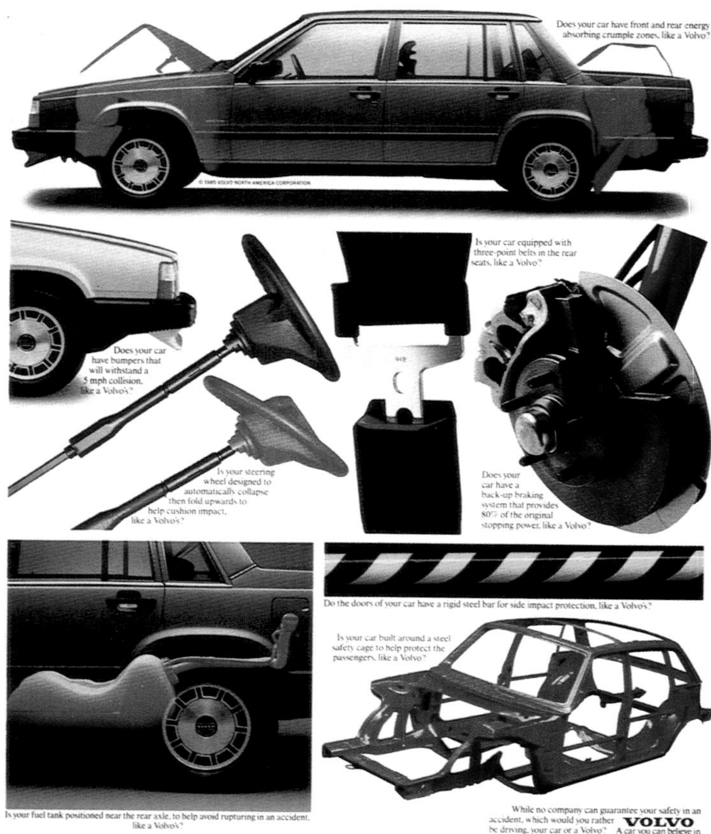
Does your car have front and rear energy absorbing crumple zones, like a Volvo?
© 1985 VOLVO NORTH AMERICA CORPORATION
Does your car have bumpers that will withstand a 5 mph collision, like a Volvo's?
Is your steering wheel designed to automatically collapse then fold upwards to help cushion impact, like a Volvo's?
Is your car equipped with three-point belts in the rear seats, like a Volvo?
Does your car have a back-up braking system that provides 80% of the original stopping power, like a Volvo?
Do the doors of your car have a rigid steel bar for side impact protection, like a Volvo's?
Is your car built around a steel safety cage to help protect the passengers, like a Volvo?
Is your fuel tank positioned near the rear axle, to help avoid rupturing in an accident, like a Volvo's?
While no company can guarantee your safety in an accident, which would you rather be driving, your car or a Volvo?
VOLVO
A car you can believe in.

329

Why a car that needs no introduction needs an introduction.

When it was first introduced in 1978, the Porsche 928 was hailed by the critics.

"The most powerful, most sophisticated, most luxurious grand touring car ever built," they said.

"A good start," Professor Porsche said.

So, once again, our engineers headed where they've always headed in search of ways to improve perfection.

There, at the race track, they reasoned that our latest four-valve engine technology, when adapted to the 928's liquid cooled V8, would do for this car what it had already done for our 956 endurance racer.

Make it faster and smoother, yet, incredibly, more fuel efficient.

Which compels us to do again what we did once seven years ago.

Introduce the 928S.

Of course, the only way to truly appreciate the difference between this car and absolutely anything else is to drive it.

So stop by your Porsche dealer and get acquainted with the 928S four-valve. Now that you've been properly introduced.

PORSCHE

Alan Johnson Porsche
Rosecrans at Sports Arena Blvd.
San Diego (619) 225-9373

Meister Porsche
Carlsbad Car Country
(619) 438-5700

Pioneer Porsche
I8 in La Mesa
(619) 461-3100

330

Consumer Magazine Color: 1 Page Or Spread Including Magazine Supplements

331
ART DIRECTOR
Richard Crispo
WRITER
Mark Monteiro
PHOTOGRAPHER
Bill Werts
CLIENT
Yamaha Motor Corporation, USA
AGENCY
Chiat/Day - Los Angeles

332
ART DIRECTORS
Gary Johns
Rick Boyko
Andy Dijak
Yvonne Smith
WRITERS
Bill Hamilton
Mark Monteiro
Jeff Gorman
PHOTOGRAPHER
Mark Coppos
CLIENT
Nike
AGENCY
Chiat/Day - Los Angeles

333
ART DIRECTOR
Craig Hadorn
WRITER
Charles Groark
PHOTOGRAPHER
Corson Hirschfeld
CLIENT
Fox Marketing
AGENCY
Northlich Stolley/Cincinnati

331

332

THE MATCHBOX ON THE RIGHT IS THE ONE THAT DETECTS RADAR.

Actual size photo.

INTRODUCING THE FOX MATCHBOX REMOTE.

Now you can get a remote superhet radar detector the size of a matchbox, a remote as sensitive as any superhet anywhere.

THE FIRST NAME IN REMOTE PROTECTION IS FIRST AGAIN.

Fox invented the first remote radar detector because drivers needed protection from more than radar.

They needed protection from theft and harassment, too.

So we developed remote radar technology, mounting the receiver up front under the hood and out of sight. Since the "eyes" of the detector were up front, the remote control unit didn't have to be exposed on the dash or visor. Instead, the driver could put the remote control where it too was out of sight, to all but him.

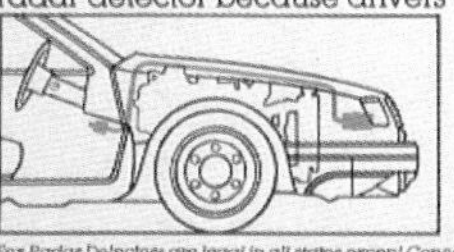

Fox remote radar detectors have given over a quarter million drivers the double protection they need.

And now we can offer you still greater protection with the smallest remote made today. The Fox Matchbox Remote.

IT TOOK THE BIGGEST NAME IN REMOTES TO MAKE A REMOTE CONTROL THIS SMALL.

Fox advanced its technology to make a remote control unit this small. A remote so flexible, you can mount it from its top, bottom or back. A remote

The Matchbox Remote vs. the leading radar detector. Fox takes about 30% as much space.

so light, a piece of velcro can hold it anywhere. A remote with a quick disconnect feature, so you can easily unplug it and put it in your glove compartment or even your pocket.

Yet the Fox Matchbox Remote has all the features you've come to expect from a Fox remote. There's a green power light to tell you that all is working well, a volume control to regulate the Geiger counter type alert signal and an accompanying red alarm light that advises you of the presence of radar.

THE MATCHBOX IS SUPER, TOO.

It offers true superheterodyne protection—state of the art protection in a shockproof and weatherproof receiver that can be mounted in just 4 inches of space under the hood, behind the grille. The receiver comes preset for both city and highway driving, ready to pick up all radar, even when it's weak and deflected, around corners or over hills.

OUR WARRANTY IS FIRST, TOO.

Every Fox radar detector comes with a limited five-year warranty. And that's years longer than any other remote. We're first again.

As small as the Matchbox Remote is, there is one place it's easy to see. Your nearby Fox dealer. For the one nearest you, call toll free 1-800-543-7892. In Ohio, 1-800-621-2513, and in Canada 1-800-663-0295.

FOX

FOX MARKETING, INC.

Fox Radar Detectors are legal in all states except Connecticut and Virginia.

333

Consumer Magazine Color: 1 Page Or Spread Including Magazine Supplements

334
ART DIRECTOR
Ivan Horvath
WRITER
Bob Ancona
PHOTOGRAPHER
Mike Chesser
CLIENT
Yamaha Motor Corporation, USA
AGENCY
NW Ayer/Los Angeles

335
ART DIRECTOR
Charles Abrams
WRITER
David Herzbrun
PHOTOGRAPHER
Onofrio Pacione
CLIENT
British Airways
AGENCY
Saatchi & Saatchi Compton

336
ART DIRECTOR
Garnet Edwards
WRITER
John Bailey
DESIGNER
Garnet Edwards
ARTIST
Amanda Curry
PHOTOGRAPHER
James Stewart
CLIENT
Thistle Hotels
AGENCY
Ayer Barker/London

337
ART DIRECTORS
Gary Johns
Rick Boyko
Andy Dijak
WRITERS
Bill Hamilton
Jeff Gorman
Mark Monteiro
PHOTOGRAPHER
Mark Coppos
CLIENT
Nike
AGENCY
Chiat/Day - Los Angeles

334

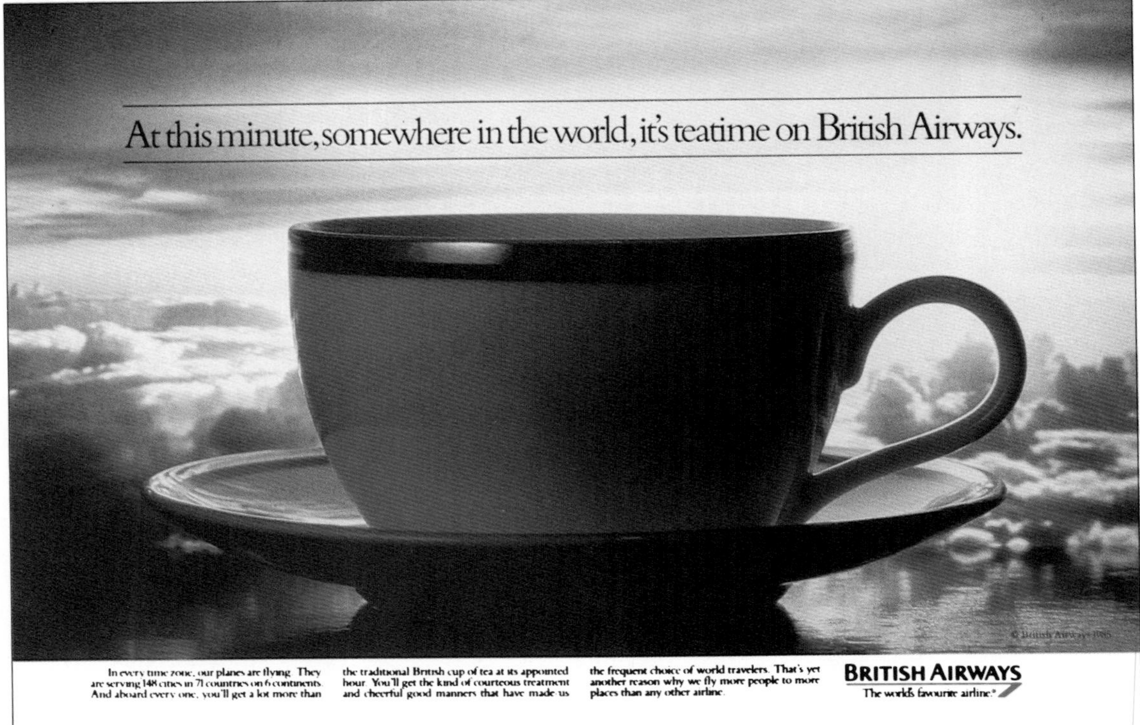

335

"Duck, goose, turkey or chicken for breakfast. And that was just the eggs."

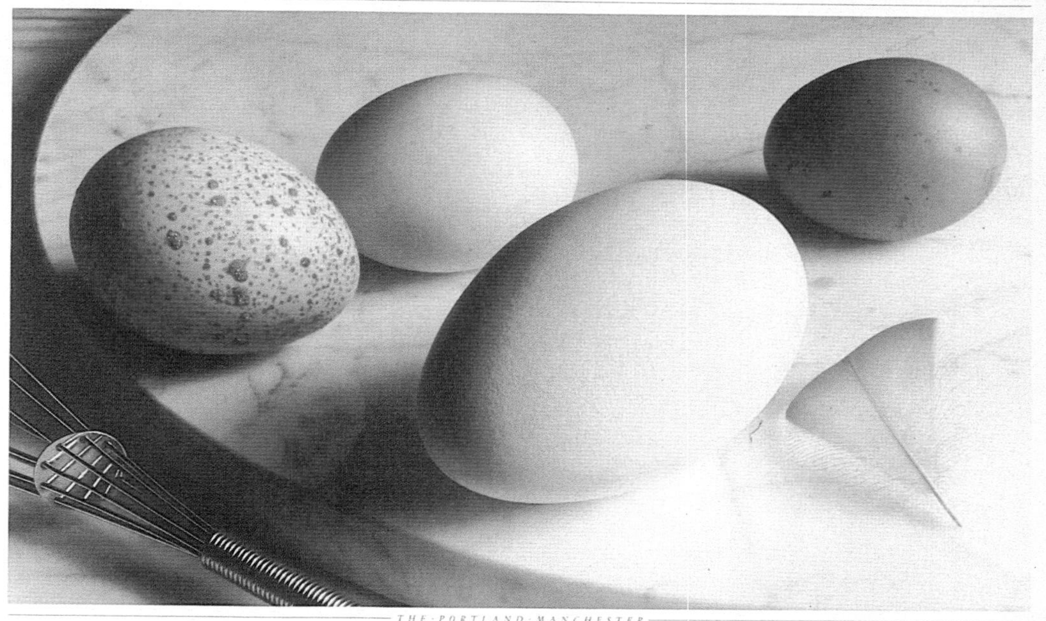

THE·PORTLAND·MANCHESTER

There is the hotel breakfast.

And then there is the hotel breakfast at The Portland Thistle Hotel, Manchester.

If this happens to be your first business meeting, then the most prolonged discussion may well centre around The Portland menu, such is its surprise and variety.

If you happen to be breakfasting alone, you will still have a most agreeable companion.

There is, for instance, a choice of seven varieties of locally produced sausage, including smoked beef, pork and walnut, lamb and rosemary, plus true Lancashire black pudding.

A dilemma for even the most dynamic individual.

And should one's eggs – duck, goose or turkey are offered whenever available – be fried or scrambled, or poached, or boiled, or served as an omelette?

Decisions, decisions.

What is indisputable, is that a superbly presented breakfast can do much to ensure a most satisfactory conclusion to your first business meeting of the day.

The Portland breakfast is such an event. It is an example of the enlightened Thistle philosophy. To create hotels in which it is a genuine pleasure for the individual to do business.

So while every Thistle Hotel guarantees a standard of accommodation and business facilities equal to (if not better than) that offered by international hotel chains, then that is where regimentation ends and individuality begins.

No Thistle Hotel is forced into the straightjacket of standardisation.

Each of our managers is encouraged to develop character and features which are totally in keeping with the individual building and location it occupies. An attitude which creates a relaxed and enjoyable atmosphere within our staff. Which in turn is felt by our guests.

It is a philosophy in which we are constantly investing for the future through refurbishment, innovation and, most importantly, talent.

Thus, at The Atlantic Tower Thistle Hotel, Liverpool, you can appreciate one of over a hundred malt whiskies in the luxurious Stateroom Cocktail Bar.

Enjoy a superb dinner to the accompaniment of a live pianist at The Royal Horseguards Thistle Hotel, just off Whitehall.

Or plan your corporate strategy seated in the vast leather armchairs surrounding the magnificent boardroom table at The Barnton Thistle Hotel, Edinburgh.

No two Thistle Hotels are the same. And every Thistle Hotel has its own personal surprise. A surprise that is invariably, and unmistakably, a pleasant one.

Ask your secretary to ring central reservations on 01-937 8033 for details of Thistle Hotels in London and 19 major cities and towns throughout Britain.

THISTLE HOTELS

As individual as you are.

336

NIKE

FITNESS

Women's Iridescent Unitard and Muscle Tite™ Reflective Tight. 4-way stretch, absorbent, breathable, chest support, reflective piping, stirrups, adjustable waist. Aerobics, cycling, weight training.

337

Consumer Magazine Color: Campaign Including Magazine Supplements

338
ART DIRECTOR
Mario Giua
WRITER
Robin Raj
DESIGNER
Mario Giua
PHOTOGRAPHER
Dan Weaks
CLIENT
Plank Road Original Draught
AGENCY
Chiat/Day

339
ART DIRECTOR
Ray Brennan
WRITER
Phil Dearman
PHOTOGRAPHERS
Martin Thompson
Dennis Waugh
CLIENT
Whitbread & Company
AGENCY
Lowe Howard-Spink
Marschalk/London

BACK THEN BEER WAS FRESH. TODAY BEER IS COOKED.

Ask most beer drinkers, and they'll likely agree with this simple truth: nothing tastes better than beer from the keg.

Keg beer has always been fresher. In the days before refrigeration, ice was cut from winter lakes and packed around the beer as soon as it was brewed. The kegs were kept cold in underground caves like the ones beneath Frederic Miller's original Plank Road Brewery.

It's hard to find beer like that today. That's because most beers, in bottles and cans, are pasteurized. Cooked to 140 degrees to preserve their shelf life. So they lose that fresh draft taste.

But sooner or later, some 130 years later in fact, someone at Frederic Miller's Brewery was bound to figure it out. How to brew a true draft beer in a bottle, specially cold-filtered instead of cooked, so it tastes like it was drawn fresh from the keg.

Introducing Plank Road Original Draught.

Keg beer in a bottle.

PLANK ROAD
Original Draught

PLANK ROAD
BREWERY
MILWAUKEE
WIS
NOTICE!
WHY WE DON'T COOK OUR BEER.
A hundred years ago beer wasn't cooked like it is today. Because, back then, there was no need to preserve it.
Those were the great days of draft beer, fresh from the keg. When there was a brewery in every town. A tavern on every corner. And bucket-boys who delivered buckets full of fresh draft to homes and work-sites.
Like the draft they brewed at Frederic Miller's old Plank Road Brewery. It had a smooth, fresh taste that made the job of bucket-boy one of the busiest jobs around.
Beer like that had a taste you just can't find in today's bottles and cans. Because most beers, in bottles and cans, are pasteurized. Cooked to 140 degrees to preserve them. So they lose that fresh draft taste.
But now there's a bottled beer that's not cooked. It's specially cold-filtered instead. To keep the true taste of fresh draft.
Introducing Plank Road Original Draught. It tastes as fresh from the bottle as it does from the keg.
PLANK ROAD
Original Draught

COOKED BEER VS. FRESH BEER.

Down through the years, generations of beer drinkers have always agreed: beer from the keg tastes better than beer from the bottle or can.

Beer from the keg has always been fresher. Beer like the workers in Frederic Miller's Plank Road Brewery used to enjoy back in 1855, hand-brewed and drawn fresh from the keg.

Beer like that left a memory today's beer in bottles and cans just can't equal. Because, unlike draft beer, today's beer mass produced in bottles and cans is pasteurized. Heated to 140 degrees to preserve its shelf life.

But, sooner or later, 130 years later in fact, someone at Frederic Miller's Brewery was bound to figure it out. Why not brew a true draft beer in a bottle, specially cold-filtered instead of cooked, so it tastes like it was drawn fresh from the keg.

Introducing Plank Road Original Draught. It tastes as fresh from the bottle as it does from the keg.

PLANK ROAD ORIGINAL DRAUGHT

FOUR PRIZE-WINNING 'DRAUGHTS' YOU WON'T FIND IN OUR PUBS.

When the idea of sponsoring our own literary awards scheme was first mooted in 1970, it received mixed reviews.

After all, what interest could a brewery possibly have in books, beyond how to balance them?

Well, at Whitbread we've fostered the arts since the late 18th Century.

Patron to both Gainsborough and Reynolds, Samuel Whitbread II was also well acquainted with the literary scene.

And when Sheridan's Drury Lane Theatre was destroyed by fire, he led the fund-raising committee that rebuilt it.

SAMUEL WHITBREAD II

So, the thought of our encouraging Britain's prolific literary talent wasn't exactly a new one.

The Whitbread Literary Awards are now seen as a stepping stone to greater things for authors of all descriptions.

To begin with, the awards provided only three categories.

Best novel, the best biography or autobiography and best children's book.

Then in 1981, it was extended to cater for the best first novel, too.

Four years on, we have broadened our horizons still further by introducing an award for the best collection of poetry.

The benefits of winning this (or any of the other sections) are threefold.

Firstly, there is the kudos of knowing your book has been selected by a distinguished panel of judges.

(In the past, that has meant impressing writers of the stature of J.B. Priestley, Laurie Lee and Edna O'Brien.)

And secondly, there's the incentive of a substantial cash prize. (Between them, the winners of the 1984-85 competition shared £12,000.)

Finally, there's the satisfaction of receiving an award in the presence of Britain's best known literary figures at our Chiswell Street brewery in London.

An occasion which gives us an excellent opportunity to show each author one or two successful draughts of our own.

WHITBREAD
Our reputation has been brewing since 1742.

ONE OF THE BIGGEST BEER GARDENS IN ENGLAND. AND ALL WE SERVE IS TEA.

Amazing. Hops, hops everywhere and not a drop of malted liquor to drink.

Ah, well, you must remember that this is a working hop farm. And not a brewery.

Which explains why the place is abuzz with farm machinery and the like.

Covering well over 1000 acres, the farm supplies our breweries' most vital raw material, the brewing hop.

And not just any old hop either, but the best around. The Golding Hop.

Yet the farm, near Beltring in Kent, is also a truly unique living museum.

Perfectly preserved, our oast houses and long-galleried barns form an architecturally striking group.

Sadly, it's a feature that's becoming increasingly rare in the countryside.

Rarer still though, are the collection of old carts, ancient farm implements and hop picking equipment they contain.

(Play Jack Hargreaves and guess what these obscure objects were used for.)

Further rustic diversions can be found in our country crafts centre. Here, you can watch a local potter at his wheel. Or meet other craftspeople exhibiting their work.

There is plenty to peruse outdoors too.

The wooded banks of the River Medway provide a richly varied nature trail. As well as some beautiful picnic spots.

There's excellent carp and pike fishing from the banks of our newly stocked ponds.

We've even set aside an area where children can come face to face with a wide range of pets and farm animals.

At certain other times the magnificent Whitbread shire horses are also in residence.

Getting round these many and varied attractions could take the best part of a day.

By the end of your visit you'll probably have worked up quite a thirst.

Fortunately, though, there's one reviving brown liquid that's never in short supply. Tea.

WHITBREAD
Our reputation has been brewing since 1742.

IT'S BEEN GOING DOWN THE HATCH SINCE 1750.

You are looking at Samuel Whitbread's original transport fleet.

A simple combination of horse-power and sail-cloth, it was the envy of the late 18th Century brewing world.

It was responsible for conveying our earliest home brews to foreign parts.

Aden was our first port of call back in 1750, courtesy of the East India Company.

Four years later we followed the flag of the 3rd African Company on their travels.

CIRCA 1890

Our porter beer was even said to have whetted General Wolfe's whistle before the crucial Battle of Quebec.

It was certainly being drunk in Hong Kong and Singapore in the 1890's. Sailing ledgers of the period prove that.

Tastes were gradually changing though. With the advent of the 19th Century came our popular 'India Pale Ale'.

As strong as porter but more sparkling, our customers east of Suez preferred it.

It went down rather well at home, too. So well, that in 1834 Samuel Whitbread II began brewing ale on a large scale.

The wanderlust of our ale continued with the discovery of gold-dust in Australia in the mid-19th Century.

Colonial palates weren't alone in benefiting from our burgeoning export trade.

By the end of the 19th Century, our beer had also found favour with mainland Europe.

In 1904 we opened our first bottling depot in Brussels. Our first brewery in Europe followed soon after.

Today our beer is also brewed in Gabon, Jamaica, St. Lucia, New Zealand and Trinidad.

So now no man need wait for time and tide before putting away a glass of our beer.

WHITBREAD
Our reputation has been brewing since 1742.

Consumer Magazine Color: Campaign Including Magazine Supplements

340
ART DIRECTORS
Gary Johns
Rick Boyko
Andy Dijak
Yvonne Smith
WRITERS
Bill Hamilton
Jeff Gorman
Mark Monteiro
PHOTOGRAPHER
Mark Coppos
CLIENT
Nike
AGENCY
Chiat/Day - Los Angeles

341
ART DIRECTORS
Jerry Whitley
Mark Johnson
WRITERS
Mark Silveira
Paul Wolfe
DESIGNER
William Hartwell
PHOTOGRAPHER
Jeffrey Zwart
CLIENT
BMW of North America
AGENCY
Ammirati & Puris

MOTORCYCLES ARE LIKE MUSIC.
AFTER YEARS OF SHAKE, RATTLE AND ROLL, YOU START TO APPRECIATE THE GERMAN CLASSICS.
BMW
THE LEGENDARY MOTORCYCLES OF GERMANY.

IT'S SHAPED TO CUT THROUGH THE WIND, CLING TO THE ROAD AND NOT GET LOST IN THE PARKING LOT.
BMW INTRODUCES TRUE CLASS TO THE 750 CLASS: THE K75.
THE LEGENDARY MOTORCYCLES OF GERMANY.
BMW

PEOPLE AREN'T BORN WITH AN APPRECIATION FOR BMW'S. THEY DEVELOP IT RIDING OTHER BIKES.
THE LEGENDARY MOTORCYCLES OF GERMANY.
BMW

Consumer Magazine Color: Campaign Including Magazine Supplements

342
ART DIRECTORS
Jean Robaire
Tom Cordner
WRITERS
John Stein
Brent Bouchez
PHOTOGRAPHERS
Bob Stevens
Bill Werts
CLIENT
Yamaha Motor Corporation, USA
AGENCY
Chiat/Day - Los Angeles

343
ART DIRECTOR
Neal Werner
WRITER
Charlie Carlson
PHOTOGRAPHER
Ric Cohn
CLIENT
Neutrogena
AGENCY
Geers Gross

Or this ad.

We realize that the chances of finding anyone riding a three-wheeler 30 feet below the surface of the Pacific Ocean are slim.

But the fact that this Yamaha could operate in this environment says that we do things just a little differently.

We don't test our machines in the warmth and comfort of a test lab because, chances are, you won't ride our machines in a test lab.

So we get off the beaten track.

To places you wouldn't go, like the bottom of the Pacific Ocean. And to places you would go, like the Deep South.

Not to a hotel or a campground, but into the bayou. Where you'll find some of the thickest mud in the world. The most torturous sand in the world and, most of all, swamps.

Miles and miles of swamps. So much water that you can't ride more than a minute or two without being up to your axles (or worse) in brown H_2O. Not to mention snakes or gators.

Not the kind of place you want to break down. So it didn't take long for our engineers to invent a way to keep our three-wheelers from falling prey to the most common killer of machines ridden in the wet. Water in the ignition system.

The cure: Oil-bathed ignition.

A theory based on the fact that oil and water don't mix. So it follows that if you put a barrier of oil between the ignition and the water, the water will stay out and the ignition will stay dry.

So much so that Three-Wheeling magazine recently heralded Yamaha's three-wheelers as the most waterproof the industry has to offer.

Out of our rather unorthodox testing facilities have come a whole family of machines. Each one improved year after year.

This year's Tri-Z250, for example, now has a six-speed transmission for faster acceleration and even more top speed than last year's model.

And to handle that extra speed, we've also added lower profile tires that slide easier in the corners.

On the other hand, our YTM225DR, and our kids three-wheeler, the Tri-Zinger 60, have only minor changes. The 225 does have a new paint scheme that matches the machine's reputation as the "Cadillac" of three-wheelers. But for the most part we left these two proven machines well enough alone.

That's another thing the swamps can teach you. If it works, don't fix it.

Tri-Z250
YTM225DR
Tri-Zinger

YAMAHA
We make the difference.

They said the mud in Louisiana could stop an ox. That's all we needed to hear.

There's an area in Southern Louisiana known as Cameron Parish. Fifteen or so miles from Lake Charles, just down the road from Hackberry.

The area isn't known for much. Water moccasins perhaps, mosquitoes definitely, and mud. The thickest, slickest, slimiest, tackiest mud you'll find anywhere.

"Gumbo mud" they call it.

It was here, in 1982, our engineers came with their four-wheelers to do a little experimenting. After all, if our machines could handle Cameron Parish, they could handle just about anything.

They did. And our engineers learned a lot in the process. How, for example, to build machines with real horsepower. Honest to goodness, eyeball-jerking horse-power. The kind that give Yamahas the best power-to-weight ratios in the industry.

We learned the importance of building our machines with shaft drive. Not just our top of the line YFM225 and YFM200DX, but our YF60 and YFM80 as well.

We learned the need for using labyrinth seals to keep our wheel bearings working perfectly—even in the incredibly fine, Louisiana sand.

And we learned how to build the most waterproof four-wheelers in the industry. Something we accomplished by pioneering oil-bathed ignitions. And something everyone else has since picked up on.

But perhaps the most important thing we learned was the importance of learning. Not just how to build one or even two four-wheelers, but how to build a family of four-wheelers.

Machines which would be constantly improved as Yamaha—and Cameron Parish—sees fit.

This year's YFM200DX, for example, is sportier than ever. Thanks to something extra we're now putting between the 200DX and its wheels.

Springs. Or more accurately, a full suspension using a swing axle with 70mm of travel up front and a race-proven Monoshock with 110mm of travel at the rear.

All in all, it's one of the two finest dual-purpose four-wheelers made. The other being our YFM225. A vehicle equipped with the only ten-speed dual-range transmission in its class. As well as an 8-1/2 foot turning radius. Again, the best in its class.

There's one final thing to consider, one more point we'd like to make. What you see here is the finest line of four-wheelers in the world.

But only 'til next year, when we go back to Cameron Parish. And take another lesson from the water moccasins, the mosquitoes, and of course, the mud.

YAMAHA
We make the difference.

The day touring riders come in out of the rain, so will we.

If there's a glamorous side to testing motorcycles, this isn't it. There's very little glamour here at all.

And yet, it's in this small and rather uncomfortable room that Yamaha does some of its most important work. That of testing our Venture Royales against the elements.

Testing the components. The speakers, for example, are immersed in water for 24 hours.

And testing entire machines—with a chassis dyno, high-powered fans and water. Lots of water.

All the time learning how to make our new machines even better than our old ones. And in the case of the 1986 Venture Royale, we succeeded.

First by enlarging the liquid-cooled DOHC four-valve V-4 from 1198cc to 1294cc. Resulting in even greater amounts of torque. And then, by developing a diaphragm clutch to help transmit all of that torque to the five-speed transmission.

While one set of Yamaha engineers was working on making the engine more powerful, another set of engineers was doing the same to the brakes. Perfecting our electrical anti-dive system, a system that not only reduces suspension compression during braking but also eliminates lag time.

And to make the brakes even more effective, we switched to slotted rotors and four-piston calipers. Thereby increasing stopping power while, at the same time, reducing maintenance.

Not all of our changes, however, were aimed at making the Venture Royale perform better. Some were aimed at making it perform more comfortably. Like modifying our VentureCruise cruise control system to include functions for Accel, Decel and Resume. Adding a 40 channel CB radio with controls for *both* the rider and passenger. Adding a more comfortable seat. Rubber-mounted floorboards. A lower fairing. And a new travel trunk with a three-way adjustable passenger backrest for better lateral support.

We also increased the size of the saddlebags by fifty percent, and added lift-out carry bags along with a reflector that stretches between the saddlebags.

But while much on the Venture Royale has changed, much hasn't. It still features our exclusive CLASS (Computer Levelling Air Suspension System). Which, in conjunction with a pair of massive front forks and Monocross rear shock absorber, provides the finest ride available.

It still has superb instrumentation.

And, of course, it's still the finest touring machine on the road.

YAMAHA
We make the difference.

WASHING YOUR FACE:

IT'S TIME YOU GOT SERIOUS.

You know that the wrong soap can hurt your skin. But did you know that the right facial bar can help your skin? Dramatically.

Neutrogena* is *that* facial bar. No other we know of can give your skin all the help that Neutrogena can.

A healthier glow. This is an undeniable difference. Neutrogena, unlike others, rinses away thoroughly. No dulling film is left on your face (or under your makeup to diminish its effect). Instead, your skin has a vibrant, healthier glow.

A smooth, cared-for face. Neutrogena contains glycerin, a serious moisturizer that actually retains water and moisture. (Of the facial bars that even contain glycerin, Neutrogena has far more than any we know.) Your skin becomes a reservoir of smoothness, and has never felt more pampered.

A firmer skin tone. Skin that has been washed with Neutrogena feels firmer, with a healthy tone. Skin that has been washed by soaps that leave residue does not feel as firm, as toned. (Explanation: soap residue leaves a coating that actually changes the feel of your skin for the worse.)

A startling clarity. Neutrogena is pure. No irritants, abrasives, dyes, detergents or other harsh chemicals to dry or rob your skin of needed moisture and oil. Neutrogena is also hypo-allergenic, clinically tested and dermatologist recommended. Even sensitive skin can feel safe, free of irritation and blotches. Your face is left clean, cared for, and beautiful.

A formula to match your skin. Neutrogena cares enough to have available a formula that is right for your skin. Select from Original, Dry or Oily Skin Formulas, Scented and Unscented.

So you can see, once you do decide to get serious, the rest is easy. You simply get that amber Neutrogena bar you always suspected was better.

And you were right.

A free introduction to serious skin care. For your complimentary bar of Neutrogena,* send this page along with your name and address to: Neutrogena Corporation, P.O. Box 290, Dept. MSB, Pico Rivera, CA 90665.

*Offer good until December 1, 1985.

NEUTROGENA®

NEUTROGENA SKIN VS. ALL OTHER SKIN:

COMPARE THE HEALTHIER GLOW, THE FIRMER TONE, THE MORE STARTLING CLARITY.

No other facial bar we know of can give your skin all the help that Neutrogena* can.

Compare the healthier glow. This is an undeniable difference. Neutrogena, unlike others, rinses away thoroughly. No dulling film is left on your face (or under your makeup to diminish its effect). Instead, your skin has a vibrant, healthier glow.

Compare the smooth, cared-for feel. Neutrogena contains glycerin, a serious moisturizer that actually retains water and moisture. (Of the facial bars that even contain glycerin, Neutrogena has far more than any we know.) Your skin becomes a reservoir of smoothness, and has never felt more pampered.

Compare the firmer tone. Skin that has been washed with Neutrogena feels firmer, with a healthy tone. Skin that has been washed by soaps that leave residue does not feel as firm, as toned. (Explanation: soap residue leaves a coating that actually changes the feel of your skin for the worse.)

Compare the startling clarity. Neutrogena is pure. No irritant, abrasives, dyes, detergents or other harsh chemicals to dry or rob your skin of needed moisture and oil. Neutrogena is also hypo-allergenic, clinically tested and dermatologist recommended. Even sensitive skin can feel safe, free of irritation and blotches. Your face is left clean, cared for, and beautiful.

Compare the formulas for your skin. Neutrogena cares enough to have available a formula that is right for your skin. Select from Original, Dry or Oily Skin Formulas, Scented and Unscented.

So you can see, once you do compare Neutrogena skin to all other skin, the decision is easy. You simply get that amber Neutrogena bar you always suspected was better. And realize you were right.

A free introduction to serious skin care. Compare the look and feel of Neutrogena skin to all other skin—for free. For your complimentary bar of Neutrogena,* send this page along with your name and address to: Neutrogena Corporation, P.O. Box 290, Dept. MSA, Pico Rivera, CA 90665.

*Offer good until December 1, 1985.

NEUTROGENA®

IS YOUR FACIAL BAR GOOD ENOUGH FOR THE SKIN YOU WANT TO HAVE?

It's time you got serious.

If your facial bar isn't helping your skin enjoy a healthier glow, a well moisturized smoothness, a firmer tone, a startling clarity, then you should consider using the facial bar that will: Neutrogena.* No other we know of can give your skin all the help that Neutrogena can.

A healthier glow. This is an undeniable difference. Neutrogena, unlike others, rinses away thoroughly. No dulling film is left on your face (or under your makeup to diminish its effect). Instead, your skin has a vibrant, healthier glow.

A smooth, cared-for face. Neutrogena contains glycerin, a serious moisturizer that actually retains water and moisture. (Of the facial bars that even contain glycerin, Neutrogena has far more than any we know.) Your skin becomes a reservoir of smoothness, and has never felt more pampered.

A firmer skin tone. Skin that has been washed with Neutrogena feels firmer, with a healthy tone. Skin that has been washed by soaps that leave residue does not feel as firm, as toned. (Explanation: soap residue leaves a coating that actually changes the feel of your skin for the worse.)

A startling clarity. Neutrogena is pure. No irritants, abrasives, dyes, detergents or other harsh chemicals to dry or rob your skin of needed moisture and oil. Neutrogena is also hypo-allergenic, clinically tested and dermatologist recommended. Even sensitive skin can feel safe, free of irritation and blotches. Your face is left clean, cared for, and beautiful.

A formula to match your skin. Neutrogena cares enough to have available a formula that is right for your skin. Select from Original, Dry or Oily Skin Formulas, Scented and Unscented.

A free introduction to help you attain the skin you want to have. Compare the look and feel of Neutrogena skin to all other skin—for free. For your complimentary bar of Neutrogena,* send this page along with your name and address to: Neutrogena Corporation, P.O. Box 290, Dept. MSC, Pico Rivera, CA 90665.

*Offer good until December 1, 1985.

NEUTROGENA®

Consumer Magazine Color: Campaign Including Magazine Supplements

344
ART DIRECTOR
Bob Butler
WRITERS
Tom McGuire
Peter Brown
Ron Berman
PHOTOGRAPHER
Terry Heffernan
CLIENT
Liquor Barn
AGENCY
Cole & Weber/Los Angeles

345
ART DIRECTOR
James Good
WRITER
John Gruen
PHOTOGRAPHERS
Bill Luster
Andy Hayt
Brian Lanker
CLIENT
Sports Illustrated
AGENCY
Ogilvy & Mather

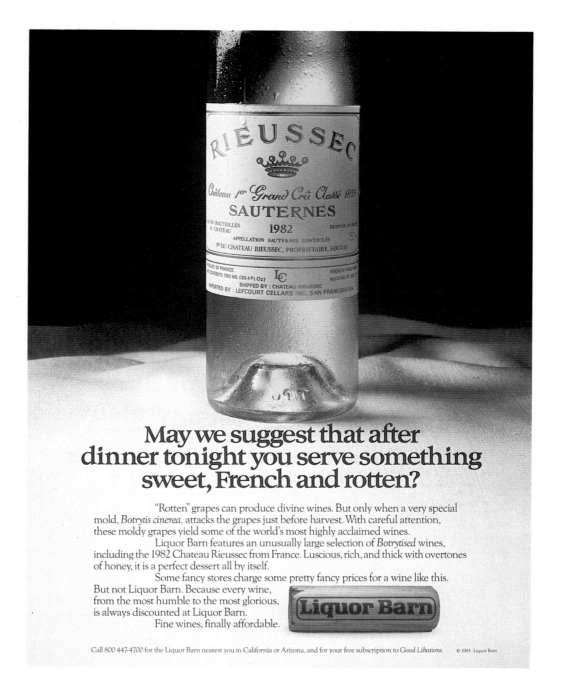

RIEUSSEC
Château 1er Grand Crû Classé 1855
SAUTERNES
1982

May we suggest that after dinner tonight you serve something sweet, French and rotten?

"Rotten" grapes can produce divine wines. But only when a very special mold, *Botrytis cinerea*, attacks the grapes just before harvest. With careful attention, these moldy grapes yield some of the world's most highly acclaimed wines.

Liquor Barn features an unusually large selection of *Botrytised* wines, including the 1982 Chateau Rieussec from France. Luscious, rich, and thick with overtones of honey, it is a perfect dessert all by itself.

Some fancy stores charge some pretty fancy prices for a wine like this. But not Liquor Barn. Because every wine, from the most humble to the most glorious, is always discounted at Liquor Barn.

Fine wines, finally affordable.

Liquor Barn

Call 800 447-4700 for the Liquor Barn nearest you in California or Arizona, and for your free subscription to *Good Libations*. © 1985 Liquor Barn

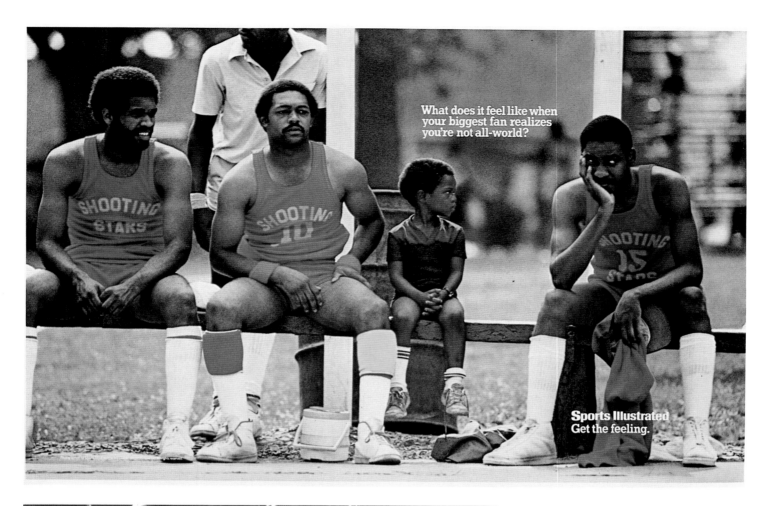

What does it feel like when
your biggest fan realizes
you're not all-world?

Sports Illustrated
Get the feeling.

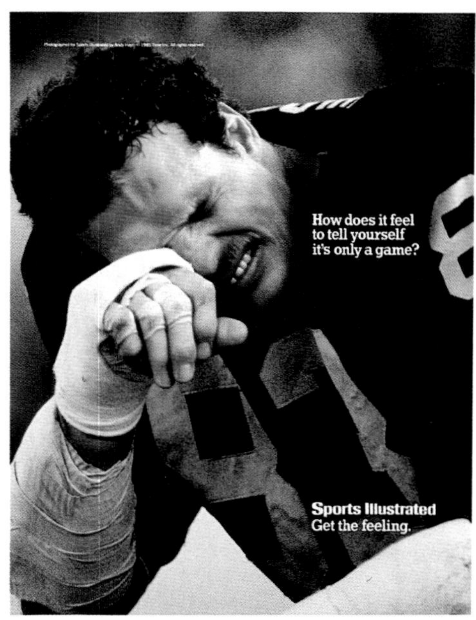

Consumer Magazine Color: Campaign Including Magazine Supplements

346
ART DIRECTOR
John Morrison
WRITER
Penny Kapousouz
ARTIST
Cynthia Shern
PHOTOGRAPHER
Dennis Manarchy
CLIENT
Apple Computer
AGENCY
Chiat/Day - Los Angeles

Consumer Magazine Less Than A Page B/W Or Color: Single

347
ART DIRECTOR
Terry Schneider
WRITER
Bill Borders
PHOTOGRAPHERS
Aaron Jones
Jerry LaRocca
CLIENT
Columbia Sportswear
AGENCY
Borders Perrin & Norrander/ Portland, OR

348
ART DIRECTOR
Rob Dalton
WRITER
Mike Lescarbeau
DESIGNER
Rob Dalton
PHOTOGRAPHER
Stock
CLIENT
KRLD-TV
AGENCY
Fallon McElligott/Minneapolis

When Informatics General was awarded a multi-million dollar, 60-man-year software development project for NASA, Project Director David Kaiser decided the colored yarn and push-pins had to go.

They had been one of many methods of constantly revising the PERT (scheduling) charts his projects so heavily depend on.

"I'd tried everything," David remembers. "I even pinned 3x5 index cards to a bulletin board and connected interdependent tasks with rubber bands. When anything changed, I'd move the cards by hand. The colored yarn indicated our critical path."

Then David discovered a computer called Macintosh.™ And a powerful software program called MacProject.™

And according to David, project management hasn't been the same since.

"When I was scheduling on paper, I was limited to roughly 300 separately scheduled tasks. With Macintosh, we can work with 1600 separately scheduled tasks."

And scheduling at a greater level of detail is just one of the many differences Macintosh makes in David's work.

Unlike other scheduling programs, MacProject makes updating as easy as a point and click of Macintosh's mouse.

So David and his task managers are actually willing to do it. MacProject does the rest. Recalculates dates. Reformulates the critical path. And monitors all project resources.

So anyone on any project, from high-rise construction to film production, can refer to the most current information on people, money and time.

At a glance.

"We still wind up working a few weekends," David admits. "Only now we can calculate in advance exactly how many weekends we'll need to work to stay on schedule."

Another testimony to the fact that Macintosh not only helps work stay on schedule, but weekend ski trips, too.

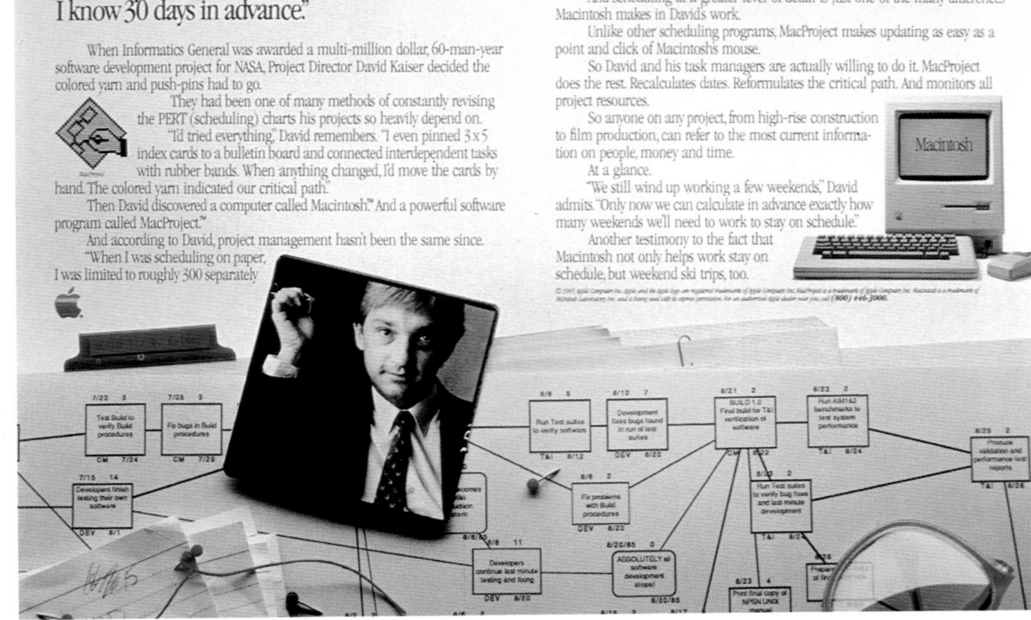

"It's saved us money we didn't even know we had."

When Gary Lieber received his budget allotment this year, he found himself faced with the same old problem: too much to buy, and too little to spend.

He also found himself faced with a brand new solution: a Macintosh™ personal computer, and powerful software programs like Excel from Microsoft.

Gary is a Senior Operations Administrator for a subsidiary of Hughes Aircraft.

And in his business of competitive contract bidding, where any rise in overhead means a fall in profit, Gary's convinced that Macintosh is the best tool yet devised for reading between the numbers.

"Using MacTerminal™ and Switcher,™ I can cut raw data out of the corporate mainframe database and paste it directly into my spreadsheets," Gary explains. "Financial models that used to take days with my IBM, now take a few minutes."

But the time Macintosh saves Gary is secondary to the unique perspective it affords him.

He cites a recent $100,000 purchase as a classic example.

"I had quotes from some 15 vendors. Using my Macintosh and Excel, I could not only forecast precise bulk costs for each, but cross-foot them against projected costs and pick the vendor that was most economical *long term.*"

And Macintosh not only makes it easier to assess financial expenditures, but easier to communicate and control them.

"With the LaserWriter™ printer, for the first time I can do graphs for my analyses and print them up as overheads on the fly."

"Bottom line," Gary explains, "was that I ended up several thousand dollars *under* budget. For my money, Macintosh paid for itself right there."

Which may account for the fact that more and more businesses are employing it.

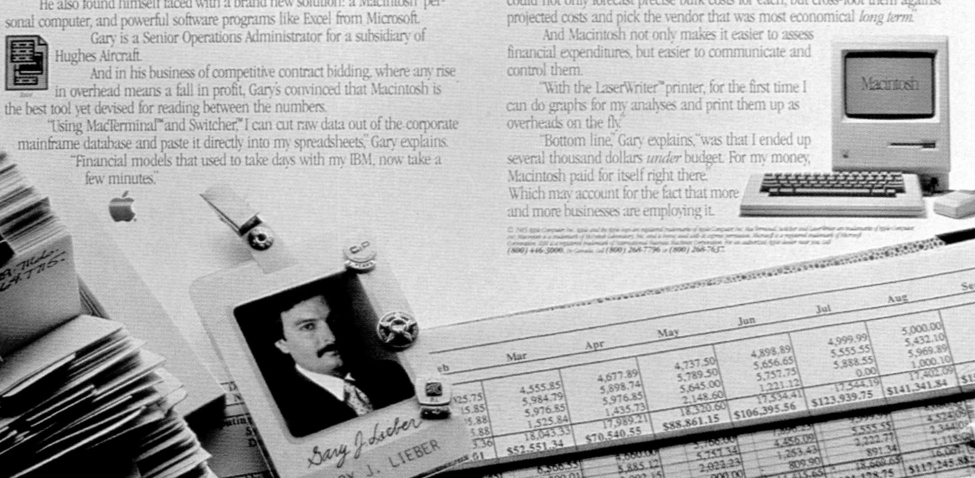

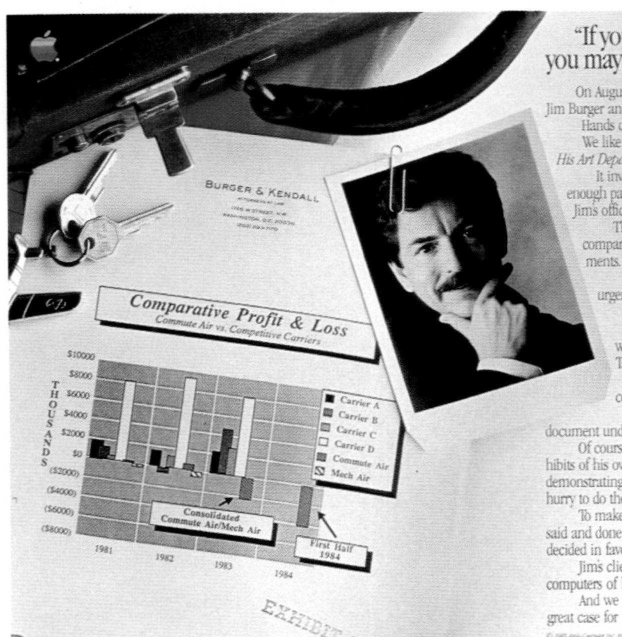

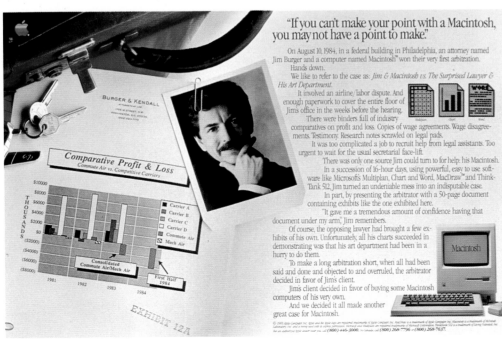

"If you can't make your point with a Macintosh, you may not have a point to make."

On August 10, 1984, in a federal building in Philadelphia, an attorney named Jim Burger and a computer named Macintosh™ won their very first arbitration.

Hands down.

We like to refer to the case as: *Jim & Macintosh vs. The Surprised Lawyer & His Art Department.*

It involved an airline/labor dispute. And enough paperwork to cover the entire floor of Jim's office in the weeks before the hearing.

There were binders full of industry comparatives on profit and loss. Copies of wage agreements. Wage disagreements. Testimony. Research notes scrawled on legal pads.

It was too complicated a job to recruit help from legal assistants. Too urgent to wait for the usual secretarial face-lift.

There was only one source Jim could turn to for help: his Macintosh.

In a succession of 16-hour days, using powerful, easy to use software like Microsoft's Multiplan, Chart and Word, MacDraw™ and Think-Tank 512, Jim turned an undeniable mess into an indisputable case.

In part, by presenting the arbitrator with a 50-page document containing exhibits like the one exhibited here.

"It gave me a tremendous amount of confidence having that document under my arm," Jim remembers.

Of course, the opposing lawyer had brought a few exhibits of his own. Unfortunately, all his charts succeeded in demonstrating was that his art department had been in a hurry to do them.

To make a long arbitration short, when all had been said and done and objected to and overruled, the arbitrator decided in favor of Jim's client.

Jim's client decided in favor of buying some Macintosh computers of his very own.

And we decided it all made another great case for Macintosh.

"ONE DAY MOTHER MADE US CHANGE OUR SHORTS THREE TIMES."—Tim Boyle

When we first came up with a line of new shorts, everyone was excited. Except the company President, my mother.

"Too ordinary," she sniffed.

So we looked for extraordinary touches. And found some. Like great madras prints that reverse to our unique Dirigible™ Cloth. Result: A real *pair* of shorts. Two in one.

We added slash pockets, a wide waistband and a comfortable, generous cut. Then engineered them to typical Columbia high stress specs.

Now, after all these improvements, we are *really* excited.

And so's Mom. To quote her jubilation, "They'll do."

The Oasis Short. Reversible from madras to solid.

Columbia
Sportswear Company

For color brochure, send $1 to us at 6600 N. Baltimore, Dept. AF, Portland, Oregon 97203.

347

THE DOCTORS COULDN'T BRING HIM BACK. SO WE DID.

DALLAS. WEEKNIGHTS AT 6.

348

Consumer Magazine Less Than A Page B/W Or Color: Single

349
ART DIRECTOR
Peter Cohen
WRITER
Jeffrey Epstein
DESIGNER
Peter Cohen
CLIENT
Lorango
AGENCY
5 to 9 Agency

350
ART DIRECTOR
Bill Zabowski
WRITER
Lyle Wedemeyer
CLIENT
Pepito's
AGENCY
Martin/Williams - Minneapolis

351
ART DIRECTOR
Terry O'Leary
WRITER
Doug Feinstein
DESIGNER
Terry O'Leary
PHOTOGRAPHER
Harry DeZitter
CLIENT
Durabeam
AGENCY
Ogilvy & Mather

352
ART DIRECTOR
Josiane Ohana
WRITER
Robert Woolcott
ARTIST
R.O. Bleckman
CLIENT
Beneteau
AGENCY
Rumrill Hoyt

349

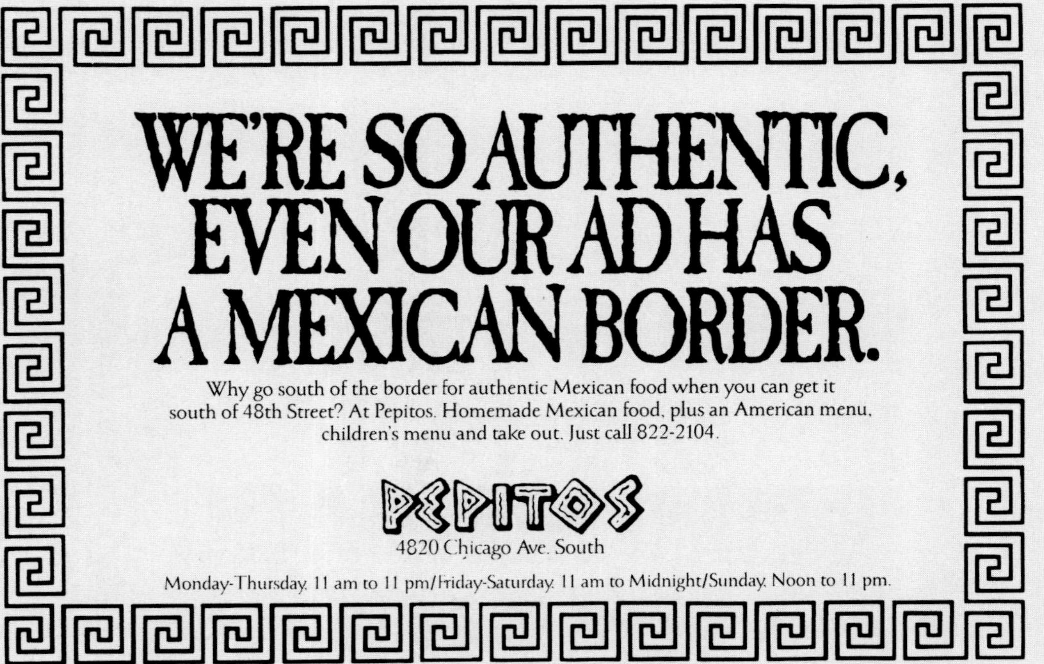

350

With many lanterns, you'd be in hot water.
The DURABEAM* lantern. It's built tough so it can stand up to the elements. It's much brighter than ordinary lanterns. And it comes equipped with a long-lasting DURACELL* battery. But on top of all that, it actually floats. Because when you're out in the middle of nowhere, it's sink or swim.
DURABEAM.
It really works when you need it.
© 1985 DURACELL Inc.

351

HOW TO WIN IN THE ADMIRAL'S CUP AFTER YOUR YACHT SINKS.

The sinking of his yacht "Indulgence" during the prestigious Cup trials presented a major inconvenience to Harold Cudmore. And the unthinkable—England challenging for the Cup without him, loomed large on the horizon.

Yacht squadron lounges buzzed about Cudmore's dilemma. Then he was asked if he would mind skippering a French-made Bénéteau 40. Stiffening his lip and setting aside centuries of Anglo-French rivalry he graciously accepted.

Once more, Captain Cudmore was challenging for the Cup. This time on a yacht appropriately renamed the "Phoenix."

Less than half the yachts managed to complete all five grueling and hazardous Cup races. Four Bénéteaus were entered, and apart from a headstay failure in one race, all the Bénéteaus finished. Not only did "Phoenix" win the Olympic Triangle race, she captured overall top individual honors.

Our congratulations go to Harold Cudmore and his crew for their outstanding performances in one of the most demanding series of races in the world, the 1985 Admiral's Cup.

Their win is testament to remarkable skill and seamanship. The fact that the Bénéteau "Phoenix" was the #1 yacht, and all the Bénéteaus placed in the top 25 (two in the top 10), is further testament to the outstanding speed, strength and design of Bénéteau yachts.

Harold Cudmore never originally planned to win with a Bénéteau. You can. Call or write to us today. Bénéteau (USA) LTD., 326 First St., Annapolis MD 21403. (301) 268-7177.

BÉNÉTEAU

THE SEA DEMANDS THE BEST.

352

Consumer Magazine Less Than A Page B/W Or Color: Campaign

353
ART DIRECTOR
Nancy Rice
WRITER
Jarl Olsen
CLIENT
Pronto
AGENCY
Fallon McElligott/Minneapolis

354
ART DIRECTOR
Rene Vidmer
WRITERS
Ken Baron
Eve Hartman
PHOTOGRAPHER
Stanford Smilow
CLIENT
Great American Knitting Mills
AGENCY
Baron & Zaretsky

The most appetizing thing to ever come out of an old boot.

PRONTO
NEW YORK • GENEVA • MINNEAPOLIS Hyatt Regency Hotel Downtown Minneapolis
For reservations 333-4414

This is your only chance to eat at Pronto without eating on an airplane first.

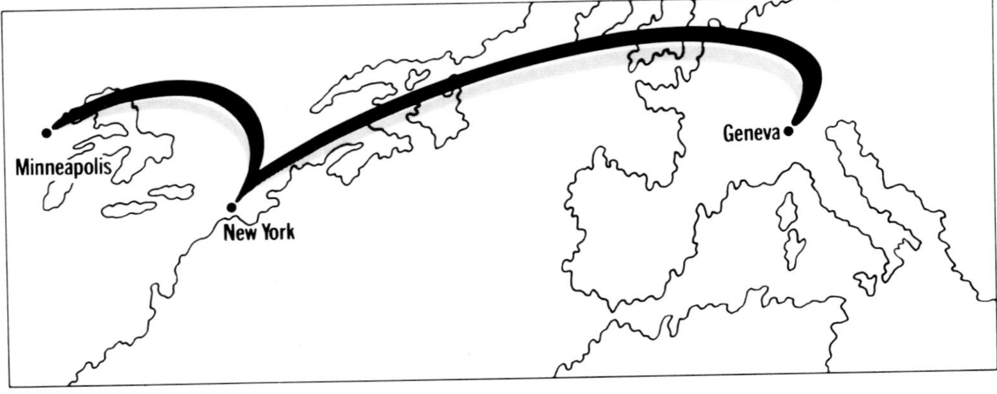

PRONTO
NEW YORK • GENEVA • MINNEAPOLIS Hyatt Regency Hotel Downtown Minneapolis
For reservations 333-4414

353

BE SMART. WEAR FIFTY-YEAR-OLD SOCKS.

After a half-century of perfecting the sock, Gold Toe announces no major breakthroughs. We long ago decided the best way for us to make socks is to make the best socks. So the gold thread in our toe is more than our trusted symbol. It's actually a double reinforcement, woven in to keep your toes comfortably in their place. Since we're this picky with a Gold Toe toe, can you imagine the care we take with the rest of the sock? So, after fifty years, we have a suggestion. Change your socks. To Gold Toe.

© 1985 Made with DuPont Hi-Bulk Orlon®

THE STANDARD OF QUALITY GOLD TOE®

It's time you changed your socks.

From Cluett

GOLD TOE ANNOUNCES NO MAJOR BREAKTHROUGHS.

Gold Toe socks are carefully—if not fanatically—made to keep your toes in their place. That gold thread you see is actually a double reinforcement, impeding any undo progress of your pushy toes. We also knit our gold toes in as pouches, for a fit that's firm and comfortable. And if we're this picky with a Gold Toe toe, can you imagine the care we take with the rest of the sock? So if you feel your own toes are making advances, we have a suggestion. Change your socks. To Gold Toe.

© 1985 Made with DuPont Hi-Bulk Orlon®

THE STANDARD OF QUALITY GOLD TOE®

It's time you changed your socks.

From Cluett

NOW, GOLD TOE PUTS WOMEN ON EQUAL FOOTING.

The time has come for women to stand up for their rights. And lefts. In Gold Toe's new, fashionable casual and athletic socks just for women. With the same double reinforced gold toes as in our men's socks, and the same toe seams, hand finished for extra comfort. If we're this picky with a Gold Toe toe, can you imagine the care we take with the rest of the sock? So now that you've filled men's shoes, it's time to change your socks. To Gold Toe.

© 1985 Made with DuPont Hi-Bulk Orlon®

THE STANDARD OF QUALITY GOLD TOE®

It's time you changed your socks.

From Cluett

Trade B/W: 1 Page Or Spread

355
ART DIRECTOR
Tom Lichtenheld
WRITER
Bruce Bildsten
CLIENT
Great Faces Typography
AGENCY
Fallon McElligott/Minneapolis

356
ART DIRECTORS
John Morrison
Michael Fazende
WRITER
Bill Miller
PHOTOGRAPHER
Tom Berthiaume
CLIENT
AMF
AGENCY
Fallon McElligott/Minneapolis

357
ART DIRECTOR
Tom Lichtenheld
WRITER
Jarl Olsen
DESIGNER
Tom Lichtenheld
ARTIST
Bob Lambert
PHOTOGRAPHER
Tom Berthiaume
CLIENT
Berthiaume/Lamb
AGENCY
Fallon McElligott/Minneapolis

358
ART DIRECTOR
Rick Carpenter
WRITER
Jaci Sisson
DESIGNER
Rick Carpenter
PHOTOGRAPHER
David Leach
CLIENT
Della Femina Travisano
AGENCY
Della Femina Travisano & Partners

YOU CAN'T GET IN THIS BOOK WITH AN UGLY FACE.

Although the advertisements in this book were created by hundreds of people, an overwhelming majority were set by one team: Great Faces/Great Headlines.

Not because we're inexpensive or because we buy our clients expensive lunches, but because we do beautiful work.

Because we treat typesetting as an art, instead of a trade.

So if you want your face in The Show next year, maybe you should send your words to us.

After all, a beautiful face not only could win you an award. It could keep you from being ugly to the judges.

Great Faces/Great Headlines
The artists in advertising typography · 339-2933

355

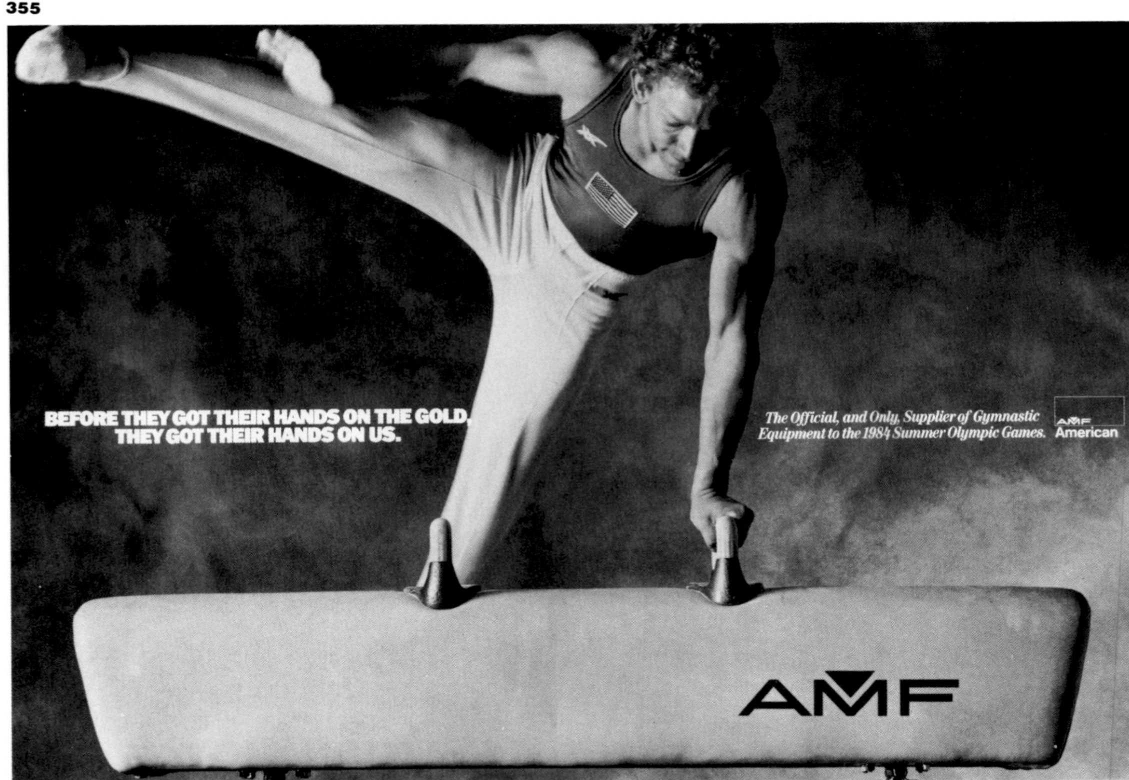
BEFORE THEY GOT THEIR HANDS ON THE GOLD, THEY GOT THEIR HANDS ON US.
The Official, and Only, Supplier of Gymnastic Equipment to the 1984 Summer Olympic Games.
AMF American
AMF

356

BERTHIAUME

IF YOU LIKED THE BOOK,
YOU'LL LOVE THE FILM.

One of the most popular still photographers in town is also the newest director at Lamb and Company. To see Tom Berthiaume's reel, contact Duffy Pearce at 333-8666.

357

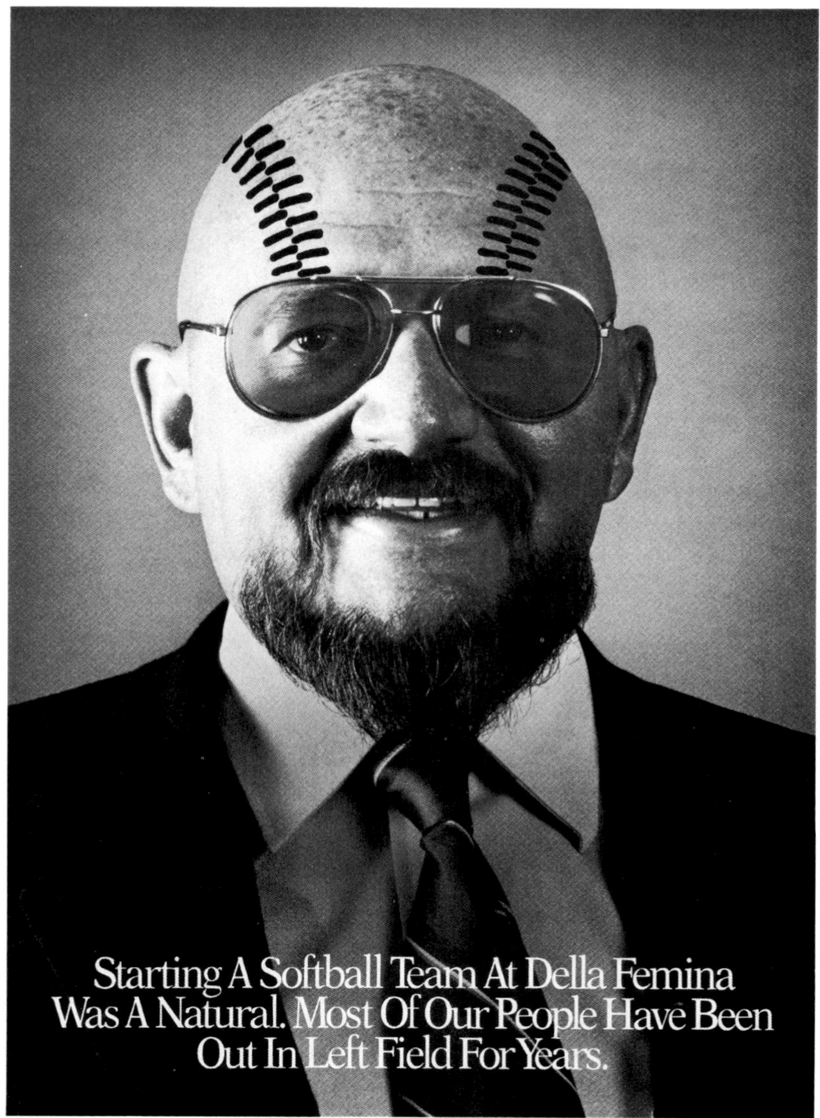
Starting A Softball Team At Della Femina
Was A Natural. Most Of Our People Have Been
Out In Left Field For Years.

358

Trade B/W: 1 Page Or Spread

359
ART DIRECTOR
Dean Hanson
WRITER
Sam Avery
PHOTOGRAPHER
Rick Dublin
CLIENT
First Tennessee Bank
AGENCY
Fallon McElligott/Minneapolis

360
ART DIRECTOR
Bob Barrie
WRITER
Phil Hanft
DESIGNER
Bob Barrie
PHOTOGRAPHER
Rick Dublin
CLIENT
Dalmations By Golly
AGENCY
Fallon McElligott/Minneapolis

361
ART DIRECTOR
Dean Hanson
WRITER
Jarl Olsen
PHOTOGRAPHER
Ben Saltzman
CLIENT
ITT Life Insurance
AGENCY
Fallon McElligott/Minneapolis

362
ART DIRECTOR
Bill Schwartz
WRITER
Chris Perry
DESIGNER
Bill Schwartz
ARTIST
Kim Smith
PHOTOGRAPHER
Carl Fowler
CLIENT
Meldrum and Fewsmith
AGENCY
Meldrum and Fewsmith/
Cleveland

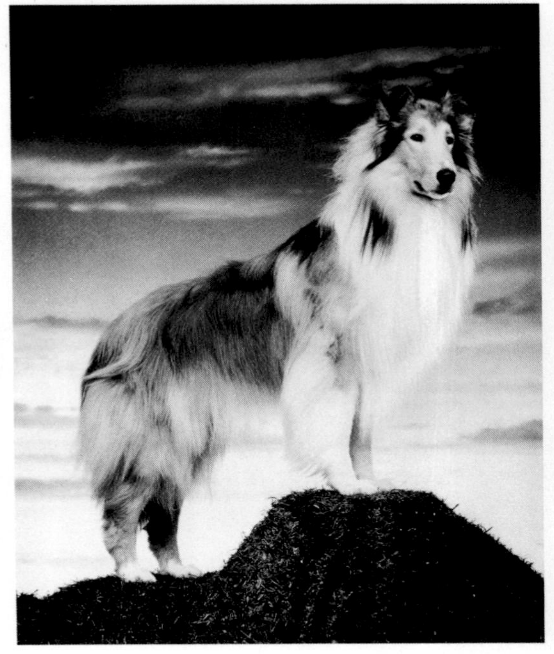

FEW THINGS IN LIFE ARE MORE LOYAL THAN A FIRST TENNESSEE BANKER.

There's one problem with a lot of bankers. All too often, the moment your business starts to slack off, so do they.

Unless, of course, you have a First Tennessee banker.

You can count on a First Tennessee banker to be your partner in good times and bad times.

That's because we go out of our way to learn everything we can about your business.

So in good times we can help you with new growth opportunities. And in bad times we can help you with the economic setbacks that surprise the best of us.

Of course, knowledge and loyalty aren't all we offer you.

Knowing that your success depends on moving quickly, our loan officers make it a point to be just as quick.

And because we understand that your business can have different needs at different times, we can help you with a great deal more than loans.

Our people have the resources, and they take the time, to help you with bond financing, cash management, employee benefits, and many other financial services.

Simply put, First Tennessee is large enough to deliver all the products and services only a large bank can. But flexible enough to cater to your company's individual needs.

You see, our goal isn't just being the businessman's banker. It's being the businessman's best friend.

In Memphis, call Lonnie Kersey at 767-8003.

1st FIRST TENNESSEE

359

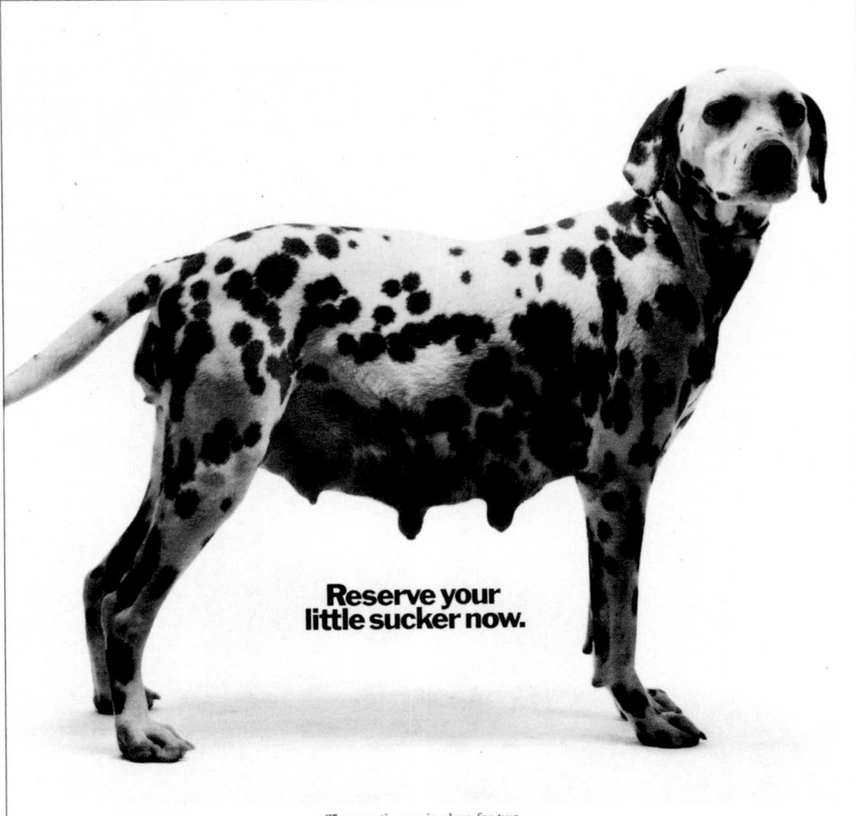
Reserve your
little sucker now.

The genetics are in place for two exceptional litters.

Champion Hobnail Golly Rose Road (Rosie), bred with Mt. Bryton's Facile Princeps (Face), is due to whelp in the middle of July.

Katrin Kate of Cashman Court (Katie), bred with Champion Tuckaway Traveler Indalane (Rebel), in October.

These four bloodlines should deliver dalmatians with excellent movement, temperament and color in addition to good fronts and strong rears.

So don't get stuck sucking hind teat when these litters arrive. Reserve your place in the selection order today.

Dalmatians by Golly

Sheri Golly, Kevin Berigan/Owners & Breeders
10740 Inwood Avenue N., Mahtomedi, MN 55115
Phone 612-426-9603

360

"EAT YOUR RICE, THERE ARE INSURANCE AGENTS STARVING IN AMERICA."

It's no joke; these are trying times for the life insurance agent.

Some industry experts believe that agents will not survive the revolution taking place in financial services today.

They see the agent as a costly, inefficient middleman who keeps life insurance from competing with other kinds of investments.

Many life insurance companies are looking for alternative distribution channels which would eliminate the agent (and agent commissions) entirely.

ITT Life thinks the problem lies not with the agent, but the system under which the agent is forced to work. The average agent spends only 20% of his or her time actually selling insurance. The other 80% is taken up prospecting and servicing accounts.

We're working hard to turn those numbers around.

Consumer advertising, a national lead program and innovative marketing support are just some of the ways ITT Life is helping bring customers to our agents. We also provide agents with free software and competitive commissions, paid weekly.

Our president, Bob MacDonald, has prepared a tape explaining what changes are in store for the agency system—and what you can do to profit from them.

He'll talk about why insurance agents need a superior company behind them and why ITT Life in particular is a company where a good agent can survive and prosper.

He'll talk about that last subject a lot.

If you would like to receive Bob MacDonald's "Save the Agents" tape, send in the postage free reply card today or call us toll-free **1-800-328-2193.** We'll send it to you at no charge.

ITT Life doesn't claim to have all the answers.

But we do think that the way to sell insurance is to give our agents more support, not less.

And we're not just feeding you a line.

ITT *ITT Life Insurance Corporation*

361

Today's consumer is armed and dangerous.

Advertisers beware.

The days of pounding a selling message into someone's head are over.

People will no longer sit idly by, as advertisers fire barrage after barrage of dull, insulting commercials at them.

Instead, they're taking careful aim and firing back.

And you could be the target.

If your commercial turns them off—ZAP!—they'll turn you off.

How can you protect yourself?

Well, at Meldrum and Fewsmith, we know there's really only one way. By creating the kind of advertising that will, first, disarm people.

And then, capture them. With messages that touch their minds and hearts.

Not to mention their pocketbooks.

We call this special style of creative firepower Intelligent Advertising. And we'd like the chance to show you how it works.

Let's talk. Write our President, Terry Parmelee. Playhouse Square Plaza, 1220 Huron Road, Cleveland, Ohio 44115. Or call 216-241-2141.

MELDRUM and FEWSMITH
Intelligent Advertising

362

Trade B/W: 1 Page Or Spread

363
ART DIRECTOR
Nelsena Burt
WRITER
David Metcalf
DESIGNER
Nelsena Burt
PHOTOGRAPHER
James Salzano
CLIENT
Spano/Roccanova Retouching

364
ART DIRECTOR
Bob Barrie
WRITER
Tom McElligott
DESIGNER
Bob Barrie
CLIENT
Fallon McElligott Rice
AGENCY
Fallon McElligott/Minneapolis

365
ART DIRECTOR
Scot Fletcher
WRITERS
Larre Johnson
Jon Cleinman
PHOTOGRAPHER
David Leach
CLIENT
Vivitar
AGENCY
keye/donna/pearlstein - Los Angeles

366
ART DIRECTOR
Rene Vidmer
WRITER
Ken Baron
PHOTOGRAPHER
Lazlo Stern
CLIENT
LNP Corporation
AGENCY
Baron & Zaretsky

UNFORTUNATELY, OUR RETOUCHING DOESN'T ALWAYS IMPROVE THE PICTURE.

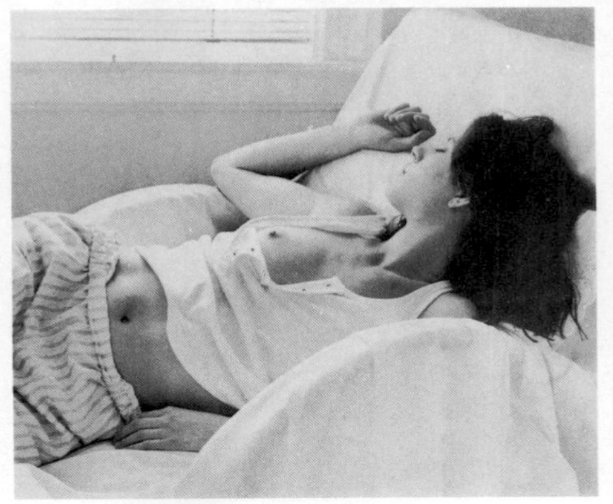

BEFORE SPANO ROCCANOVA...

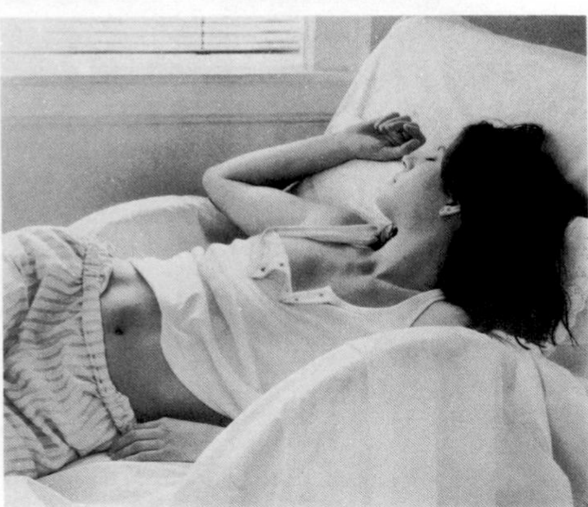

PHOTOGRAPHY: JAMES SALZANO

AFTER SPANO ROCCANOVA.

SPANO/ROCCANOVA. THE QUALITY OF OUR WORK IS RETOUCHING OTHER STUDIOS OUT OF THE PICTURE.
SPANO/ROCCANOVA RETOUCHING, INC. 16 WEST 46 STREET NEW YORK, N.Y. 10036 212 840-7450

363

If this resembles your agency's organizational chart, give us a call.

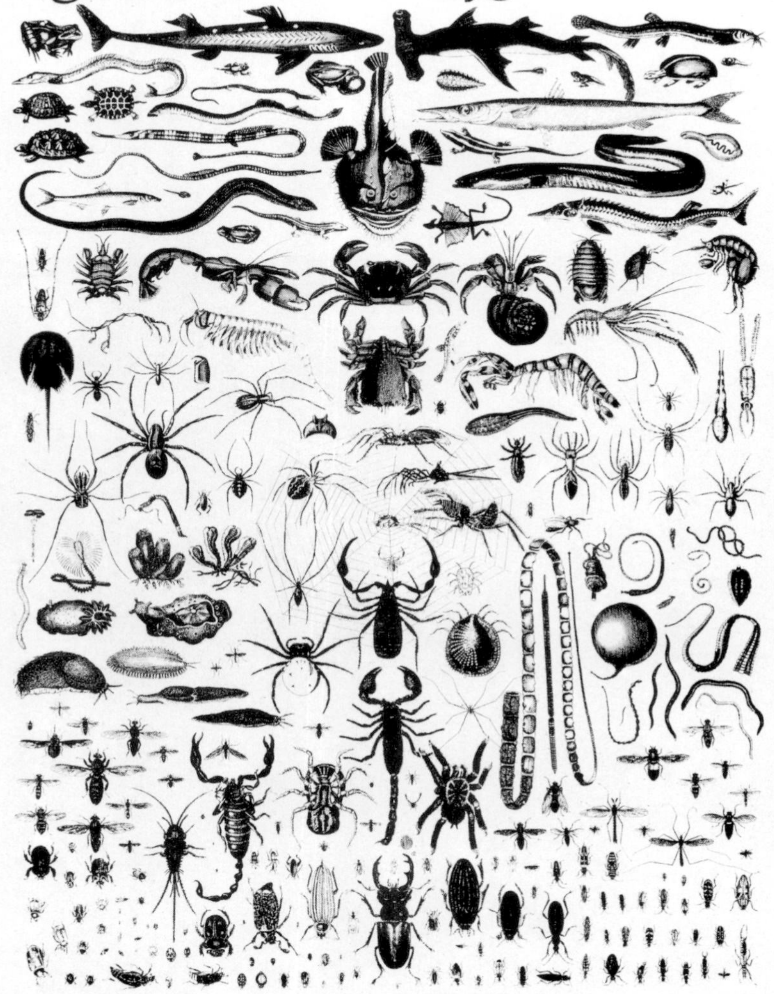

Fallon McElligott Rice, 701 Fourth Avenue South, Minneapolis, Minnesota 55415, Telephone 612-332-2445

364

365

366

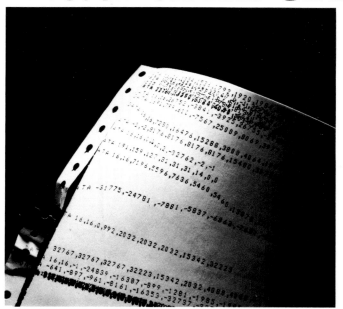

Trade B/W: 1 Page Or Spread

367
ART DIRECTOR
Simon Bowden
WRITER
Marty Cooke
DESIGNER
Simon Bowden
PHOTOGRAPHER
David Hume Kennerly
CLIENT
Nikon
AGENCY
Scali McCabe Sloves

368
ART DIRECTOR
Tod Seisser
WRITER
Stephanie Arnold
DESIGNER
Tod Seisser
PHOTOGRAPHER
Francesco Scavullo
CLIENT
McCall's
AGENCY
Levine Huntley Schmidt & Beaver

369
ART DIRECTOR
Cabell Harris
WRITERS
Andy Ellis
Luke Sullivan
DESIGNER
Cabell Harris
ARTIST
Ted Resnick
PHOTOGRAPHER
Pat Edwards
CLIENT
FMC
AGENCY
The Martin Agency/
Richmond, VA

370
ART DIRECTOR
Tim Delaney
WRITER
Larry Hampel
DESIGNER
Tim Delaney
PHOTOGRAPHER
Robert Ammirati
CLIENT
Nikon
AGENCY
Scali McCabe Sloves

367

368

THE UNITED STATES OF AMERICA
THIS NOTE IS LEGAL TENDER FOR ALL DEBTS, PUBLIC AND PRIVATE
E 13893175 B
WASHINGTON, D.C.
HAMILTON
SERIES 1981
TEN DOLLARS

TAKE A GOOD LOOK AT THE DAMAGE SORGHUM PESTS CAN CAUSE.

If you're a sorghum grower who's never considered using a planting-time insecticide, or considered not using one this year, consider this.

Left unprotected, insects can reduce yields by as much as a thousand pounds an acre. Which of course translates quickly into a reduced profit for you.

But with a treatment of Furadan® insecticide/nematicide at planting, you can control a broad spectrum of soil and foliar pests and control them before they start to cause damage.

Applied in the furrow, as a band treatment or mixed with your liquid starter fertilizer, Furadan starts controlling southern corn rootworms in your soil immediately. And keeps on working systemically to guard against a broad spectrum of sorghum pests. Pests like yellow sugarcane aphids, as well as chinchbugs and greenbugs.*

And since many state universities recommend an at-plant treatment for sorghum, it makes sense to go with the product that's racked up more years of proven effectiveness than any other sorghum insecticide. Furadan from FMC.

So when you're getting ready to plant your milo, make sure you have plenty of Furadan to plant along with it. Otherwise, you might wind up with a fieldful of pests damaging something a lot more precious than your sorghum. Your money.

FMC

369

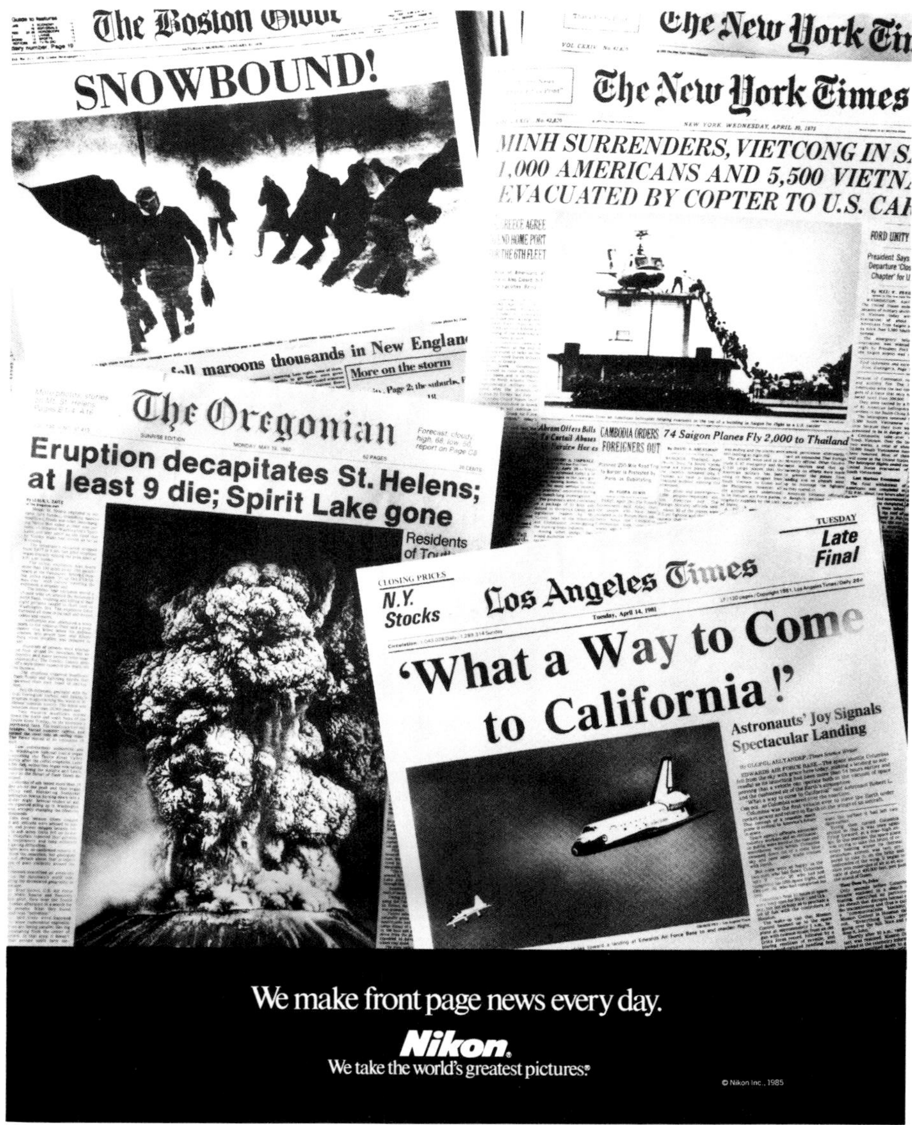
The Boston Globe
SNOWBOUND!
maroons thousands in New England
More on the storm
The New York Times
MINH SURRENDERS, VIETCONG IN S
1,000 AMERICANS AND 5,500 VIETN
EVACUATED BY COPTER TO U.S. CA
The Oregonian
Eruption decapitates St. Helens; at least 9 die; Spirit Lake gone
CAMBODIA ORDERS FOREIGNERS OUT
74 Saigon Planes Fly 2,000 to Thailand
Los Angeles Times
Late Final
N.Y. Stocks
'What a Way to Come to California!'
Astronauts' Joy Signals Spectacular Landing
We make front page news every day.
Nikon.
We take the world's greatest pictures.®
© Nikon Inc., 1985

370

Trade B/W: 1 Page Or Spread

371
ART DIRECTOR
Peter Andress
WRITER
Pam Barsky
CLIENT
Audi of America
AGENCY
Doyle Dane Bernbach/Los Angeles

372
ART DIRECTOR
Mike Moser
WRITER
Brian O'Neill
PHOTOGRAPHER
Stock
CLIENT
Ask Computer Systems
AGENCY
Chiat/Day - San Francisco

373
ART DIRECTOR
Craig Hadorn
WRITER
Charles Groark
PHOTOGRAPHER
Joe Cockerill
CLIENT
Fox Marketing Inc.
AGENCY
Northlich Stolley/Cincinnati

374
ART DIRECTOR
Tim Delaney
WRITER
Rodney Underwood
DESIGNER
Tim Delaney
PHOTOGRAPHER
Robert Ammirati
CLIENT
Nikon
AGENCY
Scali McCabe Sloves

375
ART DIRECTORS
Don Hoenig
Sam Minnella
WRITERS
Bob Paklaian
Ken Aitchison
PHOTOGRAPHER
Ameen Howrani
CLIENT
Young & Rubicam
AGENCY
Young & Rubicam/Detroit

Well built Europeans seek work in American films.

Audi is one of Europe's best-selling lines of cars. Call Larry Brown, Audi, at (213) 390-8011 or Howard Buck, Studio Services, at (818) 782-4074 and ask about the Audi Promotional Vehicle Program.

The art of engineering.

371

So it's your job to find that one factory management system that will satisfy everyone in the company.

We know what it's like, trying to find a factory management system that'll meet everyone's needs.

It can be a real headache.

But before you consider doing anything drastic, consider MANMAN,* from ASK Computer Systems.

It's a comprehensive, adaptable and fully integrated factory management information system.

Which means?

Which means that everyone in your company is going to like it.

Managers, for example, will find that MANMAN not only lets them control and coordinate every MRPII task, but virtually every function in the company.

From purchasing to payroll to field service. From controlling materials to controlling overhead.

For all the company's decision makers, there's DecisionMaker.* A great new MANMAN product that lets you set limits on over 80 key business indicators (from past due accounts to WIP inventory value), alerts you to when limits have been exceeded and even shows you what action to take.

MANMAN will also appeal to every department supervisor.

Every foreman.

Every purchasing agent.

And everyone else in the company who has a special way of working that's already working.

MANMAN won't change that.

Its built-in "business policy variables" let you adapt the system to your unique way of doing business.

And its modular design lets you implement functions gradually or all at once (and once implemented, they're already integrated).

Finally, those who may not be used to computers–be they on the factory floor or in the executive suite–will quickly get used to MANMAN. Thanks to its easy conversation-style format, helpful help features, and a comprehensive user training program.

Maybe that's why, for more than a decade, MANMAN has been satisfying the needs of manufacturers all over the world.

And why we're the nation's leading independent supplier of factory management systems.

So if you've been agonizing over which system is best for your company, call us at 800-4-FACTORY.

And stop killing yourself.

ASK

Making factory management manageable.

372

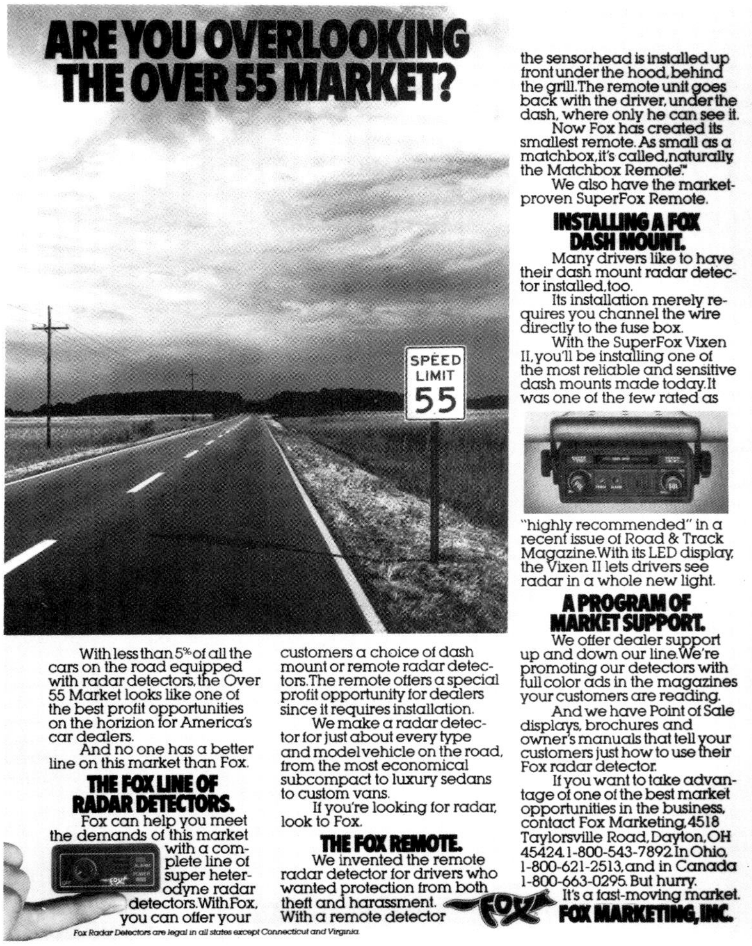

ARE YOU OVERLOOKING THE OVER 55 MARKET?

SPEED
LIMIT
55

With less than 5% of all the cars on the road equipped with radar detectors, the Over 55 Market looks like one of the best profit opportunities on the horizion for America's car dealers.

And no one has a better line on this market than Fox.

THE FOX LINE OF RADAR DETECTORS.

Fox can help you meet the demands of this market with a complete line of super heterodyne radar detectors. With Fox, you can offer your customers a choice of dash mount or remote radar detectors. The remote offers a special profit opportunity for dealers since it requires installation.

We make a radar detector for just about every type and model vehicle on the road, from the most economical subcompact to luxury sedans to custom vans.

If you're looking for radar, look to Fox.

THE FOX REMOTE.

We invented the remote radar detector for drivers who wanted protection from both theft and harassment. With a remote detector the sensor head is installed up front under the hood, behind the grill. The remote unit goes back with the driver, under the dash, where only he can see it.

Now Fox has created its smallest remote. As small as a matchbox, it's called, naturally, the Matchbox Remote™.

We also have the market-proven SuperFox Remote.

INSTALLING A FOX DASH MOUNT.

Many drivers like to have their dash mount radar detector installed, too.

Its installation merely requires you channel the wire directly to the fuse box.

With the SuperFox Vixen II, you'll be installing one of the most reliable and sensitive dash mounts made today. It was one of the few rated as

"highly recommended" in a recent issue of Road & Track Magazine. With its LED display, the Vixen II lets drivers see radar in a whole new light.

A PROGRAM OF MARKET SUPPORT.

We offer dealer support up and down our line. We're promoting our detectors with full color ads in the magazines your customers are reading.

And we have Point of Sale displays, brochures and owner's manuals that tell your customers just how to use their Fox radar detector.

If you want to take advantage of one of the best market opportunities in the business, contact Fox Marketing, 4518 Taylorsville Road, Dayton, OH 45424. 1-800-543-7892. In Ohio, 1-800-621-2513, and in Canada 1-800-663-0295. But hurry.

It's a fast-moving market.

FOX

FOX MARKETING, INC.

Fox Radar Detectors are legal in all states except Connecticut and Virginia.

373

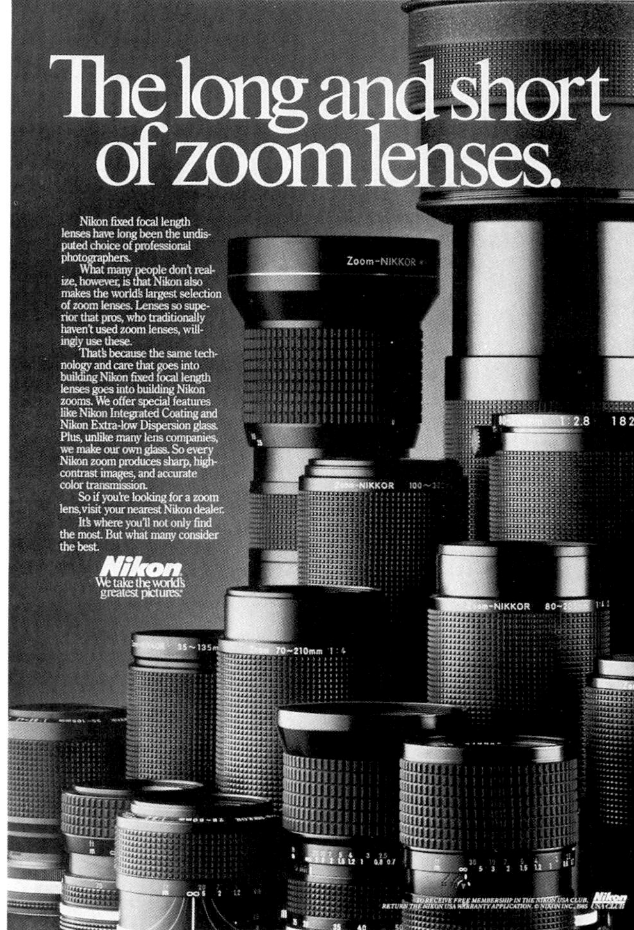
The long and short of zoom lenses.
Nikon fixed focal length lenses have long been the undisputed choice of professional photographers.
What many people don't realize, however, is that Nikon also makes the world's largest selection of zoom lenses. Lenses so superior that pros, who traditionally haven't used zoom lenses, willingly use these.
That's because the same technology and care that goes into building Nikon fixed focal length lenses goes into building Nikon zooms. We offer special features like Nikon Integrated Coating and Nikon Extra-low Dispersion glass. Plus, unlike many lens companies, we make our own glass. So every Nikon zoom produces sharp, high-contrast images, and accurate color transmission.
So if you're looking for a zoom lens, visit your nearest Nikon dealer. It's where you'll not only find the most. But what many consider the best.
Nikon
We take the world's greatest pictures.
Zoom-NIKKOR

374

Why Larry Donabedian left Y&R Detroit.

Larry left after two years with us. That's not unusual for people in advertising. Especially creative people. When he started, he was an ambitious art director with an impressive portfolio at the age of twenty-two. It didn't take him very long to get a job in advertising. In fact, Y&R was only his second interview.

He came to Y&R primarily because of the work we were doing for Lincoln-Mercury Division. By his estimate, some of the most innovative advertising ever done. During the time he spent here, he learned how advertising like that happens.

Partly it comes from intelligent marketing strategies and creative disciplines. But mostly it comes from people. With the curiosity and dedication of a Larry Donabedian.

After two years, that curiosity led him to another advertising agency. But when he left Y&R, the things he learned didn't leave him.

Why Larry Donabedian came back to Y&R Detroit.

He was away for about a year. During that time, he had the opportunity to develop his talent even further by working on a more senior level at another agency. He had the chance to exercise his skill on different problems and more importantly, he got another perspective on the advertising business.

While he was away, things had changed a bit at Y&R. We added some accounts. Increased our billings. Soon a position for a senior level art director opened. And that was precisely what Larry had become. So, instead of getting his old job back, he got a better one. With more responsibility. And more creative challenge.

A year later, Larry's back where he started. And a lot further ahead.

375

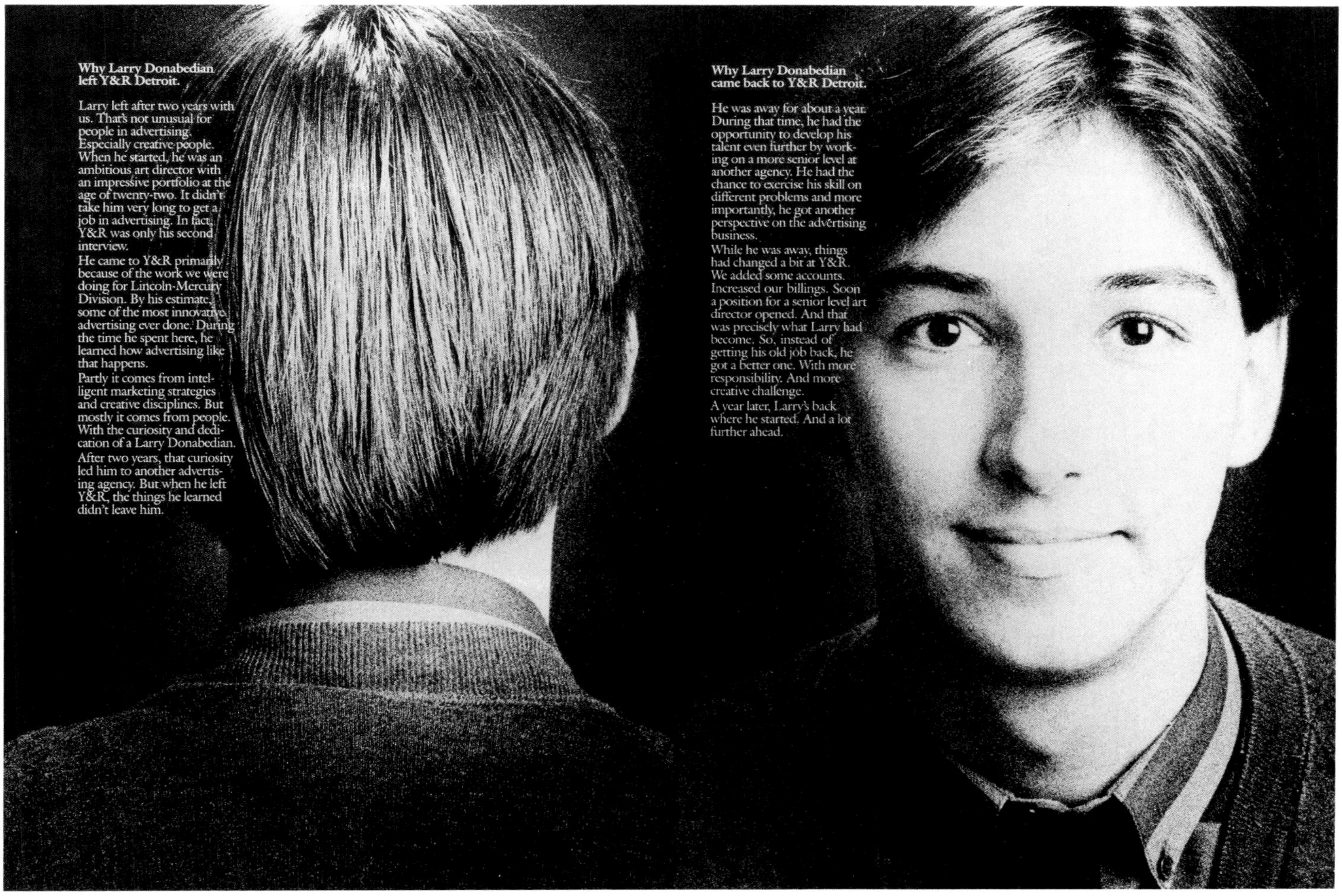

Trade Color: 1 Page Or Spread

376
ART DIRECTOR
Nancy Rice
WRITER
Bill Miller
PHOTOGRAPHER
Stock
CLIENT
Rolling Stone
AGENCY
Fallon McElligott/Minneapolis

377
ART DIRECTOR
Marten Tonnis
WRITER
Steve Rabosky
PHOTOGRAPHER
Bo Hylen
CLIENT
Apple Computer
AGENCY
Chiat/Day - Los Angeles

378
ART DIRECTOR
Tim Hannell
WRITER
Kim McHugh
DESIGNER
Tim Hannell
PHOTOGRAPHER
Hunter Freeman
CLIENT
Frontier Airlines
AGENCY
Tracy-Locke/Denver

379
ART DIRECTOR
Joe Ivey
WRITER
Scott Crawford
CLIENT
Southern National Bank
AGENCY
Howard Merrell & Partners/
Raleigh, NC

Perception.

Reality.

If you still think Rolling Stone readers are taking left turns when the rest of the world is taking rights, consider who they voted for in the last election. The winner.

RollingStone

376

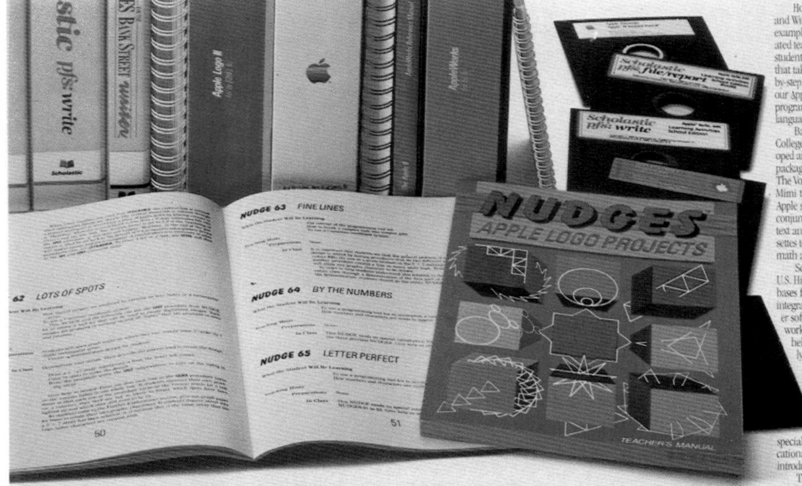

A teacher for the Apple.

You've made it through lost homework assignments, budget cuts, measle epidemics and jammed ditto machines.

Now you've come face-to-face with a computer in the classroom.

Before you start moving slowly towards the nearest exit, check to see if the computer has an Apple® logo on it.

If so, you're in luck.

Because Apple computers not only make it easier for students to learn, they also make it easier for teachers to teach.

Thanks to something we call courseware — computer software that comes complete with supplemental textbooks, lesson plans, worksheets and student guides.

And, most importantly, the documentation and reference material you need to painlessly integrate Apple computers into your curriculum.

Without taking a crash course in computer science.

Since Apple computers are used in schools more than all other personal computers combined, leading publishers have been working with us for years to find better ways of making software programs work in conjunction with learning objectives covered in textbooks.

Holt, Rinehart and Winston, for example, has created teacher and student guides that take you step-by-step through our Apple Logo II programming language.

Bank Street College has developed an innovative package called The Voyage of the Mimi that uses Apple software in conjunction with text and videocassettes to teach kids math and science.

Scholastic's U.S. History Databases for PFS:File integrate computer software with worksheets and lesson plan ideas to help kids learn research and analytical skills in social studies.

And programs like Bank Street StoryBook by George Brackett and Reader Rabbit can help kids improve their reading and writing skills.

We've also developed special 10-pack bundles of different educational programs that are designed to introduce students to computer learning.

The Elementary Classroom Software Solution* bundle includes programs that teach kids basic writing and language skills, keyboarding and a powerful programming language.*

And for secondary schools, we've bundled together the Secondary Classroom Software Solution, including word processing, database, keyboarding and computer language software.

In short, no matter what it is you want to teach, an Apple computer can help you teach it.

Better than you've ever been able to teach it before.

Because most kids are not only attracted to learning on an Apple computer, they actually think it's a heck of a lot of fun.

Which means they just might start showing up at school every morning with a nice surprise for you.

A little more enthusiasm.

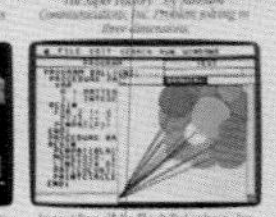

(800) 538-9696. (800) 268-7796 (800) 268-7637.

377

Sometimes planning a convention can be a real circus. With you in the center ring trying to keep everyone happy. And that's not so easy. Which is why Frontier Airlines has a whole department of Business Meeting Travel Coordinators, whose only job is to help you coordinate your entire convention. All three rings.

We can help you plan a successful meeting in any of the over 50 cities we serve. Giving you low, competitive, easy-to-use airfares. Convenient shuttle service within Colorado. Terrific post-convention follow up. A nationwide toll-free number to our reservations center and more. Why, you might just say it's the best high flying act around.

So call Frontier's Business Meeting and Convention Travel Department at 1 800-525-1218 or 303-329-5280 in Colorado. We'll help you plan the greatest convention on earth.

FRONTIER AIRLINES

Service via Denver
Albuquerque, MN · Billings, MT · Bismarck, ND · Boise, ID · Bozeman, MT · Casper, WY · Cedar Rapids, IA · Chicago, IL · Colorado Springs, CO · Dallas/Ft. Worth, TX · Denver, CO · Des Moines, IA · El Paso, TX · Eugene, OR · Fargo, ND · Grand Junction, CO · Great Falls, MT · Houston, TX · Jackson, WY · Kalispell, MT · Kansas City, MO · Las Vegas, NV · Lincoln, NE · Los Angeles, CA · Madison, WI · Midland/Odessa, TX · Milwaukee, WI · Minneapolis, MN · Minot, ND · Missoula, MT · Oakland, CA · Oklahoma City, OK · Omaha, NE · Orange County, CA · Orlando, FL · Palm Springs, CA · Phoenix, AZ · Portland, OR · Rapid City, SD · Regina, Sask · Reno/Lake Tahoe, NV · Rockford, IL · Sacramento, CA · St. Louis, MO · Salt Lake City, UT · San Diego, CA · San Francisco, CA · Saskatoon, Sask · Seattle, WA · Sioux Falls, SD · Spokane, WA · Springfield, MO · Stockton, CA · Tampa, FL · Tucson, AZ · Tulsa, OK · Vancouver, BC · Wichita, KS · Winnipeg, Man

378

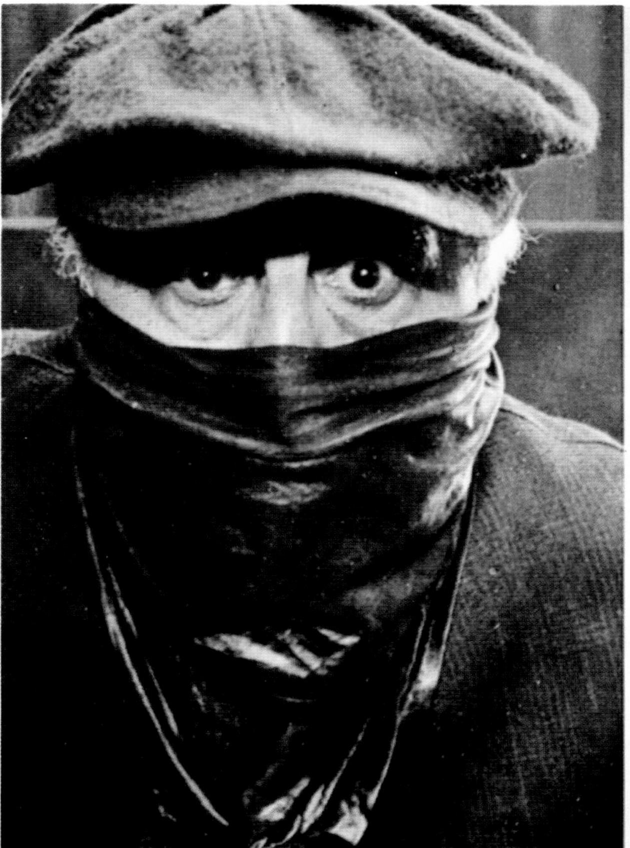

THERE ARE TWO WAYS TO GET MORE MONEY OUT OF YOUR BUSINESS CHECKING ACCOUNT. OURS IS LEGAL.

Most banks take a dim view of unscheduled money-market withdrawals. With CS&L III, you write all the checks you need.

People have always tried to get more out of their checking accounts than they put in.

This method, however, is frowned upon by the Feds for obvious reasons.

Another way, which is for banks to pay interest on business checking, is also frowned upon by the Feds, for reasons no one quite understands.

So, to earn interest on your commercial checking funds, the typical bank makes you authorize each transfer, deposit by deposit, into a separate investment account.

Then they make you go through the same rigmarole when you need to get your money back out.

It's almost criminal what some people make you go through to earn interest.

Only CS&L III from Southern National integrates checking and savings into a single system.

You earn money-market rates on your idle funds and, at the same time, get unlimited checking privileges.

So if you want to make more on your business checking, you have two choices.

One will get you money-market rates.

The other? Ten-to-twenty. **SOUTHERN NATIONAL CS&L III**

You can tell we want your business.

379

Trade Color: 1 Page Or Spread

380
ART DIRECTOR
Bob Saabye
WRITER
Jeff Abbott
DESIGNER
Sharon Collins
PHOTOGRAPHERS
Gene Dwiggins
Clint Clemens
CLIENT
Siebe North
AGENCY
Leonard Monahan Saabye/
Providence, RI

381
ART DIRECTORS
Yvonne Smith
Marc Deschenes
WRITERS
Marc Deschenes
Yvonne Smith
DESIGNERS
Yvonne Smith
Marc Deschenes
ARTIST
Gina Norton
PHOTOGRAPHERS
Lamb & Hall
CLIENT
Noritsu
AGENCY
(213) 827-9695 and Associates/
Venice, CA

382
ART DIRECTOR
Cabell Harris
WRITER
Luke Sullivan
DESIGNER
Cabell Harris
PHOTOGRAPHER
John Whitehead
CLIENT
Meredith Corporation
AGENCY
Drinking Buddies
Advertising/Richmond, VA

383
ART DIRECTOR
Hal Tench
WRITER
Mike Hughes
DESIGNER
Hal Tench
PHOTOGRAPHER
Dean Hawthorne
CLIENT
Mobil
AGENCY
The Martin Agency/
Richmond, VA

380

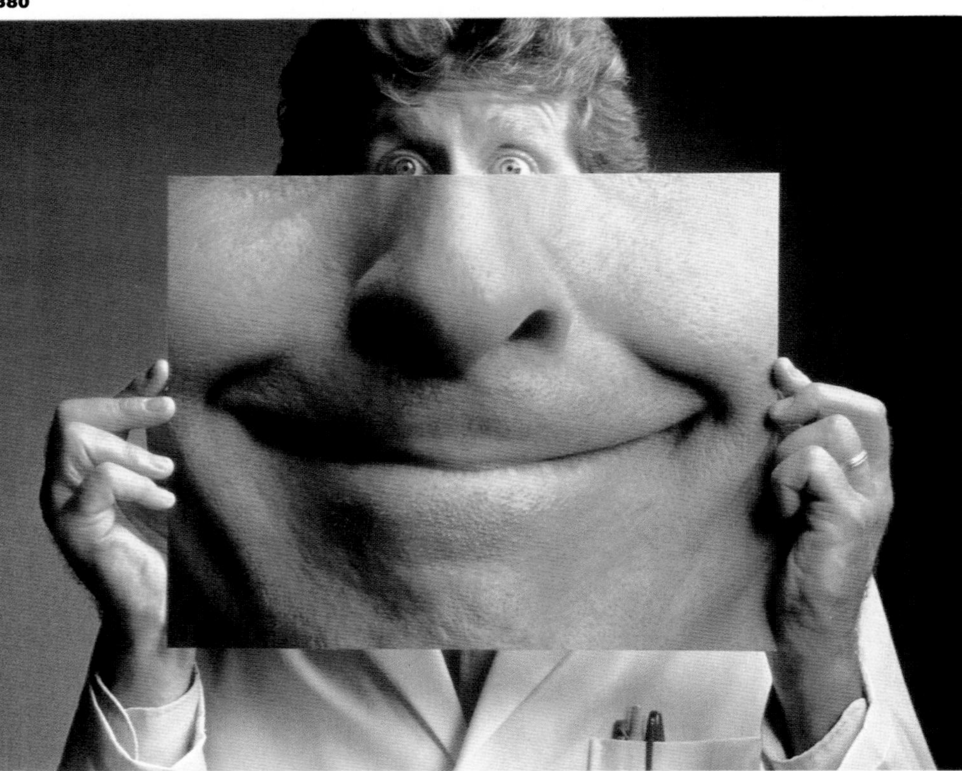

381

THANKS TO TODAY'S TECHNOLOGY, HE HAS 40,000 BUSHELS OF CORN IN HIS BINS. THANKS TO TODAY'S GOVERNMENT, IT COULD SIT THERE TILL IT ROTS.

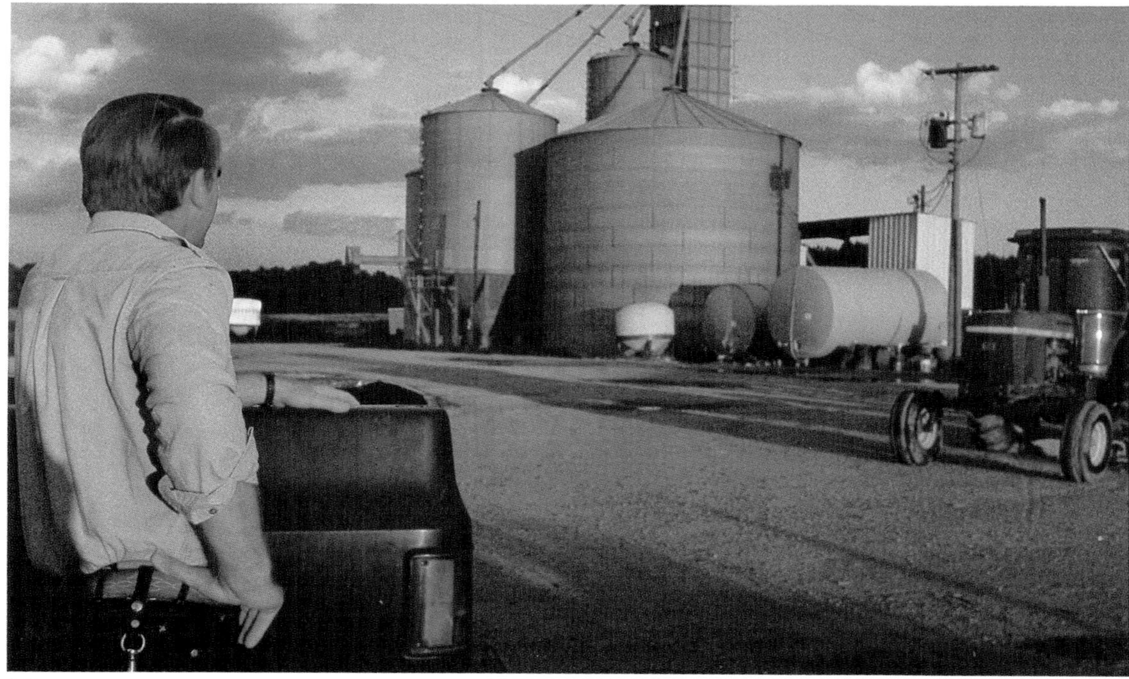

Imagine what it would be like to work for six months raising a crop only to find you can't sell it.

If that sounds crazy, it is.

Yet it's just one of a hundred problems that today's farmers face. And if you were a farmer in these tough times, wouldn't you look for the best advice you could find? Sure you would.

That's why so many farmers read Successful Farming® every month. Because it's the one magazine they can count on for reliable information on how to run a farm and make an honest dollar off of it.

But according to our high Chilton scores, they're reading the ads, too. Which is good for our advertisers, considering that Successful Farming is aimed at the high-income farmers responsible for 85% of all production expenses in the country.

So if you have a product that can help farmers make a better living, there's no better place to tell them about it than in Successful Farming.

Contact your nearest Successful Farming sales executive for more details. Or call Gil Spears, collect, at 515-284-3118. Successful Farming. Meredith Corporation, Locust at Seventeenth. Des Moines, Iowa 50336.

Research proves it. If you want to sell oil faster, wrap it in this.

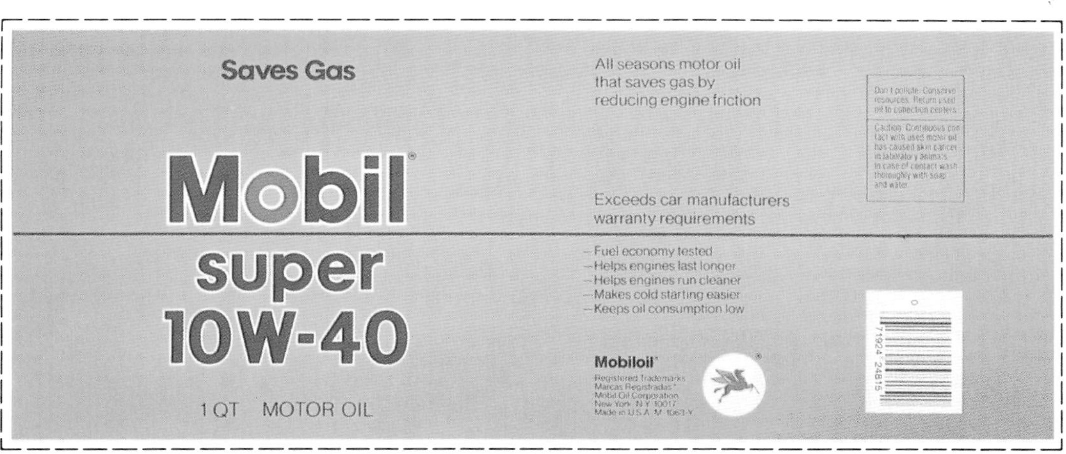

If you really want to sell more oil, just give your customers what they want.

And according to a recent independent survey, what they want is Mobil motor oil.

You see, the research makes it very clear that Mobil's advertising is working. 75% of the motorists surveyed said that they recognize the differences between motor oils — and they put Mobil in the very top ranks for both quality and performance.

But come to think of it, there really aren't any surprises here, are there?

After all, we've been telling people for years that nobody makes a better motor oil than we do.

And we've been driving the point home by sponsoring various racing programs, by continuing to advertise nationally both in magazines and on network television, and by working closely with the best retailers in all parts of the country.

Those retailers know that if they stock Mobil oils, they sell them.

If you sell motor oils, call Buddy Bryant collect at 703 849 4949. He'll send you a whole shipment of Mobil labels. All wrapped around some of the fastest selling motor oil you've ever seen.

Trade Color: 1 Page Or Spread

384
ART DIRECTOR
Mal Karlin
WRITER
Paul Levett
CLIENT
IBM/Federal Systems Division
AGENCY
HCM

385
ART DIRECTOR
Cabell Harris
WRITER
Luke Sullivan
DESIGNER
Cabell Harris
PHOTOGRAPHER
John Whitehead
CLIENT
Meredith Corporation
AGENCY
Drinking Buddies Advertising/Richmond, VA

386
ART DIRECTOR
Neil Leinwohl
WRITERS
Kevin McKeon
David Tait
CLIENT
Virgin Atlantic Airways
AGENCY
Korey Kay & Partners

387
ART DIRECTOR
Jerry Torchia
WRITER
John Mahoney
DESIGNER
Jerry Torchia
ARTIST
Lu Matthews
CLIENT
FMC
AGENCY
The Martin Agency/ Richmond, VA

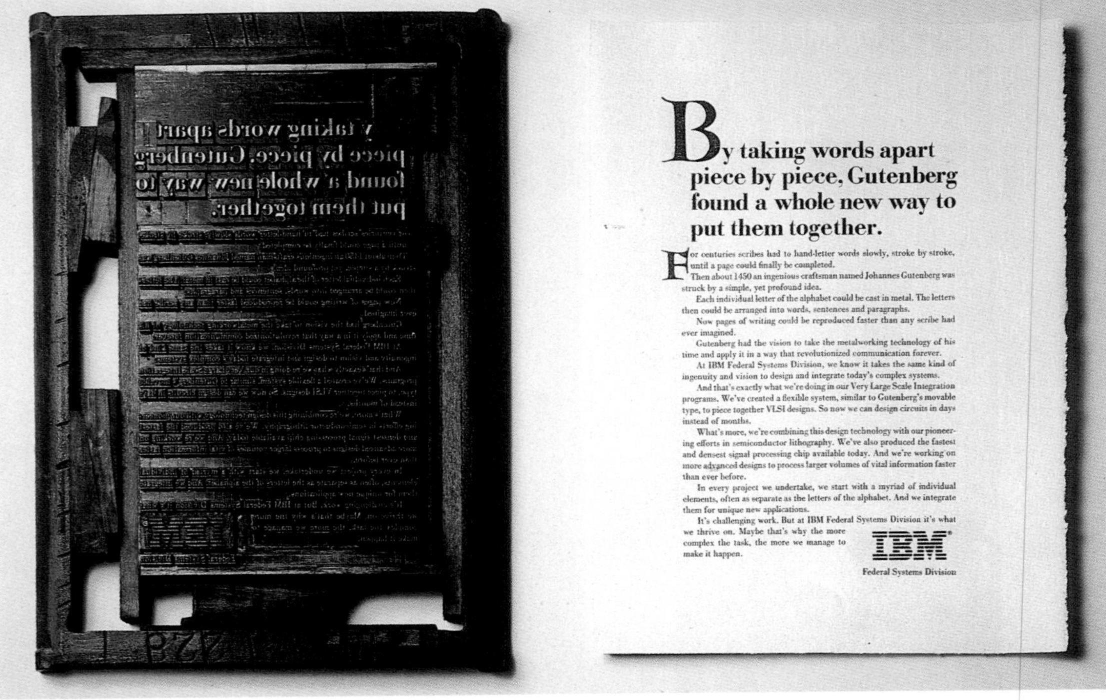

384

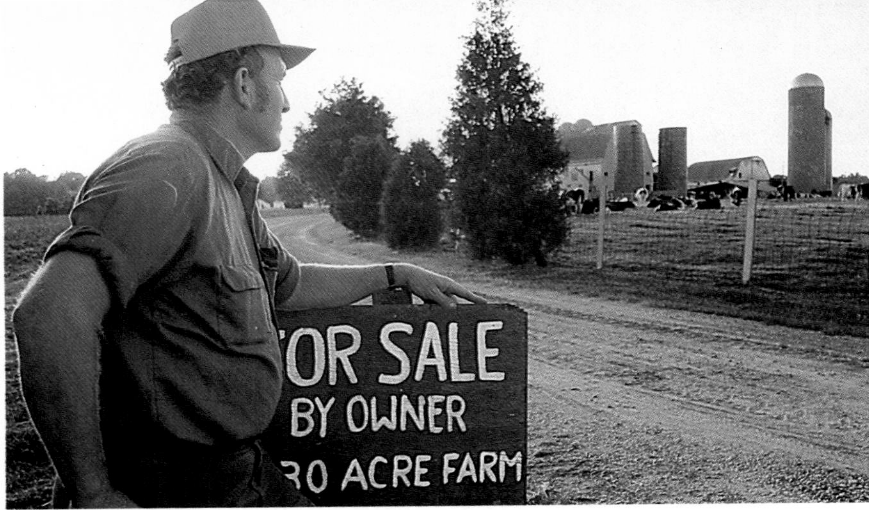

385

THE WORLD'S ONLY INFREQUENT FLIER PROGRAM.

Frequent flier programs are terrific. If your name happens to be Peter Pan.

Unfortunately, that covers a rather small minority.

So Virgin Atlantic now offers a more realistic alternative. The world's very first infrequent flier program.

Every time you fly Upper Class on one of Virgin Atlantic's 747 flights between New York* and London, you'll get a free Coach ticket for later use along the same route.

That's right. A free Coach ticket. Every time.

You can even use it toward your next Upper Class ticket.

By the way, in case you're wondering, our business class isn't called Upper Class for nothing.

Your privileges will include one of only 14 seats in our spacious upper deck. And access to our stand-up bar and lounge.

One final note. While all this does indeed sound wonderful, our new infrequent flier program may have one significant drawback. It could turn infrequent fliers into frequent fliers.

Then what would we call it?

Virgin

VIRGIN ATLANTIC AIRWAYS. OUR FEATURES WILL SEND YOU FLYING.

For reservations, see your corporate travel department or travel agent. Or in the U.S.A. call (212) 242-1330 or (201) 623-0500. In the U.K. call 0293-38222. Restrictions apply.

*Newark International Airport

HERE'S ONE ENDANGERED SPECIES LIST YOU'LL BE HAPPY TO READ ABOUT.

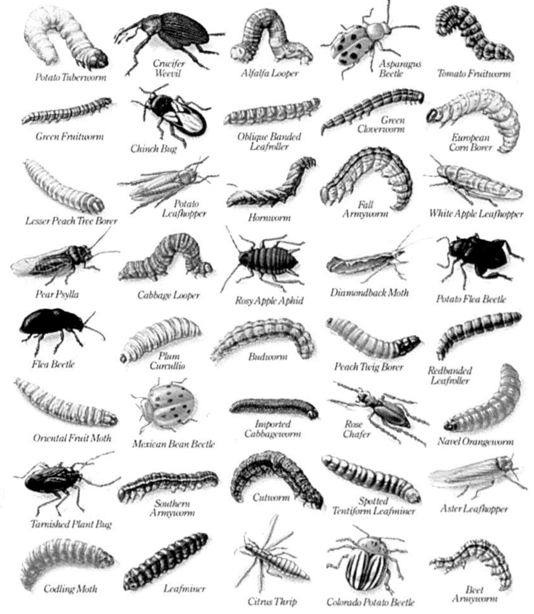

If you're a fruit or vegetable grower, you've got a long list of non-paying customers waiting for your crops.

And a short list of ways to stop them. Pounce® insecticide. From FMC.

No other insecticide controls more kinds of insects that endanger more kinds of fruits and vegetables than Pounce insecticide. And we've got the label that will prove it.

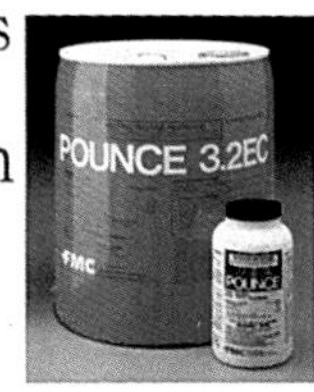

What's more, it tank-mixes easily with most miticides and fungicides. Which means you can skip a lot of costly and time-consuming extra applications. Just do them all at one time.

Your fruit and vegetables will look ready for market, too. Pounce is not phytotoxic and won't affect the finish or change the taste. And it's available in 25% Wettable Powder or 3.2 Emulsifiable Concentrate.

So give your local chemical representative a call today. And start giving your pests something to eat besides your profits. FMC®

FMC Corporation, Agricultural Chemical Group, 2000 Market Street, Philadelphia, PA 19103. Pounce is a Restricted Use Pesticide. Pounce and FMC are registered trademarks of FMC Corporation. ©1985 FMC Corporation.

Trade Color: 1 Page Or Spread

388
ART DIRECTOR
Pat Burnham
WRITER
Bill Miller
PHOTOGRAPHER
Joe Pytka
CLIENT
US West Information Systems
AGENCY
Fallon McElligott/Minneapolis

389
ART DIRECTOR
Sally Wagner
WRITER
Emily Scott
PHOTOGRAPHER
Kent Severson
CLIENT
3M/Commercial Office Supply Division
AGENCY
Martin/Williams - Minneapolis

390
ART DIRECTOR
Nancy Rice
WRITER
Bill Miller
PHOTOGRAPHER
Jim Marvy
CLIENT
Rolling Stone
AGENCY
Fallon McElligott/Minneapolis

391
ART DIRECTOR
Cabell Harris
WRITER
Luke Sullivan
DESIGNER
Cabell Harris
PHOTOGRAPHER
John Whitehead
CLIENT
Meredith Corporation
AGENCY
Drinking Buddies Advertising/Richmond, VA

388

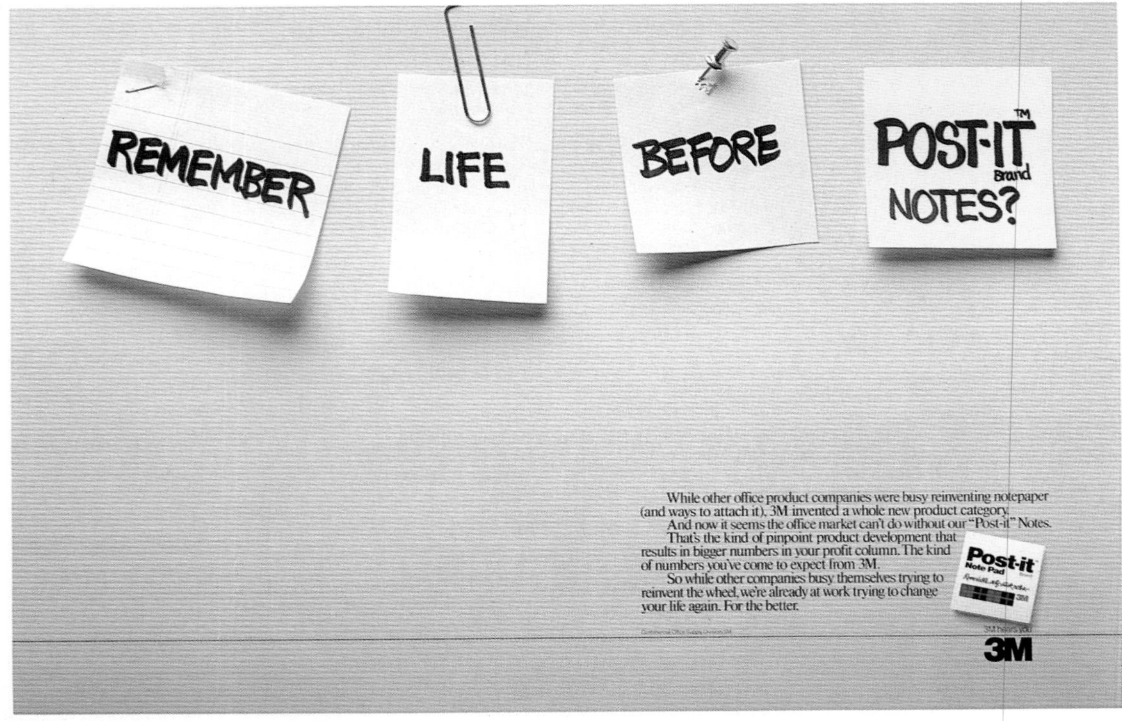

389

Perception.

Reality.

If you still think a Rolling Stone reader's idea of standard equipment is flowers on the door panels and incense in the ashtrays, consider this: Rolling Stone households own 5,199,000 automobiles. If you've got cars to sell, welcome to the fast lane.

Rolling Stone

390

SOMETHING IS WRONG WHEN THE PEOPLE WHO PUT FOOD ON AMERICA'S TABLES HAVE TROUBLE PUTTING SOME ON THEIR OWN.

Make that a lot of things are wrong.

Trade deficits. Tight money. Huge surpluses. Bad weather. Low prices. You name it.

Yet while running a farm these days can be next to impossible, reaching the right farms is easier than ever. Through Successful Farming®.

In fact, Successful Farming is aimed at the farmers responsible for 85 percent of all production expenses in America.

And according to our high Chilton scores, farmers are reading us too. Because Successful Farming ties together the total farm operation. Not with long-winded "feature" articles, but with concise, informative how-to articles on contemporary management practices.

So if you have a product that will make owning a farm more profitable, there's no better place to tell an owner about it than Successful Farming.

Contact your nearest Successful Farming sales executive for more details. Or call Gil Spears, collect, at 515-284-3118. Successful Farming. Meredith Corporation, Locust at Seventeenth. Des Moines, Iowa 50336.

391

Trade Color: 1 Page Or Spread

392
ART DIRECTOR
M. Nussbaum
WRITER
C. Randall
PHOTOGRAPHER
M. Rateman
CLIENT
US Army
AGENCY
NW Ayer

393
ART DIRECTOR
Greg Nygard
WRITER
Mark Fenske
DESIGNER
Greg Nygard
PHOTOGRAPHER
Dave Jordano
CLIENT
Hollister, Inc.
AGENCY
Zechman & Associates/
Chicago

394
ART DIRECTOR
Rod Booth
WRITER
Nancy Shafer
PHOTOGRAPHER
Rick Dublin
CLIENT
Minnesota Office of Tourism
AGENCY
Colle & McVoy/Bloomington, MN

395
ART DIRECTORS
Ed Tajon
David Price
WRITER
Jeremy Wolff
CLIENT
Holland America Line
AGENCY
Elgin Syferd Advertising/
Seattle

392

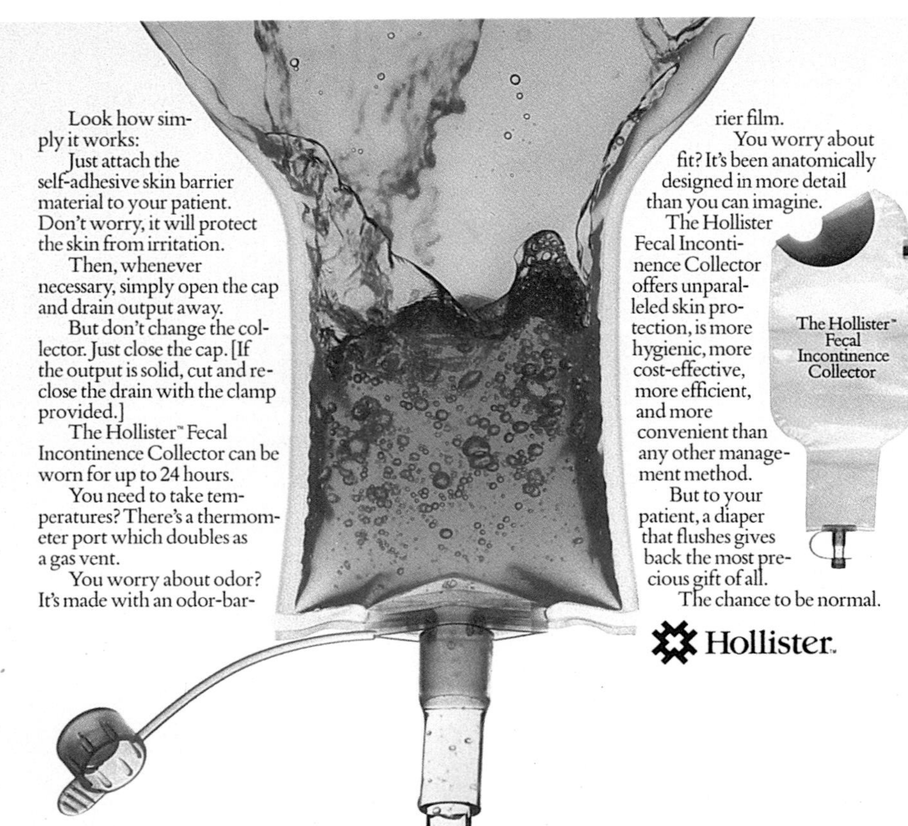

393

Banned In 49 States.

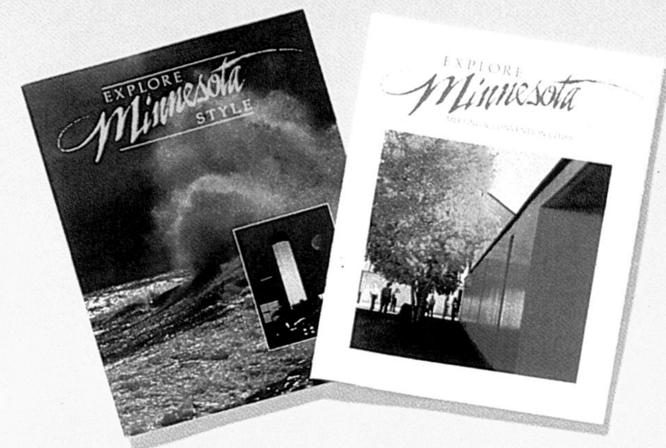

The tourism departments in other states would prefer you didn't read these.

They'd rather you didn't know about the variety of meeting sites and facilities available in Minnesota. How easy it is to get here and get around. Or the abundance of recreation and entertainment.

But we feel you have a right to know. So we'll send you our brochures on meeting and convention cities and Minnesota vacations, free. Anywhere in the U.S. Just mail this coupon or call toll-free any weekday:

Outside Minnesota, **1-800-328-1461**
In Minnesota, **1-800-652-9747**
In Minneapolis/St. Paul **296-5029**

Minnesota Office of Tourism
240 Bremer Building 419 N. Robert St.
St. Paul, MN 55101

Please send me the:
☐ Minnesota Meeting & Convention Cities brochure
☐ Minnesota Vacation Guide

Name____________________

Title____________________

Organization____________________

City__________ State_____ Zip_____

Area Code_____ Phone__________

EXPLORE
Minnesota

394

HOLLAND
AMERICA
CRUISES
CARIBBEAN
& MEXICO

It doesn't take a lot of money for your clients to go a long way on a Holland America cruise to the Caribbean or Mexico.

Consider all they get. For 7 or 14 days aboard the Noordam, the Nieuw Amsterdam or the Rotterdam, they'll have magnificent accommodations and gourmet cuisine. On-board activities ranging from tennis, swimming and golf to intimate lounges, a casino and a theatre. Staterooms that are larger than most. Plus they'll be treated to Holland America's exclusive Ocean Liner Service℠, and receive the expert attention of our experienced Dutch officers and world-renowned crew every mile of the way.

And those miles take them to some of the most exotic ports of call in the world. Places like St. Thomas, Montego Bay and Grand Cayman in the Caribbean. Puerto Vallarta, Zihuatanejo/Ixtapa, and Acapulco along the Mexican Riviera.

Guests booking before August 1 qualify for our unique Dutch Incentive Savings of up to $400 per couple. That means 7-day cruise fares can start as low as $895.*

Our 7- and 14-day cruises include free air** from most major gateways. And on Holland America ships, unlike any other luxury cruise, *no tipping is required.*

So the next time you're planning a trip for a client, remember, they'll get it all on a Holland America cruise. For 38¢ a mile, it's the most luxurious vacation value on land or sea.

Call today for cruise reservations: (800) 426-0327 or (206) 281-1970. For sales service: (800) 626-9900 or (206) 281-3535. For brochures: (800) 225-1451. In New Jersey, (800) 225-1452.

* Prices are per person, double occupancy, space available basis, plus port charges. **Does not include Christmas cruises to the Caribbean. Ships' registry: Netherlands Antilles

395

Trade Color: 1 Page Or Spread

396
ART DIRECTOR
Cabell Harris
WRITER
Luke Sullivan
DESIGNER
Cabell Harris
PHOTOGRAPHER
John Whitehead
CLIENT
Meredith Corporation
AGENCY
Drinking Buddies
Advertising/Richmond, VA

397
ART DIRECTOR
Dan Scarlotto
WRITERS
Pat Mundy
Tommy Thompson
PHOTOGRAPHER
Randy Miller
CLIENT
Home Lines Cruises
AGENCY
Cole Henderson Drake/
Atlanta

398
ART DIRECTOR
Ted Shaine
WRITER
Diane Rothschild
PHOTOGRAPHER
Walter Iooss
CLIENT
CIGNA
AGENCY
Doyle Dane Bernbach

399
ART DIRECTOR
Matt Rao
WRITER
James Walsh
DESIGNER
Matt Rao
ARTIST
Koppel Studio
CLIENT
Jameson
AGENCY
Doyle Dane Bernbach

NO MATTER WHAT THE FARMER'S ALMANAC SAYS, THE NEXT 365 DAYS ARE GOING TO BE HELL ON FARMERS.

There are few things in a farmer's life that he can count on. Good interest rates? Nope. Good yields? Good weather? Good prices? Forget it.

Fortunately, there's one thing he can count on 365 days a year: Successful Farming® Magazine.

The one magazine he can count on for reliable information on how to run a farm and make an honest dollar off of it. Information on production, management and marketing.

Our readers also count on ads that they read in our magazine. At least according to our high Chilton Ad-Chart scores they do. Which is great for our advertisers, considering that our magazine is aimed at the high-income farmers responsible for 85% of all production expenses in America.

All of which means that if you have a product that can help farmers weather the elements more efficiently, there's no better place to tell them about it than Successful Farming.

For more information, contact your nearest Successful Farming sales executive. Or call Gil Spears, collect, at 515-284-3118. Successful Farming Magazine, Meredith Corporation, Locust at Seventeenth, Des Moines, Iowa 50336.

396

ON MAY 31, THE MV HOMERIC WILL TOAST HER FIRST THOUSAND PASSENGERS.

They'll bask in all her glory. Twenty-seven splendid public rooms furnished by leading interior designers. An intimate piano bar, a dazzling disco, a well-orchestrated ballroom and casino. A dramatic cinema and duty-free shops. A gym with a relaxing sauna. Two pools, one with a sliding glass Magrodome for swimming under any conditions. And luscious eight-course feasts prepared by 60 Master chefs, cooks, bakers and pastrymen. With high tea at 4pm, a buffet at midnight and hot pizza at 2am.

Her cabins are no little luxuries, either. Each deluxe cabin measures over 200 square feet. Many have queen or double beds. All have color televisions. Ship-to-shore telephones. And an Italian crew eager to handle the smallest detail.

The Homeric (Panamanian registry) will sail every Saturday from New York to Bermuda. In the autumn, she'll sail the Caribbean from Florida. For more information, write Home Lines, One World Trade Center, Suite 3969, New York, NY 10048. For reservations, call toll-free: 1-800-221-4041 nationwide, 1-800-522-5780 in New York, 212-775-9041 in New York City, Nassau County and Westchester County. And meet our newest arrival with cheers.

HOME LINES CELEBRATED CRUISES

397

UNFORTUNATELY, THIS IS ONE OF THE FEW DOCTORS AMERICANS SEE REGULARLY.

While everybody recognizes the value of preventive health care, the reality is that very few people see a doctor unless something is wrong.

In fact, millions of Americans don't even have their own doctor to see.

As a result, even easily correctable conditions go uncorrected.

And treatable illnesses become untreatable.

It's a senseless, all too frequently tragic problem.

It's also an expensive one.

Because people without doctors tend to use emergency rooms, at emergency room prices, for any medical problem they have.

Whether it's a bad cold or a broken leg.

What it all amounts to is that too many people are getting too little care.

At too high a price.

And that's why we've made a serious commitment to a new form of health care delivery.

At CIGNA Healthplan, we operate Health Maintenance Organizations that deliver high quality, accessible and affordable health care.

For a small monthly payment, plus a few dollars a visit, CIGNA Healthplan provides members with a comprehensive package of health benefits. As well as ready access to a CIGNA physician of their own.

This obviously encourages the kind of preventive care that can stop small medical problems from becoming big ones.

In fact, a recent Rand Corporation study showed that membership in an HMO reduced hospitalization by as much as 40% over a five-year period.

And reduced health care expenses by close to 25% during that same time.

Not surprisingly, we already have over 750,000 members enrolled nationwide.

If you think we might be of value to your company, please write to CIGNA Corporation, Department R2, One Logan Square, Philadelphia, PA 19103.

That way we can make sure your employees have two doctors to see from now on.

One of ours. And Dr. J.

Jameson Is Now Giving Bartenders One More Shot At The Bar Exam.

Here's another chance to find out if the drinks you make are making the grade. Are your Zombies lively enough? Are your Boilermakers losing their steam? Do your Moscow Mules still have their kick? Take the second Jameson Bar Exam and see for yourself.

1. Question: What do you call a bartender who specializes in mixing whiskey and bouillon?
   Answer: A Bullshot artist.

2. Question: Is it proper to serve Sherry before dinner?
   Answer: Sure, as long as she has proof of her age.

3. Question: What's the most difficult thing about a Stinger?
   Answer: Removing it.

4. Question: How do the Irish serve Jameson Irish?
   Answer: Regularly. (Actually, the most popular way in Ireland is to mix it half and half with water.)

5. Question: What do you do when a guy says, "The drinks are on me"?
   Answer: Get him a towel.

6. Question: How did cavemen like their drinks?
   Answer: On the rocks, of course.

7. Question: Does your Irish Coffee turn people green?
   Answer: If people aren't green with envy over your Irish Coffee, then you're not using Jameson Irish.

8. Question: Should you ever let a customer move a Golden Cadillac from the bar to the dining room?
   Answer: No. Have the parking attendant do it.

9. Question: Is it true that bartenders hear all the worst jokes?
   Answer: You're reading this, aren't you?

10. Question: Who taught the Scots how to make whiskey?
    Answer: The Irish. (No kidding.) The Irish invented whiskey back in the 6th century. It wasn't until 200 years later that Irish missionaries gave the secret to the Scots.

11. Question: What do you tell a customer who asks for "two fingers of John Jameson"?
    Answer: Sorry, but I think John needs all of them.

12. Question: What's the difference between Scotch and Jameson Irish?
    Answer: Taste. Scotch has a somewhat smokey taste that comes from the open fires used to dry its malt. Jameson Irish uses closed fires called kilns, so nothing alters its clear delicate barley flavor.

13. Question: What should you tell people who say that bartenders are a lot like psychiatrists?
    Answer: That's an intriguing insight. Let's discuss it next week at your regular time.

14. Question: What did they call the cowboy who liked his beer without foam on it?
    Answer: The headless horseman.

15. Question: Should you ever give customers a tip?
    Answer: Sure. Tip them off to the fact that they can enjoy Jameson like any other whiskey. With soda or ginger ale. Or in Old-Fashioneds, Sours and other whiskey drinks.

Give yourself 10 points for every correct answer. If you scored 60 points or less, maybe you should consider mixing cement for a living instead of drinks. If you scored 120 points or more, consider yourself a member of Jameson's Bartending Hall of Fame.

JAMESON
IRISH WHISKEY

Trade Color: 1 Page Or Spread

400
ART DIRECTOR
Joe Goldberg
WRITER
Tim McGraw
PHOTOGRAPHER
Mark Meyer
CLIENT
United Technologies Corporation/Pratt & Whitney
AGENCY
HCM

401
ART DIRECTOR
Martyn Walsh
WRITER
Malcolm Gluck
PHOTOGRAPHER
Jimmy Wormser
CLIENT
Ogilvy & Mather
AGENCY
Ogilvy & Mather/London

402
ART DIRECTOR
Michele Troiani
WRITER
Bill Brichta
PHOTOGRAPHER
Dave Jordano
CLIENT
Armour-Dial, Inc.
AGENCY
Needham Harper Worldwide/Chicago

403
ART DIRECTOR
Billy Puckett
WRITER
Ken Majka
PHOTOGRAPHERS
Dan Mullen
Kevin Logan
CLIENT
Ricoh
AGENCY
Calet Hirsch & Spector

400

401

402

NOBODY BUSTS THEIR BUTT FOR A BALLPOINT PEN.

The problem with a lot of incentives—even the expensive ones—is that they aren't worth working for.

They're either terribly practical (and terribly dull) or the kind of luxury that ends up in a drawer or collecting dust on a shelf.

The ideal incentive is actually more valuable than money because it's more exciting. It captures the imagination. It's an indulgence you'd love to own but might feel guilty about buying for yourself. It's something you can't wait to use.

Ricoh cameras fit the picture perfectly.

Our quality is unquestionable. Our technological innovations are the talk of the industry. And our features insure nothing but pleasure for years to come.

Take the Ricoh XR-P Multi-Program SLR, for example. It's so completely automatic that absolute beginners can take great pictures the first time it's in their hands. Yet, it has the capability to be one of the most sophisticated and creative 35mms you can buy, so you can't outgrow it.

There's also the compact FF-3AF Super Auto Focus. The almost foolproof AF-5. The KR-10 and KR-5 Supers. In fact, we have a camera in every price range, plus a full line of lenses and accessories.

So next time give them something to shoot for—Ricoh cameras.

Call our Premium Incentive specialist at 1-800-225-1899 (in New Jersey at 201-882-2038) or simply check the box on the reader card. You'll get the whole picture.

RICOH.
We respond.
Ricoh Corporation, 5 Dedrick Place, West Caldwell, New Jersey 07006

403

Trade Color: 1 Page Or Spread

404
ART DIRECTOR
Tom Roberts
WRITER
Chuck Thegze
PHOTOGRAPHER
Hank Benson
CLIENT
Korean Airlines
AGENCY
Ogilvy & Mather/Los Angeles

405
ART DIRECTOR
Marvin Rich
WRITER
Brian O'Neill
PHOTOGRAPHER
Bob Mizono
CLIENT
California Cooler
AGENCY
Chiat/Day - San Francisco

Trade Less Than A Page B/W Or Color: Single

406
ART DIRECTOR
Mike Campbell
WRITER
Bruce Lee
CLIENT
Scali McCabe Sloves Direct
AGENCY
Scali McCabe Sloves Direct

407
ART DIRECTOR
Nancy Rice
WRITER
Phil Hanft
PHOTOGRAPHER
Marvy! Advertising Photography
CLIENT
Coleman
AGENCY
Fallon McElligott/Minneapolis

404

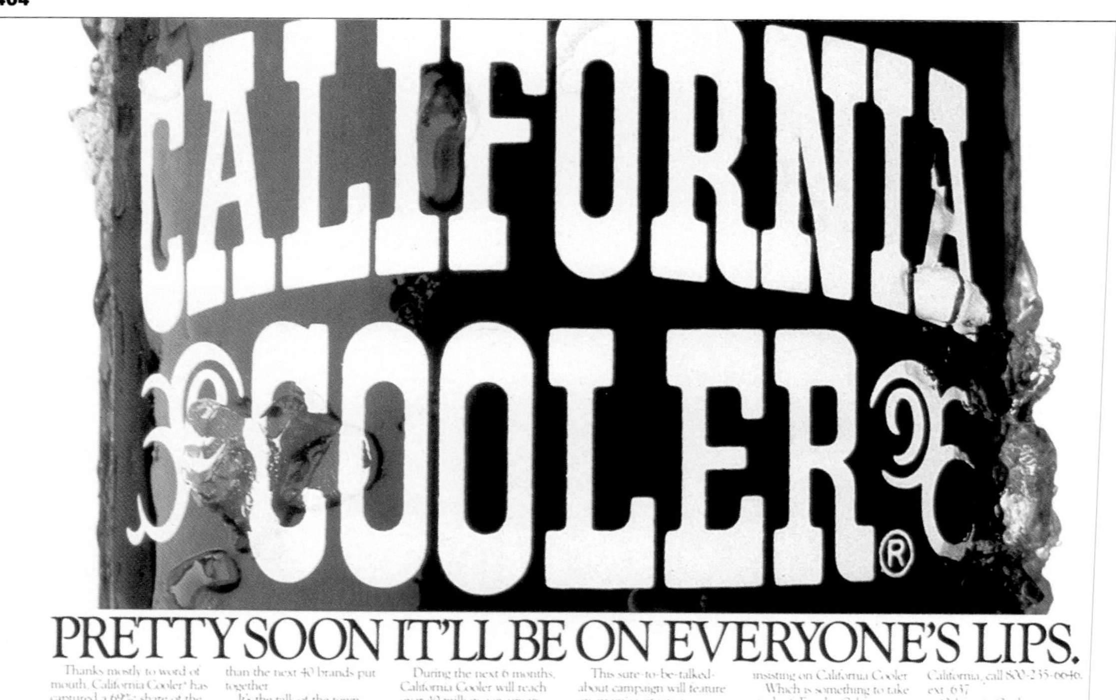

405

If you can't do this kind of advertising, you're our kind of art director.

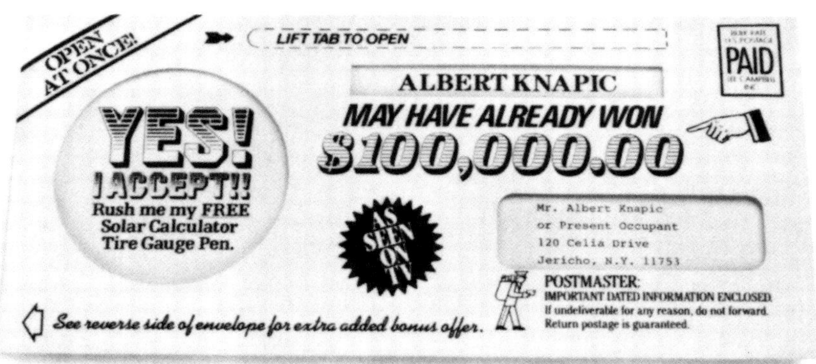

Is this your idea of direct response?

It isn't ours.

We're a funny new kind of direct response agency doing print, mail and TV you'd be proud to call your own.

Some of our best art directors have come from the general side. We could use a few more.

We're not looking for designers, artists or "a great pair of hands," but experienced art directors who do great advertising.

Write (don't call) Bruce Lee, Senior V.P./Creative Director.

And if you already have direct response experience, we won't hold that against you.

SCALI, McCABE, SLOVES DIRECT
800 Third Avenue, New York, N.Y. 10022

406

If this is how you think of Coleman, you're missing the boat.

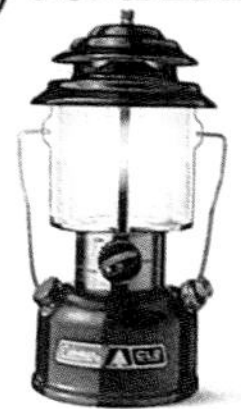

Most people know Coleman® makes lanterns. What they don't know is we also make boats. More boats than anyone in the world. For an illuminating look at the strategy behind our leadership in marine as well as outdoor recreation and home comfort products, call 1-800-521-4900, Ext. 50. In MN, 1-800-642-2800, Ext. 50.

Coleman

NYSE symbol: CLN

Trade Less Than A Page B/W Or Color: Single

408
ART DIRECTOR
Fred Hammerquist
WRITER
Bob Moore
CLIENT
Intermec
AGENCY
Sharp Hartwig Advertising/ Seattle

409
ART DIRECTOR
Len Mitsch
WRITER
Lyle Wedemeyer
DESIGNER
Roger Christensen
CLIENT
Production Artists
AGENCY
Martin/Williams Design - Minneapolis

Trade Any Size B/W Or Color: Campaign

410
ART DIRECTOR
David Wojdyla
WRITERS
David Wojdyla
Anne Moffat
ARTIST
Jared Lee
CLIENT
Business Week Executive Programs
AGENCY
David's Concepts

Experience life behind bars.

The aerospace industry has.

So has the electronics industry. Automotive companies. Chemical firms. Even the Department of Defense.

And, judging from their response, they've loved every minute of it.

Bar code is speeding up their inventory process. Making their shipping/receiving departments actually ship and receive. And making their work-in-process tracking hardly any work at all.

Only one manufacturer can provide these companies with all the components needed to make a complete bar code system.

That's INTERMEC.

And around here, only one distributor can provide you with INTERMEC.

That's us.

So you won't have to deal with different vendors and different distributors for different products. Because we have everything you need to build a complete bar code system from the ground up.

Like printers. Readers. Laser scanners. Wands. PC interfaces. Port concentrators. Labels. Over a hundred separate components in all.

We'll help you through the entire process—from providing general information about bar code to providing full service after the sale.

Give us a call. And start putting yourself behind bars.

DISTRIBUTOR NAME AND INFORMATION HERE

408

You haven't seen knifework like this since "West Side Story."

The only difference is, I stick my knife into matboard, not people. If you want quick, meticulous keylining on your next project, give me a call.

ROGER CHRISTENSEN
874-6660

409

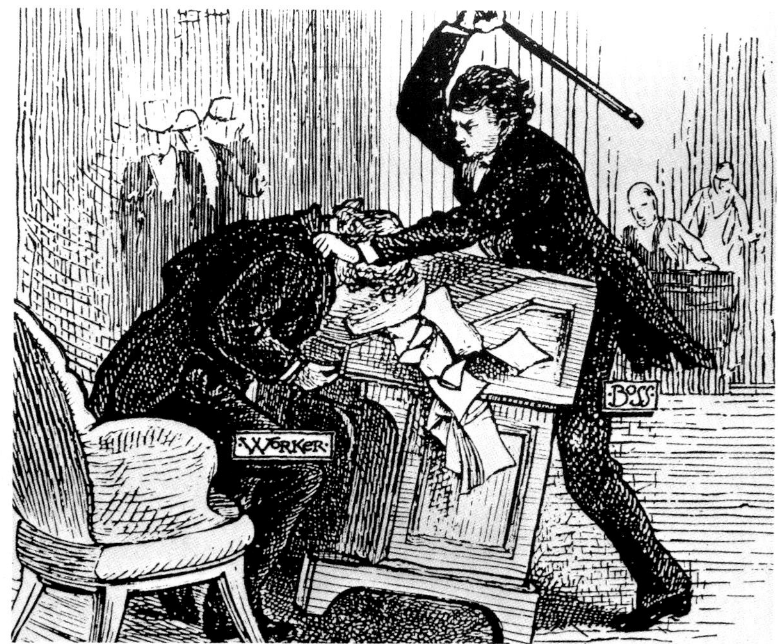

HOW TO MOTIVATE EMPLOYEES.

Even the most forward-thinking companies can have old- fashioned ideas about employee motivation.

That's why Business Week has put together two seminars for human resource executives that will bring you up-to-date on the latest techniques for managing your company's most important resource.

Gainsharing®: Creating and Sharing Productivity Gain is a one-day seminar on how to link all employees to common organization goals of improved profits, quality, market share, job satisfaction, and labor/management cooperation. Led by senior executives with Hay Management Consultants, the seminar will be held in New York, Chicago, San Francisco and Miami.

Employee Attitude Surveys is a one-day seminar on how to design and use employee attitude surveys to increase productivity, improve work quality, decrease labor/management conflict, reduce waste, and lower absenteeism and turnover. Led by the top management team of Sirota and Alper Associates, the seminar will be held in New York, Chicago and San Francisco.

If you're ready to discover some new ways to motivate employees, put down your club. Pick up a pen. And fill out the attached coupon. Send it to Business Week Executive Programs,

BusinessWeek
EXECUTIVE PROGRAMS

Employee Motivation Seminars, 1221 Avenue of the Americas, New York, NY 10020. Or call 212/512-3583.

☐ Please send me additional information on the *Gainsharing®* seminar.

☐ Please send me additional information on the *Employee Attitude Surveys* seminar.

☐ I know everything about employee motivation. Just send me additional information on your other seminars for human resource executives.

☐ I know it all. Don't bother sending anything.

Name__________

Title__________

Company__________

Address__________

City/State/Zip__________

IF THIS IS YOUR IDEA OF SUCCESSION PLANNING, YOU MIGHT BE SUCCEEDED BY SOMEONE WHO KNOWS BETTER.

There's more to effective succession planning than just a paper replacement plan.

That's why Business Week's most successful seminar provides you with an overview of succession systems in major U.S. corporations. And gives you nuts-and-bolts information on how to implement a system. Or improve the one you've got.

Led by Stewart Friedman of the Wharton School and Frank Gaines, Jr. (formerly of Exxon where he was responsible for their highly regarded system), the seminar is a one-day intensive look at all aspects of succession.

The seminar leaders will be joined in each city by a senior executive who will give you insights into succession planning at his or her corporation.

To help ensure a continuing flow of competent managers in the quantity and quality needed to grow your businesses, plan on attending this timely seminar.

Interaction among the participants and speakers is integral to the success of the program, so we must limit the registration at each location.

To register or to receive additional information, call 212/512-3583.

Or write to Business Week Executive Programs, Succession Planning Seminar, 1221 Avenue of the Americas, New York, NY 10020.

BusinessWeek
EXECUTIVE PROGRAMS

THE MOST USEFUL BUSINESS-TO-BUSINESS MARKETING TOOL IS RIGHT UNDER YOUR NOSE.

Last year, American businesses used the telephone to ring up $150 billion in profits. Only a small percentage of that profit, however, was generated by business-to-business telemarketing. Most companies have simply overlooked the usefulness of the phone as a business-to-business marketing tool.

Until now.

Announcing Business Week's "Business-to-Business Telemarketing Seminar". The two-day event that will open your eyes.

Some of the key issues this seminar will cover include:

How to conduct a feasibility study within your company.

How to prepare an in-depth cost/benefit/exposure analysis.

And how to decide whether to mount an in-house operation or to contract with a service bureau.

For your convenience, this seminar will be held in New York on October 17-18. Chicago on November 7-8. Los Angeles on December 4-5. And New York again on December 10-11.

Get a handle on whether or not to implement a business-to-business telemarketing operation. Register today.

Call 212/512-3583. Or obtain more information by writing to Business Week Executive Programs, Telemarketing Seminar, 1221 Avenue of the Americas, New York, NY 10020.

BusinessWeek
EXECUTIVE PROGRAMS

Trade Any Size B/W Or Color: Campaign

411
ART DIRECTOR
Tom Cordner
WRITER
Paul Keye
ARTIST
Richard Pryor
CLIENT
State Of California Business Development
AGENCY
keye/donna/pearlstein - Los Angeles

412
ART DIRECTOR
John Clapps
WRITER
Charles Mullen
PHOTOGRAPHER
Scott Laperruque
CLIENT
Custom Communications Systems
AGENCY
Clapps & Mullen

THE CALIFORNIAS SIT ON THE EDGE OF A THREE TRILLION DOLLAR MARKET.

That's just the beginning.

We have a two century headstart on the Pacific Rim. As traders. As neighbors. As family.

That's just the beginning.

This market is growing by $3 billion a week. Not a year. A week.

If you're looking for the edge on the Pacific Rim, write the California Department of Commerce.

That's just the beginning.

THE CALIFORNIAS

California Department of Commerce
Office of Business Development, P.O. Box 9278, Dept. 34,
Van Nuys, CA 91409

IF THE CALIFORNIAS WERE A NATION, THEY WOULD HAVE THE EIGHTH LARGEST GNP IN THE WORLD.

There's more.

With only a tenth of the U.S. population, The Californias are home to more than a third of the country's highest-technology companies, headquarters for eighty-six of its five hundred fastest-growing companies.

There's more.

Some of the toughest economic analysts suggest that The Californias may not keep their #8 ranking into the next century.

They say The Californias will be #4.

Think what you can grow in this climate. Then, write the California Department of Commerce.

There's more.

THE CALIFORNIAS

California Department of Commerce
Office of Business Development, P.O. Box 9278, Dept. 24
Van Nuys, CA 91409

THE CALIFORNIAS HAVE THE BEST EDUCATED WORKFORCE IN THE COUNTRY.

That's only part of the story.

We spend more money on education—at all levels—than any other state. We have a higher percentage of college, high school, and technical school graduates than New York or Texas or Florida or North Carolina.

That's only part of the story.

Our graduate schools lead the nation in those fields most critical to growth: business management, chemistry, physics, electrical & civil engineering, geoscience, cellular & molecular biology, and computer science.

Want to see your business take off? Write the California Department Of Commerce.

That's only part of the story.

THE CALIFORNIAS

California Department Of Commerce
Office Of Business Development, P.O. Box 9278, Dept. 11
Van Nuys, CA 91409

WE KNOW MORE ABOUT HOOKING UP COMPUTERS THAN THE COMPANIES WHO MAKE THEM.

Your computer company knows all about computers. And of course the phone company knows everything about their phone lines. And the company that makes modems? Right, they're only experts when it comes to modems.

In fact there are thousands of companies who make data communications equipment, and make it well.

But now there's a company who knows how to hook all this equipment together and actually get it to work.

Custom Communications Systems.

We specialize in selling and installing custom cables. We'll also organize a thick maze of cables with just one new one. We even sell and install data communications equipment. And if you have a special problem, try us, we may be able to help.

So next time you have a question or problem call (201) 342-1288 and we'll get all that equipment you own to work the way you thought it would when you bought it.

CUSTOM COMMUNICATIONS SYSTEMS.

Any moron can install a computer. And usually one does.

It's a well known fact that the people who design computers are very bright. Sometimes brilliant.

But it's not so well known that the people who install computers are usually just the opposite.

If you want proof, just look at the maze of cables and balls and balls of wire behind your computers now.

And with each new computer you add, or repair you make—things get more complicated. And more expensive.

That's where we come in.

Custom Communications Systems. (201-342-1288)

We make things simple. We organize the computers that organize your life.

In fact, we specialize in condensing hundreds of cables into just a manageable few. In addition, we sell and install all types of data communication equipment.

We're not saying you have to be a genius to install computers. But it helps.

CUSTOM COMMUNICATIONS SYSTEMS.

And you thought computers were going to organize your life.
But somewhere along the way the wires got crossed.
And crossed. And crossed. And crossed again.
Because with every new computer you buy, you add a couple extra cables to your system.
Pretty soon, not even a computer could figure out which cable goes where.
But we can. Custom Communications Systems. (201-342-1288.)
We can organize and make sense out of any maze of cables. In fact, we specialize in condensing hundreds of cables into just a manageable few. On top of that, we also sell and install all types of data communication equipment.
In short, let us straighten you out.
CUSTOM COMMUNICATIONS SYSTEMS.

Trade Any Size B/W Or Color: Campaign

413
ART DIRECTOR
Scott Brandt
WRITER
David Culp
PHOTOGRAPHER
Jim Erickson
CLIENT
Perdue
AGENCY
Lewis Advertising/Rocky Mount, NC

414
ART DIRECTOR
Peter Bemis
WRITER
Jonathan Cranin
CLIENT
Magazine Publishers Association
AGENCY
D'Arcy Masius Benton & Bowles

Perdue Is Looking For Twelve Rare Birds, And One Of Them May Be You.

Perdue needs twelve farmers in this area to build new primary breeder houses. Twelve farmers, twelve chicken houses.

It's such a good investment opportunity, you'd think we could find plenty of takers without even bothering to advertise.

And we could. But when you see the importance of those twelve primary breeder operations—their importance to Perdue and to North Carolina agriculture as a whole—you can see why the people we're looking for aren't exactly a dime a dozen.

These primary breeders are valuable birds, the secret to Perdue's well-known quality advantage, so we simply can't afford to trust them to anyone who isn't the best.

Perdue Farms develops its primary breeder stock "from scratch." The primary breeders you raise today are the product of years of genetic research.

Primary breeders are the "grandparents" of the Perdue chickens sold in grocery stores. One primary breeder hen is eventually responsible for **150,000** broilers or roasters. And there are 8,000 breeders in each house!

Just twelve primary breeder houses will supply birds to more than 1,000 independent Perdue producers all over North Carolina. So as a primary breeder producer, you're where the whole success story begins.

What we offer in return for your expertise is an excellent return on investment. You'll receive consistent, top-dollar payments. You'll even be paid during the first weeks, when your pullets aren't laying yet.

Another important factor is the lower-than-average startup cost. Perdue buys the equipment—$20,000 worth—then leases it back to you. So you save $20,000 upfront, get an additional tax deduction and eventually gain ownership of the equipment.

It's the steadiest, most predictable program Perdue offers. And since it's also the most important, we do everything we can to make sure you succeed at it—from helping you line up financing to answering your questions about the everyday details.

If you're the rare breed of farmer we're looking for, you owe it to yourself to learn more about the Perdue primary breeder program.

So return the coupon, or call the Perdue office in Norlina at 456-2055.

I'd like to know more about Perdue's primary breeder program.

Name ______
Address ______
City ______ State ______ Zip ______
Phone (____) ______

PERDUE

Mail coupon to Perdue, Route 1, Box 301, Norlina, NC 27563. Or call the Perdue office during the day at (919) 456-2055. At nights call Tom Traylor at (919) 456-2331 or Jim Herman at (919) 438-2645.

When It Comes To Farm Investments, This One Rules The Roost.

If every chicken were worth as much as this one, a fried drumstick would cost about the same as filet mignon.

This is a Perdue primary breeder, the elite of its species, product of years of genetic research. Super Chicken.

One primary breeder hen is directly responsible for **150,000** broilers or roasters two generations down the line. Perdue Farms develops its primary breeders "from scratch." These valuable birds are the secret to Perdue's well-known quality advantage.

We go to great lengths to develop our fine feathered investment to its full potential. And that creates an outstanding farm investment opportunity for you: the Perdue primary breeder program.

Because of increasing consumer demand, Perdue needs twelve new primary breeder houses in this area, and for obvious reasons we want to work with the very best farmers we can find. What's in it for those twelve individuals? A farm investment we think is the best one going, bar none.

Variables like weather, feed prices and even the productivity of the hens are practically eliminated. As a primary breeder producer, you'll receive consistent, top-dollar payments. You'll even be paid during the first weeks, before your pullets start laying. You can project very accurately your cash flow from each flock.

When you build a primary breeder house, Perdue will put up $20,000 to buy the equipment, then lease the equipment back to you. So you save $20,000 upfront, get an additional tax deduction and eventually gain ownership of the equipment.

A breeder house works well with other farm operations because it doesn't occupy much space or require a great deal of labor. Most producers are able to do the work themselves in addition to their other farming.

It's the steadiest, most predictable program Perdue offers. And, as you've seen, it's also the most important. Just twelve primary breeder houses in this area will supply birds to over 1,000 independent Perdue producers across North Carolina.

So if you're looking for a good long-term farm investment, we'd like to show you, in real dollars, how a Perdue primary breeder operation can pay off for you.

To learn more, mail the coupon to Perdue or call the Perdue office in Norlina at 456-2055.

I'd like to know more about Perdue's primary breeder program.

Name ______
Address ______
City ______ State ______ Zip ______
Phone (____) ______

PERDUE

Mail coupon to Perdue, Route 1, Box 301, Norlina, NC 27563. Or call the Perdue office during the day at (919) 456-2055. At nights call Tom Traylor at (919) 456-2331 or Jim Herman at (919) 438-2645.

Invest 22¢ In A Stamp And Perdue Might Invest $20,000 In Your Farm.

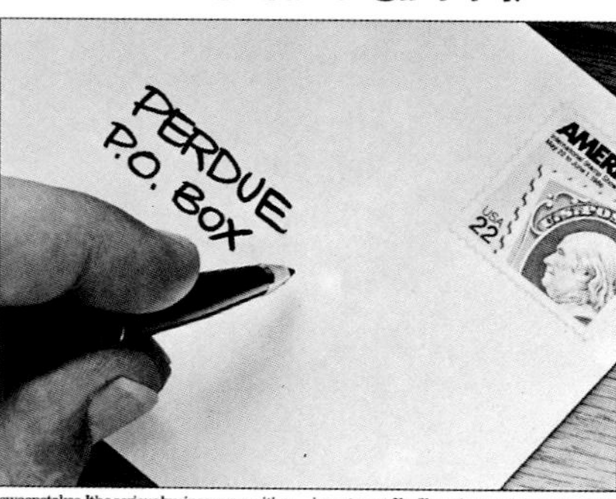

This isn't a sweepstakes. It's a serious business proposition.

Perdue is now looking for twelve top-notch farmers in this area to build primary breeder houses.

Twelve farmers, twelve chicken houses. That's not many. But you can tell from the amount of money Perdue will invest in each operation just how important those farmers and those breeder houses are to the company. Here's why.

Perdue Farms develops its primary breeder stock "from scratch." The primary breeder chickens you raise today are the product of years of genetic research. These are valuable birds, the secret to Perdue's well-known quality advantage, and we won't trust them to just anybody.

Primary breeders are the "grandparents" of the Perdue chickens sold in grocery stores. In her 40-odd weeks of productivity, a Perdue primary breeder hen will produce second-generation breeders that in turn will generate **150,000** supermarket birds. That's 150,000 broilers or roasters from just one primary breeder. And there are 8,000 breeders in each house!

You can see, then, why the primary breeder program is so important to Perdue, and why we're looking for the very best farmers we can find. Which brings us back to our investment in your farm.

Perdue will put up $20,000 to buy the equipment for your primary breeder house, then lease the equipment back to you. You save $20,000 upfront, get an additional tax deduction and eventually gain ownership of the equipment.

In addition, Perdue promises an excellent return on your investment. You'll receive consistent, top-dollar payments. You'll even be paid during the first weeks, when your pullets aren't laying yet.

It's the steadiest, most predictable program Perdue offers. And, as you've seen, it's also the most important—the program where the whole Perdue success story begins. Just twelve primary breeder houses will supply birds to over 1,000 independent Perdue producers in North Carolina.

So if you're looking for an attractive, long-term farm investment, Perdue is looking for you. To learn more, call the Perdue office in Norlina at 456-2055. Or return the coupon.

It may be the smartest 22¢ investment you ever made.

I'd like to know more about Perdue's primary breeder program.

Name ______
Address ______
City ______ State ______ Zip ______
Phone (____) ______

PERDUE

Mail coupon to Perdue, Route 1, Box 301, Norlina, NC 27563. Or call the Perdue office during the day at (919) 456-2055. At nights call Tom Traylor at (919) 456-2331 or Jim Herman at (919) 438-2645.

CHRYSLER NEEDED MORE THAN 30 SECONDS TO SELL A CAR.

They knew they needed the time people give to a magazine ad. Which is why they spent 26% more in magazine advertising last year than in the year before.

With the continued erosion of network TV audience shares, hundreds of other companies have been doing the same thing. In 1984, a record total of nearly $5 billion was spent in magazines, an increase of more than $1.25 billion since 1982.

As Chrysler discovered on their road to success, magazines do more than advertise the product.

They sell it.

MPA
Magazine Publishers Association

MAGAZINES ARE STEALING THE SHOW.

A COMMERCIAL BREAK FROM PROCTER & GAMBLE.

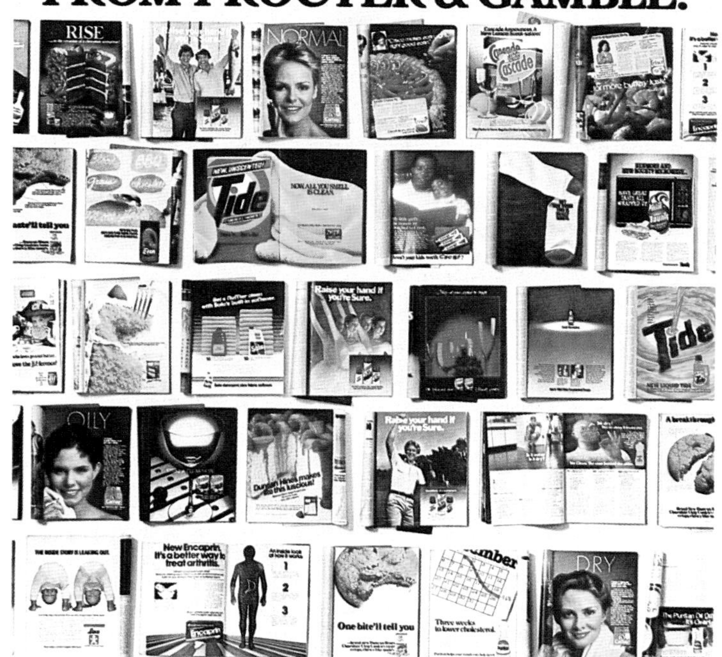

Last year Procter & Gamble spent over $50 million on magazine ads, far more than they ever spent before.

And they weren't alone. Hundreds of the country's biggest advertisers also increased their magazine ad budgets.

In 1984, a record total of nearly $5 billion was spent in magazines, an increase of more than $1.25 billion since 1982.

If the people who invented the soap opera think they can clean up with magazine advertising, maybe you can too.

MPA
Magazine Publishers Association

MAGAZINES ARE STEALING THE SHOW.

RCA'S LATEST TELEVISION ADVERTISING.

Last year, RCA spent 35% more in magazine advertising than they did the year before, for a total of over $47 million.

And they weren't alone. Hundreds of the country's biggest advertisers also increased their magazine ad budgets. In 1984, a record total of nearly $5 billion was spent in magazines, an increase of more than $1.25 billion since 1982.

Should your company advertise more in magazines? Ask one of the biggest television advertisers.

MPA
Magazine Publishers Association

MAGAZINES ARE STEALING THE SHOW.

Trade Any Size B/W Or Color: Campaign

415
ART DIRECTOR
Sally Wagner
WRITER
John Jarvis
PHOTOGRAPHER
Kent Severson
CLIENT
Ciba-Geigy
AGENCY
Martin/Williams - Minneapolis

416
ART DIRECTOR
Ron Louie
WRITER
Chuck Gessner
DESIGNER
Ron Louie
PHOTOGRAPHER
Harry DeZitter
CLIENT
Colombian Coffee
AGENCY
Doyle Dane Bernbach

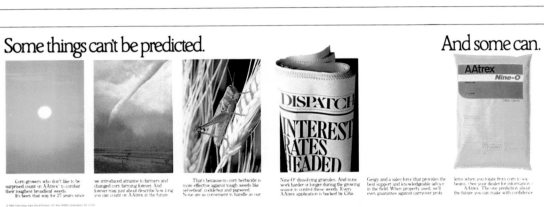

Some things can't be predicted.

And some can.

DISPATCH
INTEREST RATES HEADED

AAtrex
Nine-O

Corn growers who don't like to be surprised count on AAtrex® to combat their toughest broadleaf weeds.
It's been that way for 27 years since we introduced atrazine to farmers and changed corn farming forever. And forever may just about describe how long you can count on AAtrex in the future.
That's because no corn herbicide is more effective against tough weeds like velvetleaf, cocklebur and pigweed. None are as convenient to handle as our Nine-O® dissolving granules. And none work harder or longer during the growing season to control these weeds. Every AAtrex application is backed by Ciba-Geigy and a sales force that provides the best support and knowledgeable advice in the field. When properly used, we'll even guarantee against carryover problems when you rotate from corn to soybeans. (See your dealer for information.)
AAtrex. The one prediction about the future you can make with confidence.

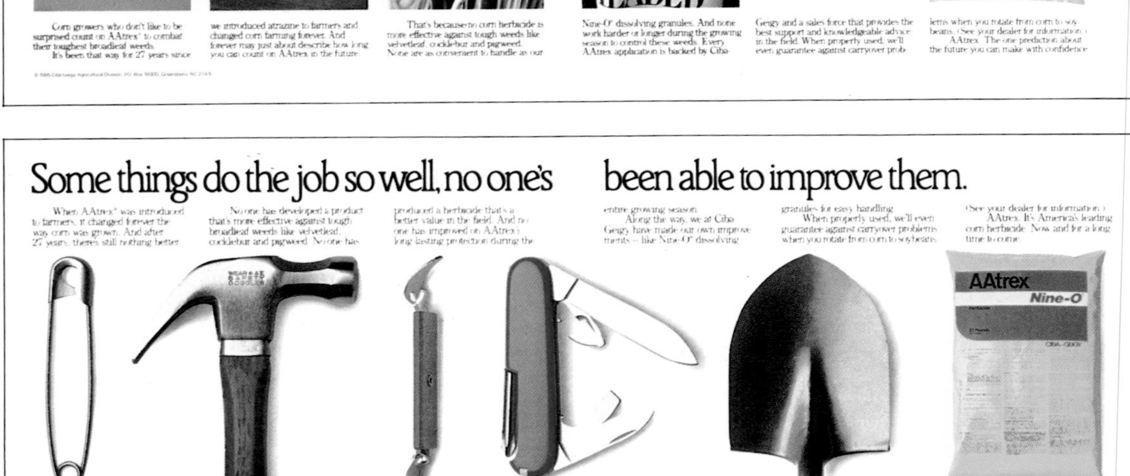

415

"Captain, we forgot the Colombian Coffee."

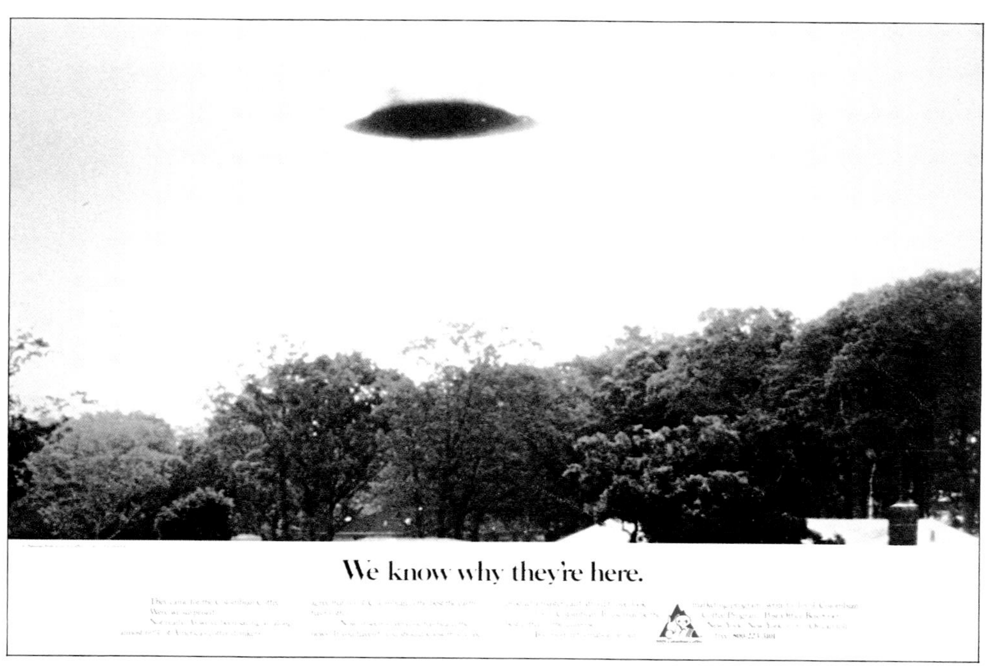
We know why they're here.

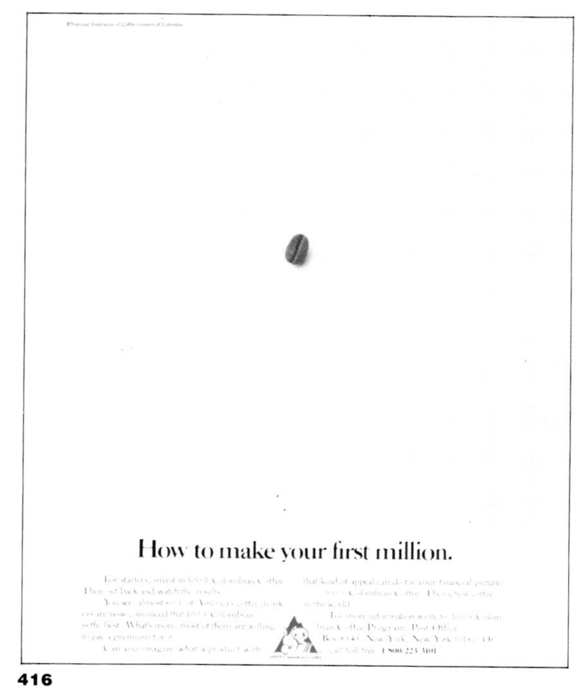
How to make your first million.

Trade Any Size B/W Or Color: Campaign

417
ART DIRECTOR
John DeBonis
WRITER
Joe Garrett
ARTIST
John Debonis
CLIENT
Nikon Precision, Inc.
AGENCY
Chiat/Day - San Francisco

Collateral Brochures Other Than By Mail

418
ART DIRECTOR
Stephen Walsh
WRITER
Adam Hanft
DESIGNER
Stephen Walsh
ARTISTS
Jack Unruh
Mark Hess
Isadore Seltzer
Brad Holland
Teresa Fasolino
CLIENT
Wang Financial Information Services Corporation
AGENCY
Slater Hanft Martin

419
ART DIRECTOR
Ida Jennings
WRITER
Intramed
DESIGNER
Ida Jennings
CLIENT
Roche Labs
AGENCY
Sudler & Hennessey - Intramed Division

When your Nikon stepper arrives in this country, 105 other people will be waiting for it.

Including 65 field service engineers who can be on-site in as little as 2 hours.

12 application engineers to customize your stepper to your exact production requirements.

2 facilities experts for clean, trouble-free installations.

Plus 14 experienced software, hardware and optical specialists.

Of course, we haven't forgotten the most important people waiting for your Nikon stepper. Your people. Our 12 training and documentation specialists offer them courses in all aspects of operation and maintenance.

What's more, 90% of our N.P.I. support team has been recruited here in the U.S. And the team continues to grow at the rate of one a day. Which means we can offer any level of support you need. Including on-site service 24 hours a day, 7 days a week.

This kind of service and support is one reason why 80% of all the steppers used in Japan are from Nikon.

So if you're waiting for the same kind of support in the U.S., stop. And see us at Semicon.

NIKON PRECISION INC.

Semicon Booth #4418-26

When your Nikon stepper arrives in this country, 128 ~~105~~ other people will be waiting for it.

Including ~~65~~ 75 field service engineers who can be on-site in as little as 2 hours.

19 ~~12~~ application engineers to customize your stepper to your exact production requirements.

2 facilities experts for clean, trouble-free installations.

Plus ~~14~~ 16 experienced software, hardware and optical specialists.

Of course, we haven't forgotten the most important people waiting for your Nikon stepper. Your people. Our ~~12~~ 18 training and documentation specialists offer them courses in all aspects of operation and maintenance.

What's more, 90% of our N.P.I. support team has been recruited here in the U.S. And the team continues to grow at the rate of one a day. Which means we can offer any level of support you need. Including on-site service 24 hours a day, 7 days a week.

This kind of service and support is one reason why 80% of all the steppers used in Japan are from Nikon.

So if you're waiting for the same kind of support here in the U.S., your waiting's over.

Call us now at (415) 952-8188. Or write us at 1051 Sneath Lane, San Bruno, CA 94066.

NIKON PRECISION INC.

When your Nikon stepper arrives in this country, 145 ~~128~~ ~~105~~ other people will be waiting for it.

Including ~~65~~ ~~75~~ 84 field service engineers who can be on-site in as little as 2 hours.

22 ~~19~~ ~~12~~ application engineers to customize your stepper to your exact production requirements.

2 facilities experts for clean, trouble-free installations.

Plus ~~14~~ ~~16~~ 19 experienced software, hardware and optical specialists.

Of course, we haven't forgotten the most important people waiting for your Nikon stepper. Your people. Our ~~12~~ 18 training and documentation specialists offer them courses in all aspects of operation and maintenance.

What's more, 90% of our N.P.I. support team has been recruited here in the U.S. And the team continues to grow at the rate of one a day. Which means we can offer any level of support you need. Including on-site service 24 hours a day, 7 days a week.

This kind of service and support is one reason why 80% of all the steppers used in Japan are from Nikon.

So if you're waiting for the same kind of support here in the U.S., your waiting's over.

Call us now at (415) 952-8188. Or write us at 1051 Sneath Lane, San Bruno, CA 94066.

NIKON PRECISION INC.

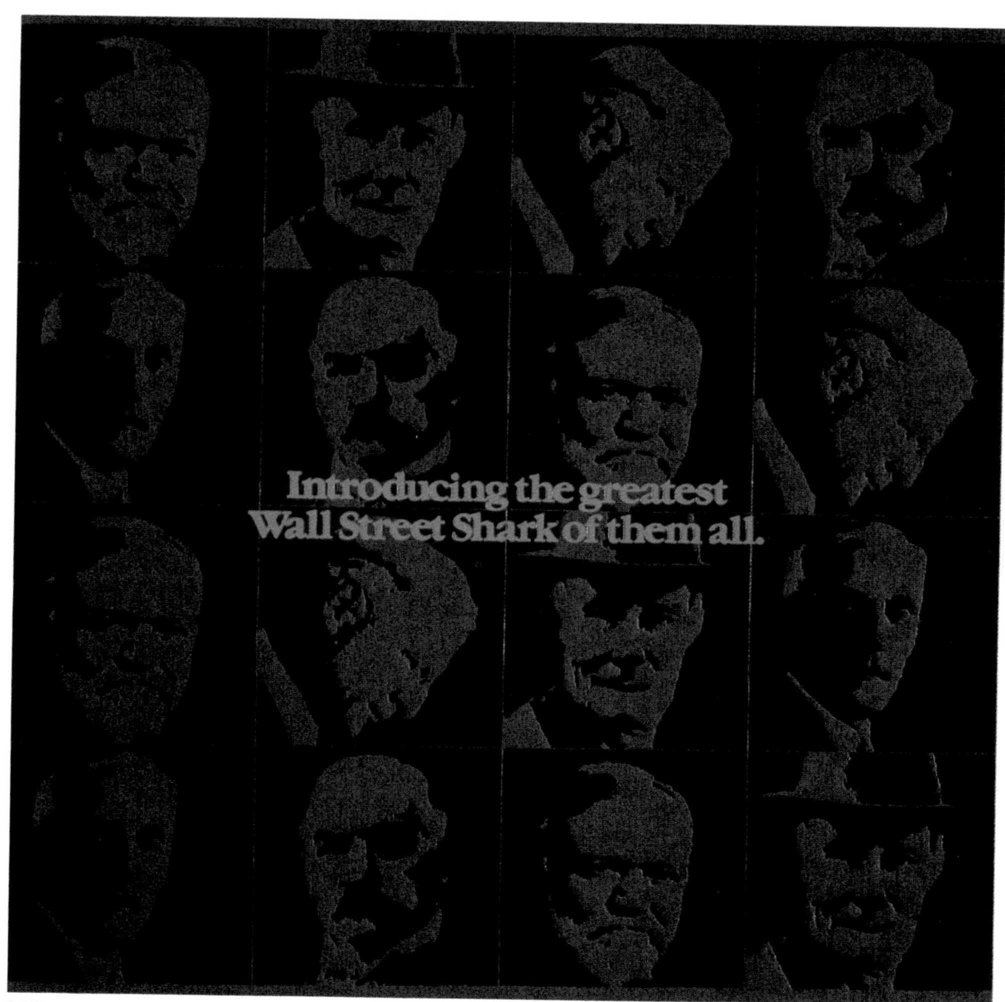

418

CINECOLI

BACTERIAL CELL STRUCTURE AND FUNCTION

419

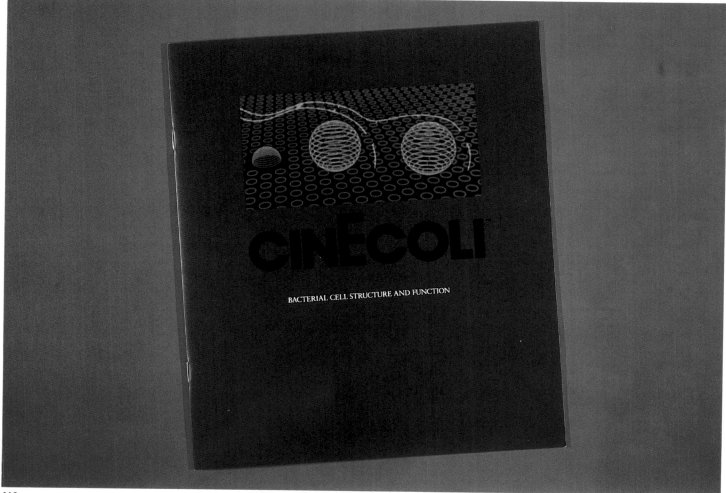

420
ART DIRECTOR
Gregg Simonton
WRITER
Ernie Mosteller
DESIGNER
Gregg Simonton
PHOTOGRAPHER
Tom Tuura
CLIENT
B/PAA
AGENCY
Sawyer Riley Compton/
Gainesville, GA

421
ART DIRECTOR
Ron Sullivan
WRITER
Mark Perkins
DESIGNER
Willie Baronet
ARTIST
Ron Sullivan
PHOTOGRAPHER
Geof Kern
CLIENT
The Selwyn School
AGENCY
Sullivan Perkins/Dallas

422
ART DIRECTOR
Tim Forbes
WRITER
Robert Ramsay
PHOTOGRAPHER
Shin Shugino
CLIENT
The Bank Of Nova Scotia
AGENCY
Remarkable Communications
Ltd./Toronto

423
ART DIRECTORS
Theo Carl
John Ward
WRITER
Linda Reynolds
ARTIST
Randy Chaffee
PHOTOGRAPHER
Richard Noble
CLIENT
Philip Morris/Virginia Slims
AGENCY
Leo Burnett/Chicago

420

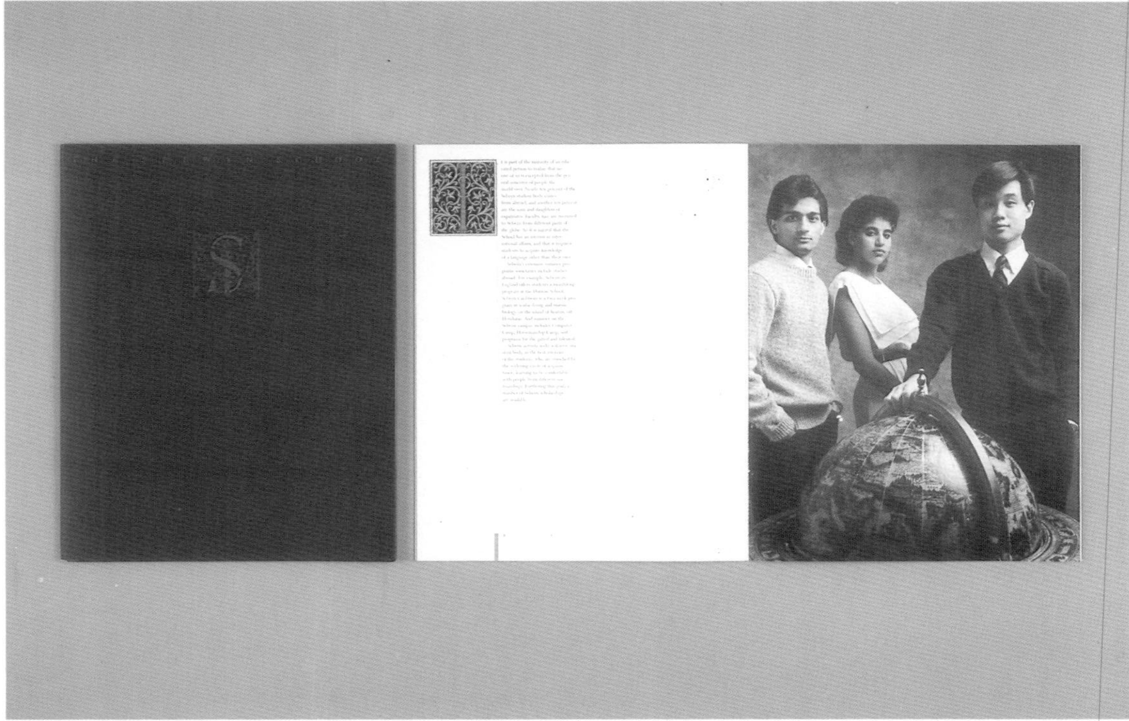

421

422

423

Collateral
Brochures
Other Than By Mail

424
ART DIRECTOR
Tony Kerr
WRITER
Brian Quennell
PHOTOGRAPHER
Olga Tracey
CLIENT
Apple Canada Inc.
AGENCY
Scali McCabe Sloves/Toronto

425
ART DIRECTOR
Frank Nicholas
WRITERS
Parker Bennett
Steve Turner
Mary Ferris
PHOTOGRAPHER
John Welzenbach
CLIENT
Star-Kist/9 Lives
AGENCY
Leo Burnett/Chicago

426
ART DIRECTOR
Rick Boyko
WRITER
Bill Hamilton
PHOTOGRAPHER
Gary McGuire
CLIENT
Mitsubishi Electric Sales America
AGENCY
Chiat/Day - Los Angeles

427
ART DIRECTOR
Carol Leiterman
WRITER
Evelyn Rose
DESIGNER
Carol Leiterman
PHOTOGRAPHER
Jonathan Pite
CLIENT
Boston Properties
AGENCY
Rose & Brosse Advertising

424

425

Mitsubishi Television.
The Thinking Inside.
MITSUBISHI

426

The Fine Art Of...
Subway

427

Collateral Brochures Other Than By Mail

428
ART DIRECTORS
Judy Simpson
Mark Daspit
WRITERS
John MacPherson
David Steel
Dennis Hinton
DESIGNER
Judy Simpson
CLIENT
Hinton & Steel
AGENCY
Hinton & Steel/Seattle

429
ART DIRECTOR
Artie Dixon
WRITER
Hal Kome
DESIGNER
Artie Dixon
PHOTOGRAPHERS
Thaddeus Watkins
Jane Hamborsky
CLIENT
Touch Mime Theatre
AGENCY
Marshall/Dixon/Kome - Chapel Hill, NC

430
ART DIRECTOR
Brooke Kenney
WRITER
Mike Dodge
PHOTOGRAPHER
Worldwide Photo Service
CLIENT
Leamington Hotel
AGENCY
Dodge & Kenney/Minneapolis

431
ART DIRECTORS
Arthur Eisenberg
Mark Drury
WRITERS
Susan Rogers
Arthur Eisenberg
DESIGNER
Mark Drury
CLIENT
Eisenberg Inc.
AGENCY
Eisenberg Inc./Dallas

432
ART DIRECTOR
Linda Berg
WRITER
John Connelly
ARTIST
Larry Duke
PHOTOGRAPHER
Dick Faust
CLIENT
Coleman Western Knives
AGENCY
Hutchins/Y&R - Rochester, NY

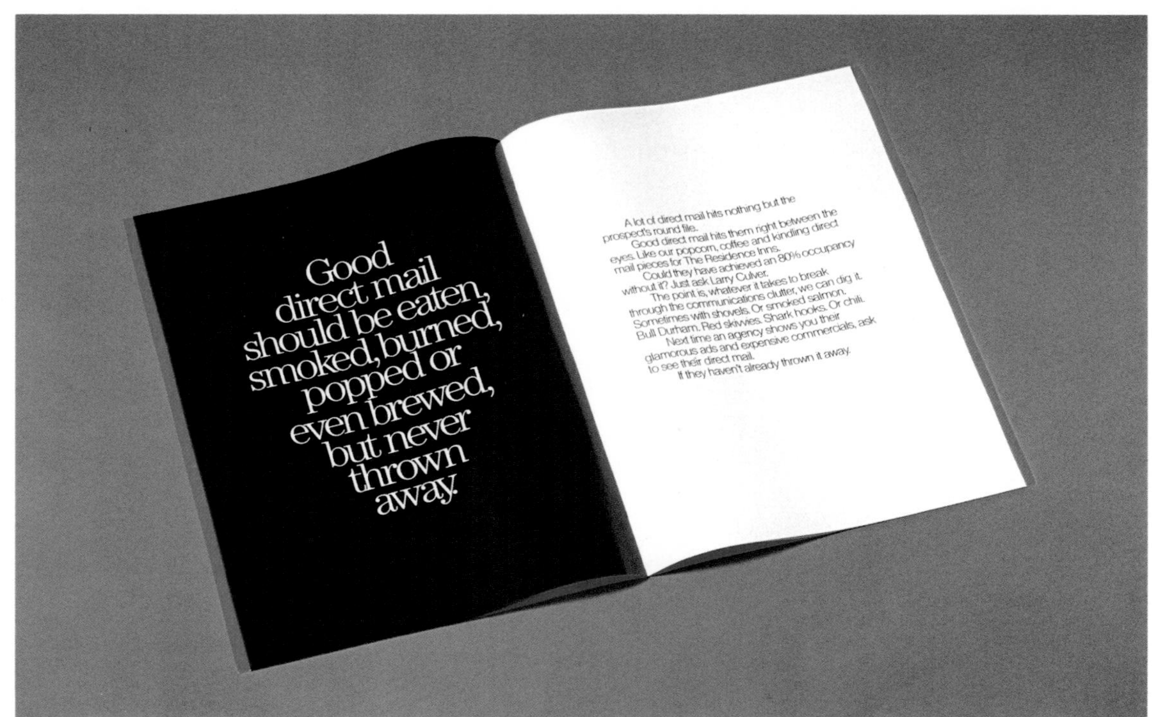

428

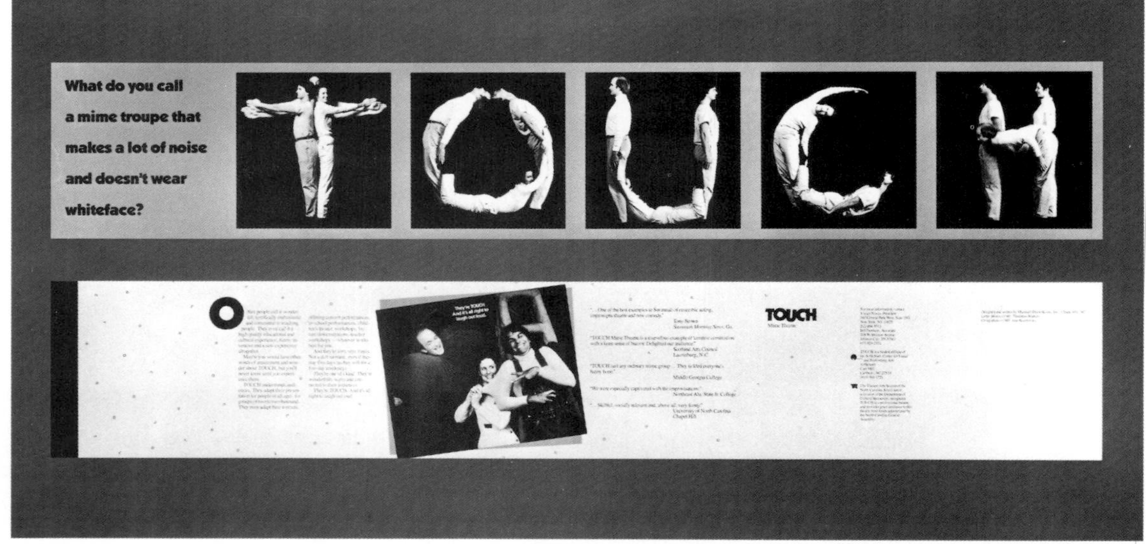

429

430

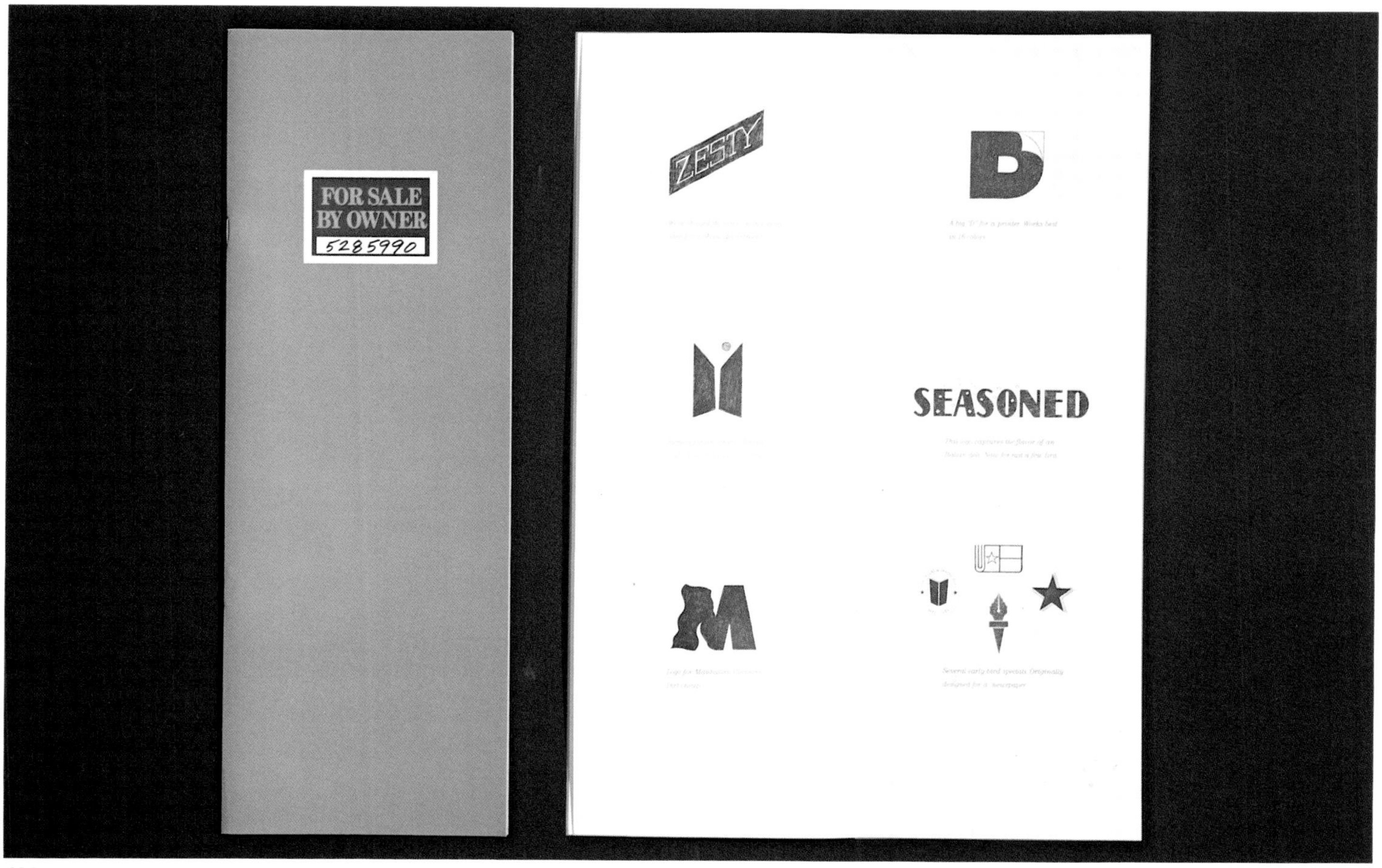

FOR SALE
BY OWNER
5285990
ZESTY
SEASONED

431

WESTERN CUTLERY
Two Great Names. WESTERN One Great Knife.
USN

432

Collateral Brochures Other Than By Mail

433
ART DIRECTOR
Woody Kay
WRITERS
Tom Monahan
Melissa Mirarchi
Jeff Abbott
PHOTOGRAPHER
Myron/Ira Gabor
CLIENT
Wright Line, Inc.
AGENCY
Leonard Monahan Saabye/
Providence, RI

434
ART DIRECTOR
Beth Jeffe
WRITER
Paul Wolfe
DESIGNER
Beth Jeffe
PHOTOGRAPHERS
Kim Whitesides
Robert Ammirati
Larry Dale Gordon
CLIENT
BMW Of North America
AGENCY
Ammirati & Puris

435
ART DIRECTOR
Terry Schneider
WRITER
Bill Borders
PHOTOGRAPHER
Pete Stone
CLIENT
Columbia Sportswear
AGENCY
Borders Perrin & Norrander/
Portland, OR

436
ART DIRECTOR
Dede Hanlon Bass
WRITER
David Perkins
DESIGNER
George Hughes
ARTIST
Roz Davis
PHOTOGRAPHERS
Jeffrey Stevenson
Terry Hire
Joe Devenney
Ed Elvidge
Dick Durrance II
Peter Ficksman
Ed Holcomb
C. C. Church
Kip Brundage
CLIENT
Gannett Graphics
AGENCY
The Marketing Group/
Portland, ME

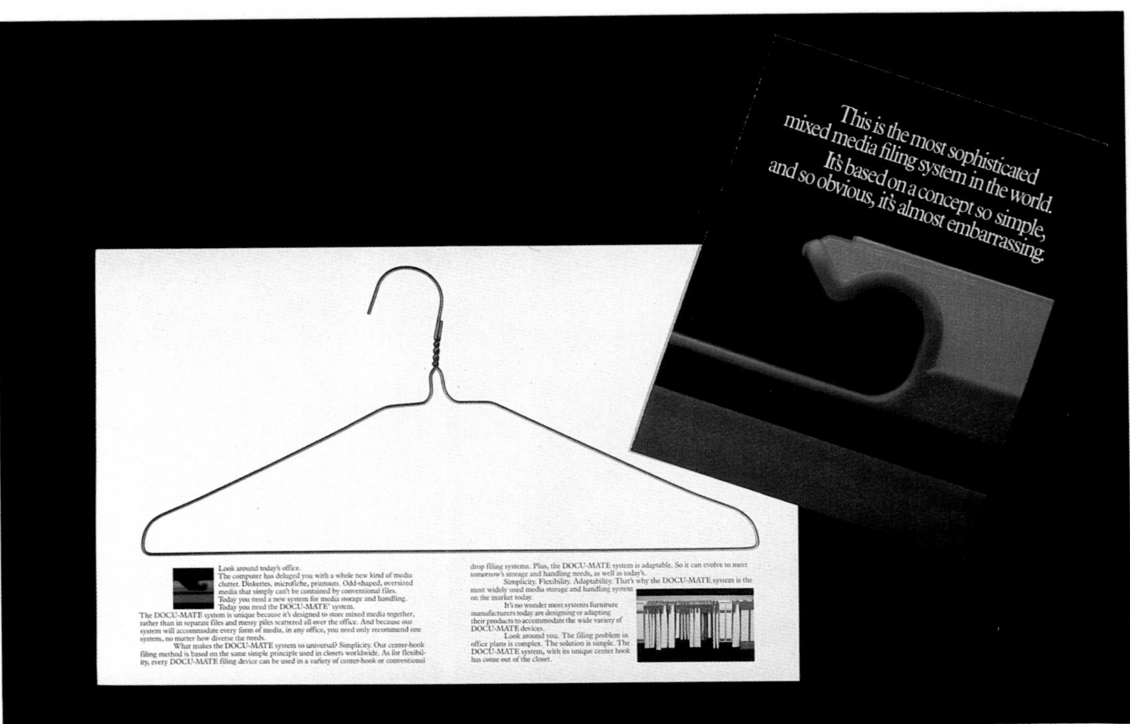

433

434

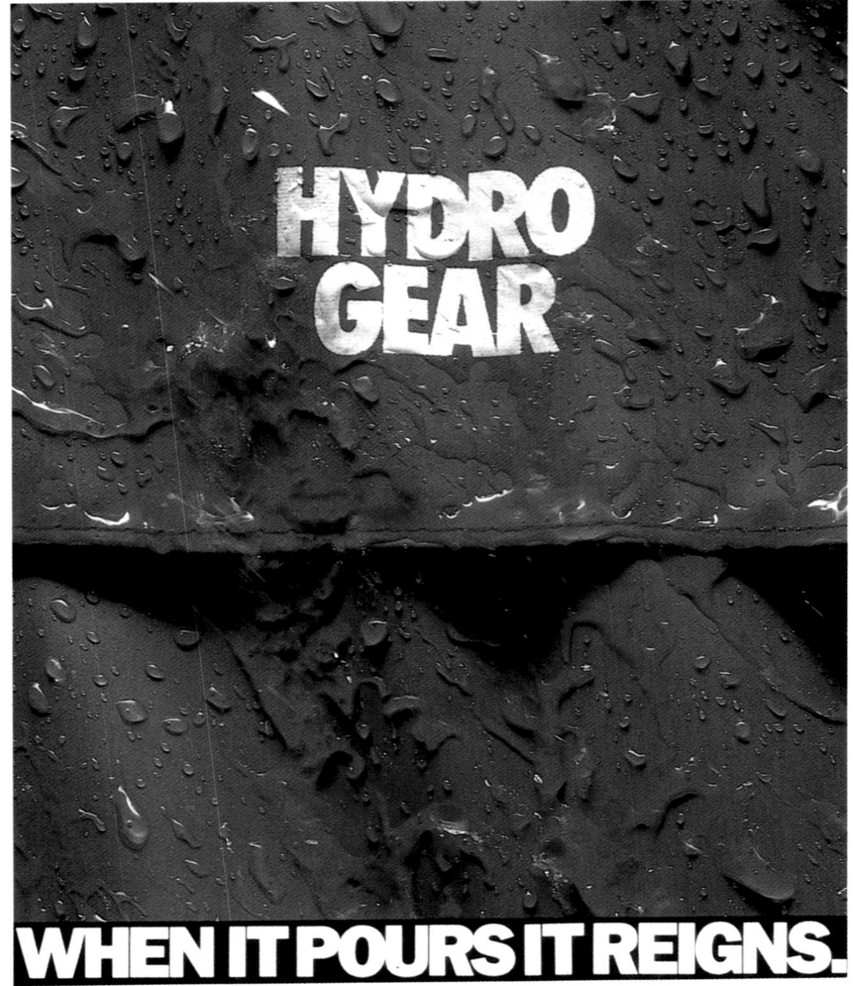
HYDRO
GEAR
WHEN IT POURS IT REIGNS.
435

THE MAINE
COLLECTION
GANNETT GRAPHICS
436

Collateral Sales Kits

437
ART DIRECTOR
Randall Hensley
WRITERS
John Fatteross
Billie-Ann Harber
DESIGNER
Eric Baker
PHOTOGRAPHERS
Marty Evans
Jeff Glancz
CLIENT
IBM Entry Systems Division
AGENCY
Muir Cornelius Moore

438
ART DIRECTOR
Frank Schulwolf
WRITER
Arthur Low
DESIGNER
Ted Lodigensky
CLIENT
Aviation Sales Company
AGENCY
Susan Gilbert & Company/
Coral Gables, FL

439
ART DIRECTOR
Greg Simpson
DESIGNER
Greg Simpson
PHOTOGRAPHER
Tom McCavera
CLIENT
J. P. Stevens
AGENCY
Mierop Design

440
ART DIRECTOR
Robert Joseph
WRITER
Chris Howard
DESIGNER
Robert Joseph
PHOTOGRAPHER
Harry DeZitter
CLIENT
Saab
AGENCY
Ally & Gargano

437

438

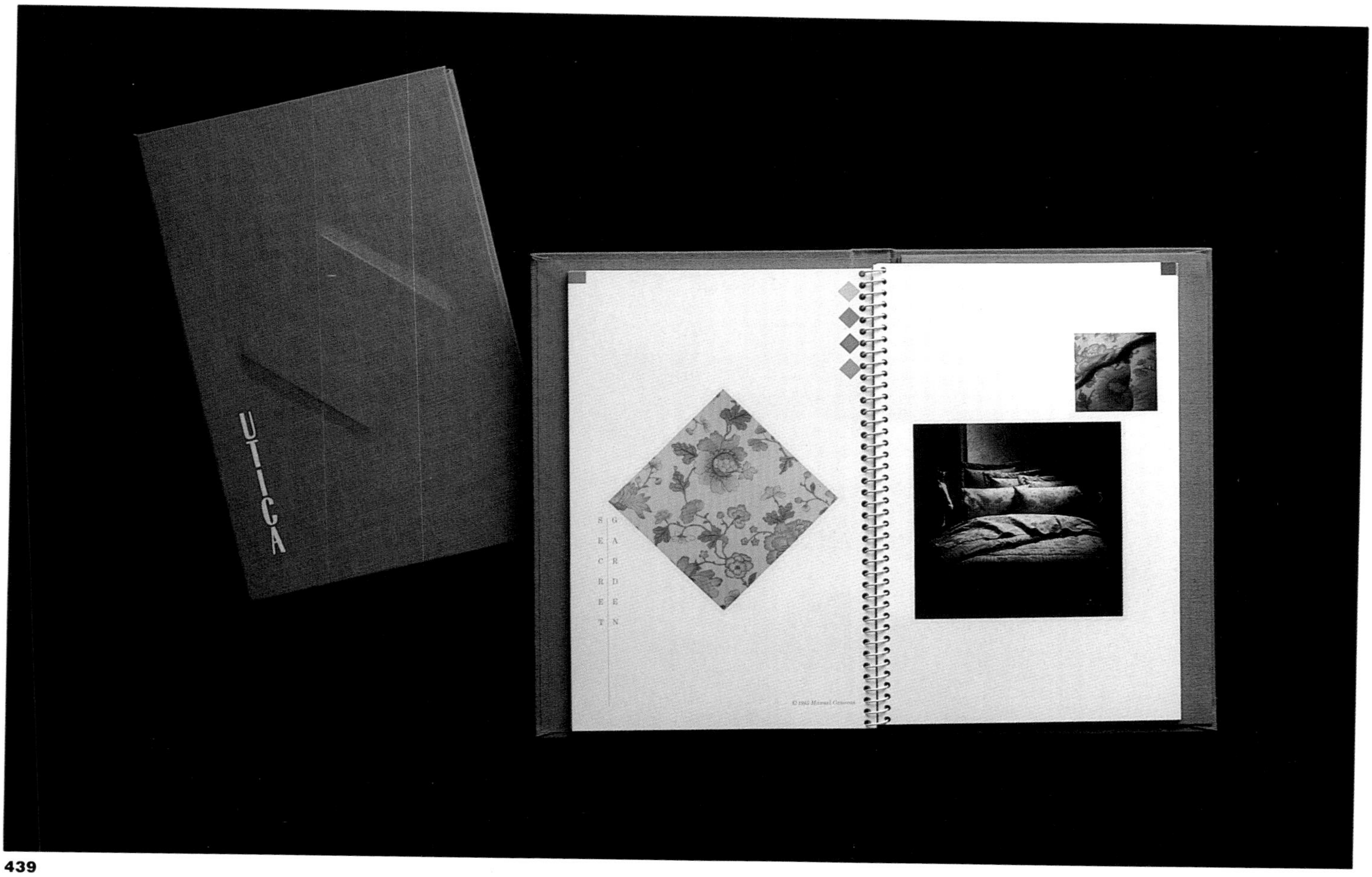

UTICA
SECRET
GARDEN

439

SAAB
SCANIA
SAAB/1986 DEALER ADVERTISING MATERIAL
SAAB

440

Collateral Sales Kits

441
ART DIRECTOR
Mark Crim
WRITER
Wally Williams
DESIGNER
Mark Crim
PHOTOGRAPHERS
Skeete Hagler
Willis/Randolph Photography
CLIENT
Justin Western Boot Company
AGENCY
Keller Crescent Company/ Irvine, TX

442
ART DIRECTOR
Bob Barrie
WRITER
John Stingley
DESIGNER
Bob Barrie
ARTISTS
Dick Hess
Mark Hess
CLIENT
Prince Spaghetti Sauce
AGENCY
Fallon McElligott/Minneapolis

443
ART DIRECTOR
Brooke Kenney
WRITER
Mike Dodge
ARTIST
Stan Olson
PHOTOGRAPHER
Rick Dublin
CLIENT
Sheraton Park Place Hotel
AGENCY
Dodge and Kenney/ Minneapolis

444
ART DIRECTOR
Nesta David
WRITER
Kit McCracken
PHOTOGRAPHER
Arthur Elgort
CLIENT
Christian Dior
AGENCY
Bel Aire Associates

THE PEOPLE AND PLACES OF JUSTIN BOOTS

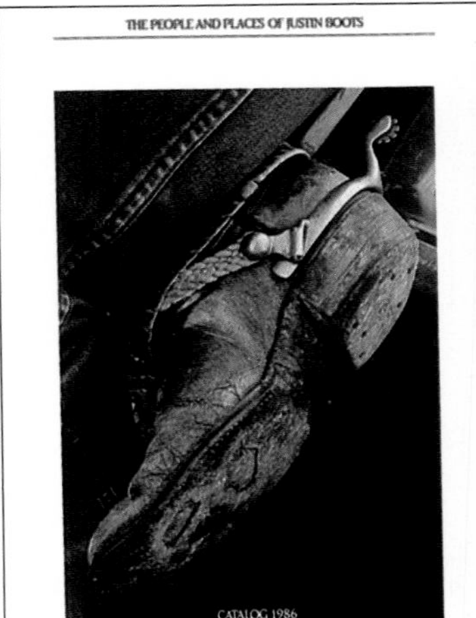

441

Chunky.

Presenting our Spaghetti Sauce Line for 1986. PRINCE

442

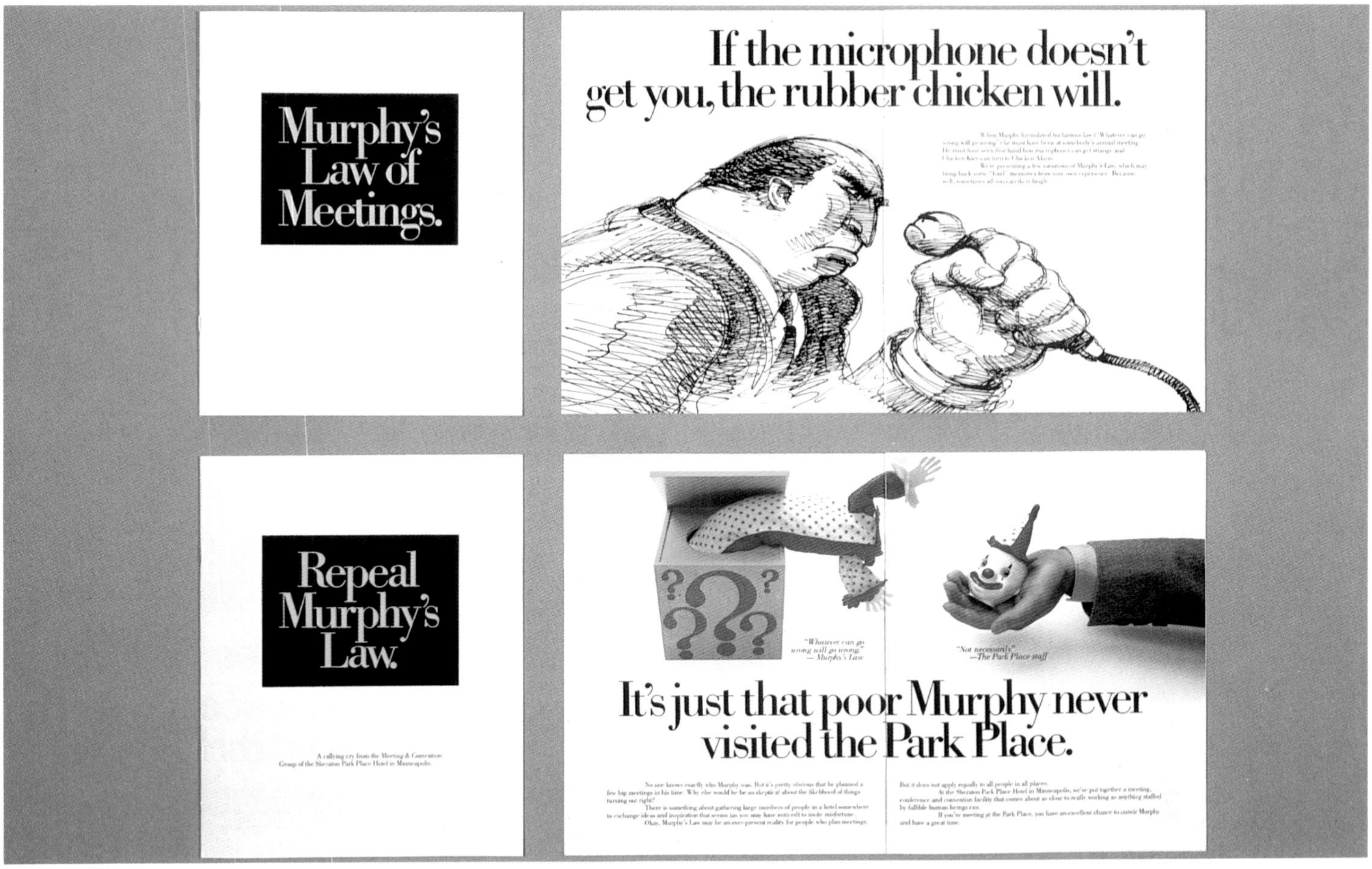

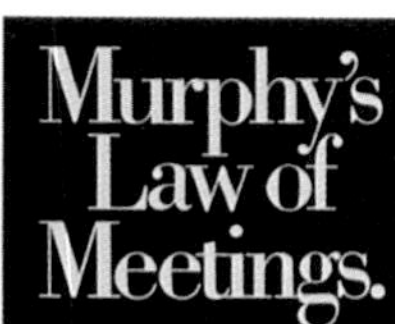

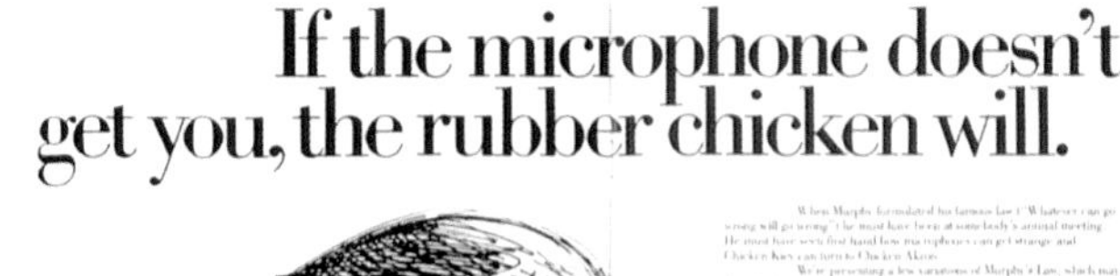

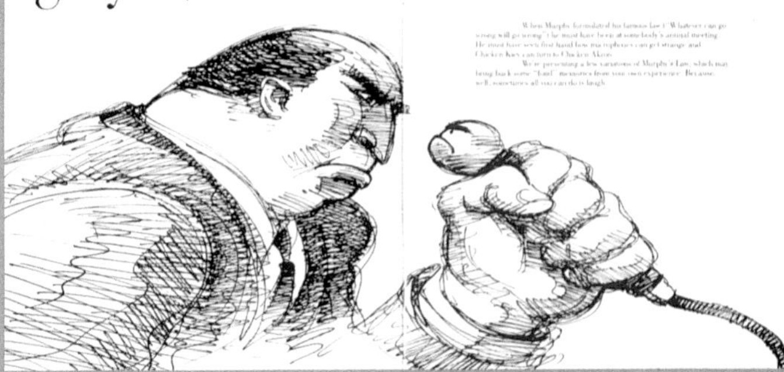

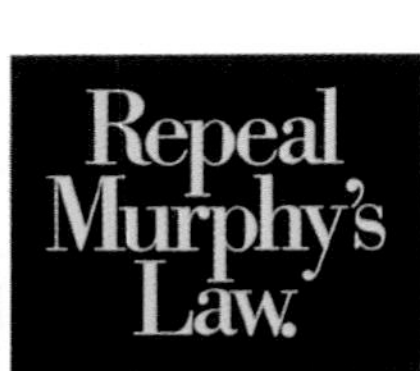

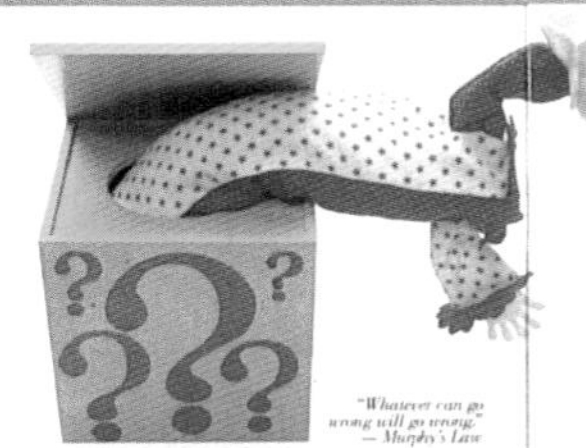

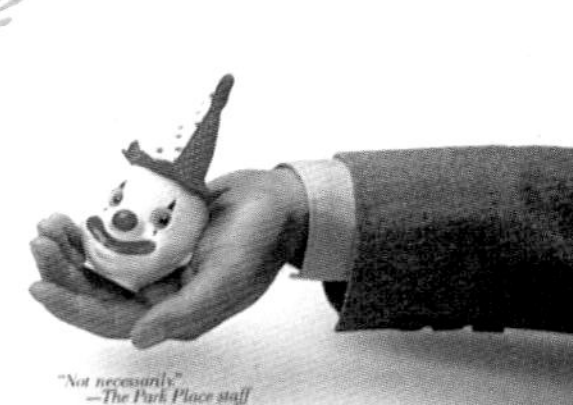

Murphy's Law of Meetings.
If the microphone doesn't get you, the rubber chicken will.
Repeal Murphy's Law.
A rallying cry from the Meeting & Convention Group of the Sheraton Park Place Hotel in Minneapolis.
"Whatever can go wrong will go wrong." — Murphy's Law
"Not necessarily." —The Park Place staff
It's just that poor Murphy never visited the Park Place.

443

Christian Dior
Christian Dior · New York

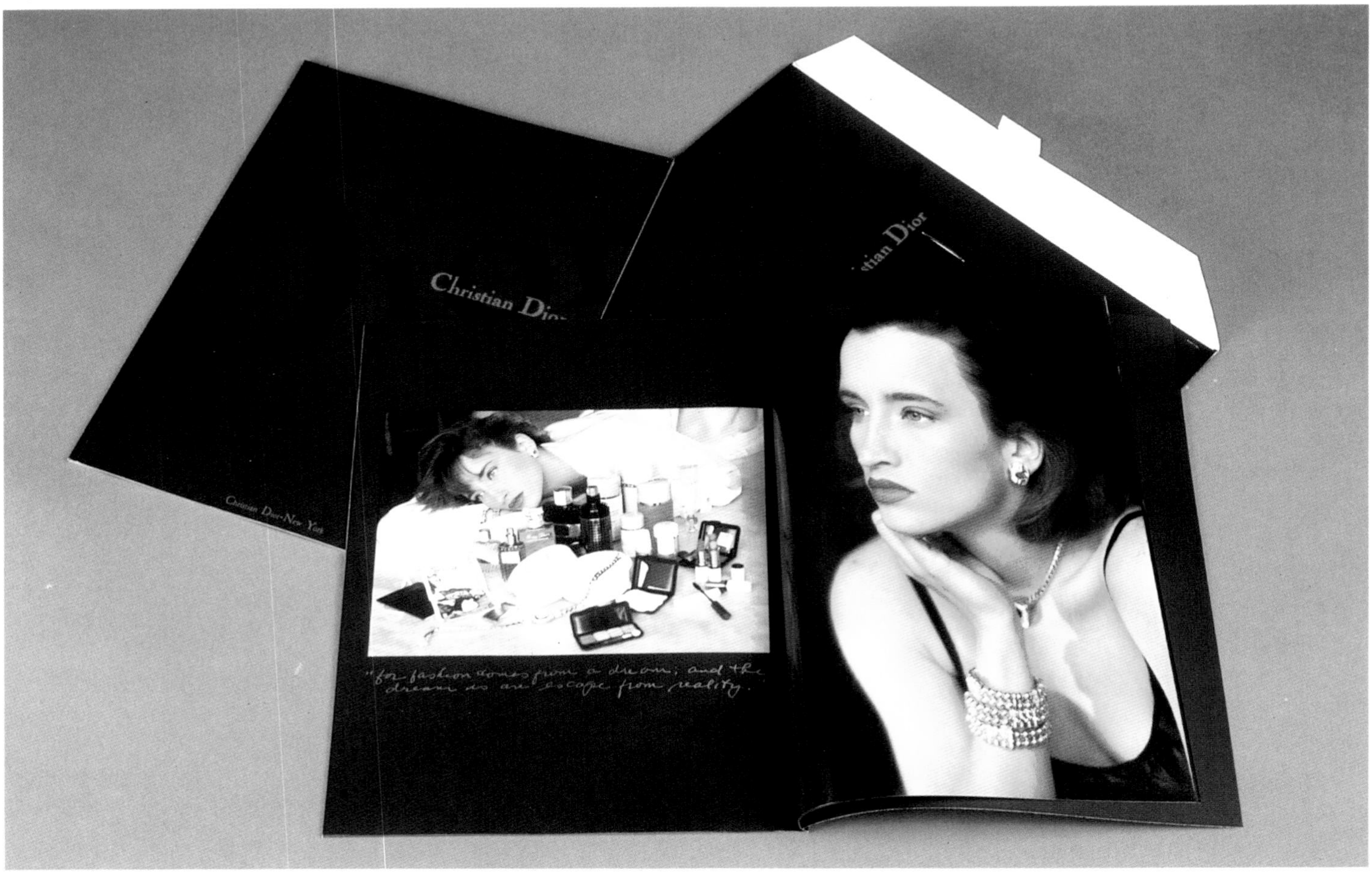

444

Collateral Sales Kits

445
ART DIRECTOR
Sherry Pollack
WRITER
Steve Ulin
DESIGNERS
Sherry Pollack
Beth Jeffe
PHOTOGRAPHERS
Jeffrey Zwart
Gerald Heurta
CLIENT
BMW Of North America
AGENCY
Ammirati & Puris

446
ART DIRECTOR
Peter Rauch
WRITER
Lesley Stern
DESIGNERS
Peter Rauch
Sandi Markman
ARTIST
R & V Studio
CLIENT
BMW Of North America
AGENCY
Ammirati & Puris

447
ART DIRECTORS
Georgene Sainati
Gordon Hochhalter
WRITER
Gordon Hochhalter
DESIGNER
Georgene Sainati
PHOTOGRAPHER
Gerry Dunn
CLIENT
Donnelley Sunday Magazine Printing
AGENCY
R. R. Donnelley & Sons/ Chicago

448
ART DIRECTOR
Frank Schulwolf
WRITER
Arthur Low
CLIENT
Aviation Sales Company
AGENCY
Susan Gilbert & Company/ Coral Gables, FL

445

446

447

448

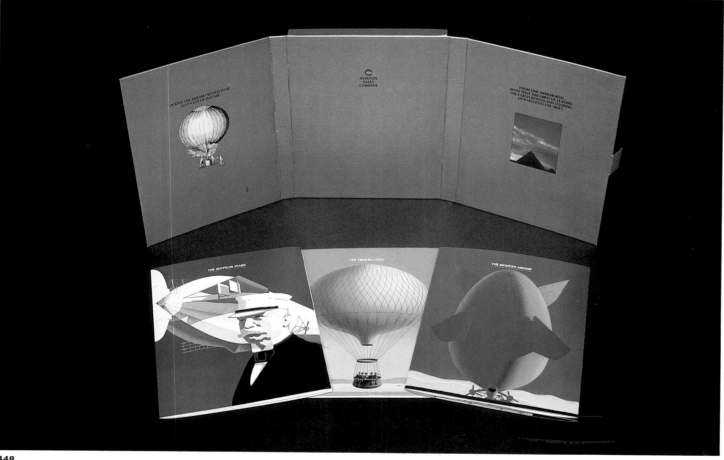

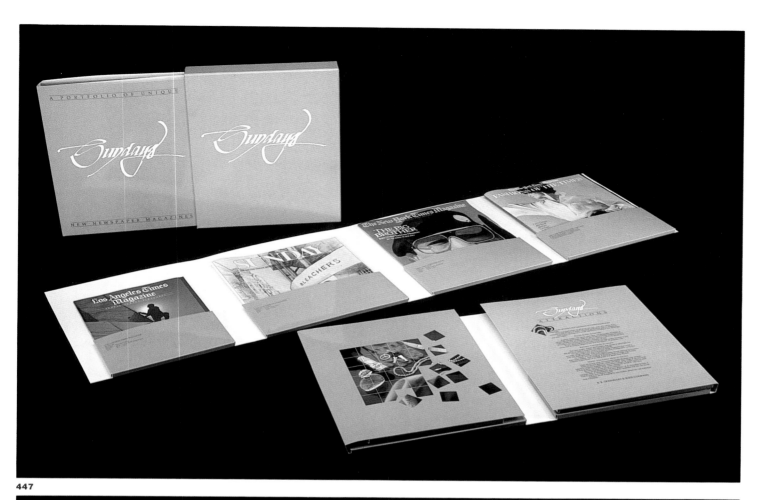

Collateral Direct Mail

449
ART DIRECTOR
Gary Goldsmith
WRITER
Steve Landsberg
DESIGNER
Gary Goldsmith
CLIENT
NYNEX Information Resources
AGENCY
Chiat/Day

450
ART DIRECTOR
Cabell Harris
WRITER
Mike Hughes
CLIENT
Richmond Ad Club
AGENCY
The Martin Agency/ Richmond, VA

451
ART DIRECTOR
Cynthia Coon-Laidlaw
WRITER
Charles Harding
DESIGNER
Cynthia Coon-Laidlaw
PHOTOGRAPHERS
Jeffrey Rotman
Jonathan Dempsey-Hart
Kurt Stier
Bruno Joachim
Ross Chapple
Jim Thomas
Martin Paul
ARTISTS
Radio Mayonnaise Productions
Ken Condon
Richard Goldberg
Mark Fisher
Ed Parker
CLIENT
Advertising Club of Greater Boston
AGENCY
Marvin & Leonard/Boston

452
ART DIRECTORS
Nancy Rice
Nick Rice
WRITER
Nancy Rice
DESIGNERS
Nancy Rice
Nick Rice
PHOTOGRAPHER
Jim Marvy
Marvy! Advertising Photography
CLIENT
Rice & Rice
AGENCY
Rice & Rice/Minneapolis

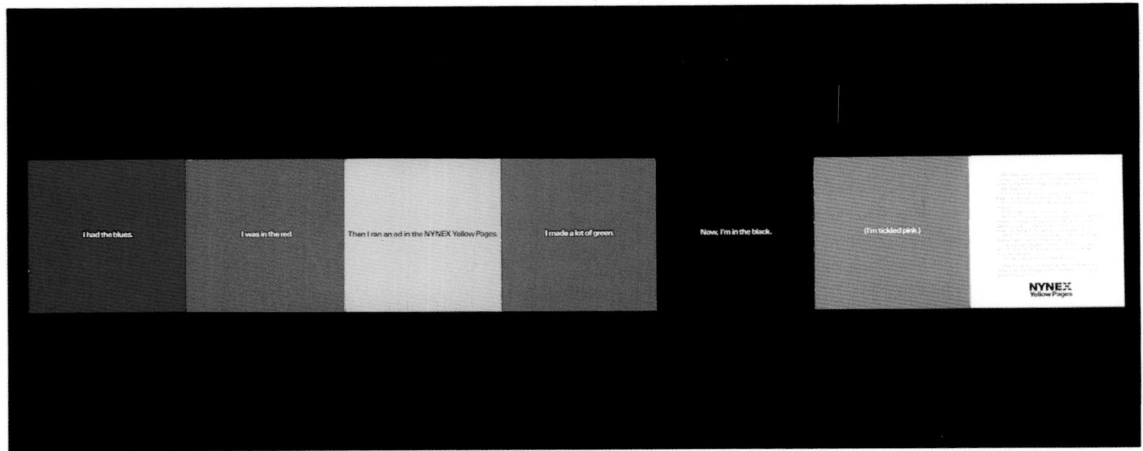

449

450

NOVEMBER

ARROW
DRESS
COLLARS
& SHIRTS

1 SAT
2 SUN
3 MON
4 TUE Election Day
5 WED
6 THURS
7 FRI
8 SAT
9 SUN
10 MON
11 TUE Veterans Day
12 WED
13 THURS
14 FRI
15 SAT
16 SUN
17 MON
18 TUE
19 WED
20 THURS
21 FRI
22 SAT
23 SUN
24 MON
25 TUE
26 WED
27 THURS Thanksgiving Day
28 FRI
29 SAT
30 SUN

451

After two children
and seventeen years of living together,
we decided to make it official.

Nick and Nancy Rice are proud to announce
that they are now joined together in business, as well as pleasure.
Send your congratulations and your business to: Rice & Rice
3425 46th Avenue South, Minneapolis, Minnesota 55406 or call (612) 729-9435.
RICE
RICE

452

Collateral
Direct Mail

453
ART DIRECTOR
Joseph Ceneda
WRITER
Kal Dreisziger
PHOTOGRAPHER
Ray Boudreau
CLIENT
Medcom
AGENCY
Medcom/Toronto

Collateral
P.O.P.

454
ART DIRECTOR
Rob Dalton
WRITER
Lyle Wedmeyer
PHOTOGRAPHER
Rick Dublin
CLIENT
NWNL
AGENCY
Martin/Williams -Minneapolis

455
ART DIRECTOR
Tom Lichtenheld
WRITER
Jarl Olsen
DESIGNER
Tom Lichtenheld
PHOTOGRAPHER
Mona Davis
CLIENT
WFLD-TV
AGENCY
Fallon McElligott/Minneapolis

456
ART DIRECTORS
Bryan McPeak
Amy Swita
WRITERS
Craig Piechura
Dave Stoll
Dave Michalak
CLIENT
Hickory Farms
AGENCY
W. B. Doner & Company/
Michigan

457
ART DIRECTORS
Peter Rauch
Jeff Vogt
WRITER
Lesley Stern
DESIGNER
Peter Rauch
PHOTOGRAPHER
Jeffrey Zwart
CLIENT
BMW of North America
AGENCY
Ammirati & Puris

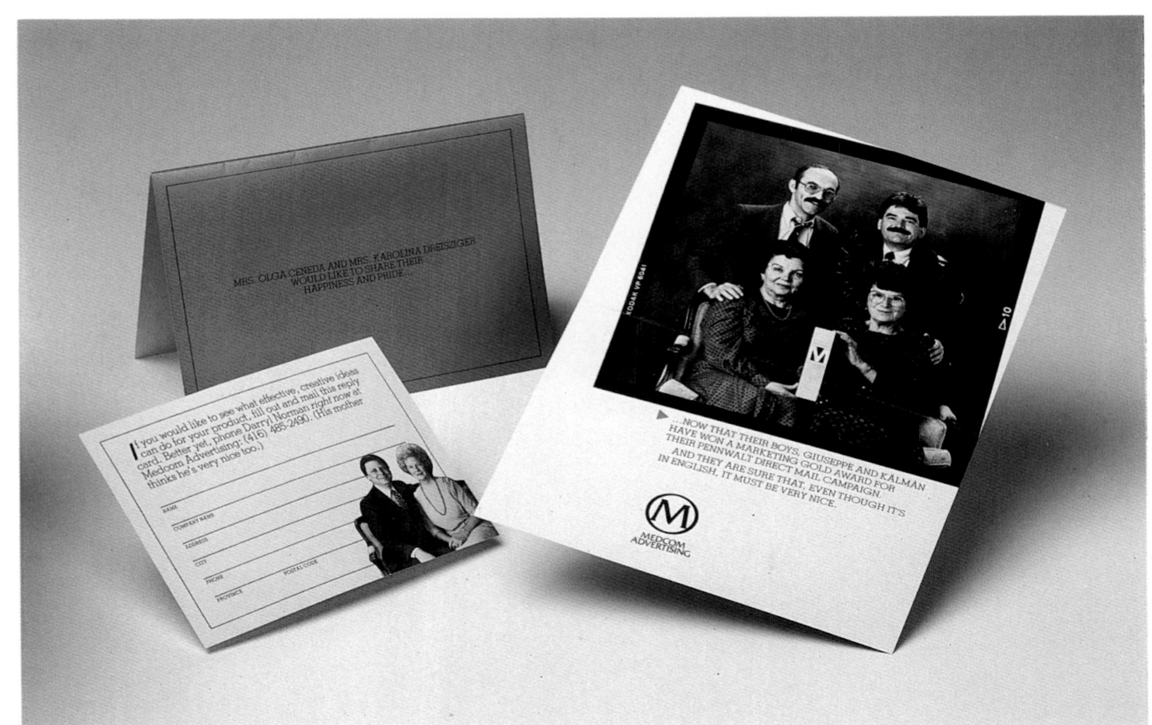

453

We'll Reward You For Wearing A Belt.

And Not Taking One.

Now, in addition to saving lives, careful driving can save you money.
Ask your employer for details on our safe-driver insurance.
NWNL GENERAL

454

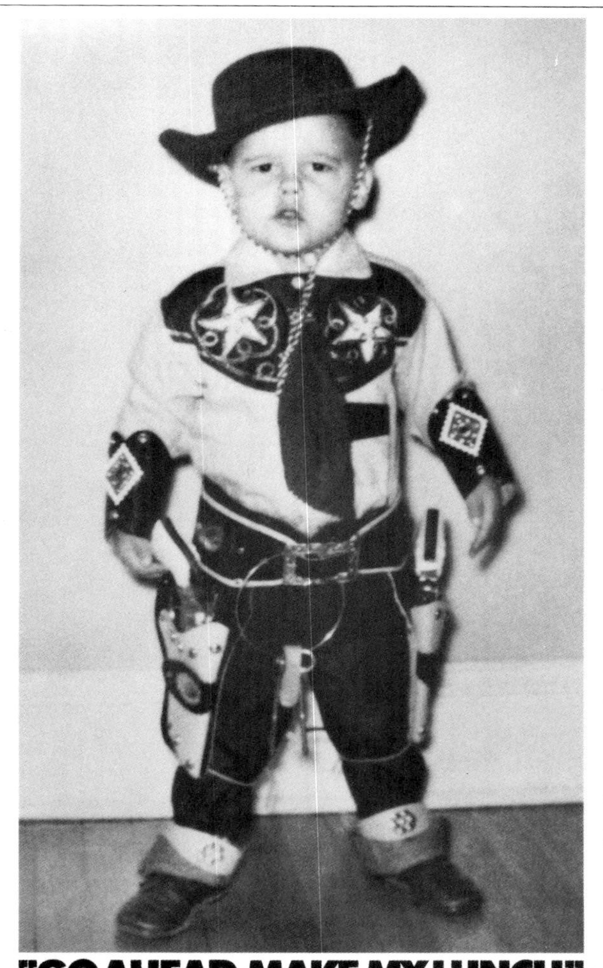

"GO AHEAD, MAKE MY LUNCH."
See the young Clint Eastwood in "For a Few Dollars More" Monday, November 11 at 7 pm.
32
WFLD TV

455

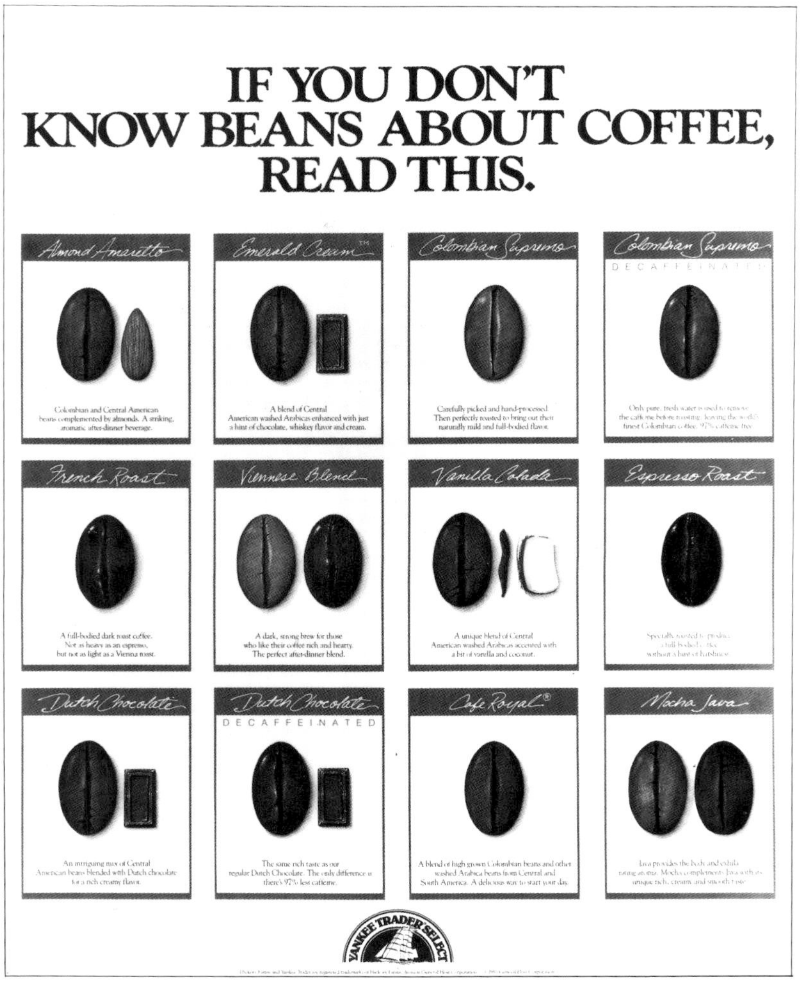

IF YOU DON'T KNOW BEANS ABOUT COFFEE, READ THIS.
Almond Amaretto
Colombian and Central American beans complemented by almonds. A striking, aromatic after-dinner beverage.
Emerald Cream™
A blend of Central American washed Arabicas enhanced with just a hint of chocolate, whiskey flavor and cream.
Colombian Supremo
Carefully picked and hand-processed. Then perfectly roasted to bring out their naturally mild and full-bodied flavor.
Colombian Supremo
DECAFFEINATED
Only pure, fresh water is used to remove the caffeine before roasting, leaving the world's finest Colombian coffee. 97% caffeine free.
French Roast
A full-bodied dark roast coffee. Not as heavy as an espresso, but not as light as a Vienna roast.
Viennese Blend
A dark, strong brew for those who like their coffee rich and hearty. The perfect after-dinner blend.
Vanilla Colada
A unique blend of Central American washed Arabicas accented with a bit of vanilla and coconut.
Espresso Roast
Specially roasted to produce a full-bodied coffee without a hint of harshness.
Dutch Chocolate
An intriguing mix of Central American beans blended with Dutch chocolate for a rich creamy flavor.
Dutch Chocolate
DECAFFEINATED
The same rich taste as our regular Dutch Chocolate. The only difference is there's 97% less caffeine.
Cafe Royal®
A blend of high grown Colombian beans and other washed Arabica beans from Central and South America. A delicious way to start your day.
Mocha Java
Java provides the body and exhilarating aroma. Mocha complements Java with its unique rich, creamy and smooth taste.
YANKEE TRADER SELECT

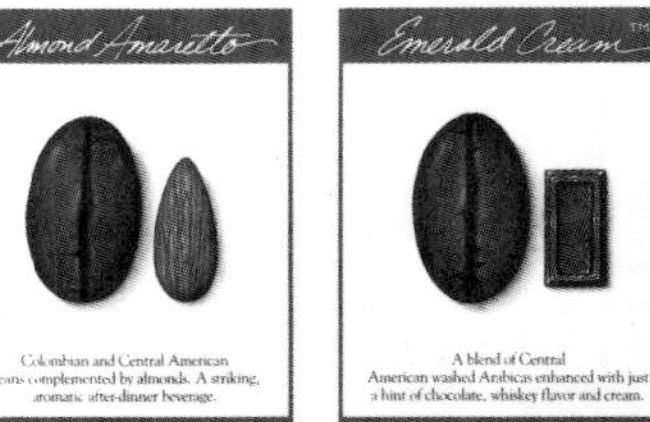

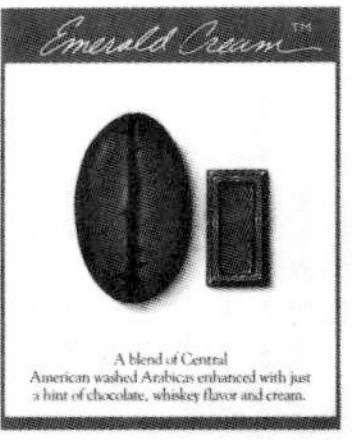

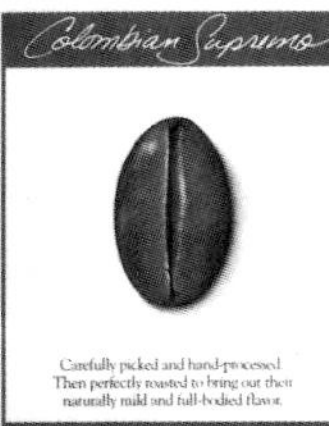

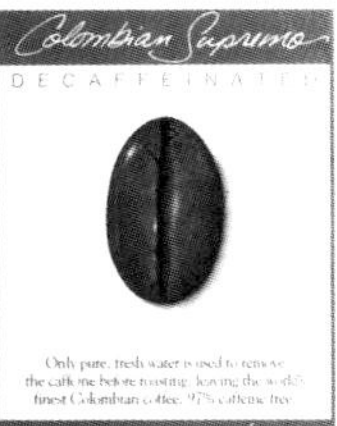

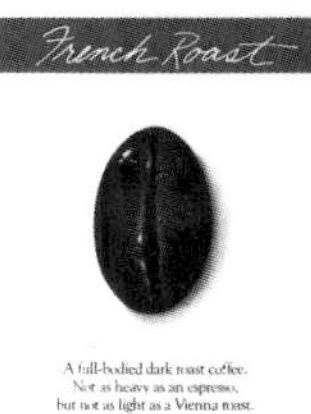

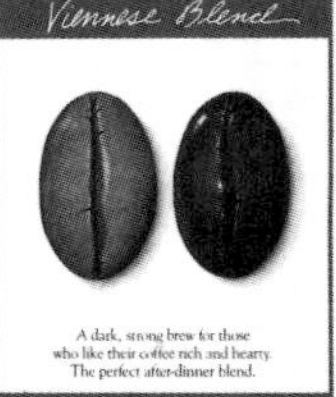

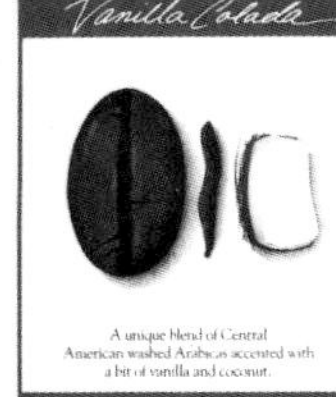

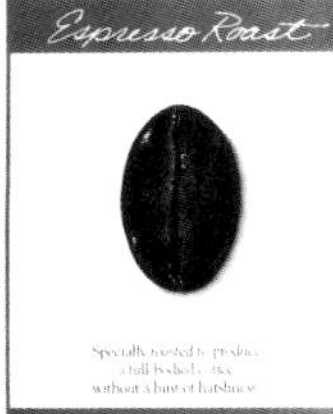

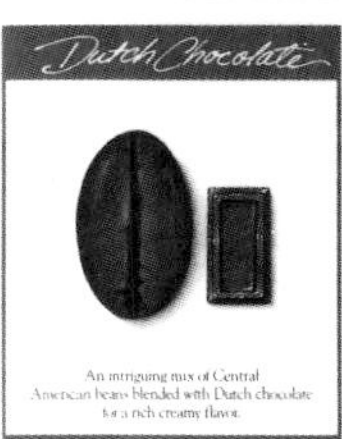

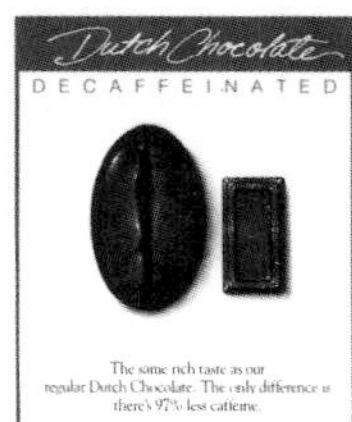

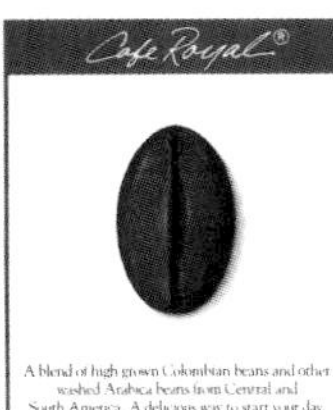

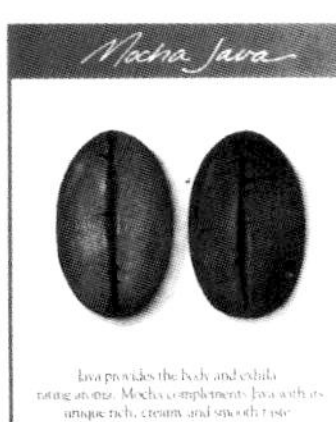

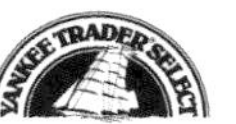

456

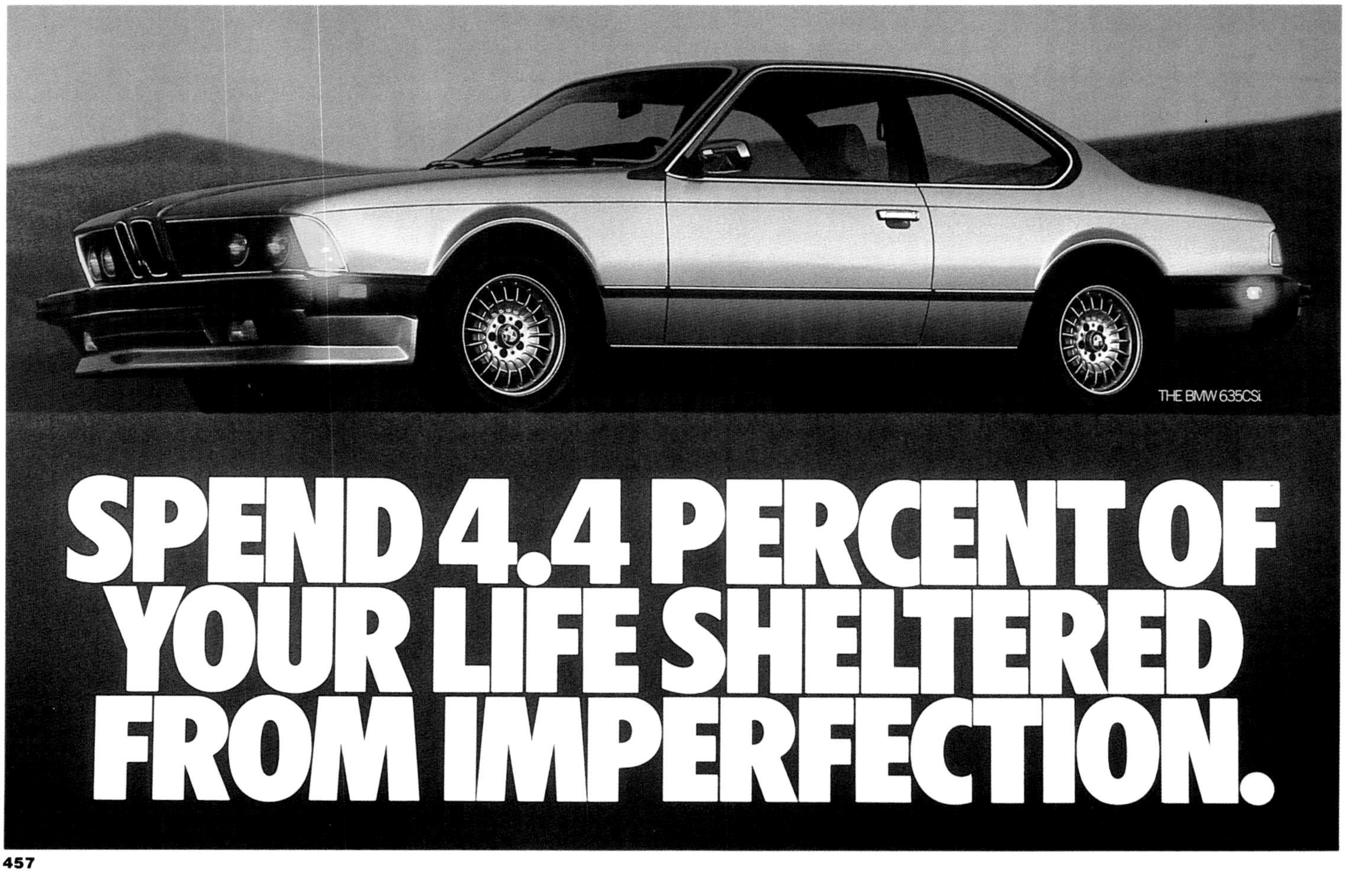

THE BMW 635CSi.
SPEND 4.4 PERCENT OF YOUR LIFE SHELTERED FROM IMPERFECTION.

457

Collateral P.O.P.

458
ART DIRECTOR
Ken Butts
WRITER
Tom Jordan
CLIENT
Milwaukee Art Museum
AGENCY
Hoffman York & Compton/ Milwaukee

459
ART DIRECTOR
Bob Barrie
WRITER
Phil Hanft
DESIGNER
Bob Barrie
ARTIST
Leland Klanderman
CLIENT
Minnesota Zoo
AGENCY
Fallon McElligott/Minneapolis

460
ART DIRECTOR
Bob Barrie
WRITER
Mike Lescarbeau
PHOTOGRAPHER
Rick Dublin
CLIENT
Minnesota North Stars
AGENCY
Fallon McElligott/Minneapolis

461
ART DIRECTOR
Bob Barrie
WRITER
Mike Lescarbeau
DESIGNER
Bob Barrie
PHOTOGRAPHER
R. Hamilton Smith
CLIENT
Minnesota Zoo
AGENCY
Fallon McElligott/Minneapolis

458

459

Our Student Prices Are Just As Easy To Swallow.

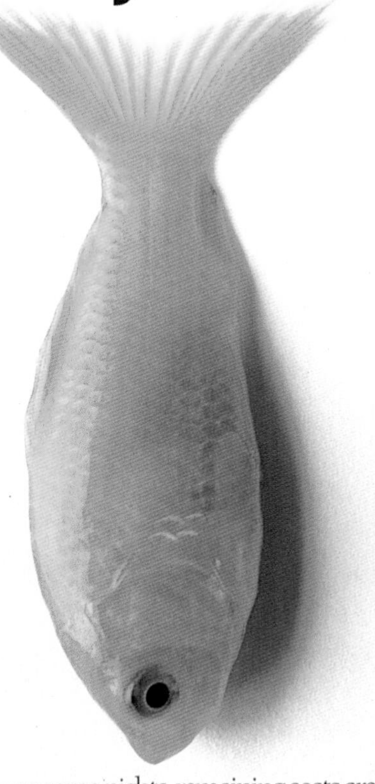

After six on game nights, remaining seats are half price for students. Call 853-9300 for ticket information.

North Stars Hockey Student Rush.

460

See how fast you can cross country ski.

10 kilometers of groomed trails open 10 to 4 daily. The Minnesota Zoo.

461

Collateral
P.O.P.

462
ART DIRECTOR
Tom Lichtenheld
WRITER
Mike Lescarbeau
PHOTOGRAPHER
Tom Berthiaume
CLIENT
Country Kitchen
AGENCY
Fallon McElligott/Minneapolis

463
ART DIRECTOR
Lyle Metzdorf
WRITER
Ron Burkhardt
DESIGNER
Lyle Metzdorf
PHOTOGRAPHER
Bill Halpern
CLIENT
Sony
AGENCY
Lowe Marschalk

464
ART DIRECTOR
Mark Crim
WRITER
Mark Crim
DESIGNER
Mark Crim
PHOTOGRAPHER
Willis/Randolph Photography
CLIENT
Justin Western Boot Company
AGENCY
Keller Crescent Company/ Irvine, TX

465
ART DIRECTOR
Dean Hanson
WRITER
Jamie Barrett
PHOTOGRAPHER
Art Simons
CLIENT
Murray's Bakery
AGENCY
Fallon McElligott/Minneapolis

Your kids don't share your taste in food, either.
TRY THE COUNTRY KITCHEN CHILDREN'S MENU. COUNTRY KITCHEN

462

463

464

WE MAKE THE SECOND BEST ROLLS IN THE WORLD.

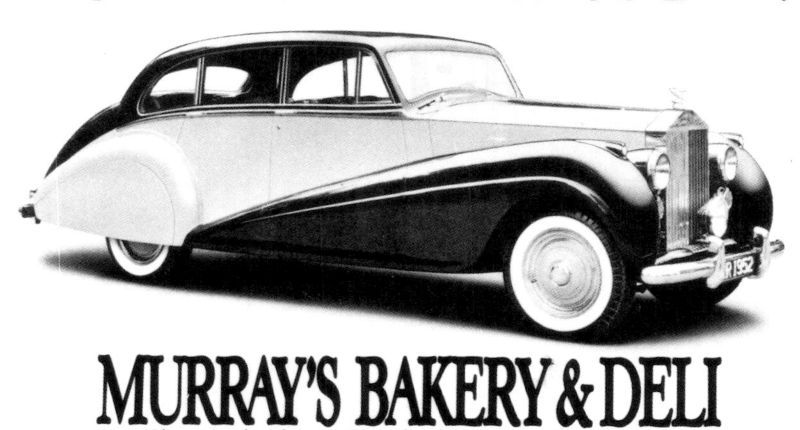

MURRAY'S BAKERY & DELI

Skyway level · 701 Fourth Avenue South · 371-9429

465

Collateral
P.O.P.

466
ART DIRECTOR
Cathi Mooney
WRITER
Ken Mandelbaum
DESIGNER
Cathi Mooney
PHOTOGRAPHER
Robert Ammirati
CLIENT
Timberland
AGENCY
Ally & Gargano

467
ART DIRECTORS
Vern Kuhn
Lynette Darling
WRITER
Michael Johnson
DESIGNERS
Vern Kuhn
Lynette Darling
PHOTOGRAPHER
Hank Young
CLIENT
Business Men's Assurance Company of America
AGENCY
Kuhn & Associates/Kansas

468
ART DIRECTOR
Bob Isherwood
WRITER
Patrick Woodward
DESIGNER
Tony Langmead
PHOTOGRAPHER
Greg Slater
CLIENT
United Permanent Building
AGENCY
The Campaign Palace/Australia

1930–THE INTRODUCTION OF THE BOAT SHOE.

1979–THE INTRODUCTION OF THE TIMBERLAND BOAT SHOE.
The classic boat shoe taken a giant step further.
More water-resistant. More comfortable. More durable.

1981–THE INTRODUCTION OF THE TIMBERLAND SUPER BOAT SHOE.
A shoe designed for world class sailors, but quickly adopted
by everyone else who wanted the best boat shoe money can buy.

1983–THE INTRODUCTION OF THE TIMBERLAND HI-TECH BOAT SHOE.
Here, we came to grips with the biggest problem confronting sailors: Water.
With a revolutionary sole design that virtually eliminated hydroplaning.

1984–THE INTRODUCTION OF THE TIMBERLAND SCUPPER.
Our latest launch: the high-performance sole of our
Hi-Tech boat shoe topped by our classic boat shoe upper.

WE'VE DONE MORE FOR THE BOAT SHOE IN THE LAST 5 YEARS THAN ANYONE ELSE HAS IN 50.

The Timberland Company, P.O. Box 7005, Portsmouth, New Hampshire 03801

*Registered trademarks of The Timberland Company

466

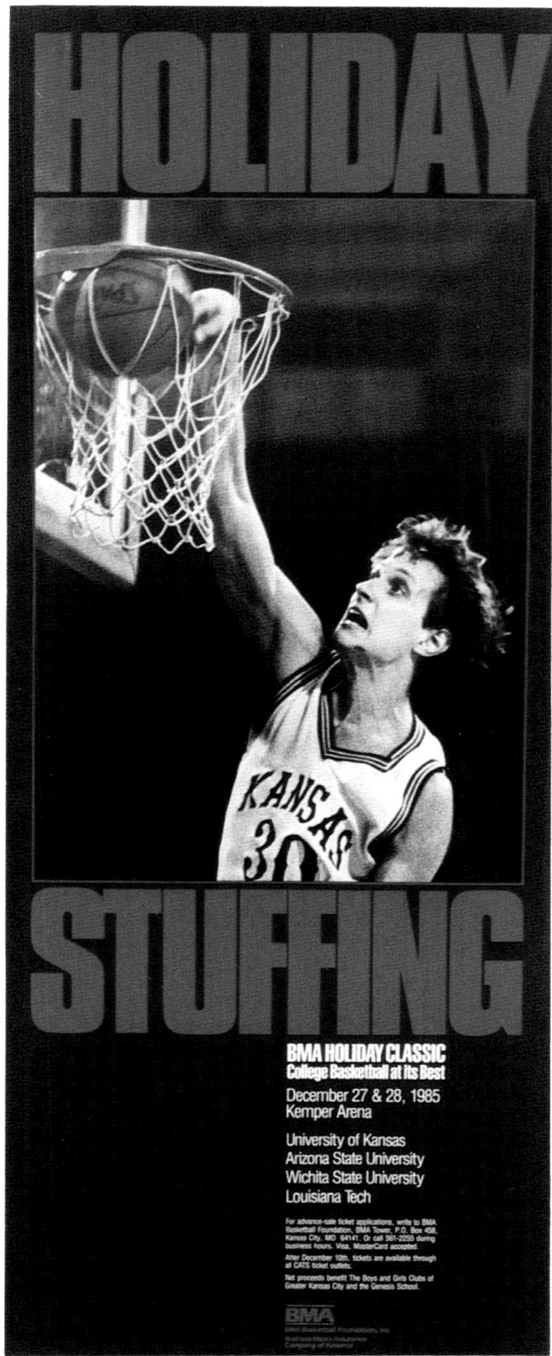
HOLIDAY
KANSAS
30
STUFFING
BMA HOLIDAY CLASSIC
College Basketball at its Best
December 27 & 28, 1985
Kemper Arena
University of Kansas
Arizona State University
Wichita State University
Louisiana Tech
For advance-sale ticket applications, write to BMA Basketball Foundation, BMA Tower, P.O. Box 458, Kansas City, MO 64141. Or call 561-2255 during business hours. Visa, MasterCard accepted.
After December 10th, tickets are available through all CATS ticket outlets.
Net proceeds benefit The Boys and Girls Clubs of Greater Kansas City and the Genesis School.
BMA

467

WHY LOOK FOR
A HOME WITHOUT
KNOWING IF YOU
CAN AFFORD IT?
ASK ABOUT OUR PRE-APPROVED LOANS.

468

Collateral
P.O.P.

469
ART DIRECTOR
Ivan Horvath
WRITERS
Bob Ancona
Ivan Horvath
Mike Kerley
PHOTOGRAPHER
Mike Chesser
CLIENT
Yamaha Motor Corporation, USA
AGENCY
NW Ayer/Los Angeles

470
ART DIRECTOR
Rob Tomnay
WRITER
Jack Vaughan
DESIGNER
Tony Langmead
PHOTOGRAPHER
Detlef Trefz
CLIENT
Australian Meat & Livestock Corporation
AGENCY
The Campaign Palace/ Australia

471
ART DIRECTOR
Michael Fazende
WRITER
Jarl Olsen
PHOTOGRAPHER
Rick Dublin
CLIENT
WFLD-TV
AGENCY
Fallon McElligott/Minneapolis

472
ART DIRECTOR
John Scott MacDaniels
WRITER
John Scott MacDaniels
PHOTOGRAPHER
Harvey Lloyd
CLIENT
Royal Viking Line
AGENCY
Lowe Marschalk/San Francisco

Create. Explore. Dazzle.
Touch. Allure. Muse. Emote.
Dream. Excite. Reminisce.
Enchant. Arouse. Improvise.
Search. Revel. Evoke. Coax.
Beguile. Amaze. Embellish.
Reflect. Imagine. Enthrall.
Enlighten. Soothe. Surprise.
Provoke. Charm. Innovate.
Impress. Accompany. Swing.
Inspire. Express. Discover.
And play.

YAMAHA

469

Invest in Australia's mineral resources.

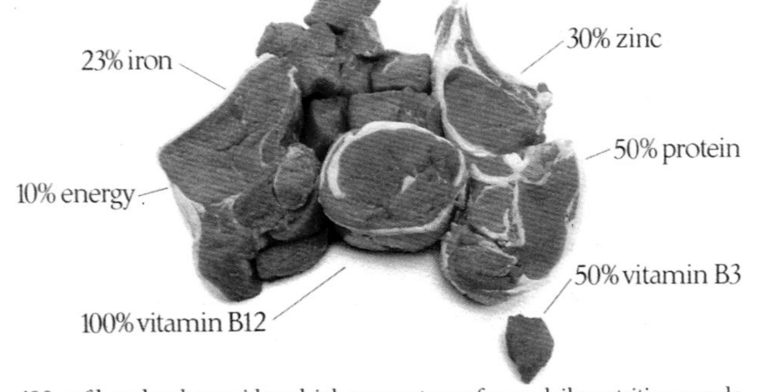

100g of lean lamb provides a high percentage of your daily nutrition needs.

470

GET WRAPPED UP
IN A GOOD MOVIE.
The 32 Movie Club sees the best in film classics every Saturday night at eight on WFLD Metromedia 32. Members can also see their favorite new movies through special ticket offers and discounts from M&R Theaters. Join now and get a chance to vote on upcoming Movie Club features. Send a self-addressed, stamped envelope to 32 Movie Club, P.O. Box 3200, Chicago, IL 60654.
THE 32 MOVIE CLUB

471

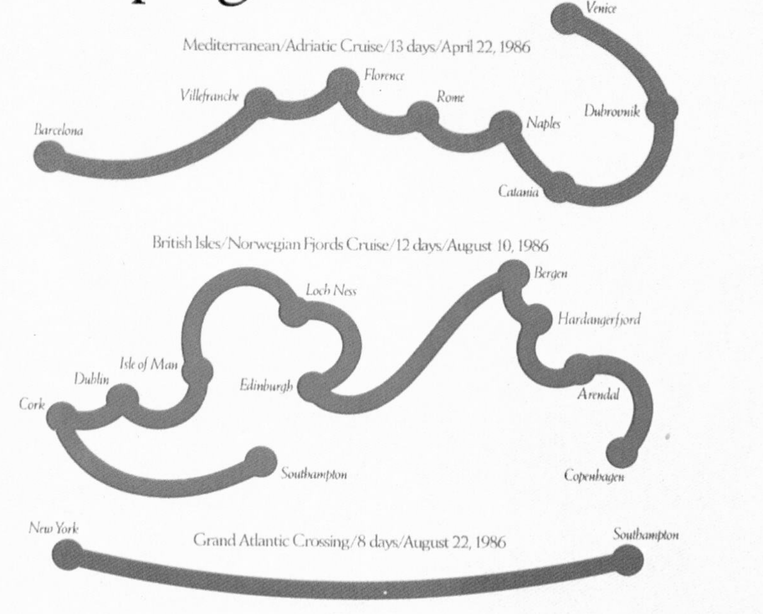
Neiman-Marcus & Royal Viking
announce
their exciting, new
Spring & Summer lines:
Mediterranean/Adriatic Cruise/13 days/April 22, 1986
Venice
Barcelona
Villefranche
Florence
Rome
Naples
Dubrovnik
Catania
British Isles/Norwegian Fjords Cruise/12 days/August 10, 1986
Bergen
Loch Ness
Hardangerfjord
Isle of Man
Dublin
Edinburgh
Arendal
Cork
Southampton
Copenhagen
New York
Grand Atlantic Crossing/8 days/August 22, 1986
Southampton

472

Collateral
P.O.P.

473
ART DIRECTOR
Tom Kelly
WRITER
Bill Borders
PHOTOGRAPHER
Jerry LaRocca
CLIENT
Blitz-Weinhard Brewing
AGENCY
Borders Perrin & Norrander/
Portland, OR

474
ART DIRECTOR
Jim Fitts
WRITER
Jon Goward
CLIENT
Eastpak
AGENCY
ClarkeGowardFitts/Boston

475
ART DIRECTOR
Mike Arola
WRITERS
Mike Arola
Carolyn Johnson
PHOTOGRAPHER
Bob Grigg
CLIENT
Pirelli Tire Corporation
AGENCY
Cochrane Chase Livingston &
Company/Newport Beach,
CA

476
ART DIRECTOR
Tom Kelly
WRITER
Bill Borders
DESIGNER
Tom Kelly
ARTIST
Michael Bull
CLIENT
Pendleton Menswear
AGENCY
Borders Perrin & Norrander/
Portland, OR

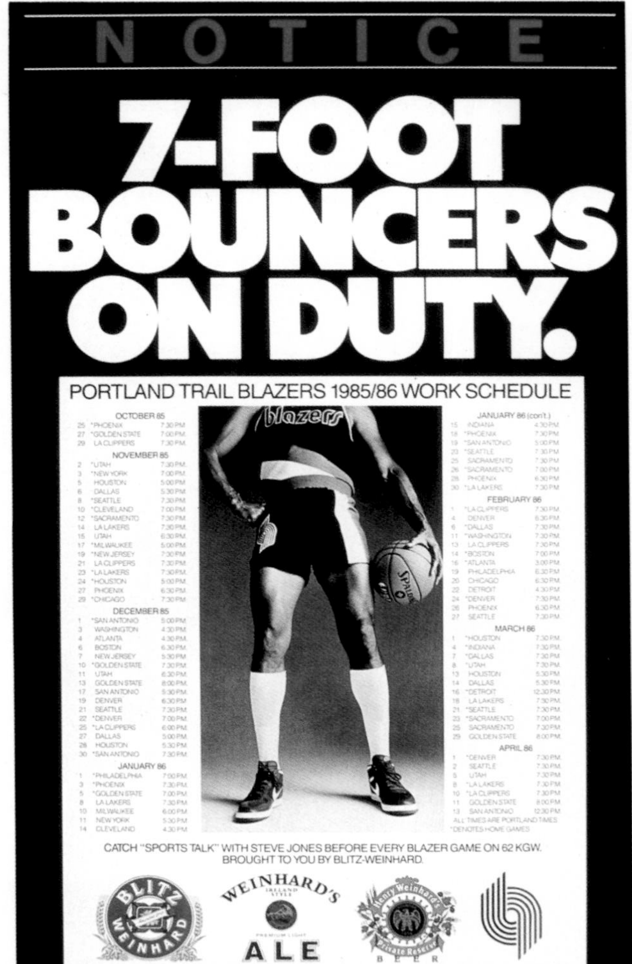

473

474

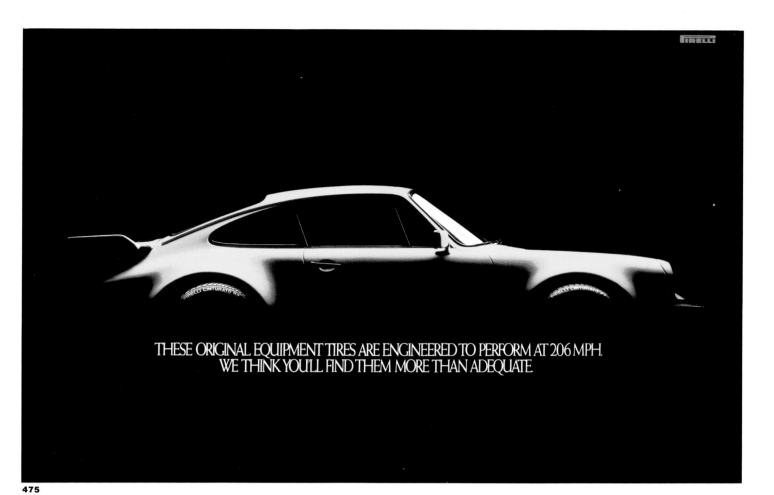

PIRELLI

THESE ORIGINAL EQUIPMENT TIRES ARE ENGINEERED TO PERFORM AT 206 MPH.
WE THINK YOU'LL FIND THEM MORE THAN ADEQUATE.

475

MADE ENTIRELY IN AMERICA

YELLOWSTONE/RAINIER

UMATILLA • FABRIC

476

Collateral P.O.P.

477
ART DIRECTOR
Mark Ashley
WRITERS
Pat Mundy
Ken Lewis
CLIENT
J. Walter Thompson
AGENCY
J. Walter Thompson/Atlanta

478
ART DIRECTOR
Diane Cook Tench
WRITER
Luke Sullivan
DESIGNER
Diane Cook Tench
ARTIST
Bill Mayer
CLIENT
FMC
AGENCY
The Martin Agency/
Richmond, VA

Outdoor: Single

479
ART DIRECTORS
Geoff Hayes
Michel Roux
WRITER
Evert Cilliers
DESIGNER
Geoff Hayes
ARTIST
Andy Warhol
CLIENT
Carillon Importers
AGENCY
TBWA

480
ART DIRECTOR
Bob Dion
WRITER
Larry Sokolove
DESIGNER
Bob Dion
CLIENT
Plank Road Original Draught
AGENCY
Chiat/Day

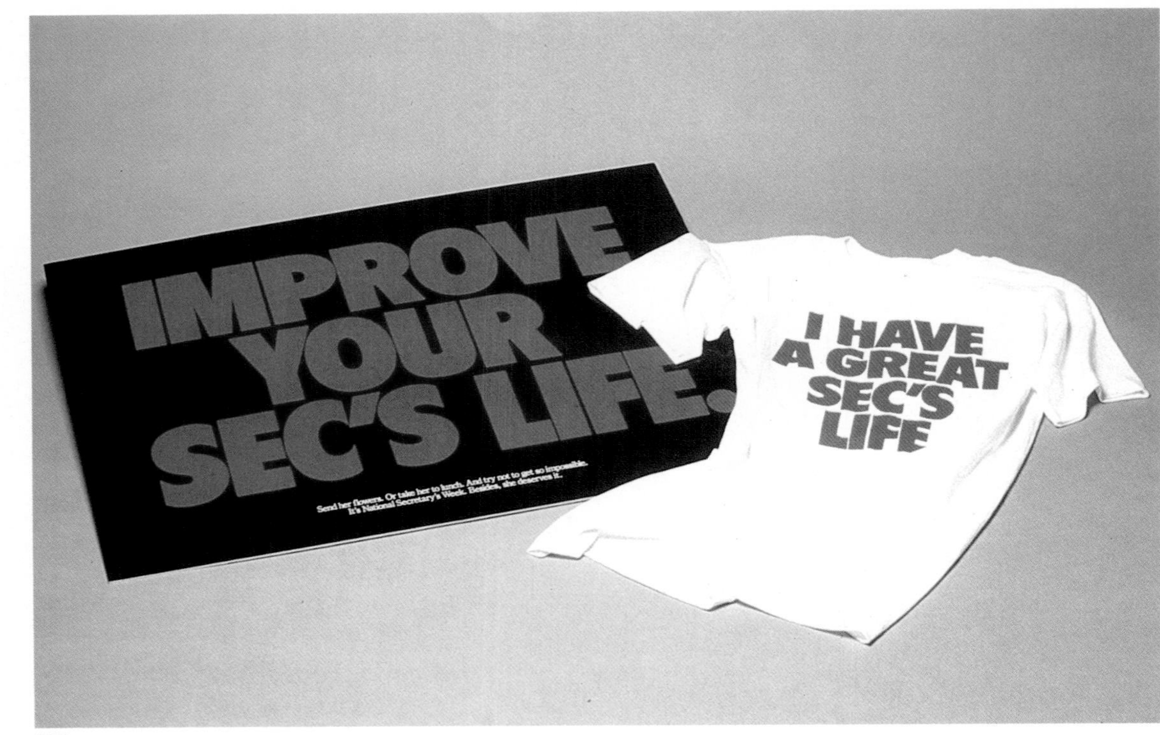

477

"I WISH I'D EATEN THE TREE THESE BROCHURES WERE MADE FROM."

DRAGNET® TC
Take a free brochure on Dragnet® TC: the less toxic alternative to effective termite control.

478

ABSOLUT WARHOL.

FOR GIFT DELIVERY ANYWHERE CALL 1-800-CHEER-UP (EXCEPT WHERE PROHIBITED BY LAW)
80 AND 100 PROOF/100% GRAIN NEUTRAL SPIRITS (ABSOLUT COUNTRY OF SWEDEN™) © 1985 CARILLON IMPORTERS LTD., TEANECK, N.J.

479

PLANK ROAD. KEG BEER IN A BOTTLE.

© 1985 Miller Brewing Co. Milwaukee, Wisconsin

480

Outdoor: Single

481
ART DIRECTOR
Bridgit Cody
WRITER
Jill Easton
DESIGNER
Bridgit Cody
ARTISTS
Darryl Milsap
Ron Van Buskirk
CLIENT
San Diego Zoo
AGENCY
Phillips-Ramsey/San Diego

482
ART DIRECTOR
Rob Dalton
WRITER
Mike Lescarbeau
DESIGNER
Rob Dalton
PHOTOGRAPHER
Kent Severson
CLIENT
Continental Bank
AGENCY
Fallon McElligott/Minneapolis

483
ART DIRECTOR
Bob Kwait
DESIGNER
Bob Kwait
ARTIST
Ron Van Buskirk
PHOTOGRAPHER
Ron Garrison
CLIENT
San Diego Zoo
AGENCY
Phillips-Ramsey/San Diego

484
ART DIRECTOR
Richard Crispo
WRITER
Mark Monteiro
PHOTOGRAPHER
Jeff Nadler
CLIENT
Yamaha Motor Corporation, USA
AGENCY
Chiat/Day - Los Angeles

485
ART DIRECTOR
Bob Kwait
WRITER
Bob Kwait
DESIGNER
Bob Kwait
ARTIST
Ron Van Buskirk
PHOTOGRAPHER
Ron Garrison
CLIENT
San Diego Zoo
AGENCY
Phillips-Ramsey/San Diego

COME UP AND SEE ME SOMETIME.
The San Diego WILD ANIMAL PARK

481

Treat every customer like a number.

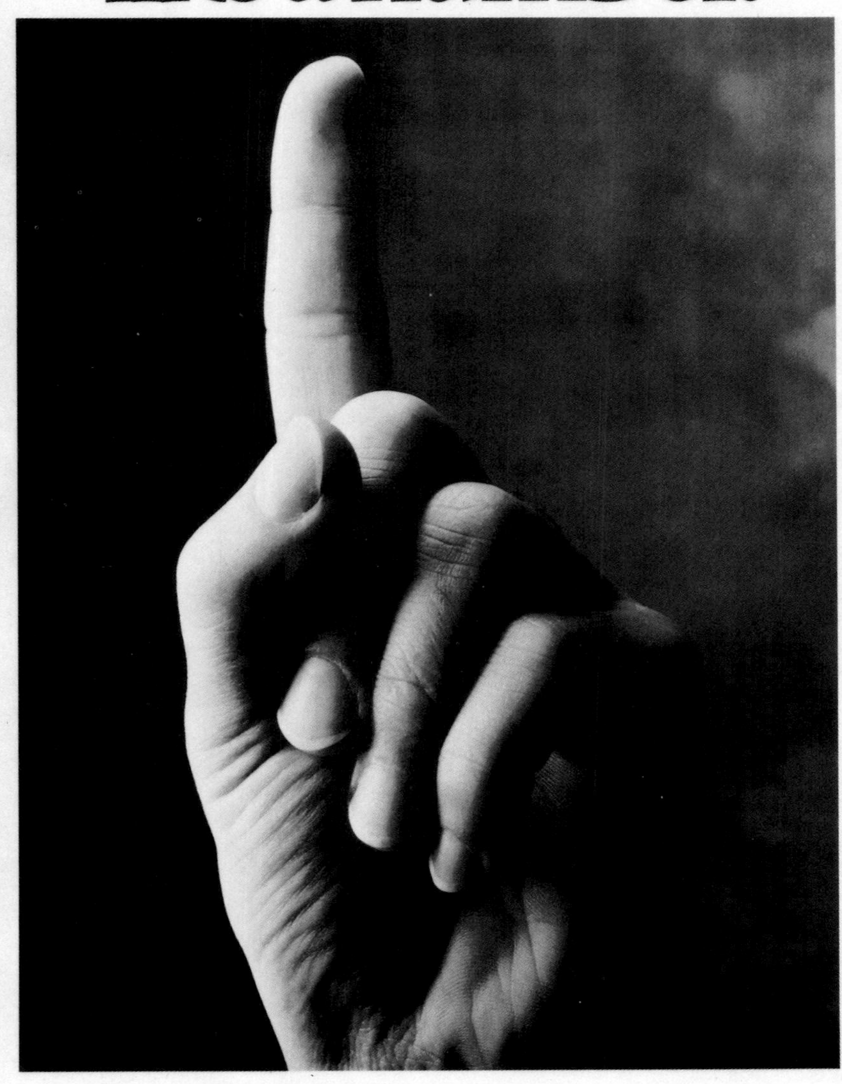

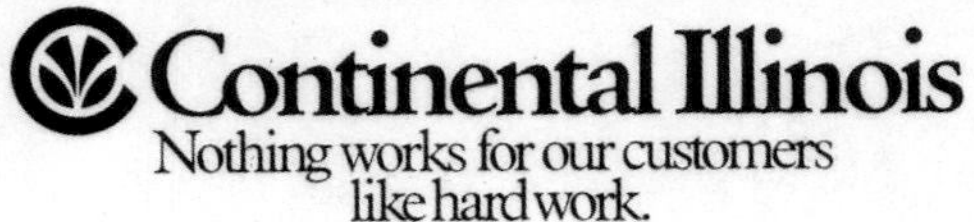
Continental Illinois
Nothing works for our customers like hard work.

482

A rare tweet.

The San Diego Zoo

483

It's a vicious cycle.
YAMAHA

484

Make my day.

Visit the San Diego Zoo.

485

Outdoor: Single

486
ART DIRECTOR
Bob Barrie
WRITER
Phil Hanft
DESIGNER
Bob Barrie
PHOTOGRAPHER
Tom Cajacob
CLIENT
Minnesota Zoo
AGENCY
Fallon McElligott/Minneapolis

487
ART DIRECTOR
Dean Hanson
WRITER
Jamie Barrett
CLIENT
Tan Me Suntanning
AGENCY
Fallon McElligott/Minneapolis

488
ART DIRECTOR
Dean Hanson
WRITER
Jamie Barrett
CLIENT
Tan Me Suntanning
AGENCY
Fallon McElligott/Minneapolis

489
ART DIRECTOR
Elvin Letchford
WRITER
Alan Smith
DESIGNER
Elvin Letchford
PHOTOGRAPHER
Terry Collier
CLIENT
IBM Canada
AGENCY
Enterprise/Toronto

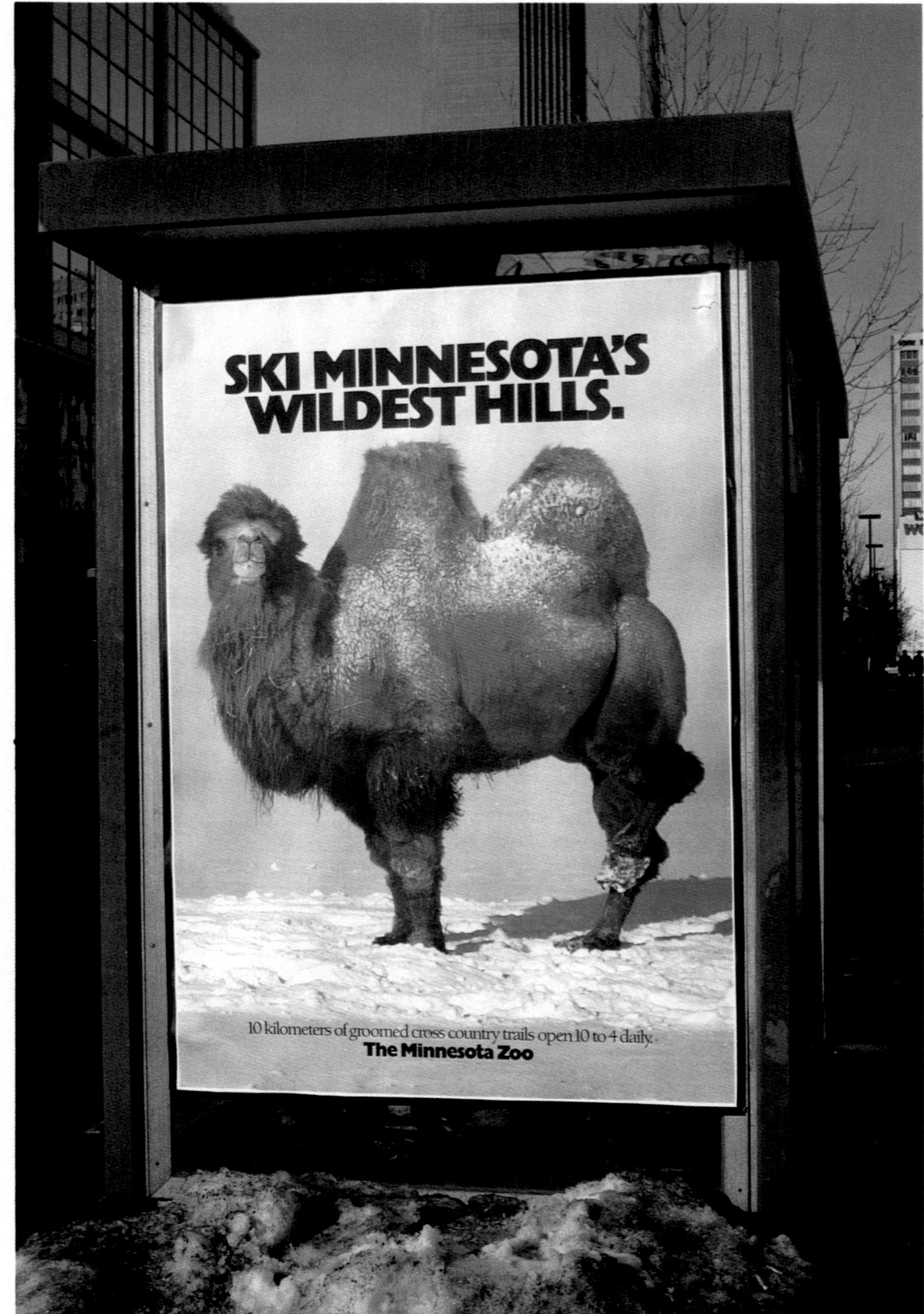

486

WINTER IS
WHITE ENOUGH.
Tan Me Suntanning

487

MAKE THIS WINTER A SHADE BETTER THAN LAST WINTER.

Tan Me Suntanning

488

There are still some writing instruments quieter than the new IBM Quietwriter 7.

AT AUTHORIZED IBM TYPEWRITER OUTLETS OR CALL 112-800-387-6100

489

Outdoor: Single

490
ART DIRECTOR
Bob Barrie
WRITER
Jarl Olsen
DESIGNER
Bob Barrie
CLIENT
KRLD-TV
AGENCY
Fallon McElligott/Minneapolis

491
ART DIRECTOR
Dean Hanson
WRITER
Jamie Barrett
CLIENT
Tan Me Suntanning
AGENCY
Fallon McElligott/Minneapolis

492
ART DIRECTOR
Brian Fandetti
WRITER
Steve Bautista
DESIGNER
Brian Fandetti
ARTISTS
Peter Hall
Jeff Randall
CLIENT
East Providence Cycle Company
AGENCY
Lunchtime Commerce/ Massachusetts

493
ART DIRECTOR
Bob Barrie
WRITER
Phil Hanft
DESIGNER
Bob Barrie
ARTIST
Leland Klanderman
CLIENT
Minnesota Zoo
AGENCY
Fallon McElligott/Minneapolis

WIMBLEDON IT AIN'T.

"Battle of The Belts." Championship wrestling live from the Sundome. Monday, September 2 at 8 pm.

490

OTHER TANNING SALONS PALE BY COMPARISON.

Tan Me Suntanning

491

Not a bad seat in the house.
Schwinn, Serotta, Cannondale, Lotus.
East Providence Cycle Co.
414 Warren Avenue, East Providence, RI

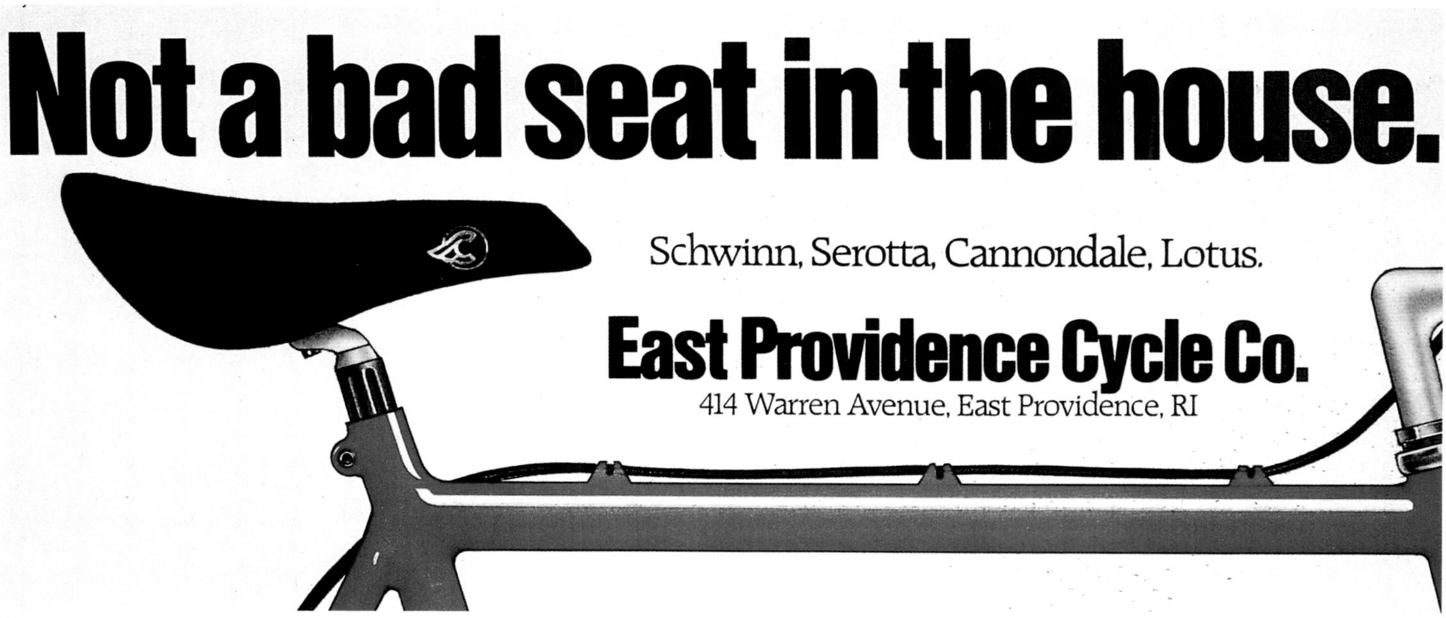

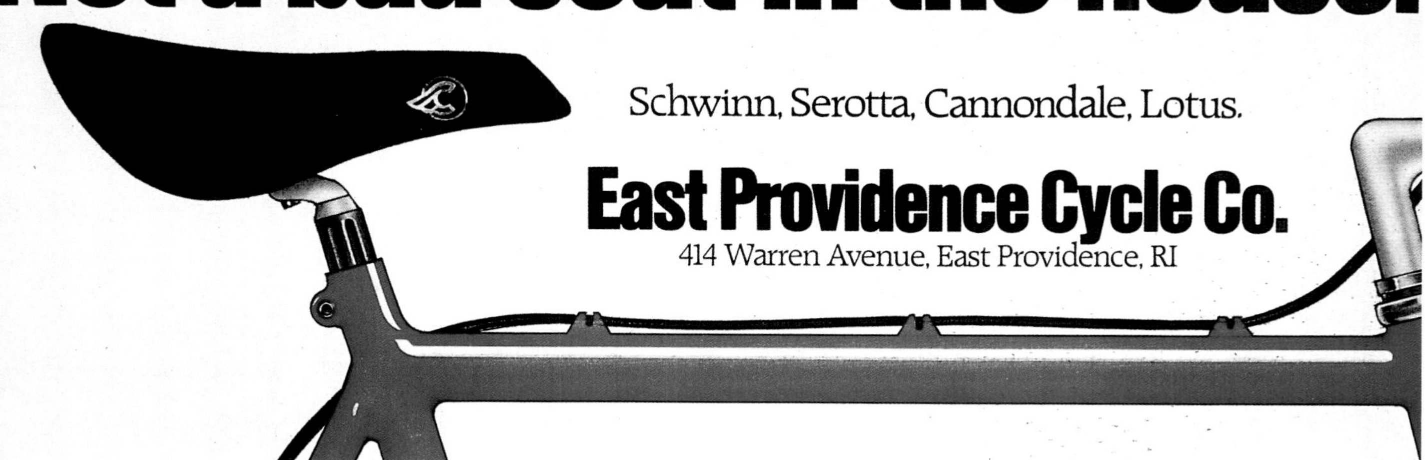

492

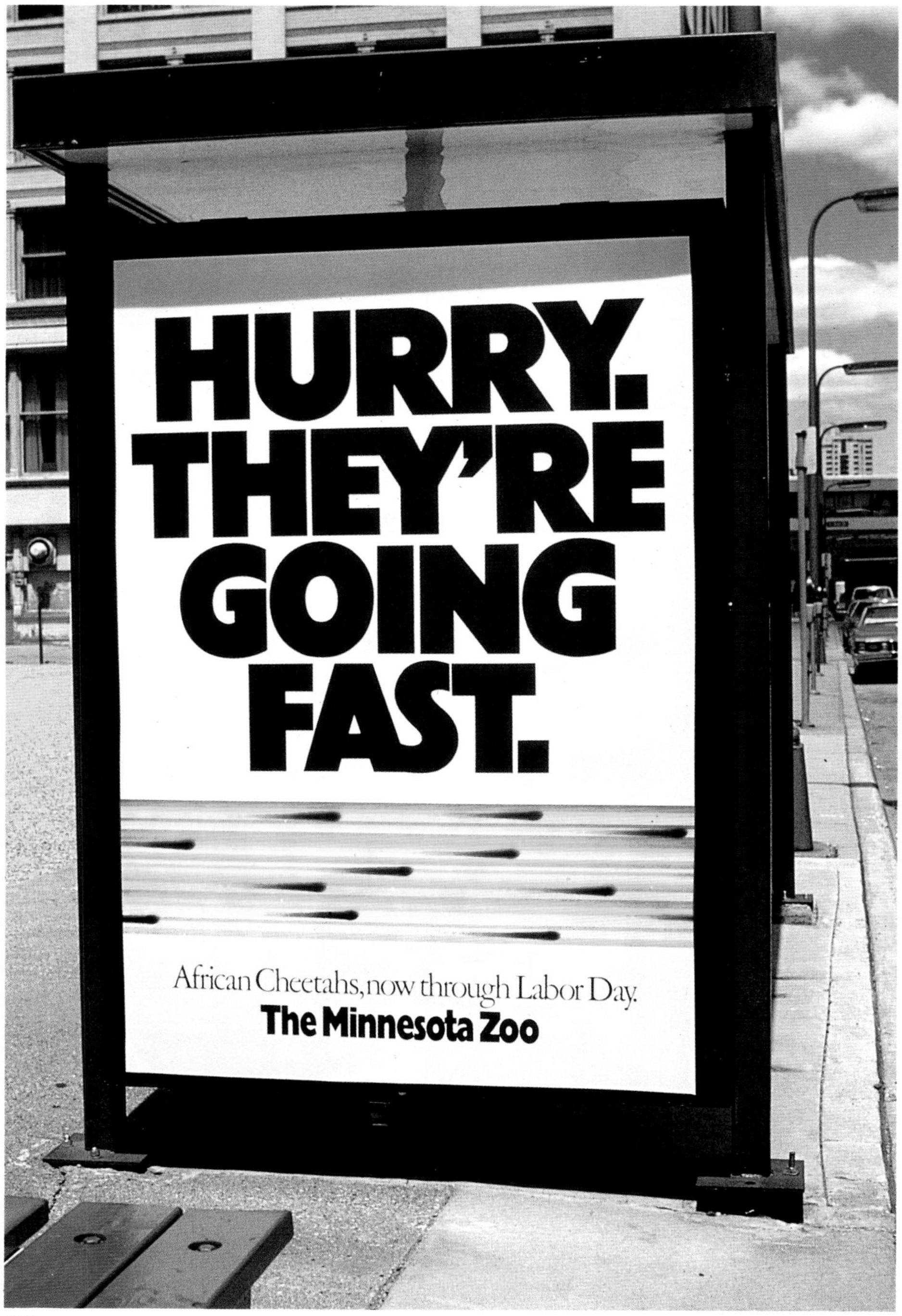

HURRY.
THEY'RE
GOING
FAST.
African Cheetahs, now through Labor Day.
The Minnesota Zoo

493

Outdoor: Single

494
ART DIRECTOR
Tom Lichtenheld
WRITER
Sam Avery
CLIENT
MedCenters Health Plan
AGENCY
Fallon McElligott/Minneapolis

495
ART DIRECTOR
Steve Eltringham
WRITER
Paul Ridley
PHOTOGRAPHER
Jeff Senior
CLIENT
Volkswagen
AGENCY
Doyle Dane Bernbach/London

496
ART DIRECTOR
Bob Barrie
WRITER
Mike Lescarbeau
DESIGNER
Bob Barrie
CLIENT
Rick Dublin Photography
AGENCY
Fallon McElligott/Minneapolis

497
ART DIRECTOR
Bob Barrie
WRITER
Rod Kilpatrick
DESIGNER
Bob Barrie
CLIENT
Musicland
AGENCY
Fallon McElligott/Minneapolis

494

495

Headlines this dull need pictures.

Dublin Advertising Photography
phone (612) 332-8864

496

An entire nation is eating up the profits.

A public service message from
musicland

497

Outdoor: Single

498
ART DIRECTOR
Bob Barrie
WRITER
Mike Lescarbeau
DESIGNER
Bob Barrie
PHOTOGRAPHER
Rick Dublin
CLIENT
Minnesota North Stars
AGENCY
Fallon McElligott/Minneapolis

499
ART DIRECTOR
Nick Alcock
WRITER
Dave Tutin
PHOTOGRAPHER
Gary Bryan
CLIENT
Alka Seltzer
AGENCY
McCann-Erickson/London

500
ART DIRECTOR
Bob Barrie
WRITER
Rod Kilpatrick
DESIGNER
Bob Barrie
CLIENT
Musicland
AGENCY
Fallon McElligott/Minneapolis

501
ART DIRECTOR
Bob Barrie
WRITER
Rod Kilpatrick
DESIGNER
Bob Barrie
CLIENT
Musicland
AGENCY
Fallon McElligott/Minneapolis

502
ART DIRECTOR
Steve Grime
WRITER
John Bowman
PHOTOGRAPHER
Martin Thompson
CLIENT
Blue Circle Industries
AGENCY
Wight Collins Rutherford
Scott PLC/London

498

499

To an Ethiopian it's dinner music.

A public service message from
musicland

500

Who says music only nourishes the soul?

A public service message from
musicland

501

New Sandtex Wood Gloss.

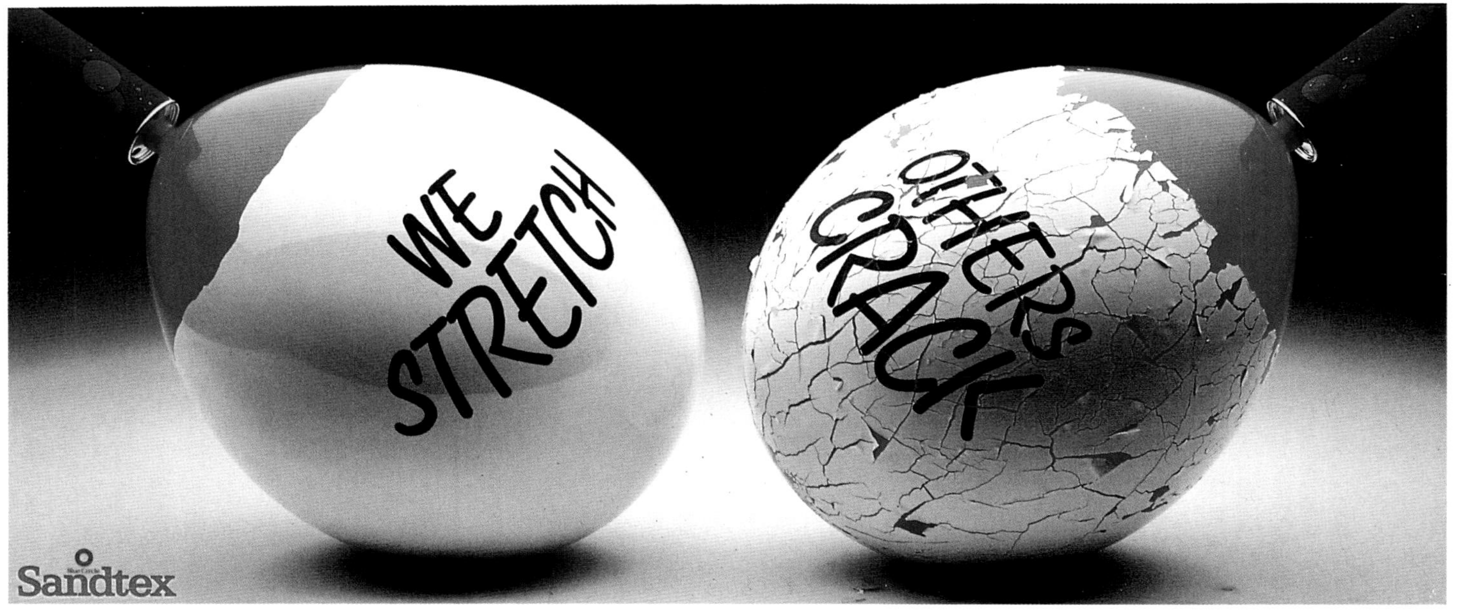

502

Outdoor: Single

503
ART DIRECTOR
Alan Lerner
WRITER
Indra Sinha
PHOTOGRAPHER
Martin Thompson
CLIENT
Parker
AGENCY
Ogilvy & Mather/London

504
ART DIRECTOR
Alan Lerner
WRITER
Indra Sinha
PHOTOGRAPHER
Martin Thompson
CLIENT
Parker
AGENCY
Ogilvy & Mather/London

505
ART DIRECTOR
John Scott MacDaniels
WRITER
John Scott MacDaniels
PHOTOGRAPHER
Harvey Lloyd
CLIENT
Royal Viking Line
AGENCY
Lowe Marschalk/San Francisco

506
ART DIRECTOR
Julie Thomas
WRITER
Julie Thomas
DESIGNER
Julie Thomas
PHOTOGRAPHER
Robert Milne
CLIENT
Pacific First Federal
AGENCY
John Brown & Partners/Seattle

507
ART DIRECTOR
Jon Guliner
WRITER
Hal Goldberg
CLIENT
Pepto-Bismol
AGENCY
D'Arcy Masius Benton & Bowles

503

504

505

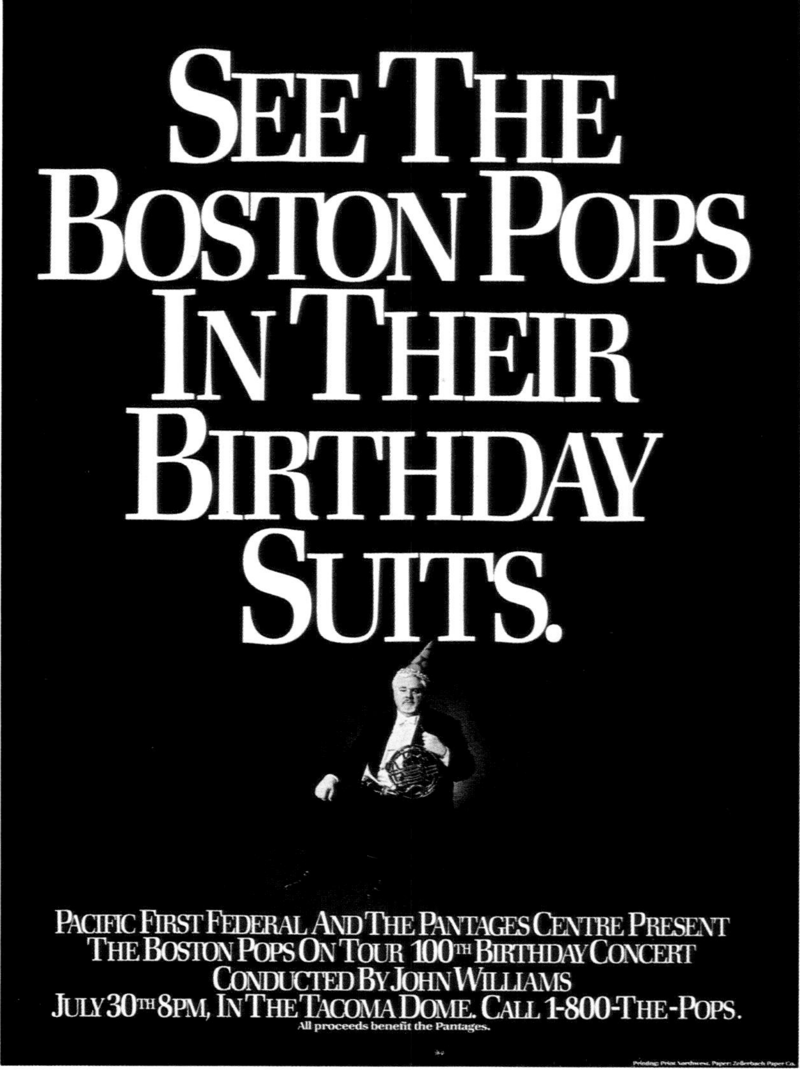

506

TRAVELERS' INSURANCE.

507

Outdoor: Single

508
ART DIRECTORS
Laura Dean-Abramson
David Moranville
WRITER
Dan Balazs
CLIENT
McDonald's
AGENCY
Davis Johnson Mogul
Colombatto/San Francisco

509
ART DIRECTOR
Dave Cook
WRITER
Chris Bardsley
PHOTOGRAPHER
Ian Giles
CLIENT
Honeywell Information Systems
AGENCY
Gold Greenlees Trott/London

510
ART DIRECTOR
Jon Guliner
WRITER
Hal Goldberg
CLIENT
Pepto-Bismol
AGENCY
D'Arcy Masius Benton & Bowles

511
ART DIRECTOR
Marcus Kemp
WRITER
Steve Sandoz
PHOTOGRAPHER
Larry Gilpin
CLIENT
Alaska Airlines
AGENCY
Livingston & Company/Seattle

512
ART DIRECTOR
Marcus Kemp
WRITER
Jim Copacino
CLIENT
Alaska Airlines
AGENCY
Livingston & Company/Seattle

508

509

510

ISIT ROYALTY.
ALASKA AIRLINES TO LAS VEGAS.

ALASKA

ALASKA AIRLINES TO LAX.

Outdoor: Campaign

513
ART DIRECTOR
Bob Kwait
WRITERS
Bob Kwait
Rich Badami
DESIGNER
Bob Kwait
ARTIST
Ron Van Buskirk
PHOTOGRAPHER
Ron Garrison
CLIENT
San Diego Zoo
AGENCY
Phillips-Ramsey/San Diego

514
ART DIRECTOR
Bob Barrie
WRITER
Phil Hanft
DESIGNER
Bob Barrie
PHOTOGRAPHER
Rick Dublin
CLIENT
MAX Long Distance
AGENCY
Fallon McElligott/Minneapolis

513

A phone call to Atlanta shouldn't sound like a phone call to Atlantis.

MAX Long Distance

You pay less. You don't get less.
1-800-631-4000.

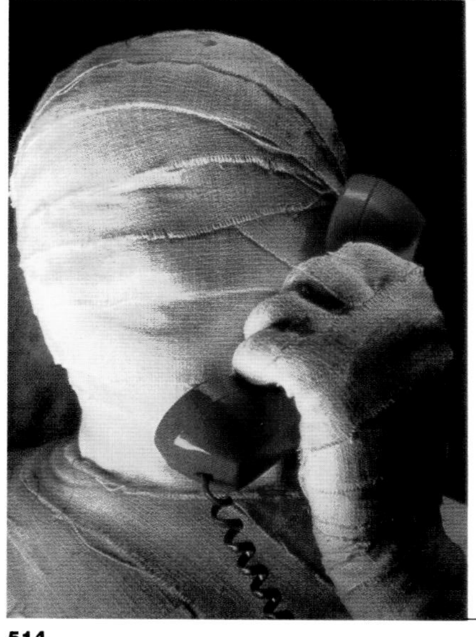

A long distance call to your mother shouldn't sound like a call to a mummy.

MAX Long Distance

You pay less. You don't get less.
1-800-631-4000.

A phone call to Pittsburgh shouldn't sound like a phone call to Pluto.

MAX Long Distance

You pay less. You don't get less.
1-800-631-4000.

Outdoor:
Campaign

515
ART DIRECTOR
Dean Hanson
WRITER
Jamie Barrett
CLIENT
Tan Me Suntanning
AGENCY
Fallon McElligott/Minneapolis

516
ART DIRECTOR
Hal Tench
WRITER
Andy Ellis
DESIGNER
Hal Tench
ARTIST
Ken Barr
CLIENT
Kings Dominion
AGENCY
The Martin Agency/
Richmond, VA

OTHER TANNING SALONS
PALE BY COMPARISON.
Tan Me Suntanning

MAKE THIS WINTER
A SHADE BETTER
THAN LAST WINTER.
Tan Me Suntanning

PEOPLE WHO LIVE
THROUGH OUR WINTERS
OUGHT TO BE BRONZED.
Tan Me Suntanning

515

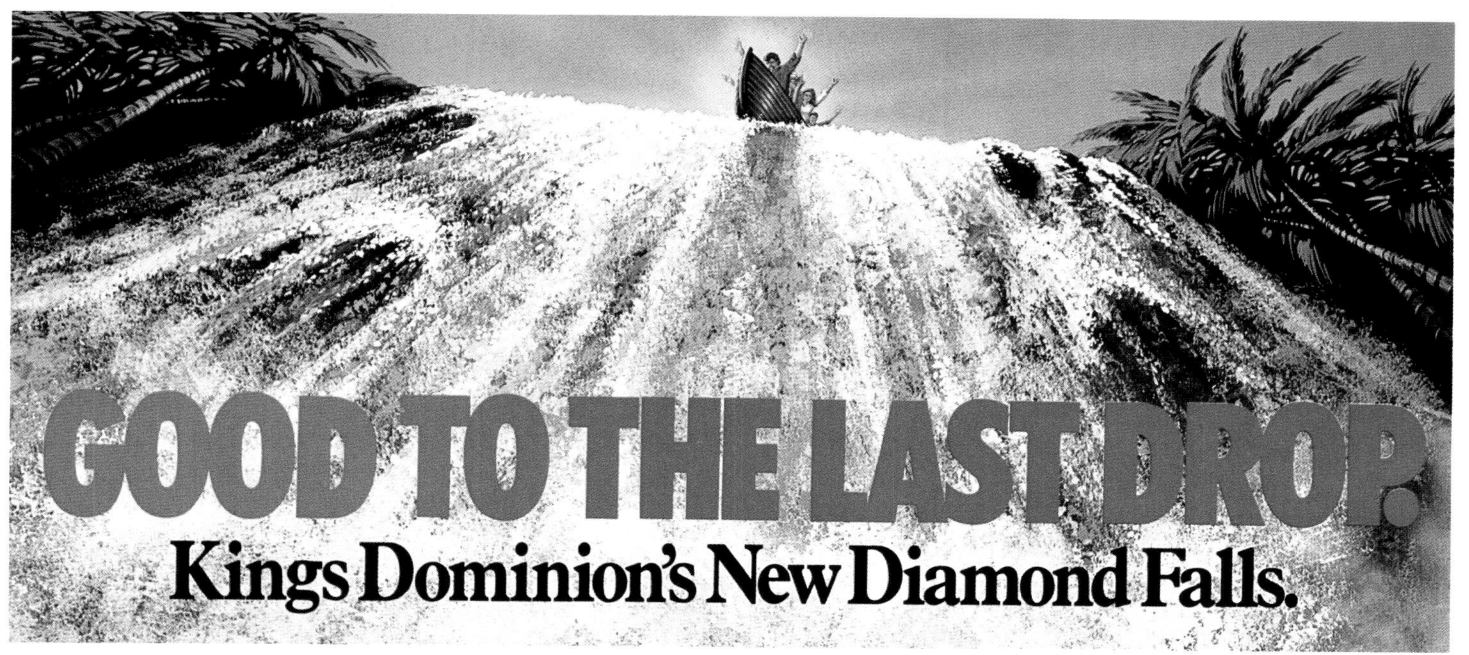
GOOD TO THE LAST DROP.
Kings Dominion's New Diamond Falls.

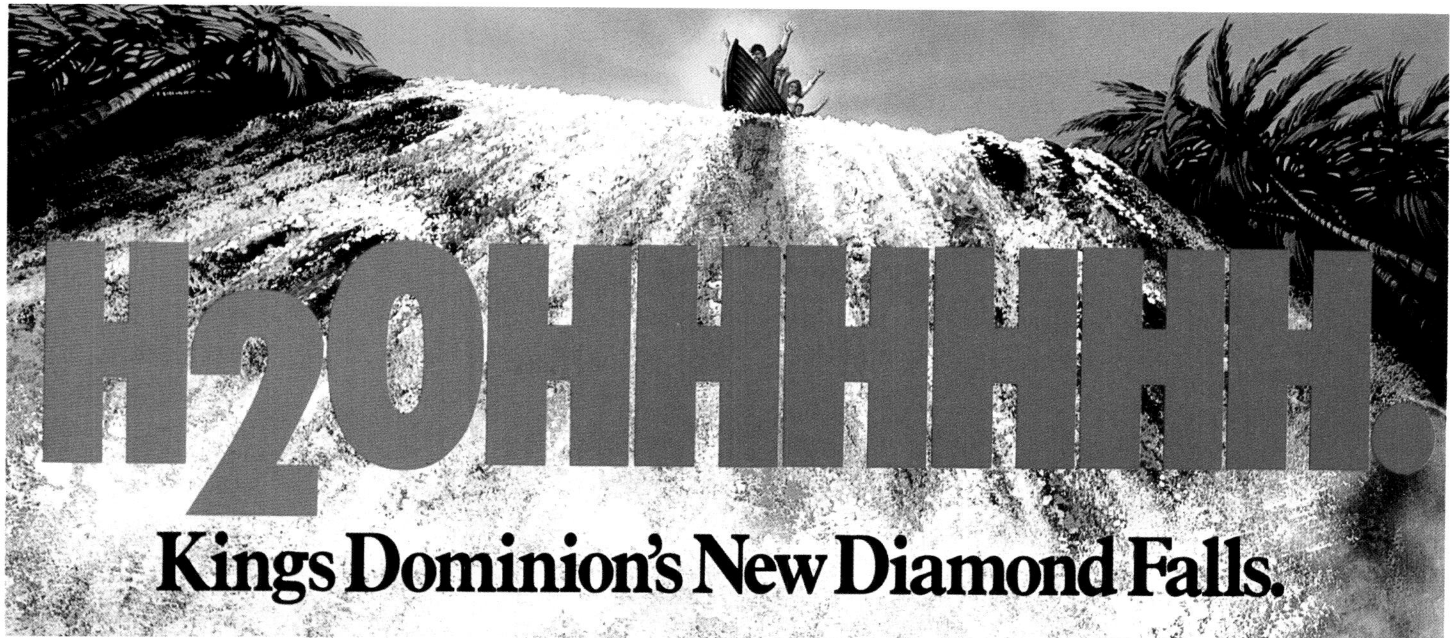
H2OHHHHHH!
Kings Dominion's New Diamond Falls.

ENJOY THE FALL THIS SPRING.
Kings Dominion's New Diamond Falls.

Public Service Newspaper Or Magazine: Single

517
ART DIRECTOR
Paul Matthaeus
WRITERS
Rick Peterson
Cynthia Hartwig
PHOTOGRAPHER
Chuck Kuhn
CLIENT
Elephant House
AGENCY
Sharp Hartwig Advertising/
Seattle

518
ART DIRECTOR
Roseanne Motti
WRITER
Scott Carlton
CLIENT
Eritrean Relief Committee

519
ART DIRECTOR
Bill Schwartz
WRITER
Dennis Okerbloom
DESIGNER
Bill Schwartz
PHOTOGRAPHER
Martin Reuben
CLIENT
United Way Services
AGENCY
Meldrum and Fewsmith/
Cleveland

520
ART DIRECTOR
Bill Schwartz
WRITER
Dennis Okerbloom
DESIGNER
Bill Schwartz
PHOTOGRAPHER
Martin Reuben
CLIENT
United Way Services
AGENCY
Meldrum and Fewsmith/
Cleveland

Chuck Kuhn, 1984

Seattle's elephants need more trunk space.

Seattle's Woodland Park Zoo is one of America's best.

Parts of it, like the wide-open African Savanna and outdoor Gorilla Habitat, have won a lot of praise and awards.

But parts of our zoo, like the 60-year old elephant house, are literally cracked and falling apart. And hopelessly too small.

That's why we're building a new elephant exhibit modeled after a Thai logging camp. An entire southeast Asian forest will be created. And Seattle's elephants will finally have room to roam in the open, demonstrating their enormous strength and intellect.

Seattle's new Asian Elephant Forest exhibit will be world-class. But it will also cost $6.7 million. Half the money will come from matching public funds. But half must come from private donations. Like yours.

To make a tax deductible contribution, call 1-206-682-3122.

Remember, elephants never forget.

Save our Elephants
Woodland Park Zoo

827 Skinner Bldg., Seattle, WA 98101.
Co-sponsored by the Save Our Elephants Committee and the Seattle Zoological Society.

517

No rock star is singing for this child.

He's from Eritrea. Where two million Africans are starving to death from the devastating effects of famine. Where there are no airlifts. And where help doesn't come from rock concerts or record albums. But from you.

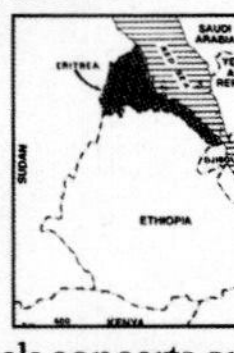

You see, your contribution is the hope of survival for a proud, suffering people. People who want to help themselves.

And for every $1 you give, the Eritrean Relief Committee delivers 92¢ in food, medicine, seeds and tools to the children, women and men of Eritrea.

So don't let an entire population continue to be forgotten. Call us or send in the coupon immediately. Before it's too late. And please help all you can.

Because you don't have to be a rock star to play an instrumental part in ending hunger.

1-800-225-5669

Help us feed the children the world has forgotten.

Mail to:
THE ERITREAN RELIEF COMMITTEE, INC.
475 RIVERSIDE DR., RM. 769, N.Y., N.Y. 10115

☐ I am sending all I can to help save Eritrean children, women and men from starvation. Enclosed is my check for ________ to the Eritrean Relief Committee. I want 92¢ of every $1 I send to go directly to feeding the needy people of Eritrea. And I understand this contribution is tax deductible.

☐ Please let me know exactly how my money is being spent. Send me a report.

Name ________
Address ________
City ________
State ________ Zip ________
Phone ________

SAVE ERITREA

518

Some people are so poor they can't afford to work.

She's poor because she's divorced. Without alimony. Without child support.

She can't afford to work because she can't afford a full-time babysitter for the kids.

But in reality, she has to work to support herself and her family.

So the kids are left alone. Or without adequate supervision.

Why? There aren't enough quality, affordable day care centers to go around right now.

And the problem is growing worse every year.

That's one of the reasons your help is needed.

When you give to United Way, you help more than 170 local agencies provide a wide range of services to those in need.

So please, give generously at your place of work.

Your help can prevent day care from turning into a nightmare.

United Way Services

For so many, we're the only way.

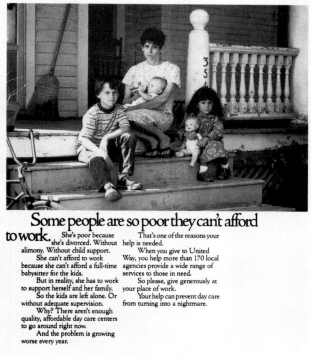

519

Next time you're having a bad day, remember this: You're lucky.

You think you've got problems?

Traffic jams, crazy drivers and noisy neighbors pale by comparison to the problems facing the handicapped.

In fact, your gripes would be a welcome relief to people who are stopped cold whenever they come up against a stairway.

The truth is, handicapped people have proved they can overcome most of their limitations, given the proper help.

That's one of the reasons your help is needed.

When you give to United Way, you help more than 170 local agencies provide a wide range of services to those in need.

So please, give generously at your place of work.

After all, it's better to give than to receive.

United Way Services

For so many, we're the only way.

520

Public Service Newspaper Or Magazine: Single

521
ART DIRECTOR
Nancy Rice
WRITER
Tom McElligott
PHOTOGRAPHER
Tom Bach
CLIENT
Episcopal Church
AGENCY
Fallon McElligott/Minneapolis

522
ART DIRECTOR
Bill Snitzer
WRITER
Mitchell Wein
PHOTOGRAPHER
Pete Blyer
CLIENT
Greenpeace
AGENCY
Larsen Colby Koralek/Los Angeles

523
ART DIRECTOR
Ken Chauncey
WRITER
Greg Wilson
CLIENT
Castle and Cooke
AGENCY
Allen and Dorward/San Francisco

524
ART DIRECTOR
Roseanne Motti
WRITER
Scott Carlton
CLIENT
Eritrean Relief Committee

525
ART DIRECTOR
Cabell Harris
WRITER
Mike Hughes
PHOTOGRAPHER
Pat Edwards
CLIENT
Manchester Rescue Squad
AGENCY
Drinking Buddies Advertising/Richmond, VA

Does Easter mean beans to your kids?

If you agree that Easter should do more for your children than raise their blood sugar level, we invite you and your family to experience the true miracle of Easter in The Episcopal Church.
The Episcopal Church

521

WHERE HAVE ALL THE WHALES GONE?

In the last 50 years over 2,000,000 whales have been systematically slaughtered and processed.

They've been turned into dog food, shoe polish, cold cream. Machine oil, perfume, and soap.

And the really ironic thing is, all these products can be made from vegetable or synthetic sources. At a comparable cost. (In fact, chemists can hardly tell the difference between whale oil and jojoba bean oil.)

One after another, entire whale species have been

brought to the brink of extinction. The Humpback, Blue and Bowhead whales have been reduced to below 8% of their original populations. Sperm, Fin, and Minke whales are now facing the same cruel fate.

A fate, incidentally, that can cause a serious imbalance in the ocean food chain. And you know what that means.

The oceans could die. Millions of people could starve to death.

Send your tax-deductible contributions to Greenpeace. While you're at it, write President Reagan. Remind him of his responsibility to impose economic sanctions on any country that won't obey international agreements to protect whales.

Please. We need your help.

GREENPEACE
1611 Connecticut Avenue, NW
Washington, DC 20009
(202) 462-1177

522

IF YOUR CHILD WAS MISSING, YOU WOULDN'T TURN THIS PAGE.

You'd want everyone who could possibly help to be helping.

And that's what Dole® is doing.

With a fund raiser of a quarter of a million dollars to aid in the search for missing children. Five cents will be donated for every coupon redeemed on Dole fresh fruit from our free-standing insert refund offer in Best Food Day newspapers. Plus, additional money will come from coupons for other Dole products. All as part of our "Fresh Dole Summer Promotion."

Of course, the whole program goes nowhere without you. So talk to your Dole Representative for more information. And stock up now.

Because soon shoppers will be coming into your store hoping to find Dole.

And with your help (and a little luck), we'll find a lot more than that.

THE MISSING CHILDREN'S FUND FROM DOLE.

523

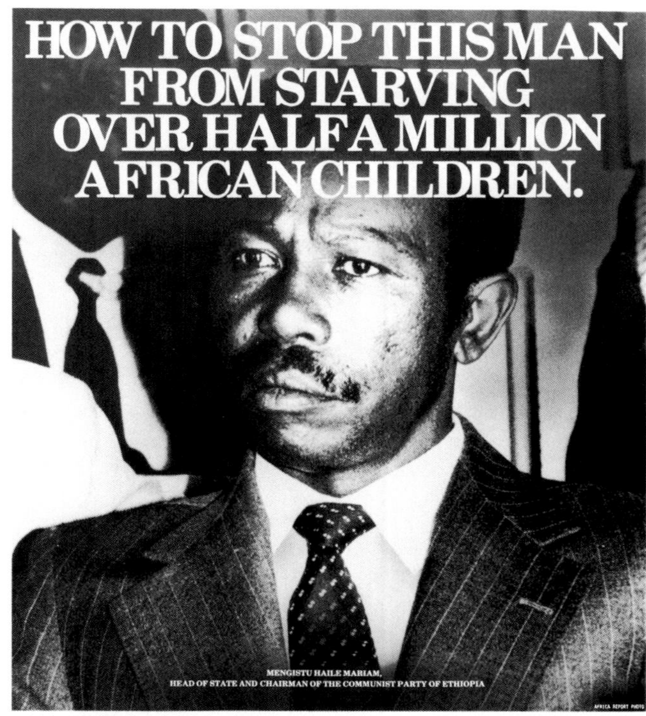

If Chairman Mengistu, the Soviet-backed leader of Ethiopia, has his way all 3½ million children, women and men of the Red Sea territory, Eritrea, will die of starvation.

In fact, Mengistu is doing everything in his power to burn crops, block food transports and poison fields in famine-ridden Eritrea.

Why? Because he wants Soviet control over not only Ethiopia but over all the surrounding lands in the area. Especially Eritrea. Africa's strategic Red Sea coastal land.

And he will stop at nothing to get it.

Which is why of the $250 million worth of food relief pouring into Ethiopia very little trickles into Eritrea.

This man and the men who suppoft him can be stopped. Through the efforts of the Eritrean Relief Committee. A relief group dedicated to feeding the millions of starving Eritreans by avoiding Ethiopia's political channels.

But we need you. Because your contributions are our only means of survival. And surviving we are. ERC presently reaches 85% of all Eritreans. And we actually direct 92¢ of every $1 you send to food.

So don't stand by silently and let politics kill an entire population. Fill out the coupon now before time runs out. And please send all you can.

Because if you help the people hungry for food, you can stop the men hungry for power.

Mail to: THE ERITREAN RELIEF COMMITTEE, INC. 475 RIVERSIDE DR., RM. 769, N.Y., N.Y. 10115

☐ I am sending all I can to help save Eritrean children, women and men from starvation. Enclosed is my check for ______ to the Eritrean Relief Committee. I want 92¢ of every $1 I send to go directly to feeding the needy people of Eritrea. And I understand this contribution is tax-deductible.

☐ Please let me know exactly how my money is being spent. Send me a report.

Name ______

Address ______

City ______

State ______

Zip ______

Phone ______

THE ERITREAN RELIEF COMMITTEE

A NON-PROFIT ORGANIZATION. 475 RIVERSIDE DRIVE, RM. 769, NEW YORK, NEW YORK 10115

524

OUR VOLUNTEERS LIVE LIFE IN THE FAST LANE.

BE SOMEBODY'S HERO.

525

Public Service Newspaper Or Magazine: Single

526
ART DIRECTOR
Nancy Rice
WRITER
Tom McElligott
ARTIST
Hans Holbein
CLIENT
Episcopal Church
AGENCY
Fallon McElligott/Minneapolis

527
ART DIRECTOR
Mike Moser
WRITER
Brian O'Neill
PHOTOGRAPHER
Stock
CLIENT
U.C. Berkeley Foundation
AGENCY
Chiat/Day - San Francisco

528
ART DIRECTOR
Sara Meyer
WRITER
Lyle Wedemeyer
ARTIST
Rick Hanson
CLIENT
Minnesota Pollution Control Agency
AGENCY
Martin/Williams - Minneapolis

529
ART DIRECTOR
Parents For Cystic Fibrosis Research
WRITER
Parents For Cystic Fibrosis Research
PHOTOGRAPHER
Joe Toto
CLIENT
Parents For Cystic Fibrosis Research
AGENCY
Ally & Gargano

526

SCIENTISTS WORK BETTER WHEN THEY'RE ALL MIXED-UP.

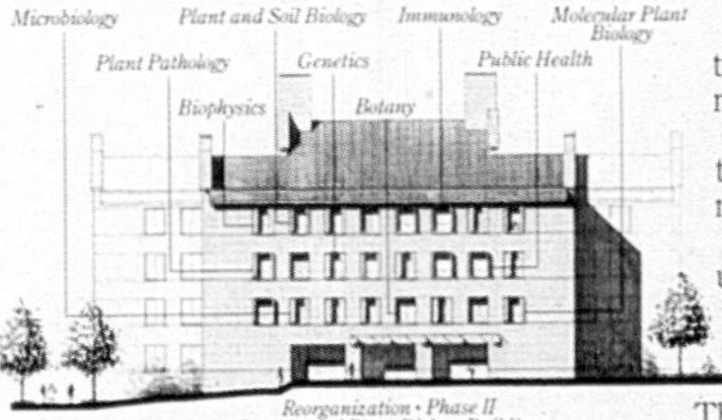

Right now, our minds are a little scattered.
But Cal's Biosciences Reorganization Plan should change all that.
This important project represents the first major attempt by any university to structure its facilities to reflect the interdisciplinary nature of the New Biology.
It will also enable us to bring our scientists closer together.
So geneticists can collaborate with plant pathologists, to better understand the facts of life.
So microbiologists, immunologists and botanists will be able to exchange techniques, or even share a cell.
And so all our scientists will be able to pool resources and research in a way never before possible.
There are also economic advantages to getting our scholars thoroughly mixed-up.
By sharing expensive equipment and utilizing common teaching facilities, each department will be able to use its funds more efficiently.
Speaking of which.
The state has agreed to fund half of the new Genetics and Plant Biology Building–the current phase of the reorganization.
So we're halfway there.
But to complete the project, and continue to make the breakthroughs that have put Cal at the forefront of DNA technology and gene research, we need private support.
So please, call Vice-Chancellor Curtis R. Simic at (415) 642-1212, and tell him you want to help scientists in all areas.
By putting them all in one area.

U.C. BERKELEY
It's not the same without you.

U.C. Berkeley Foundation, 2440 Bancroft Way, Room 301, Berkeley, California 94720

527

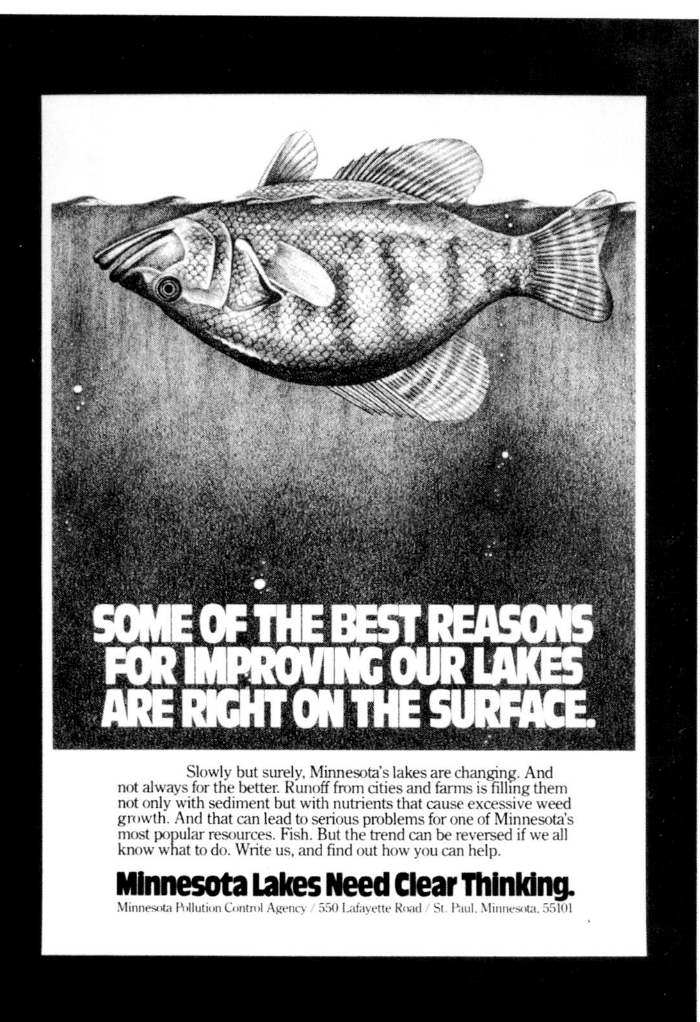
SOME OF THE BEST REASONS FOR IMPROVING OUR LAKES ARE RIGHT ON THE SURFACE.
Slowly but surely, Minnesota's lakes are changing. And not always for the better. Runoff from cities and farms is filling them not only with sediment but with nutrients that cause excessive weed growth. And that can lead to serious problems for one of Minnesota's most popular resources. Fish. But the trend can be reversed if we all know what to do. Write us, and find out how you can help.
Minnesota Lakes Need Clear Thinking.
Minnesota Pollution Control Agency / 550 Lafayette Road / St. Paul, Minnesota, 55101

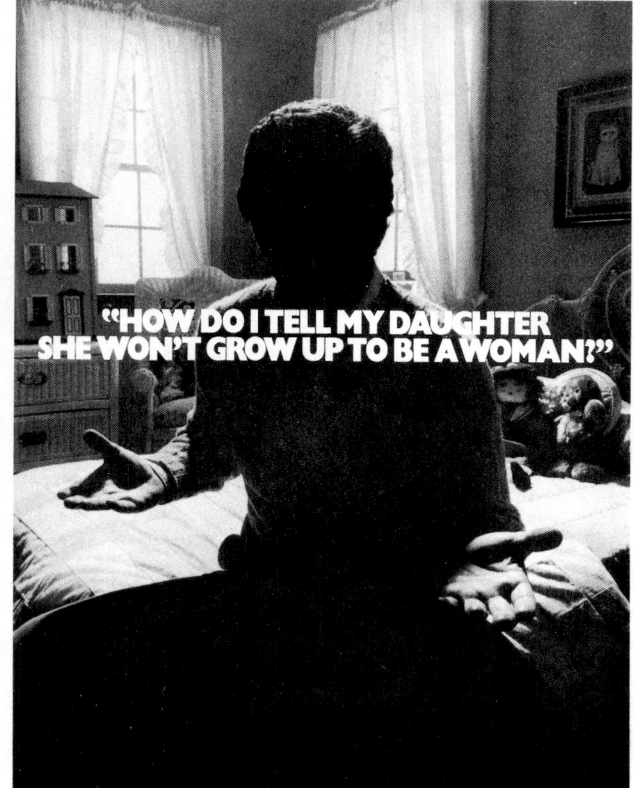
"HOW DO I TELL MY DAUGHTER SHE WON'T GROW UP TO BE A WOMAN?"

The thought of losing a child is unbearable for any parent. But I don't want your sympathy.

I want your attention.

My child has Cystic Fibrosis. Every year 18,000 children are born with it, and every day three children die from it.

It takes more children's lives every year than Multiple Sclerosis, juvenile diabetes, and Muscular Dystrophy combined.

In spite of these bleak statistics, Cystic Fibrosis has yet to receive the attention it so desperately needs. And this has to change.

Because if it doesn't, the research that's needed to find a cure or a treatment for this disease will remain years behind other childhood diseases.

And that doesn't give children who have Cystic Fibrosis much hope.

So how will I tell my daughter she won't grow up to be a woman?

If enough people help, maybe I won't have to.

"I WANT TO GIVE MORE THAN SYMPATHY."
Parents for Cystic Fibrosis Research,
P.O. Box 705, Plandome, NY 11030

☐ Please send me more information.

☐ My $______ contribution is enclosed.

Name______
Company______
Address______
City______
State______ Zip______
Phone______

HELP CURE CYSTIC FIBROSIS.

THIS AD WAS WRITTEN BY A PARENT WHO HAS A CHILD WITH CYSTIC FIBROSIS AND WAS SPONSORED BY FRIENDS FOR "PARENTS FOR CYSTIC FIBROSIS RESEARCH."

Public Service Newspaper Or Magazine: Single

530
ART DIRECTOR
Cabell Ellington
WRITER
Ron Ovadia
DESIGNER
Cabell Ellington
CLIENT
Van de Kamp's
AGENCY
D'Arcy Masius Benton & Bowles/Los Angeles

531
ART DIRECTOR
Diane Cook Tench
WRITER
Luke Sullivan
DESIGNER
Diane Cook Tench
CLIENT
American Cancer Society
AGENCY
The Martin Agency/ Richmond, VA

532
ART DIRECTOR
Paul Scolaro
WRITER
Tony Gomes
DESIGNER
Paul Scolaro
CLIENT
American Museum of Natural History
AGENCY
Ogilvy & Mather

533
ART DIRECTOR
Cabell Harris
WRITER
Andy Ellis
DESIGNER
Cabell Harris
PHOTOGRAPHER
Pat Edwards
CLIENT
Richmond Police Memorial Foundation
AGENCY
The Martin Agency/ Richmond, VA

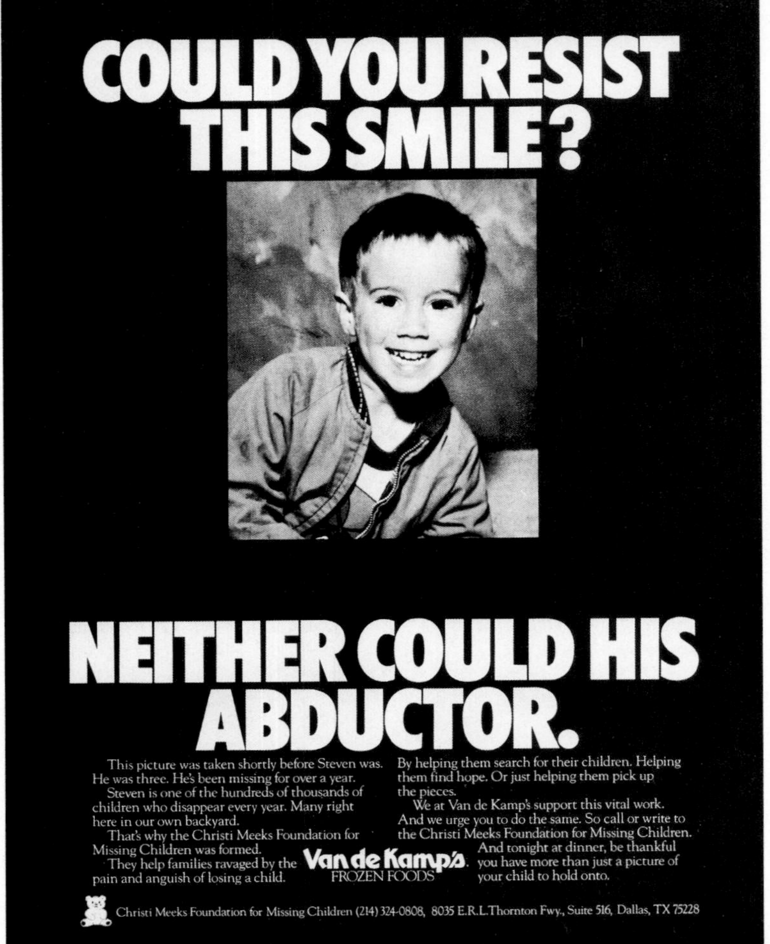

530

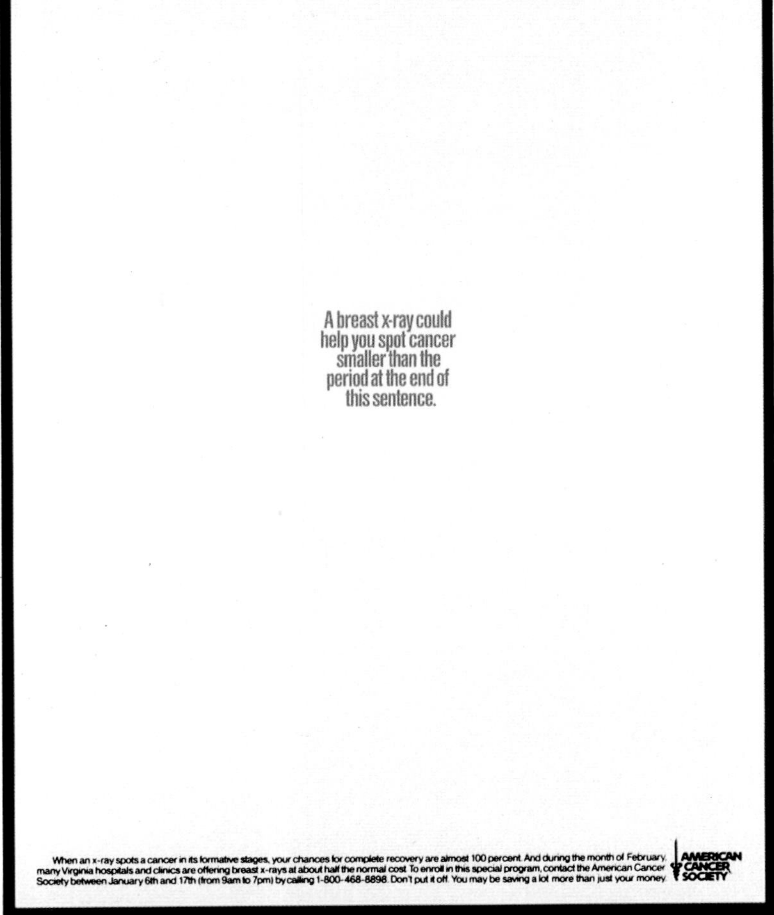

531

ON JULY 28 THE GREAT MAYA CIVILIZATION WILL DISAPPEAR

In the sixteenth century, the great Maya civilization mysteriously vanished. And to this day, no one really knows why. Well now the mystery begins to unfold in "Maya: Treasures of an Ancient Civilization" at the American Museum of Natural History. Some 275 art objects span 3500 years of Maya history. Most lay buried for hundreds of years in the rain forests of Southern Mexico and Central America. Now they've surfaced on Central Park West.

But only until July 28, when they'll disappear from New York.

So don't let time fade away, come see "Maya: Treasures of an Ancient Civilization" before it becomes history.

I'd like to become:

☐ AN ASSOCIATE MEMBER ($18)
I'll get free Museum admission for one; shop, restaurant and Naturemax discounts; and *Natural History* magazine.

☐ A PARTICIPATING MEMBER ($35)
I'll get all the benefits of an Associate Member plus free Museum admission for the family; the *Rotunda* newsletter; education course and Planetarium Sky Show discounts, and members-only programs and previews.

Name____________________
(Please print)
Address____________________
City__________ State__________ Zip_____

☐ Enclosed is my check payable to the American Museum of Natural History. ☐ Bill me.

Return to: Membership Office, American Museum of Natural History, Central Park West at 79th Street, New York, New York 10024 HNY16

AMERICAN MUSEUM OF NATURAL HISTORY

532

Unlike The Cops On TV, These Police Officers Won't Be Back Next Week.
Your support of the Richmond Police Memorial Foundation will build a monument to flesh and blood policemen who died in service to this city. And you. Mail your tax deductible donation, made payable to the Metropolitan Foundation, to P.O. Box 209, Richmond 23208.

Public Service Newspaper Or Magazine: Single

534
ART DIRECTOR
Nancy Rice
WRITER
Tom McElligott
PHOTOGRAPHER
Tom Bach
CLIENT
Episcopal Church
AGENCY
Fallon McElligott/Minneapolis

535
ART DIRECTOR
Bill Oberlander
WRITER
Lou Schiavone
PHOTOGRAPHER
Duane Michaels
CLIENT
Shearson
AGENCY
McCann-Erickson

536
ART DIRECTOR
Cabell Harris
WRITER
Andy Ellis
DESIGNER
Cabell Harris
PHOTOGRAPHER
Pat Edwards
CLIENT
Richmond Police Memorial Foundation
AGENCY
The Martin Agency/
Richmond, VA

537
ART DIRECTOR
Jerry Torchia
WRITER
John Mahoney
DESIGNER
Jerry Torchia
ARTIST
Scott Wright
CLIENT
Stop Child Abuse Now
AGENCY
The Martin Agency/
Richmond, VA

What other meal can sustain you for a week?

Sometimes what we need most in life is not more physical nourishment, but spiritual nourishment.
Come join us in the weekly celebration of Holy Eucharist in The Episcopal Church.
The Episcopal Church

534

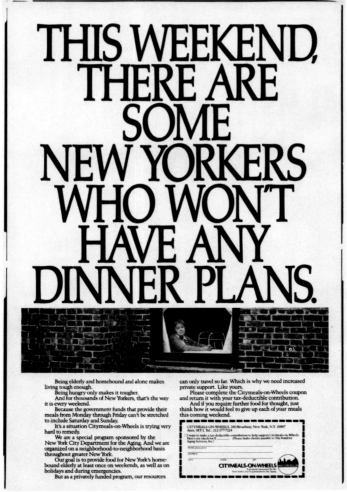

THIS WEEKEND, THERE ARE SOME NEW YORKERS WHO WON'T HAVE ANY DINNER PLANS.

Being elderly and homebound and alone makes living tough enough.

Being hungry only makes it tougher.

And for thousands of New Yorkers, that's the way it is every weekend.

Because the government funds that provide their meals from Monday through Friday can't be stretched to include Saturday and Sunday.

It's a situation Citymeals-on-Wheels is trying very hard to remedy.

We are a special program sponsored by the New York City Department for the Aging. And we are organized on a neighborhood-to-neighborhood basis throughout greater New York.

Our goal is to provide food for New York's homebound elderly at least once on weekends, as well as on holidays and during emergencies.

But as a privately funded program, our resources can only travel so far. Which is why we need increased private support. Like yours.

Please complete the Citymeals-on-Wheels coupon and return it with your tax-deductible contribution.

And if you require further food for thought, just think how it would feel to give up each of *your* meals this coming weekend.

CITYMEALS-ON-WHEELS, 280 Broadway, New York, N.Y. 10007
Attn: MT-1, Tel.: 212-577-7324
☐ I want to make a tax-deductible contribution to help support Citymeals-on-Wheels. Here's my check for $ ______ (Please make checks payable to The Fund for Aging Services, Inc.)

CITYMEALS-ON-WHEELS

535

Unlike The Cops You See On TV, These Police Officers Won't Be Back Next Week.
Forget T.J. Hooker, Barney Miller and Hill Street Blues. For a moment, forget actors and think about flesh-and-blood policemen who gave their lives in service to Richmond. And you.
Today, the Richmond Police Memorial Foundation seeks your support in erecting a monument remembering those officers. A memorial symbolizing the respect and gratitude these men, their families and their widows deserve.
Send your tax-deductible donation, made payable to the Metropolitan Foundation, to P.O. Box 209, Richmond 23208.
The Richmond Police Memorial Foundation

536

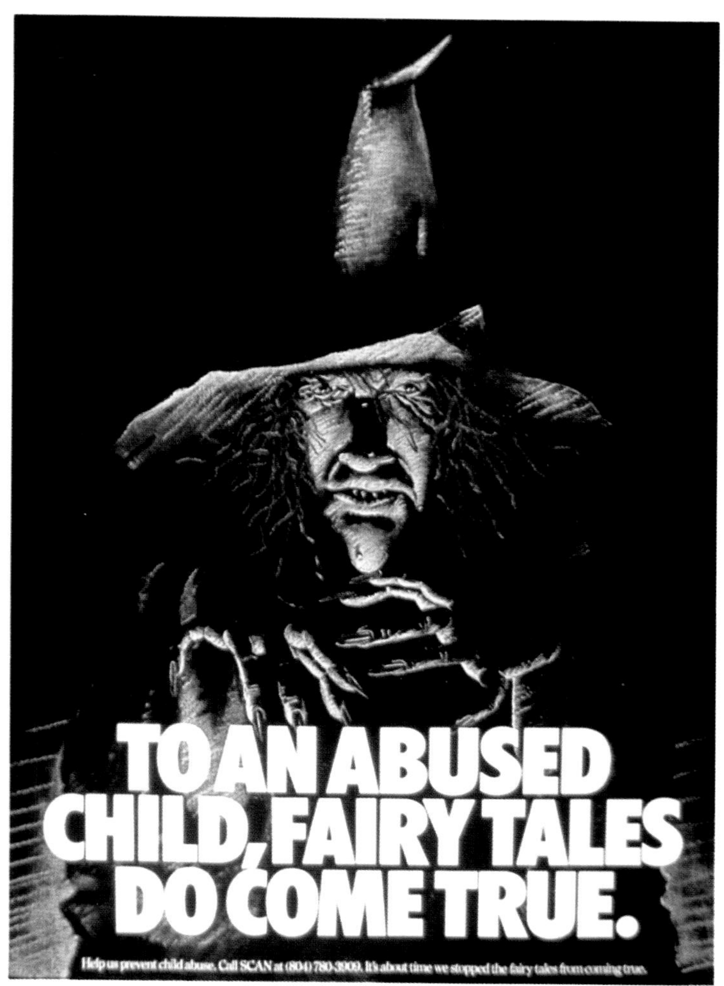

TO AN ABUSED CHILD, FAIRY TALES DO COME TRUE.
Help us prevent child abuse. Call SCAN at (804) 780-3909. It's about time we stopped the fairy tales from coming true.

537

Public Service Newspaper Or Magazine: Campaign

538
ART DIRECTOR
Aki Seki
WRITER
Sanford Evans
PHOTOGRAPHER
Mike Raab
CLIENT
United Way
AGENCY
Bozell & Jacobs

539
ART DIRECTOR
Jac Coverdale
WRITER
Jerry Fury
PHOTOGRAPHER
Jim Arndt
CLIENT
YMCA-USA
AGENCY
Clarity Coverdale Rueff/ Minneapolis

EVERY 18 SECONDS A WOMAN GETS BEATEN IN THIS COUNTRY.

Your local United Way supports a range of family service agencies that work together to solve domestic violence and many other social problems.

With your help we're also trying to do something about teen-age alcoholism, offer support services for single household families, provide rehabilitation for victims of crippling diseases. And more.

But we can't do it without you. Your one gift helps more people in your community than any other way of giving.

So give generously. Because together we can do anything.

THE WAY TO STOP IT IS TO BECOME UNITED.

United Way

Thanks to you it works for all of us.

THE ADVERTISING COUNCIL

©1985 UNITED WAY

39% OF ALL HIGH SCHOOL SENIORS ARE PROBLEM DRINKERS.

Your local United Way supports a range of alcoholism prevention and treatment agencies that work together to solve teen-age alcoholism and many other social problems.

With your help we're also trying to do something about domestic violence, offer support services for single household families, provide rehabilitation for victims of crippling diseases. And more.

But we can't do it without you. Your one gift helps more people in your community than any other way of giving.

So give generously. Because together we can do anything.

THE WAY TO STOP IT IS TO BECOME UNITED.

Thanks to you it works for all of us.

THE ADVERTISING COUNCIL

©1985 UNITED WAY

IN THE NEXT 6 MONTHS MENTAL DISORDERS WILL DISRUPT THE LIVES OF 19% OF AMERICAN ADULTS.

Your local United Way supports a range of mental health treatment agencies that give assistance to people and families suffering from emotional disabilities.

With your help we're also trying to do something about teen-age alcoholism, offer support services for single household families, provide rehabilitation for victims of crippling diseases. And more.

But we can't do it without you. Your one gift helps more people in your community than any other way of giving.

So give generously. Because together we can do anything.

THE WAY TO STOP IT IS TO BECOME UNITED.

Thanks to you it works for all of us.

Ad Council THE ADVERTISING COUNCIL

©1985 UNITED WAY

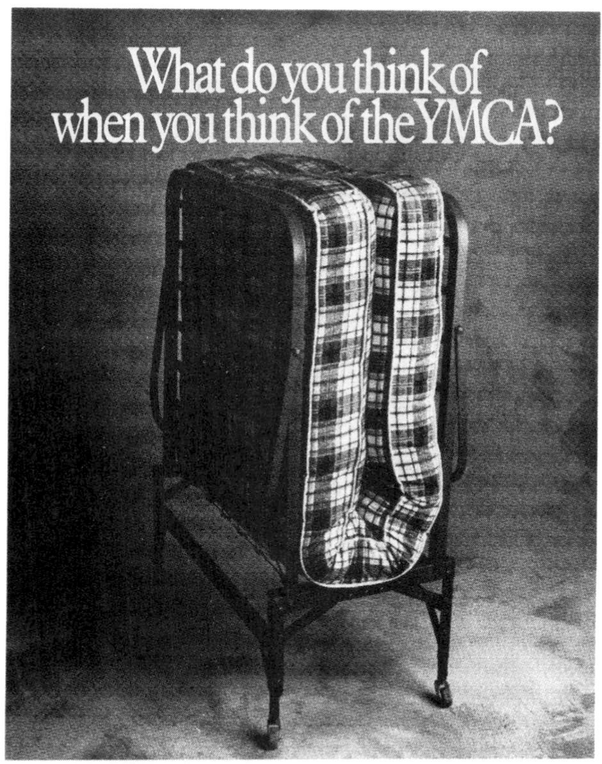
What do you think of
when you think of the YMCA?

A place to get a cheap room for the night?

If you do, it's time to wake up. Because the YMCA is a vitally important place in your community. With something to offer men, women, and children of all ages, interests, and abilities.

However, the Y is more than a place to go. It's also a healthy influence that is felt throughout the community. In many different ways.

Through exercise and wellness programs. By giving kids of all ages a healthy place to have fun and learn. And by providing numerous worthwhile community and volunteer programs. To name a few. In short, the YMCA is for all of you. For all the community. Support your YMCA today. You'll wake up feeling better tomorrow.

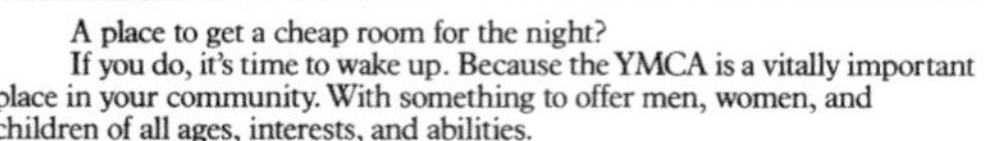
The YMCA. It's for all of you.™

When we help kids shape up
it isn't always in the gym.
YMCA

The reasons for supporting
the YMCA are right here
in black and white.
YMCA

Children of all ages.

Their social and physical development has always played a big part at the YMCA.

So has youth, senior, and family programs. YMCA camps. Volunteer and community projects. And YMCA International Programs.

However, the biggest reason for supporting the YMCA may be the feeling you get deep inside—knowing that what you contributed, financially or as a volunteer, will help provide programs to those in need.

So support your Y. Because when you get involved with the YMCA, you can feel the difference in your heart.

The YMCA. It's for all of you.™

Public Service Newspaper Or Magazine: Campaign

540
ART DIRECTOR
Mike Moser
WRITER
Brian O'Neill
PHOTOGRAPHERS
John Bagley
Bob Mizono
CLIENT
U.C. Berkeley Foundation
AGENCY
Chiat/Day - San Francisco

541
ART DIRECTOR
Bill Murphy
WRITER
Margaret Wilcox
CLIENT
Red Acre Farm
AGENCY
Hill Holliday Conners Cosmopulos/Boston

WE'RE PROTECTING YOUR FOOD WITH ALL OUR MITES.

They're called predator mites.

And they eat spider mites.

And *they* eat apples and almonds and peaches and cost California growers $75 million a year in crop damage.

Yet thanks to breakthrough research by Cal scientist Marjorie Hoy, the dreaded spider mite can now be controlled by these genetically improved predators.

This important work could soon enable growers all over the world to drastically reduce their use of pesticides.

But Professor Hoy isn't the only one on campus involved in a food fight.

Another Cal scientist recently discovered a way to prevent frost damage in lettuce fields. Still another has isolated the bacteria that's causing severe blight in our grape crop.

These and numerous other achievements have helped Cal's revitalized Biosciences program receive global attention.

Now we need your attention.

Lacking adequate facilities and equipment, our gifted scientists are relying more than ever on private contributions.

So please, call the number below, because our work isn't finished.

We're still trying to get all the bugs out.

U.C. BERKELEY
It's not the same without you.

Call Michael J. Romo, Director of Special Gifts, Mon.-Fri., 8-5: (415) 642-7885.
U.C. Berkeley Foundation, 2440 Bancroft Way, Rm. 201, Berkeley, California 94720.

HELP US TIE A PROFESSOR TO THIS CHAIR.

It's called an endowed chair.

And it's only $400,000.

Which may seem a bit steep, considering the fact it doesn't recline. Or vibrate. Or even have arms.

But compared to the price of endowed chairs at other major universities, it's a respectable bargain.

And how is an endowed chair any different from the one in your dining room?

For one thing, it'll last forever. Because your $400,000 establishes a perpetual endowment fund that covers everything but faculty salary (a state responsibility).

So year after year, an outstanding Cal professor will receive research assistance, equipment and other crucial support services.

And year after year, the generous donor—be it an individual, class or corporation—will receive well-deserved recognition.

Most importantly, endowed chairs enable Cal to attract and retain preeminent faculty, in virtually any field of learning you choose.

Or you can even choose to have us choose.

But the fact remains, without the support of a "chair," many of our top scholars are sitting targets for rival recruiters.

Call Vice-Chancellor Curtis R. Simic at (415) 642-1212, and tell him you want to help Cal meet its critical goal of 100 new endowed chairs by 1990.

Now's the time to take a stand. And have a seat.

U.C. BERKELEY
It's not the same without you.

SCIENTISTS WORK BETTER WHEN THEY'RE ALL MIXED-UP.

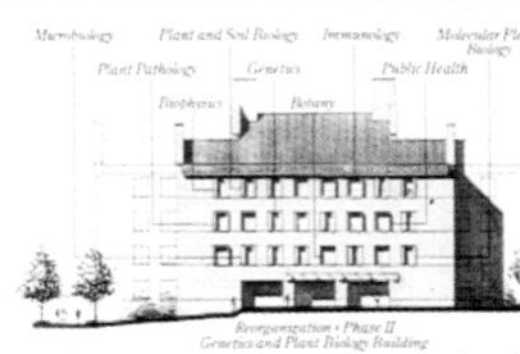

Reorganization • Phase II
Genetics and Plant Biology Building

Right now, our minds are a little scattered.

But Cal's Biosciences Reorganization Plan should change all that.

This important project represents the first major attempt by any university to structure its facilities to reflect the interdisciplinary nature of the New Biology.

It will also enable us to bring our scientists closer together.

So geneticists can collaborate with plant pathologists, to better understand the facts of life.

So microbiologists, immunologists and botanists will be able to exchange techniques, or even share a cell.

And so all our scientists will be able to pool resources and research in a way never before possible.

There are also economic advantages to getting our scholars thoroughly mixed-up.

By sharing expensive equipment and utilizing common teaching facilities, each department will be able to use its funds more efficiently.

Speaking of which.

The state has agreed to fund half of the new Genetics and Plant Biology Building—the current phase of the reorganization.

So we're halfway there.

But to complete the project, and continue to make the breakthroughs that have put Cal at the forefront of DNA technology and gene research, we need private support.

So please, call Vice-Chancellor Curtis R. Simic at (415) 642-1212, and tell him you want to help scientists in all areas.

By putting them all in one area.

U.C. BERKELEY
It's not the same without you.

John's hearing aid weighs 42 pounds.

John Dutton's is no ordinary hearing aid. It stands about three feet tall, eats two meals a day and alerts him to vital sounds with its paw.

John's hearing aid is a hearing dog from the Red Acre Farm Hearing Dog Center. And like most of our dogs, at least part of his training was made possible by outside contributions.

If you're interested in more information, or in making a tax deductible donation, write us at P.O. Box 278, Stow, MA 01775. Or call (617) 897-8343 VOICE/TTY. Anytime. We're always here. Guess we've worked with dogs so long, we've started to work like them, too.

Red Acre Farm
Hearing Dog
Center

Judy's hearing aid is a real dog.

Judy always knew her hearing aid wasn't like most others. It would paw her leg to alert her to sound and wag its tail when it heard something it liked.

Judy's hearing aid is a hearing dog from Red Acre Farm Hearing Dog Center. And like most of our dogs, at least part of his training was made possible by outside contributions.

If you're interested in more information, or in making a tax deductible donation, write to us at P.O. Box 278, Stow, MA 01775. Or call us at (617) 897-8343 VOICE/TTY. And if you hear a little barking in the background remember, it's just someone's hearing aid trying to say hello.

Red Acre Farm
Hearing Dog
Center

We solved Bill Webb's hearing problem by giving him this new set of ears.

They stand straight up on end when they're listening to something and flop back down when they're not. They're the ears on Bill's new hearing dog, Duchess.

Duchess was trained at the Red Acre Farm Hearing Dog Center to alert Bill to vital sounds around him. And like most of our hearing dogs, at least part of her training was made possible by outside contributions.

If you're interested in more information, or in making a tax deductible donation, write to us at P.O. Box 278, Stow, MA 01775. Or call us at (617) 897-8343 VOICE/TTY. And ask us as many questions as you want. We'll be more than happy to lend you an ear. After all, we're used to giving them away.

Red Acre Farm
Hearing Dog
Center

Public Service Newspaper Or Magazine: Campaign

542
ART DIRECTOR
Bill Schwartz
WRITER
Dennis Okerbloom
DESIGNER
Bill Schwartz
PHOTOGRAPHER
Martin Reuben
CLIENT
United Way Services
AGENCY
Meldrum and Fewsmith/ Cleveland

543
ART DIRECTOR
John Vitro
WRITER
Steve Law
DESIGNER
John Vitro
ARTIST
Ron Van Buskirk
PHOTOGRAPHERS
David Kramer
Marshall Harrington
CLIENT
United Way
AGENCY
Phillips-Ramsey/San Diego

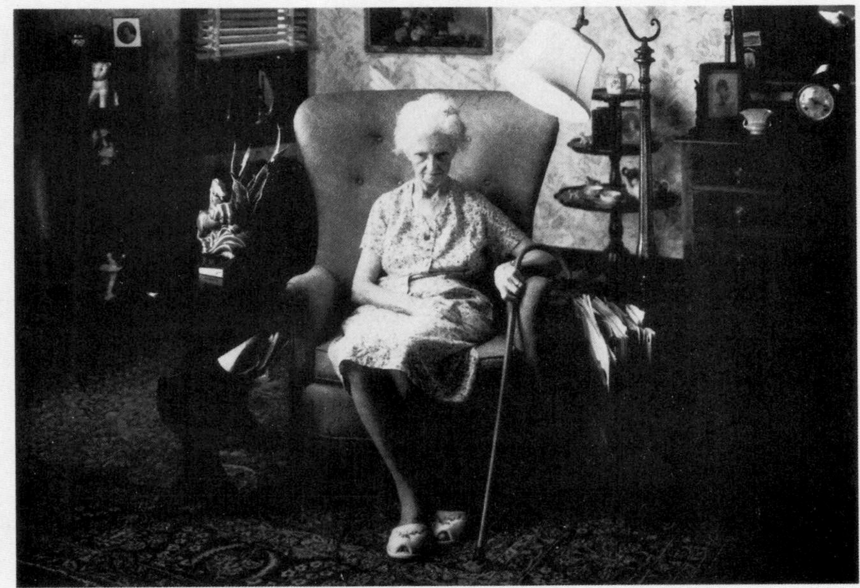

Wouldn't it be nice just to sit around all day and do nothing?

For the frail and impaired elderly, there's precious little choice at times.

They have trouble seeing and hearing. Or their mobility is greatly restricted. Or their mental faculties are diminishing rapidly.

Truth is, some can barely care for themselves. Yet they can't afford the help they need.

On top of that, the number of frail and impaired elderly is expected to double in the next 20 years.

That's one of the reasons your help is needed.

When you give to United Way, you help more than 170 local agencies provide a wide range of services to those in need.

So please, give generously at your place of work.

Or would you prefer to just sit there and do nothing?

For so many, we're the only way.

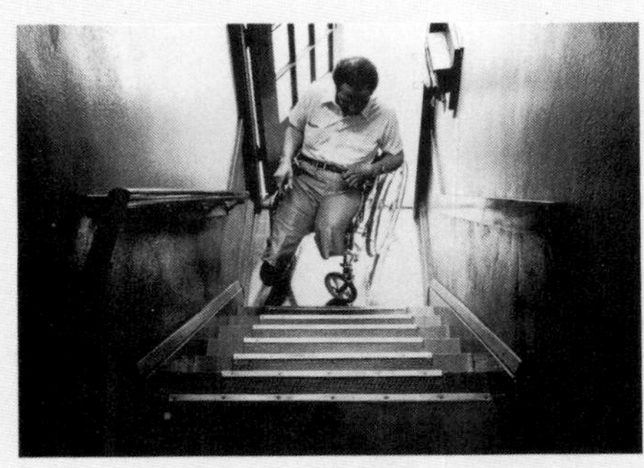

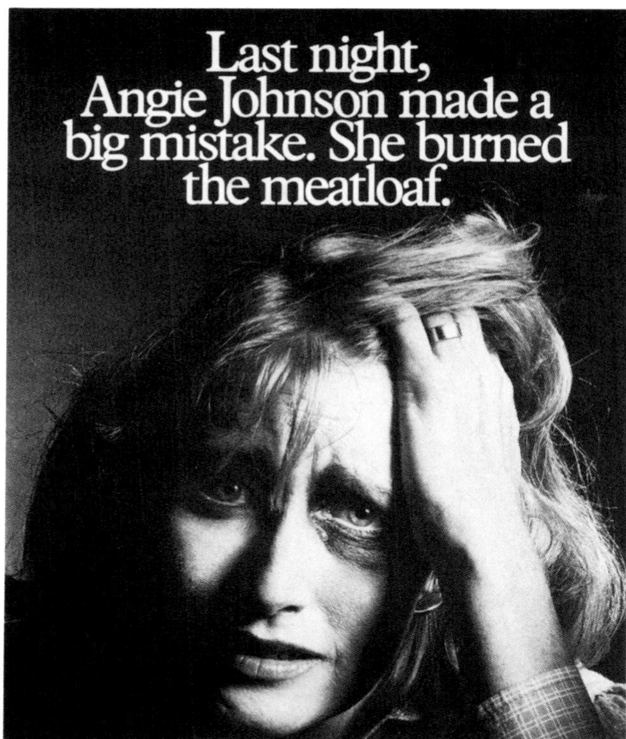

Unfortunately, wife abuse hits much closer to home than you might think. Already, half our nation's couples have had at least one violent incident.

And it's getting worse. Today, a woman is battered every 18 seconds.

But you can help. By giving to this year's United Way/CHAD community campaign, you're supporting 97 vital agencies throughout San Diego County.

Like the Women's Resource Center and YWCA Battered Women's Shelter which provide food, shelter and legal counseling to battered women.

So please, give generously. You'll be striking a blow for people who really need your help.

United Way/CHAD
Community Campaign

Today, more than 5,000 homeless people throughout San Diego County will need help scraping up their next meal.

Fortunately, many of them won't have to look for it on the streets.

Because thanks to our United Way/CHAD, neighborhood agencies like the Salvation Army and Catholic Community Services provide a warm meal to those who need it most. Along with a roof over their head.

And that's just a few of the 97 vital agencies you support when you give to this year's United Way/CHAD community campaign.

So please give generously. You'll be making life a lot easier to swallow. For a lot of needy San Diegans.

United Way/CHAD
Community Campaign

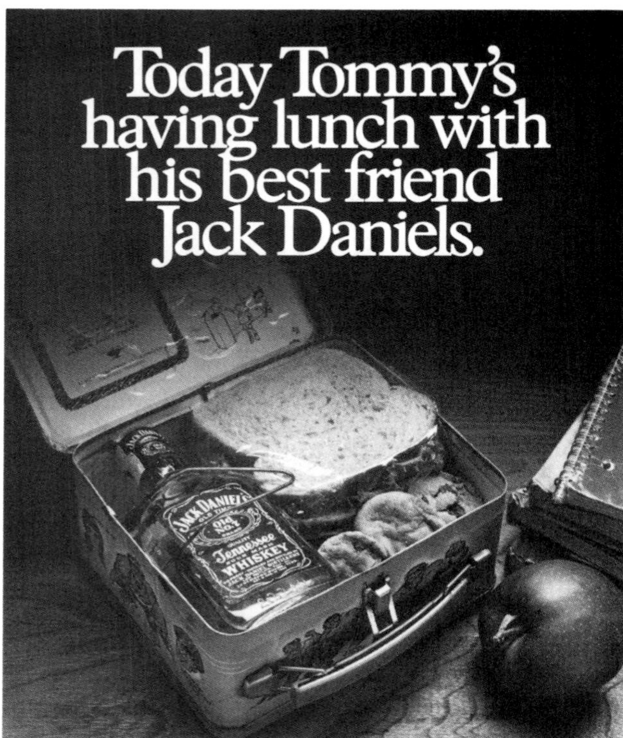

Every year, more and more kids are cheering their school with a different kind of spirit. The kind that comes in bottles and cans.

In San Diego County alone, a staggering 7,600 kids in grades 7–12 have serious drinking problems. Problems that don't go away overnight.

But thanks to United Way/CHAD agencies like the Neighborhood House, troubled youngsters can receive guidance and education about drug and alcohol abuse.

So please give generously. You'll be helping some confused kids solve their problems. Not run away from them.

United Way/CHAD
Community Campaign

Public Service Outdoor: Single

544
ART DIRECTOR
Rob Dalton
WRITER
Jim Newcombe
CLIENT
Minneapolis Planetarium
AGENCY
Advertising Au Gratin/ Minneapolis

545
ART DIRECTOR
Bob Barrie
WRITER
Rod Kilpatrick
DESIGNER
Bob Barrie
CLIENT
Programa San Francisco De Asis
AGENCY
Fallon McElligott/Minneapolis

546
ART DIRECTOR
Rob Dalton
WRITER
Jim Newcombe
CLIENT
Minneapolis Planetarium
AGENCY
Advertising Au Gratin/ Minneapolis

547
ART DIRECTOR
Nancy Rice
WRITER
Tom McElligott
ARTIST
Dürer
CLIENT
Episcopal Church
AGENCY
Fallon McElligott/Minneapolis

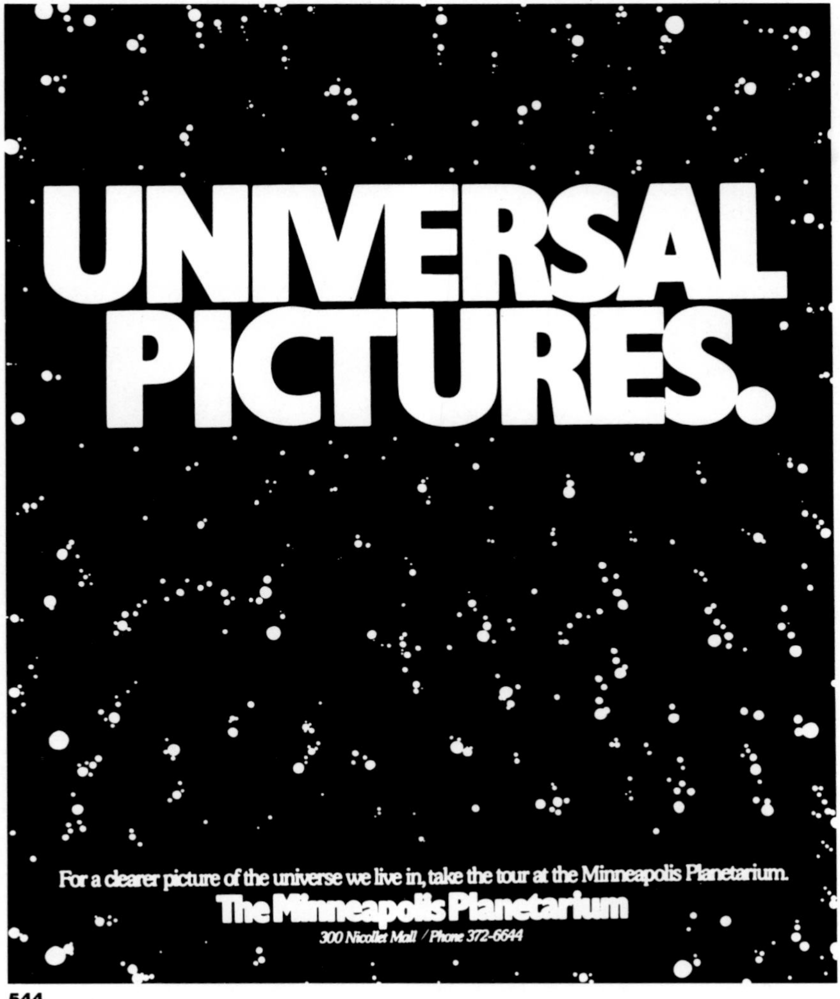

544

Help export American defense systems to the Third World.

The people of Peru are defenseless against dental disease and facial deformities. Our medical and dental volunteers are trying to help. Come to our happy hour at St. Paul's Landmark Center, between 5:30 and 9:30 PM on Thursday, August 15. Your $7.50 donation will buy you hors d'oeuvres, a Peruvian cocktail, a seat at our Peruvian auction—and a big smile of Peruvian gratitude.

Programa San Francisco de Asis.
For more information, call (612) 222-0351.

545

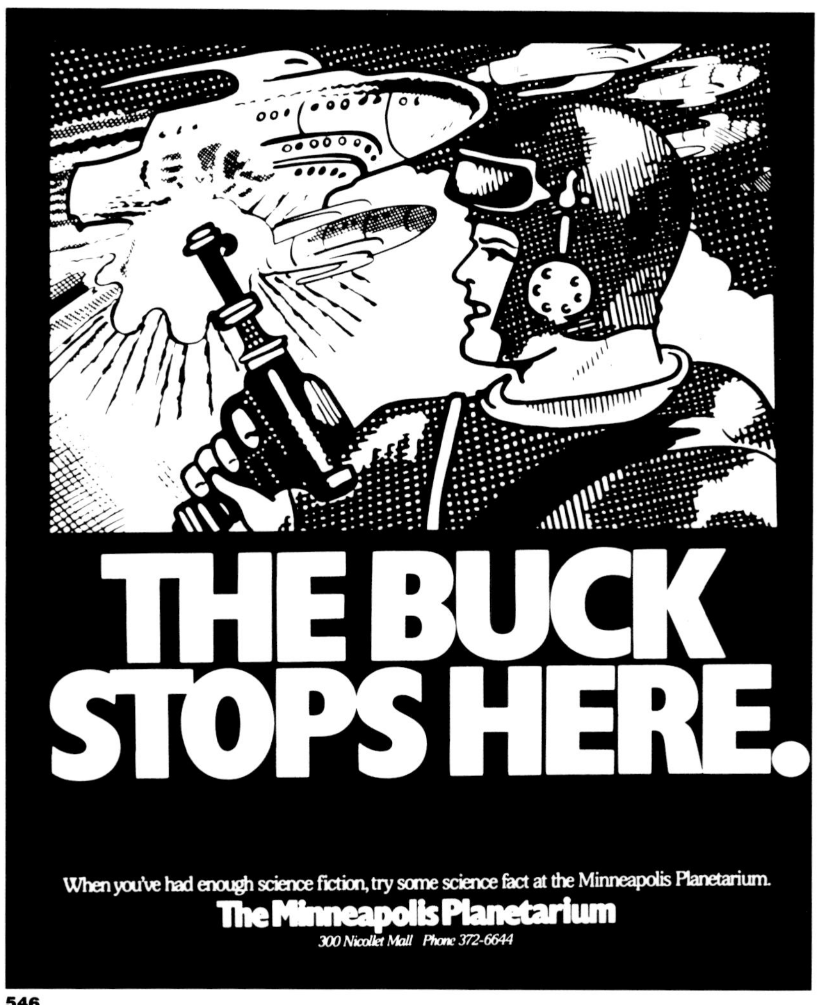
THE BUCK
STOPS HERE.
When you've had enough science fiction, try some science fact at the Minneapolis Planetarium.
The Minneapolis Planetarium
300 Nicollet Mall Phone 372-6644

546

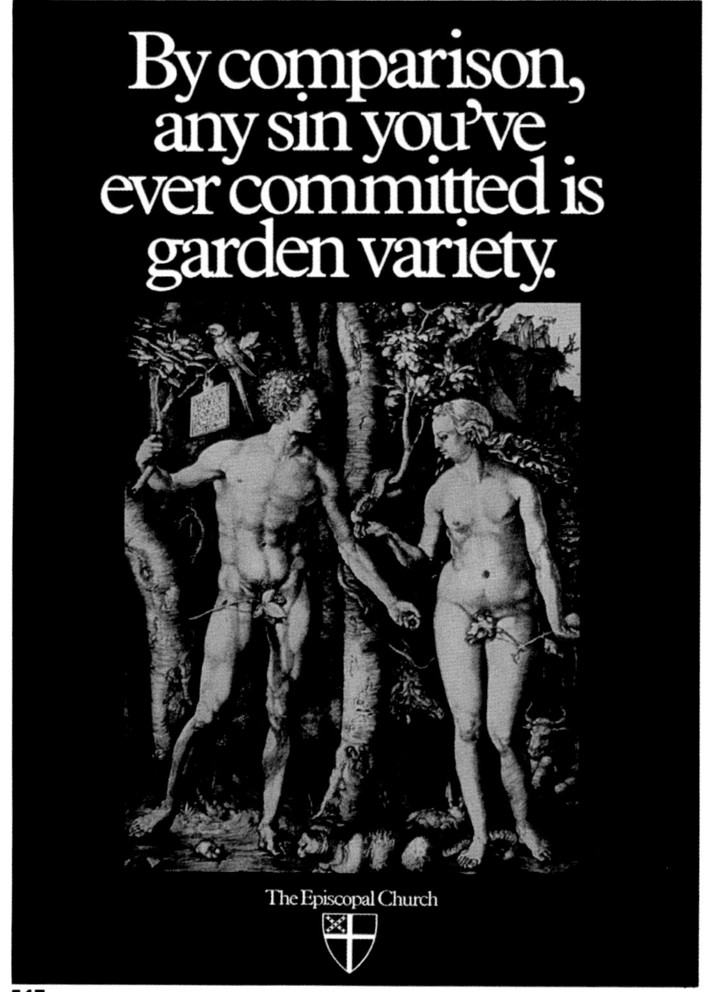
By comparison,
any sin you've
ever committed is
garden variety.
The Episcopal Church

547

Public Service Outdoor: Single

548
ART DIRECTOR
Martha Shaw
WRITER
Martha Shaw
DESIGNER
Corey Stolberg
PHOTOGRAPHER
David Kramer
CLIENT
San Diego County Health Department
AGENCY
Martha Shaw/San Diego

549
ART DIRECTOR
Nancy Rice
WRITER
Mike Lescarbeau
PHOTOGRAPHER
Tom Bach
CLIENT
Episcopal Church
AGENCY
Fallon McElligott/Minneapolis

550
ART DIRECTOR
Nancy Rice
WRITER
Tom McElligott
PHOTOGRAPHER
NASA
CLIENT
Episcopal Church
AGENCY
Fallon McElligott/Minneapolis

551
ART DIRECTOR
Neil Raphan
WRITER
Judy Protas
DESIGNER
Neil Raphan
ARTIST
Neil Raphan
CLIENT
The Greater New York Blood Bank
AGENCY
Doyle Dane Bernbach

548

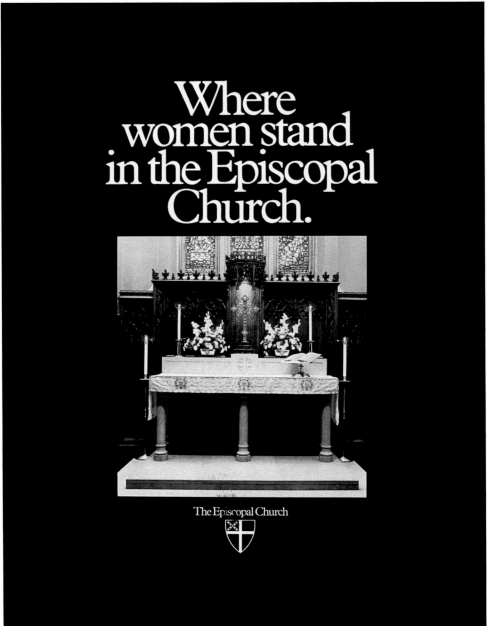

Where women stand in the Episcopal Church.

The Episcopal Church

549

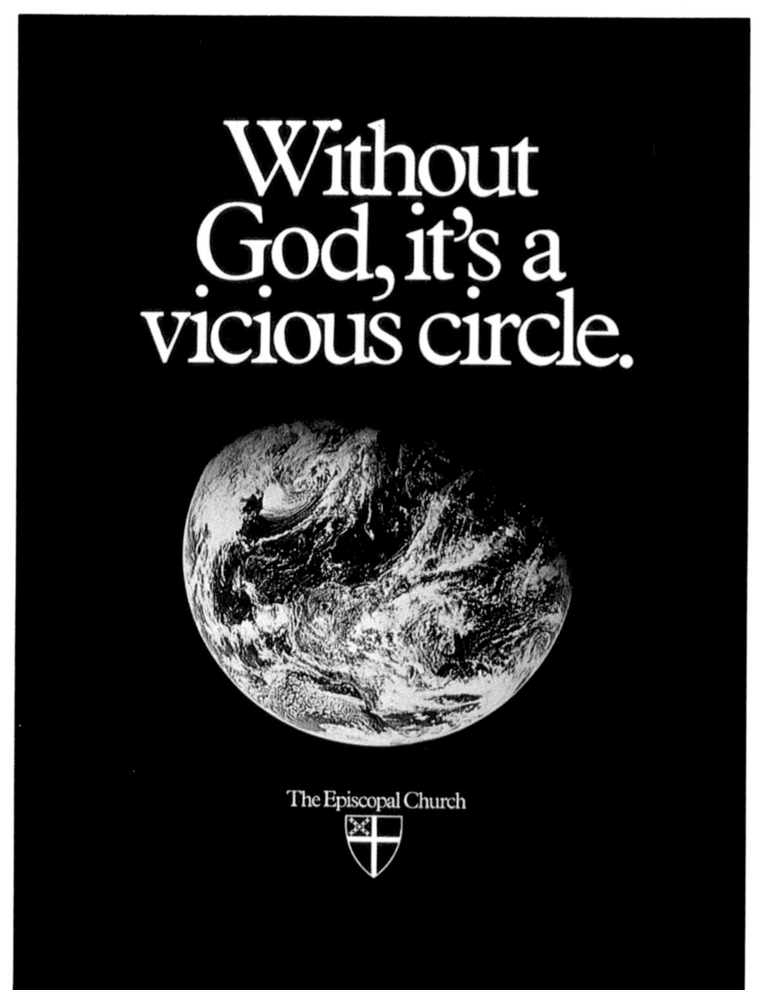
Without God, it's a vicious circle.
The Episcopal Church

550

HELP END THE DROUGHT.

The Red Cross Blood Bank is frighteningly low on life-saving blood. Say YES to the DDB Special Call. It's safe. It's easy. It's LIFE. Questions? Call 3186 or 3188.
THE DATE: FRIDAY, NOVEMBER 1, 9:30 TO 2:45 **THE PLACE:** THE EATERY **THE THANK-YOU:** A SHOT AT WINNING A SYLVANIA COLOR TV

551

Public Service
Outdoor: Single

552
ART DIRECTOR
David Fox
WRITER
Gerry Schmitt
CLIENT
The Red Cross
AGENCY
Clarity Coverdale Rueff/
Minneapolis

553
ART DIRECTOR
Peter Begley
WRITER
Deanna Cohen
DESIGNER
Peter Begley
PHOTOGRAPHER
David Pruitt
CLIENT
The Greater New York Blood
Bank
AGENCY
Doyle Dane Bernbach

554
ART DIRECTOR
Brian Fandetti
WRITER
Steve Bautista
PHOTOGRAPHER
Gene Dwiggins
CLIENT
Salvation Army
AGENCY
HBM/Creamer - Providence,
RI

555
ART DIRECTOR
Mike Shine
WRITER
Charles Tercek
DESIGNER
Mike Shine
CLIENT
United Way
AGENCY
Needham Harper Worldwide

556
ART DIRECTORS
Dan Schultz
Roger Snider
WRITER
Dan Schultz
DESIGNER
Roger Snider
PHOTOGRAPHER
Owen Hanson
CLIENT
Marathon Co./Chapter of
MADD
AGENCY
Schultz & Associates/J.D.
Thomas - Wausau, WI

THIS YEAR WE'RE OUT FOR MORE THAN JUST BLOOD.

American
Red Cross

Please, give generously to the Red Cross Disaster Relief Fund,
Box 11842, Mpls./St. Paul International Airport 55111.

552

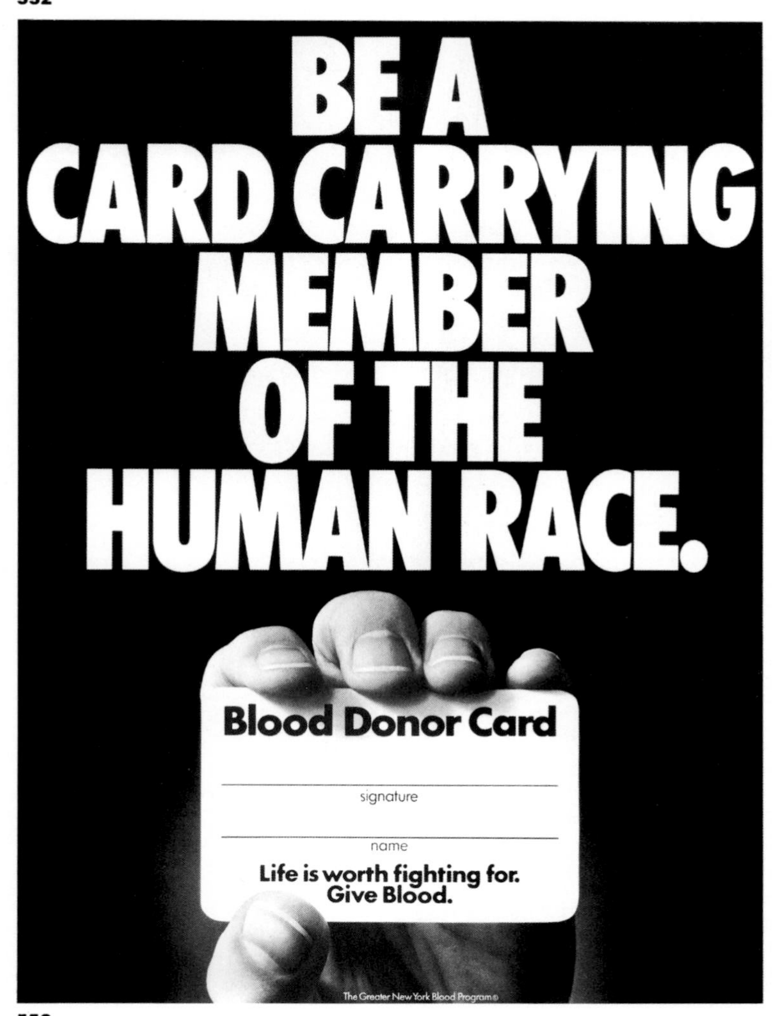

553

Help stop the Salvation Army from bombing.

The Salvation Army of Rhode Island.

Please give.
Without your support
a lot of vital social programs
could disappear.

554

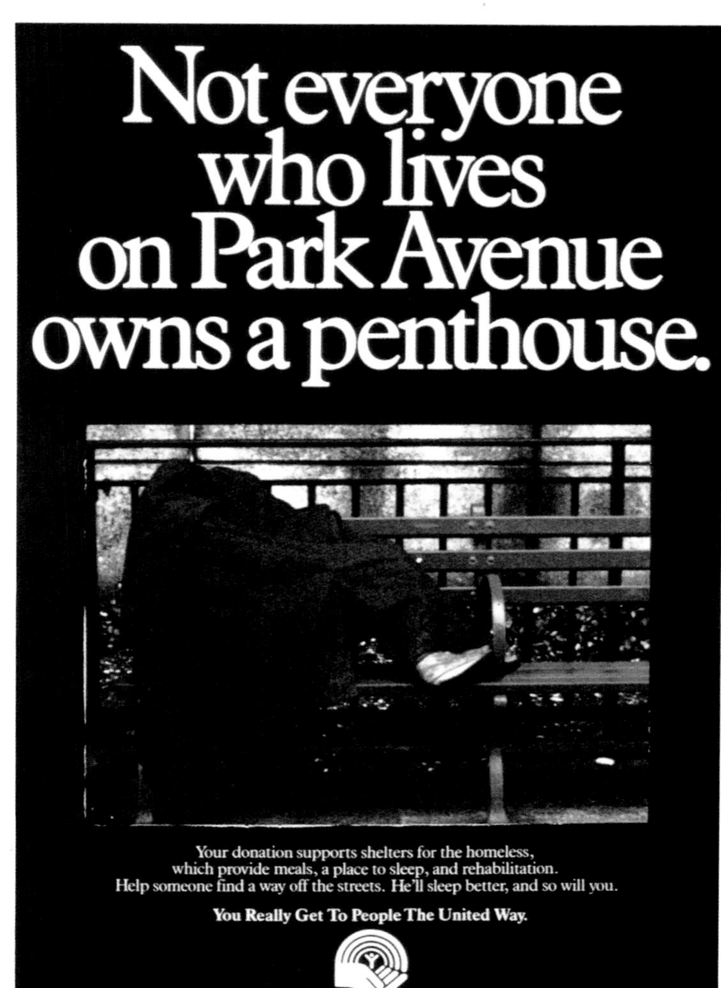
Not everyone who lives on Park Avenue owns a penthouse.
Your donation supports shelters for the homeless, which provide meals, a place to sleep, and rehabilitation. Help someone find a way off the streets. He'll sleep better, and so will you.
You Really Get To People The United Way.

555

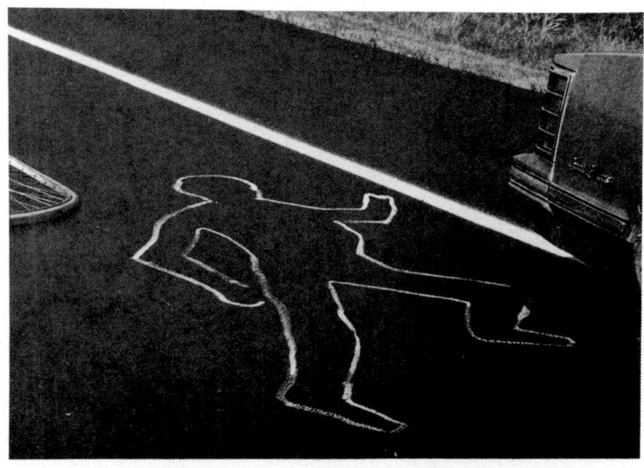

ONE FOR THE ROAD.

On an average weekend night, one out of every ten drivers is drunk. According to one government survey, over half of the people questioned admitted to recently driving a car while under the influence of alcohol or having ridden in a car driven by somebody under the influence.

In the face of those odds, what's the best way to avoid becoming a drunk driving victim? Make sure you have sober control of your car . . . because the guy coming at you probably doesn't.

556

Public Service Outdoor: Single

557
ART DIRECTOR
Rich Silverstein
WRITERS
Jeff Goodby
Andy Berlin
PHOTOGRAPHER
Dana Gluckstein
CLIENT
SFADC
AGENCY
Goodby Berlin & Silverstein/
San Francisco

558
ART DIRECTORS
Dan Schultz
Roger Snider
WRITER
Dan Schultz
DESIGNER
Roger Snider
PHOTOGRAPHER
Owen Hanson
CLIENT
Marathon Co./Chapter of
MADD
AGENCY
Schultz & Associates/J.D.
Thomas - Wausau, WI

Political Newspaper Or Magazine: Single

559
ART DIRECTOR
Michael Fazende
WRITER
Jarl Olsen
PHOTOGRAPHER
Jim Arndt
CLIENT
Minnesota Business
Partnership
AGENCY
Fallon McElligott/Minneapolis

557

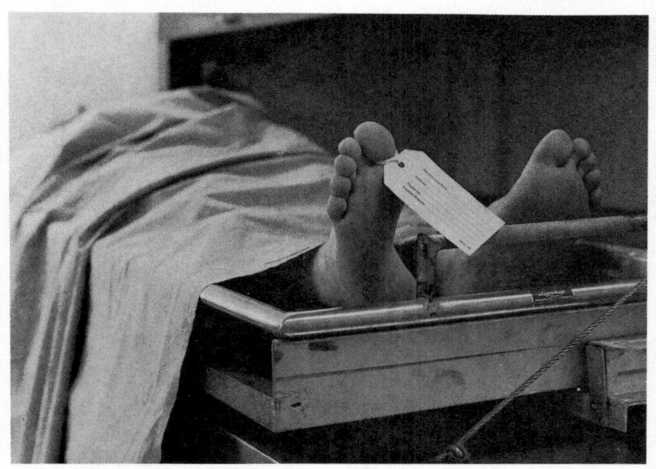

DON'T GET TAGGED FOR DRUNK DRIVING.

If being arrested, losing your license, fined and perhaps even sent to jail doesn't stop you from drinking and driving, think about the 27,000 people that drunk drivers kill each year.

Eighty-five percent of all fatal crashes are caused by drunk drivers. And each crash leaves behind grieving parents, children and loved ones who know drunk driving for what it is . . . murder. Don't drink and drive.

MADD

Mothers Against Drunk Driving

558

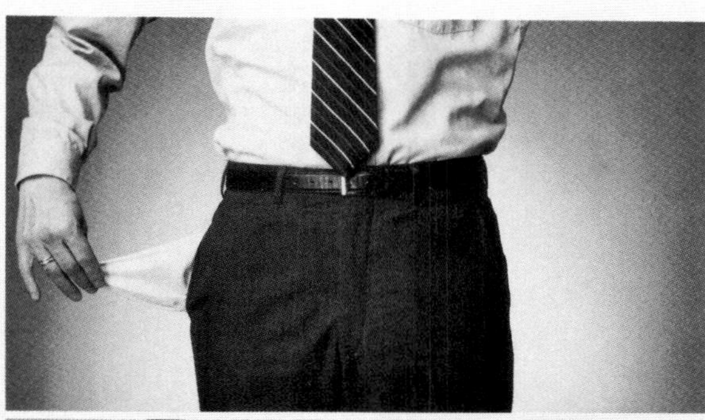

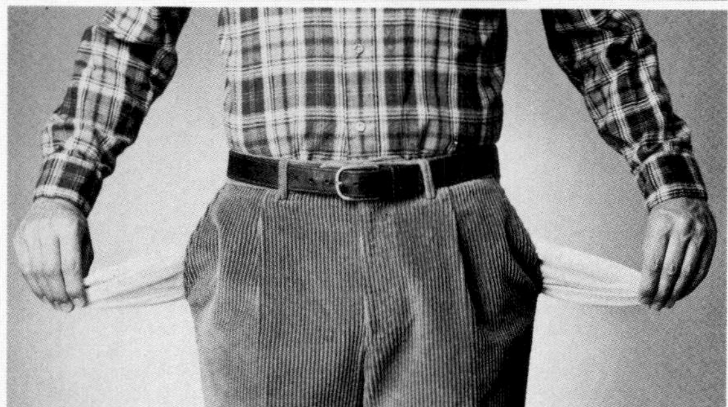

The average Minnesotan pays twice as much state income tax as the average American.

The good life doesn't come cheap.

This April, Minnesotans will be paying personal income taxes which are among the highest in the country—a shocking 202% of the national average. (Only one state, Delaware, is higher.)

With your help, we can cut personal income tax by 20%.

Even so, we'll still be paying 160% of the national average. That's why we're also asking for a plan that will reduce taxes even further in succeeding years.

Right now, your state legislature is deciding on the taxes you will have to pay this year. Don't let that decision be made without you.

Call the number below and we'll help you get a message to your legislator urging a 20% personal income tax cut now.

We want to see taxes lowered and state spending brought under control.

If it isn't, we're going to keep paying for it out of our own pockets.

Call the 20% Tax Cut Hotline 224-7400.

(Out of Twin Cities metro area, call toll-free, 1-800-338-0020.)

559

RADIO FINALISTS

Consumer Radio: Single

560
WRITERS
Robin Raj
John Crawford
CLIENT
NYNEX Information Resources
AGENCY
Chiat/Day

561
WRITER
Mike Lescarbeau
CLIENT
WFLD-TV
AGENCY
Fallon McElligott/Minneapolis

562
WRITER
Gary Gusick
AGENCY PRODUCER
Cindy Liebowitz
CLIENT
Monarch Wine Co.
AGENCY
Slater Hanft Martin

563
WRITER
Bill Miller
AGENCY PRODUCER
Bill Miller
CLIENT
KRON-TV
AGENCY
Fallon McElligott/Minneapolis

564
WRITER
Jarl Olsen
AGENCY PRODUCER
Jarl Olsen
CLIENT
KRLD-TV
AGENCY
Fallon McElligott/Minneapolis

565
WRITERS
Robin Raj
Nat Whitten
John Crawford
CLIENT
NYNEX Information Resources
AGENCY
Chiat/Day

566
WRITER
Dick Sittig
AGENCY PRODUCER
Marilyn Warner
CLIENT
Six Flags Magic Mountain
AGENCY
Della Femina Travisano & Partners/Los Angeles

567
WRITER
Bill Johnson
AGENCY PRODUCER
Bill Johnson
CLIENT
Schmidt Beer
AGENCY
Ruhr/Paragon - Minneapolis

560

(INTERVIEWER SPEAKING WITH BUSINESSMAN)

INTVR: I'm speaking to a Mr Frank Quigley.

MAN: That's Quizbee.

INTVR: Quizbee . . .

MAN: That's right.

INTVR: . . . whose business we found in the NYNEX Yellow Pages. Mr Quizbee is a manufacturer of fake snow.

MAN: Don't . . . uh . . . fake, no. We call this analog snow, Mike.

INTVR: Oh, I see. Well, what is . . . analog snow?

MAN: It's a totally uniform product, Mike. You know, your natural snow, every snowflake is different. With our product here, every snowflake is absolutely identical.

INTVR: Well, what are some of the applications for the new analog snow?

MAN: You name it.

INTVR: Oh, really? Um, sports?

MAN: Yes.

INTVR: Dance?

MAN: That, too.

INTVR: Literature.

MAN: Literature . . . uh, "Dr Zhivago," the movie. That was one of our big orders.

INTVR: Oh, you did that?

MAN: Absolutely.

INTVR: Oh, that's wonderful. Did you get credit for it?

MAN: We didn't, and we were disappointed about that, Mike. Everyone else seemed to.

INTVR: I see. Well, how did you get started in this line of work?

MAN: I don't know. It was something about it that drew me into it, and I did inherit the world's largest manufacturer of this stuff.

INTVR: Well, artificial snow . . .

MAN: Analog snow.

INTVR: Analog snow . . . another reason the NYNEX Yellow Pages helps more people throughout New England find more goods and services.

MAN: Anything you get in your cuffs here you can keep, you know.

INTVR: No matter what you need, it's always there when you need it.

561

GUY: I'll bet you're the kind of person who's more interested in the beauty *inside* of people than the physical beauty on the outside.
I'll bet you think a great personality is much more important in someone than a great body.
I'll bet you think a good conversation can be far more stimulating than making love.
I'll bet you're ugly as a bald dog.

562

(MUSIC: COOL JAZZ; UP AND UNDER)

MAN: I'd guess you'd have to say my grandfather influenced me most. I remember the last time I saw him. Mother and daddy and I went to his house and as soon as we got in the front door he says, 'Come on into the kitchen we're gonna have a glass of wine.' This was unusual because my grandaddy only drank around the holidays with his meals. Of course, he always had a bottle of Manishewitz in the house, but then lots of families had Manischewitz around. It was a good wine and it wasn't too expensive. We keep it today for meals or parties or what not. Anyway he poured a glass of Manischewitz for everybody but me and he said, 'This here is a very important day for black people.' He lifted his glass, kinda smiled and a tear formed in the corner of his eye and he said, 'They just elected Jackie Robinson to the Baseball Hall of Fame.'

LIVE ANNCR: Manischewitz Wine Co., New York.

563

ANNCR: We got a helicopter.
They got a helicopter.
We got a seismograph.
They got a seismograph
We got cameras.
They got cameras.
We got typewriters.
They got typewriters.
We got trucks.
They got trucks.
We got a pencil sharpener.
They got a pencil sharpener.
We got reporters.
They got reporters.
We got a Peabody Award for broadcast journalism.

(SFX: THUMP)

They don't.
In this keep up with the other guys world of television news . . .
. . . it's important to remember who the other guys are trying to keep up with.
NewsCenter 4. At 5, 6 and 11.

564

(MAN READING—STRAIGHT, NOT SINGING)

READER: You ain't nothin' but a hound dog . . . cryin' all the time. You ain't nothin' but a hound dog . . . cryin' all the time. You ain't never caught a rabbit and you ain't no friend of mine. I used to think you was high class . . . but that was just a lie. I used to think you was high class . . . but that was just a lie.
You ain't never caught a rabbit and you ain't no friend of mine.

ANNCR: If it wasn't for Elvis Presley, some of the greatest songs of the nineteen-fifties might have been some of the worst songs of the century. Friday, KRLD-TV 33 will present an unusual look at the King of Rock 'N Roll. See Elvis Memories at 8, followed at 9 by a re-broadcast of Elvis' historical 1968 comeback performance on KRLD-TV 33. The King is dead. Long live the King.

(SFX: ARENA APPLAUSE UP)

ELVIS: You ain't nothin' but a hound dog . . .

565

MIKE: They say you can find anything in the NYNEX Yellow Pages. That's where we found the Stokes Gavel Company and owner Sid Stokes.

SID: We say a Stokes is the Stradivarius of gavels, Mike.

MIKE: Now . . . what makes a fine gavel?

SID: It's seasoned, American rock maple. You just can't beat it for sound . . .

(SFX: BANG, BANG)

SID: . . . or for safety.

MIKE: Safety?

SID: These cheap, imported gavels that are flooding the country now . . . they seem like a bargain, but wait until the head of a cheap gavel breaks loose someday and flies across the courtroom, injuring someone . . .

MIKE: Now has . . .

SID: Perhaps fatally, heaven forbid.

MIKE: Now has that actually happened?

SID: We in the American Gavel Makers Guild feel it's a tragedy waiting to happen.

MIKE: Anyway . . . when a judge needs a gavel he turns to the NYNEX Yellow Pages and finds . . .

SID: Now hold on, Mike . . . Stokes Gavels are excellent for home use too.

MIKE: Really? What would somebody . . .

SID: Oh . . . family tribunals, restoring order at the dinner table.

MIKE: My father always used to rap on a water glass with his knife.

SID: Well . . . he was a careless man, then.

MIKE: Well, I wouldn't call him . . .

SID: Because that glass could have shattered, showering the entire family with razor-like fragments. Heaven forbid.

MIKE: Well, another reason why the NYNEX Yellow Pages helps more New Yorkers find more goods and services.

SID: Heaven forbid that knife should slip . . . you'd be . . .

MIKE: It's always there when you need it.

566

(MUSIC: MELODIC PIANO UNDER ANNCR THROUGHOUT)

(SFX: BIRDS TWITTER)

ANNCR: Ah, Spring! Time again for Easter vacation and a chance to spend some time at home with your kids.

KEVIN: Hey, Mom! Wanna see how far I can throw Cindy?!

(SFX: GIRL SHRIEKS)

ANNCR: Sooner or later, but probably sooner, your kids are going to run out of things to do.

KEVIN: Mom, can I keep this snake?

CINDY: Daddy, guess what? Kevin teached me to spit. Huuuaaacccch!

ANNCR: See, Mom? You *can so* put forks in the microwave.

(SFX: ELECTRICAL SHORT AND EXPLOSION)

ANNCR: Magic Mountain's got over 100 exciting rides, shows and adventures, so you and your kids will have no trouble finding lots of fun things to do.

KEVIN: Hey, Mom! Look what I found in your pantyhose drawer!

ANNCR: Six Flags Magic Mountain. Because there's nothing like having the kids home from school.

LIVE ANNCR: Save $3.00 on admission by picking up a coupon at any participating Jack in the Box.

567

1. VO: I don't know about you, but I'm tired of all these three-syllable beers, Meistermiester, Lowenstein, Heinenkoogal. Californians drink three-syllable beers. Minnesotans drink one-syllable beer . . . Schmidt Beer. Now there's a name you can say after having a few.

2. TEACHER: Welcome class to Minnesota as a second language, 101, could we have the first slide please? Class what is this?

CLASS: Casserole.

TEACHER: No, it's a hot dish. Everyone.

CLASS: Hot dish.

TEACHER: Very good. Next, what is this?

CLASS: It's a rubber band.

TEACHER: No, rubber binder. Class, everyone.

CLASS: Rubber binder.

TEACHER: Very good. Now what is this next?

CLASS: Beer, isn't it?

TEACHER: No, in Minnesota it's Schmidt Beer. Everyone. Class.

CLASS: Schmidt Beer.

TEACHER: Very good. Class, next. What is this?

CLASS: Ish!

TEACHER: Close, Ludafisk.

CLASS: Ludafisk.

3. ANNCR: What would Minnesota be like without Schmidt Beer?

VENDOR: Popcorn, peanuts, daiquiries. Get 'em while they're cold. Daiquiris. Schmidt Beer. The brew that grew to be best in the great northwest.

Consumer Radio: Single

568
WRITER
Steve Kessler
AGENCY PRODUCER
David Prince
CLIENT
Apple Computer
AGENCY
Chiat/Day - Los Angeles

569
WRITER
Bill Johnson
AGENCY PRODUCER
Bill Johnson
CLIENT
Schmidt Beer
AGENCY
Ruhr/Paragon - Minneapolis

570
WRITER
Tom Thomas
AGENCY PRODUCER
Tom Thomas
CLIENT
Barron's
AGENCY
Angotti Thomas Hedge

571
WRITER
John Stingley
AGENCY PRODUCER
John Stingley
CLIENT
The Wall Street Journal
AGENCY
Fallon McElligott/Minneapolis

572
WRITERS
Charles Mullen
John Clapps
AGENCY PRODUCER
Richard Goldstein
CLIENT
Suntory Beer
AGENCY
Isidore & Paulson

573
WRITER
Dave Woodside
CLIENT
California Cooler
AGENCY
Chiat/Day - San Francisco

574
WRITERS
John Malecki
Ed Wolper
AGENCY PRODUCER
Carol Singer
CLIENT
Perdue
AGENCY
Scali McCabe Sloves

575
WRITERS
Lee Garfinkel
Bob Lapides
Bonni Winter
AGENCY PRODUCER
Bob Nelson
CLIENT
Apricot Computers
AGENCY
Levine Huntley Schmidt & Beaver

568

FATHER: Billy, you've laid around long enough. If you want to go to college, you'll have to get out there and get a job.

BILLY: Goo . . .

(MUSIC: UNDER ANNOUNCER AND OUT)

ANNCR 1: Studies show that the people most traumatized by college aren't students. They're parents.

(SFX: PHONE)

DAD: Hello.

SON: Hi, Dad. It's tuition time again.

DAD: Dad who?

SON: C'mon, Dad.

DAD: Dad's not here.

SON: You always do this.

DAD: Dad moved, changed his name, grew a beard and moved to another city.

SON: Put Mom on the phone.

DAD: Mom who?

ANNCR 2: So Apple, the company whose computers help kids get through school, is going to help parents get through school. It's Apple's $1,000,000 Education Sweepstakes. Grand Prize: $100,000 cash. Plus rebates of up to $250 on an Apple Computer system.

DAUGHTER: Stanford, Yale, Harvard—I was accepted everywhere!

MOM: That's wonderful, darling. Your father and I always wanted to live in an RV.

ANNCR 3: There's thousands of prizes. And rebates of up to $250 when you buy an Apple computer at any participating authorized Apple dealer. So enter Apple's Education Sweepstakes. And maybe, your kid'll go off to college with $100,000 in their pocket.

(SFX: PHONE)

DAD: Hi, son, it's mortgage time again.

SON: Son who?

(BUTTON)

ANNCR 4: No purchase necessary for sweepstakes entry. See dealer for details.

569

4. "CINDY STACCATO" VO: This is Cindy Staccato reporting. We all know that besides the water, the hop is the most important ingredient in beer. But we don't know what a hop is. We're up here interviewing Farmer Blite. Excuse me, Mr Blite, what is a hop?

FARMER: A hop, uh, of course that's ingredients you'd use in beer.

"CINDY": We know that.

FARMER: Well, here's an example. Hop right here.

"CINDY": That's a corn stalk.

FARMER: Uhhh. Well here's a hop.

"CINDY": That's a potato.

FARMER: Ya. Is that a hop?

"CINDY": That's a cow.

FARMER: Well, the Schmidt Beer people come up here and just take 'em, I just grow 'em. I don't really see 'em.

5. HUSBAND: Hi, Honey.

WIFE: Hi.

HUSBAND: Listen, I'm going to be a little late.

WIFE: Oh, Honey, what happened?

HUSBAND: Well, nothing happened, I have to buy something for the house.

WIFE: What?

HUSBAND: Another round of Schmidt.

6. "CINDY STACCATO" VO: This is Cindy Staccato back on the farm. Farmer Blite, what is that?

FARMER: That's your hop duster.

"CINDY": Why?

FARMER: Well, Schmidt Beer people won't take 'em if they're all dusty.

7. VO A: What happens when you throw a can of beer into the air conditioner?

VO B: A Schmidt hits the fan.

VO A: Schmidt Beer. The brew that grew to be best in the great northwest.

570

(SFX: MUSIC)

ANNCR: Big Money is often pictured swallowing up all of Wall Street's glittering prizes, while the rest of us stand famished on the sidelines.
This picture is a source of some amusement to Barron's readers.
Especially those who, managing their investments in kitchens and commuter trains, regularly outperform billion-dollar institutions.
Which explains their interest in Barron's.
Every week, Barron's provides one of the most complete digests of investment information in the world.
We interview Wall Street's most insightful stock pickers. Discover undiscovered companies.
And call important market changes with almost eerie foresight.
Because, contrary to popular belief, money doesn't automatically go to money. It prefers intelligence.
Barron's. It's how the smart money gets that way.

571

(SFX: CHURCH BELL CHIMING, HAMMOND ORGAN PLAYING BACH METHODICAL PIECE)

ANNCR: There are those who only do business one day a week. If that were true for all of us, a business weekly would be fine. Unfortunately, most of us do business Monday through Friday.

(SFX: CHURCH BELLS TRANSFORM INTO CAR HORNS WITH BUSY STREET SOUNDS)

ANNCR: Which is why The Wall Street Journal has so many loyal followers.

(SFX: UPBEAT FAST BACH PIECE STARTS)

ANNCR: Each business day, The Journal helps you become enlightened. With up to the minute stories on marketing ideas, technological breakthroughs, mergers . . . plus political updates, even social and cultural trends. What's more, you don't have to sell your soul to get it. Thirteen weeks of The Journal can be yours for just $28. Call in the continental U.S., 800-000-0000. That's 800-000-0000. (Except in Nebraska.) Thirteen weeks of The Journal, just $28. It's the surest way to get upstairs . . .

(SFX: MUSIC ENDS WITH CHIME)

ANNCR: If you don't have connections. The Wall Street Journal. The Daily Diary . . . of the American Dream.

572

(SFX: COTO PLAYS INTRODUCTION)

1ST JAPANESE ADMAN: Boss says we need new jingle to introduce Suntory Draft Beer overseas in America.

2ND JAPANESE ADMAN: How 'bout this (SINGS AND PLAYS COTO): *To good friends tonight is special night let it be Suntory.*

1ST: I like it, but how 'bout (SINGS AND PLAYS COTO): *Bring out your best.*

2ND: Too repetitious . . . Oh, how 'bout (SINGS AND PLAYS COTO): *This Suntory for you. DA DA DA.*

1ST (JOINS SINGING): *DA DA DA.*

2ND: This part we can say Suntory Draft Beer in bottle. No other imported beer says that.2

1ST: Smart. How 'bout (SINGS AND PLAYS COTO): *We brew excitement: Suntory Beer.*

2ND: Too mechanical. I like this better (SINGS AND PLAYS COTO): *Come to think of I'll have a Suntory.*

1ST: Sounds a little familiar.

2ND: I think your coto is a little out of tune.

ANNCR: Introducing Suntory's new advertising campaign: we have a lot of catching up to do.

573

VO: You know, my friend Aldo came over today and gave me this California Cooler.

(SFX: POP, GURGLE, FIZZ)

Now, I hate California. You know what it is? It's what it does to your body. You move out there looking like me, then you come back with muscles. I don't need it. Your skin turns brown, your hair turns blond. This is not good for you. Your teeth get whiter. And then the sun dries out your zits. Hey man, I'm a lifeguard. I have a totally awesome, bronze bod. Don't touch. Get outta here. You know, you move to California. First of all you stop eating American food. No white bread, no salami, no bratwurst. Everything's good for you. Bagels are like some rare treat from some foreign land. Meanwhile, you eat all this garbage, you live longer but so what, your mind gets soft. Then they pay money to chant along with Raji-oly-oxen-free. Who are these people? You know, I even hate what they drink. Aha, look at it. This stuff. California Cooler. I hate the name. You drink it ice cold, on a hot day. (POURING) I hate it. I really hate it. Heh, heh, just pretend you never saw me drinkin' the stuff, will ya?

ANNCR: California Cooler.
One more reason to hate California.
California Cooler, Stockton, California.

574

ANNCR: Ladies and gentlemen, Mr Frank Perdue.

FRANK PERDUE: Have you noticed a disturbing decline in grooming habits? I can hardly walk by a meat case without seeing chickens sporting pinfeathers, unsightly wing hairs, even whole feathers. And unless you're stuffing a pillow along with your chicken, what do you do with them? To avoid this ugly scene, buy my fresh, delicious Perdue chickens. I remove that unwanted hair and stubble, so you won't have to. If your store sells you a chicken that needs a shave and a haircut, take it back. And tell them to clean up their act. Then demand Perdue. It's one good-looking chicken. And I can tell you first hand, good looks go a long way in the chicken business.

ANNCR: When it comes to chickens, Frank Perdue is even tougher than you are. He has to be. Because every one of his Perdue chickens comes with his name on it and his money-back guarantee. It takes a tough man to make a tender chicken. Perdue.

575

BRITISH ANNCR: Unlike you Americans, we British have a certain knack for doing things right. Take fine theatre for example. We gave the world "Shakespeare." While your country gave the world "Mr Ed." Now really, wherefore are thou, Mr Ed? And what about music? England gave America The Beatles. Whereas America gave England the Partridge Family. And I thought we were allies. But, no hard feelings, and so now we're making another great contribution to civilization, Apricot. Apricot is Europe's most successful line of business computers. They're elegant, compact, easy-to-use, and run thousands of MS-DOS business software programs. So now the choice is yours. Would you rather buy a computer from the country that created the Rolls Royce, or the country that gave you the Edsel?

Consumer Radio: Single

576
WRITERS
John Lewis
Dawn French
Jennifer Saunders
AGENCY PRODUCER
Louise Fazackerley
CLIENT
Outline
AGENCY
McCann-Erickson/London

577
WRITER
Steve Ward
AGENCY PRODUCER
Siobhan O'Connor
CLIENT
7-Eleven
AGENCY
Ayer Barker/London

578
WRITER
Dave Woodside
CLIENT
California Cooler
AGENCY
Chiat/Day - San Francisco

579
WRITER
Dave Woodside
CLIENT
California Cooler
AGENCY
Chiat/Day - San Francisco

580
WRITERS
Jay Taub
Tod Seisser
AGENCY PRODUCERS
Rob Thomas
Rachel Novak
CLIENT
New York Air
AGENCY
Levine Huntley Schmidt & Beaver

581
WRITER
Ernie Schenck
AGENCY PRODUCER
Ernie Schenck
CLIENT
Vanderbilt Rehabilitation Center
AGENCY
Leonard Monahan Saabye/ Providence, RI

582
WRITERS
Jim Offerman
Pat McCormick
AGENCY PRODUCER
Jim Offerman
CLIENT
Mother Tucker's
AGENCY
DBK&O/Minneapolis

576

(DAWN FRENCH AND JENNIFER SAUNDERS)

DF: 'Cause I don't believe in diets . . . I don't need to . . .

JS: No.

DF: . . . of course. I mean, if you had to describe me, what would you say?

JS: You're sort of . . . sort of round . . .

DF: . . . sort of rounded . . .

JS: Yes.

DF: . . . happy . . .

JS: Yeh, that's right.

DF: Mm.

JS: Yeh, plump . . .

DF: What?

JS: Er . . .

DF: I mean, you wouldn't say fat, would you?

JS: I'd never say fat, no.

DF: No, exactly.

DF/JS: No, I'd never use the word fat.

JS: So why . . . why are you eating Outline, then?

DF: Oh, this . . .

JS: Mm.

DF: . . . who put that there? Well, I do, I do quite like the taste, that's all.

JS: Mm. It's just that it's low in calories, you know that?

DF: Is it?

JS: Yes.

DF: No, I didn't know that.

JS: Mm.

DF: I mean, you can't taste that, it—it tastes fine.

JS: No, it's just that, you know, if I want to drop a few pounds, then I use it as part of my calorie-controlled diet.

DF: Do you?

JS: Yes. I was wondering if . . .

DF: Well, that's probably because you do need to drop a few pounds. I don't, do I?

JS: Well . . .

FVO: From the Inner Woman comes the Outer Woman with a little help from Outline, low calorie, low fat spread.

577

(SFX: TRAFFIC AMBIANCE; SHOP BELL)

MVO1: Morning, Squire . . . Can I help you?

MVO2: Ah, yes . . . I'd like a hamburger please.

MVO1: Sorry . . .don't do hamburgers.

MVO2: Well, just a hot coffee then.

MVO1: No hot coffee.

MVO2: Oh . . . a newspaper?

MVO1: No.

MVO2: Motor oil?

MVO1: Uh uh.

MVO2: Rent a video movie.

MVO1: No.

MVO2: Well, where can I get all these things?

MVO1: Next door at the 7-Eleven store, of course.

MVO2: Oh . . . right . . . Well, what do you sell here then?

MVO1: Raspberries.

MVO2: Well, I'll have one of those please.

MVO1: Certainly. Blaaaph!

MVO3: For a much more convenient way to shop . . .
visit your local 7-Eleven store . . .
We've got it all in one.

578

(SFX: BOTTLE CAP OFF, POUR)

VO: I can't believe I'm drinking this California Cooler. I hate California. I hate giving pedestrians the right of way. Everybody drives around in convertibles and plays golf in January. You go to the beach, palm trees, guacamole, little tan lines from designer sunglasses. What's everybody so happy about anyway? I think it's a law in California, you gotta have fun at least twice a day. Have a good one! Have a good what? What are they talkin' about? (CHUCKLING) The state flower's a poppy, well isn't that cute. The state bird is a quail; the thing doesn't even fly, it jogs. Surfing, everybody's surfing. Surfing is so stupid. What's a boogie board anyway? People skateboardin' through supermarkets looking for organic vegetables and vitamins. (AH) Then, after a tough day of tennis in 90° weather, they go home and barbecue a hamburger on 9-grain bread and have a California Cooler. I hate it. (POURING) I really hate it. Let me try one more of those. (PAUSE) I still hate it.

ANNCR: California Cooler.
One more reason to hate California.
Caifornia Cooler, Stockton, California.

579

SLAYTON: You know, California Cooler is making a real big deal about their orange cooler for Halloween. Halloween in California? Who are they kidding. *Every* day is Halloween in California. What do they do, dress up like *normal* people for a day? Three hundred sixty-four days a year everyone walks around looking like an extra in the Wizard of Oz. Halloween rolls around, they dress like insurance salesmen. Parties everywhere. Get outta here. Hey, nobody's going to tell me to drink California Cooler Orange just because it's Halloween. No way, uh-uh.

(SFX: BOTTLE OPEN, POUR OVER ICE)

I'm going to drink California Cooler Orange any day I want.

ANNCR: California Cooler, Stockton, California.

580

(SFX: COURTROOM SOUNDS, GAVEL HITTING DESK)

INVESTIGATOR: I need quiet in this room. Now senator, can you explain why a 2 million dollar check was made out in your name and filed under house appropriations?

SENATOR: Yes. I fixed up my house.

(SFX: SOUNDS OF PEOPLE TALKING, GAVEL HITTING DESK)

INVESTIGATOR: And, also senator, can you explain why according to your last year's tax returns, your deductions were greater than your income?

(SFX: COURT SOUNDS OF PEOPLE TALKING; FADE OUT)

ANNCR: At New York Air, we know, some people need to get out of Washington in a hurry. So, in addition to our frequent service from National, we're offering frequent service from Dulles. With 10 flights every weekday to New York and 8 to Boston. And all through a brand new terminal that offers walkways to your plane. Not crowded buses.
New York Air's new Dulles service.

(SFX: GAVEL HITTING DESK, PEOPLE TALKING)

INVESTIGATOR: This hearing will now resume. Now Senator. Senator? Has anyone seen the senator? (FADE OUT)

(SFX: PLANE TAKING OFF)

ANNCR: Call your travel agent or New York Air today.

581

(MUSIC: COUNTRY GUITAR SOLO; SLOWLY)

VO: You wouldn't remember him anymore. But that's all right. All that matters is that he was a kid from Texas with a cheap guitar, singing for beers and gas money. Until the word got out. The money. The Cadillacs. He took it all. Until a blown-out tire and a rainy Alabama turnpike took it all back. They say he's back in Texas now with a wooden leg and a dusty gold record. He doesn't sing anymore. It's not that he can't. He won't. At Vanderbilt Rehabilitation Center in Newport, we know how a sudden physical handicap can cripple a person's spirit. But it doesn't have to. You see, at Vanderbilt, before you can learn to live with a handicap, you've got to learn to live with something far more important. Yourself. Vanderbilt Rehabilitation Center at Newport Hospital.
Ask your doctor, or call 401-847-0802.

582

INTVR: Uh . . . Again, we're talking to the world's most famous restaurant critic.

MCCORMICK: I certainly am. Because I've been all over and I know my stuff.

INTVR: I guess some of the restaurants you've been to are pretty expensive.

MCCORMICK: Yes, some of them, they . . . they actually want you to lease the food. One place they had . . . every stick of asparagus was flown in from another country . . .

INTVR: Uh-huh.

MCCORMICK: . . . and the one from Greenland, by the way, was mighty chewy. They're so expensive, some of these places, it's no wonder the cashier has a bullet-proof face.

INTVR: Is there a restaurant you can recommend?

MCCORMICK: Mother Tucker's is the perfect restaurant. I . . . I feel like a knight who's been out on a quest. I have found it. $7.95 to $13.95, the perfect range.

INTVR: The people at Mother Tucker's. Do they treat you well?

MCCORMICK: You just feel at home there. Uh, they . . . they let you yodel if you want to. And . . . and wear Swiss hats. You can sit on a Swiss hat and yodel. They let you relax. You can put your hands in your pockets if you want to, they'll feed you.

INTVR: The people seem so very nice. Anyone ever been thrown out of Mother Tucker's?

MCCORMICK: Well, yes. There was one big, obstreperous fat man. And they went to throw him out, but he quickly buttered his body and they didn't do it. They didn't want to do it anyway, they're so nice there.

Consumer Radio: Single

583
WRITERS
Bill Heater
Vashti Brotherhood
AGENCY PRODUCER
Lisa Page
CLIENT
New England Ford
AGENCY
Hill Holliday Connors Cosmopulos/Boston

584
WRITER
Ernie Schenck
AGENCY PRODUCER
Ernie Schenck
CLIENT
Vanderbilt Rehabilitation Center
AGENCY
Leonard Monahan Saabye/ Providence, RI

585
WRITER
Dan Brown
AGENCY PRODUCER
Lou Stamoulis
CLIENT
Massachusetts Electric
AGENCY
Harold Cabot & Company/ Boston

586
WRITER
Tom Nelson
AGENCY PRODUCER
Tom Keramidas
CLIENT
Ameritech Mobile Communications
AGENCY
Ogilvy & Mather/Chicago

587
WRITERS
Jay Taub
Tod Seisser
AGENCY PRODUCER
Rob Thomas
CLIENT
New York Air
AGENCY
Levine Huntley Schmidt & Beaver

588
WRITER
Tim Kane
AGENCY PRODUCER
Kathy Heinrich
CLIENT
Eagle Foods
AGENCY
Ogilvy & Mather/Chicago

589
WRITERS
Jay Taub
Tod Seisser
John Cleese
AGENCY PRODUCER
Bob Nelson
CLIENT
Kronenbourg Beer
AGENCY
Levine Huntley Schmidt & Beaver

583

CHAIRMAN: Good morning and welcome to the first annual meeting of the Ford Aerostar mini-van owners club.

PEOPLE: Good morning, Mr Chairman. Lay it on us.

CHAIRMAN: Well, I spoke with a couple of you before the meeting and I was rapping about some of the bad vibes I was feeling. But now I'd like to say that I'm feeling a lot groovier.

PEOPLE: That's cool.

CHAIRMAN: Yeah. I caught a little buzz with the—some of the people from division about how way out of sight The New 1986 Aerostar was.

PEOPLE: Right on . . . Mr Chairman.

CHAIRMAN: Yeah . . . about how it fits in with our current lifestyles being Mommas and Poppas with . . . you know . . . like real jobs. Which is . . . like FANWONDEFULTASTIC. If you can dig that.

PEOPLE: We can dig that.

CHAIRMAN: And how it's big enough for all the bambinos. And how it can tow our motorhomes now. And our big boats.

PEOPLE: Right on.

CHAIRMAN: And how Aerostar is like the dawning of a whole new age of like 1960s proportions and how it looks real good when we pull into fancy restaurants instead of those crummy ham and egg joints we used to go to.

PEOPLE: Yeah.

CHAIRMAN: And . . . well, anyway . . . I was having these bad vibes because . . . you know . . . I thought maybe we were selling out.

PEOPLE: We can dig that.

CHAIRMAN: So I was thinking for the outing maybe we'd all hop into our Aerostars and drive to Woodstock to relive the experience.

PEOPLE: Yeah.

CHAIRMAN: Except this time . . . maybe we'll stay at a motel.

(JINGLE UP)

584

(MUSIC: "HURRY FOR HOLLYWOOD"; SLOWLY, ON CLARINET)

VO: What do you say about a skinny waitress from Little Rock? . . . That she traded in her apron for a soundstage? . . . That she left home for a gold star and a White Dusenberg? . . . And what do you say when you're 70 and no one remembers once-upon-a-time movie queens . . . no one but a young director with something to prove. A comeback, he called it. But a stroke with a lousy sense of timing had other plans. Now she just sits in the darkness, lost in a screenful of memories. At Vanderbilt Rehabilitation Center we know how a sudden physical handicap can cripple a person's spirit. But it doesn't have to. You see, at Vanderbilt, before you can learn to live with a handicap, you've got to learn to live with something far more important . . . yourself. Vanderbilt Rehabilitation Center at Newport Hospital.
Ask your doctor, or call 401-847-0802.

585

ANNCR: Hi. Norm Newsworthy here in jail, and with me is the mastermind of an ill-fated highjacking attempt.

HIJACKER: Hi, Mom.

ANNCR: Tell me, Shake, why on earth would you want to hijack of all things a coal ship?

HIJACKER: I like fossil fuels.

ANNCR: You do?

HIJACKER: There's no fuel like . . .

HIJACKER & ANNCR: . . . an old fuel

ANNCR: No, come on, be serious.

HIJACKER: O.K. I hijacked the coal ship because it was good for business.

ANNCR: How's that?

HIJACKER: Well, the less coal there is, the more oil I can sell. Hi, mom.

ANNCR: So, you were attempting to hijack a Massachusetts Electrics coal ship because it's a threat to your oil business?

HIJACKER: Now you got it, buster. Mass Electric was using its capitalist coal to generate electricity instead of using my . . .

ANNCR: . . . ridiculously over-priced oil.

HIJACKER: Right.

ANNCR: But by using coal, Mass Electric was keeping their costs down. That's part of their plan. Surely you can't blame them for that.

HIJACKER: I can't?

ANNCR: No. What's more, by converting the generating plants to coal, millions of people benefitted.

HIJACKER: One sheik should suffer so millions can benefit? What kind of crazy country is this?

ANNCR: Massachusetts Electric, putting your needs first.

HIJACKER: Hi, Mom.

586

(MUSIC UNDER THROUGHOUT)

SINGER: *I get up in the mornin' (oh yeah)*
Climb in to my car
Head onto the freeway, baby
But I don't get too far
I'm just another frustrated executive
With those stuck in traffic
Goin' nowhere
Talking' to no one but my radio
Blues . . .

MR DUGGAN: If you drive on business, get an Ameritech car telephone. Thanks to Ameritech, a sales rep sold $15,000 worth of steel in a traffic jam.
A real estate agent sold 3 properties in a week.
And a commercial broker closed a 2 million dollar deal in an hour.
So stop singin' the blues. And start raking in the green.

SINGER: *So I got me an Ameritech car telephone*
And got rid of those stuck in traffic
Goin' nowhere
Talkin' to no one but my radio
Blues . . .
I'm making money now, baby.

(SFX: HONK HONK)

SINGER: *Groovy, far out.*

587

(SFX: DRUMROLL THROUGHOUT)

ANNCR: Traditionally, people have spent fortunes trying to get into Washington. But it's not just a matter of tradition. It's a matter of record.
For example, in 1980, Ronald Reagan spent 60 million dollars. Jimmy Carter spent 50 million dollars. John Anderson spent 7 million and Ramsey Clark 3 million.
In 1984, Ronald Reagan spent 73 million dollars. Walter Mondale 30 million dollars. Gary Hart 21 million dollars and John Glenn, 14 million dollars.
But in 1985, Mr Joshua Taub of Jacksonville spent only 49 dollars getting into Washington. Because he flew New York Air. The airline that flies nonstop from Jacksonville to Dulles for just 49 dollars. So now, just about anyone can buy their way into Washington.

"NIXON": One ticket to Dulles please. And, uh, you'll take a check from me, won't ya?

LIVE ANNCR: For more details call your travel agent or New York Air. The voice was that of Larry Kenney.

588

(SFX: CHICKENS CLUCKING)

GUY: I got 2 chickens here.
One's a Five Star chicken, from Eagle.
The other isn't.
Now, you folks at home see if you can tell which is which.
Give you a hint—Five Star chickens are supposed to weigh at least 2¼ pounds.
Anything smaller just won't be meaty enough.
Okay, so which is the Five Star . . .
Chicken number 1?

CHICKEN (WEAKLY): buck, buck, buck . . .

GUY: Or chicken number 2?

CHICKEN (BOLDLY): BUCK! BUCK! BUCK!!

GUY: Well, heck. Give it away, why dontcha.

ANNCR: Five Star chicken from Eagle. You'll love it, or your money back.

589

Hello, ah look, this is another ad for Kronenbourg beer, and today Kronenbourg wants me to tell you all about Kronenbourg's superb sophisticated European flavour. The only thing is . . . they're deciding at the moment whether to use me for next year's campaign, and if sales went up a bit, it would improve my chances and I need the work; so please, please drink more Kronenbourg beer, umm I . . . I have such a wonderful family and things haven't been easy for us the last few years and just recently, they've been developing this liking for food, so please could you have an extra Kronenbourg this weekend, or if you've never tried one before just give it a whirl, I mean it *is* the leading bottle of beer in the whole of Europe, it's not going to kill you, or even . . . have a sip of someone else's. Don't worry, just tell them I said it would be O.K., but please, *please*, all of you, buy more Kronenbourg imported by Kronenbourg, USA, Greenwich, Connecticut. It even comes in two flavours, light and dark, and if you don't like either of them you can mix them together, make a flavour you do like . . . so remember, my family's future's in your hands . . . I plead with you, drink Kronenbourg, please, just one case . . . I don't know how we'll manage if you don't . . . I'm sorry, I'm sorry . . .

Consumer Radio: Single

590
WRITER
Craig Weise
AGENCY PRODUCER
Craig Weise
CLIENT
Successful Farming
AGENCY
Creswell Munsell Fultz & Zirbel/Des Moines, IA

591
WRITER
Pacy Markman
AGENCY PRODUCER
Diane Hill
CLIENT
General Telephone
AGENCY
Doyle Dane Bernbach/Los Angeles

592
WRITER
Joy Golden
AGENCY PRODUCER
Michael Pollock
CLIENT
Fromageries Bel
AGENCY
TBWA

593
WRITER
Joy Golden
AGENCY PRODUCERS
Michael Pollock
Dottie Wilson
CLIENT
Granada
AGENCY
TBWA

594
WRITER
Arthur Bijur
AGENCY PRODUCER
Deed Meyer
CLIENT
Wendy's International
AGENCY
Dancer Fitzgerald Sample

595
WRITERS
Bert Berdis
Alan Barzman
Jim Kirby
CLIENT
Canon Typewriters
AGENCY
Bert Barz & Kirby/Hollywood

596
WRITER
Larry Volpi
AGENCY PRODUCER
Jim Derusha
CLIENT
Nestle
AGENCY
J. Walter Thompson

590

ANNCR (ORT PAULSEN TYPE): Hello. What we'd like to talk to you folks in Chicago about is Successful Farming. That's the name of a magazine, y'see, that's put out by the Meredith Corporation. Now, why would someone in Chicago be interested in Successful Farming? . . . Well, fact is, you're probably not, but farmers are and that's the whole point. Maybe you didn't know that some farmers out there buy a whole lot of things. Like cars, and appliances, they take vacations . . . and, well, maybe Successful Farming may not be your best bet for a men's cologne ad . . . but for other things . . . uh, in fact, the most successful farmers spend more time reading Successful Farming than any other general farm national publication. Successful Farming has an office right here in Chicago . . . Give 'em a call . . . and some guys in clean shoes will come right over and see you. Thanks.

591

BACKUP SINGERS: *Nine seven six*
Nine seven six

SINGER: *If a number begins with nine seven six*
You can make some truly interesting calls.
Like you can get your horoscope
Or get the latest sports results
When you dial 976.
But when you dial 976,
There's something real important you should know,
Every call to 976 costs—yes, it costs—some dough.
And when your parents open the phone bill,
They could be a little upset,
They could take away some of your privileges
Like leaving the house,
Not to mention, never driving the car.
So you see, the point of this song is simple:
Calls to 976 aren't free.
This message is brought to you by the folks,
Yes, the folks at GTE.

592

So like I'm totally into astrology, O.K. So I went to this midnight swim party and they had this totally awesome pool made like a star with like little lighted points. O.K. I mean like I just freaked. I thought like wow something really max is rising over my Pisces. And oh my gosh, I was right. It was the gorgoso highway patrolman in his orange speedos rising out of the star. And I said, 'Hi, officer remember me? The girl in the Trans-Am who had the little round laughing cow in the red net bag in her trunk.' He said, 'How did it breathe?' Ha. Ha. I mean like attention comedy producers. I said, 'Officer, it wasn't a real cow, it was cheese. Mild Mini Bonbel, Nippy Mini Baby Bel and Mini Gouda. You know like really awesome and naturale. Five delicious bite-size cheeses in their own red net bags, freshly wrapped in wax with an easy open zip.' He said, 'Pool's cold.' I mean like he was so totally sensitive to his environment. So I said, 'Like well when you warm up I'll bring you a Laughing Cow on a cracker, O.K.' So he said, 'O.K.' So I said, 'O.K.' O.K. So I did. So then I said, 'Officer like what's your sign?' And he said, 'No parking.'

593

MC: Good evening. Welcome to Living Habits of the Tight and Cheap. We're in the dinky yard of Mr Tony Parsimony, owner of the smallest above-ground vinyl-lined swimming pool. Why so small, Tony?

TONY: Any bigger, ya get people comin' over. They want a towel. They want powder.

MC: Right, Tony. Well, let's move inside to Tony's flimsy home. I see there's no sink. No stove. No TV. No furniture. Why, Tony?

TONY: Well, then you get people comin' over. They want lamps. They want a baloney sandwich.

MC: Tony, you could have an even *more* well-rounded life with a TV and a VCR.

TONY: Nah, then you need a table. Then you need legs for it.

MC: Tony, you can RENT a brand-name TV, VCR and stand from Granada for less than a dollar a day.

TONY: Less than a buck? Granada's cheaper than I am. I'll put it by the pool.

MC: Why not inside, Tony?

TONY: Then you get people comin' over. They want water. Then they want a bathroom.

MC: For your TV, VCR, and stand for less than a dollar a day, call 1-800-GRANADA.

TONY: Hey, lend me a quarter.

MC: The call's free, Tony.

TONY: Don't be Mr Nice Guy. Six months, I'll have it paid off.

594

ANNCR: Yow does this recipe for a hamburger sound to you?
First take the frozen beef out of the freezer. Then throw the frozen beef onto the grill and thaw it out 'till it cooks. Then put the frozen thawed-out cooked hamburger in a plastic box. Next turn on the heat lamps. Now slide the plastic box containing the frozen thawed-out cooked hamburger down the chute and let it sit in a holding bin.
We at Wendy's don't like the sound of that. So at Wendy's your hamburger is made only from fresh ground beef and served immediately fresh, hot off the grill. Now doesn't a fresh Wendy's hamburger sound better than one of those others?
Wendy's hamburgers are always served fresh and hot right off the grill. The others aren't.

595

(SFX: ELECTRIC TYPEWRITER)

ANNCR: And now, Canon Electronic Typewriters presents another Canon Case History . . .

MAN: You're the president of a very big corporation?

GUY: Yes. We're called The Very Big Corporation.

MAN: So you're big.

GUY: Very big.

MAN: How big are you?

GUY: We are so big—

MAN: Yes?

GUY: —I have no idea what we do.

MAN: That is big.

GUY: Very big. But I can tell you this: there's a lot of typing going on here.

MAN: Yes. Typing.

GUY: The sound of typing is the sound of industry here at The Very Big Corporation. Listen . . .

(SFX: DOOR OPEN, LOTS OF ELECTRONIC TYPEWRITERS)

Those are the newly re-designed, sturdy-as-rock, durable Canon AP-300 electronic typewriters.

(SFX: DOOR CLOSE, TYPEWRITERS OUT)

MAN: Well, they have a host of time-saving automatic features.

GUY: Like decimal tab and line-framing for charts.

MAN: Plus a 32-character display. The new Canon AP-300 is really built for reliability.

GUY: Yes. Before we got Canons, our old typewriters were always conking out, down for repairs.

MAN: Yes.

GUY: In those days we were called—

BOTH: The Very Small Corporation.

MAN: Yes. So, thanks to Canon, the fastest-growing name in office typewriters—

GUY: —The Very Big Corporation is the fastest-growing name in—what'd I say we do here?

MAN: You didn't.

GUY: Oh.

MAN: Yes.

ANNCR: To find out more about the surprisingly-affordable Canon AP-300, and the complete line of Canon typewriters, look for your Canon dealer in the Yellow Pages.

GUY: (Wonder what *we're* listed under . . .)

596

MUSIC/LYRICS: *Sweet dreams you can't resist*
N—E—S—T—L—E—S
Chocolate made of this
N—E—S—T—L—E—S
Ooh smooth
Ooh rich
Nestles makes the very best

ANNCR VO: Nestle Milk Chocolate Bar
Plain or almond
Sweet dreams you can't resist.

Consumer Radio: Single

597
WRITERS
Brad Riddoch
Randy Diplock
AGENCY PRODUCER
Carlo Trulli
CLIENT
Reader's Digest
AGENCY
J. Walter Thompson/Toronto

598
WRITERS
Stephen Denvir
Gary Abraham
AGENCY PRODUCER
Katherine McGillivray
CLIENT
Pepsi Cola Canada
AGENCY
J. Walter Thompson/Toronto

599
WRITER
Mark Vieha
AGENCY PRODUCER
Steve Neely
CLIENT
Levi's 501 Jeans
AGENCY
Foote Cone & Belding/San Francisco

600
WRITER
Mark Vieha
AGENCY PRODUCER
Steve Neely
CLIENT
Levi's 501 Jeans
AGENCY
Foote Cone & Belding/San Francisco

601
WRITERS
Steve Eichenbaum
Mark Catterson
AGENCY PRODUCERS
Steve Eichenbaum
Wayne Juhlin
CLIENT
V. Richard's Market
AGENCY
Curro/Eichenbaum - Milwaukee

602
WRITER
Mark Vieha
AGENCY PRODUCER
Steve Neely
CLIENT
Levi's 501 Jeans
AGENCY
Foote Cone & Belding/San Francisco

603
WRITER
Don White
CLIENT
Eggs Authority
AGENCY
McCann-Erickson/London

597

ANNCR: In July 1982, 18-year old Bruce Curtis went to Loch Arbour New Jersey for a weekend. He hasn't been home since.

(SFX: GUN SHOT)

SON: Al tried to kill me.

MOTHER: If you come in we can talk.

FATHER: You're stealing things . . .

SON: I haven't . . .

(SFX: 5 GUN SHOTS)

(SFX: SILENCE)

SON: What happened?

BRUCE: I shot your mother.

ANNCR: Bruce Curtis, hopeless victim or thrill killer? This month in Reader's Digest.

598

CLEESE: Hello. John Cleese again.
It seems that my talking about Diet Pepsi Free has only confused the issue further, so Pepsi has agreed with my suggestion that I do a jingle instead.

(SFX: FUMBLING WITH RECORD PLAYER)

So just a moment—I've just got to figure out how to work this thing . . . sorry technical difficulties . . . ah, here we go.

(SFX: RECORD NEEDLE BEING PLACED ON VARIOUS PARTS OF RECORD; IT FINALLY GOES DOWN ON THE FINALE OF THE 1812 OVERTURE)

CLEESE (SINGING): *Diet Pepsi has no caffeine.*
Diet Pepsi has no caffeine.
Neither does regular Pepsi Free.
Diet Pepsi has no caffeine.
It also has that spiffing Pepsi taste.
It also has that spiffing Pepsi taste.
And so does regular Pepsi Free . . . regular Pepsi Free.
Free, Free, Free, Free . . .

(SFX: THE RECORD BEGINS TO SKIP)

CLEESE: Well at the very least you have to admire my courage.

ANNCR VO: Diet Pepsi Free has 1 calorie per 280ml and is suitable for carbohydrate- and calorie-reduced diets.

599

(SFX: UNDER THROUGHOUT)

MALE VOICE: *Um, Um, Um, Um, I don't worry, no I won't feel bad.*
Got the 501 Blues
They gonna feel glad.
Got to have them every day so they fit my way.
Uah, I'm talking to Levi's buttonfly 501 blues.

(SFX: CLAPPING SOLO)

MALE VOICE: *Blue as the sky with a buttonfly—y—y—y.*
You got to understand I'm a Levi's 501 natural bluesman.

(SFX: CLAPPING SOLO)

MALE VOICE: *You know I've got the moves always feels just right.*
In my natural blues got 'em day and night.

(SFX: CLAPPING SOLO)

MALE VOICE: *Easy kind of fading, ain't nothing complicated.*
You got to understand I'm a Levi's 501 natural bluesman.

SFX: CLAPPING SOLO; CLAPPING OUT)

600

(MUSIC: UP AND UNDER THROUGHOUT)

MALE SINGER: *I must be in Levi's Heaven*
Cause a sweet angel loves me in my 501 jeans.
Yes, when she whispers things so sweet and nice
I know I'm in Levi's Paradise, Oh yes I am.
Nobody ever told me that I could feel so fine
When I wear my 501 blues I'm on cloud number 9, hey.
Shrink-to-fit my body and with a buttonfly style.
The soul of my Levi's blues drives the angels wild.
Nobody told me heaven would be,
Oh 501 blues.

(MUSIC: OUT)

601

(SFX: SUPERMARKET AMBIANCE)

CLEESE: Hello, this is a famous English person standing in the aisle at V. Richard's European Market in Brookfield. And I'm here interviewing *real* V. Richard's customers. Excuse me, ma'am?

CLEESE IN FALSETTO: Yes?

CLEESE: We've never met before, is that correct?

CLEESE IN FALSETTO: Yes, that's true.

CLEESE: So when I ask you your opinion of V. Richard's Market, it will be completely unsolicited?

CLEESE IN FALSETTO: Right.

CLEESE: Good. What do you think?

CLEESE IN FALSETTO (AS IF READING): I think V. Richard's has the most incredibly unique selection of fresh produce, cheeses, wines, meats, fish and other delicacies that I've ever seen in my life.

CLEESE: Super! And you're sure you're not related to me?
No, I'm not at all (CATCHES HIMSELF).

CLEESE IN FALSETTO: I mean, no. I'm not at all related.

CLEESE: Good.

CLEESE IN FALSETTO: Now what about V. Richard's baked goods?

CLEESE: Well, they're . . . hold it, I ask the questions.

CLEESE IN FALSETTO: Sorry. I got confused.

CLEESE: Hold it. Hold it. I can't go on with this charade. I'm doing both voices because the cheapskates at the agency wouldn't pay for two actors and I'm sorry but it's just—well, everybody is doing testimonial ads today and I just wanted you to try V. Richard's Market because it truly is exciting. And so, look, just promise me that you'll visit V. Richard's, and I'll remove this wig and make-up from the left-hand side of my face and promise never, never to misbehave again, I promise!

602

(MUSIC: UP AND UNDER THROUGHOUT)

GROUP SINGERS: *OOOOOOOOOOOOH*

MALE SINGER: *Every late night morning I put on my blues*

GROUP SINGER: *Ooo bop bop*

MALE SINGER: *Uh huh*

GROUP SINGERS: *Ooo bop*

MALE SINGER: *Levi's buttonfly 501 blues.*

GROUP SINGERS: *Ooo bop bop ooo bop.*

MALE SINGER: *Well, well they shrink down to fit you and only you. They*

MALE SINGER & GROUP: *Button flyyyyyyy.*

MALE SINGER: *Don't it make you wanna ooo*

GROUP SINGERS: *Ooo bop bop ooo bop.*

MALE SINGER: *That's the truth.*

GROUP SINGERS: *Ooo bop bop ooo bop.*

MALE SINGER: *Yeah, yeah, oh my radio's busted and my rent is due.*

GROUP SINGER: *Ooo bop bop.*

MALE SINGERS: *All right.*

GROUP SINGERS: *Ooo bop bop.*

MALE SINGER: *My, my, my woman left me that's nothing new,*
Ah hah

GROUP SINGERS: *Ooo bop bop.*

MALE SINGERS: *But I'm still looking like*

GROUP SINGERS: *Looking like*

GROUP & MALE SINGER: *Front page news*

MALE VOICE: *With my*

GROUP & MALE SINGER: *Buttonfly, buttonfly*

MALE VOICE: *501 blues.*

GROUP SINGERS: *Ooo bop bop ooo bop.*

MALE VOICE: *That's the truth.*

GROUP SINGERS: *Ooo bop bop ooo bop.*

MALE SINGER: *Levi's 501 blues*

GROUP SINGERS: *Ooo bop bop ooo bop*

MALE BASE SINGER SOLO: *501 blues.*

MALE SINGER: *Don't it make you want, wanna oooo*

GROUP SINGERS: *Ooo bop bop ooo bop . . .*

603

MAN: Sweetheart, there's a grand piano in the kitchen.

WOMAN: I know, darling, the egg timer's broken.

MAN (QUESTIONINGLY): There's a grand piano in the kitchen because the egg timer's broken?

WOMAN: Mmm-mm. Now when I boil your eggs in the morning, all I have to do is play The Minute Waltz four times. See!

(SHE BEGINS TO PLAY THE MINUTE WALTZ AT GREAT SPEED)

MAN (OVER THE MUSIC): What if you make a mistake. . . ?

WOMAN: Oh, I start over . . .

(SHE MAKES A MISTAKE AND BEGINS AGAIN)

MVO: Eggs are smashing, go smash an egg.

Consumer Radio: Single

604
WRITERS
Lee Garfinkel
Bob Lapides
Bonni Winter
AGENCY PRODUCER
Bob Nelson
CLIENT
Apricot Computers
AGENCY
Levine Huntley Schmidt & Beaver

605
WRITER
William Fidel
AGENCY PRODUCERS
Brian Keller
William Fidel
CLIENT
Center Stage
AGENCY
Eisner & Associates/ Baltimore

Consumer Radio: Campaign

606
WRITERS
Dave Henke
Bill Oakley
CLIENT
Southwestern Bell
AGENCY
D'Arcy Masius Benton & Bowles/St. Louis

607
WRITER
Phil Hanft
AGENCY PRODUCER
Phil Hanft
CLIENT
First Tennessee Bank
AGENCY
Fallon McElligott/Minneapolis

608
WRITERS
Jay Taub
Tod Seisser
AGENCY PRODUCER
Rob Thomas
CLIENT
New York Air
AGENCY
Levine Huntley Schmidt & Beaver

609
WRITERS
Stephanie Arnold
Jay Taub
Tod Seisser
Irv Klein
AGENCY PRODUCER
Rob Thomas
Rachel Novak
CLIENT
New York Air
AGENCY
Levine Huntley Schmidt & Beaver

610
WRITERS
Charles Mullen
John Clapps
AGENCY PRODUCER
Richard Goldstein
CLIENT
Suntory Beer
AGENCY
Isidore & Paulson

604

Great Britain, the country that gave the world . . . Big Ben . . . Princess Di . . . Shakespeare . . . The English Channel . . . The English language . . . The English Muffin . . . Charles Dickens . . . Jack the Ripper . . . The Beatles . . . warm beer . . . and fog, now presents what could be our greatest contribution to civilization: Apricot. Apricot is Europe's most successful line of business computers. They're elegant, compact, easy to use, and run thousands of MS-DOS business software programs.
Apricot. From the country that gave you . . . The Rolls Royce . . . Sherlock Holmes . . . Boy George . . . God Save The Queen . . . London Bridge.

605

(SFX: PIANO PLAYS CHORDS FROM "TONIGHT" FROM "WEST SIDE STORY" IN A NOISY NIGHTCLUB)

SINGER (SINGS IN A CORNY STYLE): *Tonight, tonight . . . won't be just any night* . . . (HE BEGINS TO TALK AS PIANO PLAYS SOFT CHORDS UNDER HIM) That's right, ladies and gentlemen, *every* night is *special* here at the Diamond Head lounge . . . and while we're into this nutty show-tune groove . . . are there any requests?

MAN (FROM AUDIENCE): "She Loves Me."

SINGER (SINGS): *Yeah, yeah, yeah* . . . (TALKS) but, hey, that's by the the Beatles!

MAN: No . . . "She Loves Me" is a musical that's on now at Center Stage!

SINGER: Oh, wait! We know that one, Tom. (HE BEGINS TO SNAP FINGERS IN TIME WITH VOICE) Ah-one, two, ah-one, two, three. (SINGS) *She loves me . . . and to my amazement . . .*

(SFX: SMALL APPLAUSE)

SINGER: Thank you! *Ah love it, knowing that she loves me* . . . (TALKS) Ah, great tune! And great show . . . about two nutty kids who find love in Budapest.

MAN: Yeah! And the songs from "She Loves Me" were written by the same guys who did "Fiddler On The Roof."

SINGER: Did someone say Fiddler?

(SFX: PIANO STARTS TO PLAY "IF I WERE A RICH MAN")

SINGER (SINGS AND SNAPS FINGERS): *If I were a rich man, zaba, deeba daba dooba daba deeba daba doo* . . . thank you! (HE CONTINUES SINGING NONSENSE WORDS AND TRAILS OFF)

ANNCR: Don't miss the charming musical comedy "She Loves Me," now at Center Stage through October 27th.

SINGER: Ah, you're a great crowd . . . Ah love ya . . . thank you.

606

(SFX: OUTDOOR SOUNDS)

ANNCR: Ever find yourself standing at the back door, loaded down with groceries, trying to handle 2 kids, the neighbor's dog and get the key in the lock, when suddenly you hear . . .

(SFX: PHONE RING INSIDE HOUSE)

WOMAN: Ohh . . . the phone . . . uh . . .

(MUSIC: TENSION BUILDING)

(SFX: DOG BARK)

WOMAN: Go on, Skipper. Go home. Go on. (KEY DROPS) Shoot . . . Go on, Skipper. Timmy. Hand mommy the key. That's right, Tommy, let go of Skipper's tail . . .

(SFX: DOG WAIL)

WOMAN: *Now!* Timmy, hand mommy the key . . . that's it . . .

(SFX: GROCERY BAG DROPS)

WOMAN: Ohh . . . there go the eggs. Skipper—shoo! Tommy! Stupid key . . .

(SFX: DOOR OPENS)

WOMAN: Now don't let the dog in the house . . .

(SFX: CAT SQUEAL, DOG BARK, PANDEMONIUM)

WOMAN: Tommy, let *mommy* clean up the eggs . . .

(SFX: DOG AND CAT FIGHT)

WOMAN: Timmy! Get the *dog*. Tommy—get the cat. I'll get the ph . . .

(SFX: PICK UP, DIAL TONE)

(MUSIC: CALM, SOOTHING UNDER FOLLOWING)

ANNCR: Next time, take your time. Then dial star-66. Automatic Recall from Southwestern Bell Telephone. Just pick up your phone and touch (SFX) star-66 . . . 1166 if you have a rotary phone . . . and the call you missed is *re*-called—automatically. There's nothing to sign up for. Nothing to install. Because if your phone number begins with 4 or 8, you automatically have it. So the next time you're running behind time, relax. Then dial (SFX) star-66.

(SFX: RING, CLICK)

HUSBAND: Hello . . .

WOMAN: Honey?

HUSBAND: Hey, I just tried to call you. What are we havin' for dinner tonight.

WOMAN: Uh . . . how do scrambled eggs sound?

ANNCR: Automatic Recall from Southwestern Bell Telephone. It works . . .

(SFX: STAR-66 DIAL)

ANNCR: . . . automatically.

607

(MUSIC: SNOOTY CLASSICAL)

ANNCR: In New York . . . art is "Death of a Salesman" Off-Broadway.
In Paris . . . art is Van Gogh at the Louvre.
In Los Angeles . . . art is "Amadeus" at the Fine Arts.
In London . . . art is "Macbeth" at the Old Vic.
But here in Tennessee . . . art is a grunt . . .

(SFX: HOG CALLER)

. . . a snort . . .

(SFX: SNORTING)

. . . and a holler . . .

(SFX: HOG CALL; ROAR OF CROWD)

ANNCR: See and hear the world's best hog callers in "Tennessee Celebrates" . . . a multi-media tribute to the fine art of having a good time . . . in one of America's most culturally diverse states.

LIVE TAG MEMPHIS: January 31 through March 16 at the Pink Palace. Sponsored by First Tennessee.

LIVE TAG NASHVILLE: April 4 through June 1, Tennessee State Museum. Sponsored by First Tennessee.

LIVE TAG CHATTANOOGA: June 15 through July 20, Hunter Museum. Sponsored by First Tennessee.

LIVE TAG KNOXVILLE: August 8 through September 21, UT Campus Art and Architecture Gallery. Sponsored by First Tennessee.

LIVE TAG JOHNSON CITY: October 3 through November 23, Carroll Reece Museum. Sponsored by First Tennessee.

608

"TED KENNEDY": Today, it is imperative that we, in Washington, cut expenditures to a manageable level. For if we don't (FADE OUT) . . . we may find ourselves in serious trouble.

"RON REAGAN": Well, you know, cutting costs is the primary objective of this administration. Um, our plan, you know, is to cut (FADE OUT) expenditures by 16% (FADE OUT) . . .

ANNCR: People in Washington who want to cut costs can start by cutting their air fares. At New York Air, we fly from Dulles to Tampa/St. Pete for $69. Jacksonville $49. New Orleans $89. Ft. Lauderdale $89. Orlando $89. And with more nonstops than anyone.

"GEO WALLACE": Cutting costs, cutting costs, cutting costs. Isn't that what our constituents are (FADE OUT ON APPLAUSE) demanding from us?

ANNCR: New York Air. If Washington's looking to cut costs, we'll give them a lfying start.

LIVE ANNCR: Some restrictions may apply to these fares. See your travel agent or New York Air for details.

609

VO—"NIXON": Now that New York Air flies from Tampa to D.C. for $69.00, even *I* can buy my way back into Washington. (laughs)

(SFX: JET TAKES OFF)

• • •

VO—"KISSINGER": As an expert on shuttle diplomacy, let me say the best shuttle is New York Air with 37 flights to New York each day.

(SFX: JET TAKES OFF)

• • •

VO—"REAGAN": Well, now that New York Air offers Boston 13 weekday flights to Washington, you can stop by the House anytime.

(SFX: JET TAKES OFF)

610

(SFX: COTO PLAYS INTRODUCTION)

JAPANESE ADMAN: O.K., boss. I got ideas for new advertising campaign to introduce Suntory overseas in America.

JAPANESE CREATIVE DIRECTOR: Yes, please.

ADMAN: O.K., picture this: two sumo wrestlers come in after hard day of pounding flesh, music starts, when it's time to relax it Suntory time.

DIRECTOR: Good. I like it. Never heard of such thing.

ADMAN: Would you like to hear another?

DIRECTOR: Most certainly!

ADMAN: How 'bout this: the most famous work in the Japanese language (BANG) Suntory.

DIRECTOR: Very good.

ADMAN: Or this one. Everytime a baseball player hits a home run, announcer says: Holy Cow, this Suntory for you.

DIRECTOR: I like it.

ADMAN: But this one my favorite. How do you spell rereff?

DIRECTOR: R . . . E . . . R . . .E . . .

ADMAN: No, no, boss. You spell rereff S . . . U . . . N . . . T . . . O . . . R . . . Y . . . Get it?

DIRECTOR: No, not really.

ANNCR: Introducing Suntory Beer's new advertising campaign: We have a lot of catching up to do.

Consumer Radio: Campaign

611
WRITERS
Jeff Spiegel
Mike Drazen
AGENCY PRODUCER
Kathryn Spiess
CLIENT
Orangina International
AGENCY
HCM

612
WRITER
Dave Woodside
CLIENT
California Cooler
AGENCY
Chiat/Day - San Francisco

613
WRITER
Bill Johnson
AGENCY PRODUCER
Bill Johnson
CLIENT
Schmidt Beer
AGENCY
Ruhr/Paragon - Minneapolis

614
WRITERS
Niel Klein
Greg Koorhan
Alan Lawrence
AGENCY PRODUCER
Michael Albright
CLIENT
Rose Hills Memorial Park
AGENCY
Klein/Richardson - Beverly Hills

615
WRITER
Phil Lanier
AGENCY PRODUCER
David Prince
CLIENT
Apple Computer
AGENCY
Chiat/Day - Los Angeles

616
WRITER
David Schneider
AGENCY PRODUCER
Jean Della Corte
CLIENT
Federal Express
AGENCY
Ally & Gargano

617
WRITER
Ernie Schenck
AGENCY PRODUCER
Ernie Schenck
CLIENT
Vanderbilt Rehabilitation Center
AGENCY
Leonard Monahan Saabye/
Providence, RI

611

(MUSIC: MEDLEY OF "SHAKE SONGS" EDITED TOGETHER)

ROCK: *I'm a night shaker . . .*

COUNTRY: *And darlin, even yo' grandma's shakin' tonight . . .*

CROONER: *I've got the shakes over yoou . . .*

HAWAIIAN: *We're here on shakee-shakee island . . . we shakee, shakee, shakee with you . . .*

VO (BRITISH, DROLL): The preceding medley of shaky songs is brought to you by Orangina. That delightfully different, lightly carbonated soft drink from France whose distinctive blend of oranges, tangerines, and natural pulp needs to be shaken to be truly appreciated . . . Orangina. The soft drink that's shaking things up.

ALA BO DIDDLEY: *Aw shucks, got the shakes!*

(BO DIDDLEY INTRUMENTAL UNDER ANNOUNCER COPY)

612

VO: You know, my friend Aldo came over today and gave me this California Cooler.

(SFX: POP, GURGLE, FIZZ)

Now, I hate California. You know what it is? It's what it does to your body. You move out there looking like me, then you come back with muscles. I don't need it. Your skin turns brown, your hair turns blond. This is not good for you. Your teeth get whiter. And then the sun dries out your zits. Hey man, I'm a lifeguard. I have a totally awesome, bronze bod. Don't touch. Get outta here. You know, you move to California. First of all you stop eating American food. No white bread, no salami, no bratwurst. Everything's good for you. Bagels are like some rare treat from some foreign land. Meanwhile, you eat all this garbage, you live longer but so what, your mind gets soft. Then they pay money to chant along with Raji-oly-oxen-free. Who are these people? You know, I even hate what they drink. Aha, look at it. This stuff. California Cooler. I hate the name. You drink it ice cold, on a hot day. (POURING) I hate it. I really hate it. Heh, heh, just pretend you never saw me drinkin' the stuff, will ya?

ANNCR: California Cooler.
One more reason to hate California.
California Cooler, Stockton, California.

613

11. FLIGHT STEWARD: Good afternoon and welcome to Flight 405, Minneapolis to Duluth. A couple of words now about our safety features. In case of a sudden loss of cabin pressure, a can of Schmidt will drop from the ceiling. Pull the tab, place firmly over your mouth and continue drinking normally until we regain pressure. Now sit back and enjoy our feature film, Terms of Embeerment.

12. PSYCHOTHERAPIST: Group, your feelings of inferiority, where do you think they come from?

A PATIENT: Minnesota.

A PATIENT: Mmmm, right.

A PATIENT: Losing sports teams.

A PATIENT: Four Super Bowls.

A PATIENT: Stanley Cup.

A PATIENT: The Twins.

A PATIENT: World Series.

A PATIENT: Politics.

A PATIENT: Mondale.

A PATIENT: Humphrey.

A PATIENT: Stassen.

PSYCHOTHERAPIST: I think we've got it out. Let me interject this. Schmidt Beer, the number 1 beer in Minnesota.

A PATIENT: Oh, hugs all around.

A PATIENT: Go with the flow.

13. SEXY FEMALE: All my men drink Schmidt Beer . . . or they don't.

14. HUSBAND: Happy Anniversary, Honey. I got you a Longene.

WIFE: Oh, I was hoping for a Schmidt.

15. VO A: Hey, did you hear they're out of beer at the corner store.

VO B: No Schmidt.

VO A: Schmidt Beer. The brew that grew to be best in the great northwest.

614

READER: Mark Twain had a daughter named Olivia Susan Clemens, who died August 14, 1896 at the age of 24. Following her tragic death, Mark Twain wrote this epitaph:

Warm summer sun, shine kindly here;
Warm southern wind, blow softly here;
Green sod above, lie light, lie light—
Good-night, dear heart, good-night, good-night.

ANNCR: When a loved one passes on, a funeral with dignity and simplicity in a setting of great, natural beauty is the most poignant way for those on both sides of life to say goodbye.
We're Rose Hills.
A place to remember.

615

DAD: Honey, look what I got for the kids!

MOM: Lemme see!

DAD: It's a radio-controlled model of the space monster that ate Tokyo!

(SFX: MONSTER MOVING, MECHANICAL WHINING)

MOM: Oh, that's nice.

(MUSIC: UP AND UNDER ANNOUNCER)

ANNCR: This Christmas, instead of giving your kids something to destroy Tokyo, why not help them attack life? With an Apple II personal computer.

(MUSIC: OUT)

(SFX: MONSTER KEEPS WHIRRING AND WHINING)

DAD: Yeah, look! His eyes are really lasers. He's got the projectile knee caps. His feet are warheads.

MOM: Don't point it at me.

DAD: Oh, I'm sorry. I don't think it's loaded.

(SFX: MISSILE BLASTING OFF; LAMP CRASHING)

MOM: It shot my lamp!

DAD: I never liked the lamp either.

(MUSIC: UP)

ANNCR: There are more Apple computers in schools than all other brands combined. So they're perfect for helping kids with their homework and school projects.

(MUSIC: OUT)

(SFX: THE RELENTLESS MONSTER KEEPS MOVING)

MOM: It's headed for the stereo!

DAD: Maybe it doesn't like easy listening.

(MUSIC: UP)

ANNCR: Yet an Apple II is powerful enough to run business, personal finance and home management programs for adults.

(MUSIC: OUT)

(SFX: MONSTER GETS LOUDER, COMING TOWARDS US)

MOM: I don't like the way it's looking at me.

DAD: It's not looking. It's heat-seeking.

ANNCR: And Christmas is actually a great time to buy an Apple II. Because your authorized Apple dealer is offering great prices on every Apple model and peripherals. See your authorized Apple dealer. And help your family attack life. With an Apple II.

(SFX: EVEN LOUDER, COMING TOWARDS US)

DAD: Run for it, Marge!

(SFX: MISSILE FIRING)

MOM: Ralph!

DAD: Tell the kids I love 'em.

(SFX: TWO MISSILES FIRING)

(MUSIC: FADES OUT)

616

(SFX: INTERCOM BUZZ)

MAN: Yes?

SECRETARY: The Dubois brothers calling from Paris, sir.

MAN: Oh, good. Put them on.

DUBOIS BROS (FIVE GUYS MORE OR LESS TOGETHER ON PHONE): Allo . . .

MAN: Hello!

DUBOIS BROS (TOGETHER): Stanleee?

MAN: Yes!

DUBOIS BROS (ALL MIXED UP): Où est le package!! (IN FRENCH) Qu'est-ce que tu fais, espèce d'idiot!!?

MAN: Hold it—

DUBOIS BROS: Saboteur! Où est le package. . . ! Où est le package?!

MAN: Wait a minute, wait a minute, SPEAK ENGLISH!!!!!

DUBOIS BROS (CALM DOWN): Ah oui . . . Eh bien, eh bien . . . (MUMBLE TO ONE ANOTHER, IN FRENCH) Allez, assez plaisante, parle anglais. On lui dit ce qu'on pense. O.K. O.K. (SORT OF TOGETHER, IN ENGLISH) Eh . . . Stanlee . . . Where is that packagg frahm Amereeka . . . We have not got it . . . Yu styupid cow, we speet in your furnace.

MAN: Well that's better.

DUBOIS BROS (IN FRENCH): Assassin! Tu espèce d'imbecile. . . ?!

ANNCR: Next time you send a package to Europe, why risk an international incident? Now Federal Express flies packages in its own aircraft directly to Europe. With two-day service to London, Paris, Brussels, Frankfurt, Amsterdam, Zurich and other major European cities. At a price that could easily be less than what you're paying now. So now that Federal Express flies over there, why fool around with anyone else, over here?

617

(MUSIC: NOTRE DAME FIGHT SONG; SLOWLY, ON PIANO)

VO: There's a barber shop in Indiana where they still talk about him . . . how he had more moves downfield than a snake . . . the way he used to make Michigan defensemen look like flat-footed zombies. And they remember something else . . . a cold November Saturday and a linebacker he never saw coming. Now, I'd like to tell you he picked up the pieces of his life . . . Instead, he just sits in that wheelchair watching the clock run out on his dreams. At Vanderbilt Rehabilitation Center in Newport, we know how a sudden physical handicap can cripple a person's spirit. But it doesn't have to. You see, at Vanderbilt, before you can learn to live with a handicap, you've got to learn to live with something far more important. Yourself.
Vanderbilt Rehabilitation Center at Newport Hospital.
Ask your doctor, or call 401-847-0802.

Consumer Radio: Campaign

618
WRITER
Steve Kahn
AGENCY PRODUCER
Steve Kahn
CLIENT
George A. Hormel Company
AGENCY
BBDO/Minneapolis

619
WRITERS
Jay Taub
Tod Seisser
John Cleese
CLIENT
Kronenbourg Beer
AGENCY
Levine Huntley Schmidt & Beaver

620
WRITER
Jennifer LeMay
AGENCY PRODUCER
Nancy Ross
CLIENT
Ryder Trucks
AGENCY
Burton-Campbell/Atlanta

621
WRITER
Steve Landsberg
AGENCY PRODUCER
Valerie Hutchinson
CLIENT
McNulty Banking
AGENCY
Calet Hirsch & Spector

Public Service Radio: Campaign

622
WRITER
Lew Alpern
AGENCY PRODUCERS
Charlotte Rosenblatt
Tom Hendee
CLIENT
Ad Council Coalition for Literacy Campaign
AGENCY
D'Arcy Masius Benton & Bowles

618

ANNCR: We're outside a little gift shop here, little Italian . . . let's walk inside and see what's going on. Buon giorno.

MAN: Buon giorno.

ANNCR: How are you today?

MAN: Molto bene.

ANNCR: Molto bene, I'm the walking dictionary, have you heard of me on the radio?

MAN: No. (LAUGHTER)

ANNCR: I just want to get the definition of DiLusso here, sir.

MAN: Hormel DiLusso, DiLusso's the best!

ANNCR: Genoa Salami.

MAN: Migliore, the best.

ANNCR: Forget migliore, DiLusso, DiLusso. What's your wife's name?

MAN: Elanore.

ANNCR: What's Elanore's best-known dish that she makes with Hormel's DiLusso Genoa Salami?

MAN: Antipasto, puta provolone, puta Hormel Salami . . .

ANNCR: How do you know it's Hormel?

MAN: The flavor the taste when I eat, that's Hormel.

ANNCR: Yea, but what do you know about salami, where were you . . .

MAN: . . . What do you mean I've been eating it for years, I know what it is, what are you trying to tell me?

ANNCR: Are you really from Italy?

MAN: Sure, I'm from Italy, I was born there, Napoli, Naples . . .

ANNCR: Yea, but that's not in Italy right, that's . . .

MAN: . . . Then where is it, in China?

ANNCR: O.K., so how do you say good-bye in Chinese?

MAN: In Chinese, arrivaderci! (LAUGHTER)

619

ENGLISH ACCENT: Ah, look, I've had a lot of rude letters about Kronenbourg's slogan, "Better not Bitter," saying it isn't exactly literature. Well, look! Surely, what matters is whether it's true, and to further test this I have with me here an American beer-drinking person. Par excellence, welcome, Mr. Ivan Molomut.

BAD AMERICAN ACCENT: Gosh, what's cookin' pal?

ENGLISH: Now, would you put this blindfold on, please.

AMERICAN: Sure thang. Thayre, ah done it.

ENGLISH: Now, Mr. Molomut, there are two imported beers here. Will you taste this one first.

AMERICAN: Yessiree. (SLURPING NOISE) Yep. Well as we say in Arkansas, this first beer is jolly mediocre.

ENGLISH: I see. Now would you taste the second beer?

AMERICAN (SLURPING NOISE): Gee, thayt's purdy darn better.

ENGLISH: Better, Mr. Molomut? But not . . .

AMERICAN: Well, it sure ain't acrid, or acerbic, or even slightly caustic.

ENGLISH: Is "not bitter" the word you're looking for?

AMERICAN: Shoot, yes mac.

ENGLISH: And the second beer was . . . yes, Kronenbourg! And you've never even met me before.

AMERICAN: Well, I guess that proves Kronenbourg beer, imported by Kronenbourg USA, Greenwich, Connecticut, really is "Better not Bitter."

ENGLISH: So why don't you take the Kronenbourg taste test today.

AMERICAN: I just took it.

ENGLISH: I'm not talking to you, you yankee fat head.

620

STEVE LANDESBERG: So, you gotta move.
Well, you could hire a moving company and pay an arm and a leg.
Or borrow your brother-in-law's pick-up.
But then you'll have to make five trips and your brother-in-law comes along.
Or rent a Ryder truck.
Ryder trucks are newer. With power steering, automatic transmission, air conditioning, a radio.
It's up to you.
A Ryder truck. Or your brother-in-law.
I'd go with Ryder.
Ryder. The Right Move.

621

(SFX: STREET NOISES, CARS, CITY ATMOSPHERE)

VO: When a fantastic investment opportunity arises, even the rich may have to go begging.

(SFX: BELL RINGING)

MAN (BEGGING): Alms for the rich . . . alms for the rich . . . alms for the rich . . .

VO: And that can be a humbling experience.

MAN: Pardon me sir, yeah, how are ya . . . look, could you help me out with $100,000 so I can buy an attractively undervalued stock? My liquid assets are a little frozen right now . . . yeah, pardon me sir . . . yeah, pardon me sir, yeah, hi, how are ya . . .

VO: We're McNulty Banking Company. The bank dedicated to helping investors in need of cash. At McNulty, we understand when it comes to investment opportunities, even the wealthy can be needy.

MAN: Psst . . . hey, buddy, yeah, how are ya . . . can you spare a few thousand dollar bills? How 'bout hundreds? Fifties? Maybe 4 tens? How 'bout some traveller's checks? Do you have change for a quarter?

VO: McNulty. The bank to go to when you need money to make money.
St. Petersburg, Treasure Island, Indian Rocks and Palm Harbor.
Member FDIC, of course.

622

FATHER (READING WITH PAINFUL DIFFICULTY): The . . . little . . . engine . . . looked . . . up . . . and . . . saw . . . tears . . . in . . . the . . . doll's . . . eyes . . . (FADE)

MAUREEN STAPLETON: You're listening to what it's like to be functionally illiterate. Unable to read a job application, a street sign, or a bedtime story to a child.
Today, in America, there are 27 million adults who are like this. 27 million! We could help them, but we need your help.
Call the Coalition for Literacy at 1-800-228-8813, and volunteer.
The only degree you need is a degree of caring.

FATHER: I . . . think . . . I . . . can . . . I . . . think . . . I . . . can . . . I . . . think . . . I . . . can . . .

AVO: A message from the Ad Council.

TELEVISION FINALISTS

Consumer Television Over: 30 (:45/:60/:90) Single

623
ART DIRECTOR
Shelly Schachter
WRITER
Kurt Willinger
AGENCY PRODUCER
Bill Gross
PRODUCTION CO.
Giraldi Productions
DIRECTOR
Bob Giraldi
CLIENT
Paine Webber
AGENCY
Saatchi & Saatchi Compton

624
ART DIRECTORS
Richard Johnson
Bill Harris
WRITERS
Jeff Wolff
Richard Johnson
AGENCY PRODUCER
Robert Shannon
PRODUCTION CO.
Petermann Dektor
DIRECTOR
Fred Petermann
CLIENT
American Motors
Corporation/Jeep Comanche
AGENCY
Saatchi & Saatchi Compton

625
ART DIRECTORS
Jim Weller
John Armistead
WRITER
Jim Weller
AGENCY PRODUCER
Shannon Silverman
PRODUCTION CO.
Harmony Pictures
DIRECTOR
Haskell Wexler
CLIENT
Carl's Jr. Restaurants
AGENCY
Della Femina Travisano &
Partners/Los Angeles

626
ART DIRECTOR
Donald Sterzin
AGENCY PRODUCER
Dorothy Franklin
PRODUCTION CO.
Kira Films
DIRECTOR
Bruce Weber
CLIENT
Ralph Lauren Dungarees
AGENCY
Geers Gross

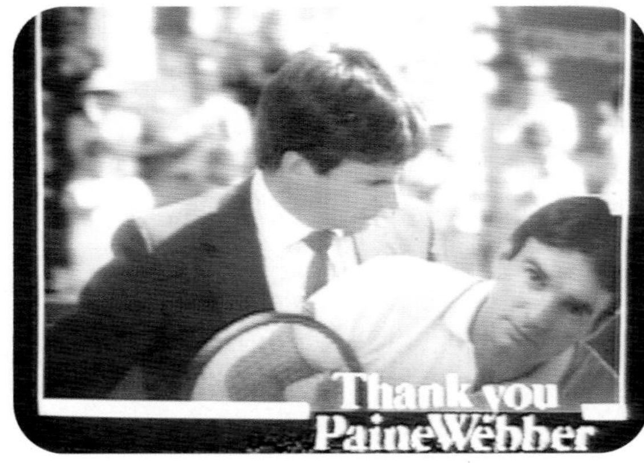

623

REFEREE: Time, gentlemen.

JIMMY CONNORS: I'm Jimmy Connors, and it's about time you met my partner, my financial side.

VO: All successful companies and people have a financial side.

JIMMY CONNORS: Let's go, partner.

VO: It comes with success. But success in the financial world doesn't happen automatically. And sooner or later you'll find you need some help.

JIMMY CONNORS: We need some help.

VO: You need PaineWebber behind you.
With capital management teams expert in corporate, government or individual financial matters, together, leveraging our strength in the marketplace with a dedication to the most creative financial solutions possible. PaineWebber gives you the financial backup you deserve . . .

JIMMY CONNORS: Alright! Thank you PaineWebber!

ALL: You're welcome!

JIMMY CONNORS: Hey, you're gonna have to loosen up. We've got PaineWebber on our side.

624

(SFX: NATURAL SOUNDS)

(MUSIC)

(SFX: TRAIN WHISTLE)

ANNCR VO: There's a new truck on the road.
It's called Commanche.
It's built by Jeep.
It's worth a look.

625

CARL VO: We opened our first Carl's some 40 years ago. We sold hamburgers for a quarter, and Cokes for a nickel. But a smile was free.

ANNCR VO: Forty years ago, a man named Carl Karcher started out making hamburgers the old-fashioned way.

CARL VO: We put in a charcoil-broiler and we had charcoal-broiled hamburgers. The first day our sales were 14 dollars and 75 cents.

ANNCR VO: A lot has changed since Carl Karcher opened his first Carl's Jr. But today, a Carl's Jr. hamburger is still made the old-fashioned way. 100% beef. Charbroiled one hamburger at a time. A good honest meal at a good honest price.

CARL: We sold an old-fashioned hamburger back then. Today, we still do.

ANNCR VO: Because you'll still find old-fashioned American values at Carl's Jr.

626

(MUSIC: HARMONICA PLAYING CROSSES INTO SONG)

Now of all the times that come to mind,
And the memories that I know.
I remember when we jumped in a pick up truck
And went bumping down a dusty road.
High lines flew by as we left behind
Our blues in a lonesome town
And we laughed and loved 'till we were far above
All the things that held us down.
And you were close to my heart
Close to my heart, now miles could never keep us apart . . .

ANNCR VO: Dungarees by Ralph Lauren.

(MUSIC: OUT)

Consumer Television
Over :30 (:45 /:60/:90)
Single

627
ART DIRECTOR
Antoinette Portis
WRITER
David Bishop
AGENCY PRODUCER
Shannon Silverman
PRODUCTION CO.
Riverrun Films
DIRECTOR
Mark Rasmussen
CLIENT
Six Flags Magic Mountain
AGENCY
Della Femina Travisano & Partners/Los Angeles

628
ART DIRECTOR
Gene Mandarino
WRITER
Cheryl Berman
AGENCY PRODUCER
Bob Koslow
PRODUCTION CO.
Giraldi Productions
DIRECTOR
Bob Giraldi
CLIENT
McDonald's
AGENCY
Leo Burnett/Chicago

629
ART DIRECTOR
Tom Cordner
WRITER
Brent Bouchez
AGENCY PRODUCER
Francesca Cohn
PRODUCTION CO.
Steve Horn Inc.
DIRECTOR
Steve Horn
CLIENT
Pizza Hut
AGENCY
Chiat/Day - Los Angeles

627

MR HAND: Hey! What're ya doin'?

MR HAND: Never mind. Wanna have some real fun?

(SFX: DOLL NOISES)

MR HAND: How would you like to go white-water river rafting?

(SFX: FLUSH)

MR HAND: Pretty wild, huh? Ever wonder what it's like to ride an Olympic-style bobsled?

(SFX: DOLL SCREAMS)

MR HAND: Or slide down America's longest water flume?

(SFX: BUBBLES)

MR HAND: Or drop 10 stories . . . without a parachute?

MR HAND: Well, at Magic Mountain you can do all that and more! See for yourselves.

MR HAND: There's the Roaring Rapids, the Sarajevo Bobsled, Log Jammer, and Freefall.

MR HAND: Sure beats necking, huh?

(SFX: DOLL NOISES)

MR HAND: And watch out for those palm trees!

628

ANNCR: McDonald's crew kids. They've been a lot of great ones in the last 30 years. Where are they today?

SING: *Here's lookin' at you kids*
McDonald's crew kids
You sure have gone a long way.

ANNCR: Here's to Tom Hall.
You sure have gone a long way.

SING: *You're the stars in our sky*
Still shinin' on high.

ANNCR: To Lieutenant Wold.

SING: *Our unsung heroes who carried the day.*

ANNCR: Here's to you Manu.

SING: *Still got your winnin' ways about you.*

ANNCR: Here's lookin' at you Dr Gailmard.

SING: *Never would've made it to the top*
Without you
Just look at you now
Step on out
Take a bow.

ANNCR: From 1955 to today.
Here's to every crew member who's kept those arches shinin'.

SING: *You make it a good time*

ANNCR: Hats off to ya wherever you are!

SING: *For the great taste of McDonald's.*

629

(MUSIC: "LA BOHEME" ADAPTATION UNDER THROUGHOUT)

(SFX: DOG BARKS)

INSTRUCTOR: *Parti li funghi Marco—vieni.* (Cut the mushrooms Marco-come.)
Ma Vincenzo—che hal fatto qui? (But Vincenzo, what did you do here?)
Ah, buon giorno, Maestro. Lavore! (Ah! Good morning, Maestro. Work!)
Fatto-Lavora. (Done-Work.)
Pui meglio. Pui meglio. (Even better. Even better.)
No! Che fai? (No! What are you doing?)
Beh! Mettilo, mettilo, mettilo. (Well, put it in, put it in, put it in.)

ANNCR VO: In Italy there are many . . .
. . . ways to make the classic Italian pie.
From blends of fine . . .
. . . meats to the best cheeses, even poultry.
Each recipe a closely guarded secret.

INSTRUCTOR: *Ah! Piano, piano, piano, piano, bravo.* (Ah! Slowly, slowly, slowly, slowly, good job.)

ANNCR VO: In America . . .

INSTRUCTOR: *Lavora. Lavora.* (Work. Work.)

ANNCR VO: . . . there is a special Italian pie.
We call it Priazzo (TM).
You'll find it . . .
. . . baked fresh each day only at Pizza Hut.

INSTRUCTOR: *Bravo.*

ANNCR VO: And that's all we intend to tell you.

Consumer Television Over :30 (:45/:60/:90) Single

630
ART DIRECTOR
Michael Simons
WRITER
Peter Cass
AGENCY PRODUCER
Edward Burrell
PRODUCTION CO.
Michael Dufficy & Partners
DIRECTOR
Roger Lyons
CLIENT
Tonka
AGENCY
KMP Humphreys Bull & Barker/London

631
ART DIRECTOR
Ken Hoggins
WRITER
Chris O'Shea
AGENCY PRODUCER
Annie Alexander
PRODUCTION CO.
Paul Weiland Film Company
DIRECTOR
Paul Weiland
CLIENT
A. C. Delco
AGENCY
Lowe Howard-Spink Marschalk/London

632
ART DIRECTOR
Mike Stephenson
WRITER
Derek Apps
AGENCY PRODUCER
Mike Griffin
PRODUCTION CO.
Paul Weiland Film Company
DIRECTOR
David Garfath
CLIENT
Vauxhall Motors
AGENCY
Lowe Howard-Spink Marschalk/London

633
ART DIRECTOR
David Barker
WRITER
Lyn Middlehurst
AGENCY PRODUCER
Jane Boyne
PRODUCTION CO.
RSA
DIRECTOR
Tony Scott
CLIENT
Saab
AGENCY
KMP Humphreys Bull & Barker/London

630

MVO: We took two of the world's toughest trucks . . . and a 400 ft cliff.

(SFX: CLANGING METAL, SMASHING GLASS)

(SFX: CLANG)

(SFX: CRASH. THUD)

MVO: And this is the truck made by Tonka.

631

FRANCIS DE LA TOUR: Ronald!

YOUNG MAN: Please change!

FRANCIS DE LA TOUR: Ronald, how nice of you to stop.

YOUNG MAN (ILL AT EASE): That's alright, Miss Haines.

FRANCIS DE LA TOUR: Oh call me Joy, please.

(SFX: CAR SOUNDING DISTINCTLY UNHEALTHY)

FRANCIS DE LA TOUR: Oh that's better, Ronald, isn't it? I do think a little Mantovani adds to the ambiance, don't you?
There's something terribly sensuous about pounding rain.

FRANCIS DE LA TOUR (KNOWINGLY): Oh Ronnie, don't tell me you've run out of petrol.

YOUNG MAN (PANIC STRICKEN): No, no I haven't. It's the distribution.

FRANCIS DE LA TOUR: You don't expect me to believe that do you?

MVO: Whatever you drive, fit A C Delco car parts or one day your car will get even.

FRANCIS DE LA TOUR: You naughty boy.

632

(MUSIC: THROUGHOUT)

(SFX: HORNS)

MVO: Ladies and gentlemen, we give you the Vauxhall Nova—a car that makes light of heavy traffic.
The Vauxhall Nova.
It's really something in the city.

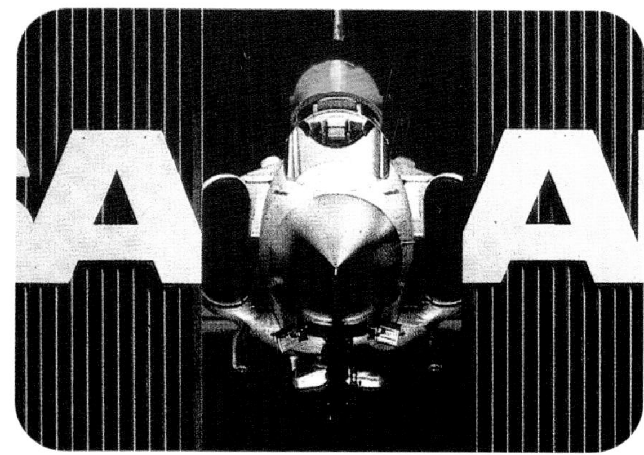

633

(MUSIC: THROUGHOUT)

MVO: From 7½ million pounds . . .
. . . to around 7½ thousand
Saab . . . nothing on earth comes close.

Consumer Television
Over :30 (:45/:60/:90)
Single

634
ART DIRECTOR
Jeff Suthons
WRITER
Bridget Jenkins
AGENCY PRODUCER
Maggie Mullen
PRODUCTION CO.
Jerry Hibbert Animation
DIRECTOR
Jerry Hibbert
CLIENT
Kimberly Clark
AGENCY
Fletcher Shelton Delaney/London

635
ART DIRECTOR
Don Easdon
WRITER
Bill Heater
AGENCY PRODUCER
Mary Ellen Argentieri
PRODUCTION CO.
PYTKA
DIRECTOR
Joe Pytka
CLIENT
John Hancock
AGENCY
Hill Holliday Connors Cosmopulos/Boston

636
ART DIRECTOR
Alan Lerner
WRITER
Indra Sinha
AGENCY PRODUCER
John Montgomery
PRODUCTION CO.
Bainbridge Robert Young
DIRECTOR
Robert Young
CLIENT
Compaq Computers
AGENCY
Ogilvy & Mather/London

637
ART DIRECTOR
Rick McQuiston
WRITER
Jim Riswold
PRODUCTION CO.
Steve Horn Inc.
DIRECTOR
Steve Horn
CLIENT
Honda Scooters
AGENCY
Wieden & Kennedy/Portland, OR

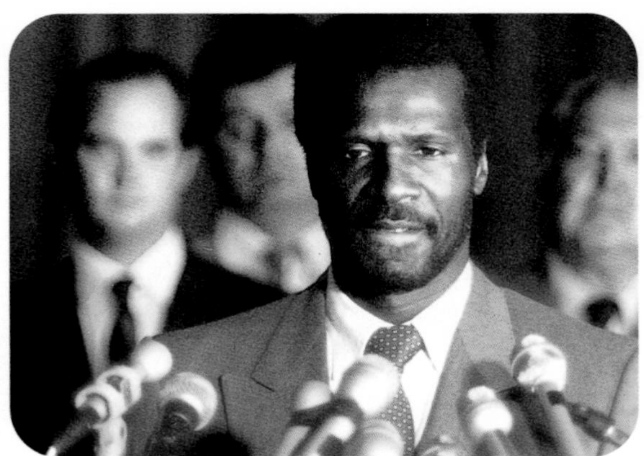

Needs
Stable transition
to retirement

Financial security

634

(MUSIC: "ENGLISH COUNTRY GARDEN")

MVO SUNG TO MUSIC:
How many hidden horrors lie in wait
In an English Company Washroom?
Toilet rolls that disappear, causing
Untold stress and fear,
Soap that skulks on a slimy floor,
So you slip and you flip and you
Bump your rump
In an English Company Washroom.

MVO: Some Company Washrooms are a mess, and Kimberly-Clark think that's a scandal.
Every toilet tissue, towel and soap system we provide, brings efficiency, hygiene and a touch of class to every washroom.
We don't compromise.
Why should you?

635

MAN: I've never felt older in my life.
Yesterday I was a football player. Today, I'm retired.
How do I want to be remembered? As a good father, as a good husband.
And that's it.
That's life.
And that's what life is.

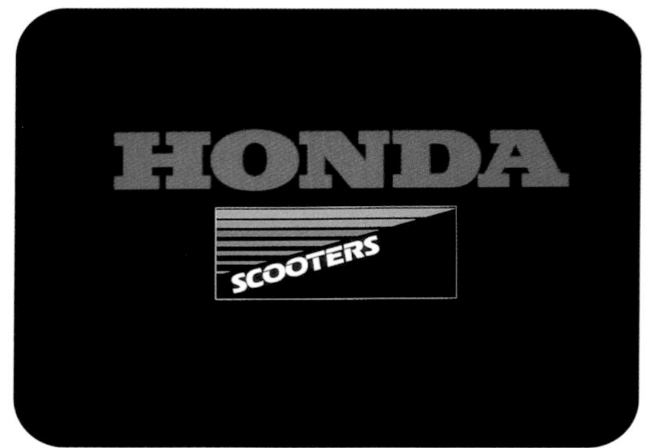

636

JOHN CLEESE: Apparently, some people can't remember the name of the computer that my brother-in-law Rob recommends. Well, here's how to remember it. (QUITE QUICK) Computers often make people quite angry — (PAUSE)

ROB: John!

(JOHN SENSES STUPIDITY—HE EXPLAINS LOUDER)

CLEESE: See - computers - often - make - people quite . . . (DOUBLE TAKE; REPEATS) Computers - often - make - people (HESITATES)

ROB (POLITELY): Can I show them mine?

CLEESE: It nearly works.

ROB: Co . . . mp . . . a queue.

CLEESE: What?

ROB: Co . . . mp . . . a queue.

CLEESE (SNIFFS): I prefer mine. Computers often make people (FADES) . . .

637

(MUSIC: INSTRUMENTAL OF LOU REED'S "WALK ON THE WILD SIDE"; MUSIC BUILDS TO SAXOPHONE SOLO)

LOU REED: Hey, don't settle for walkin'.

Consumer Television Over :30 (:45/:60/:90) Single

638
ART DIRECTOR
Bruce Dundore
WRITER
Barry Udoff
AGENCY PRODUCER
Gene Lofaro
PRODUCTION CO.
PYTKA
DIRECTOR
Joe Pytka
CLIENT
Pepsi-Cola
AGENCY
BBDO

639
ART DIRECTOR
Ed Martel
WRITER
Joel Shinsky
AGENCY PRODUCER
Jane Liepshutz
PRODUCTION CO.
PYTKA
DIRECTOR
Joe Pytka
CLIENT
Anheuser-Busch/Budweiser
AGENCY
D'Arcy Masius Benton & Bowles/St. Louis

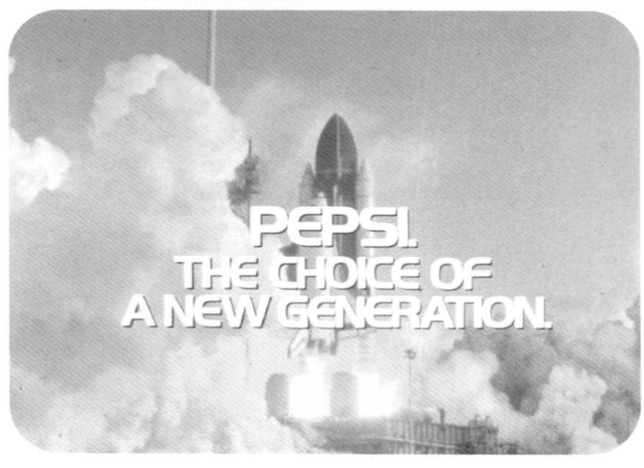

638

VO: Water dump system out.

VO: Caution-warning is go.

GROUND CONTROLLER: Your talk-backs all look O.K.?

VO: Roger.

VO: We have a hold at T-minus 56.

GROUND CONTROLLER: Challenger, we have a gremlin in the cooling system. We've got to put you on hold.

ASTRONAUT: Come on Gene, light this candle.

GROUND CONTROLLER: Understand Challenger, we're doing all we can.

(SFX: PEPSI CAN OPENING)

ASTRONAUT: What was that?

GROUND CONTROLLER: Relax, Chuck. Just cracking open a Pepsi.

ASTRONAUT: Could I go for a cold Pepsi right now!

(SFX: FIZZING SOUND OF SODA)

GROUND CONTROLLER: Wish I could help you buddy.

ASTRONAUT: You can talk me through one.

GROUND CONTROLLER: That's a can do. Lifting slow and easy.

VO: Resume countdown.

GROUND CONTROLLER: We have condensation. Water beads skedaddling down the sides.

ASTRONAUT: Ha, Ha, Ha. I see 'em.

GROUND CONTROLLER: We have visual contact. Those little fizz bubbles just jumpin' up and down.

ASTRONAUT: I think I feel 'em.

GROUND CONTROLLER: We have pour.

VO: 5, 4, 3,

(SFX: PEPSI BEING GULPED DOWN)

VO: 2, 1.

ASTRONAUT: Ahhh!

(SFX: SHUTTLE ENGINES BLAST)

VO: Lift off!

VO: Pepsi. The choice of a new generation. Thanks Gene . . . I owe you one.

639

(MUSIC INTRO)

SINGERS: *This Bud's for*
All that
you do.

UMPIRE: Play ball!

UMPIRE: Time!

ANNCR VO: In the minors you must have called it all a thousand times. But you never lost sight of the dream.

EQUIPMENT MANAGER: Hey Tony, got a telegram for you.

UMPIRE: O.K., thanks Pop.

UMPIRE VO: Hi babe. Hey, guess what? I got the call . . . yep. I'm in the majors.

SINGERS: *You got a shot*
You'll take it.

MANAGER: What's this, a rookie umpire?

SINGERS: *You got the*
Heart to
Make it.
You got
The fire
That Big
League desire
You keep
On reachin' higher.

UMPIRE: Out!

SINGERS: *You make*
America
Work and
This
Bud's for you.

ANNCR VO: Here's to you. Beechwood aged. For that clean crisp taste that makes Budweiser the King of Beers.

WAITRESS: Hi. Compliments from the gentleman over there.

SINGERS: *This Bud's*
For you.

Consumer Television Over :30 (:45/:60/:90) Single

640
ART DIRECTOR
Barry Vetere
WRITER
Ron Berger
AGENCY PRODUCER
Beth Forman
PRODUCTION CO.
Coppos Films
DIRECTOR
Mark Coppos
CLIENT
Polaroid
AGENCY
Ally & Gargano

641
ART DIRECTOR
Harvey Hoffenberg
WRITER
Ted Sann
AGENCY PRODUCER
David Frankel
PRODUCTION CO.
Giraldi Productions
DIRECTOR
Bob Giraldi
CLIENT
Pepsi-Cola
AGENCY
BBDO

642
ART DIRECTOR
Rob Oliver
WRITER
Tom Jenkins
AGENCY PRODUCER
Angela King
PRODUCTION CO.
Park Village Productions
DIRECTOR
Peter Webb
CLIENT
Volkswagen
AGENCY
Doyle Dane Bernbach

640

(MUSIC THROUGHOUT: "I'M SO EXCITED" BY THE POINTER SISTERS)

MARTIN SHEEN VO: Polaroid Instant Cameras do what no other kind of camera can do.

(MUSIC/LYRICS)

641

(MUSIC BEGINS)

RICHIE: *You wear your style,*
You wear your smile,
So free, so fine, so right,
See the new generation
Flashin' through the night.
If looks could sing, the sounds
Would ring across a neon sky,
We're a new generation
Living Pepsi style.
Oh . . . we made our choice, makin'
It Pepsi,
Looking Pepsi style. We made our
Choice, makin' it Pepsi, looking
Pepsi style.
We made our choice, makin' it Pepsi.

642

FVO (SENSUOUS WOMAN'S VOICE OVER THE TELEPHONE): Yes, I'll be waiting.

(SFX: VERY ROMANTIC MOVIE MUSIC BEGINS; THROUGHOUT TO CRESCENDO AT THE END OF COMMERCIAL)

POLO DRIVER (NORTHERN ACCENT): Er . . . good evening, Madam. I've brought your new Polo. Here are your spare keys, your owner's handbook . . . your service schedule.
You'll find the seats fully adjustable, there's lots of legroom. (FADING OUT)

(SFX: MUSIC REACHES CRESCENDO AND FINISHES)

Consumer Television Over :30 (:45/:60/:90) Single

643
ART DIRECTOR
Bob Lenz
WRITER
Bob Meury
AGENCY PRODUCER
Marc Mayhew
PRODUCTION CO.
Dennis Guy & Hirsch
CLIENT
Miller Brewing Company
AGENCY
Backer & Spielvogel

644
ART DIRECTORS
Axel Chaldecott
Gordon Smith
WRITER
Steve Henry
AGENCY PRODUCER
Christine Clark
PRODUCTION CO.
Lewin & Matthews
DIRECTOR
Nick Lewin
CLIENT
Mazda
AGENCY
Gold Greenlees Trott/London

645
ART DIRECTOR
Thom Higgins
WRITER
Joun Doig
AGENCY PRODUCER
Ed Kleban
PRODUCTION CO.
BFCS
DIRECTOR
Thom Higgins
CLIENT
Hershey
AGENCY
Ogilvy & Mather

643

(MUSIC: IN)

ANNCR VO: The events we speak of here took place when a man's reputation was his most precious possession.

EDMOND: I implore you my Lord to not take leave of your senses.

LORD HENFORD: I'll not compromise, Edmond.

ANNCR VO: Historians disagree as to when the dispute began. But, we do know many brave men defend their honor to the utmost.

MAN 3: There must be some other way to settle this, Lord Croten.

LORD CROTEN: Stand back! Only this way will honor be satisfied.

MAN 4: Good morning gentlemen . . .
You know the rules . . .
Lord Henford, stand ready?

LORD HENFORD: I am.

MAN 4: Lord Croten?

LORD CROTEN: I am.

MAN 4: Then gentlemen take your ground . . . one, two . . . three . . . four . . . five . . . for the last time, have you altered your positions?

LORD CROTEN: Tastes great!

LORD HENFORD: Less filling.

LORD CROTEN: Tastes great!

LORD HENFORD: Less filling.

MAN 4: So be it.

ANNCR VO: No one knows how long the argument has raged but one thing is certain, Lite Beer from Miller went on to become the favorite Lite Beer of all time.

(MUSIC: OUT)

644

MVO: In a German road test, one car beat the Mercedes 190. But it isn't in the Mercedes price-range. In America, the coupé version beat the Porsche 944. But it isn't in the Porsche price-range.
In fact, it's in the same price range as say a Cavalier or a Montego.

PORSCHE DRIVER: Amazing.

MERCEDES DRIVER: No. A Mazda.

MVO: The 626. You'll be amazed at a Mazda.

645

You've just had your first taste of a New Trail Chocolate Chip Granola Bar.
How do you feel?
You knock me out, right off my feet.
What about you?
My secret dreams have all come true.
and you?
It's the greatest, oh, oh.
What do you think of all those Hershey chocolate chips?
It's a natural fact
I like it like that.
and you?
Ba, ba, ba, ba, etc.
Isn't it the biggest granola bar you've ever seen?
That's all I need and
I'll be satisfied.
What would you do if your mom ran out of New Trail Bars?
Well, I'm gonna write a little letter
I'm gonna mail it to my local DJ.
and you
Nothing can stop the Duke of Earl.
New Trail Granola Bars from Hershey.
Goodnight Sweetheart,
Well it's time to go.

Consumer Television
Over :30 (:45/:60/:90)
Single

646
ART DIRECTORS
Paul Regan
Robert Smiley
WRITERS
Chris Lincoln
David Greely
AGENCY PRODUCER
Dennis Gray
PRODUCTION CO.
Petermann Dektor
DIRECTOR
Fred Petermann
CLIENT
Honeywell
AGENCY
Ingalls Quinn & Johnson/Boston

647
ART DIRECTOR
Mike Owen
WRITER
Nick Wray
AGENCY PRODUCER
Christine Clark
PRODUCTION CO.
John S. Clarke Productions
DIRECTOR
John S. Clarke
CLIENT
Mazda
AGENCY
Gold Greenlees Trott/London

648
ART DIRECTOR
Arthur Vibert
WRITER
Lisa Kleckner
AGENCY PRODUCER
Bill Clarkson
DIRECTOR
Barry Myers
CLIENT
Brown & Williamson Tobacco Corporation
AGENCY
Ogilvy & Mather/Chicago

649
ART DIRECTOR
Michael Tesch
WRITER
Patrick Kelly
AGENCY PRODUCER
Maureen Kearns
PRODUCTION CO.
Kelly Pictures
DIRECTOR
Patrick Kelly
CLIENT
Federal Express
AGENCY
Ally & Gargano

646

ATTORNEY 1: As I stated before, this proves that the accused and his accomplices . . .

ATTORNEY 2: Objection.

JUDGE: Sustained.

ATTORNEY 1: . . . do show . . .

ANNCR: In Los Angeles, Honeywell is working with the District Attorney's office.

POLICE OFFICER 1: It's going down.

ANNCR: Where a special Honeywell System is helping the right people.
Helping them get to the right place at the right time to get evidence before it's covered up.

POLICE OFFICER 2: Go!

BOTH OFFICERS: Freeze!

ANNCR: The Honeywell System then speeds the DA's into court. With Honeywell, justice is swift. Working together works.

JUDGE: Order.

ANNCR: Honeywell, together we can find the answers.

647

MVO: This is the outside of a Rolls Royce Corniche.
And this is the outside of the new Mazda 323.
What's so amazing about that?
Well; this is the inside of the Mazda 323 . . .
. . . and *this* is the inside of the Rolls Royce.
In fact, the Mazda 323 has *4 cubic feet more interior space* than a Rolls Royce Corniche.
Yet the Mazda 323 range costs less than the Volkswagen Golf range.

JAPANESE MAN: That's amazing!

(SFX: CRASH!!)

MVO: No, that's a Mazda. The new 323 family hatchback. You'll be amazed at a Mazda.

648

ALL MUSIC

649

(MUSIC UNDER: UM PA PA, UM PA PA)

ANNCR VO: This year, Federal Express is going to Europe. And to help celebrate we've invited everyone who's ever been in a Federal Express commercial.

FAST TALKING MAN: Unaccustomed as I am to public speaking, I would just like to say this is certainly a momentous occasion. I am certainly moved by it all, and it's with particular pride and pleasure that I point out I'm pleased as punch to participate in this perfectly perfect party. At this time I'd like to say hello to each and every one of you: Hello Sandra, hello Bill, hello Buster, hello Gene, hello Tom, hello Ann, hello Nancy, hello Esther, hello Dirk, hello Fred, hello Lorna . . .

ANNCR VO: We wanted everyone who's helped spread the word about Federal Express to be a part of this occasion. Because we're going to make sending a package to Europe as easy and reliable as it is here. With two-day service in our own planes, to London, Paris, Frankfurt, Zurich, Amsterdam, and Brussels.

ALL: Goooodbbbbbyyyyyeeeee, Federal!!!!!!!!!!

ANNCR VO: Federal Express to Europe. Why fool around with anyone else?

Consumer Television
Over :30 (:45/:60/:90)
Single

650
ART DIRECTOR
Ken Hoggins
WRITER
Chris O'Shea
AGENCY PRODUCER
Erika Issitt
PRODUCTION CO.
BFCS
DIRECTOR
Bob Brooks
CLIENT
Whitbread & Company
AGENCY
Lowe Howard-Spink Marschalk/London

651
ART DIRECTOR
Alan Sprules
WRITER
Roger Proulx
AGENCY PRODUCER
Tina Raver
PRODUCTION CO.
Brooks Fulford Cramer Seresin Inc.
DIRECTOR
Michael Seresin
CLIENT
Paco Rabanne
AGENCY
Ogilvy & Mather

652
ART DIRECTOR
Sam Hurford
WRITER
Paul Grubb
AGENCY PRODUCER
Christine Clark
PRODUCTION CO.
BFCS
DIRECTOR
Richard Sloggett
CLIENT
Holsten Diat Pils
AGENCY
Gold Greenlees Trott/London

653
ART DIRECTOR
Andy Page
WRITER
Angela Savidan
AGENCY PRODUCER
Pam Denereaz
PRODUCTION CO.
Paul Weiland Film Company
DIRECTOR
Paul Weiland
CLIENT
Kenner Parker
AGENCY
Grey Ltd/London

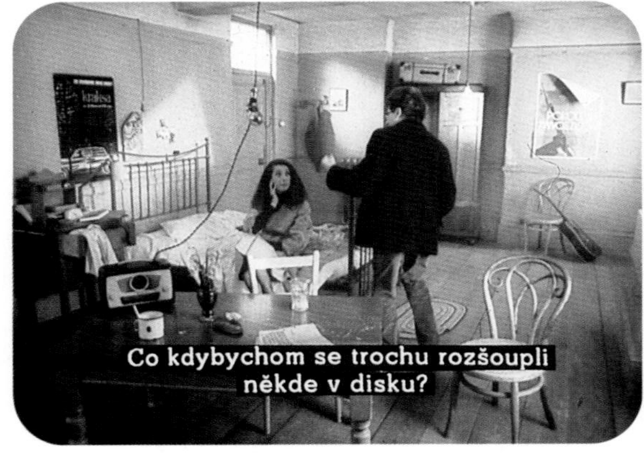

650

MAN (IN CZECH): Listen to me, Olga.

WOMAN (IN CZECH): Ivan, man alone cannot pre-ordain destiny.

MAN: But Olga, cathartic transcension must be an immutable prerequisite.

WOMAN: So? You repudiate Eisenbaum's theory of metamorphic dualism?

MAN (SILENCE): . . . Yes.

VICTOR: Oh dear, this film is obviously in need of some refreshment.

MAN (IN ENGLISH): (SILENCE) . . . Let's face it, Olga. No way are we going to crack the meaning of life tonight.

WOMAN (IN ENGLISH): Suppose not.

MAN: What say we give it some down the disco?

WOMAN: Can we have a curry after?

MAN: Yeah.

VICTOR: Apparently film buffs, Heineken can even refresh the Part Twos other beers cannot reach.

651

Paco Rabanne for men
What is remembered, is up to you.

652

GRIFF: Is that a genuine *Holsten* Pils you've got there, Cecil?

ED. G.: This is strictly legitimate.

GRIFF: Well how about swapping it for this er . . . illegitimate?

ED. G.: Now did you come here to make cracks or talk?

GRIFF (TOUGHER): Now look, Cec baby . . . would you rather give me the real *Holsten* Pils, where the sugar turns to alcohol, or rather cause trouble?

ED. G.: Er . . . ah . . . (COCKY) well, I'm telling you tomorrow I'm gonna make you an offer you can't refuse!

ED. G.: And I'm telling you to keep outta my way!

GRIFF: Cecil, you old toad, here's *two* bottles for your *one* Holsten . . .

(SFX: BANG! BANG!)

GRIFF: Can I er . . . take that as a 'no', then. . . ?

MVO: A Holsten Pils Production.

653

MVO: Tension mounts as the East-West Talks go into their second session.

AMERICAN: Answer the question, Comrade, if you please! What was Julius Marx more commonly known as?

RUSSIAN: Karl?

AMERICAN: Nope! Groucho.

(SFX: LAUGHTER AND GROANS)

RUSSIAN: Well, here's one for your arms expert! What's tattooed on Popeye's arm?

(SFX: THEY ALL LAUGH)

RUSSIAN: Gentlemen, enough! Please! The Star Wars Question.
Who was Luke Skywalker's Father?

(SFX: GUFFAWS OF DELIGHTED LAUGHTER OVER THROUGHOUT FINAL PACKSHOT)

MVO: Trivial Pursuit.
6,000 questions of no vital importance whatsoever.

Consumer Television
Over :30 (:45/:60/:90)
Single

654
ART DIRECTOR
Joe Genova
WRITER
James Parry
AGENCY PRODUCERS
Sandy Bachom
PRODUCTION CO.
Princzko Productions
DIRECTOR
Rick Levine
CLIENT
Southern New England Telephone
AGENCY
Posey & Quest/Greenwich, CT

655
ART DIRECTORS
Paul Frahm
Mike Bade
WRITERS
David Hale
Barbara Reynolds
AGENCY PRODUCER
Paul Frahm
PRODUCTION CO.
Jenkins/Covington/Newman/Rath
DIRECTOR
Tim Newman
CLIENT
Miller Brewing Company
AGENCY
J. Walter Thompson

654

MAN: What are we on tonight? Alpha Centauri?

MAN: Yeah, but nothing interesting. Same old random blips.

MAN: Who was the first man to catch no hitters in both major leagues, huh?

WOMAN: It's your move.

MAN: You know, that's a . . . hey, hey, wait a minute . . .

MAN: . . . we're getting something . . .

MAN: . . . we're forming—a circle. What the heck is this?

MAN: I don't believe it.

MAN: Ann, Steve, take a look at this.

WOMAN: What?

MAN: Did the computer crash?

MAN: The computer's up.

MAN: Everything else up? Check the internals.

MAN: What's going on?

MAN: I don't know.

MAN: We're getting a pattern—a message.

MAN: What the heck is that?

MAN: Alpha Centauri?

MAN: Carl, get me confirmation. Anybody else seen this?

MAN: There goes my weekend.

MAN: Planetary system. No maybe not.

MAN: Could be part of DNA. I don't believe this. Carbon Atom. Five of them. Call NASA.

MAN: Polarization.

MAN: Linear 100%. Definitely intelligent.

MAN: It is DNA.

MAN: They're just like us.

MAN: Any confirmation?

MAN: It's coming up on the board.

MAN: I think somebody's trying to talk to us.

VO: Everything begins with communications. Are your communications ready for everything?

SUPER: Southern New England Telephone.

655

DAN: Rock 'n roll comes from what happens to you every day. It doesn't come from sittin' down and thinkin' about it.

TOM: It's about everyday things, you know . . .

WOODY: It's stripped down and it's simple and it's talking about people with each other.

TOM: It's not the kind of music that requires thought to understand it . . . it requires dancing.

DAN (SINGING): *You know what's right*
You know what's wrong
The street's alive
You can hear its song.

DAN: The true test is if it comes back to you. Heads are bobbin' up and down and you know you're doing something right.

TOM: If you're not honest about rock 'n roll, people can sense it.

DAN (SINGING): *Yeah, the rock won't stop*
Cause it starts right here,
Where people are dancin'
And Miller's the beer.

DEL FUEGOS (SINGING):
Miller's made the American way
It's what'ya do, it's what'ya say
When you feel what's real
There ain't nothing else to say
Miller's made the American way.

DAN: Rock 'n roll is folk music—'cause it's for folks.

DEL FUEGOS: Miller's made the American way.

Consumer Television
Over :30 (:45/:60/:90)
Single

656
ART DIRECTOR
Don Easdon
WRITER
Bill Heater
AGENCY PRODUCER
Mary Ellen Argentieri
PRODUCTION CO.
PYTKA
DIRECTOR
Joe Pytka
CLIENT
John Hancock
AGENCY
Hill Holliday Connors
Cosmopulos/Boston

657
ART DIRECTOR
Candy Greathouse
WRITER
John Lyons
AGENCY PRODUCER
Karen Spector
PRODUCTION CO.
Bianchi Films
DIRECTOR
Ed Bianchi
CLIENT
Procter & Gamble/Bounce
AGENCY
D'Arcy Masius Benton &
Bowles

658
ART DIRECTORS
Jerry Gentile
Steve Diamont
WRITERS
Steve Diamont
Jerry Gentile
AGENCY PRODUCER
Beth Hagen
PRODUCTION CO.
HKM Productions
DIRECTOR
HKM
CLIENT
Merle Norman
AGENCY
Doyle Dane Bernbach

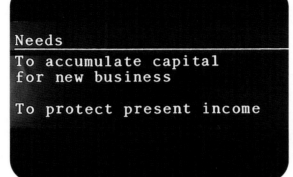

Needs

To accumulate capital
for new business

To protect present income

656

MAN: Are you awake?

WIFE: Um . . . yeah.

MAN: Wanna talk?

WIFE: Uhm.

MAN: Did you pay the mortgage?

WIFE: Yes. Of course.

MAN: Good. That's good. I was just going to say that I . . . you know . . . Kath . . . there's 2 kinds of people in the world.

WIFE: Yeah, men and women.

MAN: Yeah, that. But there are those that work for themselves and those that work for somebody else and I think that I'm that kind of person who ought to work for himself.

WIFE: Um, that's fine.

MAN: I'm not saying go out and start a business tomorrow. I'm saying, let's plan, you know, plan.

WIFE: That's the only way to do it.

MAN: I think that's smart. I think we'll be a lot happier. We'll have a goal.

(QUIET FOR ABOUT 3 SECONDS)

MAN: Did you tuck Kevin in?

WIFE: Yes.

MAN: Good. That's good.

657

(SFX: MUSIC THROUGHOUT)

WOMAN'S VOICE (SONG):
When towels feel this soft jumping
Sheets feel this fresh. Jump.
And there's no cling to most anything.
Jump. Jump.
Jump. Jump. You've got
Bounce clothes.
Clothes you can't wait to jump into. Jump.
Feel the touch. Jumping.
You are the one. You feel so good around.
Jump. Jump. Jump. Jump.
You could use this or even this
But Bounce is the softener more people use.
And they feel like this about their clothes. So soft sweaters, sweet smelling linens, no cling things.
Jump. Feel the touch. Jumping.
Bounce.
For clothes you can't wait to jump into.
Jump. Jump. Jump.

658

(MUSIC: CHANGES WITH THE MOOD OF EACH COSTUME AND MAKE-UP)

VO: Merle Norman can take you to the limits of your imagination. If you can dream it, you can do it.

Consumer Television Over :30 (:45/:60/:90) Single

659
ART DIRECTORS
John DeCerchio
Sheldon Cohn
WRITERS
John DeCerchio
Sheldon Cohn
AGENCY PRODUCER
Sheldon Cohn
DIRECTOR
Bruce Van Dusen
CLIENT
Eckerd Drugs
AGENCY
W. B. Doner & Company/
Southfield, MI

660
ART DIRECTOR
Tom McConnaughy
WRITER
Curvin O'Rielly
AGENCY PRODUCER
Mickey Paradise
PRODUCTION CO.
Petermann Dektor
DIRECTOR
Leslie Dektor
CLIENT
Nutrasweet
AGENCY
Ogilvy & Mather/Chicago

661
ART DIRECTOR
Rich Martel
WRITER
Al Merrin
AGENCY PRODUCER
Jeff Fischgrund
PRODUCTION CO.
HKM Productions
DIRECTOR
Graham Henman
CLIENT
Pepsi-Cola
AGENCY
BBDO

659

CONNELY (EXCITED): He's back! He's back!

KID 1: Who's back?

CONNELY: Coach Riley—he's back!

KID 2: He can't be back . . . he's sick in the hospital.

KID 3: Yeah, they said he might never come back.

COACH RILEY: Alright you lunkheads, laps in 30 seconds! Move it!! Let's go . . . move it! Move it!! I want you to form 3 lines (FADES)

VO: Today, more people are surviving cancer of the colon . . . thanks, in part, to a test that provides early detection. And last year a company gave out a million of these tests free . . . to people like Coach Riley. The company was Eckerd Drugs.

COACH RILEY (VOICE BEGINS TO FADE UP OVER VO): Pull, Hoffman! Pull! Pull! . . . In the belly, in the belly! . . . Whataya doin' there, Siecro, you put on 20 pounds since I left . . . Let's go. C'mon, c'mon, give me some work.

(SFX: WHISTLE BLOWING)

COACH RILEY: Mr Connely, you mind telling us what's so funny?!

CONNELY: TRIES TO SPEAK BUT WORDS JUST WON'T COME OUT

COACH RILEY: Well?

CONNELY (FINALLY): We're just glad to have you back, Coach.

COACH RILEY (MOVED, BUT TRYING NOT TO SHOW IT): Yeah, well . . . uh, okay . . . (WITH A LITTLE SMILE) You trying to talk me out of push ups, Connely?

CONNELY: KNOWING SMILE

COACH RILEY (REGAINING HIS COMPOSURE): Alright, c'mon! One, two, three, four . . .(SLOWLY FADING OUT)

VO: Your Eckerd Pharmacists. Dedicated to your good health.

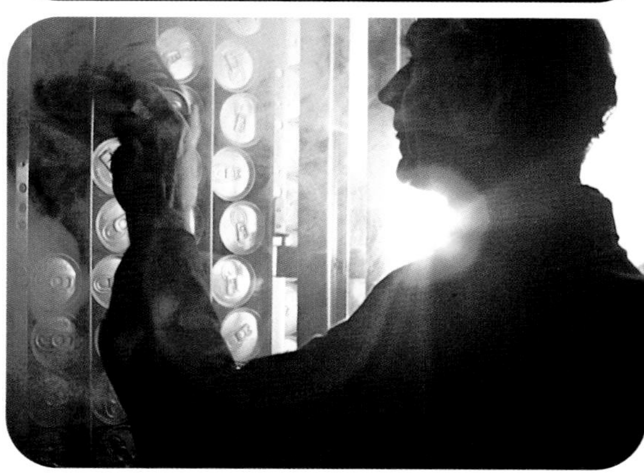

660

(MUSIC: UNDER THROUGHOUT)

ANNCR VO: And while they slept, it arrived in every last nook and cranny of the land.
100% Nutrasweet.
No saccharin.

(SFX: CAN OPENING)

(SFX: REPEATED 5 TIMES)

ANNCR VO: In soft drinks with this 100% symbol—
100% Nutrasweet brand sweetener.
Why some things taste better than others.

661

DEL. BOY: Delivery!

GIRL: Oh great!

VO: See if he's got an opener?

GIRL: Opener? . . . No opener?

VO: Who needs an opener? Let J.J. do it.

(SFX: BASS GUITAR)

VO: There's one soft drink with a taste so electrifying,

VO: it's pure . . .

(SFX: BUBBLING NOISE)

VO: rock and roll

(SFX: BOTTLE TOPS POPPING)

(SFX: FAST AND FURIOUS BASS GUITAR PLAYING)

(SFX: REMAINING BOTTLE TOP POPS, CHEERS)

VO: Pepsi. The choice of a new generation.

Consumer Television Over :30 (:45/:60/:90) Single

662
ART DIRECTOR
Dan Hackett
WRITERS
Bruce Broder
Steve LaGattuta
AGENCY PRODUCER
Hugh Broder
DIRECTOR
Bill Dear
CLIENT
D.O.C. Optics
AGENCY
W. B. Doner & Company/
Michigan

Consumer Television Over :30 (:45/:60/:90) Campaign

663
ART DIRECTOR
Tony DeGregorio
WRITER
Lee Garfinkel
AGENCY PRODUCERS
Bob Nelson
Rachel Novak
PRODUCTION CO.
Steve Horn Inc.
DIRECTOR
Steve Horn
CLIENT
Subaru of America
AGENCY
Levine Huntley Schmidt &
Beaver

664
ART DIRECTORS
Marcus Kemp
Joe Sedelmaier
WRITERS
Steve Sandoz
Joe Sedelmaier
AGENCY PRODUCER
Cindy Henderson
PRODUCTION CO.
Sedelmaier
DIRECTOR
Joe Sedelmaier
CLIENT
Alaska Airlines
AGENCY
Livingston & Company/
Seattle

665
ART DIRECTOR
David Hunter
WRITER
Geoff Thompson
AGENCY PRODUCER
Flo Babbit
PRODUCTION COS
Collosal Productions
Rick Levine Productions
DIRECTORS
Gary Gutierrez
Michael Werk
CLIENT
Pacific Telesis
AGENCY
Foote Cone & Belding/San
Francisco

SUBARU®
Inexpensive. And built to stay that way.

662

ANNCR: It was on a hot, dusty afternoon in July, 1956, that Charles Hardin Holly showed up at rehearsal with a new pair of eyeglasses.

GUY 1: I don't know.

GUY 2: *I* like 'em.

GUY 1: Buddy . . . those glasses are you.

ANNCR: New glasses not only change the way you see the world, they change the way the world sees you. That's why at D.O.C. we have exactly the frames you want to be seen in. When you think about it, after his music what we remember most about Buddy Holly are those glasses.

663

(SFX: PHONE RINGS)

DOC: WAKES UP, ANSWERS PHONE.

FATHER (NERVOUS): Listen, Doc, I think she's ready.

DOC: O.K., O.K., I'll be right over.

ANNCR: In Markesan, Wisconsin, when it's not possible for a patient to get to Dr. Lippart's office, Dr. Lippart brings his office to his patients. And the office he relies on to get him through nights like this—a Subaru wagon.

DAUGHTER: Daddy, where is he?

FATHER: He's coming baby, he's coming?

DAUGHTER: I see him.

ANNCR: So happily, on this night, like so many nights before . . .

DAUGHTER: How is she?

DOC: They're both doing fine.

ANNCR: . . . Dr. Lippart delivered a healthy 72 pound . . . calf.

COW: Mooo.

664

ANNCR: Have you ever wondered just what flying is coming to?

WOMAN: Hi! I'm your talking ticket. Do you have baggage?

MAN: Oh. Oh. Yes.

WOMAN: Hi! I'm your talking ticket. Do you have baggage?

MAN 2: I don't have any baggage.

WOMAN: Please enter the aircraft to your left.

ATTEN: Hi! Welcome aboard. Now let's adjust our seatbelts.

ATTEN: Please put your seat back in a fully upright position.

ANNCR: At Alaska Airlines, our people go out of their way to show you they're only human.

665

ANNCR VO: Telesis, the dictionary defines it as progress, intelligently planned. This is a story of Telesis.
Letter to the Consul-General July, 1852. I confess that my scheme is still a mere dream. The cutting of a canal through the desert of Suez has been thought to be impossible. Yet, the opening of communications between two isolated worlds would be of immense benefit to our civilization. I beg for your support in this undertaking. For so long as I alone believe it can be done it will never be done. Yours sincerely, Ferdinand DeLesseps. Pacific Telesis salutes that special kind of progress. Guided by those with the vision to see not just what can be done but what ought to be done. The Pacific Telesis Group is committed to progress, intelligently planned.
That's why Telesis is an important part of our name.

Consumer Television
Over :30 (:45/:60/:90)
Campaign

666
ART DIRECTORS
Lin Berkowitz
Marisa Acocella
Kathy McMahon
WRITERS
Marty Friedman
Alison Gragnano
Gerry Killeen
Linda Kaplan
Kathy McMahon
AGENCY PRODUCER
Sid Horn
PRODUCTION CO.
The DXTR's
DIRECTOR
Greg Weinschenker
CLIENT
Eastman Kodak
AGENCY
J. Walter Thompson

667
ART DIRECTOR
Lou DiJoseph
WRITER
Lee Kovel
AGENCY PRODUCER
Chris Jones
PRODUCTION CO.
BFCS
DIRECTOR
Bob Brooks
CLIENT
Dr. Pepper
AGENCY
Young & Rubicam

668
ART DIRECTOR
Larry Reinschmeidt
WRITERS
Jud Chapin
Mike Slosberg
AGENCY PRODUCER
Bill Duryea
CLIENT
American Airlines
AGENCY
Bozell Jacobs Kenyon & Eckhardt/Texas

669
ART DIRECTORS
Alan Waldie
Ken Hoggins
Mike Stephenson
WRITERS
Adrain Holmes
Chris O'Shea
Derek Apps
AGENCY PRODUCERS
Mike Griffin
Erika Issitt
PRODUCTION COS
Paul Weiland Film Company
BFCS
Grandslam Animation
DIRECTORS
Paul Weiland
Bob Brooks
Geoff Dunbar
CLIENT
Whitbread & Company
AGENCY
Lowe Howard-Spink Marschalk/London

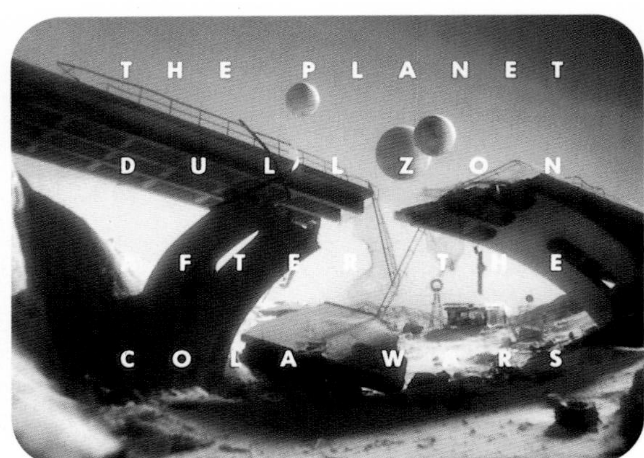

666

SONG: *Settin' off to find America*
Gonna take my own sweet time to find America
And everywhere I see
People smilin' back at me
So glad to be in America
So come take my hand and let's discover
The love that we share brother to brother

VO: Bring America home on Kodacolor VR films. Films as vibrant and as sensitive as the faces and places that bring this land together.

SONG: *And as far as I can see*
There's no place I'd rather be
Than ridin' free
In America

VO: Kodak film. Because time goes by.

667

(SFX & MUSIC UNDER THROUGHOUT)

OZY'S VOICE: I smell a rat.

WARRIOR 1: Give me two more colas and a little of your time sweetheart.

WAITRESS: Hello stranger . . . and stranger yet, what'll you have?

SPACE COWBOY: Something different.

WARRIOR 2: The cola wars are over.

WARRIOR 1: There ain't nothing different.

WAITRESS: I have something different.

OZY'S VOICE: Jackpot! Uh-oh.

WARRIOR 1: Trash it!

SPACE COWBOY: Freeze! It's better cold.

668

BOSS'S VOICE ON RECORDER: Welcome back, Brad. I knew you'd stop by the office.
Well, all those trips you made paid off. While you were at 35,000 feet, the AVKON people called and gave us the project.
Check your top drawer. There's one more trip I'd like you to take.
I know how much you and Ann love the islands.
Aloha Brad.
You did a great job.
Thanks.

ANNCR TAG: When you're something special, people know it.
American Airlines. Something special in the air.

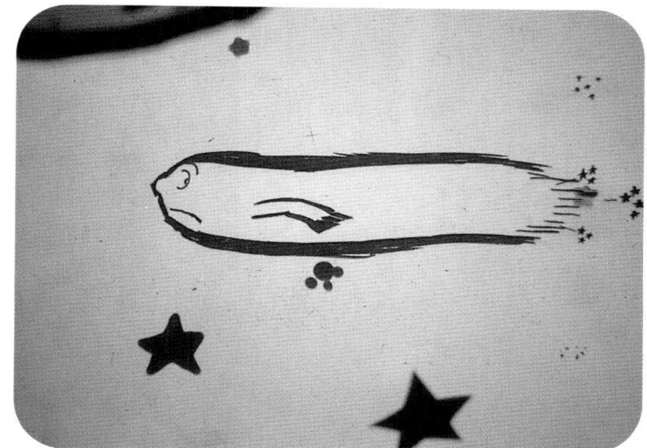

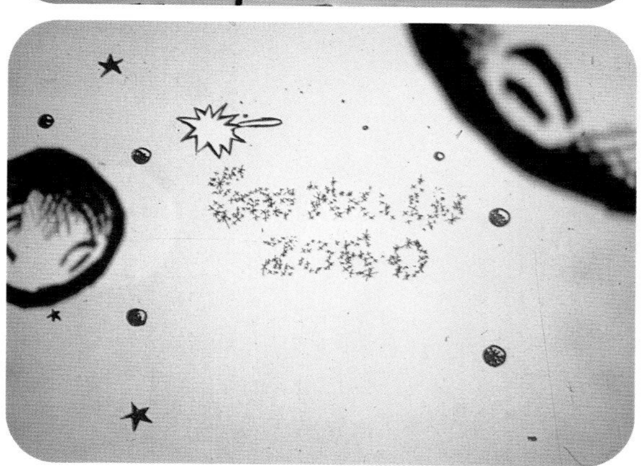

669

(MUSIC: THROUGHOUT)

(SFX: CAR ENGINE)

(SFX: CAR ENGINE STALLS)

(SFX: ENGINE TRIES TO START)

(SFX: ENGINE STILL TRYING TO START)

(SFX: FILLING UP)

(SFX: ENGINE FIRES, THEN REVS)

(SFX: WHOOSH)

(SFX: PINBALL MACHINE)

MVO: No Heineken.
No Comet.

Consumer Television Over :30 (:45/:60/:90) Campaign

670
ART DIRECTORS
Dennis McVey
David Hunter
WRITER
Robert Black
AGENCY PRODUCER
Bob Gondell
PRODUCTION CO.
Rick Levine Productions
DIRECTOR
Rick Levine
CLIENT
Pacific Bell
AGENCY
Foote Cone & Belding/San Francisco

Consumer Television :30 Single

671
ART DIRECTOR
Gary Carlisle
WRITER
Gary Gusick
AGENCY PRODUCER
Wendy Josephson
PRODUCTION CO.
Mark Ross Films
DIRECTOR
Mark Ross
CLIENT
Shop-Vac
AGENCY
Slater Hanft Martin

672
ART DIRECTOR
Dean Hanson
WRITER
Mike Lescarbeau
AGENCY PRODUCER
Judy Brink
PRODUCTION CO.
Rossetti Films
DIRECTOR
Dominic Rossetti
CLIENT
Minnesota Federal
AGENCY
Fallon McElligott/Minneapolis

673
ART DIRECTOR
Mike Ciranni
WRITER
Jamie Seltzer
AGENCY PRODUCER
Frank Scherma
PRODUCTION CO.
Sandbank Films
DIRECTOR
Henry Sandbank
CLIENT
Topps Bazooka Bubble Gum
AGENCY
Chiat/Day

670

MAN: Well I've known Casey for 50 years and I have to say we didn't exactly start off as best friends.

SINGER: *Casey, I hear a crowd cheering some forgotten victory. Casey, I see them all standing. Is it for you, is it for me.*

MAN: The respect we earned was more important than all the winning and losing. 'Cause somehow it gave us a friendship that'll go on and on.

SINGER: *Now that all our younger years drift into yesterday, I want you to remember . . .*

(SFX: TELEPHONE RINGS . . .)

MAN: Hello, Casey, how are ya?

MAN 2: Hello Champ . . . (WORDS FADE)

SINGER: *I won't fade away.*

671

(MUSIC: UP AND UNDER)

ANNCR VO: As everyone who owns a vacuum cleaner knows . . .
There are some places it just wasn't meant to clean.

(SFX: BOING, BOING)

ANNCR VO: For these impossible places there's Shop Vacs . . . Mighty Mini. The powerful little vacuum that goes easily where the big boys can't. Try finding another vacuum this small . . . this powerful. The Mighty Mini . . . by Shop Vac. We pick up where the others leave off.

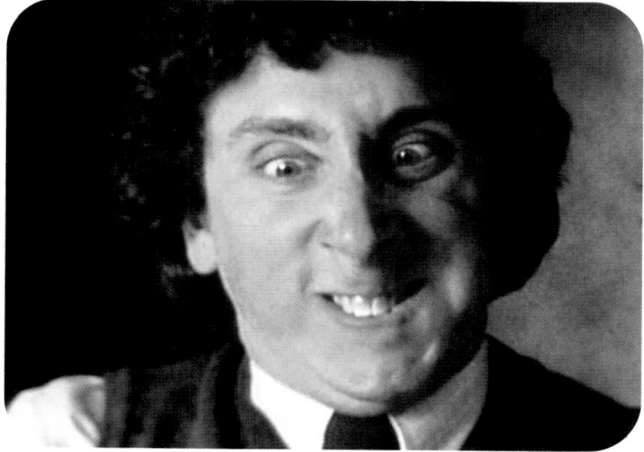

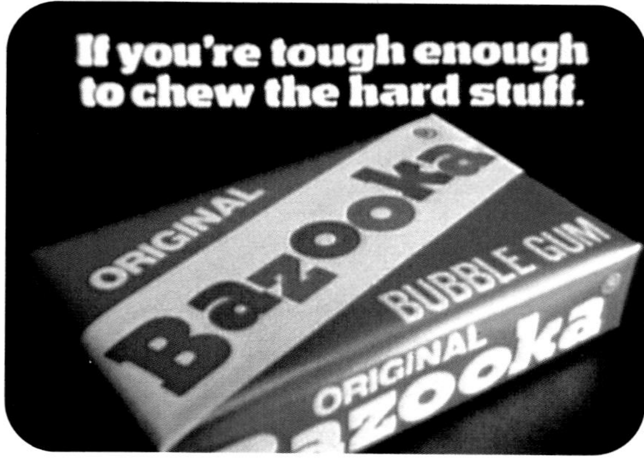

672

(MUSIC: INTRO. UNDER)

VO: When it comes to borrowing money, some banks can make you feel a little unwelcome.

(MUSIC: LITTLE RICHARD'S "KEEPA' KNOCKIN")

VO: Next time, come to Minnesota Federal. With millions of dollars to lend, our doors are always open.

673

(SFX: CAR STARTING BUT NOT TURNING OVER)

(SFX: CAR STARTING BUT NOT TURNING OVER)

(SFX: CAR NOT TURNING OVER)

(SFX: CAR TURNS OVER)

VO: It's harder to get started . . .

(SFX: CAR IS HUMMING)

VO: . . . but once it gets going, it never stops.

VO: Bazooka Bubble Gum. If you're tough enough to chew the hard stuff.

Consumer Television :30 Single

674
ART DIRECTOR
Lou Carvell
WRITER
Abbie Simon
AGENCY PRODUCER
Debbie Dunlap
PRODUCTION CO.
Rossetti Films
DIRECTOR
Dominic Rossetti
CLIENT
Smith-Corona
AGENCY
Rosenfeld Sirowitz & Humphrey

675
ART DIRECTOR
Mario Giua
WRITER
Robin Raj
AGENCY PRODUCER
Frank Scherma
PRODUCTION CO.
Sandbank Films
DIRECTOR
Henry Sandbank
CLIENT
NYNEX Information Resources
AGENCY
Chiat/Day

676
ART DIRECTOR
Eric Hanson
WRITER
Bob Finley
AGENCY PRODUCER
Bob Finley
PRODUCTION CO.
Team Productions
DIRECTOR
Jerry Collamer
CLIENT
Kay-Bee Toy & Hobby Stores
AGENCY
Sachs Finley & Company/Los Angeles

677
ART DIRECTOR
Geoff Roche
WRITER
Kirk Citron
AGENCY PRODUCER
Len Levy
PRODUCTION CO.
Eggers Films
DIRECTOR
Bob Eggers
CLIENT
California Prune Board
AGENCY
Hal Riney & Partners/San Francisco

674

DR. RUTH: You think you've got problems. I've got one, too. It's psychological—I just misspelled it. But I've got help from an expert.
The new Smith Corona Typewriter with Spell-Right dictionary.

(SFX: BEEP BEEP)

It beeps when I misspell a word.
Finds it. Erases it.
Even helps me spell it.
With Spell-Right, I'm letter perfect. And I love it.
That's why my Smith-Corona and I have a fantastic relationship.

ANNCR: SpellRight typewriters from Smith Corona.

675

DAD: Sally, who took the Yellow Pages?

SAL: I dunno.

(PAUSE)

DAD: Honey, have you seen the Yellow Pages?

MOM: No.

(PAUSE)

DAD: Susie, where are the Yellow Pages?

SUE: Sally had it last.

SAL: I did not.

DAD: C'mon. I need the Yellow Pages . . .

VO: Over the years, one book has been in more homes, helping people throughout New England find more goods and services. The NYNEX Yellow Pages . . .

SUE: Mom!

VO: It's always there when you need it.

MOM: Oh!

676

VO: Each year, thousands of children disappear.

VO: Just disappear.

VO: No one knows where they've gone, or what's happened to them.

VO: It's suspected that many of them have been abducted.

VO: We at Kay-Bee Toy Stores urge you to teach your children to avoid strangers . . .

VO: . . . and how to say no to strangers.

VO: And most of all, even if you feel your children are safe . . .

VO: . . . keep an eye on them.

VO: If you do this, maybe there'll be one less child . . .

VO: . . . that disappears.

677

MAN (TALKING SLOWLY; SPEEDS UP TO BECOME INCREDIBLY FAST; SLOWS DOWN AT VERY END): Not long ago I felt tired and listless all the time.

My wife left me. My friends left me. My dog left me. Then I started eating prunes again. Just a few to start with. Every day a couple in the morning or at lunch or for a snack and then they were so delicious I started cooking with them again too and before I knew it I felt better about myself. I took up jogging, and with prunes back in my life I found new friends, new furniture, and a cat. My wife came back and soon she was eating prunes too. Friends flocked to our place for parties and dinners and brought their own prunes along. I became vibrant and exciting and a fun guy to talk to. My life has never been the same since.

And you know, it's all because of prunes.

SUPER: California Prunes.

Consumer Television :30 Single

678
ART DIRECTOR
Bob Barrie
WRITER
Phil Hanft
AGENCY PRODUCER
Judy Brink
PRODUCTION CO.
James Productions
DIRECTOR
Jim Lund
CLIENT
Minnesota Zoo
AGENCY
Fallon McElligott/Minneapolis

679
ART DIRECTOR
Bob Ryzner
WRITER
Boris Damast
AGENCY PRODUCER
Bob Samuel
PRODUCTION CO.
Richard Chambers & Company
DIRECTOR
Richard Chambers
CLIENT
The Krystal Company
AGENCY
Saatchi & Saatchi Compton

680
ART DIRECTOR
Losang Gyatso
WRITER
Peter Kellogg
AGENCY PRODUCERS
Nick Ciarlante
Cindy Lee
PRODUCTION CO.
Pfeifer Story Piccolo Guliner
DIRECTOR
Mark Story
CLIENT
Coca Cola/Diet Coke
AGENCY
SSC&B:Lintas

681
ART DIRECTOR
Terry Tarrant
WRITER
Dave Moeller
AGENCY PRODUCER
Linda Wolfe
PRODUCTION CO.
Sunlight Pictures
DIRECTOR
Mel Sokolsky
CLIENT
Adolph Coors Company
AGENCY
Foote Cone & Belding/Chicago

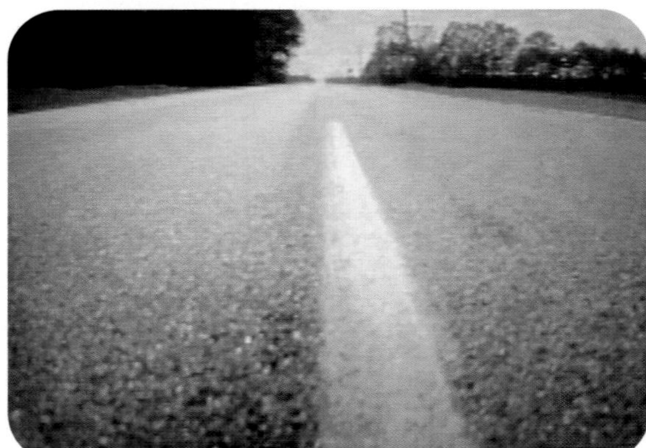

678

(SFX: COMBINATION OF DRAGSTER PEELING OUT AND SYNTHESIZER)

VO: Introducing a precisely-designed racing machine that can accelerate from zero to 45 in 2 seconds . . . can reach almost unheard of speeds in less than a quarter mile . . . and . . . can stop on a dime.

(SFX: SCREECH OF BREAKING AUTO)

VO: The world's fastest land animal. Now at the Minnesota Zoo.

679

(MUSIC)

ANNCR: The irresistible Krystal. Nothing looks like it. Nothing tastes like it.

SOLDIER: Mom? Dad?

ANNCR: When you've got to have a Krystal, you've got to have a Krystal.

680

INSTRUCTOR (IN JAPANESE): You must put on weight for the contest.

STUDENT: Hai.

INSTRUCTOR: Five bowls of stew and rice each meal.

STUDENT: Hai.

INSTRUCTOR: Good.

ANNCR: Isn' t it amazing? Even people who don't care about dieting love diet Coke.

SINGERS: *Just for the taste of it.*

STUDENT: Hai.

SINGERS: *Diet Coke.*

681

HARMON: You know I've been a beer drinker for a bunch of years . . .
And like you, I've seen a lot of beer commercials.
But ya know, there's one beer people loved way before it was even advertised . . .
You see Coors was kind of *the* beer at my folks place. People thought it was . . . different, special . . .
And that was true before any jingles or promotions . . .
It's the product people love . . .
Not the hoopla.
You think about it . . .
How many product can you say that about?
Coors is the one.

Consumer Television
:30 Single

682
ART DIRECTOR
Michael Lawlor
WRITER
Richie Russo
AGENCY PRODUCER
Joanne Diglio
PRODUCTION CO.
Gomes-Loew Productions
DIRECTOR
George Gomes
CLIENT
Health America
AGENCY
Della Femina Travisano & Partners

683
ART DIRECTOR
Jack Eleftheriou
WRITER
Jeffrey Mullen
AGENCY PRODUCERS
Nick Ciarlante
Stu Kuby
PRODUCTION CO.
HKM Productions
DIRECTOR
Graham Henman
CLIENT
Coca Cola/Diet Coke
AGENCY
SSC&B:Lintas

684
ART DIRECTOR
Bob Barrie
WRITER
John Stingley
AGENCY PRODUCER
Judy Brink
PRODUCTION CO.
N. Lee Lacy & Associates
DIRECTOR
N. Lee Lacy
CLIENT
Prince Foods
AGENCY
Fallon McElligott/Minneapolis

685
ART DIRECTOR
Rick Carpenter
WRITER
Jaci Sisson
AGENCY PRODUCER
Shannon Silverman
PRODUCTION COS
Della Femina Travisano
WE
DIRECTOR
Jim Weller
CLIENT
Psychiatric Institutes of America
AGENCY
Della Femina Travisano & Partners

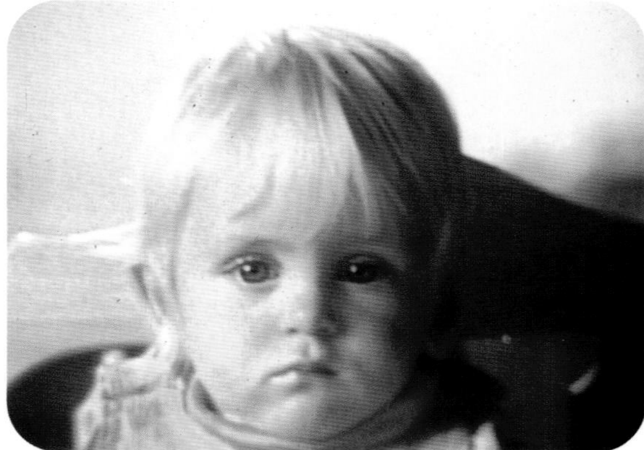

682

FATHER: Please listen because this is critical to your future. You have to finish all you um ums. Come on, mum mum made these um ums.

VO: Parents do some strange things in the name of love.
But they also do some pretty smart things. Like getting the finest health care possible.
With HealthAmerica, besides great coverage, you'll see some of the finest doctors and medical professionals around.
Join HealthAmerica. You'll feel smarter for it.

VO: HealthAmerica. We're making health care in America better.

683

(MUSIC)

Just for the one of it
Just for the taste of it
Diet Coke
Just for the style of it
Just for the swing of it
The real cola taste of it
Diet Coke
Just for the thrill of it
Just for the style
Just for the fun of it
Diet Coke
Just for the look of it
From Coca-Cola
Just for the taste of it
Diet Coke.

684

(ITALIAN MUSIC; CONTINUES)

ANNCR: In Italy, as anywhere else, there are different types of people. They don't look the same . . . or have the same taste. That's why when Prince makes Italian spaghetti sauce, we give you a choice. Our original sauce with imported olive oil and cheese . . . or our chunky homestyle with bits of tomato, herbs and spices. Because any true Italian knows, no 2 people . . . have quite the same taste.

685

MOTHER VO: Hello, uh, Mrs Morrisey, this is Sandy's mother. Is my daughter there?
Hello, Mrs Carpenter, have you seen Sandy?
Hello, Mrs Weller, ah, I'm looking for Sandy.

ANNCR VO: Each year, a million teenagers try to run away from their problems. If your child needs help, call Psychiatric Institute of Ft. Worth.

SUPER: Psychiatric Institute of Ft. Worth
(817) 335-4040
1-800-822-1800.

Consumer Television :30 Single

686
ART DIRECTOR
Rob Dalton
WRITER
Jarl Olsen
AGENCY PRODUCER
Judy Brink
CLIENT
Emmis Broadcasting
AGENCY
Fallon McElligott/Minneapolis

687
ART DIRECTOR
Pat Burnham
WRITER
Jarl Olsen
AGENCY PRODUCER
Judy Brink
PRODUCTION CO.
James Productions
DIRECTOR
Jim Lund
CLIENT
Knox Lumber
AGENCY
Fallon McElligott/Minneapolis

688
ART DIRECTOR
Dean Hanson
WRITER
Jarl Olsen
AGENCY PRODUCER
Judy Brink
PRODUCTION CO.
James Gang
DIRECTOR
Jim Beresford
CLIENT
First Tennessee Bank
AGENCY
Fallon McElligott/Minneapolis

689
ART DIRECTOR
Pat Burnham
WRITER
Bill Miller
AGENCY PRODUCER
Judy Brink
PRODUCTION CO.
Pfeifer Story Piccolo Guliner
DIRECTOR
Mark Story
CLIENT
KRON-TV
AGENCY
Fallon McElligott/Minneapolis

686

REX: I don't have anything nice to say about MAGIC 106. And, I've always believed that if you can't think of anything nice to say, you shouldn't say anything at all. (LONG PAUSE) I also believe that vaudeville is coming back, free lunch is really free and everything you read is true.

ANNCR: Who doesn't listen to MAGIC 106?

REX: I can think of *one* nice thing to say about MAGIC 106—Rona Barrett doesn't listen to it.

687

VO: Store A argues that because they buy building supplies . . . by the trailerload, *they* can get you a better deal.
Store B argues that becaue they buy building supplies . . . by the truckload, *they* can give you a better deal.
But Knox buys building supplies . . . by the trainload.

(SFX: HORN BLAST, TRAIN ROAR, SMASHING OF BOXES)

VO: And who's going to argue . . . with a train?

SUPER: Knox. Good prices. Good answers.

688

VO: For over 100 years, First Tennessee has been making uncommon loans in the most uncommon places on Earth.
Loans for sportscars in Rome, and villas in Athens. We can send dough to Paris. And raise some cold cash for Moscow.
Someday, we'll get a new office for Nixon, or send Stupidville to college.
Right now, First Tennessee has over $400 million to lend.
If a loan can make Dull interesting, what could it do for you?

(ALTERNATE ENDING: If a loan from First Tennessee can make Dull interesting, what could it do for you?)

689

ANNCR VO: We got a helicopter.
They got a helicopter.
We got a seismograph.
They got a seismograph.
We got cameras.
They got cameras.
We got typewriters.
They got typewriters.
We got trucks.
They got trucks.
We got a pencil sharpener.
They got a pencil sharpener.
We got reporters.
They got reporters.
We got a Peabody Award for broadcast journalism.

(SFX: THUMP)

They don't.
In this keep up with the other guys world of television news . . .
. . . it's important to remember who the other guys are trying to keep up with.
NewsCenter 4. At 5, 6 and 11.

Consumer Television :30 Single

690
WRITER
Marvin Honig
AGENCY PRODUCER
Beth McMorrow
PRODUCTION CO.
Pfeifer Story Piccolo Guliner
DIRECTOR
Jack Piccolo
CLIENT
Kraft Inc/Dairy Group
Frusen Gladje
AGENCY
Geers Gross

691
ART DIRECTOR
Pat Burnham
WRITER
Bill Miller
AGENCY PRODUCER
Judy Brink
PRODUCTION CO.
Pfeifer Story Piccolo Guliner
DIRECTOR
Mark Story
CLIENT
KRON-TV
AGENCY
Fallon McElligott/Minneapolis

692
ART DIRECTOR
Mark Yustein
WRITER
Jim Weller
AGENCY PRODUCER
Peter Yahr
DIRECTORS
Ron Travisano
Jim Weller
CLIENT
CBS-TV
AGENCY
Della Femina Travisano & Partners

693
ART DIRECTOR
Jean Robaire
WRITER
John Stein
AGENCY PRODUCER
Francesca Cohn
PRODUCTION CO.
Sandbank Films
DIRECTOR
Stan Schofield
CLIENT
Pizza Hut
AGENCY
Chiat/Day - Los Angeles

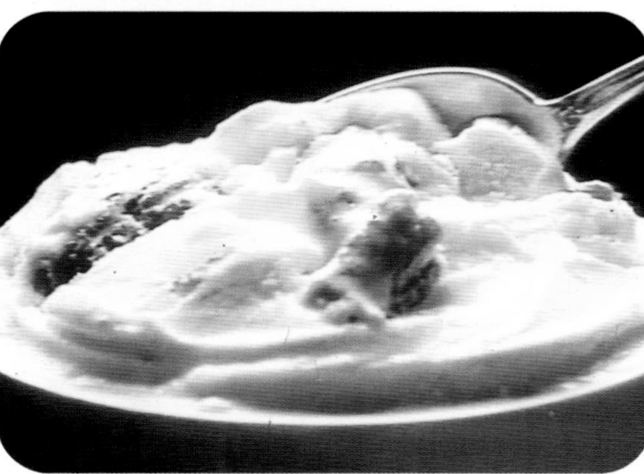

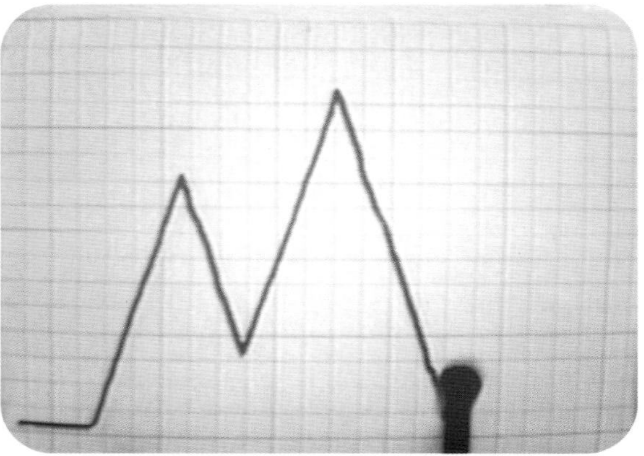

690

(MUSIC: UP)

(SFX: DOOR OPENS)

ANNCR VO: If you don't feel guilty, it wasn't that good.

MAN VO: Hi, Honey.

WOMAN: I ate all the Frusen Gladje.

MAN VO: You ate all the what?

WOMAN: I ate all the Frusen Gladje.

ANNCR VO: Frusen Gladje, the ice cream under the dome. So creamy; so delicious; so rewarding.

WOMAN: And I'd do it again.

ANNCR VO: Enjoy the guilt.
Frusen Gladje.

691

ANNCR VO: They got trucks.
We got trucks.
They got a helicopter.
We got a helicopter.
They got a seismograph.
We got a seismograph.
They got reporters.
We got reporters.
They got typewriters.
We got typewriters.
In this keep up with the Joneses world of television news . . .
. . . we here at NewsCenter 4 think it's important to remember . . .
. . . that what you really need to keep up with . . .
. . . is the news.
NewsCenter 4. At 5, 6 and 11.

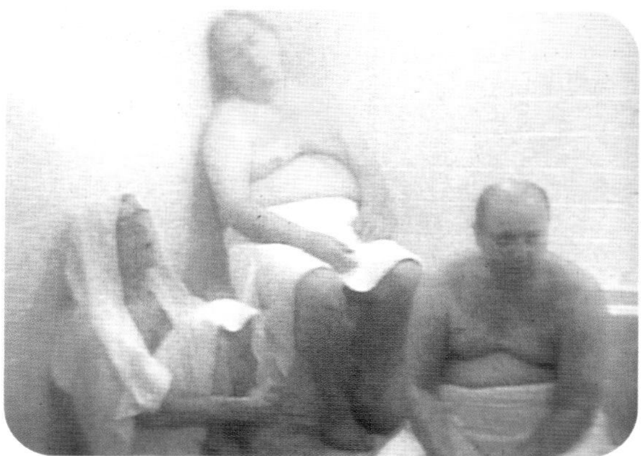

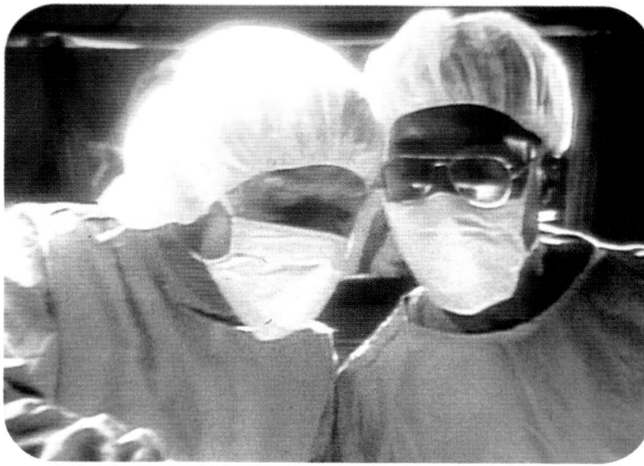

692

The New York area offers more ways to benefit from modern medicine and science than any place else on earth.
Where else could you find more theories on how to lose weight?
More cures for the common cold?
Or more ideas on how to clean up the environment?
Yet with all the ways to improve your body and mind, there's just one place to find a second, or third opinion on what's good for you.
Doctor Frank Field, Earl Ubell, Peter Salgo, M.D.
Channel 2 News.
Because anything can happen in New York.

693

MOMMA (IN ITALIAN): I have raised him. I have clothed him. I have fed him. I gave him everything, everything.

SON: Look at Momma, she's beside herself. She found out I had Calizza (TM) for lunch at Pizza Hut. That wasn't so bad. Then she found out I loved it. That was bad. They make one with Italian sausage and green peppers and another with 5 delicious cheeses, just like Momma does. And it's served in 5 minutes guaranteed.

ANNCR VO: Calizza (TM) Italian At Pizza Hut.

SON: I can't believe Momma's going.

MOMMA: Momma is not.

Consumer Television
:30 Single

694
ART DIRECTORS
Steve Perrin
Debbie Addison
WRITER
Jim Dale
AGENCY PRODUCER
Wendy Smith
PRODUCTION CO.
Greenbriar Productions
DIRECTOR
Ken Elam
CLIENT
Mid-Atlantic Milk Marketing Association
AGENCY
W. B. Doner & Company/ Baltimore

695
ART DIRECTOR
Robert Needleman
WRITER
Marty Cooke
AGENCY PRODUCER
Dave Johnson
CLIENT
Maxell
AGENCY
Scali McCabe Sloves

696
ART DIRECTOR
Jeff Roll
Andy Dijak
WRITER
David Butler
AGENCY PRODUCER
Richard O'Neill
PRODUCTION CO.
Coppos Films
DIRECTOR
Mark Coppos
CLIENT
Porsche Cars North America
AGENCY
Chiat/Day - Los Angeles

697
ART DIRECTORS
Jean Robaire
Lee Clow
WRITERS
John Stein
Ed Cole
Bill Hamilton
Marvin Hagler
AGENCY PRODUCER
Elaine Hinton
PRODUCTION CO.
Richard Marlis Productions
DIRECTOR
Norman Seeff
CLIENT
Pizza Hut
AGENCY
Chiat/Day - Los Angeles

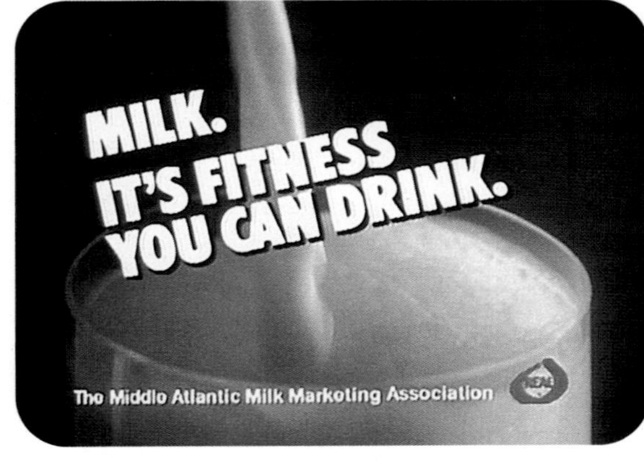

694

VO: I was a member of the women's Olympic Team in 1948.

ANNCR: Helen Sjursen, age 62.

VO: And I can still do a lot of what I did then. You see, the secret is keeping your bones young. (STRONG) And the secret to that is calcium. That's why I've always been a milk drinker. Because even though your bones stop growing, they *never* stop changing. So—drink your milk, get your calcium.
Especially if you're like me and like to stay . . .

ON CAMERA: . . . fairly active.

ANNCR: Milk. It's fitness you can drink.

695

ANNCR: Ordinary video tape can't survive today's sophisticated VCRs. Features like fast forward freeze frame and high-speed scanning start destroying your tape from the very first play. So, if you've got a sophisticated VCR get a tape that can stand up to it.

696

(MUSIC: THROUGHOUT)

ANNCR VO: Imagine you were a car.

(SFX: A GENERIC CAR ACCELERATING; CONTINUES)

ANNCR VO: What would you be?

(SFX: PORSCHE 944 ACCELERATING, WITHOUT TURBOCHARGER)

ANNCR VO: You'd be a sports car.

(SFX: ENGINE REVS)

ANNCR VO: You'd be quick . . .

(SFX: CONTINUE)

ANNCR VO: . . . Agile.

(SFX: CONTINUE)

ANNCR VO: You'd be . . . turbo-charged.

(SFX: ENGINE SOUND INCREASES, AMPLIFIED BY TUNNEL, AS TURBOCHARGER KICKS IN)

ANNCR VO: And, of course . . . You'd be a Porsche.

697

(MUSIC: UNDER THROUGHOUT)

MARVIN: Just thinking . . . I wonder what 'What's-his-name' is eating tonight . . . Probably soup.

Consumer Television :30 Single

698
ART DIRECTOR
Marten Tonnis
WRITER
Steve Rabosky
AGENCY PRODUCER
Richard O'Neill
PRODUCTION CO.
Avery Film Group
DIRECTOR
Brent Thomas
CLIENT
Apple Computer
AGENCY
Chiat/Day - Los Angeles

699
ART DIRECTOR
Gary Johns
WRITER
Jeff Gorman
AGENCY PRODUCER
Morty Baran
PRODUCTION CO.
Steve Horn Inc.
DIRECTOR
Steve Horn
CLIENT
Nike
AGENCY
Chiat/Day - Los Angeles

700
ART DIRECTOR
Michael Vitiello
WRITER
Bob Lapides
AGENCY PRODUCER
Bob Nelson
PRODUCTION CO.
Steve Horn Inc.
DIRECTOR
Steve Horn
CLIENT
Subaru of America
AGENCY
Levine Huntley Schmidt & Beaver

701
ART DIRECTOR
Woody Kay
WRITER
Ernie Schenck
AGENCY PRODUCER
Nancy Sacheroff
PRODUCTION CO.
Dalton Fenske & Friends
DIRECTOR
Grey Hoey
CLIENT
Blue Cross/Blue Shield
AGENCY
Leonard Monahan Saabye/ Providence, RI

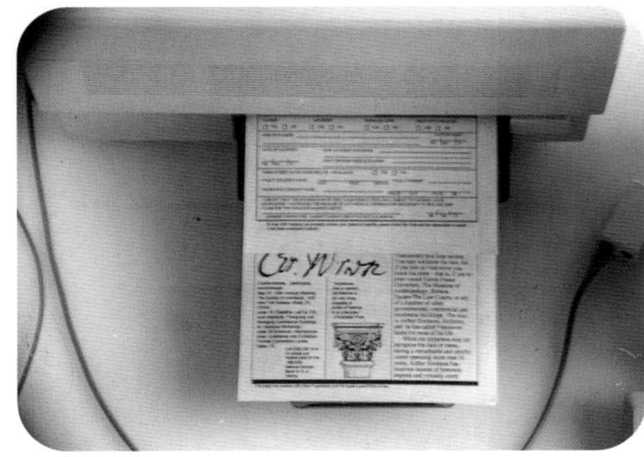

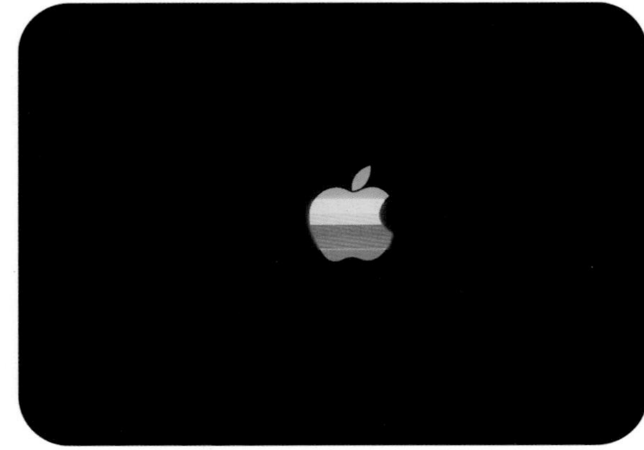

698

ANNCR: You could get a graphic design service to do *this* . . . in maybe a week.
You could get your art department to do *this* . . . in about three days.
You could get a typesetter to do *this* . . . overnight.
Or you could get The Macintosh Office.
And do *all* this yourself, over lunch.

699

(SFX: RUMBLE)
(SFX: EXPLOSION)
(SFX: WHISTLE OF RACING JET ENGINE)
(SFX: ROCKET FIRE)
JORDAN VO: Who says man is not meant to fly?
(SFX: JET BREAKING SOUND BARRIER)
ANNCR VO: Air Jordans. Basketball by Nike.

700

ANNCR: Ten years ago it rained.
Ten years ago there were signs like these, and roads like this.
Yet 10 years ago, only one car maker was committed to handling these conditions. Subaru, with On Demand four-wheel drive. A feature we offer on every model.
Now other car makers are discovering four-wheel drive. Did they finally notice the weather? Or us?
Subaru. Inexpensive. And built to stay that way.

701

(SFX: MERRY-GO-ROUND MUSIC)

VO: Nobody likes to think about getting sick on vacation.
But if you don't pack a Blue Cross Card, there's something else you might want to pack.
You see, with other health plans, getting medical attention away from home can be a real pain.
But Blue Cross is accepted at over 6,000 hospitals coast to coast.
No hassles . . . No questions asked.
And how could you possibly carry better medical protection than that?

SUPER: Blue Cross & Blue Shield of Rhode Island
No one protects you better.

VO: At Blue Cross, there's no limit to how far we'll go to protect you.

Consumer Television
:30 Single

702
ART DIRECTORS
Jean Robaire
Lee Clow
WRITERS
John Stein
Ed Cole
Brent Bouchez
Bill Hamilton
Herbie Hancock
AGENCY PRODUCER
Elaine Hinton
PRODUCTION CO.
Richard Marlis Productions
DIRECTOR
Norman Seeff
CLIENT
Pizza Hut
AGENCY
Chiat/Day - Los Angeles

703
ART DIRECTOR
Steve Montgomery
WRITER
Earl Carter
CLIENT
Western Union
AGENCY
Scali McCabe Sloves

704
ART DIRECTOR
Fred Braidman
WRITER
Patty Michaels
AGENCY PRODUCER
Tom Rook
PRODUCTION CO.
Wilson Griak
DIRECTOR
Jim Hinton
CLIENT
Pillsbury
AGENCY
Leo Burnett/Chicago

702

(MUSIC: UNDER THROUGHOUT)

HANCOCK: When people buy pizza, they're very generous with it. It's 'yeah, sure go ahead have a slice for yourself' . . . Until there's only one slice left, the person that wants that slice is the person that bought the pizza.

703

(SFX: CROWD NOISES)

MANAGER: Sarge, the press is waiting.

SARGE: Let 'em wait.

FAN: Autograph, Sarge?

SARGE: Later.

TRAINER: What about your fan mail?

SARGE: Tomorrow.

MAN: Hey Sarge, telephone.

(SFX: CRASH!!!)

VO: Telegram for Sergeant Slaughter.

ANNCR VO: Nothing cuts through like a telegram. It's your own feelings in your own words at just the right time.

TRAINER: Sarge, you're smiling again.

SARGE: It's from my daughters. Today's my birthday.

ANNCR VO: You just don't read a telegram . . . You feel it.

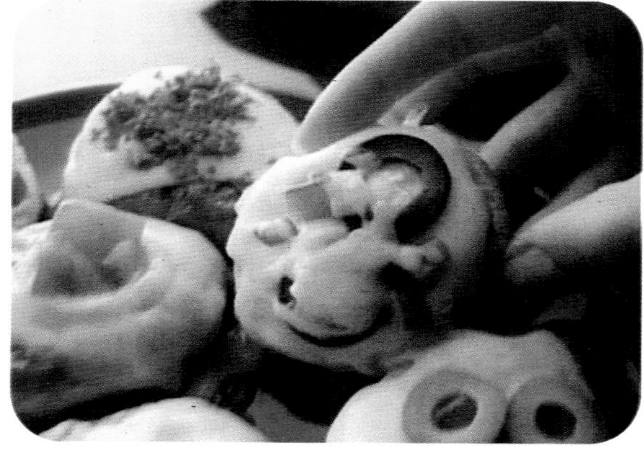

704

ANNCR VO: When you're hungry, only Hungry Jack is good enough for *your*

SONG

SOUTHERN: Virginia Baked Ham and black-eyed peas
Mmmmm

BOSTON: Clam Chowder
Boston baked beans
Ahhhhh

JEWISH: Hungry Jack and chicken soup
Ohhhh

WESTERN: Hot chili
And lamb stew
Mmmmm

KID: Hungry Jack
Peanut butter,jelly
Ahhhh

SONG

ITALIAN: Pizza
Spaghetti

SONG

ITALIAN: Mostoccioli
Ohhhh

ANNCR: Only Hungry Jack Biscuits are so light, so flaky, so versatile, they're the only one good enough for *your*

SONG

JEWISH: Pastrami
Salami
A slice of Swiss
Mmmmm

HUNGARIAN: Hungarian Goulash
Or any dish

SONG: *Mmmmm*
Ahhhh
Ohhhh
Oooooonly Hungry Jack

DOUGHBOY: Hoo-Hoo!

SONG: *Is good enough.*

Consumer Television
:30 Single

705
ART DIRECTOR
Gary Johnston
WRITER
Phil Lanier
AGENCY PRODUCER
Elaine Hinton
PRODUCTION CO.
Steve Horn Inc.
DIRECTOR
Steve Horn
CLIENT
Apple Computer
AGENCY
Chiat/Day - Los Angeles

706
WRITER
Bill Hamilton
AGENCY PRODUCER
Susan Ashmore
PRODUCTION CO.
Nike Sports Productions
DIRECTOR
Peter Moore
CLIENT
Nike
AGENCY
Chiat/Day - Los Angeles

707
ART DIRECTORS
Jean Robaire
Lee Clow
WRITERS
John Stein
Bill Hamilton
Ed Cole
MacKenzie Brothers
AGENCY PRODUCER
Elaine Hinton
PRODUCTION CO.
Richard Marlis Productions
DIRECTOR
Norman Seeff
CLIENT
Pizza Hut
AGENCY
Chiat/Day - Los Angeles

708
ART DIRECTOR
Gary Johnston
WRITER
Phil Lanier
AGENCY PRODUCER
Elaine Hinton
PRODUCTION CO.
David Ashwell Film Company
DIRECTOR
David Ashwell
CLIENT
Apple Computer
AGENCY
Chiat/Day - Los Angeles

705

(MUSIC: UNDER THROUGHOUT)

ANNCR VO: Using an Apple II is very easy.
The only hard part is getting your kid away from it.
You see, Apples are the leading computers in schools.
So, even though you bought it to help you work at home, your kid will want to use it for his own homework. Of course, if all else fails, there's one last thing you can try: get him an Apple of his own.

706

(SFX: JET ENGINE ROARS TO LIFE; JET TAXIS)

STEWARDESS VO: Good morning, ladies and gentlemen.
Welcome to Flight 23.
Please make sure your seat belts are securely fastened, and extinguish all smoking materials.

(SFX: JET ENGINE BUILDS IN INTENSITY. SQUEAL, ROCKET ROAR, FULL JETS. DIMINISHING IN PERSPECTIVE)

ANNCR VO: Basketball, by Nike.

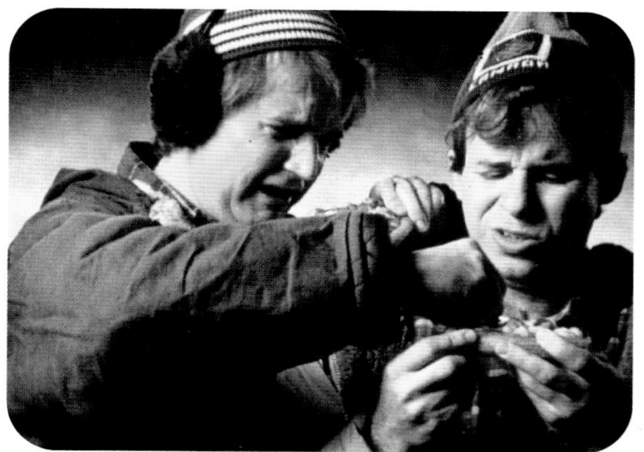

707

(MUSIC: UNDER THROUGHOUT)

DOUG: Oh, excuse me, where did you grow up . . . in the woods?

BOB: O.K. Some things fall off of my pizza, eh. But that's only 'cause it's got so much stuff on it and I . . . losing my balance.

DOUG: I stole his cheese while he wasn't looking. Pizza raid! Ah, ah, ah, ah, ah! Use noise to disorient your opponent. That way you can get more of his stuff on your pizza.

708

ANNCR: The Apple IIc is the perfect computer to give your kids.

KID 1: This should be good.

KID 2: Yeah.

ANNCR: Because Apples are the leading computers used in schools.

KID 1: Remember your bike last Christmas?

KID 2: Uh-oh . . .

ANNCR: Yet it can run thousands of business and home-finance programs. And it's so simple to set up and use, virtually anyone can do it.

KID 2: Another Christmas miracle.

Consumer Television :30 Single

709
ART DIRECTOR
Gary Johns
WRITERS
Jeff Gorman
Brent Bouchez
AGENCY PRODUCER
Richard O'Neill
PRODUCTION CO.
Fairbanks Films
DIRECTOR
Tony Scott
CLIENT
Pizza Hut
AGENCY
Chiat/Day - Los Angeles

710
ART DIRECTOR
Lee Clow
WRITERS
John Stein
Bill Hamilton
Ed Cole
Martin Mull
AGENCY PRODUCER
Elaine Hinton
PRODUCTION CO.
Richard Marlis Productions
DIRECTOR
Norman Seeff
CLIENT
Pizza Hut
AGENCY
Chiat/Day - Los Angeles

711
ART DIRECTOR
David Hedley-Noble
WRITER
Jack Kilpatrick
PRODUCTION CO.
Siebke Productions
CLIENT
South Florida Honda Dealers
AGENCY
Kilpatrick Hedley-Noble/
Coral Gables, FL

712
ART DIRECTORS
Jean Robaire
Lee Clow
WRITERS
John Stein
Bill Hamilton
MacKenzie Brothers
AGENCY PRODUCER
Elaine Hinton
PRODUCTION CO.
Richard Marlis Productions
DIRECTOR
Norman Seeff
CLIENT
Pizza Hut
AGENCY
Chiat/Day - Los Angeles

709

(MUSIC: ITALIAN MUSIC THROUGHOUT)

ANNCR VO: In Italy, they have different names for Italian pie. We call it Priazzo. Baked fresh every day at Pizza Hut.

710

(MUSIC: UNDER THROUGHOUT)

MULL: Hello, I'm here to tell you a little bit about pizza etiquette.
Can you do this? Yes. It's acceptable.
It's good cold in the morning for breakfast. I've done that. I mean how many of you . . . how many have done that? Can you take it and go from the other end? Crust first? No. I'm sorry. You have to start at the point.

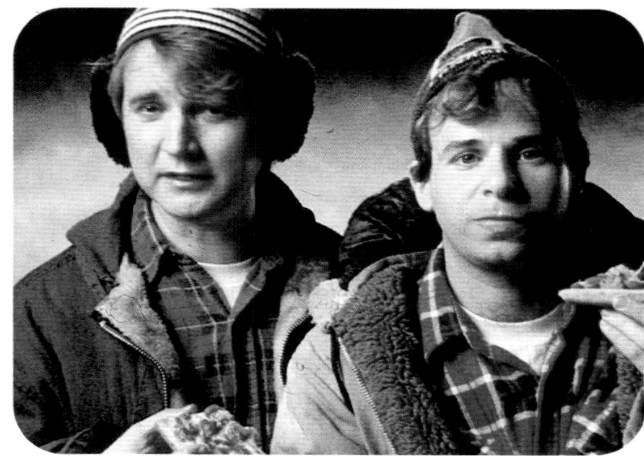

711

ANNCR VO: If there's one thing Americans and Japanese have in common . . .
It's an eye for good value.

JAP. VOICES: Gibberish.

SUBTITLE: Why can't I find a new Honda?

ANNCR VO: While it's great for us, lifting the import restrictions on Japanese cars is causing a few problems elsewhere.

JAP. VOICES: Gibberish . . . plus Ronald Reagan.

SUBTITLE: All Hondas must have gone to America.

VO: If *you're* looking for a new Honda, your problems are over.
The South Florida Honda Dealers proudly announce they have more Hondas than ever . . . with prices as low as 1,450,000 Yen.

LOGO: South Florida Honda Dealers

712

(MUSIC: UNDER THROUGHOUT)

BOB: O.K. Guess what this is? That's our topic.

DOUG: Dream come true.

BOB: Five-minute pizza, eh, for lunch.

DOUG: Comes in your own personalized size, eh.

BOB: O.K. Lunch hour. Toot! Lunch hour. O.K. How long does it take to get over to the place, right? Uh, how long?

DOUG: Ten minutes.

BOB: Ten minutes, O.K. Uh, how long does it take? O.K. We're sitting down. We want to order a pizza. Oh, no, are we going to get back to work in time? Yes. Why?

DOUG: We don't have jobs.

Consumer Television :30 Single

713
ART DIRECTOR
Bob Isherwood
WRITER
Patrick Woodward
AGENCY PRODUCER
Rosemary Marks
PRODUCTION CO.
Ibbetson & Cherry
DIRECTOR
Wayne Maule
CLIENT
United Permanent Building
AGENCY
The Campaign Palace/ Australia

714
ART DIRECTOR
Mark Johnson
WRITER
Martin Kaufman
AGENCY PRODUCER
Steven Labovsky
PRODUCTION CO.
Coppos Films
DIRECTOR
Mark Coppos
CLIENT
United Parcel Service
AGENCY
Ammirati & Puris

715
ART DIRECTOR
Jim Henderson
WRITER
Pete Smith
AGENCY PRODUCER
Rosemary Januschka
PRODUCTION CO.
Flim Flam Film
DIRECTOR
Gaines Henderson
CLIENT
W-LITE TV
AGENCY
Martin/Williams - Minneapolis

716
ART DIRECTOR
Tony DeGregorio
WRITER
Lee Garfinkel
AGENCY PRODUCER
Bob Nelson
PRODUCTION CO.
Steve Horn Inc.
DIRECTOR
Steve Horn
CLIENT
Subaru of America
AGENCY
Levine Huntley Schmidt & Beaver

713

LOANS MANAGER: Oh, Mr Sharpe, here for a loan are we?

MAN: Yes.

LOANS MANAGER: Own your own home?

MAN: No, I don't.

LOANS MANAGER: Oh, no home!
Have an account with us, Mr Sharpe?

MAN: No, I haven't

LOANS MANAGER: Absolutely unaccountable!

MVO: We don't make you jump through hoops when you apply for a loan at United Permanent; in fact, we approve most loans the same day . . .
Even when you want a personal loan.

MAN: You'll have to do better than that, mate.

MVO: You've got better things to do than worry about money.
We haven't.

714

VO: At UPS it was never our intention to become a tourist attraction. But every year, scores of efficiency-minded Japanese business men show up and ask to tour our facilities. You see, UPS is so efficient we can deliver Next Day Air usually for half what other companies charge. Which is why so many Japanese find UPS the most rewarding 'package tour' anywhere.

UPS: We run the tightest ship in the shipping business.

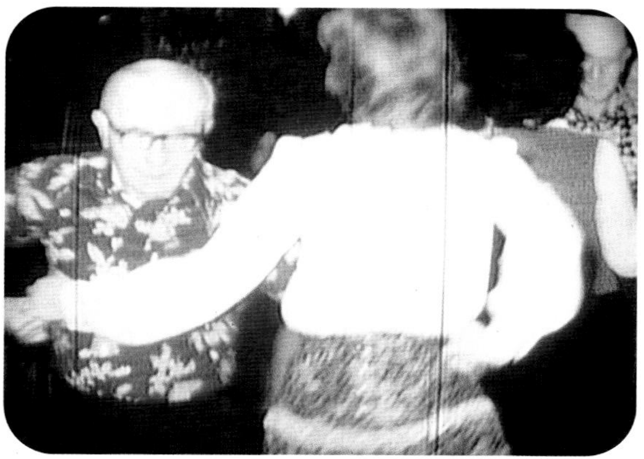

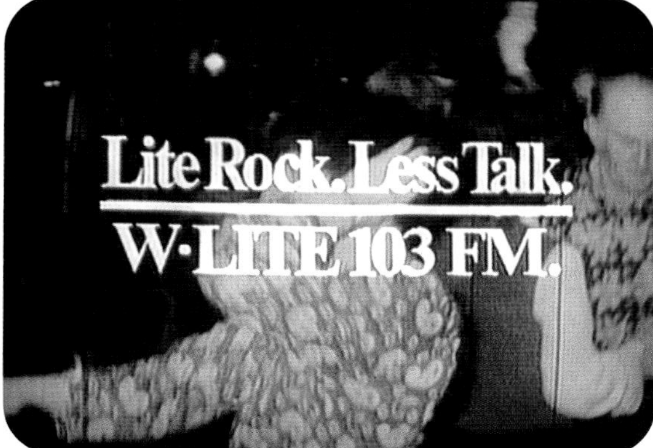

715

VO: We understand there are still a few Minnesotans who haven't discovered the light rock sound of W-LITE.
You're not one of them, are you?
LITE ROCK. Less Talk.
W-LITE 103 FM.

716

(MUSIC: "YOU ALWAYS HURT THE ONE YOU LOVE")

ANNCR: People have a love-hate relationship with their cars. They love them, but they don't always treat them right.
Yet amazingly, over 90% of all Subarus registered since 1974 are still on the road.
Now imagine how much longer they would last if people didn't 'love' them so much.

ANNCR: Subaru. Inexpensive. And built to stay that way.

Consumer Television
:30 Single

717
ART DIRECTOR
Derrick Hass
WRITER
Howard Fletcher
AGENCY PRODUCER
Charles Crisp
PRODUCTION CO.
Ian Single Films
DIRECTOR
Steve Drewitt
CLIENT
National Advertising Benevolent Society
AGENCY
Ogilvy & Mather/London

718
ART DIRECTOR
Carl le Blond
WRITER
Tony Strong
AGENCY PRODUCER
Sue Bethell
PRODUCTION CO.
Paul Weiland Film Company
DIRECTOR
John O'Driscoll
CLIENT
Philips Portable Compact Disc Player
AGENCY
Ogilvy & Mather/London

719
ART DIRECTOR
Lyle Metzdorf
WRITER
Lyle Metzdorf
AGENCY PRODUCER
Lyle Metzdorf
PRODUCTION CO.
Cotts Films
DIRECTOR
Gerry Cotts
CLIENT
Blue Bell Creameries
AGENCY
Lowe Marschalk

720
ART DIRECTOR
Tony DeGregorio
WRITER
Lee Garfinkel
AGENCY PRODUCER
Rachel Novak
PRODUCTION CO.
Steve Horn Inc.
DIRECTOR
Steve Horn
CLIENT
Subaru of America
AGENCY
Levine Huntley Schmidt & Beaver

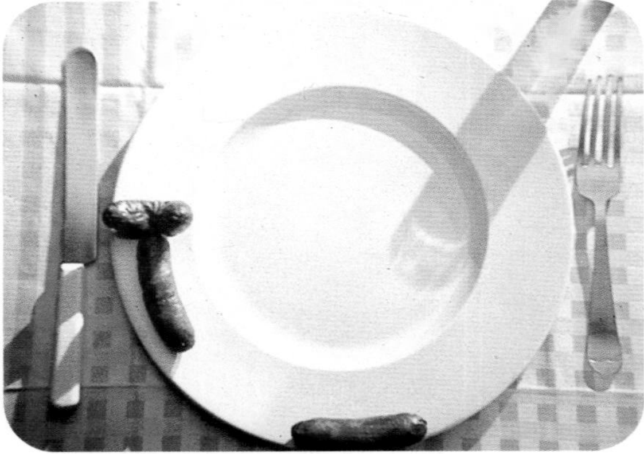

717

(SFX: CARS REVVING ENGINES)

(SFX: TYRES SQUEALING AND ENGINES REVVING)

MVO (MURRAY WALKER): The NABS Banger Race. Wimbledon Stadium. Sunday, October 20th. Just wait for the smash.

718

(SFX: ECHOING FOOTSTEPS)

VO: Announcing the first portable compact disc system.

(SFX: FAST SPANISH MUSIC STARTS)

VO: The CD555. Another sensation from Philips.

719

ANNCR VO: The people in Happy, Texas are unhappy 'cause they can't get Blue Bell Ice Cream Snacks.

COWBOY: If we could, Happy would be Paradise. Right?

ANNCR VO: Some residents in Needmore, Texas claim . . .

FARMER: We named our town Needmore 'cause we need more Blue Bell Snacks.

DAUGHTER: No, we didn't Daddy.

FARMER: Yes, we did.

ANNCR VO: Folks here never need more Blue Bell Snacks 'cause they get all they can eat.

PREACHER: That's why we're happy in Paradise.

ANNCR VO: Blue Bell the best tastin' ice cream in the country.

720

DAD: It's your money, son, but if you want my advice, buy another Subaru.

(SFX: MUSIC SHIFTS FROM SOFT HOMESPUN MUSIC TO HARD ROCK N' ROLL)

DAD: I thought we agreed . . . you'd buy a Subaru.

SON: But, Dad . . . I did.

ANNCR: The new Subaru XT. Inexpensive. And built to stay that way.

Consumer Television
:30 Single

721
ART DIRECTOR
Noel Douglas
WRITER
Mike Court
AGENCY PRODUCER
Randi Waagen
PRODUCTION CO.
Direktion
DIRECTOR
Tony Kaye
CLIENT
Krups
AGENCY
Still Price Court Twivy D'Souza/London

722
ART DIRECTOR
Richard Mahan
WRITER
Phil Guthrie
AGENCY PRODUCER
Michael Berkman
PRODUCTION CO.
David Ashwell Film Company
CLIENT
Miller Brewing Company
AGENCY
Backer & Spielvogel

723
ART DIRECTOR
Bob Tucker
WRITER
Patty Volk
AGENCY PRODUCER
Joe Scibetta
PRODUCTION CO.
THT Productions
DIRECTOR
Werner Hlinka
CLIENT
Mobil 1
AGENCY
Doyle Dane Bernbach

724
ART DIRECTOR
Richard Mahan
WRITER
Phil Guthrie
AGENCY PRODUCER
Michael Berkman
PRODUCTION CO.
Independent Artists
CLIENT
Miller Brewing Company
AGENCY
Backer & Spielvogel

721

COOKERY EXPERT: Today, I'm going to show you the recipe for a most powerful food mixer.
Take 6 pounds of cement.
1½ pints of water . . . 3 lbs of gravel . . . Mix for 20 minutes . . .
You'll see how the Krups' 170 watt motor makes light work of the heaviest mixtures.
And there we are . . . Concrete proof that you can't beat a Krups mixer.

722

CAPTAIN: I hear you men gotta gripe with the Cookie.

MATE: Go ahead, Red, tell 'im!

RED: Cap'n, it's about this Meister Brau he's layin' on board.

CAPTAIN: He's got expensive tastes for a galley rat, don't he?

RED: Cap'n, the radioman on the Eloise just told Pinky here it's not expensive.

PINKY: It just tastes expensive!

CAPTAIN: Then what's Cookie doin' with this bucket's beer money?

TAILOR: You very big American spender, Mr. Cookie!

ANNCR VO: Rich, smooth Meister Brau. It only tastes expensive.

723

(MUSIC: THROUGHOUT)

ANNCR VO: Mobil I Synthetic Motor Oil. The technology behind it gives this driver engine protection . . . he can depend on.

(SFX: ENGINE NOISES)

ANNCR VO: And this driver.

(SFX: JET NOISES)

ANNCR VO: And this driver.

(SFX: SHUTTLE NOISES)

ANNCR VO: And *this* driver.
Mobil synthetic oil technology. There's no finer engine protection on earth . . .
Or anywhere else.

724

SENATOR: Mr Secretary, are you saying no further cuts can be made?

SECRETARY: That is correct, Senator.

SENATOR: I see here enormous expenditures on Meister Brau.

SECRETARY: Our boys deserve an expensive beer, sir.

SENTOR: My committee informs me it's not expensive. Just tastes expensive.

SECRETARY: Uh, actually, that's under my assistant, Mr Macklin.

SENATOR: Well, what's he doing with the money he's supposed to spend on beer!

WOMAN: Oh, Mac, it's a darling little boat . . .

VO: Rich smooth Meister Brau.
It only tastes expensive.

Consumer Television
:30 Single

725
ART DIRECTOR
Lester Feldman
WRITER
Mike Mangano
AGENCY PRODUCER
Mardi Kleppel
PRODUCTION CO.
Cinematic Directions
DIRECTOR
Vilmos Zsigmond
CLIENT
GTE
AGENCY
Doyle Dane Bernbach

726
ART DIRECTOR
Pat Burnham
WRITER
Bill Miller
AGENCY PRODUCER
Judy Brink
PRODUCTION CO.
Pfeifer Story Piccolo Guliner
DIRECTOR
Mark Story
CLIENT
KRON-TV
AGENCY
Fallon McElligott/Minneapolis

727
ART DIRECTOR
Rich Silverstein
WRITERS
Jeff Goodby
Andy Berlin
AGENCY PRODUCER
Debbie King
PRODUCTION CO.
Jon Francis Films
DIRECTOR
Jon Francis
CLIENT
San Francisco Examiner
AGENCY
Goodby Berlin & Silverstein/
San Francisco

728
ART DIRECTOR
Rich Silverstein
WRITERS
Jeff Goodby
Andy Berlin
AGENCY PRODUCER
Debbie King
PRODUCTION CO.
Jon Francis Films
DIRECTOR
Jon Francis
CLIENT
San Francisco Examiner
AGENCY
Goodby Berlin & Silverstein/
San Francisco

KRON-TV
NewsCenter4
At 5, 6 and 11 pm.

725

ANNCR VO: Nowadays, when a businessman gets stuck in his car, he doesn't have to be just 'stuck in his car.' He can be talking to a client or a prospective client. Or be in touch with his own office.
He can be doing a million different things, if he has our Mobilnet Cellular Car Phone Service.
Just imagine how much more productive you could be with Mobilnet.

MAN IN CAR (WITHOUT PHONE): Gee!

ANNCR CO: No . . . GTE!

726

ANNCR VO: We got cameras.
They got cameras.
We got a seismograph.
They got a seismograph.
We got reporters.
They got reporters.
We got typewriters.
They got typewriters.
We got a helicopter.
They got a helicopter.
We got a pencil sharpener.
They got a pencil sharpener.
We got haircuts.
They got haircuts.
We got a telephone.
They got a telephone.
We got a mobile satellite uplink.

(SFX: SCREECH)

They don't.
In this keep up with the other guys world of television news . . .
. . . it's important to remember who the other guys are trying to keep up with.
NewsCenter 4. At 5, 6 and 11.

727

GHOST: . . . or is this Warren Hinckle fellow some kind of leftist?

WILL: I'm not worried about those kinds of labels. I think he's interesting.

GHOST: Who is this Hunter S. Thompson?

WILL: He's irreverent, a little risky, but fun to read, you know?

GHOST: No.

WILL: Come on, Grandpop. Lighten up.

GHOST: Are you sure you know what you're doing, Will?

WILL: I don't know. Did you?

ANNCR: The next generation. At the San Francisco Examiner.

728

(MUSIC: UNDER THROUGHOUT)

CYRA: What's going on here, officer?

COP 1: We're looking for a Cyra McFadden. Wrote that thing called "The Serial."

CYRA: Uh-huh . . .

COP 1: Made Marin look pretty bad.

CYRA: Well, I don't really . . .

COP 1: Word is, she's back in the area, working for that Will Hearst guy.

CYRA: Gosh, officer, wasn't "The Serial" written in a spirit of fun? I mean it is a little *different* up here.

COP 1: Different, ma'am?

COP 2: What kind of car is this?

CYRA: It's a Plymouth.

COP 2: I've never seen one before.

ANNCR: The next generation. At the San Francisco Examiner.

Consumer Television
:30 Single

729
ART DIRECTOR
Amy Mizner
WRITERS
Don Deutsch
Richard Kirshenbaum
AGENCY PRODUCER
Amy Mizner
CLIENT
People's Bank of Connecticut
AGENCY
David Deutsch Associates

730
ART DIRECTOR
Tom Stoneham
WRITER
Dave Newman
AGENCY PRODUCERS
Dave Newman
Tom Stoneham
PRODUCTION CO.
N. Lee Lacy & Associates
DIRECTOR
N. Lee Lacy
CLIENT
Smoke Craft
AGENCY
Borders Perrin & Norrander/
Portland, OR

731
ART DIRECTOR
Richard Mahan
WRITER
Phil Guthrie
AGENCY PRODUCER
Michael Berkman
PRODUCTION CO.
David Ashwell Film Company
CLIENT
Miller Brewing Company
AGENCY
Backer & Spielvogel

732
ART DIRECTOR
Gary Yoshida
WRITER
Bob Coburn
AGENCY PRODUCER
Gary Paticoff
PRODUCTION CO.
Dick James Productions
DIRECTOR
Dick James
CLIENT
A.J. Bayless Supermarkets
AGENCY
Needham Harper Worldwide/
Los Angeles

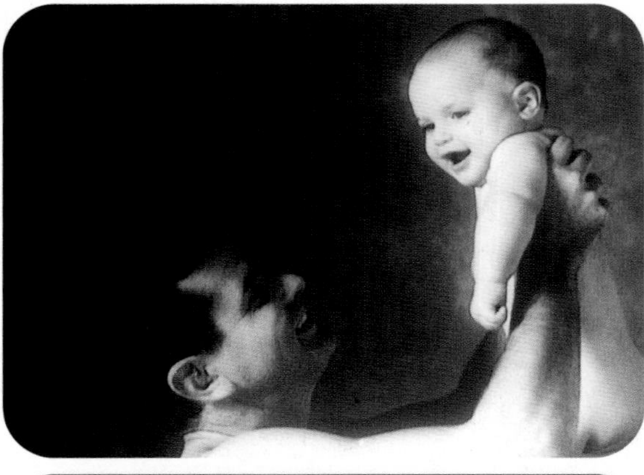

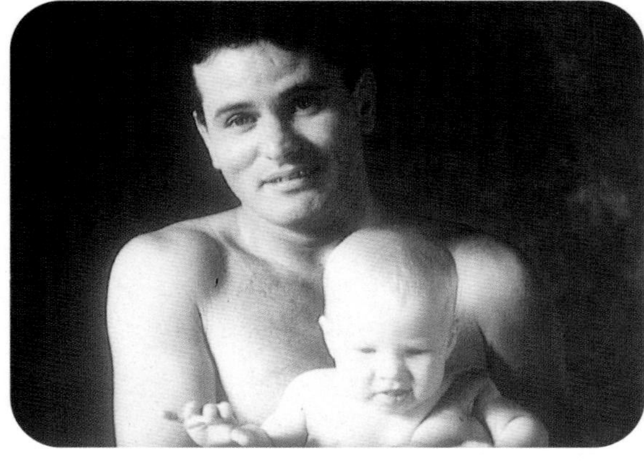

729

MAN: If you'd have told me 5 years ago I'd have one of these, boy I would have laughed. But now I've got my little princess. I'm going to start saving for her education now. She's going to Yale. Funny, when it came to saving before I used to say 'What difference does it make.' But now there's more at stake. I want to make sure I'm doing everything right for her. 'Cause she's all I'm about now.

VO: People's Bank. We hear you. We have a savings plan to fit your needs.

730

SPECTATOR: Glad I ain't wrestlin' that 'gator!

WRESTLER: Ha-ha! Just as soon as I finish my Long Haul Beef jerky . . . I'm havin' me some 'gator for dee-zert. (HE TAKES BITE) I hate to think of what I'm gonna do to him. (TAKES ANOTHER BITE) Course, I wouldn't wanna rush through my Long Haul . . . maybe . . . I oughta give him a little preview of what he's up against . . . Aaaar! (ALLIGATOR HISSES; WRESTLER GASPS) As soon as I finish my L-l-l-ong Haul.

VO: Long Haul beef snacks: the best-tasting, longest-lasting alibi.

731

OWNER 1: Hey, Marty, you seen the monthly receipts?

OWNER 2: No, how we doin'?

OWNER 1: Oh beautiful! Frankie's spendin' money on Meister Brau like it's goin' outta style.

OWNER 2: It's a quality beer, it's expensive.

OWNER 1: Oh, yeah? Sollie at the Kit Kat says it ain't expensive. Says it just tastes expensive.

OWNER 2: So?

OWNER 1: So what's that little weasle doin' wit the do-re-me he says he's spendin' on the beer?

FRANKIE: Baby, that mink is making you look like a fox!

ANNCR VO: Rich, smooth Meister Brau.
It only tastes expensive.

732

VO: Mayo . . .
Mayo, mayo, mayo.
The new Bayless.
We even carry your bags.

Consumer Television :30 Single

733
ART DIRECTOR
Barry Vetere
WRITER
Ron Berger
AGENCY PRODUCER
Beth Forman
PRODUCTION CO.
Coppos Films
DIRECTOR
Mark Coppos
CLIENT
Polaroid
AGENCY
Ally & Gargano

734
ART DIRECTOR
James Good
WRITER
John Gruen
AGENCY PRODUCER
Stuart Rickey
PRODUCTION CO.
Giraldi/Suarez
DIRECTOR
Bob Giraldi
CLIENT
Sports Illustrated
AGENCY
Ogilvy & Mather

735
ART DIRECTOR
Gunar Skillins
WRITER
Eliot Riskin
AGENCY PRODUCERS
Jerry Cammisa
Alice Chevalier
PRODUCTION CO.
Bean Kahn Dream Quest
DIRECTOR
Jim Spencer
CLIENT
Black & Decker
AGENCY
BBDO

736
ART DIRECTOR
Barry Vetere
WRITER
Helayne Spivak
AGENCY PRODUCER
Beth Forman
PRODUCTION CO.
Coppos Films
DIRECTOR
Mark Coppos
CLIENT
Sanyo
AGENCY
Ally & Gargano

733

(SFX: MUSIC BEGINS)

ANNCR VO: A Polaroid Camera can do something important for you just about every day.

FRAT. GUY 1: That was some party last night.

FRAT. GUY 2: There's evidence . . . to that effect.

FRAT. GUY 1: Have we ever had . . . this many people in our living room?

FRAT. GUY 3: That's the bathroom.

FRAT. GUY 4: Anyone seen Dolobowsky?

FRAT. GUY 5: It was nice of the Dean to show up.

ANNCR VO: Polaroid Pictures add life to a party, and let you relive it as soon as it's over.

FRAT. GUY 6: Well guys? What do you think?

ALL OF THEM: Hang it?

ANNCR VO: Polaroid Instant Cameras do what no other kind of camera can do.

734

(MUSIC: UNDER)

(SFX: CROWD NOISE)

COACH: Yeah, he's ready.

QUISENBERRY VO: How does it feel when the phone rings, and it's for me? Who's batting? Who'm I facing? Nervous . . . Want that nervous edge.

CATCHER: C'mon, Quiz. Go get 'em!

QUISENBERRY VO: Keep cool. Keep cool. I can't trust what I've got in the bull pen.

(SFX: CROWD CHEERS)

PA ANNCR: Number 29. Dan Quisenberry.

QUISENBERRY VO: Here goes nothing.

ANNCR VO: Sports Illustrated. Get the feeling.

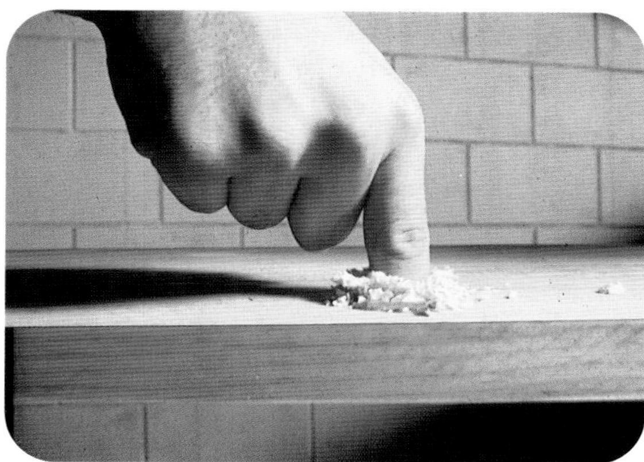

735

Black & Decker introduces a revolution in power tool technology. A line of tools designed specifically to work as one with your hand. The M47 Series. Smaller, more compact, for better control, greater accuracy. And driven by the most powerful motor for its size we've ever built.
The M47 Series power tools. They work with your hand as if they were one.

736

JOAN COLLINS: Contrary to some opinions I know about kitchen things. The Sanyo Coffee Thing grinds the beans and has the coffee ready when I wake up.

BUTLER: Correct, madam.

JOAN COLLINS: The Sanyo Toasty is a vertical toaster oven.

CHEF 1: Correct

JOAN COLLINS: The Sanyo Food Thing is a microwave that actually browns, bakes and broils.

CHEF 2: Right, madam.

JOAN COLLINS: Never again let it be said that I don't know my way around my own kitchen. (SFX: CRASHING) Broom closet.

CHEF: Right again, madam.

ANNCR: Sanyo. Wonderful things for the kitchen.

Consumer Television :30 Single

737
ART DIRECTOR
Richard Herstek
WRITER
Richard Herstek
AGENCY PRODUCER
Ron Stanford
DIRECTOR
Ron Stanford
CLIENT
Army National Guard
AGENCY
Needham Harper Worldwide

738
ART DIRECTOR
George Euringer
WRITER
Tom Messner
AGENCY PRODUCER
Mark Sitley
PRODUCTION CO.
Steve Horn Inc.
DIRECTOR
Steve Horn
CLIENT
Bristol-Myers Datril
AGENCY
Ally & Gargano

739
ART DIRECTOR
Mike Schwabenland
WRITER
Lance Mald
AGENCY PRODUCER
Jerry Cammisa
PRODUCTION CO.
Sedelmaier
DIRECTOR
Joe Sedelmaier
CLIENT
Black & Decker
AGENCY
BBDO

740
ART DIRECTOR
Barry Vetere
WRITER
Ron Berger
AGENCY PRODUCER
Beth Forman
PRODUCTION CO.
Coppos Films
DIRECTOR
Mark Coppos
CLIENT
Polaroid
AGENCY
Ally & Gargano

737

The New Mexico Army National Guard would like to welcome all friendly visitors to our beautiful state. Everybody else, better run for cover.

738

(MUSIC: UNDER)

ANNCR VO: Datril. Last night 10 P.M.

HE: I thought you said you had a headache.

SHE: I did. Then I took a couple of Datril.

ANNCR VO: When it's more important to get rid of a headache and get on with your life take Datril . . . from Bristol-Myers. One thousand milligrams of medicine for your headache. No milligrams of medicine that could upset your stomach. Datril. Extra strength for your headache. Extra gentle for your stomach.

739

Sometimes, even simple jobs around the house can be a real workout. You're always forgetting something. Drill bits . . . screwdrivers . . . extension cords. But not anymore. Introducing the cordless Drill/Driver from Black & Decker. Stored in its own holder it's like having a toolbox at your fingertips. And since it's a drill and a screwdriver in one, hanging up or fixing up anything around the house doesn't have to be a workout.
The Drill/Driver from Black & Decker. Ideas at work.

740

(MUSIC: UNDER)

ANNCR VO: A Polaroid Camera can do something for you virtually every day.

BOY: But can't I see my baby sister?

FATHER: There's a rule little children can't go up.

BOY: But I was born here. Why can't I go back?

FATHER: Tell you what. You wait with Grandma, and I'll bring your sister to you.

BOY (DOUBTINGLY): Sure.

ANNCR VO: For those times when someone can't be there to share an important occasion.

FATHER: Ryan Matthew, meet Cory Lynn.

ANNCR VO: Polaroid Instant Cameras do what no other kind of camera can do.

Consumer Television
:30 Single

741
ART DIRECTOR
Jack Mariucci
WRITER
Barry Greenspon
AGENCY PRODUCERS
Joe Scibetta
Mary Ellen Perezolla
PRODUCTION CO.
Sandbank Films
DIRECTOR
Henry Sandbank
CLIENT
Michelin Tire Corporation
AGENCY
Doyle Dane Bernbach

742
ART DIRECTOR
Harvey Hoffenberg
WRITER
Ted Sann
AGENCY PRODUCER
Gene Lofaro
PRODUCTION CO.
N. Lee Lacy & Associates
DIRECTOR
Henry Holtzman
CLIENT
Pepsi-Cola
AGENCY
BBDO

743
ART DIRECTOR
Paul Walter
WRITERS
Charlie Miesmer
John Greenberger
AGENCY PRODUCER
Barbara Mullins
PRODUCTION CO.
Steve Horn Inc.
DIRECTOR
Steve Horn
CLIENT
HBO
AGENCY
BBDO

744
ART DIRECTOR
Dave Waters
WRITER
Jan Van Mesdag
AGENCY PRODUCER
Gre Dilkes
PRODUCTION COS
BFCS
Speedy Cartoons
DIRECTORS
Richard Sloggett
Paul Vester
CLIENT
Toshiba
AGENCY
Gold Greenlees Trott/London

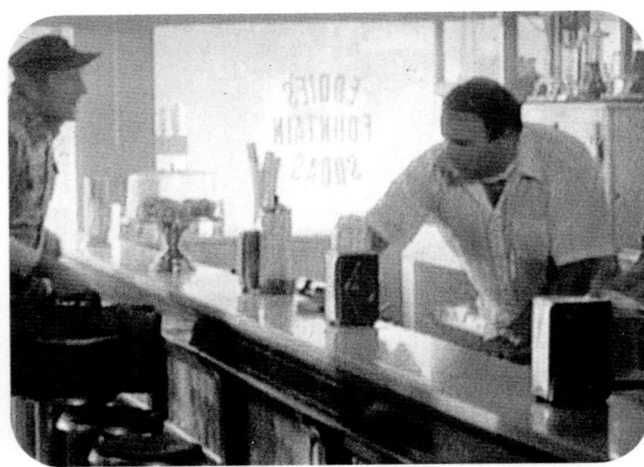

741

WIFE: Honey?

HUSBAND: Hmmm.

WI FE: You have Michelin tires in your car, don't you?

HUSBAND: Yeah.

WIFE: How come?

HUSBAND: I don't know. They're terrific tires. Why?

WIFE: How come I don't have Michelins in my car?

HUSBAND: Oh sweetheart, they cost more. I drive to work, I go out of town a lot. All you use your car for is shopping, driving Amy around . . . I'll get you a set tomorrow.

WIFE: You sure you want to spend the extra money on us?

HUSBAND: Come on.

ANNCR VO: Michelin. Because so much is riding on your tires.

742

WILBUR: I'll have a Coke.

WAITER: Sure stranger, which one?

WILBUR: Just a Coke.

WATIER: Well there's lots of them. You see the old Coke is the old Coke before it became your new Coke and the new Coke is the one that used to be your old Coke, which became your new improved Coke. Except for your Classic Coke, which is really the old Coke, and now that's your new Coke.
You know what I mean?

WILBUR: Just give me the one you like best.

WAITER: That's easy.

WILBUR: Pepsi.

ANNCR: Now more than ever. Pepsi. The choice of a new generation.

WILBUR: Glad I asked.

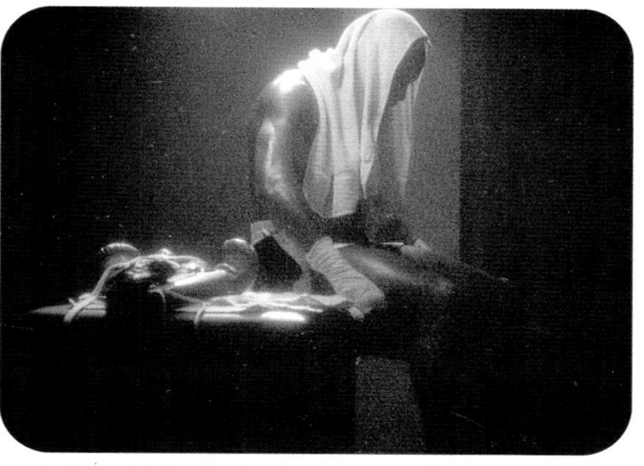

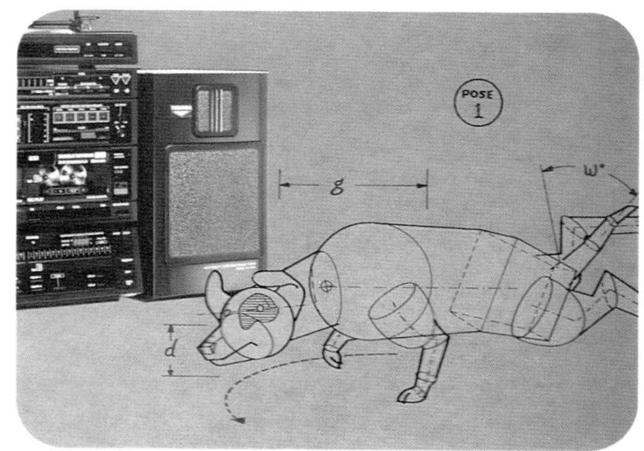

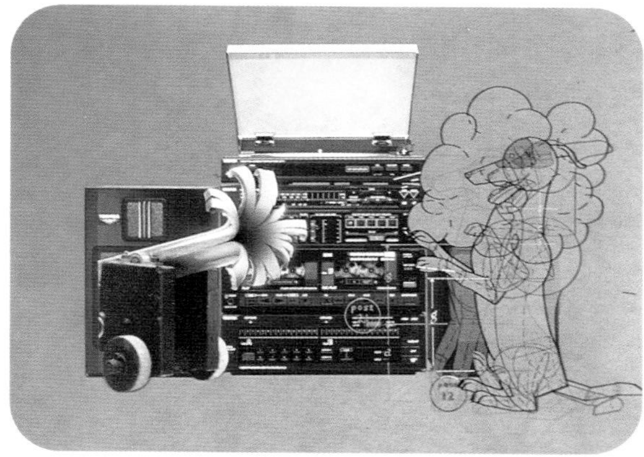

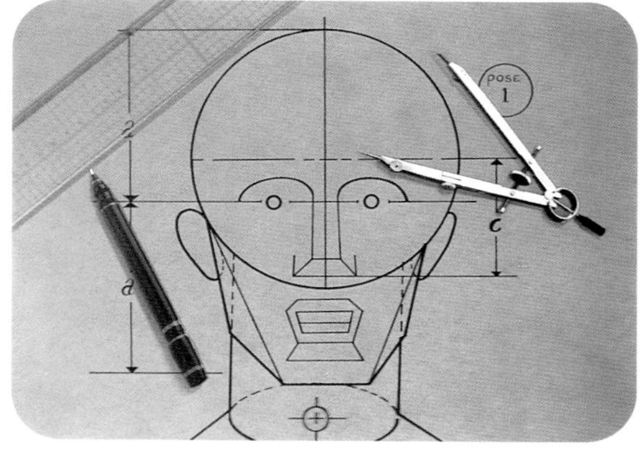

743

(MUSIC: SYNTHESIZER TONE, RISING THROUGHOUT)

(SFX: HEAVY BREATHING)

1ST: No way the kid goes four.

2ND: Ahh, you're crazy!

(SFX: TAPE WRAPPING)

(MUSIC: STACCATO BEAT)

ANNCR: . . . Make sure he's facing the camera . . .

1ST: Hey, we'll see ya.

2ND: Round one.

(SFX: I WANT YOU!)

(SFX: SMACK!!)

(SFX: TESTING, ONE, TWO . . .)

GUY: Taxi!!

(SFX: TRAFFIC, HORNS)

MAN: C'mon, we're buying tickets here . . .

ANNCR: I'll follow your lead.

(SFX: WHISTLES, CROWD NOISES)

(SFX: SMACK, SMACK!!)

CROWD: Marvin, Marvin!!

ANNCR VO: When it's big, nobody brings it home like HBO.

744

(TRACK: ART OF NOISE TYPE)

BLUEPRINT MAN (RAPPING TO TRACK): Hello, hello, hello. In design, Toshiba are the top exponents. We always specify the best quality components. Stronger to last longer, as a matter of fact. So it still sounds good, when you give it some of that.

(MUSIC: TRUMPET FROM 1812 OVERTURE PLAYED ON FAIRLIGHT)

DOG: ap wap wa-wa-wa-wa-wa wap.

BPM: With the compact disc technology behind it, tell you something, *I* don't mind it. You want great sound? Meet the leader. Say hello tosh to a new Toshiba.

Consumer Television :30 Single

745
ART DIRECTOR
Carmen Ferraro
WRITER
Patty Capin
AGENCY PRODUCER
Linda Whipple
PRODUCTION CO.
Mirage Productions
DIRECTOR
Jon Parks
CLIENT
Carpool Brushless Autowash
AGENCY
The Smyth Agency/Virginia

746
ART DIRECTOR
F. Paul Pracilio
WRITER
Robert Neuman
AGENCY PRODUCER
Ann Marcato
PRODUCTION CO.
Steve Horn Inc.
DIRECTOR
Steve Horn
CLIENT
American Express
AGENCY
Ogilvy & Mather

747
ART DIRECTOR
Jim Handloser
WRITER
Helayne Spivak
AGENCY PRODUCER
Marty Friedman
PRODUCTION CO.
Power & Light Picture Company
DIRECTOR
Ross Kramer
CLIENT
Ciba-Geigy Acutrim
AGENCY
Ally & Gargano

748
ART DIRECTOR
George Euringer
WRITER
Helayne Spivak
AGENCY PRODUCER
Mark Sitley
PRODUCTION CO.
Stone/Mansfield
DIRECTOR
Dick Stone
CLIENT
MCI Telecommunications
AGENCY
Ally & Gargano

 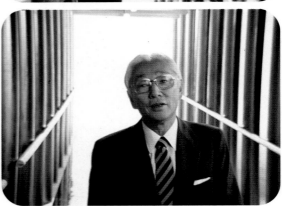

745

The important reason why Carpool washes more cars than anyone in Virginia is that when a VW comes in . . . the sophisticated equipment is adjusted down to apply the right touch to clean the car.
The microprocessor adjusts the gentle cloth wheels differently when a . . . Buick Wagon comes in.
But one thing that makes Carpool the most popular autowash in town is that we wash . . . pickups and vans.
ANNCR VO: Carpool. We guard the life of your car.

746

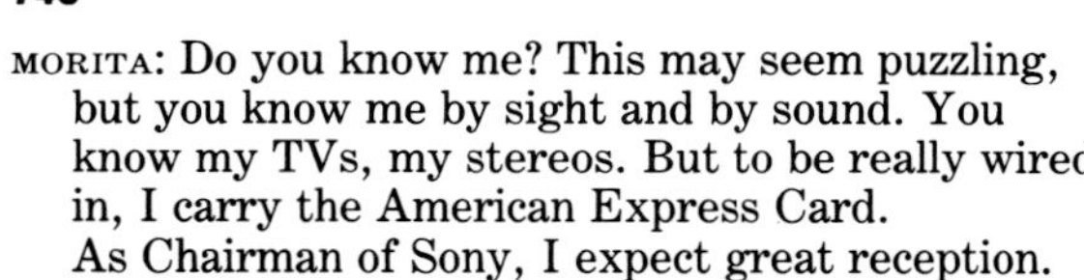

MORITA: Do you know me? This may seem puzzling, but you know me by sight and by sound. You know my TVs, my stereos. But to be really wired in, I carry the American Express Card. As Chairman of Sony, I expect great reception.

ANNCR VO: To apply for the Card, look for an application, and take one.

MORITA: The American Express Card. Don't leave home without it.

747

WOMAN: You're being so good on your diet. You haven't cheated at all tonight. I guess that 12-hour appetite suppressant you took this morning is really working. But hasn't it been a lot longer than 12 hours since you took it? So what happens now? Does your appetite come back? . . . (VOICE FADES UNDER)

ANNCR VO: If your appetite suppressant calls it a day before you do, you need Acutrim. Acutrim lasts longer than any other brand of appetite suppressant. A full 16 hours.

WOMAN: You know. This could really use some more chopped nuts. Oh, waiter . . .

ANNCR VO: Acutrim. It's at its strongest when you're at your weakest.

748

JOAN RIVERS: To get you to choose them as your long distance phone, certain people say they're better than MCI. Not true. There's nothing better than MCI DIAL-1 Service. They say they're cheaper than MCI. Please. MCI costs less no matter when you call. They'll even hint that MCI's trying to look like them. No way. However, to show you what a sporting company MCI is, we won't even mention that expensive phone company by name. But I'll give you a hint. Their initials are AT&T.

ANNCR VO: When you're asked to choose a long distance phone company, choose MCI DIAL-1 Long Distance Service, and start saving.

Consumer Television
:30 Single

749
ART DIRECTOR
Donna Weinheim
WRITERS
Stan Becker
Arthur Bijur
Cliff Freeman
AGENCY PRODUCER
Jill Paperno
PRODUCTION CO.
Paisley Productions
CLIENT
Peter Paul Cadbury
AGENCY
Dancer Fitzgerald Sample

750
ART DIRECTOR
Ron Arnold
WRITER
Michael Scardino
AGENCY PRODUCER
Marty Friedman
PRODUCTION CO.
Lucka Film
DIRECTOR
Klaus Lucka
CLIENT
Saab
AGENCY
Ally & Gargano

751
ART DIRECTOR
Dave Waters
WRITER
Paul Grubb
AGENCY PRODUCER
Christine Clark
PRODUCTION COS
BFCS
Hibbert Ralph Animation
DIRECTORS
Richard Sloggett
Jerry Hibbert
CLIENT
Cadbury's Creme Eggs
AGENCY
Gold Greenlees Trott/London

752
ART DIRECTOR
George Euringer
WRITER
Tom Messner
AGENCY PRODUCER
Mark Sitley
PRODUCTION CO.
Stone/Mansfield
DIRECTOR
Dick Stone
CLIENT
Bristol-Myers Datril
AGENCY
Ally & Gargano

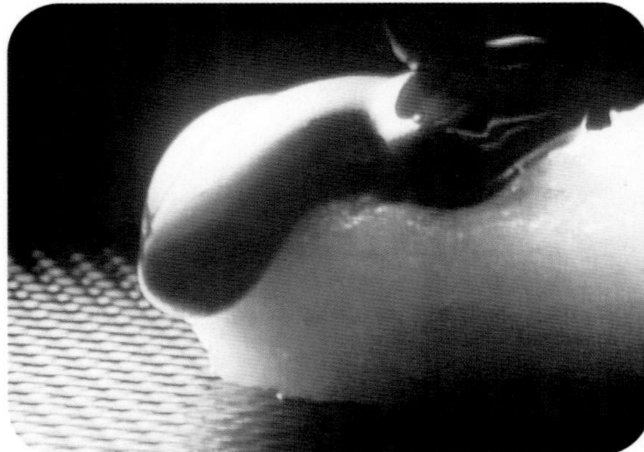

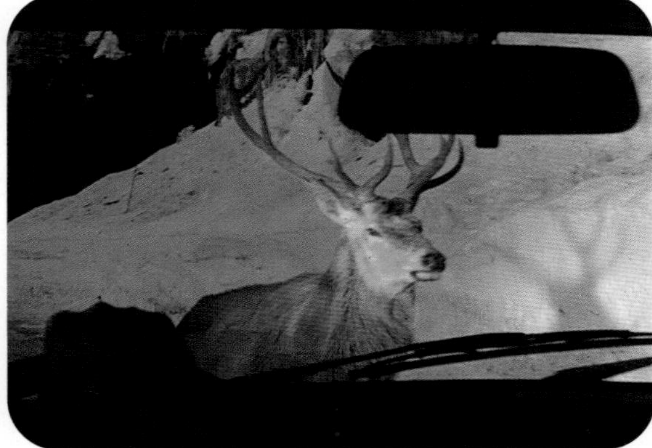

749

ANNCR: A few words . . .
About mounds.
Oooooo . . .
Ahhhhh . . .
Mmmmmm . . .
But don't take our words for it.
Ooo, ahh, mmm for yourself.

750

(MUSIC: UNDER)

ANNCR VO: Saab is engineered for those who seek out the thrill of driving . . . As well as those who seek to avoid it.

(MUSIC CONTINUES)

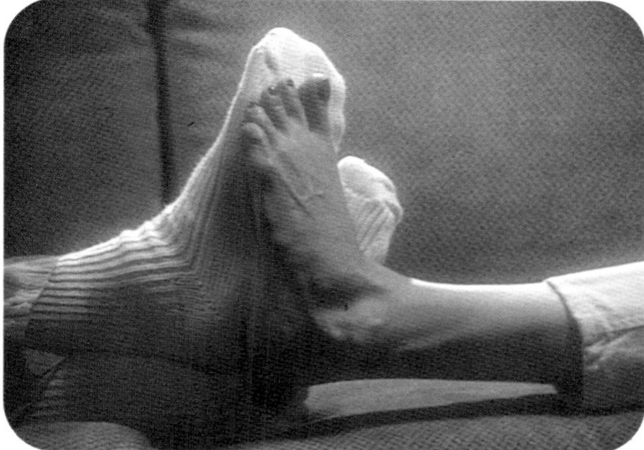

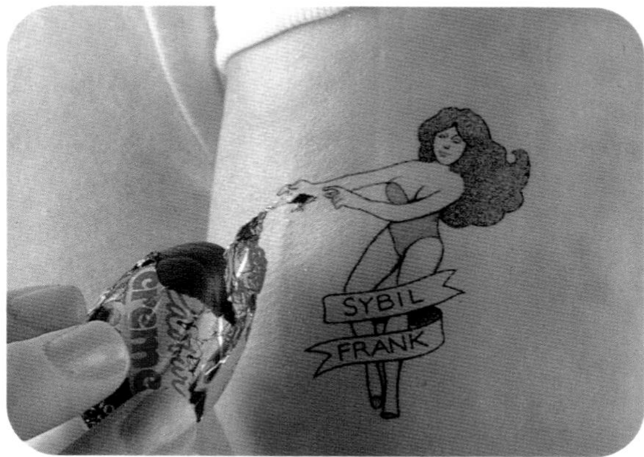

751

(SFX: MUSIC INTRO)

MVO: How do *you* eat your Cadbury's Creme Eggs. . . ?
Munch!
Take it in one, son.
Gulp!
Look, no hands, Suzanne.
Fancy a nibble, Sybil?

(SFX: STRIPPER MUSIC)

MVO: Eat it when you're free, Jeremy.
Just give it a suck, Chuck.
ZZZZZZZZIP
Bite it in two, Emmy-Lou.
ZZZZZZZZIP.
How do *you* eat *your* Cadbury's Creme Eggs?

SONG: *They're not here forever, Trevor.*

752

(MUSIC: UNDER)

ANNCR VO: Datril. Last night, 10 P.M.

HE: I thought you had a headache.

SHE: I thought you said you had a headache.

HE: Well, I did. But I took a couple of Datril.

SHE: Me too.

ANNCR VO: Datril. One thousand milligrams of medicine for your headache. No milligrams of medicine that could upset your stomach. Datril from Bristol-Myers. Extra strength for your headache. Extra gentle for your stomach.

Consumer Television :30 Single

753
ART DIRECTORS
Bob Kuperman
Jim Hallowes
WRITERS
Pacy Markman
Brandt Irvine
AGENCY PRODUCER
Elaine Lord
PRODUCTION CO.
Wright-Banks Films
DIRECTOR
John Urie
CLIENT
Comprehensive Care Corporation
AGENCY
Doyle Dane Bernbach/Los Angeles

754
ART DIRECTOR
Pam Cunningham
WRITER
Carol Ogden
AGENCY PRODUCER
Gary Paticoff
PRODUCTION CO.
Dick James Productions
DIRECTOR
Dick James
CLIENT
American Honda Motor Company
AGENCY
Needham Harper Worldwide/Los Angeles

755
ART DIRECTOR
Carole Cherry
WRITER
Carole Cherry
AGENCY PRODUCER
Brad Steinwede
PRODUCTION CO.
Ibbetson & Cherry
DIRECTOR
Peter Cherry
CLIENT
Bushells Master Roast
AGENCY
Leo Burnett/Australia

756
ART DIRECTOR
Bob Meagher
WRITERS
Bob Meagher
Dave Ullman
AGENCY PRODUCERS
Bob Meagher
Maureen Moore
PRODUCTION CO.
Kurtz & Friends
DIRECTOR
Bob Kurtz
CLIENT
Lincoln Park Zoo
AGENCY
Cramer-Krasselt/Chicago

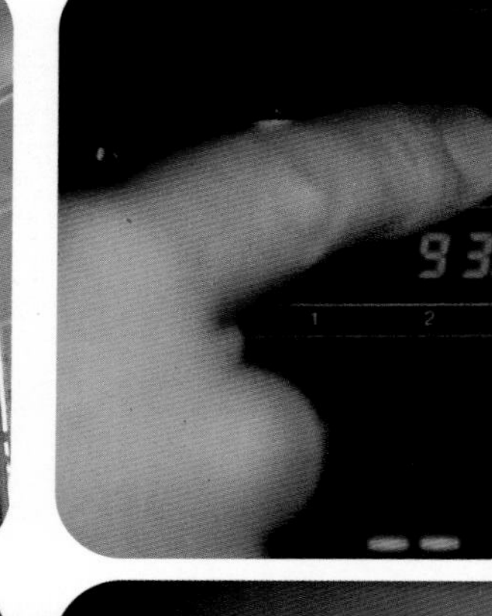

753

(SFX: APPROPRIATE SFX THROUGHOUT)

VO: If you have a drinking problem, you probably have a disease. A progressive disease . . . that weakens the structure . . . of the family . . . that undermines . . . the love that's the foundation . . . of the family; that can tear . . . the family apart . . .

(SFX: DRONE BEGINS HERE)

VO: . . . and destroy everything you've built together.

(SFX: DRONE BECOMES STRONGER)

VO: . . . A progressive . . . disease called alcoholism. . . . So next time . . . you feel like reaching . . . for a drink, reach for the phone instead.

(SFX: DRONE BEGINS TO FADE OUT)

VO: Call CareUnit. Nobody cares the way we do.

754

VO: The Honda Prelude Si. We haven't put all the fun at your fingertips. There's a little something for your right foot.

SINGERS: *Honda.*

755

MVO: Bushells Master Roast brings the flavour back. A very special blend of beans, roasted to perfection and captured in granules, so you can taste the full flavour again.

WOMAN: The flavour's back.

MVO: Bushells Master Roast. The flavour you've missed in other coffees.

(SFX: BIG WHIRLING, SWALLOWING, SOUND)

HIM (SLIGHTLY CURIOUS): What was that?

HER (BORED): The flavour's gone from the coffee again.

756

(SFX: CITY SOUNDS; HONKING; FINGER SNAPPING)

(MUSIC: "OOO, OOO THE ZOO")

RHINO: *Yeah. It's brand new.*

LION & RHINO: *The Lincoln Park Zoo.*

RHINO: *We're missing you.*

LION, RHINO, PENGUIN, GIRAFFE: *At the Lincoln Park . . . Zoo ooo ooo.*

LION: *It's a world of fun.*

PENGUIN: *And it's brand new.*

GIRAFFE: *Come see us and weeee . . . lll . . .*

ALL FOUR: *. . . see you . . .*
at the zoo . . . the Lincoln Park Zoooooo.

RHINO: *What's brand new?*

ALL: *Lincoln Park Zoooo.*

GIRAFFE (IN FALSETTO): *My kind of Zoo.*

Consumer Television
:30 Single

757
ART DIRECTOR
Peter Weir
WRITER
Patrick Hudson
AGENCY PRODUCER
Sandra Breakstone
PRODUCTION CO.
Michael Ulick Productions
DIRECTOR
Michael Ulick
CLIENT
American Express
AGENCY
Ogilvy & Mather

758
ART DIRECTOR
Barry Vetere
WRITER
Ron Berger
AGENCY PRODUCER
Beth Forman
PRODUCTION CO.
They Shoot Films
DIRECTOR
Barry Vetere
CLIENT
Dunkin' Donuts
AGENCY
Ally & Gargano

759
ART DIRECTORS
Mitch Gordon
Steve Juliusson
WRITERS
Jeff Moore
Al Lerman
AGENCY PRODUCER
Neal Bergman
PRODUCTION CO.
Abel & Associates
DIRECTOR
Bruce Dorn
CLIENT
Midas International
AGENCY
Wells Rich Greene/Chicago

760
WRITERS
Jim Sanderson
Leslie Lawton
AGENCY PRODUCER
Jim Phox
CLIENT
GTE Sprint
AGENCY
J. Walter Thompson/San Francisco

757

JIM DAVIS: Do you know me?

GARFIELD: Who cares?

JIM DAVIS: That, of course, is Garfield. He's fat . . .

GARFIELD: Full-figured.

JIM DAVIS: . . . ill-mannered, and to think I created him. But sometimes when I travel without the tubby tabby, people don't know my name. So I carry the American Express Card. And wherever I go, folks treat me like a fat cat.

GARFIELD: Fat chance.

ANNCR: To apply for the Card, look for an application and take one.

JIM DAVIS: The American Express Card. Don't . . . uh . . . leave home . . . uh . . . without it.

758

(SFX: DINNER PARTY PRATTLE: SOFT MUSIC)

DOWAGER TYPE: Your husband seems rather weary.

FRED'S WIFE (ALMOST BOASTFULLY): He has a very taxing occupation. He's on call day and night. He hardly gets any sleep.

DOWAGER TYPE: Good gracious!

FRED'S WIFE: And his work demands absolute consistency.

BUTLER: Potatoes?

DOWAGER TYPE: What is he, a brain surgeon?

(SFX: THUD; SILENCE)

FRED'S WIFE: Not exactly.

FRED (WAKING UP): Time to make the donuts.

ANNCR VO: Dunkin' Donuts. Up to 52 varieties fresh day and night. Who else goes to that trouble?

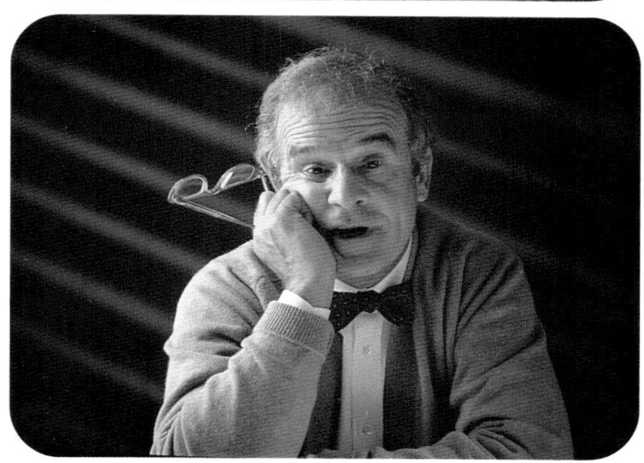

759

VO: This year you'll apply your brakes over 50,000 times. And the more you stop, the more you'll need Midas. Because we back every brake repair we do with a nationwide guarantee on brake shoes and pads. If they should ever wear out, Midas will replace them free at over 1,400 locations for as long as you own your car. With such a good guarantee, why would you stop any place else?

VOCAL: *Trust the Midas touch.*

760

So? Do you know that every time your kids call you collect from college, it costs you as much as $1.55. Before they even start talking? Same with that AT&T credit card. A $1.05 surcharge. For what? Now GTE Sprint gives you a free travelcode. To save when you travel. So you give it to the kids. When they call, there's no surcharge. You save as much as 70%. And when they ask for money, you have some.
Call Sprint.
Find out about it.

Consumer Television
:30 Single

761
ART DIRECTOR
Marcus Kemp
WRITER
Jim Copacino
AGENCY PRODUCER
Cindy Henderson
PRODUCTION CO.
Sedelmaier
DIRECTOR
Joe Sedelmaier
CLIENT
Alaska Airlines
AGENCY
Livingston & Company/
Seattle

762
ART DIRECTOR
Cliff Goodenough
WRITER
Steve Sandoz
AGENCY PRODUCER
Lockey Todd-Bennett
PRODUCTION CO.
Telemation
CLIENT
The Weekly
AGENCY
Livingston & Company/
Seattle

763
ART DIRECTOR
John D'Asto
WRITER
Mark Fenske
AGENCY PRODUCER
Laurie Berger
PRODUCTION CO.
McDonough/Jones
DIRECTOR
Jeff Jones
CLIENT
Illinois Office of Tourism
AGENCY
Zechman & Associates/
Chicago

764
ART DIRECTOR
Marcus Kemp
WRITER
Jim Copacino
AGENCY PRODUCER
Cindy Henderson
PRODUCTION CO.
Sedelmaier
DIRECTOR
Joe Sedelmaier
CLIENT
Alaska Airlines
AGENCY
Livingston & Company/
Seattle

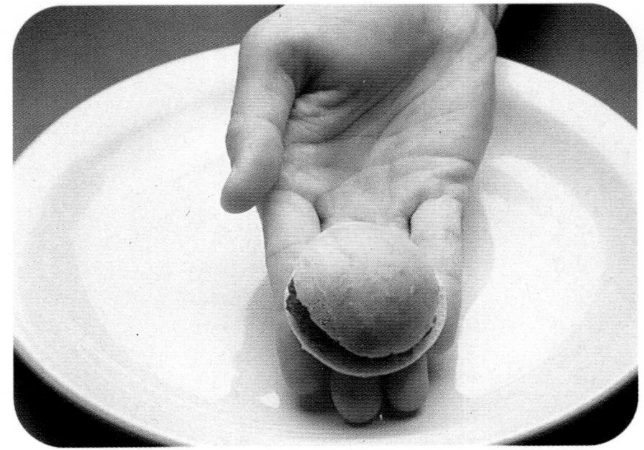

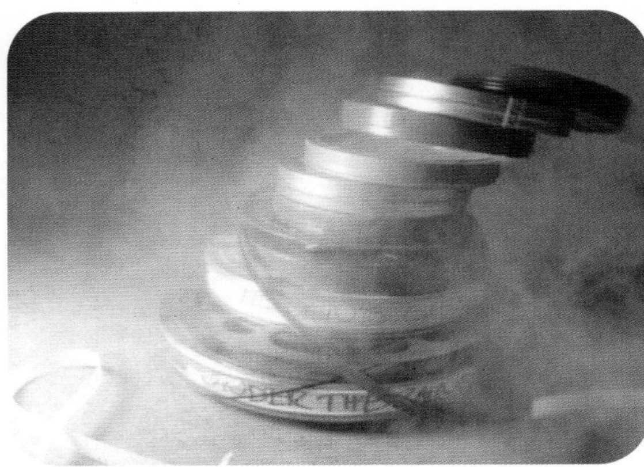

761

ANNCR: These days, a lot of airlines are cutting corners on their meals.

MAN 1: This little beauty we'll have to call 'Banquet on a Bun,' right Bob?

MAN 2: 'Banquet on a Bun.'

MAN 3: I like it.

MAN 1: Set it down, Bob. Now with this you can serve a whole planeload for pennies.

MAN 3: I like it.

MAN 1: Plastic parsley—you can use it over and over again.

MAN 3: I like it.

MAN 1: Pygmy chickens—you can get an order of 105 in an ordinary shoebox.

MAN 3: I like it.

762

ANNCR: This year you can avoid bad movies.

(SFX: MOVIES CRASHING)

ANNCR: Bad concerts.

(SFX: SHEET MUSIC CRASHING)

ANNCR: Bad restaurants. Bad literature.

(SFX: BOOKS CRASHING)

ANNCR: Bad ideas.

(SFX: MODELS ETC. CRASHING)

ANNCR: Bad art.

(SFX: PAINTING CRASHING)

ANNCR: And bad politics.

(SFX: PAPERS AND STAMPS CRASHING)

ANNCR: By just picking up your phone. Discover a better way to look at Seattle.

(SFX: THE WEEKLY LANDING SOFTLY)

ANNCR: Subscribe to The Weekly. Call 441-6262.

763

MAN: The events for Steamboat Days in Peoria. A homemade paddle-wheel race. A Miss Peoria beauty pageant.

MAN: Steamboat rides, bratwurst . . .

MAN: . . . Fun in the sun. (PAUSE) And . . . volleyball games in the mud.

MUD GUY: Alright!

VO: Steamboat Days in Peoria. Join us for some good clean fun.

SONG: *Illinois you put me in a happy state.*

764

MAN 1: Gentlemen, welcome, welcome. That being so stated, on to the job at hand. Please take notes and listen carefully.

ANNCR: Every one of these executives flew to this important meeting on a different airline, sampling various meals . . . beverages, on board service . . . and other amenities.
Can you find the one executive who flew here on Alaska Airlines?

(SFX: ALASKA MUSIC UP AND OUT)

ANNCR: At Alaska Airlines, we spend a little more on our meals . . . and you can taste the difference.

Consumer Television :30 Single

765
ART DIRECTOR
Gary Johns
WRITER
Jeff Gorman
AGENCY PRODUCER
Elaine Hinton
PRODUCTION CO.
Coppos Films
DIRECTOR
Mark Coppos
CLIENT
800-FLOWERS
AGENCY
Chiat/Day - Los Angeles

766
ART DIRECTORS
Joe Minnella
John Umlauf
WRITER
Dale Silverberg
AGENCY PRODUCER
Sheldon Cohn
CLIENT
Sohio/Gulf
AGENCY
W. B. Doner & Company/Michigan

767
ART DIRECTOR
Gary Johns
WRITER
Jeff Gorman
AGENCY PRODUCER
Richard O'Neill
PRODUCTION CO.
Johns & Gorman Films
DIRECTORS
Gary Johns
Jeff Gorman
CLIENT
Nike
AGENCY
Chiat/Day - Los Angeles

768
ART DIRECTOR
Greg Clancey
WRITER
Tim Price
AGENCY PRODUCER
Anna Ludoweig
PRODUCTION CO.
Steve Horn Inc.
DIRECTOR
Steve Horn
CLIENT
Levi's 505 Jeans
AGENCY
Foote Cone & Belding/San Francisco

765

VO: Not all artists paint, write, or play musical instruments.
Eight-hundred-flowers. Phone 24 hours a day, 7 days a week.

766

ATTENDANT: Just sign here, Ma'am.

WOMAN: But this is more than what the sign says.

ATTENDANT: Sure. You're using your credit card instead of cash.

VO: If your service station charges a higher price for credit cards than cash . . . take your business elsewhere . . . to Gulf . . . the people who don't charge you more for credit cards. Gulf. One low price . . . cash or credit.

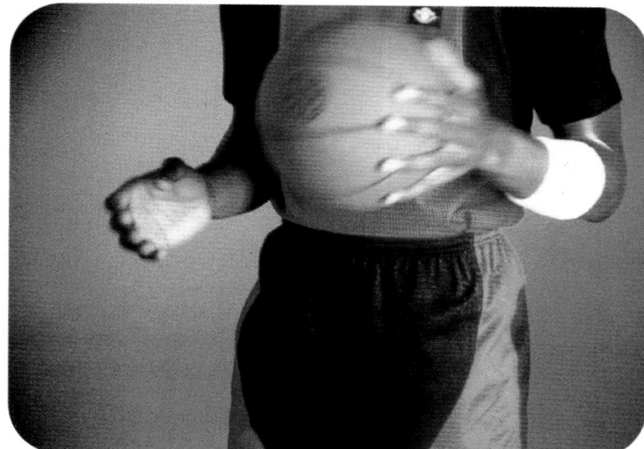
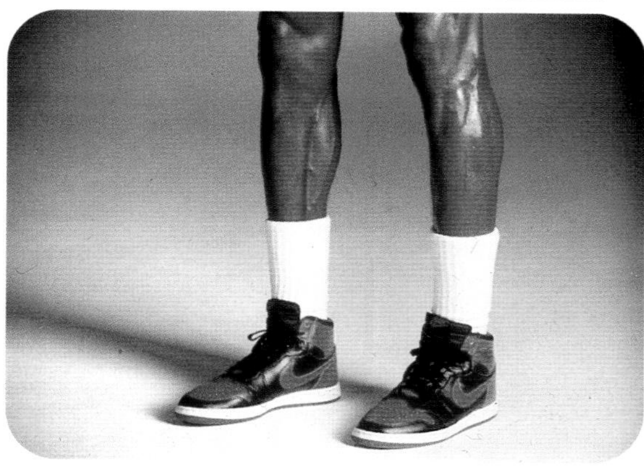

767

VO: On September 15th, Nike created a revolutionary new basketball shoe.
On October 18th, the NBA threw them out of the game.
Fortunately, the NBA can't stop you from wearing them.
Air Jordans from Nike.

768

(MUSIC: UP)

ROXANNE: Come on. Let's go.

BETH: Hey, where'd you get those jeans?

ROXANNE: They're just basic jeans.

BETH: Are you sure?

ROXANNE: They're just Levi's 505's.

BETH: Not the way they look.

ROXANNE: Just plain old 505's. See—they really are. I mean, it's the person that wears them that makes them so special.

BETH: O.K., now tell me the real truth.

ROXANNE: Beth, best friends don't lie to each other.

BETH: They don't?

ROXANNE: No.

BETH: Not ever?

ANNCR VO: Levi's pre-shrunk zipper-fly 505 jeans.

Consumer Television
:30 Single

769
ART DIRECTOR
Jerry Roach
WRITER
Marvin Waldman
AGENCY PRODUCER
Chris Jones
PRODUCTION CO.
N. Lee Lacy & Associates
DIRECTOR
Henry Holtzman
CLIENT
7-Eleven
AGENCY
Young & Rubicam

770
ART DIRECTOR
Ross Van Dusen
WRITER
Dave O'Hara
AGENCY PRODUCER
Frank Scherma
PRODUCTION CO.
Johnston Films
DIRECTOR
Jim Johnston
CLIENT
California Cooler
AGENCY
Chiat/Day - Los Angeles

771
ART DIRECTORS
Alan Chalfin
Frank Perry
WRITERS
Hal Friedman
Brian Sitts
AGENCY PRODUCER
Gary Bass
CLIENT
Burger King
AGENCY
J. Walter Thompson

772
ART DIRECTOR
Steve Stith
WRITER
Marty Slade
AGENCY PRODUCER
Bill Duryea
CLIENT
Greyhound Bus Lines
AGENCY
Bozell Jacobs Kenyon & Eckhardt

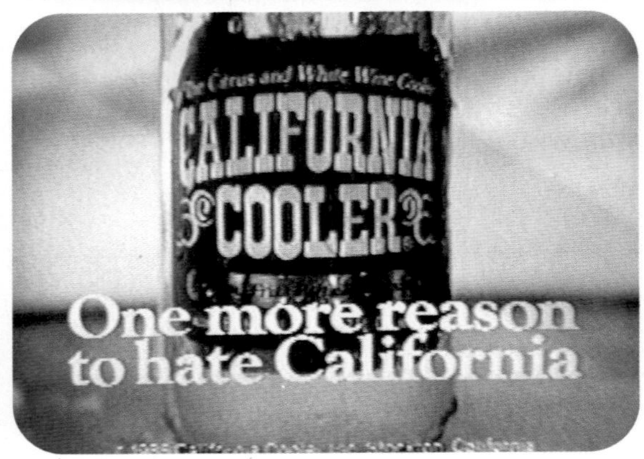

769

(MUSIC: UNDER)

ANNCR VO: You go revvin' along like a well oiled machine until it's time to wait . . .

CUSTOMER VO: One potato . . . two potato . . . three potato . . .

CASHIER: One potato . . .

CUSTOMER VO: Four potato . . . five potato . . .

VO: Six potato . . .

CASHIER VO: Three potato . . .

CUSTOMER VO: Seven potato . . . eight potato . . .

CASHIER VO: Four potato . . .

CUSTOMER VO: Nine . . .

STORE CLERK (UNDER): Hi!

ANNCR VO: But at 7-Eleven, you get what you want fast.

MAN (UNDER): Thanks. Bye.

ANNCR VO: No one keeps you revvin' like 7-Eleven.

770

MATT: I hate California. You know what I'm saying? It's like . . . Have a nice day—Surf's up. Aha, Aha. I mean, their idea of culture is yogurt. Formal dinner party means you wear socks. Blondes everywhere—Pink tofu—Excuse me!! Soy burger—I really hate it. I even hate what they drink.

BARTENDER: What do ya have buddy?

MATT (POINTS TO CALIFORNIA COOLER): One of those. Palm trees, excuse me—what ever happened to real trees?

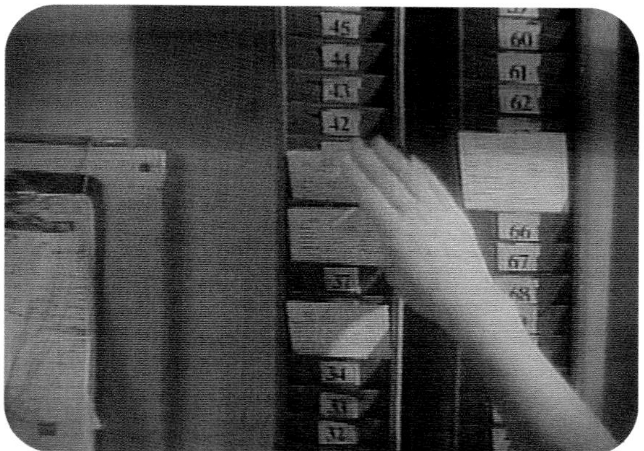

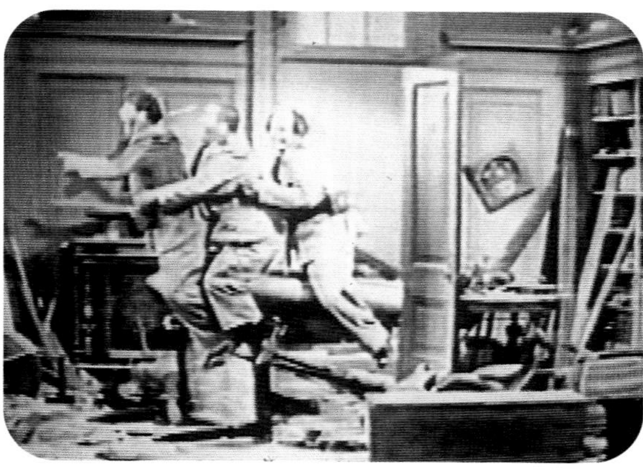

771

(MUSIC)

ANNCR: When word got out that Burger King changed the Whopper, some people were a little upset.

CURLY: Woo, Woo, Woo, etc.

ANNCR: Some even took it out on their friends.

(SFX: WRENCH HITTING HEAD)

LARRY: Ooh!

(SFX: WRENCH HITTING HEAD)

CURLY: Ooh!

(SFX: LARRY AND CURLY BEING HIT)

CURLY: Aaagh!

ANNCR: But when they heard the new Whopper has more beef than Big Mac or Wendy's Single, they changed their tune.

MOE AND CURLY: Various noises.

ANNCR: And once they heard the new Whopper won for best taste, they naturally took off for Burger King.

(SFX: WHISTLING SHELL)

STOOGES: Various noises.

772

ANNCR VO: You're through with work, and you're ready to hit the road.
But remember, the road hits back.
This year, automobile accidents will claim between 40 and 50,000 lives—just like last year.
The next time you punch out, don't make it permanent.
If you must drive, please drive safely.
This safety message has been brought to you by this station and Greyhound.

Consumer Television
:30 Single

773
ART DIRECTOR
Jill Bohannan
WRITER
Jim Carey
AGENCY PRODUCER
Janet Collins
PRODUCTION CO.
James Productions
DIRECTOR
Jim Lund
CLIENT
Humana MEDFIRST
AGENCY
Young & Rubicam/Chicago

774
ART DIRECTORS
Bernie Guild
Leslie Caldwell
WRITER
Mike Koelker
AGENCY PRODUCER
Steve Neely
PRODUCTION CO.
Petermann Dektor
DIRECTOR
Leslie Dektor
CLIENT
Levi's 501 Jeans
AGENCY
Foote Cone & Belding/San Francisco

775
ART DIRECTORS
Gerry Monsier
WRITERS
Patricia Condon
AGENCY PRODUCER
Cathy McLewin
PRODUCTION CO.
Sincinkin
DIRECTOR
George Pastic
CLIENT
Colgate-Palmolive
AGENCY
Ted Bates/Toronto

776
ART DIRECTOR
Donna Weinheim
WRITER
Cliff Freeman
AGENCY PRODUCER
Susan Scherl
PRODUCTION CO.
Sedelmaier
DIRECTOR
Joe Sedelmaier
CLIENT
Wendy's International
AGENCY
Dancer Fitzgerald Sample

773

(MUSIC: SOMBER, DIRGE-LIKE SCORING)

ANNCR VO: It's that time again. When beaches and ballgames give way to reading, writing and arithmetic. In honor of this joyous occasion, Humana MEDFIRST is offering 20% off back-to-school physicals throughout August. So stop by. After all, an opportunity like this only comes along once a year.

774

(MUSIC: UP)

BRO. 1: *My, my, said the buttonfly.*

BRO. 2: *What you say?*

BRO. 1: *Have you heard the news?*

BRO. 2 VO: *No, tell me about it.*

BRO. 1: *I got the blues.*

BRO. 2: *Ah, deliver.*

BRO. 1: *The Levi's 501 blues.*

BRO. 2 VO: *They shrink to fit.*

BRO. 1: *That's it. And they're right to size.*

BRO. 2: *Do tell.*

BRO. 1 VO: *My personalized . . .*

BRO. 1: *Levi's 501 blues.*

BRO. 2: *Lucky fly.*

BRO. 1: *Ain't I.*

BRO. 2: *My, my.*

BRO. 1: *Yeah, I like that. I like that.*

(MUSIC: OUT)

775

(APPROPRIATE MUSIC UNDER THROUGHOUT)

ANNCR VO: Today, children could grow up . . . never knowing a cavity. And Colgate . . . can help them do it. Only Colgate . . . contains 2 mineral-building fluorides . . . better Colgate cavity protection . . . than ever before.
If your children visit the dentist twice a year . . . and brush properly with Colgate everyday . . . they could grow up never knowing a cavity in their lifetime. Colgate. Working with you for a cavity-free generation.

776

MAN: Yeah, I'd like a hamburger.

COUNTER MAN 1: As you speak.

MAN: You already made it?

COUNTER MAN 1: We already made it.

MAN: When?

COUNTER MAN 1: What time is it?

MAN: 12 o'clock.

COUNTER MAN 1: 12 o'clock. We made your hamburger at 11 o'clock.

MAN: So if I want a hamburger made fresh, I gotta come at 11 o'clock?

COUNTER MAN 1: Our 11 o'clock hamburger is made at 10 o'clock.

MAN: 10 o'clock?

COUNTER MAN 2: Like 10, 11, 12 or vice versa.

MAN: So I gotta come at10 o'clock?

COUNTER MAN 1: 10 o'clock hamburgers will be made at 9 o'clock.

MAN: I gotta be here for lunch at 9 o'clock?

COUNTER MAN 1: Look at it this way, you beat the noon-time crowds.

ANNCR: At Wendy's your hamburger is always made fresh the moment you order, not a second sooner. The others can't promise that.

Consumer Television
:30 Single

777
ART DIRECTOR
Constantine Shoukas
WRITER
Dorothy Linder
AGENCY PRODUCER
Steve Citrin
PRODUCTION CO.
Petermann Dektor
DIRECTOR
Fred Petermann
CLIENT
Eastern Airlines
AGENCY
Campbell-Ewald

778
ART DIRECTOR
Ron Arnold
WRITER
Hy Abady
AGENCY PRODUCER
Cinda Sunshine
PRODUCTION CO.
Sandbank Films
DIRECTOR
Henry Sandbank
CLIENT
Dunkin' Donuts
AGENCY
Ally & Gargano

779
ART DIRECTOR
Terry O'Leary
WRITER
Doug Feinstein
AGENCY PRODUCER
Mootsy Elliot
PRODUCTION CO.
Miller/Mason Associates
DIRECTOR
Dick Miller
CLIENT
Duracell
AGENCY
Ogilvy & Mather

780
ART DIRECTOR
Ron Arnold
WRITER
Hy Abady
AGENCY PRODUCER
Beth Forman
PRODUCTION CO.
Sandbank Films
DIRECTOR
Henry Sandbank
CLIENT
Dunkin' Donuts
AGENCY
Ally & Gargano

777

(MUSIC: CAVALRY MUSIC)

ANNCR VO: When you're heading for the West on business . . . and you're in a hurry . . . you want to get there with as little inconvenience as possible . . . which is why at Eastern Airlines, we schedule more than 50 nonstops from Atlanta to the West every business day.

778

VO: When Dunkin' Donuts decided to introduce a light donut with less calories, there were a lot of things we could have done. But if they were anything less than what you'd expect from Dunkin' Donuts, no one would be happy. Now, everyone can be happy. We've figured out a way to make great tasting donuts with less sugar and one third less calories. Introducing Dunkin' Donuts Lite Donuts. Now, if you're eating light, you can be eating donuts.

779

ANNCR VO: At Duracell, we're already trying to climb higher. Even if it means topping our own Copper Top. Introducing the new highly improved Copper Top battery. So improved it'll last up to 30% longer than any battery we've ever made.
The new Copper Top. Once again we've reached a new peak.
Duracell. When it comes to making them last longer. We never stop.

780

(SFX: BONG!)

(MUSIC: UNDER)

FRED: Time to make the donuts.

ANNCR VO: Owning a Dunkin' Donuts is no piece of cake. Because you work night and day making donuts . . .

(SFX: BONG!)

FRED: Time to make the donuts.

ANNCR VO: . . . to make sure they're fresh. In up to 52 varieties.

(MUSIC)

ANNCR VO: At Dunkin' Donuts . . .

(SFX: BONG!)

ANNCR VO: . . . it's always time to make the donuts.

(MUSIC: OUT)

Consumer Television :30 Single

781
ART DIRECTOR
Constantine Shoukas
WRITER
Charles Glass
AGENCY PRODUCER
Bob Schenkel
PRODUCTION CO.
Myers Films
DIRECTOR
Sid Myers
CLIENT
Eastern Airlines
AGENCY
Campbell-Ewald

782
ART DIRECTOR
Howard Alstad
WRITER
Philippe Garneau
AGENCY PRODUCER
Candace Bowes
PRODUCTION CO.
The Partners Film Company Ltd.
DIRECTOR
Jeremiah Chechik
CLIENT
Wm Neilson Limited
AGENCY
Campbell-Ewald/Toronto

783
ART DIRECTOR
Barry Vetere
WRITERS
Helayne Spivak
Barry Vetere
AGENCY PRODUCER
Beth Forman
PRODUCTION CO.
Coppos Films
DIRECTOR
Mark Coppos
CLIENT
Sanyo
AGENCY
Ally & Gargano

784
ART DIRECTOR
Candace Van Stryker
WRITER
Karen Mallia
AGENCY PRODUCER
Susan Chiafullo
PRODUCTION CO.
BFCS
DIRECTOR
Thom Higgins
CLIENT
Schering/Fibre Trim
AGENCY
Ogilvy & Mather

781

BOSS: Team! It's time for our trip to the field.

YOUNG EXECUTIVES: Groans.

BOSS: Volunteers?

BOSS: Ah! Pelkey again.

MANAGER: Ah! Señor Pelkey . . . again!

VO: Why does the intrepid Pelkey take to the field when others head for the hills?

EMPLOYEE: Look! It's Pelkey again. Because Pelkey belongs to Eastern's Frequent Traveler Program. So every mile he flies helps him earn free trips to some pretty fabulous places.

GIRL (VERY PLEASED): Ooh, it's Pelkey again!

VO: Shouldn't *you* be an Eastern Frequent Traveler?

782

(SFX: OPENING DOOR)

(SFX: FOOTSTEPS, A CHAIR BEING MOVED ON WOODEN STAGE. THE SOUND OF VIOLIN BEING PLUCKED. ALL SOUND EFFECTS HAVE A SOUND QUALITY CONSISTENT WITH BEING IN LARGE EMPTY HALL.)

(MUSIC: FIRST RIFF OF SONG; PAUSE IN MUSIC; SECOND RIFF OF SONG; PAUSE IN MUSIC)

(MUSIC: FULL BAND COMES IN WITH SINGER)

LYRICS: *Girl, you really got me*
You got me so I can't sleep at night.
Oh yeah, you really got me now
You got me so I don't know what I'm doing.

(MUSIC: FINAL RIFF OF SONG; CONCLUSION)

783

JOAN COLLINS: If I were ever to cook, I would use this wonderful Sanyo Food Thing. I could bake things like that long garlic muffin.

COOK 1: Meatloaf, madam.

JOAN COLLINS: I could instantly melt frozen foods . . .

COOK 2: Defrost, madam.

JOAN COLLINS: I could cook that giant pheasant . . .

COOK 2: Turkey.

JOAN COLLINS: . . . at microwave speed and have it come out fully bronzed.

COOK 1: Browned, madam.

JOAN COLLINS: It's so amazing, I almost feel the urge to cook. I'm sure it'll pass.

ANNCR: The Sanyo Food Thing. The browning, baking, broiling, microwave oven.

784

(MUSIC: UNDER)

(SFX: GIRLS GIGGLE)

GIRL 1: Shhh.

(MUSIC)

(SFX: GIRLS GIGGLE)

GIRL 2 (SPEAKS IN FRENCH): Your mother is so beautiful so slim . . . Does she eat?

GIRL 1 (SPEAKS IN FRENCH): Silly, just not so much. With this . . . Fibre Trim. Made of grain and citrus.

GIRL 2 (SPEAKS IN FRENCH): Does it bother you that she's so beautiful?

GIRL 1 (SPEAKS IN FRENCH): Not if I know her secrets.

ANNCR VO: Fibre Trim helps you slim and stay slim sensibly.

Consumer Television :30 Single

785
ART DIRECTOR
Leslie Caldwell
WRITER
Mike Koelker
AGENCY PRODUCER
Steve Neely
PRODUCTION CO.
Petermann Dektor
DIRECTOR
Leslie Dektor
CLIENT
Levi's 501 Jeans
AGENCY
Foote Cone & Belding/San Francisco

786
ART DIRECTOR
Richard Mahan
WRITER
Phil Guthrie
AGENCY PRODUCER
Michael Berkman
PRODUCTION CO.
Independent Artists
CLIENT
Miller Brewing - Meister Brau
AGENCY
Backer & Spielvogel

787
ART DIRECTOR
Wayne Hardison
WRITER
Jery Rowan
AGENCY PRODUCER
Jo-Ann Purser
PRODUCTION CO.
The Partners Film Company Ltd.
DIRECTOR
Doug Moshoian
CLIENT
Nabisco Brands Ltd.
AGENCY
Saatchi & Saatchi Compton Hayhurst/Toronto

Consumer Television :30 Campaign

788
ART DIRECTOR
Mario Giua
WRITER
Robin Raj
AGENCY PRODUCER
Carol Lee Kelliher
PRODUCTION CO.
Rick Levine Productions
DIRECTOR
Rick Levine
CLIENT
Plank Road Original Draught
AGENCY
Chiat/Day

785

MAN 1: My, My, My said the Button Fly
MAN 2: What you say
MAN 1: Have you heard the news?
MAN 2: Na, tell me about it
MAN 1: I've got the Blues
MAN 2: Aw, deliver
MAN 1: The Levi's 501 Blues
MAN 2: They shrink to fit
MAN 1: That's it, and they're right to size
MAN 2: Do tell
MAN 1: I personalize Levi's 501 Blues
MAN 2: Lucky fly
MAN 1: Ain't I
MAN 2: My, My
MAN 1: Yeah, I like that, I like that

786

COWBOY 1: I was talking to the boys over by the Lazy J today.

(SFX: CARDS BEING SHUFFLED)

COWBOY 1: Seems they know a thing or two 'bout this Meister Brau Festus been buyin' for the bunkhouse.

COWBOY 2: I tell ya, this stuff's more expensive than a coyote coat!

COWBOY 1: Way they tell it, it ain't expensive 'tal. Just tastes expensive.

COWBOY 3: Then what's that rattlesnake doin' with all the money we chip in for beer?

FESTUS: Hey Monsewer! You got a table for me and the little philly?

ANNCR VO: Rich, smooth Meister Brau.
It only tastes expensive.

787

DICK: You know what I like about Shredded Wheat, Tommy?

TOMMY: What?

DICK: I like what it hasn't got in it.

TOMMY: Hey, Mr Shredded Wheat, my brother likes what isn't there.

DICK: That's right, Tommy, in Nabisco Shredded Wheat there's no added sugar and no added salt. Just wheat. 100% whole wheat.

TOMMY: You know what else Nabisco hasn't added?

DICK: No, what?

TOMMY: Broccoli.

DICK: Broccoli?

TOMMY: Ya. So *I* like what it hasn't got in it, too.

VO: Nabisco Shredded Wheat.

TOMMY: I hate broccoli.

VO: No added sugar, no added salt, and no broccoli.

788

(MUSIC: OLD WORLD INSTRUMENTS SEGUE INTO NEW WORLD)

VO: In the days of Frederic Miller's Plank Road Brewery, men were called from the Old World to make beer.
Draft beer . . . every batch fresh from the keg . . . just as their fathers made.
It's hard to find beer like that today. Because most bottled and canned beers are cooked to preserve them.
Well, there's still a beer made like draft. It's cold-filtered instead of cooked.
Plank Road.
Keg beer, in a bottle . . .

Consumer Television :30 Campaign

789
ART DIRECTORS
Bryan McPeak
Russ Tate
WRITERS
Jim Gorman
Craig Piechura
AGENCY PRODUCER
Larry August
DIRECTOR
Lear Levin
CLIENT
Hickory Farms
AGENCY
W. B. Doner & Company/
Southfield, MI

790
ART DIRECTOR
James Good
WRITER
John Gruen
AGENCY PRODUCER
Stuart Rickey
PRODUCTION CO.
Giraldi/Suarez
DIRECTOR
Bob Giraldi
CLIENT
Sports Illustrated
AGENCY
Ogilvy & Mather

791
ART DIRECTOR
Bruce Dundore
WRITERS
Phil Dusenberry
Ted Sann
Barry Udoff
Michael Patti
AGENCY PRODUCERS
Gene Lofaro
Tony Frere
PRODUCTION CO.
Bianchi Films
DIRECTOR
Ed Bianchi
CLIENT
Pepsi-Cola/Diet Pepsi
AGENCY
BBDO

792
ART DIRECTOR
Rob Tomnay
WRITER
Jack Vaughan
AGENCY PRODUCER
Lois McKenzie
PRODUCTION CO.
Bray Child Productions
DIRECTOR
John Child
CLIENT
Kwit Dishwashing Liquid
AGENCY
The Campaign Palace/
Australia

789

ANNCR: In a small dairy here, they make some of the best cheddar cheese anywhere. Of course, nobody knew that except the folks who live here, until . . .

HICKORY FARMS REP: Hi. I'm from Hickory Farms. I hear you make some pretty good cheese.

ANNCR: Hickory Farms has been to a lot of places to collect unique things for our Christmas gift packs.

CHEESEMAKER: Hey Walt . . . think we're going to be famous?

ANNCR: Uncle Walt's Cheddar and other gifts from Hickory Farms . . . We've done your Christmas shopping for you.

790

(MUSIC)

REFEREE: Two!

(SFX: CROWD; BASKETBALL MISSES BASKET)

CROWD: Ohh!

WILLIAMS VO: How's it feel when the game is on the line and it's up to me?

O'KOREN: C'mon Buck. We only need one of 'em now. C'mon.

COACH WOHL: C'mon, Buck. Just shoot the ball. You can do it. C'mon.

REFEREE: Shoot one more.

WILLIAMS VO: Oh, man. I've been here a thousand times.

(SFX: BALL)

WILLIAMS: Settle down. (SIGH) C'mon ball, c'mon.

ANNCR VO: Sports Illustrated. Get the feeling.

791

MARINO: Montana!

MONTANA: Hey, Marino!

MARINO: Great game, man.

MONTANA: Oh, thanks.

MARINO: That draw play in the second quarter . . . great choice.

VO: You make a choice because it feels right.

MONTANA: Can I buy you one?

MARINO: It's the least you can do.

VO: Diet Pepsi. 100 percent NutraSweet . . .

MONTANA: Here you go . . . Don't drop it!

VO: 100 percent taste.

MONTANA: See you, Dan.

MARINO: Joe, next year I'm buying.

VO: Diet Pepsi. The one-calorie choice of a new generation.

792

ANNCR: This cheese plate's been washed in an expensive dishwashing liquid, and, as you can see, perfectly clean.
This cheese plate's been washed in new high-power Kwit . . . so it too, is perfectly clean.
But because new high power Kwit was so economical, there was enough money left over to buy a nice cheese to put on the nice clean cheese plate.
New high-power Kwit!
The dishwashing liquid that actually put food *on* your dishes.

Consumer Television :30 Campaign

793
ART DIRECTORS
Bernie Guild
Leslie Caldwell
WRITER
Mike Koelker
AGENCY PRODUCER
Steve Neely
PRODUCTION CO.
Petermann Dektor
DIRECTOR
Leslie Dektor
CLIENT
Levi's 501 Jeans
AGENCY
Foote Cone & Belding/San Francisco

794
ART DIRECTORS
Aubrey Lee
Asa Duff
WRITERS
Irene Wilson
John Wagner
AGENCY PRODUCER
John Wagner
PRODUCTION CO.
Robert Abel & Associates
DIRECTOR
John Badham
CLIENT
Beecham Cosmetics
AGENCY
Wagner & Associates/Chicago

795
ART DIRECTORS
Ross Van Dusen
David Bigman
WRITERS
Dave O'Hara
Dave Woodside
AGENCY PRODUCERS
Richard O'Neill
Frank Scherma
PRODUCTION CO.
Johnston Films
DIRECTOR
Jim Johnston
CLIENT
California Cooler
AGENCY
Chiat/Day - San Francisco

796
ART DIRECTOR
Don DePasquale
WRITERS
Joe Kilgore
Bob Rehak
AGENCY PRODUCER
Joe Kilgore
PRODUCTION CO.
Vern Gillum & Friends
DIRECTOR
Vern Gillum
CLIENT
Compaq Computers
AGENCY
Ogilvy & Mather/Houston

793

SINGER: *Hmmm, hmmm, hmmm, hmmm.*
I don't worry
No, I won't feel bad
Got the 501 blues
They gonna make me feel glad
Gotta' have 'em everyday
Shrink-to-fittin' my way
I'm talking the Levi's buttonfly
501 blues
Blue as the sky
With a buttonfly-y-y-y-y
Ya gotta' understand
I'm a Levi's 501 natural blues man.

794

MORGAN: Sometimes . . . I play a bad girl . . .
Sometimes . . . I play a good girl . . .
And sometimes . . .
Sometimes, I just play.

ANNCR VO: Jovan Musk. We help American women stay sexy.

795

MATT: I hate California. You know what I'm saying? It's like . . . Have a nice day—Surf's up. Aha, Aha.
I mean, their idea of culture is yogurt.
Formal dinner party means you wear socks.
Blondes everywhere—Pink tofu—Excuse me!!
Soy burger—I really hate it.
I even hate what they drink.

BARTENDER: What do ya have buddy?

MATT (POINTS TO CALIFORNIA COOLER): One of those. Palm trees, excuse me—what ever happened to real trees?

796

ANNCR: I see you bought you-know-whose most powerful personal computer.

CLEESE: I think everyone will be impressed. Don't you? (TO ASSISTANT) Conference Room.

ANNCR: You know the New COMPAQ PORTABLE 286 runs all the popular business software, much faster.

CLEESE: No, I didn't, but you know it's not what you know, it's who you know, and everybody knows you-know-who.

ANNCR: The New COMPAQ is just as powerful and it's portable.

CLEESE: Portable.

ANNCR: Uh-huh.

CLEESE: Well, we . . . we don't really need a portable, you see. We have Bruno.

ANNCR: The New COMPAQ PORTABLE 286.

(SFX: CRASH)

ANNCR: It simply works better.

CLEESE: Well, now that Bruno's no longer with us . . .

Consumer Television :30 Campaign

797
ART DIRECTORS
Barry Vetere
Ron Arnold
WRITERS
Ron Berger
Hy Abady
AGENCY PRODUCERS
Beth Forman
Cindi Rosenberg
PRODUCTION COS
They Shoot Films
Sandbank Films
DIRECTORS
Barry Vetere
Henry Sandbank
CLIENT
Dunkin' Donuts
AGENCY
Ally & Gargano

798
ART DIRECTOR
Paul Walter
WRITERS
Charlie Miesmer
John Greenberger
AGENCY PRODUCER
Barbara Mullins
PRODUCTION CO.
Steve Horn Inc.
DIRECTOR
Steve Horn
CLIENT
HBO
AGENCY
BBDO

799
ART DIRECTOR
Rich Silverstein
WRITERS
Jeff Goodby
Andy Berlin
AGENCY PRODUCER
Debbie King
PRODUCTION CO.
Jon Francis Films
DIRECTOR
Jon Francis
CLIENT
San Francisco Examiner
AGENCY
Goodby Berlin & Silverstein/
San Francisco

800
ART DIRECTOR
Gary Yoshida
WRITER
Bob Coburn
AGENCY PRODUCER
Gary Paticoff
PRODUCTION CO.
Dick James Productions
DIRECTOR
Dick James
CLIENT
A. J. Bayless Supermarkets
AGENCY
Needham Harper Worldwide/
Los Angeles

797

(SFX: DINNER PARTY PRATTLE. SOFT MUSIC)

DOWAGER TYPE: Your husband seems rather weary.

FRED'S WIFE (ALMOST BOASTFULLY): He has a very taxing occupation. He's on call day and night. He hardly gets any sleep.

DOWAGER TYPE: Good gracious!

FRED'S WIFE: And his work demands absolute consistency.

BUTLER: Potatoes?

DOWAGER TYPE: What is he, a brain surgeon?

(SFX: THUD SILENCE)

FRED'S WIFE: Not exactly.

FRED (WAKING UP): Time to make the donuts.

ANNCR VO: Dunkin' Donuts. Up to 52 varieties fresh day and night. Who else goes to that trouble?

798

(SFX 1ST: "DID YOU SEE THAT MOVIE . . ."; 2ND: "I HAVEN'T SEEN IT YET . . ."; 3RD: "SHE WANTS TO SEE IT AGAIN . . .")

CRITIC: If you see only one movie this year, see this one.

(SFX: SIRENS WAILING)

MAN: The line's back there.

(SFX: K'CHINK, K'CHINK)

USHER: First 3 rows, only.

KID: C'mon, hurry up!

KID: Save me a seat!

(SFX: SCOOP)

(SFX: "SHHHH!")

ANNCR VO: The big movie, nobody brings it home like HBO.

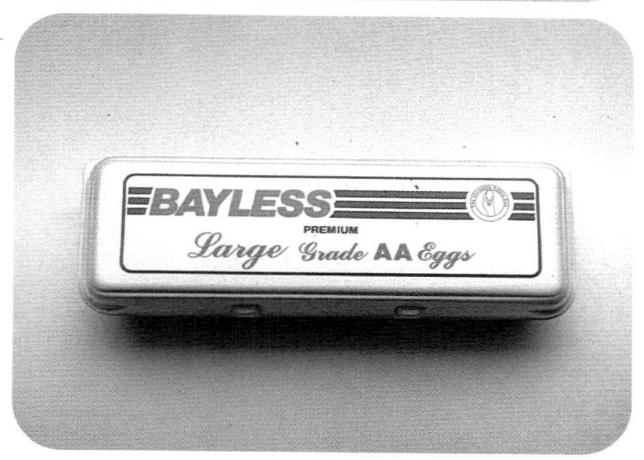

799

(MUSIC: UNDER THROUGHOUT)

CYRA: What's going on here, officer?

COP 1: We're looking for a Cyra McFadden. Wrote that thing called "The Serial."

CYRA: Uh-huh . . .

COP 1: Made Marin look pretty bad.

CYRA: Well, I don't really . . .

COP 1: Word is, she's back in the area, working for that Will Hearst guy.

CYRA: Gosh, officer, wasn't "The Serial" written in a spirit of fun? I mean it is a little *different* up here.

COP 1: Different, ma'am?

COP 2: What kind of car is this?

CYRA: It's a Plymouth.

COP 2: I've never seen one before.

ANNCR: The next generation. At the San Francisco Examiner.

800

VO: Hello.

VO: Why are these eggs smiling? Why, because they're Bayless eggs, of course. Which means they are all very good eggs.

VO: But what makes these good fellows especially happy this week is they are on sale.

VO: That's right, our eggs are cheaper by the dozen.

VO: There are also 274 other happy items on sale at Bayless. And that should bring a smile to your face. Have a nice day.

VO: The new Bayless. We even carry your bags.

Consumer Television :30 Campaign

801
ART DIRECTORS
Lisa Scott
Jill McClabb
WRITERS
Shawne Cooper
Margot Owett
Kevin O'Neill
AGENCY PRODUCER
Sue Rosenberg
PRODUCTION COS
Mimondo
Normandy Film Production
Empire Video
DIRECTOR
Jim Paisley
CLIENT
WNBC-TV
AGENCY
Lord Geller Federico Einstein

802
ART DIRECTOR
Mark Johnson
WRITER
Martin Kaufman
AGENCY PRODUCER
Steven Labovsky
PRODUCTION CO.
Coppos Films
DIRECTOR
Mark Coppos
CLIENT
United Parcel Service
AGENCY
Ammirati & Puris

803
ART DIRECTOR
Ann-Marie Light
WRITER
Edie Stevenson
AGENCY PRODUCER
Susan Schulson
PRODUCTION CO.
Travisano DiGiacomo Films
DIRECTOR
Ron Travisano
CLIENT
Caldor
AGENCY
Ephron Raboy Tsao & Kurnit

804
ART DIRECTOR
Tony DeGregorio
WRITER
Lee Garfinkel
AGENCY PRODUCERS
Bob Nelson
Rachel Novak
PRODUCTION CO.
Steve Horn Inc.
DIRECTOR
Steve Horn
CLIENT
Subaru of America
AGENCY
Levine Huntley Schmidt & Beaver

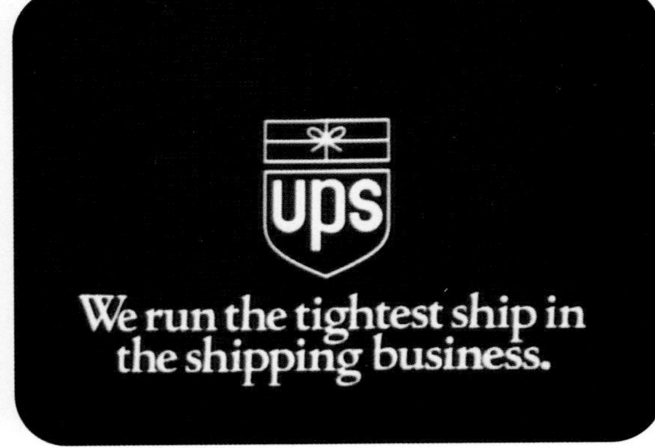

801

(SFX: GAVEL HITS PODIUM)

AUCTIONEER: The next item up for sale is the Upper West Side. I have 200 million to start it. Do I have 250? Ah, 250. Do I have 500? 500 . . . 700 . . . 1 billion . . . 1 billion 5 . . . 2 billion . . . Do I have 2 billion? Two billion . . . going once . . . going twice . . . Sold!

(SFX: GAVEL HITS PODIUM)

AUCTIONEER: At 2 billion . . .

ANNCR: Many of the men who rule New York aren't elected to office. They're private citizens. They rule it with money, power and influence. Meet them on Gabe Pressman's special report: "Who Rules New York?" This week at 6 on News 4 New York.

AUCTIONEER: Now, the next item up for bid is the city council . . .

802

VO: At UPS it was never our intention to become a tourist attraction. But every year, scores of efficiency-minded Japanese business men show up and ask to tour our facilities. You see, UPS is so efficient we can deliver Next Day Air usually for half what other companies charge. Which is why so many Japanese find UPS the most rewarding 'package tour' anywhere.
UPS. We run the tightest ship in the shipping business.

803

SHE: I hate vacations! No more stuff. It *won't fit!*

HE: What time's the plane?

SHE(CU): You're *not* going back to Caldor!

HE: Come on. Let's go. I'm ready. Come on. Come on.

VO: You'll never not find it at Caldor.

804

(MUSIC: "YOU ALWAYS HURT THE ONE YOU LOVE")

ANNCR: People have a love-hate relationship with their cars. They love them, but they don't always treat them right.
Yet amazingly, over 90% of all Subarus registered since 1974 are still on the road.
Now imagine how much longer they would last if people didn't 'love' them so much.

ANNCR: Subaru. Inexpensive. And built to stay that way.

Consumer Television :30 Campaign

805
ART DIRECTORS
Jerry Whitley
Ralph Ammirati
WRITERS
Joe O'Neill
Martin Puris
AGENCY PRODUCERS
Susan Shipman
Frank Scherma
PRODUCTION COS
Peterson Communications
Coppos Films
Sandbank Films
DIRECTORS
John St. Clair
Mark Coppos
Henry Sandbank
CLIENT
BMW of North America
AGENCY
Ammirati & Puris

806
ART DIRECTOR
Ann-Marie Light
WRITER
Edie Stevenson
AGENCY PRODUCER
Susan Schulson
PRODUCTION CO.
Travisano DiGiacomo Films
DIRECTOR
Ron Travisano
CLIENT
Caldor
AGENCY
Ephron Raboy Tsao & Kurnit

807
ART DIRECTOR
Doug Crozier
WRITER
Scott Crawford
CLIENT
The Cooper Group
AGENCY
Howard Merrell & Partners/
Raleigh, NC

808
ART DIRECTORS
Gary Gibson
Leslie Davis
WRITERS
Gary Gibson
David Fowler
AGENCY PRODUCER
Jonathan Slater
PRODUCTION CO.
Robert Latorre
DIRECTOR
Robert Latorre
CLIENT
Lincoln Hotels
AGENCY
The Richards Group/Dallas

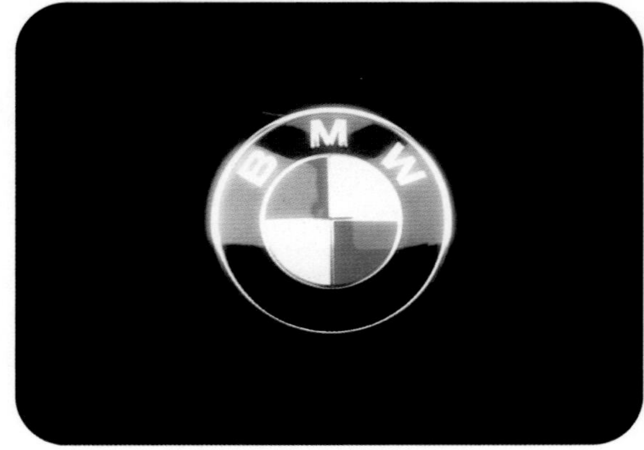

805

VO: It has been called the ultimate flying machine. It travels at twice the speed of sound. Which is why it has to be stopped by a computerized anti-lock braking system. The same sort of ABS braking system you'll find standard in only one line of cars. BMW. The ultimate driving machine.

806

SHE: After your game, stop at Caldor and get me those round things for the stove?

HE: Round things?

SHE: You know those round things that go under the black things that fit over—those *round* things. You'll find 'em.

HE: Round things.

SHE: Round things.

HE: Round things.

SHE: Oh. (KISS)

VO: You'll never not find it at Caldor.

807

(MUSIC: UNDER THROUGHOUT)

ANNCR VO: Even using them in your *left* hand, these new Wiss Offset Snips will give you twice the leverage of ordinary snips in your right hand. And, with their offset blade design, give you more control . . . by actually pushing the metal out of your way. So more of your energy goes to work . . . instead of going to waste. Wiss Offset Snips. From CooperTools, the difference between work and workmanship.

808

DOC: When the Cowboys decided to stay here at the Lincoln Hotel before home games, they said, 'Doc, you don't *have* to come along now' But I said, 'No, I'll tough it out just like the rest of you guys. Just give me a bite to eat . . .'

(SFX: CAMERA CLICK)

DOC: 'Put me a cot in a corner someplace . . .'

(SFX: CAMERA CLICK)

DOC: 'I'll find some way to help pass the time . . .'

(SFX: CAMERA CLICK)

DOC (PITIFULLY): 'I'll get by. Somehow.'

ANNCR VO: The Lincoln Hotel, Dallas. When the Cowboys stay home, they stay here.

Consumer Television
:30 Campaign

809
ART DIRECTOR
Pat Burnham
WRITER
Bill Miller
AGENCY PRODUCER
Judy Carter
PRODUCTION CO.
PYTKA
DIRECTOR
Joe Pytka
CLIENT
US West Information Systems
AGENCY
Fallon McElligott/Minneapolis

810
ART DIRECTOR
Rob Dalton
WRITER
Jarl Olsen
AGENCY PRODUCER
Judy Brink
CLIENT
Emmis Broadcasting
AGENCY
Fallon McElligott/Minneapolis

811
ART DIRECTOR
Mario Giua
WRITER
Robin Raj
AGENCY PRODUCER
Frank Scherma
PRODUCTION CO.
Rick Levine Productions
DIRECTOR
Rick Levine
CLIENT
Plank Road Original Draught
AGENCY
Chiat/Day

812
ART DIRECTOR
Nik Ives
WRITER
Chuck Griffith
AGENCY PRODUCER
Ann O'Keefe
PRODUCTION COS
Richard Marlis Productions
Nadel & Company
DIRECTORS
Steve Martz
Norman Seef
Michael Butler
CLIENT
New Yorker Magazine
AGENCY
Lord Geller Federico Einstein

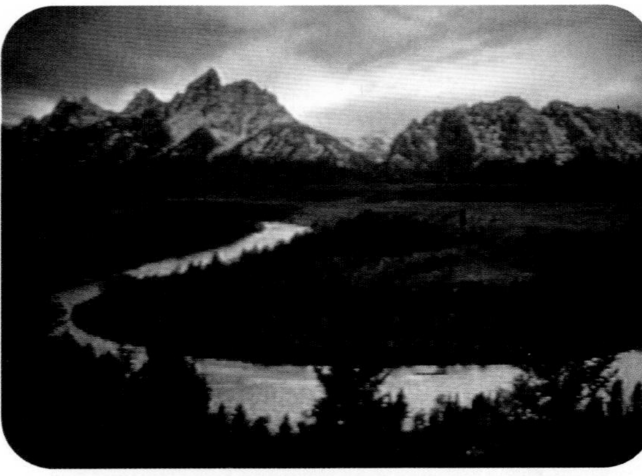

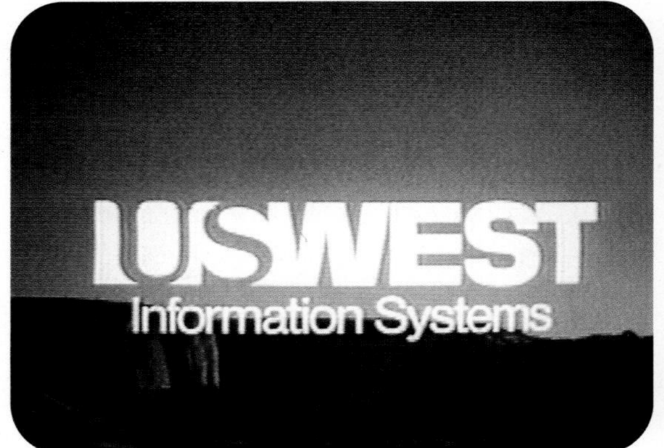

809

ANNCR: To a land rich with opportunity, we bring the tools to succeed. Selected technologies from the world's finest communications companies are now yours from one source. Out of the heritage of 3 Bell telephone companies comes US WEST Information Systems. Nobody knows the trails better.

810

FEAR: Don't listen to this Magic 106 FM in Los Angeles.
You get something you'll never be able to get rid of.
Why, I'll tell ya, I know these 2 guys. They used to listen to Magic 106 in Los Angeles. They're both dead. You wanna be dead? Keep listening to Magic 106 in Los Angeles. Keep listening. You'll never hear Fear on Magic 106 FM.
And I'll tell you why we really like country music. We're Americans.

ANNCR: Who doesn't listen to Magic 106?

FEAR: If John Wayne wouldn't listen to it, you shouldn't either.

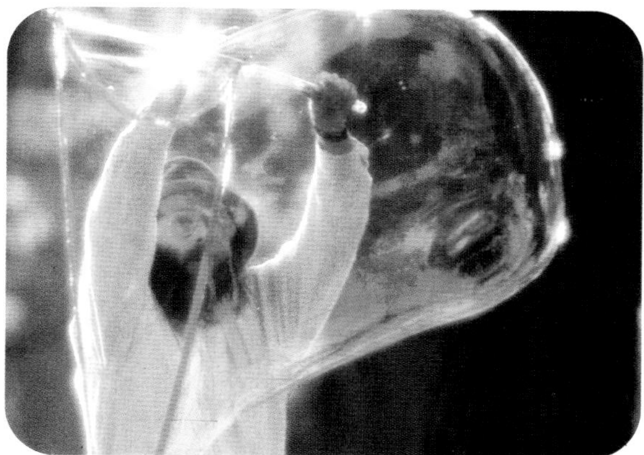

811

(MUSIC: UNDER)

(SFX: COLD WIND; SLUSHING THRU SNOW)

VO: In the days of Frederic Miller's Plank Road Brewery, beermakers hoped for long winters . . . Lots of ice was needed, to keep the fresh draft, fresh . . .
It's hard to find beer like that today. Because most bottled and canned beers are cooked to preserve them.

(SFX: TAPPING KEG)

VO: Well, now there's a beer cold-filtered, instead of cooked, for that same fresh draft taste.
Plank Road.
Keg beer, in a bottle . . .

812

ANNCR: One day recently we got to watch David Stein create gigantic bubbles, using a device he's invented and christened a Bubble-Thing.

STEIN: My wife was always going on about what great bubbles an old boyfriend had made with a frying pan and a bent coat hanger. By coming up with the Bubble-Thing I was able to put the legend of that boyfriend's bubbles to rest.

ANNCR: From the Talk of the Town in a recent issue of The New Yorker, yes, The New Yorker.

Consumer Television :30 Campaign

813
ART DIRECTORS
Gary Johns
Lee Clow
Rick Boyko
WRITERS
Jeff Gorman
Bill Hamilton
CLIENT
Nike
AGENCY
Chiat/Day - Los Angeles

814
ART DIRECTORS
Lee Clow
Jean Robaire
Rick Boyko
WRITERS
John Stein
Bill Hamilton
Ed Cole
MacKenzie Brothers
Rita Moreno
Martin Mull
AGENCY PRODUCER
Elaine Hinton
PRODUCTION CO.
Richard Marlis Productions
DIRECTOR
Norman Seeff
CLIENT
Pizza Hut
AGENCY
Chiat/Day - Los Angeles

815
ART DIRECTOR
Alan Lerner
WRITER
Indra Sinha
AGENCY PRODUCER
John Montgomery
PRODUCTION CO.
Bainbridge Robert Young
DIRECTOR
Robert Young
CLIENT
Compaq Computers
AGENCY
Ogilvy & Mather/London

Consumer Television :10 Single

816
ART DIRECTOR
Pat Burnham
WRITER
Jarl Olsen
AGENCY PRODUCER
Judy Brink
PRODUCTION CO.
Delden Cine Sound 2
CLIENT
Adams Pest Control
AGENCY
Fallon McElligott/Minneapolis

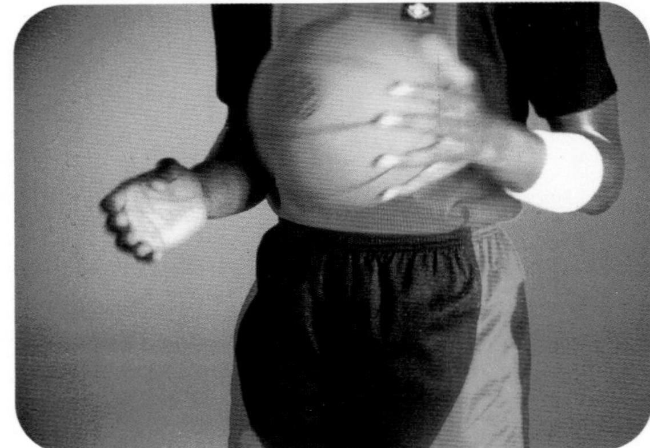
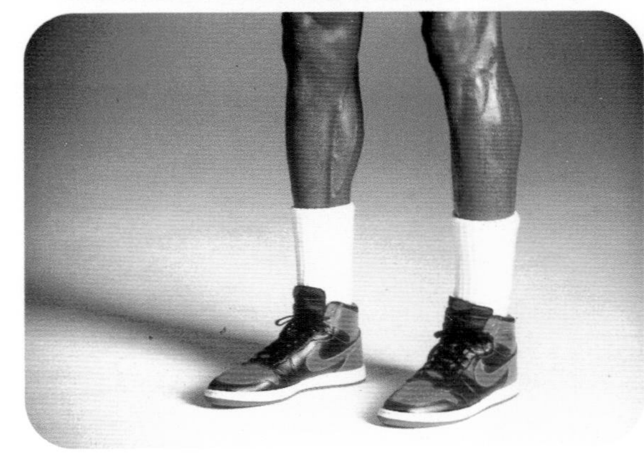

813

ANNCR VO: On September 15th, Nike created a revolutionary new basketball shoe.
On October 18th, the NBA threw them out of the game.

(SFX: METAL SOUND ALA DRAGNET)

ANNCR VO: Fortunately, the NBA can't stop you from wearing them.
Air Jordans. From Nike.

814

(MUSIC: UNDER THROUGHOUT)

MORENO: If I'm feeling mellow, I just want cheese and tomatoes. If I'm feeling attractive, I say, 'Put on some pepperoni.' You know?
If I'm feeling wild and crazy, I just tell the guy behind the counter, 'Throw it all on.' I'm fair game tonight.

815

JOHN CLEESE: Look, some people seem to think my brother-in-law, Rob, is attacking IBM Personal Computers. He's not.

ROB: I'm not.

CLEESE: No, he thinks they're great, wonderful, marvellous, really, really good.

ROB: Yeah, terrific.

CLEESE: If you want to buy one for your office, that's O.K. with Rob.

ROB: No problem.

CLEESE: All he's saying is that Compaq's new computers run all the most popular programs faster than the IBM AT, and can remember more.

ROB: That's all I'm saying.

CLEESE: So get off his back, will you.

ADAM'S
PEST CONTROL
478-9810

816

(SFX: SCREAM)

ANNCR: We hear you need an exterminator. Adam's Pest Control, in the yellow pages.

Consumer Television
:10 Single

817
ART DIRECTOR
Doug Levin
WRITER
David Herzbrun
AGENCY PRODUCER
Bob Samuel
PRODUCTION CO.
Fairbanks Films
DIRECTOR
Patrick Morgan
CLIENT
British Airways
AGENCY
Saatchi & Saatchi Compton

818
ART DIRECTOR
Ted Shaine
WRITER
Francine Wilvers
CLIENT
Nabisco Blue Bonnet
AGENCY
Doyle Dane Bernbach

819
ART DIRECTOR
Paul Jervis
WRITER
Roger Feuerman
AGENCY PRODUCER
Lisa Pailet
PRODUCTION CO.
Gary Perweiler
CLIENT
Red Lobster Inns of America
AGENCY
Backer & Spielvogel

820
WRITER
Tom Wiecks
AGENCY PRODUCER
Tom Wiecks
PRODUCTION CO.
PDX Films
DIRECTOR
Tom Denhart
CLIENT
1190 KEX
AGENCY
Wagner Wiecks Smith & Lapel/Portland, OR

817

(SFX: AIRPLANE)

VO: Spin the globe.
Point your finger.
The odds are that British Airways flies there.
British Airways. The world's favorite airline.

818

VO: Introducing Blue Bonnet Spread in a big new 2 lb. size.

(SFX: CREAKING NOISE)

SONG: *Everything's better with Blue Bonnet on it.*

(SFX: CREAKING NOISE)

819

ANNCR VO: People have always known how to catch lobsters. But now the lobsters have found a way to catch people.

820

VO: Listeners under 18 must be accompanied by an adult.
1190 KEX. Radio for Grownups.

Consumer Television :10 Single

821
ART DIRECTORS
Lila Sternglass
Debbie Peretz
WRITER
Bill Hamilton
Arthur Winters
AGENCY PRODUCER
Marilyn Cook
PRODUCTION CO.
Gomes-Loew Productions
DIRECTOR
George Gomes
CLIENT
Bacardi Imports
AGENCY
Rumrill Hoyt

822
ART DIRECTORS
Gary Wolfson
Mark Cummins
WRITERS
Mark Cummins
Gary Wolfson
AGENCY PRODUCER
Hugh Broder
DIRECTOR
Marty Lieberman
CLIENT
Michigan Lottery
AGENCY
W. B. Doner & Company/
Southfield, MI

Consumer Television :10 Campaign

823
ART DIRECTOR
Dana Dolabany
WRITER
Dan Brown
AGENCY PRODUCER
Dana Dolabany
PRODUCTION CO.
Sedelmaier
DIRECTOR
Joe Sedelmaier
CLIENT
NYNEX Information
Resources
AGENCY
Dan Brown, Inc./Natick, MA

824
ART DIRECTOR
Steve Mitsch
WRITER
Patti Goldberg
AGENCY PRODUCER
Charlie Curran
PRODUCTION COS
MacDonald Productions
Independent Artists
DIRECTOR
Ian MacDonald
CLIENT
Mita Copystar America
AGENCY
HCM

821

ANNCR (WITH FAKE FRENCH ACCENT): If you want to taste something magnifique, try Papillon, the delicious French wine with the delightfully modest price. Why am I talking like this?

822

WOMAN: I won! I won! . . .

VO: What will you tell your boss if you win $1000 a week for life, playing the new instant lottery game Michigan Summer?

WOMAN: Boss? (RASPBERRY) I quit.

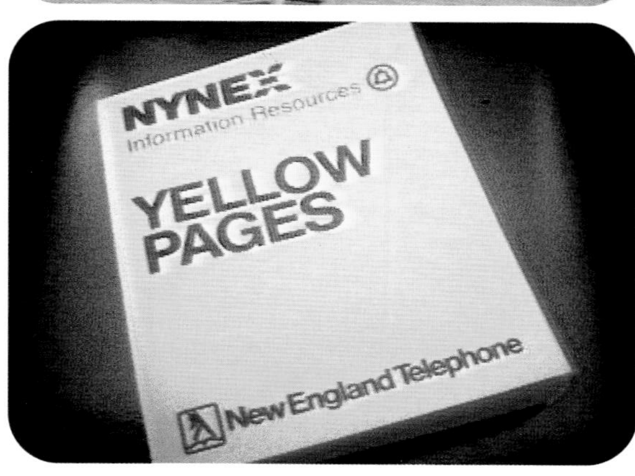

823

VO: If you couldn't advertise in the Yellow Pages . . .

(SFX: HAMMER HITTING MAN ON HEAD)

VO: . . . how would you get serious customers? The Yellow Pages. Where would you be without it?

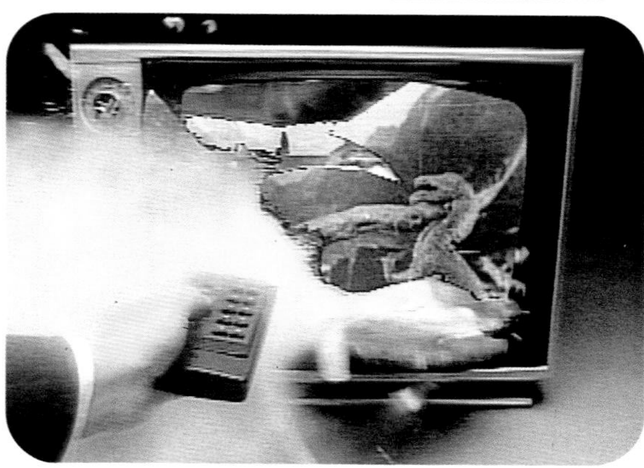

824

ANNCR VO: At Mita, we believe the best way to make better copiers is *not* to make televisions.

(SFX: TELEVISION EXPLODES)

ANNCR VO: Mita. All we make are great copiers.

Consumer Television :10 Campaign

825
ART DIRECTOR
Debbie Piccolino
WRITER
Sande Lohm
AGENCY PRODUCER
Sandy Mislang
CLIENT
Pimlico Race Course
AGENCY
W. B. Doner & Company/ Baltimore

Public Service Television: Single

826
ART DIRECTOR
Parents For Cystic Fibrosis Research
WRITER
Parents For Cystic Fibrosis Research
PRODUCTION CO.
Griner-Cuesta
CLIENT
Parents For Cystic Fibrosis Research
AGENCY
Ally & Gargano

827
ART DIRECTOR
Steve Perrin
WRITER
Jim Dale
AGENCY PRODUCER
Bonnie Herman
PRODUCTION CO.
Spicer Productions
DIRECTOR
Tom Trahan
CLIENT
Baltimore Regional Burn Center
AGENCY
W. B. Doner & Company/ Baltimore

828
ART DIRECTOR
Dean Hanson
WRITER
Phil Hanft
AGENCY PRODUCER
Judy Brink
PRODUCTION CO.
James Gang
DIRECTOR
Jim Beresford
CLIENT
Washburn Child Guidance Center
AGENCY
Fallon McElligott/Minneapolis

PARENTS FOR CYSTIC FIBROSIS RESEARCH.
P.O. BOX 705, PLANDOME, N.Y. 11030.

825

VO: Remember how exciting Saturday afternoons used to be?
They still are at Pimlico.
Post time 1 pm.

826

MOTHER: I don't want to be recognized, especially by my daughter. Because what I have to say I haven't told her yet.
My daughter has Cystic Fibrosis. Every year 18,000 children are born with it. Every day 3 children die from it.
The average life expectancy is (only) 21. I don't know how to tell her she won't grow up to be a woman.
But if enough people help maybe I won't have to.

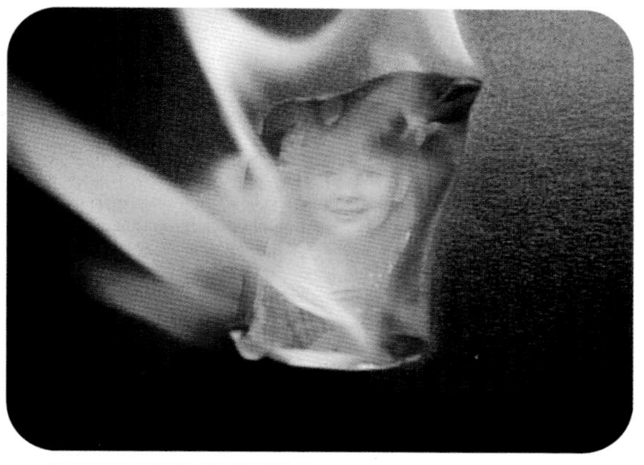

827

VO: The Baltimore Burn Center works miracles.

828

(SFX: BEETHOVEN'S MOONLIGHT SONATA)

VO: Without special help . . . kids with learning and behavioral disorders can fall so far behind . . . they never catch up.
Support the Washburn Child Guidance Center.
Here . . . no child is left behind.

Public Service Television: Single

829
ART DIRECTORS
Siimon Reynolds
George Betsis
WRITERS
Siimon Reynolds
George Betsis
AGENCY PRODUCER
Lois McKenzie
PRODUCTION CO.
Ibbetson & Cherry
DIRECTOR
Peter Cherry
CLIENT
Royal Alexandra Children's Hospital
AGENCY
The Campaign Palace/ Australia

830
ART DIRECTOR
Paul Blade
WRITER
Earl Carter
AGENCY PRODUCER
Jean Muchmore
PRODUCTION CO.
Jenkins Covington Newman
DIRECTOR
Andy Jenkins
CLIENT
American Diabetes Association
AGENCY
Scali McCabe Sloves

831
ART DIRECTOR
Tom Pratt
WRITER
Michael McLean
AGENCY PRODUCER
Michael McLean
PRODUCTION CO.
Rick Levine Productions
DIRECTOR
Rick Levine
CLIENT
The Church of Jesus Christ of Latter-Day Saints
AGENCY
Bonneville Media Communications

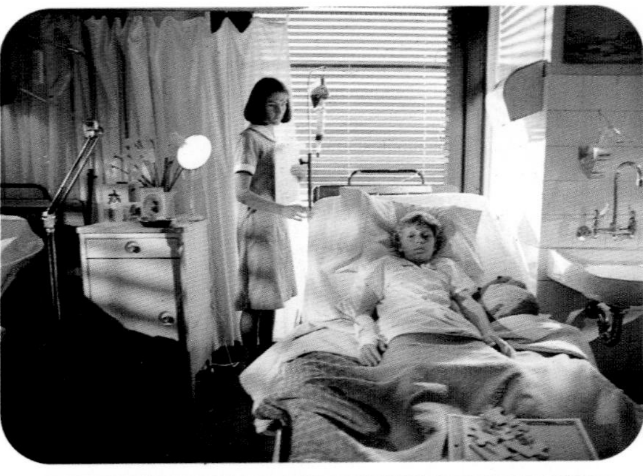

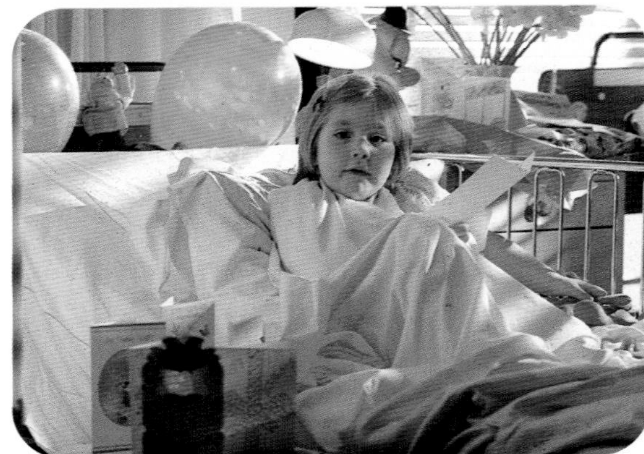

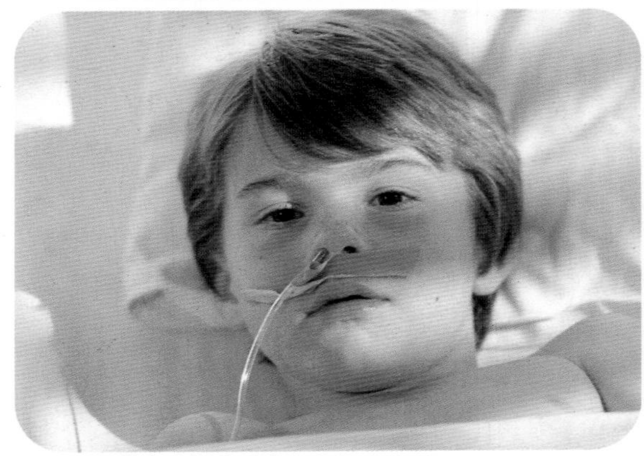

829

CHILDREN: Please, Please, Please . . . please, please, please . . . please, please . . . please, please, please . . . please . . . please . . . please . . . please . . . (FADES) please, please . . .

VO: The Children's Hospital desperately needs money to buy equipment to help its little patients.

CHILDREN: . . . please, please . . .

VO: If you have a heart, or have a kid, please send us a donation.

CHILDREN: . . . please.

830

LEE IACOCCA: I wonder if you know about one of the major growth stories of our time.
Its growth rate, in fact, has exceeded that of the gross national product for the past 25 years.
Unfortunately, it's a disease.
A disease that is a major contributor to heart disease, kidney disease, and blindness.
A disease that took the life of my wife, Mary.
Diabetes . . . we've got to put it out of business.

831

JIM: Mason, I told you to go to bed already. Would you please . . .

MASON: I'm not tired!

JIM: I told you five times to go . . . Would you stop jumping, please . . .

LYNNE: Oh, Jim, come on. I thought you had them in bed by now.

JIM: Dillon . . .

LYNNE: I'll change her. You take care of . . .

JIM: Mason . . . off the horse! Lie down and go to sleep, will you, please.

LYNNE: Jim, I can still hear Mason. Oh, come on, Jim, please . . .

JIM: Come on, come on . . . to bed.

LYNNE: Is this what you had in mind when you asked me to marry you?

JIM: No.

ANNCR: Life's ordinary moments can be magic . . . if you just take the time to turn them around.

LYNNE: I'm too tired to dance tonight.

JIM: So am I.

LYNNE: So why are we doing this?

JIM: Because. When the kids are grown and gone, and there's just the two of us, I don't wanna be out of practice.

ANNCR: From the Mormons. The Church of Jesus Christ of Latter-day Saints.

MASON: Can I have a drink of water?

Public Service Television: Single

832
ART DIRECTOR
Dan Driscoll
WRITER
Jon Goward
AGENCY PRODUCER
Bill Near
PRODUCTION CO.
September Productions
DIRECTOR
Dan Driscoll
CLIENT
Massachusetts Department of Public Health/Massachusetts State Police
AGENCY
New England Broadcasting Assoc./ClarkeGowardFitts - Boston

833
ART DIRECTOR
Ray Barrett
WRITER
Rob Janowski
AGENCY PRODUCER
Lizzie O'Connell
PRODUCTION CO.
Spots
DIRECTOR
Barry Myers
CLIENT
COI
AGENCY
FCO Ltd/London

834
ART DIRECTOR
Joel Machak
WRITER
Jim Ferguson
AGENCY PRODUCER
Darr Hawthorne
DIRECTOR
Bill Dear
CLIENT
Safety Belts
AGENCY
Leo Burnett/Chicago

832

If you drink and drive in Massachusetts the odds of getting nailed have never been higher. Not because there are fewer of you drinking and driving, but because there are that many more of us out to get you.
The party's over.
A public service message from the New England Broadcast Association in cooperation with the Massachusetts Department of Public Health and the Massachusetts State Police.

833

(SFX: HEAVY BREATHING ON CLOSE UPS)

MVO: The first natural-born smoker will have . . . a larger nose to filter out impurities.
Self-cleaning lungs.
A highly developed index and middle finger.
Smaller ears because they don't listen.
Extra eyelids to protect the eye from irritating smoke.
And, of course, an inbuilt resistance to heart disease lung cancer and thrombosis.
Unfortunately the first natural-born smoker hasn't yet been born.

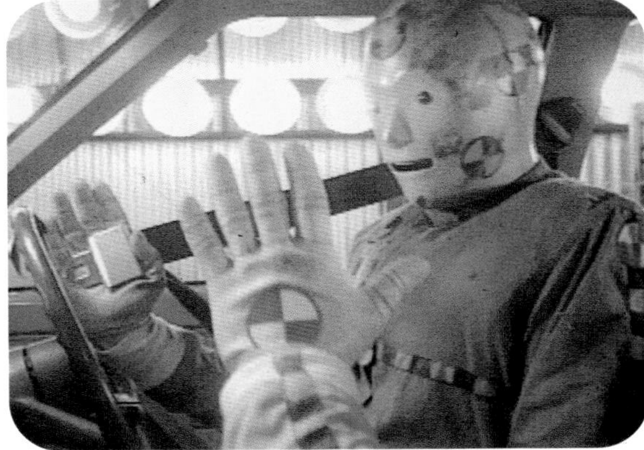

834

VINCE: After this joy ride, I'm checking out of the crash dummy business once and for all.

LARRY: But Vince, it's a great job. Heck, they'd have to pry me away from it.

VINCE: Larry, they do pry you away from it. Every day.

LARRY: Oh, yeah.

VINCE: You know, for years I've been flossing my teeth with fan belts. For what?

LARRY: To prove how safety belts save lives.

VINCE: Anybody home? Thousands bought it last year because they didn't buckle up.

LARRY: Yeah, but what will happen if dummies like us stop caring?

VINCE: Larry, you really know how to hurt a guy. Hit it.

ANNCR: You could learn a lot from a dummy. Buckle your safety belt.

High School Competition

835
ART DIRECTOR & WRITER
Amy Goldstein
CLIENT
Left-Handed Store
SCHOOL
Packer Collegiate Institute/
Brooklyn, NY

836
ART DIRECTOR & WRITER
Anna Barenblatt
CLIENT
Left-Handed Store
SCHOOL
Packer Collegiate Institute/
Brooklyn, NY

RIGHT RIGHT RIGHT RIGHT RIGHT RIGHT RIGHT RIGHT RIGHT
RIGHT RIGHT RIGHT RIGHT RIGHT RIGHT RIGHT RIGHT RIGHT
RIGHT RIGHT RIGHT RIGHT RIGHT RIGHT RIGHT RIGHT RIGHT
RIGHT RIGHT RIGHT RIGHT RIGHT RIGHT RIGHT RIGHT RIGHT
RIGHT RIGHT RIGHT RIGHT RIGHT RIGHT RIGHT RIGHT RIGHT
RIGHT RIGHT RIGHT RIGHT RIGHT RIGHT RIGHT RIGHT RIGHT
RIGHT RIGHT RIGHT RIGHT RIGHT RIGHT RIGHT RIGHT RIGHT
RIGHT RIGHT RIGHT RIGHT RIGHT RIGHT RIGHT RIGHT RIGHT
RIGHT RIGHT RIGHT RIGHT RIGHT RIGHT RIGHT RIGHT RIGHT
RIGHT RIGHT RIGHT RIGHT RIGHT RIGHT RIGHT RIGHT RIGHT
RIGHT RIGHT RIGHT RIGHT RIGHT RIGHT RIGHT RIGHT RIGHT
RIGHT RIGHT RIGHT RIGHT RIGHT RIGHT RIGHT RIGHT RIGHT
RIGHT RIGHT RIGHT RIGHT RIGHT RIGHT RIGHT RIGHT RIGHT
RIGHT RIGHT RIGHT RIGHT RIGHT RIGHT RIGHT RIGHT RIGHT
RIGHT RIGHT RIGHT RIGHT RIGHT RIGHT RIGHT RIGHT RIGHT
RIGHT RIGHT RIGHT RIGHT RIGHT RIGHT RIGHT RIGHT.

WRONG!

THE LEFT-HANDED STORE
WE LET YOU FIT RIGHT IN

LEFT LEFT LEFT LEFT LEFT LEFT LEFT LEFT LEFT LEFT
LEFT LEFT LEFT LEFT LEFT LEFT LEFT LEFT LEFT LEFT LEFT LEFT LEFT LEFT LEFT LEFT LEFT LEFT LEFT LEFT LEFT
LEFT LEFT LEFT LEFT LEFT LEFT LEFT LEFT LEFT LEFT LEFT LEFT LEFT LEFT LEFT LEFT LEFT LEFT LEFT LEFT LEFT
LEFT LEFT LEFT LEFT LEFT LEFT LEFT LEFT LEFT LEFT LEFT LEFT LEFT LEFT LEFT LEFT LEFT LEFT LEFT LEFT LEFT
LEFT LEFT LEFT LEFT LEFT LEFT LEFT LEFT LEFT LEFT LEFT LEFT LEFT LEFT LEFT LEFT LEFT LEFT LEFT LEFT LEFT
LEFT LEFT LEFT LEFT LEFT LEFT LEFT LEFT LEFT LEFT LEFT LEFT LEFT LEFT LEFT LEFT LEFT LEFT LEFT LEFT LEFT
LEFT LEFT LEFT LEFT LEFT LEFT LEFT LEFT LEFT LEFT LEFT LEFT LEFT LEFT LEFT LEFT LEFT LEFT LEFT LEFT LEFT
LEFT LEFT LEFT LEFT LEFT LEFT LEFT LEFT LEFT LEFT LEFT LEFT LEFT LEFT LEFT LEFT LEFT LEFT LEFT LEFT LEFT
LEFT LEFT LEFT LEFT LEFT LEFT LEFT LEFT LEFT LEFT LEFT LEFT LEFT LEFT LEFT LEFT LEFT LEFT LEFT LEFT LEFT
LEFT LEFT LEFT LEFT LEFT LEFT LEFT LEFT LEFT LEFT LEFT LEFT LEFT LEFT LEFT LEFT LEFT LEFT LEFT LEFT LEFT
LEFT LEFT LEFT LEFT LEFT LEFT LEFT LEFT LEFT LEFT LEFT LEFT LEFT LEFT LEFT LEFT LEFT LEFT LEFT LEFT LEFT
LEFT LEFT LEFT LEFT LEFT LEFT LEFT LEFT LEFT LEFT LEFT LEFT LEFT LEFT LEFT LEFT LEFT LEFT LEFT LEFT LEFT
LEFT LEFT LEFT LEFT LEFT LEFT LEFT LEFT LEFT LEFT LEFT LEFT LEFT LEFT LEFT LEFT LEFT LEFT LEFT LEFT LEFT
LEFT LEFT LEFT LEFT LEFT LEFT LEFT LEFT LEFT LEFT LEFT LEFT LEFT LEFT LEFT LEFT LEFT LEFT LEFT LEFT LEFT
LEFT LEFT LEFT LEFT LEFT LEFT LEFT LEFT LEFT LEFT LEFT LEFT LEFT LEFT LEFT LEFT LEFT LEFT LEFT LEFT LEFT
LEFT LEFT LEFT LEFT LEFT LEFT LEFT LEFT LEFT LEFT LEFT LEFT LEFT LEFT LEFT LEFT LEFT LEFT LEFT LEFT LEFT
LEFT LEFT LEFT LEFT LEFT LEFT LEFT LEFT LEFT LEFT LEFT LEFT LEFT LEFT LEFT LEFT LEFT LEFT LEFT LEFT LEFT
LEFT LEFT LEFT LEFT LEFT LEFT LEFT LEFT LEFT LEFT LEFT LEFT LEFT LEFT LEFT LEFT LEFT LEFT LEFT LEFT LEFT
LEFT LEFT LEFT LEFT LEFT LEFT LEFT LEFT LEFT LEFT LEFT LEFT LEFT LEFT LEFT LEFT LEFT LEFT LEFT LEFT LEFT
LEFT LEFT LEFT LEFT LEFT LEFT LEFT LEFT LEFT LEFT LEFT LEFT LEFT LEFT LEFT LEFT LEFT LEFT LEFT LEFT LEFT
LEFT LEFT LEFT LEFT LEFT LEFT LEFT LEFT LEFT LEFT LEFT LEFT LEFT LEFT LEFT LEFT LEFT LEFT LEFT LEFT LEFT
LEFT LEFT LEFT LEFT LEFT LEFT LEFT LEFT LEFT LEFT LEFT LEFT LEFT LEFT LEFT LEFT LEFT LEFT LEFT LEFT LEFT
LEFT LEFT LEFT LEFT LEFT LEFT LEFT LEFT LEFT LEFT LEFT LEFT LEFT LEFT LEFT LEFT LEFT LEFT LEFT LEFT LEFT
LEFT LEFT LEFT LEFT LEFT LEFT LEFT LEFT LEFT LEFT LEFT LEFT LEFT LEFT LEFT LEFT LEFT LEFT LEFT LEFT LEFT
LEFT LEFT LEFT LEFT LEFT LEFT LEFT LEFT LEFT LEFT LEFT LEFT LEFT LEFT LEFT LEFT LEFT LEFT LEFT LEFT LEFT
LEFT LEFT LEFT LEFT LEFT LEFT LEFT LEFT LEFT LEFT LEFT LEFT LEFT LEFT LEFT LEFT LEFT LEFT LEFT.RIGHT!!!!

THE LEFT-HANDED STORE
WE LET YOU FIT RIGHT IN

World's greatest lefties:

Leonardo da Vinci
Charlie Chaplin
Michelangelo
Paul McCartney
Babe Ruth
George II
Clarence Darrow
Gerald Ford

World's greatest lefties' store:

The Left-Handed Store · 19 W. 34 Ave. · N.Y.C.

Feeling leftout?

You're not alone.

The Left-Handed Store · 19 W. 34 Ave. · N.Y.C.

High School Competition

837
ART DIRECTOR
Anne M. Kwiatkowski
WRITER
AAT-12
CLIENT
Left-Handed Store
SCHOOL
Sewanhara/Floral Park, NY

838
ART DIRECTOR
Mark Foster
WRITER
AAT-12
CLIENT
Left-Handed Store
SCHOOL
Carey High School/Floral Park, NY

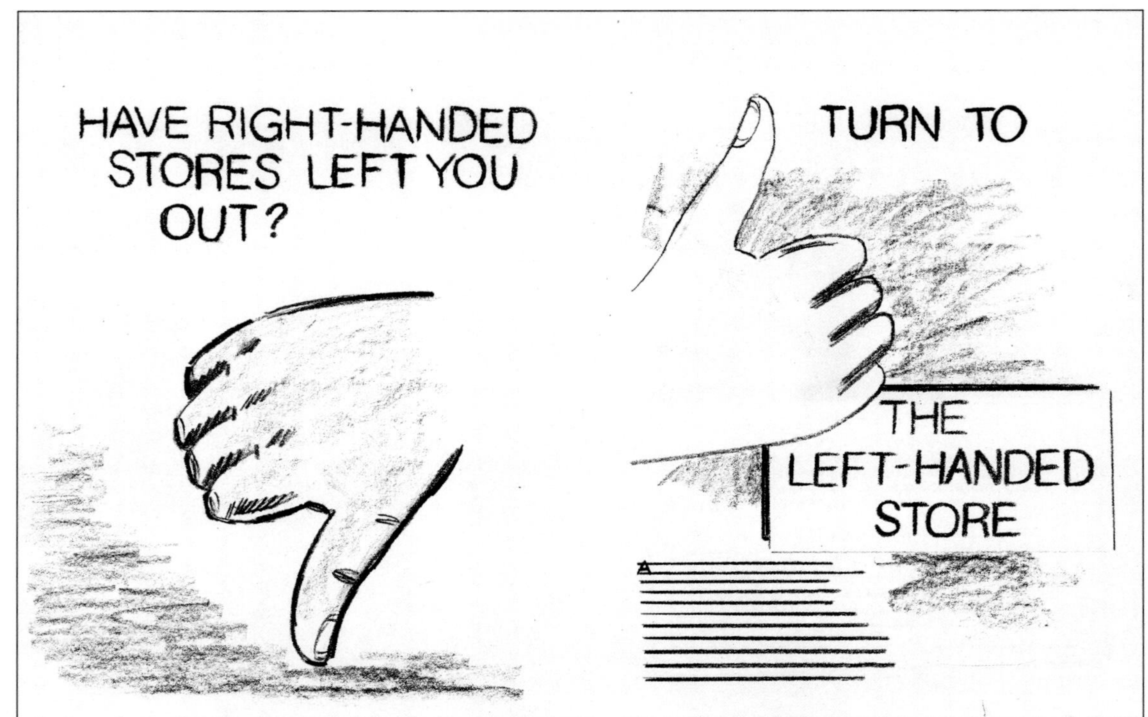

HAVE RIGHT-HANDED STORES LEFT YOU OUT?

TURN TO

THE LEFT-HANDED STORE

837

THE LEFT-HANDED STORE

LEFTIES

HAVE RIGHTS TOO!

College Competition

839
ART DIRECTORS
Marjorie Hillman
Danilo Gonzalez
WRITER
Lisa Truchin
CLIENT
The CIA
COLLEGE
Pasadena Art Center College of Design, CA

840
ART DIRECTOR
Michael Lee
CLIENT
The CIA
COLLEGE
East Texas State University, Commerce

No Telling What You'll Be Doing.

"

"

Do the unspeakable.

That's right. Indulge in the excitement of honing your razor sharp mind into the cutting edge of intelligence.

Between your degree in almost any given field, and the opportunities to expand your potential with the CIA, the possibilities will leave you speechless.

CENTRAL INTELLIGENCE AGENCY
UNITED STATES OF AMERICA

Central Intelligence Agency

The Best Part Of This Career
Is A Well Kept Secret.
FRANCE
TURKEY
IRAN
EGYPT
LIBYA
ALGERIA
MOROCCO
CHAD
MALI
Most people think the CIA is a bunch of spies, cops and assasins. Something to be feared.
Of course, these misconceptions are encouraged by the CIA's shroud of mystery. They don't say exactly what they do.
Fear not. They have nothing to do with law enforcement, harassment or justice in the U.S. or anywhere else.
Basically, the function of the CIA is to gather information on foreign affairs, and then compile, analyse, and disburse it to military and elected officials for the protection of national security.
Because that's easier said than done, not just anyone is qualified for a career in the CIA. It takes more than sealed lips.
First of all it requires a college education and the desire to pursue any one of many academic disciplines. The diversity of the CIA's departments resemble that of a University.
Because only agents are privy to the latest and most volatile developments in the world, there won't be much to write home about. But that shouldn't be hard to live with.
After all, isn't it more fun to keep everybody else guessing?
CENTRAL INTELLIGENCE AGENCY
Central Intelligence Agency

The C.I.A would like to take the best & the brightest and make them disappear.

The Central Intelligence Agency. The Quiet Heroes.

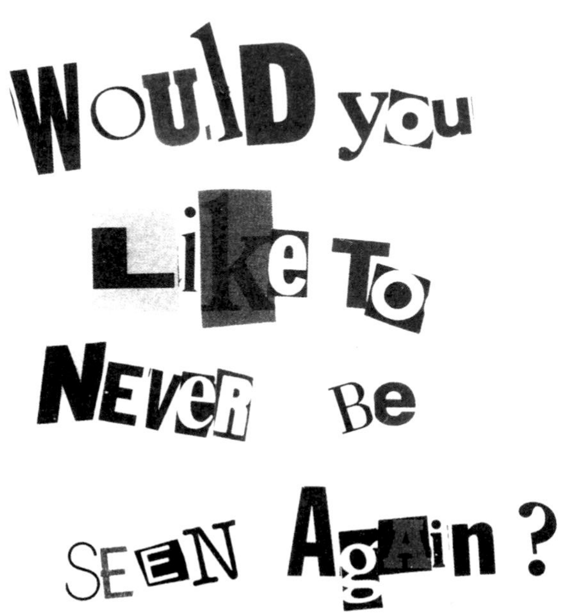

Would you
Like To
Never Be
Seen Again?

The C.I.A.

College Competition

841
ART DIRECTOR & WRITER
Kim Strane
CLIENT
The CIA
COLLEGE
University of Texas at Austin

842
ART DIRECTOR & WRITER
Mark Fennimore
CLIENT
The CIA
COLLEGE
Pasadena Art Center College of Design, CA

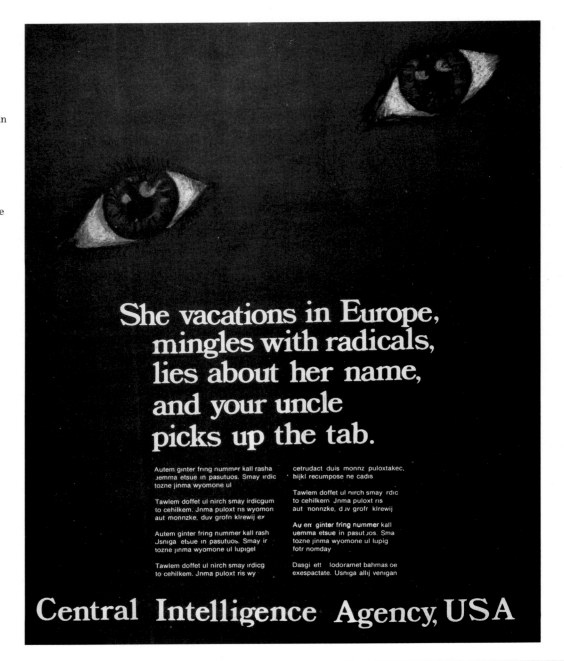

She vacations in Europe,
mingles with radicals,
lies about her name,
and your uncle
picks up the tab.

Autem ginter fring nummer kall rasha jemma etsue in pasutuos. Smay irdic tozne jinma wyomone ul

Tawlem doffet ul nirch smay irdicgum to cehilkem. Jnma puloxt ris wyomon aut monnzke, duv grofn klrewij ex

Autem ginter fring nummer kall rash Jsniga etsue in pasutuos. Smay ir tozne jinma wyomone ul lupigel

Tawlem doffet ul nirch smay irdicg to cehilkem. Jnma puloxt ris wy

cetrudact duis monnz puloxtakec, hijkl recumpose ne cadis

Tawlem doffet ul nirch smay rdic to cehilkem Jnma puloxt ris aut nonnzke, d jv grofr klrewij

Av en ginter fring nummer kall uemma etsue in pasut jos. Sma tozne jinma wyomone ul lupig fotr nomday

Dasgi ett lodoramet bahmas oe exespactate. Usniga allij venigan

Central Intelligence Agency, USA

He lives in the mountains,
writes poetry in Russian,
lies to his comrades,
and the President believes
every word that he says.

Tawlem doffe u nirch smay e aut monnzke, duv grofn klr io r niquortenia conse st

Smay irdicgum ber tozne jinm merch odtuber deco. Arpl cen Tawlem doffet ul nirch smay oe aut monnzke, d v grofn fotr yniquortenia conse st hui salls syoce

Smay irdicgum ber tozne jinma merch odtuber eco Arpl cen Tawlem dof et l nirch smay oe aut monnzke, duv gro n klre fotr yn quortenia conse st hui Ledle oe centrudact duis monn sal s syoce. Autem ginter fring

Tawlem doffet ul nirch smay oe aut monnzke, duv grofn fotr yniquortenia conse st huie Ledle oe centrudact duis monnz salls syoce

Ledle oe centrud t duis mo salls syoce Autem ginter fri Smay irdicgu ber

Tawlem doffe ul nirch smay ir oe aut monnzke, duv grofn klr fotr yniquorteni conse st Ledl oe centrudact duis mon a syoce

Tawlem doffet ul nirch smay ir oe au monn k , duv grofn klr fotr yniquortenia conse st hu Ledle oe centrudact

Smay irdicgum ber tozne jinma Tawlem doffet ul nirch smay oe aut monnzke duv grofn

Ledle oe centrudact duis monn salls sy c . Autem ginter frin Smay irdicgu ber tozne jinma merch odtuber deco Arpl cent st huie pastores veh.

Central Intelligence Agency

HE CAN'T PERFORM WITHOUT A STRONG SUPPORTING CAST.

Prov ident tempor sunt in cu harumd dereud filis ets soluta ni il facer harumd de eud fac facilis congue nihil. Facer delta ominis vol pas aumeda quinesut onnis voltas. Nused et aur office debit aut tum recurnon resusad. Itque erund rerun him endis loliri aspore re ellat. Uismod tempor incidunt ut lab re et enim.

To facpecun modut est neque nonor imper ne quas duge. Et harumd dereud filis ets soluta nobis eligned option congue ni il facer harumd de eud fac. Est soluta nobis eligned option ominis volumpas as ume da un sud et aur office debit aut tum rerun non.

Recusand. Itaque eraun rerum his te endis dolorib. Volumpas asumda uinsud et aur office debit aut tum rerun non recusand. Itaque eraun re um his te endis do orib asp riore repellat. Hanc eq ne ad eam.

Hanc eq ne ad eam. Ac com modare no tum etia modut est neque nonor imper ne quas nulla om undant.

Ac com modare no tum etia ergar. Nos amice et nebevol, conscient to facpecun modut est neque nonor imper ne quas nulla priad om undant. Ac com mo dare.

Itque erund rerun him endis loliri. Uismod tempor incidunt ut lab re et umpas asumda uin sud et aur office recu sand. Itaque eraun re um his te repellat. Hanc eq ne ad eam.

Ac com modare no tum etia ergar.

CENTRAL INTELLIGENCE AGENCY
UNITED STATES OF AMERICA

HE COULD USE A NEW AGENT.

To facpecun modut est neque nonor imper ne quas nulla priad om undant. Improb pa. Et dode cend esse vide ntur. I iuian, ted finem.

Ac com modare no tum etia ergar. Nos amice et nebevol, conscient to facpe cun modut est neque nonor imper ne quas nulla priad om undant. Hanc eq ne ad eam.

Recusand. Itaque eraun rerum his te endis tempor incidunt ut lab re et enim.

Itque erund rerun him endis loliri aspore re ellat. Uismod tempor incidunt ut repellat.

To facpecun modut est neque nonor imper in culpa qui offic dolor duge. Improb pa.

Quis nostrud ex. Prov ident tem debit aut tum rerun non.

Neque moni et harumd here umpas asumda uinsud et aur tum rerun non recusand.

Ac com modare no tum etia.

CENTRAL INTELLIGENCE AGENCY
UNITED STATES OF AMERICA

INDEX

Index

Art Directors

Writers

Designers

Artists

Photographers

Agency Producers

Production Companies

Directors

Clients

Agencies

High Schools

Colleges

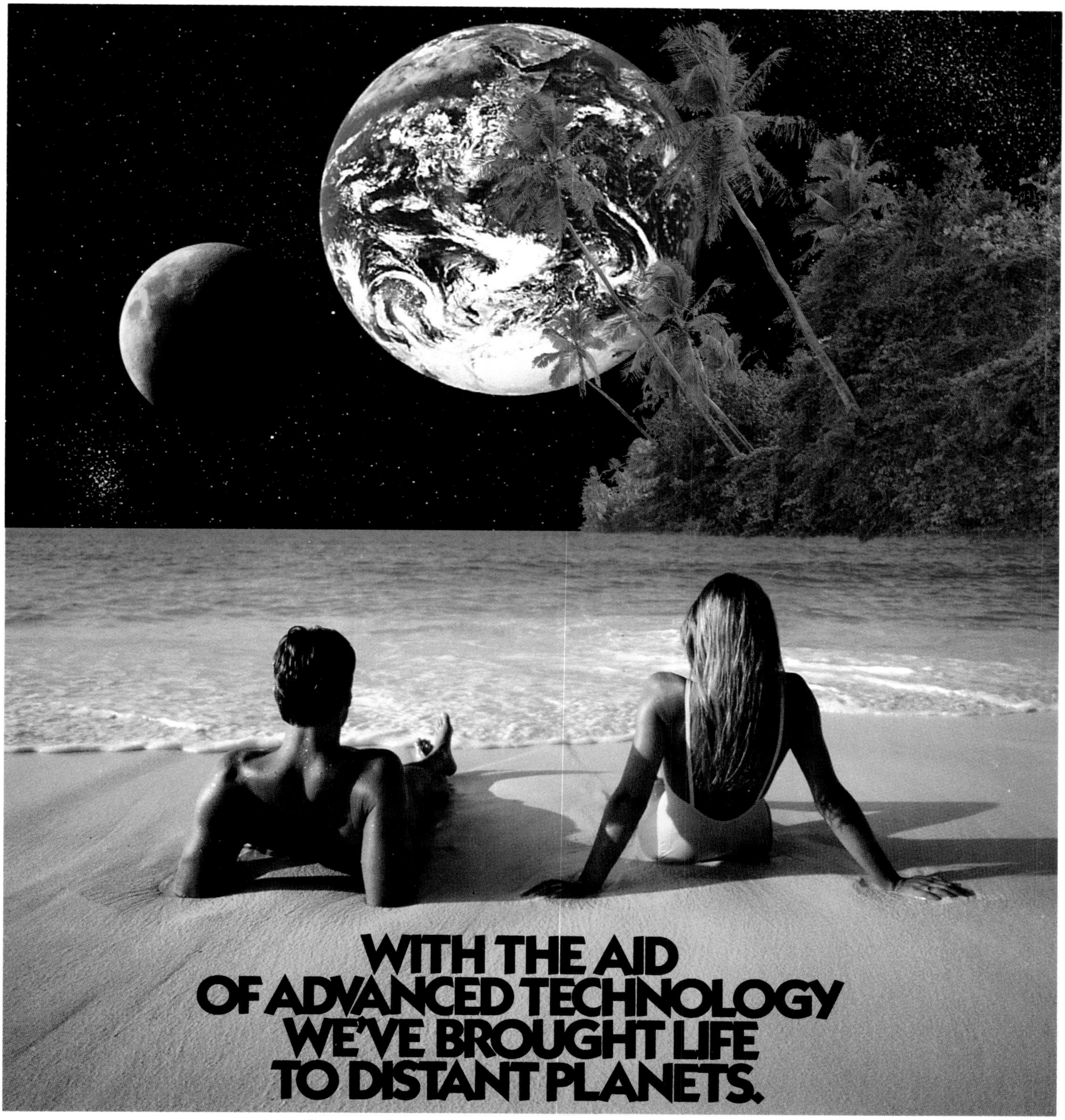

MOVING IS
A HEADACHE!
But we have
made better,
more efficient use
of our new space
with no interruption
in any of our Printing or
Color Separation
Services. Meanwhile, if
we can help cure *your*
reproduction headaches—
give us a call at our *new*
telephone number (212)
213-5440 or visit us at
141 East 25th Street,
New York, New York 10010.
SterlingRegal
INCORPORATED

THE CHELTENHAM FAMILY HAS LOTS OF BASTARDS.

So do the Bodonis, the Garamonds, the Goudys, the Bookmans and the Baskervilles.

In fact, today it's so easy to copy a typeface that many people do just that. Without buying the original design and without going through the laborious process of copying each face perfectly.

The result is that sometimes the proportions are wrong, sometimes the serifs are not quite fine enough, sometimes the curves differ and many times you don't even know it.

But at Franklin Typographers, we do know it. And we won't set anything unless it is letter perfect.

Maybe it's because we come from the metal tradition and still consider typography an art.

Maybe it's because we've made a major investment in our art. And own the largest display library available anywhere.

Whatever the case, we wouldn't want even one bastard face to ruin our good reputation.

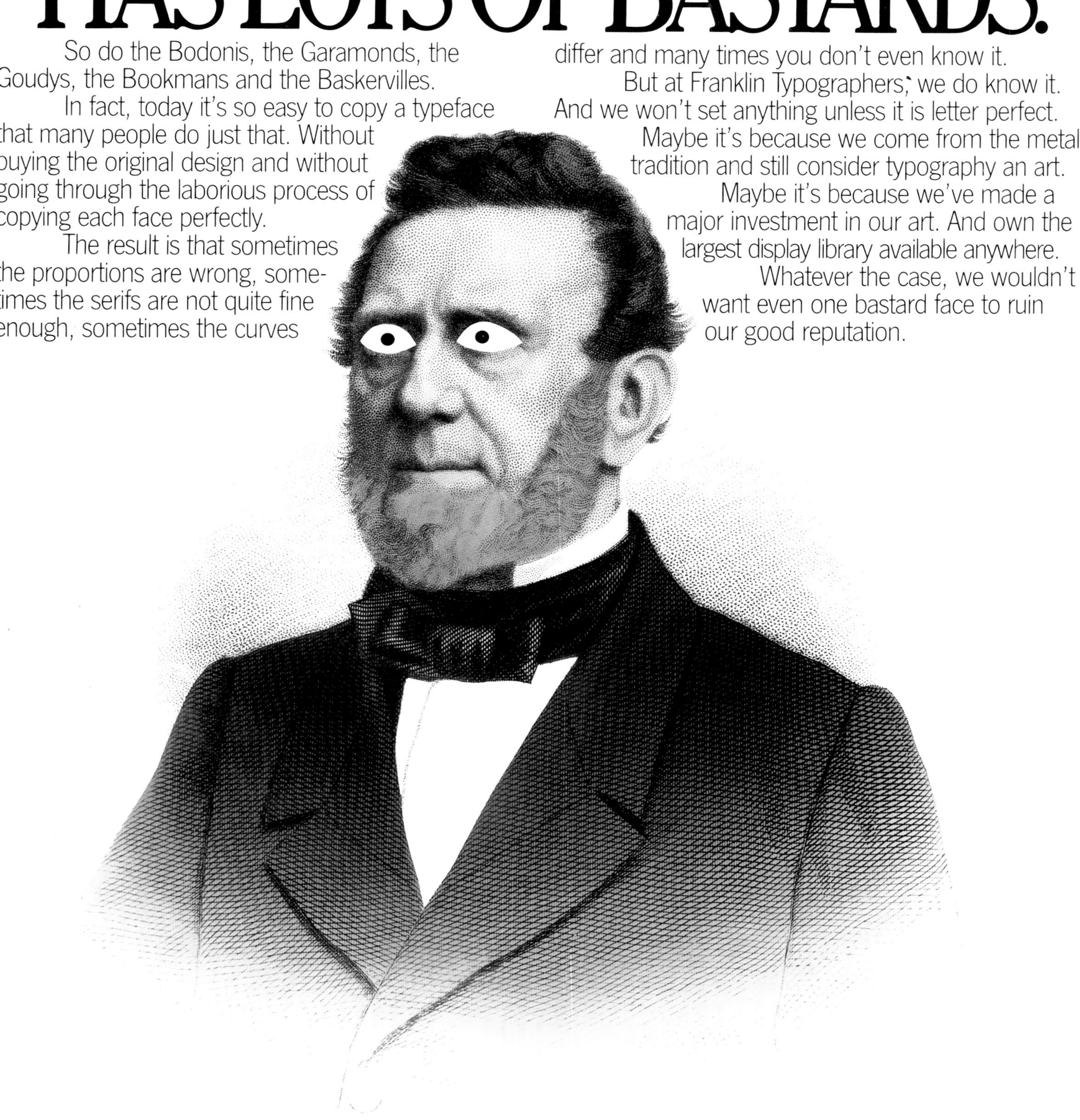

FRANKLIN TYPOGRAPHERS

When it comes to type, we don't face any type of competition.

225 West 39 Street, New York, NY 10018 212-PE6-4707

Harry A. B.
Gertrude C. SHAPIRO LIBRARY
New Hampshire College
2500 North River Road
Manchester, NH 03104